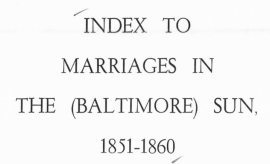

INDEX TO
MARRIAGES IN
THE (BALTIMORE) SUN,
1851-1860

Compiled by

Thomas L. Hollowak

Baltimore
GENEALOGICAL PUBLISHING CO., INC.
1978

INTRODUCTION

This book is a sequel to my previously published work, *Index to Marriages and Deaths in the (Baltimore) Sun, 1837-1850.* Although it treats only marriages, the period of coverage is extended through the year 1860. Like the previous work this index is arranged alphabetically by grooms' surnames. The second part, the Family Index, is an index to brides and to all other persons mentioned incidentally in the marriage notices.

The series of figures on the right side of each entry gives the month, day, and year of the newspaper's publication. The last number in the series refers to the page on which the notice originally appeared. The date incorporated in the main entry is the date of marriage. If the notice appeared in more than one issue of the paper, the date, or dates, of earliest issue is included at the end of the main entry and the date of latest issue extended to the right.

As with the earlier book, during the period with which we are concerned no issue of *The Sun* was produced on Sundays or the day following the Fourth of July, Thanksgiving, and Christmas.

I should like to express my gratitude to Mr. John Burgan (Chief of Central) and to Mr. Ralph Clayton (Microfilm Center), both of the Enoch Pratt Free Library, Baltimore, for permission to use the microfilm copy of the paper from which I compiled this index. I especially wish to thank, for all of her help, my secretary, Mrs. Patti Smith Matulonis.

Thomas L. Hollowak

INDEX TO MARRIAGES IN
THE (BALTIMORE) SUN, 1851-1860

(?), Charles, 12 Nov. 1856, (?) (?)	11/14/56-2
(?), Charles H., 26 Sept. 1859, Ellen Amelia Delevit	9/28/59-2
(?)-man, Michael, 7 Mar. 1860, Sarah Jane (?)	4/19/60-2
(?)-mbell, Jas. S., 20 Apr. 1852, (Mrs.) Ann Warren	4/23/52-2
(?)-mple, (?) (Gov.), 4 Aug. 1852, Kate Lowbed	8/ 6/52-2
(?)-ney, Josiah, (?) Sept. 1857, Maggie Curry	9/18/57-2
(?)-rmer, Chas., 25 Mar. 1852, (Mrs.) Lydia Hinsey	3/27/52-2
(?)-ungincke, Henry M., 5 Mar. 1860, Adelaide Wilstore	3/12/60-2
Abbat, James A., 27 Nov. 1853, Malvina A. Love	11/ 4/53-2
Abbero, Jerome, 21 Feb. 1854, Amanda S. Lamden	2/23/54-2
Abbott, Alexander, 11 Mar. 1856, Jessie E. Keavins	3/13/56-2
Abbott, Alexander, 22 Feb. 1859, Lizzy Beatty	2/24/59-2
Abbott, Benjamin, 20 Dec. 1853, Clara E. Potter, dau. of Mathias S.	12/22/53-2
Abbott, D. W., 22 Dec. 1853, Kate Wills	12/28/53-2
Abbott, Francis, 10 June 1852, Ellen V. Wichens	6/15/52-2
Abbott, James W., 16 Jan. 1852, Jane Rebecca Briggs, dau. of (Rev.) S. S.	1/17/52-2
Abbott, John N., 13 June 1858, Elizabeth A. Meriken	6/17/58-2
Abbott, John W., 12 May 1853, Mary E. Hall	5/14/53-2
Abbott, John W., 12 May 1853, Mary E. Hall, dau. of (Capt.) Warner; corrected copy	5/19/53-2
Abbott, Thomas, 5 June 1856, (Mrs.) Mary Boyer	6/ 6/56-2
Abell, Franklin M., 25 Dec. 1852, Mary Ann Medinger	4/25/53-2
Aberle, John, 25 Dec. 1851, Elizabeth Ann Smith	12/27/51-2
Abey, George, 30 Apr. 1856, Sarah Elizabeth Roten	5/ 9/56-2
Abey, Joseph W., 2 July 1860, Sophia C. Fuller	7/ 7/60-2
Abey, Michael B., 22 May 1856, Mary Ann Livingston	5/24/56-2
Abey, Wm. H., 3 Jan. 1854, Harriet J. Spedden	1/ 7/54-2
Abrahams, Wm. H., 28 Jan. 1858, Ursula Perean, Kimberly, dau. of Nathaniel	1/30/58-2
Abrams, Jacob D., 6 June 1854, Adaline Rennous	6/ 9/54-2
Achenback, Hiram H., 17 July 1860, Mary Elizabeth Shafer	7/19/60-2
Achey, Charles F., 5 Feb. 1856, Amelia S. Shultz	2/ 7/56-2
Achey, Frederick, 22 May 1856, Mary C. Brown, dau. of (Dr.) John E.	5/23/56-2
Acken, Wm. D., 17 Apr. 1855, Jane C. Moncrieff	4/19/55-2
Ackland, James, 2 Jan. 1854, Mary Catherine Kersey	1/ 4/55-2
Acomb, John W., 9 Feb. 1854, Mary Jane Paul	2/14/54-2
Acton, Elijah, 27 Sept. 1860, Camilla McCleary, dau. of James	10/ 3/60-2
Acton, Samuel G., 3 Aug. 1852, Ann Elizabeth Prentice	8/26/52-2
Adair, John, 27 Feb. 1851, Elizabeth McMurray	3/ 1/51-2
Adair, John, 24 Nov. 1853, Martha E. Gill	11/26/53-2
Adair, Joseph, 3 May 1859, Ella Giull	5/31/59-2

Adair, Robert, 31 Dec. 1850, Rachel Ann Cooksey, dau. of
    William and Mary   1/ 3/51-2
Adam, Frederick E., 28 Sept. 1859, Annie F. Lehrs   9/30/59-2
Adam, John W., 23 May 1852, Margaret C. Knight   6/ 1/52-2
Adams, Alexander S., 31 Jan. 1859, Amanda E. Reasin, dau. of
    Wm. D.   2/ 3/59-2
Adams, Anthony F., 13 Feb. 1854, Mary E. Gettier   2/14/54-2
Adams, Charles (Capt.), 9 Sept. 1858, Mary E. Keys   9/10/58-2
Adams, Charles S., 10 Oct. 1860, Elizabeth A. Waggner   10/16/60-2
Adams, Chas. A., 17 Nov. 1853, Frances E. Donnald   11/21/53-2
Adams, Dennis, 10 Mar. 1859, Margaret Howard   3/12/59-2
Adams, Frederick E., 17 Jan. 1856, Sophia D. Walstrums   1/19/56-2
Adams, George W., 2 May 1859, (Mrs.) Ellen A. Baly   5/ 5/59-2
Adams, Howard J., 17 Dec. 1857, Lizzie H. Flint, dau. of
    William   12/19/57-2
Adams, Jacob G., 19 Dec. 1854, Mary Jane Scott   12/28/54-2
Adams, James M., 25 July 1859, Elizabeth J. Clark   8/26/59-2
Adams, John E., 23 Aug. 1853, Anna E. Nickels   9/20/53-2
Adams, John E., 20 July 1856, Mary C. Wright   7/21/56-2
Adams, John H., 9 Oct. 1851, Anna E. Davis   10/14/51-2
Adams, John K., 23 May 1851, Elizabeth A. Goodman   6/ 4/51-2
Adams, John Quincy, 24 Jan. 1854, Lizzie B. Morrow, dau. of
    John   1/25/54-2
Adams, John W., 1 Dec. 1857, Julia Ann Edmonds   12/ 2/57-2
Adams, Jos. S., 25 Nov. 1852, Mary Jane Tarlton   11/27/52-2
Adams, Joseph Henry, 31 July 1855, Laura Jane Webb   8/ 2/55-2
Adams, Orson, 10 Jan. 1860, Annie L. Fisher, dau. of Thos.;
    1/17/60-2   1/18/60-2
Adams, Samuel, 19 July 1851, Margaret Ann Drapper, dau. of
    (Dr.) Simon Guthrow; 7/31/51-2   8/ 1/51-2
Adams, Samuel S., 7 Oct. 1858, Caroline V. Holt   10/13/58-2
Adams, Thomas, 5 May 1854, Jane Gregg   5/ 8/54-2
Adams, Wm. F. (Capt.), 17 Oct. 1860, (Mrs.) Anne E. Owings,
    dau. of N. D. Worthington   10/22/60-2
Adamson, Alexander, 10 May 1858, Annie M. Finley   5/12/58-2
Addison, Edwin R., 18 May 1858, Laura Stygers   5/19/58-2
Addison, Geo. C., son of Saml., 5 June 1856, Marletta Bond   6/12/56-2
Addison, Wm. W., 8 Mar. 1853, Susan Atler   3/10/53-2
Adkins, J. L. (Dr.), 12 Aug. 1852, Mary E. Hughlett   8/14/52-2
Adkinson, Lemuel, 11 Feb. 1851, Minerva E. Henderson   2/12/51-2
Adrean, Pearson, 4 Feb. 1857, (Mrs.) Catharine Ann Murphy   2/ 6/57-2
Adreon, C. C., 6 Oct. 1856, Mary E. Brickley, dau. of
    (Dr.) Geo.   10/18/56-2
Adreon, Wm. P., 31 Mar. 1856, Mary E. Galvin   4/ 9/56-2
Adres, William H., 28 Feb. 1860, Ann Boyer   3/12/60-2
Ady, William M., 19 Oct. 1858, Laura G. Eichelberger, dau. of
    Wm.   10/21/58-2
Affavroux, Epaulete A., 27 Oct. 1858, Martha J. Watts   11/ 3/58-2
Affayroux, Francis P., 22 Jan. 1851, Eliza A. O'Hara   1/28/51-2
Aftung, John, 24 June 1860, Elizabeth Ann Granger   6/26/60-2
Agin, John, 25 Aug. 1853, (Mrs.) Elizabeth Harris   8/31/53-2
Ahl, Phillip, 15 May 1853, Jane Knight   5/18/53-2
Ahlsleger, Wm., 8 Nov. 1860, Rebecca High, dau. of Joseph   11/15/60-2
Ahrens, Adolph, 26 May 1852, Anna Wetherald, dau. of Jos.   5/29/52-2
Airey, James, 9 Jan. 1853, Abbey Ann Youngman   1/14/53-2
Airey, John B., 6 Apr. 1859, Laura J. Cline   5/16/59-2
Aitken, Alex. M., 4 Sept. 1860, Emma L. Jackson, dau. of
    E. B.   9/ 6/60-2
Akehurst, Chas., 21 Aug. 1856, (Mrs.) Mary M. Hipkins   9/20/56-2
Akehurst, Chas., 23 Oct. 1856, Amanda Ann Bevans   11/28/56-2
Akers, Chas., Jr., 30 Sept. 1858, Sarah R. Orem   10/ 2/58-2
Akers, Rezin T., 2 Feb. 1860, Emily Clayridge   3/ 6/60-2
Akers, William, 22 Oct. 1857, Josephine Claridge, dau. of
    Lloyd   10/24/57-2

Akhurs, Richard H., 15 Oct. 1857, Julia A. Kidd   10/17/57-2
Akins, Henry, 16 Oct. 1856, Frances Fortune   10/18/56-2
Albach, John, 11 Apr. 1854, Emelia White, dau. of David   4/13/54-2
Alban, Noah, 9 June 1859, Mary E. Kane   6/10/59-2
Albaugh, Daniel J., 20 Apr. 1859, Mary F. Link   4/22/59-2
Albaugh, Henry C., 23 Dec. 1858, Sarah J. Hull, dau. of
   Thos. J.   12/24/58-2
Albert, Augustus, 26 May 1853, Madaline C. Hatch   5/27/53-2
Albert, Daniel, 30 Jan. 1851, Susan Zimmer   2/ 1/51-2
Albert, Michael, 13 Apr. 1858, Mary A. Hartmeyer, dau. of
   Richard   4/16/58-2
Albright, William J., 26 July 1859, Kate Breaning   7/29/59-2
Alcock, William E., 20 Dec. 1855, Mary Van Bokkelen, dau. of
   T. Byrom Grundy   12/24/55-2
Alder, Wm., 23 Sept. 1852, Ophelia Getty   9/25/52-2
Alderson, John D., 26 Nov. 1860, Anne M. Dunn, dau. of
   Thomas   12/14/60-2
Aldridge, George W., 3 Nov. 1853, Rachel Meredith   11/ 7/53-2
Aleman, John H., 7 June 1858, Harriet Cladfelter   6/ 9/58-2
Aler, John, 6 Sept. 1860, Elizabeth Trought   12/ 5/60-2
Aler, Samuel, 27 Dec. 1855, Eliza Virginia Coomes   12/31/55-2
Alexander, Elijah, 4 July 1858, Rachel Vogelman   7/ 7/58-2
Alexander, John, 18 Mar. 1851, Margaret Henderson   3/21/51-2
Alexander, P. B., 2 Jan. 1856, Mary A. Graham   1/ 4/56-2
Alexander, Robt. E., 8 Apr. 1856, Caroline A. Lucas, dau. of
   William and Sarah   4/15/56-2
Alger, Horace B., 8 Apr. 1855, Emelia Criswell   4/10/55-2
Alison, Nathaniel O., (?) Mar. 1852, Susan Hitaffer   3/17/52-2
Allard, Albert A., 1 Apr. 1860, Ann Elizabeth Wilson   4/ 4/60-2
Allard, John Edward, 20 Dec. 1853, Laura Francis Smallwood   12/23/53-2
Allard, Joseph, 19 Feb. 1852, Susan A. Baysman   2/23/52-2
Alldidise, John, 20 Dec. 1852, Sarah J. Fisher   12/24/52-2
Allen, Benjamin, 5 Sept. 1852, (Mrs.) Catharine Criswell   9/ 8/52-2
Allen, Charles, 5 June 1854, Susan J. Gregory, dau. of
   Joseph   6/ 7/54-2
Allen, E. M., 2 Dec. 1852, Sallie E. Wilson, dau. of
   William   12/11/52-2
Allen, Geraldis S., 7 Feb. 1855, Martha F. Fincher   2/10/55-2
Allen, Isaac J., 26 May 1858, Henrietta E. Rochester   5/28/58-2
Allen, James, no date given, C. M. Duering, dau. of D. F.   3/19/52-2
Allen, Jas. S., 1 Mar. 1855, Cordelia A. Wyatt   3/ 5/55-2
Allen, John, 6 Apr. 1853, Amanda Boon   4/14/53-2
Allen, Peter R., 17 Jan. 1856, Frances B. Baker   1/24/56-2
Allen, Robert, 6 Sept. 1860, Molly White   11/28/60-2
Allen, Robert J., 6 Sept. 1860, Mary Nequet, dau. of
   (Capt.) B.; corrected copy   11/29/60-2
Allen, Thomas F., 20 Nov. 1856, Martha R. Crouch   11/22/56-2
Allen, William, 23 Nov. 1858, Cornelia E. Webster   12/ 6/58-2
Allenbaugh, Wm. H., 27 Nov. 1854, Mary A. Leeden, dau. of
   Peter   11/29/54-2
Allender, Charles, 21 Aug. 1853, Mary Elizabeth Ayler   8/23/53-2
Allender, Geo. H., 28 June 1857, Alphonso Trusill   7/ 8/57-2
Allers, Harmann E., 2 Nov. 1854, Regina Ruff   11/ 6/54-2
Allgier, Amon, 17 Sept. 1855, (Mrs.) Lucy T. Culman   9/28/55-2
Allison, Philip S., 2 June 1857, Leanna Davis, dau. of
   James C.   6/ 4/57-2
Allison, Richard T., 9 Feb. 1852, Maria Key Taney, dau. of
   (Chief Justice) Roger B.   2/10/52-2
Allison, William J., 26 Feb. 1856, Elmira Sparks   3/ 1/56-2
Allon, J., 18 June 1857, Amanda M. Vanborn, dau. of James W.   6/23/57-2
Almoney, Mordecai, 29 Dec. 1853, Mary E. Warner, dau. of
   Wm. A.   12/31/53-2
Alrebt, Michael, 13 Apr. 1858, Mary A. Hartmeyer, dau. of
   Richard   4/14/58-2

Alt, John, 12 Apr. 1858, Elizabeth C. Rupert   4/15/58-2
Altemus, William E., 22 June 1858, Emilie J. Saville   10/25/58-2
Alton, Lewis H., 12 June 1855, Mary Olevia Sanner   6/16/55-2
Altrogge, William, 4 June 1854, Mary Elizabeth Breighner   6/ 8/54-2
Altvater, Charles A., 4 July 1855, Virginia A. Bruce   7/16/55-2
Altvater, William F., 4 Feb. 1851, Mary Jane McCurdy   2/20/51-2
Ambrose, Robert D., 6 Jan. 1853, Mary Jane Leonard, dau. of
   William M.   2/ 4/53-2
Amerling, Harman, 13 Feb. 1855, Sarah Sipes   2/24/55-2
Ames, Leonard H., 9 Apr. 1857, Virginia S. Joynes   4/28/57-2
Amhos, Christopher, 16 Aug. 1857, Ellen C. V. Pierce   8/19/57-2
Amhurse, Charles, 13 Oct. 1859, Mary Jane Stansbury   10/15/59-2
Amos, Benjamin, 19 Apr. 1851, Eliza Jane Robinson   4/26/51-2
Amos, Fred'k. A., 26 June 1851, Louisa W. Waters   7/ 3/51-2
Amos, L. R., 27 Nov. 1860, Mary L. Ault, dau. of Samuel, Jr. 12/18/60-2
Amos, Thomas, 18 Feb. 1858, Mary J. Slade   3/ 4/58-2
Amos, Thomas A., 23 Apr. 1856, Angaline V. Weatherill   4/25/56-2
Amos, Wm. E., 11 Sept. 1851, Anna E. Clapp   9/12/51-2
Amos, Zachariah, 29 Jan. 1855, Caroline F. Moore   2/ 9/55-2
Amoss, Benjamin, 29 Feb. 1860, Susanna Robinson   3/ 6/60-2
Amoss, E. Pearson, 21 Jan. 1858, Francina H. Wetherill   2/12/58-2
Amoss, Henry C., 7 Jan. 1860, Mary A. Frazier, dau. of
   Solomon T.   1/19/60-2
Amoss, Isaac Risteau, 27 Nov. 1860, Mary Louisa Ault   12/ 1/60-2
Amoss, James F., 18 Dec. 1855, Emma J. Murray   12/19/55-2
Amoss, Lemuel H., 23 Dec. 1851, Eliza J. Fraizier   12/25/51-2
Amoss, Oliver C., 3 Nov. 1857, Theresa C. Favour   11/ 6/57-2
Anders, Upton, 2 Nov. 1858, (Mrs.) Sarah J. Barnheart   12/ 4/58-2
Anderson, Benjamin T., 17 Oct. 1855, Mary G. Royston   10/19/55-2
Anderson, Chaney, 28 Jan. 1858, Elizabeth Garring   2/11/58-2
Anderson, Charles C., 3 Feb. 1853, Mary A. Boston   2/ 5/53-2
Anderson, Charles P., 28 July 1858, Susan Redmile   7/30/58-2
Anderson, Clifford C., 5 Jan. 1860, Corinne Cannon, dau. of
   James D.; corrected copy   1/13/60-2
Anderson, Clifford C., 5 Jan. 1860, M. Corinne Cannon, dau.
   of James B.   1/12/60-2
Anderson, Cromwell, 5 Oct. 1854, Catherine Hartman   10/13/54-2
Anderson, Edward E., 17 Nov. 1853, Catharine A. Downs   11/22/53-2
Anderson, H. Mortimer (Dr.), 25 May 1854, Julia Hand, dau.
   of Hayard E.   6/14/54-2
Anderson, Henry (Dr.), 8 Apr. 1857, Nannie E. Peterman, dau.
   of John   4/22/57-2
Anderson, Isaac J., 16 Mar. 1854, Ann Catharine Horney   3/21/54-2
Anderson, Israel, 6 Nov. 1851, (Mrs.) Emily Chance   11/ 8/51-2
Anderson, J. W., 9 Feb. 1858, C. L. Knight; 2/11/58-2   2/12/58-2
Anderson, James, 6 Aug. 1854, Catharine McKendry   8/15/54-2
Anderson, James, 14 Nov. 1860, Eleanora A. Moore   11/16/60-2
Anderson, James M., 1 Dec. 1859, Susie R. Fulton, dau. of
   J. C.; 12/ 7/59-2   12/10/59-2
Anderson, Jas., 13 Jan. 1853, Mildred Cole   3/ 9/53-2
Anderson, John Waters, 18 Sept. 1851, Elizabeth Rebecca
   Taylor, dau. of (Rev.) Wm.   9/25/51-2
Anderson, John William, 25 Oct. 1859, Mary Houlton   11/ 8/59-2
Anderson, Joseph, 28 Nov. 1852, Mary Elizabeth Smith, dau.
   of Francis   2/24/52-2
Anderson, Joseph, 15 Jan. 1856, Margaret McElroy   1/16/56-2
Anderson, Joshua, 15 Sept. 1857, Sallie Sandford   9/23/57-2
Anderson, Morris, 31 July 1853, Maria Reed   8/ 4/53-2
Anderson, R. M., 11 June 1860, A. M. Bradford   6/14/60-2
Anderson, Robert, 14 Nov. 1854, (Mrs.) Laura A. E. Gale, dau.
   of James B. Dixon   11/17/54-2
Anderson, Robert S., 27 Nov. 1856, Eliza B. Dangerfield   11/29/56-2
Anderson, Samuel, 27 Jan. 1853, Margaret Ann Beard, dau. of
   Thos. R.   2/10/53-2

Anderson, Samuel E., 24 July 1856, Fannie W. Ropes, dau. of
    (Mrs.) Archer   8/12/56-2
Anderson, William, 24 Mar. 1851, Elizabeth J. Spence   3/27/51-2
Anderson, William H., 11 Aug. 1858, Emily E. Dorsey   8/20/58-2
Anderson, Wm. H., 7 Oct. 1852, Isabella Ferrar   10/ 9/52-2
Andrew, Benjamin F., 26 Oct. 1854, Sophia Homer   10/30/54-2
Andrew, J. Hervey, 14 Nov. 1854, Mary Smith   11/16/54-2
Andrew, Samuel, 15 Oct. 1852, Lucretia Weeden   10/21/52-2
Andrews, Henry C., 8 Oct. 1857, Alice A. Gott   10/ 9/57-2
Andrews, John H., 1 Dec. 1858, Charlotte A. Richards   2/23/58-2
Andrews, John J., 1 Mar. 1857, Henrietta S. Weaver   3/ 4/57-2
Andrews, Snowden, 18 Dec. 1855, Mary C. Lee, dau. of Josiah 12/22/55-2
Andrews, Thos. Broughton, son of H. W., 10 Sept. 1855,
    Jane Smith, dau. of Joseph W.   9/14/55-2
Andrews, Wm., 20 Mar. 1856, Elizabeth A. Coale   3/22/56-2
Andrews, Wm. A., 27 Apr. 1851, Mary R. Morgan   4/29/51-2
Angel, John T., 20 Oct. 1853, Mary Jane Holbrooke   10/22/53-2
Angel, Thomas B., 12 Sept. 1859, Charlotte A. Rapley   9/14/59-2
Annesley, Robert, 7 Dec. 1858, Amanda Catharine Dickle   12/18/58-2
Anstadt, P., 22 Dec. 1853, Lizzie A. Benson   12/23/53-2
Anthony, Henry A., 31 Dec. 1850, Mary A. Stitcher   1/ 6/51-2
Anthony, James H., 18 Sept. 1856, Eliza J. Thompson, dau.
    of Parker; 9/23/56-2   9/24/56-2
Anthony, Lyscum T., 22 Feb. 1859, (Mrs.) Jemima Carpenter   2/25/59-2
Antrim, Geo. T., 19 Dec. 1854, C. J. Schumacker   12/22/54-2
Appal, William, 11 Nov. 1859, Caroline Henze, dau. of
    Augustus   12/14/59-2
Apple, Joseph H.(Rev.), 30 Mar. 1856, Elizabeth A. Gieger,
    dau. of (Rev.) Jacob   4/10/56-2
Apple, Theo., 13 Apr. 1854, Susan B. Wolff, dau. of
    (Rev.) B. C.   4/14/54-2
Appleby, Andrew J., 30 Oct. 1855, Margaret Hinkel   11/ 5/55-3
Applegarth, George W., 17 Jan. 1856, Mary Ann Skinner   1/19/56-2
Applegarth, Robert, 14 May 1854, Harriet Smith   5/17/54-2
Applegarth, Robert, 9 May 1859, (Mrs.) Mary Ann Hitzleberger 5/13/59-2
Applegarth, William, 27 Mar. 1859, Catharine Shuck, dau. of
    Michael   3/31/59-2
Appler, Arthur M., 14 Sept. 1859, Helen M. Etchison, dau. of
    Thos. H.   9/29/59-2
Appler, Orlando M., 23 Nov. 1854, Mary A. Davidson   11/27/54-2
Appold, Theodore R., 20 Oct. 1857, Kate C. Dorney, dau. of B. 10/22/57-2
Archer, Robert H., 23 Feb. 1853, Ellen H. Davis, dau. of
    (Rev.) R. H.   2/24/53-2
Archer, Robert H., 9 Nov. 1858, Mary Ringgold, dau. of Jane G. 11/10/58-2
Archer, Stevenson, 4 Jan. 1855, Blanche Franklin   1/19/55-2
Archibald, John, 7 June 1859, Indiana Hook   6/23/59-2
Ardin, D., Jr., 12 June 1853, Clara L. Stuart   9/13/53-2
Arendt, Jacob, 20 May 1856, Eliza Sheets, dau. of Jacob   5/24/56-2
Arens, Henry, 24 Nov. 1855, Emma J. Simon, dau. of Chas.   10/25/55-2
Argenti, T., 5 Oct. 1859, Ellen Kelly   10/13/59-2
Armacost, Amos, 18 Dec. 1851, Sarah Charlotte Price   12/20/51-2
Armager, John L., 6 May 1858, Rosa B. Peregoy, dau. of
    John W.   5/10/58-2
Armeger, John L., 9 Feb. 1854, Mary Ellen Hindes, dau. of
    Samuel   2/11/54-2
Armiger, Jas. R., 8 Nov. 1860, Marion Middleton, dau. of
    John W.   11/13/60-2
Armiger, John W., 23 July 1856, Sarah A. Armiger   7/25/56-2
Armiger, Joseph, 19 May 1859, Mary E. Yewell   5/20/59-2
Armiger, Joshua, 22 Oct. 1851, Sarah Elizabeth Armiger   10/24/51-2
Armour, John D., 28 June 1860, Deborah Owings, dau. of
    Wm. L.   7/ 4/60-2
Armstrong, Benjamin H., 27 Nov. 1851, Margaret A. C. Chandler,
    dau. of W. D.   12/ 2/51-2

Armstrong, Geo. W., 22 June 1856, Adeline Lauderman, dau. of
   (Capt.) James   7/ 2/56-2
Armstrong, James, 14 Mar. 1858, Eliza Griffith   3/18/58-2
Armstrong, James E. (Rev.), 1 Nov. 1855, Maggie Hickman, dau.
   of John T.   11/ 5/55-3
Armstrong, James W., 14 Sept. 1854, Catherine Burton   9/18/54-2
Armstrong, John A., 22 Mar. 1859, Margaretta McKee, dau. of
   William   3/31/59-2
Armstrong, John C., 9 Jan. 1851, Nancy Ellen Kelly, dau. of
   Martin   1/10/51-2
Armstrong, John H., 18 Mar. 1852, Esther Gregg, dau. of David   3/20/52-2
Armstrong, John L., 25 July 1854, Catherine Elenora Atweel   7/28/54-2
Armstrong, Thomas, 6 Oct. 1857, Pamela E. Lee, dau. of
   (Mrs.) Anne   10/ 8/57-2
Armstrong, William, 6 Jan. 1857, Emilie Frances Miller   1/ 8/57-2
Armstrong, Wm. K., 25 Dec. 1859, Sarah E. Wilson   1/ 2/60-2
Arnett, James, 5 July 1857, Rebecca Wrightson   7/22/57-2
Arnett, James W., 12 June 1855, Rose A. Cannon, dau. of
   (Capt.) James   6/25/55-2
Arnett, Levi, 30 Oct. 1853, Mary Jane Lightner   11/ 1/53-2
Arnold, Alexander, 3 Nov. 1858, Sarah J. Littleton   11/ 9/58-2
Arnold, Andrew J., 27 Aug. 1857, Sarah L. Wells   8/29/57-2
Arnold, George, 11 May 1854, E. M. Tilley   5/13/54-2
Arnold, George W., 8 Sept. 1860, Henrietta Gardner   9/12/60-2
Arnold, Henry, 8 Dec. 1853, Mary Ann Seymour   12/10/53-2
Arnold, Israel, 30 Dec. 1857, Martha Jane Green   2/ 3/57-2
Arnold, Jacob, 11 Nov. 1857, Sarah Allen   11/14/58-2
Arnold, John, 26 Apr. 1855, Elizabeth V. Hamilton; corrected
   copy   5/12/55-2
Arnold, John, 26 Apr. 1855, Lizzie V. Hamilton   4/27/55-2
Arnold, Mathias, 18 Oct. 1852, (Mrs.) Susan Hambleton   10/22/52-2
Arnold, Sam'l., 31 Aug. 1852, (Mrs.) Ann Maria Hopkins   9/ 1/52-2
Arnold, Samuel E., 11 Dec. 1851, Sarah Ann Champion   12/15/51-2
Arnold, Thomas H., 4 Aug. 1853, Sarah R. Waring, dau. of
   Richard H.   8/ 6/53-2
Arnold, William Henry, 13 Oct. 1852, Mary A. Bayne, dau. of
   Thomas   10/14/52-2
Arnold, Wm., 2 Sept. 1858, C. A. B. Field   9/ 3/58-2
Arringdale, Jas. M., 20 Nov. 1860, Annie E. Rose, dau. of
   (Dr.) John   11/22/60-2
Artlip, Mahlon, 16 Feb. 1854, Catharine Whalen   4/19/54-2
Artman, Wm., 23 Sept. 1857, Jennie Van Tilburgh   10/ 2/57-2
Ash, James F., 1 Aug. 1859, Emma J. Spafford   8/ 4/59-2
Ashburner, Charles H., 16 Dec. 1858, Mary Catharine Richard-
   son, dau. of George W.   12/20/58-2
Ashby, John R., 7 Oct. 1858, Laura Kennedy   10/11/58-2
Ashe, Charles V., 18 May 1851, Sina Ann Proctor   5/22/51-2
Asher, Wm., 25 Sept. 1854, Ellen E. Thompson   10/ 3/54-2
Ashley, James D., 8 Apr. 1856, Lydia A. Stephens   4/12/56-2
Ashoom, John L. A., 18 Aug. 1853, Robertanner Bean   8/20/53-2
Ashton, John A., 10 Nov. 1853, Susannah Ashton   11/16/53-2
Askens, Wm., 5 May 1858, Ann Jennes   5/ 8/58-2
Askew, J. B., 9 Dec. 1856, Mary E. Carroll   12/11/56-2
Askins, Jeremiah, 18 Oct. 1855, Jane Rebecca Reed   10/19/55-2
Askins, Josiah, 29 Jan. 1860, Isabella Cooper   1/30/60-2
Askins, Moses, 1 Nov. 1855, Hester Wilson   11/ 7/55-3
Asplin, John; no date given, Elizabeth Ann Harrington   12/11/56-2
Aspril, David T., 23 Aug. 1853, Mary Ann Jefferson, dau. of
   Purnell   8/25/53-2
Ast, Wm. F., 30 Oct. 1856, Rosa Lambert   11/ 3/56-2
Atkins, Joseph, 22 Feb. 1859, Elizabeth A. Kirby   2/23/59-2
Atkinson, Archibald (Dr.), 2 Nov. 1858, Mary Elizabeth Thomas   11/13/58-2
Atkinson, Brodnax, 6 Dec. 1859, Eliza Purviance, dau. of
   (Capt.) H. Y.   12/ 8/59-2

Atkinson, John W., 4 Dec. 1851, Maria Seacombe, dau. of
    Thomas   12/ 6/51-2
Atkinson, Joseph T., 20 Sept. 1855, Mary Isabel Conant, dau.
    of Cyrus   9/24/55-2
Atkinson, Robert (Dr.), 5 Nov. 1856, Georgiana H. Kierl, dau.
    of George H.   11/10/56-2
Atkinson, Samuel E., 16 Feb. 1860, Charlotte L. Emmart   2/18/60-2
Atkinson, William S., 15 Mar. 1853, Susan H. Gray   5/27/53-2
Atkinson, Wm. F., 4 Nov. 1851, Ann R. Altvater   11/ 5/51-2
Atwell, Daniel, 11 Sept. 1851, Rebecca Underwood   9/16/51-2
Atwell, James R., 28 Oct. 1856, Martha Smith   11/ 7/56-2
Atwood, Benjamin, 13 Oct. 1859, Catherine Barry   11/ 4/59-2
Atzs, Charles C., 2 Aug. 1852, Rebecca Cunningham   8/ 5/52-2
Aubury, Thomas, 14 May 1857, Susan Clark   5/16/57-2
Audibert, John H., 10 Sept. 1851, Mary Jane Bowlin   9/25/51-2
Audoun, Lewis, 28 Jan. 1851, Catherine Mundel Chamberlain,
    dau. of Aaron   1/29/51-2
Audoun, Lewis, 22 May 1855, Emily A. Trott   5/26/55-2
Audson, G. Walter, 23 July 1857, Mary E. C. Hearickle, dau.
    of Geo. W.   7/30/57-2
Augustus, Esau, 27 Jan. 1859, Mary Richards   2/ 5/59-2
Auld, Benjamin F., 6 July 1860, Kate A. W. Clark, dau. of
    Benj. J.   10/ 5/60-2
Auld, Haddaway, 8 Apr. 1851, Virginia Johnson   4/10/51-2
Auld, James, 28 Aug. 1856, Sarah E. Hunt, dau. of Stephen   9/ 9/56-2
Aurdibert, John H., 27 Oct. 1857, Annie E. Curtain   10/31/57-2
Austen, Edward, 20 Apr. 1858, Mary R. Morse, dau. of
    Richard C.   4/27/58-2
Austen, George, 14 June 1859, Rebecca Chandler, dau. of
    George W.   6/18/59-2
Austen, George C., 15 Apr. 1852, Ellen G. Kirby   4/17/52-2
Auster, Charles L., 24 Oct. 1860, Sophia E. Reigart, dau. of
    Henry F., niece of (Mrs.) M. J.   11/ 9/60-2
Avery, Salem, 1 Jan. 1857, (Mrs.) Lucretia Anderson   1/ 7/57-2
Axce, David, 12 Nov. 1855, Mary A. Fryer, dau. of P. R.   11/13/55-2
Axe, John C., 28 May 1855, Eliza Freelen   10/ 3/55-2
Axe, John Cunningham, 25 Mar. 1852, Caroline E. McCandless   3/30/52-2
Axer, John, 12 Apr. 1855, Rosanna Keplinger   4/14/55-2
Ayars, Jonathan D., 16 Mar. 1851, (Mrs.) Ann Jackson   3/19/51-2
Aydeloff, Peter, 28 Oct. 1851, Mary Ann Moore   11/ 1/51-2
Ayers, James H., 13 Dec. 1860, Hester Ann E. Bowley   12/15/60-2
Ayers, John, 13 Nov. 1856, Emily Miller   11/15/56-2
Babl, William W., 24 Sept. 1855, Carie Bandell   10/ 2/55-2
Bachelor, Charles, 3 Mar. 1859, Mary Taylor, dau. of Geo.   3/ 8/59-2
Bachmann, J. C. Henry, 14 Dec. 1858, M. E. K. Thompson, dau.
    of (Capt.) W. C.   12/25/58-2
Backmeister, G. C., 5 Apr. 1855, Isabel M. M'Neir, dau. of
    (Col.) Wm.   4/ 6/55-2
Bacon, T. Scott (Rev.), 1 Nov. 1858, Jane Y. Kelso, dau. of
    George Y.   11/ 2/58-2
Badders, A. J., 22 June 1854, Mary J. Pearsol   6/29/54-2
Badders, Andrew J., 16 Aug. 1855, Amanda Scarff   8/18/55-2
Badders, Henry H., 23 Sept. 1856, Edith S. Bonsall   9/25/56-2
Baden, Jeremiah, 10 Dec. 1857, Rebecca O. Wilson, dau. of
    (Rev.) Wm. T.   12/18/57-2
Badger, Thomas P., 20 Sept. 1859, Sarah V. McComas   9/26/59-2
Baer, E. Ridgely (Dr.), 10 Oct. 1854, Virginia M. Lucas   10/11/54-2
Baer, Joseph, 26 Mar. 1854, Mary Beckenheimer   3/28/54-2
Baetholick, Jonathan W., 3 Nov. 1853, Mary E. Hillery   11/ 8/53-2
Bagge, Thomas, 7 July 1853, Rosetta McCambridge   7/11/53-2
Baggs, William, 8 Feb. 1856, Sarah Greer   2/11/56-2
Bahm, Lewis, 31 Aug. 1859, Catharine Ann Epping   9/ 2/59-2
Bahr, C. (Capt.), 2 Sept. 1852, Marie Von Santen   9/ 4/52-2
Bailey, Edward A., 23 Oct. 1851, Ann Rebecca Gosnell   10/27/51-2

```
Bailey, James, 16 Nov. 1854, Martha P. Woods, dau. of N. L.      11/17/54-2
Bailey, James W., 7 Nov. 1854, Mary E. Taylor                    11/10/54-2
Bailey, John H., 31 Aug. 1858, Ann Eliza Williams                 9/10/58-2
Bailey, Lewis E., 15 July 1852, M. E. Orme                        7/16/52-2
Bailey, William, 15 Aug. 1852, Martha E. Devaughn                 8/31/52-2
Baily, Edmund J., 10 Sept. 1856, Mary E. Campbell                 9/19/56-2
Baily, Watson, 11 Nov. 1858, Martha Sheaf                        11/13/58-2
Bain, George W., 6 Mar. 1851, (Mrs.) Sarah F. Smith               3/ 8/51-2
Baird, Samuel M., 31 May 1855, Eliza J. Dunn                      6/ 5/55-2
Baish, J. H., 12 Oct. 1856, Kate E. Traver                       10/15/56-2
Baker, Alfred Creighton; no date given, Rebecca J. Fry            3/21/57-2
Baker, C. Ferreira, 18 May 1858, Victoria A. Benson               5/24/58-2
Baker, Charles H., 16 June 1853, Deborah M. Davis                 6/20/53-2
Baker, Charles L., 8 Dec. 1853, Mary A. Wilson                   12/12/53-2
Baker, Chas. H., 5 Jan. 1857, Mary A. Smith                       2/23/57-2
Baker, Davis, 23 Oct. 1855, Celia A. Brewer                      10/25/55-2
Baker, G. Alex., 12 Apr. 1860, Mary Frances Kuhn                  4/14/60-2
Baker, George, 18 Apr. 1856, Mary T. Wallace                      5/ 1/56-2
Baker, Henry, 15 July 1855, Annie M. Stewart                      7/19/55-2
Baker, Isaac Monroe, 30 Sept. 1856, Eliza Jane Sprowl, dau.
    of James                                                     10/15/56-2
Baker, James, 20 Apr. 1852, Jane Brown                            5/13/52-2
Baker, James C., 19 Feb. 1860, Regina M. Hutson                   2/21/60-2
Baker, Jesse, 9 May 1858, Mary Hedrick                            5/13/58-2
Baker, John, 6 Sept. 1851, Margaret Matilda Carter, dau. of
    Richard D.                                                   11/12/51-2
Baker, John A. J., 9 Feb. 1857, Margaret Ann Conway               2/17/57-2
Baker, John E., 5 Aug. 1852, Catharine B. Woods                  10/ 4/52-2
Baker, John G., 30 Dec. 1851, Sarah R. Hammond                    1/ 1/52-2
Baker, John H., 20 Jan. 1852, Sarah R. Ruff                       1/29/52-2
Baker, John W., 27 Nov. 1856, Emma J. Spurrier, dau. of
    Thomas                                                       11/29/56-2
Baker, Joseph, 24 July 1851, (Mrs.) Mary E. Ennis                 7/29/51-2
Baker, Lewis, 2 Mar. 1860, Hannah E. Wilson                       3/17/60-4
Baker, Marcus A., 6 Jan. 1852, Laura C. Tucker, dau. of
    (Capt.) George C.                                             1/10/52-2
Baker, Nelson, 17 Jan. 1856, Rebecca Kebble                       1/19/56-2
Baker, Perry, 29 Apr. 1858, Rebecca Johnson; 5/ 1/58-2            5/ 4/58-2
Baker, R. B., 28 Mar. 1860, Harriet A. Ways                       3/31/60-2
Baker, Samuel, 16 June 1857, Cordelia Davis                       6/20/57-2
Baker, Samuel H., 21 Nov. 1854, Annie Jackson                    11/27/54-2
Baker, Samuel O., 31 Dec. 1851, Mary A. Anderson                  1/ 1/52-2
Baker, William D., 10 Mar. 1853, Martha Sewell                    3/12/53-2
Baker, William H. K., 10 Feb. 1853, Emily E. Lee                  2/14/53-2
Baker, William Wesley, 29 Sept. 1859, Mary Elizabeth Elliott     10/ 1/59-2
Baker, Wm. C., 24 Feb. 1853, Susan Waggner                        2/26/53-2
Baker, Wm. Henry, 16 Feb. 1858, Caroline Billups                  2/23/58-2
Bailey, Jeremiah S., 31 July 1860, Sarah A. Hudnell               8/ 3/60-2
Balash, Samuel, 1 Sept. 1855, Emma Green                          9/ 4/55-2
Balden, Samuel, 22 Nov. 1857, Charlotte A. Johnson               11/25/57-2
Balderston, John C., 20 Nov. 1860, Ada Hiss, dau. of
    Jacob, Jr.                                                   11/22/60-2
Balderston, Marcellas, 8 Dec. 1857, Margaret D. Haislett         12/19/57-2
Balderston, Oliver H., 24 Oct. 1854, Sarah H. Martin, dau.
    of (Dr.) G. P.                                               10/25/54-2
Baldin, John F., 9 Nov. 1851, Jane Frances Woolen                11/12/51-2
Baldus, Gustav, 22 Nov. 1859, Mary C. R. Mitchell                11/24/59-2
Baldwin, Caleb C., 7 Aug. 1856, Martha Marriott Miller,
    dau. of James M.                                             10/28/56-2
Baldwin, John, 27 Apr. 1851, Sarah Smith                          4/29/51-2
Baldwin, John, 18 Jan. 1857, Emma Smith                           1/24/57-2
Baldwin, John M., 24 Feb. 1853, Sarah E. Hanaway                  2/26/53-2
Baldwin, John T., 10 Feb. 1852, Sarah Ann Bryan, dau. of
    Stephen                                                       2/13/52-2
```

Baldwin, Peter L., 9 Nov. 1854, Mary E. Small   11/13/54-2
Baldwin, Richard, 3 Mar. 1857, Sophronia Jane Furlong, dau.
     of (Rev.) Henry   3/ 5/57-2
Baldwin, Thomas C., 23 June 1853, Mary E. Jones   6/26/53-2
Baldwin, Wm. H., 30 Sept. 1860, Rebecca Jane Shipley   10/ 3/60-2
Baley, Watson, 11 Nov. 1858, Martha A. Sheaff   11/15/58-2
Ball, Charles, 3 Nov. 1853, Elizabeth Hirsh   11/ 4/53-2
Ball, Edgar S., 3 June 1860, Annie Elizabeth Carr, dau. of
     John and Mary Ann   6/ 5/60-2
Ball, Henry S., 25 Oct. 1860, Margaret G. Black   11/ 1/60-2
Ball, John D., 28 Jan. 1851, Margaret Zell   2/ 5/41-2
Ball, John H., 24 Nov. 1857, Catherine Carr; 11/26/57-2   11/28/57-2
Ball, S. T., 30 Sept. 1857, Anna L. Conant   10/ 6/57-2
Ball, S. T., 30 Sept. 1857, Anna L. Conant, dau. of Samuel W.;
     corrected copy   10/ 8/57-2
Ball, Stephen H., 11 June 1860, Annie R. Joiner   6/22/60-2
Ball, T. Walker, 17 Nov. 1857, Helen F. Cobb   12/ 1/57-2
Ball, Walter, Jr., 13 May 1851, Elleanor Randall, dau. of
     Nicholas Ford   5/15/51-2
Ball, William H., 11 Nov. 1857, Elizabeth J. Bankhead, dau.
     of (Gen.) James   12/ 7/57-2
Ballard, Bryan, 6 Mar. 1855, Frances A. C. Earles   3/ 8/55-2
Ballard, Cyrus, 9 Dec. 1858, Elizabeth A. Leaf   12/20/58-2
Ballard, James, 10 Sept. 1854, Rachel Ann Trip   9/23/54-2
Ballentine, John H., 8 Sept. 1859, Jeanette Boyd, dau. of
     John   9/10/59-2
Balloch, James, Jr., 5 May 1853, Catharine Jane Trimble   5/ 9/53-2
Baltzell, Charles C., 5 Aug. 1858, Mary F. Miller   8/30/58-2
Baltzell, P. C., 3 June 1857, Kate E. Dickey, dau. of
     William   6/11/57-2
Bamberger, David, 2 July 1854, Johanna Adler   7/ 6/54-2
Bamberger, Joseph C., 9 Dec. 1858, Lizzie Buckley   1/25/59-2
Bandel, George S., 12 Oct. 1852, Mary R. Pumphrey   10/13/52-2
Bandell, Michael, 12 Nov. 1852, Virginia M. Lushbaugh   11/16/52-2
Bangert, Francis S., 6 Oct. 1857, Barbara Miller   10/ 9/57-2
Bangs, Charles, 21 Dec. 1854, Rachel M. Bennett, dau. of
     John   12/23/54-2
Bangs, Charles, 7 Jan. 1858, Beckie McCann   1/12/58-2
Bangs, Charles W., 4 Oct. 1853, Catharine C. Claypoole   10/ 7/53-2
Bangs, Edward, 9 Nov. 1858, Ellen E. Thomas, dau. of Jenkin   11/10/58-2
Bankard, David, 31 Dec. 1859, Rosa Ann Mulligan   1/ 7/59-2
Bankard, Henry Nicholas, 15 Oct. 1857, Carrie Amelia Horn,
     dau. of Benjamin   10/23/57-2
Bankard, John L., 25 Aug. 1853, (Mrs.) Margaret Seltzer   8/30/53-2
Banks, A. B., 2 Jan. 1851, Margaret Ann Whiteside   1/ 7/51-2
Banks, Andrew, 21 Nov. 1860, Lizzie Godwin, dau. of D. C.   11/27/60-2
Banks, James, 26 Sept. 1860, Martha Williams   9/28/60-2
Banks, Joshua, 8 Mar. 1859, Rennis Lee   3/10/59-2
Banks, Wm. E., 17 Oct. 1854, M. Louisa Loane, dau. of Joseph   10/25/54-2
Bannan, John, 22 June 1854, Maria Tanzey, dau. of Bernard   6/24/54-2
Bannan, John J., 12 Sept. 1859, Emma Switzer   10/ 5/59-2
Bannester, William G., 24 Mar. 1857, Isabella Morris   3/26/57-2
Bansemer, G. A., 14 Dec. 1858, Susan Byers   12/16/58-2
Barbee, B. Russell, 1 May 1856, Mary E. Owens, dau. of
     (Mrs.) Eliza H.   5/ 6/56-2
Barber, Jno. O., 25 Mar. 1858, Maggie Johnston   6/16/58-2
Barber, Yates, 8 Mar. 1860, Eliza C. Morgan   3/13/60-2
Barbour, David E., 8 May 1856, Agnes R. Bowen   5/13/56-2
Barbour, Lloyd E., 8 Dec. 1859, Eliza R. Coe; 12/15/59-2   12/17/59-2
Barbour, William H., 25 Oct. 1855, Lavinia N. Marks   10/30/55-2
Barclay, Jos. Harry, 27 Apr. 1856, Mattie McCron Jenison   4/29/56-2
Barcley, Richard R., 15 June 1858, Mary V. Bowling, dau. of
     Thomas   6/17/58-2
Bardroff, Joseph B., 20 Dec. 1854, A. Marie Keplinger   12/27/54-2

Bardroff, Lewis Edward, 21 June 1859, Mary C. Treble, dau.
    of Frederick   6/27/59-2
Barenger, Francis, 7 Oct. 1852, Mary Elizabeth Burgin, dau. of
    Thomas   10/ 9/52-2
Barger, Henry, 16 June 1854, Elizabeth Anderson, dau. of Hugh 6/24/54-2
Barker, Benjamin, 15 Dec. 1859, Anna Rebecca Ogden   12/21/59-2
Barker, Edw. W., 10 Oct. 1860, S. Maggie Loughridge, dau. of
    Wm.   10/15/60-2
Barker, William, 14 Apr. 1853, Patience Jones   4/16/53-2
Barkley, George Lewis, 24 Feb. 1857, Ann Rebecca Grant, dau. of
    William and Mary Ann   7/ 4/51-2
Barling, Edward, 17 June 1858, Mary Ann Crowel; 6/24/58-2   6/25/58-2
Barling, John, 30 June 1856, Mary Barnes   7/ 1/56-2
Barnard, Leon, 18 May 1854, Mary E. Hubbell, dau. of
    (Rev.) Saml.   5/19/54-2
Barnard, Wm., 31 Dec. 1850, Mary Ann Selby   1/ 4/51-2
Barnes, A. M., 25 June 1857, S. E. James   6/27/57-2
Barnes, C. Fletcher, 15 Oct. 1857, Minnie Mylinger, dau. of
    Samuel   10/19/57-2
Barnes, Christopher B., 15 July 1860, Laura Frances Collins   10/13/60-2
Barnes, H. P., 22 June 1856, Kate A. Wyrouch   6/25/56-2
Barnes, Isaac N., 16 Jan. 1855, (Mrs.) Maria Davy   3/ 5/55-2
Barnes, James J., 13 Feb. 1853, Louisa Plummer   2/15/53-2
Barnes, Jefferson J., 23 June 1859, Emma E. Face   6/24/59-2
Barnes, Joseph A., 19 Apr. 1860, Sarah E. Wickens   4/28/60-2
Barnes, Mortimer C., 29 July 1859, Julia E. Buxton   8/ 5/59-2
Barnes, Samuel N., 18 Apr. 1852, Mary Ellen Vickars   4/23/52-2
Barnes, Winston, 28 Jan. 1858, Maria H. Elzey   2/ 3/58-2
Barnett, Andrew J., 3 Nov. 1853, H. J. Rogers; corrected copy 1/16/54-2
Barnett, Andrew J., 3 Jan. 1854, H. L. Rogers   1/14/54-2
Barnett, Dewarren E., 20 Feb. 1851, Amelia E. Marsden   2/27/51-2
Barnett, James, 2 Oct. 1859, Mary Ann Sanders   10/ 6/59-2
Barnett, Nicholas J., 29 Apr. 1852, (Mrs.) Mary A. Johnston   5/ 7/52-2
Barnett, Thomas; no date given, Catherine Ratcliffe   3/ 3/54-2
Barnett, Thomas, 8 Jan. 1855, Ann Eliza Bellis   1/23/55-2
Barnetz, George, 1 Oct. 1856, Lizzie Bittinger, dau. of
    (Gen.) Henry   10/ 3/56-2
Barney, J. Nicholson, 28 Dec. 1858, Nannie S. Dor-(?)-in,
    dau. of (Capt.) Thos. A.   12/31/58-2
Barney, Joshua, 5 Apr. 1858, Kate B. Thurston, dau. of
    Jacob Keller   4/10/58-2
Barnhill, A. H., 20 Sept. 1860, Eliza Monroe, dau. of Henry
    and Lucretia   9/24/60-2
Barnitz, Alexander H., 4 Oct. 1855, Leonora A. McFaul, dau.
    of Joseph Judick   10/13/55-2
Barns, Benjamin Franklin, 1 Apr. 1858, Mary Elizabeth White   4/ 3/58-2
Barr, S. C., 19 Dec. 1855, Mary Simson   12/21/55-2
Barranger, Edwin, son of Lewis, 5 Mar. 1860, Frances
    Spielberger, dau. of Joseph   3/12/60-2
Barrenger, Wm. Thomas, 8 Aug. 1851, Laura J. Mummy   8/ 9/51-2
Barret, Solomon, 26 Aug. 1860, Mary E. Floyd   8/27/60-2
Barrett, Clement B., 19 Oct. 1852, R. Slater League, dau. of
    Geo. Browne   10/20/52-2
Barrett, Edward, 2 July 1857, Rachel Williams   7/ 3/57-2
Barrett, Gregory, Jr., 5 Nov. 1857, Martha W. Shaw   12/23/57-2
Barrett, James F., 27 Sept. 1855, Jane Rainier   9/29/55-2
Barrett, James J., 21 Oct. 1851, Anna Lithgo   10/23/51-2
Barrett, John Latrobe, 16 Oct. 1851, Elizabeth Ann Blanchard 10/18/51-2
Barrett, John P., 17 Feb. 1857, Kate Conner   2/25/57-2
Barrett, John T., 22 Dec. 1857, Charlotte Reed   12/24/57-2
Barrett, L. Z., 17 Apr. 1860, Isabella G. McLennan   4/18/60-2
Barrett, Roswell, 2 May 1854, Sarah J. Barrett, dau. of Asa   5/ 5/54-2
Barrett, Thomas P., 15 Mar. 1857, Ann E. Legg   3/26/57-2
Barrett, Thos. H., 19 Feb. 1857, Emma M. A. Duering, dau. of
    John S.   3/ 3/57-2

```
Barrett, William D., 4 Nov. 1852, Julia C. Beehler, dau.
    of Francis                                              11/ 8/52-2
Barrington, Francis T., 11 Feb. 1858, Mary W. Taylor         2/13/58-2
Barrington, Francis T., 11 Feb. 1858, Mary W. Taylor, dau. of
    Joseph; corrected copy                                   2/15/58-2
Barroll, Chas., 4 May 1852, E. Virginia Reed                 5/27/52-2
Barroll, J. Leeds, 5 Dec. 1854, Ellenora K. Horsey, dau. of
    Thomas H.                                               12/ 6/54-2
Barroll, James W., 30 Oct. 1855, Ann E. Jenkins, dau. of M. W.  11/ 1/55-2
Barron, J. Marion, 15 May 1860, Emma Morton Bowles           5/16/60-2
Barron, John D., 26 Sept. 1858, Mary Mullins                 9/27/58-2
Barron, Nathaniel D., 15 May 1856, Susan M. Powers           5/17/56-2
Barron, Samuel Howell, 15 Nov. 1853, (Mrs.) Rebecca A. Miller,
    dau. of Jacob Myers                                     11/17/53-2
Barrow, Alexander H., 9 Oct. 1851, Mary W. Bosler, dau. of
    John                                                    10/11/51-2
Barry, Francis, 11 Jan. 1859, Henrietta Virginia Vermillion,
    dau. of Richard                                          1/22/59-2
Barry, Geo. E., 12 Jan. 1853, Ellen Emory, dau. of Henry     1/13/53-2
Barry, John J., 1 Jan. 1856, Sarah Elvira Brown              1/ 3/56-2
Barry, Llewellyn F., 14 Oct. 1858, Annie Harrison, dau. of
    Joseph, Jr.; corrected copy                             10/19/58-2
Bartholomee, John Julius, 2 Jan. 1855, Rosalie Bruhns        1/18/55-2
Bartholow, B. F., 8 Sept. 1859, Carrie R. Hay                9/12/59-2
Bartholow, J. Presley, 14 Feb. 1856, Belle Phillips          2/19/56-2
Bartholow, Lycurgus L., 22 Jan. 1856, Avis E. Denning, dau.
    of (Col.) John N.                                        1/25/56-2
Bartholow, N. J., 4 Aug. 1853, Sarah A. Phelps               8/ 6/53-2
Barthslick, Jonathan W., 2 Nov. 1853, Mary E. Hillery       11/ 3/53-2
Bartlett, Charles W., 25 Dec. 1859, (Mrs.) Margaret Newhouse,
    dau. of Jacob Penn                                      12/29/59-2
Bartlett, J. M., 21 Feb. 1856, Mary A. Inloes                3/ 1/56-2
Bartlett, James, 21 Nov. 1855, (Mrs.) Fannie A. Van Rossum,
    dau. of George Whitten                                  12/22/55-2
Barton, Jacob, 20 Feb. 1853, Martha Ann Stone                3/ 3/53-2
Barton, James, 30 May 1854, Mary E. Wiley                    6/16/54-2
Barton, James L., 29 Sept. 1853, Julia A. Pentz, dau. of
    Daniel                                                  10/ 3/53-2
Barton, John W., 1 Aug. 1859, Caroline V. Hardesty           8/ 2/59-2
Barton, Lazarus, 31 July 1853, Hannah Ann German             8/ 4/53-2
Barton, William L., 23 Dec. 1855, Fanny Kerner               1/ 3/56-2
Barton, Wm. H., 5 Aug. 1856, Eliza McGowan, dau. of John     8/ 7/56-2
Baseman, John, 28 Dec. 1852, Amelia A. E. Hipsley           12/31/52-2
Baseman, Vachel W., 4 Oct. 1853, Ann Cockey Brown, dau. of
    (Hon.) Elias                                            10/20/53-2
Basil, John, 9 Dec. 1852, Ann E. Covel                      12/11/52-2
Basil, John, Jr., 13 Jan. 1853, Julia Maria Phelps           1/20/53-2
Basman, Isaac H. (Capt.), 10 Sept. 1856, Ann H. Skillman,
    dau. of Robert and Naomi                                10/22/56-2
Bassett, John B., 19 Feb. 1852, Sarah Elizabeth Budd         2/21/52-2
Bastable, Chas., 2 Jan. 1853, Mary Magin                     1/ 8/53-2
Bastianelli, E. A., 10 Aug. 1859, Rosebelle Atwell, dau. of
    (Capt.) Benj.                                            8/13/59-2
Bastianelli, Gaetano, 13 Apr. 1858, Ady P. Masters           5/ 1/58-2
Bastien, Emile, 31 Aug. 1856, Mary Theresa Wheelan           9/ 5/56-2
Batchelor, Nathaniel, 28 May 1854, Eliza Jane Walker         5/15/58-2
Batchelor, Sam'l. K., 3 Oct. 1852, Hester Ann Forest        10/ 5/52-2
Batchelor, Wallace, 24 Apr. 1855, Mary Beatty                4/26/55-2
Bateman, Benj. M. G., 23 Oct. 1854, Laura Ann Tarr          10/25/54-2
Bateman, James H., 25 Aug. 1859, Sydndey A. Shipley          8/30/59-2
Bateman, James J., 14 Aug. 1856, Sarah A. Blair, dau. of
    Samuel                                                   8/16/56-2
Bateman, James O., 24 Feb. 1853, Sarah Elizabeth Cowman      4/ 7/53-2
Bateman, John *, 5 May 1852, Mary Rafetay                    5/ 6/52-2
Bateman, John, 13 Apr. 1857, Susan Young                     4/14/57-2
```

Bateman, John L., 8 Apr. 1855, Eliza A. Haslitt   4/11/55-2
Bateman, William, 14 Dec. 1859, Sarah J. Baker   12/17/59-2
Bates, Frederick, 6 Oct. 1853, Caroline V. Lewis, dau. of
    John   10/ 7/53-2
Bates, James, 28 July 1851, Julia Hockley   7/30/51-2
Bates, John E., 6 Jan. 1852, Charlotte J. Williams, dau. of
    Geo.   1/ 9/52-2
Battee, John, 9 Aug. 1852, Sarah A. Irons, dau. of Robert   8/10/52-2
Battee, Richard R., 16 Feb. 1854, Carrie E. L. Cochran, dau. of
    Charles, Jr.   2/17/54-2
Battees, John, 18 Oct. 1855, (Mrs.) Ann E. Evans   10/20/55-2
Battinger, William, 2 Nov. 1858, Elizabeth A. Seltzer   11/ 5/58-2
Batty, John E. L., 24 Jan. 1854, Elizabeth Francis Childs   1/31/54-2
Baughman, F. M., 28 May 1857, Eva Shaw Leader, dau. of
    Senary   5/29/57-2
Baughman, Joseph, 14 Oct. 1852, Susan Stuart   10/16/52-2
Baulinn, James G., 5 July 1855, Elizabeth Whilington   7/ 6/55-2
Baumann, Louis, 8 Apr. 1858, Catharine Buschmann   4/10/58-2
Baumgardner, William J., 6 Aug. 1857, Elizabeth Madden   9/ 4/57-2
Baumgart, Joseph, 13 June 1853, Rosalia Michael   6/26/53-2
Baumgarten, Julius, 20 Feb. 1859, Elizabeth Hexter   2/22/59-2
Bavard, James, 14 Aug. 1851, J. Street   8/16/51-2
Bawden, John H., 13 Mar. 1852, Mary Ann Robosson   3/23/52-2
Baxley, William H., 31 May 1853, M. Jane Evins   6/ 3/53-2
Baxter, James R., 24 Feb. 1856, Eliza J. Whiteside   2/27/56-2
Baxter, Jos. V., 20 Feb. 1851, Anna R. Walker   2/22/51-2
Bay, George Edward, 6 Jan. 1852, Elmira Montairdon   1/ 8/52-2
Bay, George Edward, 6 Jan. 1852, Elmira Montandon; corrected
    copy   1/ 9/52-2
Bayard, Richard B., 20 Dec. 1860, Ellen G. Howard   12/22/60-2
Bayer, A., 3 Feb. 1853, Virginia Sulzbach, dau. of Peter   2/16/53-2
Bayless, Wm. J., 20 Oct. 1858, Mary E. Sanderson, dau. of
    Geo. H.   10/22/58-2
Bayley, J., 3 May 1855, Emily J. Grinage   10/ 1/55-2
Bayley, Robert P., 6 Dec. 1859, Emma L. Dowing   12/10/59-2
Baylies, James L., 1 Nov. 1855, Sallie M. Dutton, dau. of
    (Col.) John   11/ 3/55-3
Baylor, C. G., 6 Jan. 1853, Louisa D. Wadeworth   1/10/53-2
Bayly, George R., 16 Oct. 1854, Catharine Railey   11/13/54-2
Bayly, James F., 21 June 1860, Carrie E. Polkinhorn, dau. of
    Charles   6/22/60-2
Bayly, Philip R., 13 Nov. 1859, Mary J. Beers, dau. of
    Thomas   11/16/59-2
Baymond, John A., 8 Apr. 1851, Ann Steel   4/ 8/51-2
Bayne, Alexander, 9 Dec. 1858, Charlotte Ann Heard   12/13/58-2
Bayne, William C., 22 Sept. 1857, Mary S. Pembroke   9/25/57-2
Baynes, John H., 29 Mar. 1860, Beulah J. McCay, dau. of Jas.;
    3/30/60-2   3/31/60-2
Beach, Columbus, 25 Aug. 1858, Caroline Starr   8/28/58-2
Beach, George E., 9 Feb. 1854, Mary E. Williams   2/13/54-2
Beach, Samuel, 10 June 1853, Harriet Henderson, dau. of
    David   7/ 8/53-2
Beacham, George P., 24 Feb. 1852, Elizabeth Searley   3/ 3/52-2
Beacham, James, 19 Apr. 1853, Eurath Ensor   4/21/53-2
Beacham, Jas. A., 10 Dec. 1851, Rosalba E. Foxwell   12/12/51-2
Beadenkopf, John, 7 Oct. 1852, Helena Daugherty   10/12/52-2
Beal, B. Frank, 18 Oct. 1855, Carrie E. Streeter, dau. of
    S. F.   10/19/55-2
Beal, S. M., 18 July 1860, Lida H. Milburn   7/23/60-2
Beale, William T. B., 1 Jan. 1854, Sarah A. Hurton   1/ 3/54-2
Beall, Richard J. T., 31 Mar. 1859, Annie E. Little   4/ 6/59-2
Beall, W. Francis (Dr.), 6 Dec. 1855, Harriet Annie Yearley 12/11/55-2
Bealmer, Thomas, 18 Jan. 1855, Julia A. R. Hoover   1/25/55-2
Beam, George F., 8 Jan. 1857, Susannah M. Shurtz, dau. of
    W. D.   1/10/57-2

Beam, Jacob, Jr., 17 Nov. 1853, Sarah Jane (?)-che-(?)-nu,
    dau. of Bernard   11/19/53-2
Beam, Lewis Henry, 27 Jan. 1858, Anne Bebecca Amey   2/ 2/58-2
Beam, Lewis Henry, 27 Jan. 1858, Anne Rebecca Amey; corrected
    copy   2/ 3/58-2
Beaman, W. A., 17 Mar. 1858, Laura H. Bradenbaugh   4/ 2/58-2
Bean, George L., 22 Dec. 1856, Emily L. Armitage   12/24/56-2
Bean, J. Henry, 26 Apr. 1855, Kate Kelley, dau. of Wm. P. 4/28/55-2
Bean, Jos. H., 22 May 1860, Lottie O. Byrne   5/24/60-2
Bean, Joseph A., 12 May 1856, Mary E. Armstrong   6/ 2/56-2
Bean, R. J., 19 Aug. 1857, Fannie J. Trowbridge   8/21/57-2
Bean, R. M., 17 Dec. 1856, Sarah E. Wilson   12/20/56-2
Beane, William H., 20 July 1858, Elizabeth A. Holland   7/28/58-2
Beans, Elias H., 1 Apr. 1852, Susan N. Cunningham, dau. of
    Daniel M.   4/ 5/52-2
Beard, Edward H. (Capt.), 28 Apr. 1852, Ada E. Pamburn, dau.
    of P. C.   7/ 2/52-2
Beard, G. Washington, 2 Dec. 1858, Annie V. Buckingham   12/ 6/58-2
Beard, George V., 15 Feb. 1859, Mary Moone   2/18/59-2
Beard, J. W. (Dr.), 23 Dec. 1858, Louisa G. Mezick   12/24/58-2
Beard, Robert H., 27 Dec. 1853, Ann E. Copes   12/30/53-2
Beardsley, Wm. H., 19 Sept. 1855, Maria Sophia Schiebler 9/26/55-2
Bearis, George W., 11 Jan. 1855, Elmira Crumbie   1/20/55-2
Beasley, George, 6 Jan. 1853, Eliza Ann Hood   1/ 7/53-2
Beatley, Nathaniel R., 4 June 1854, Julian Tinker   6/ 9/54-2
Beatty, Chas. W., 4 Jan. 1854, Augusta M. Schwartz, dau. of
    (Dr.) A. J.   1/ 7/54-2
Beatty, Geo. W., 3 June 1856, Mary George Heeter   6/ 5/56-2
Beatty, James, 16 Nov. 1852, Mary Louisa Goodwin, dau. of
    Lyde   11/17/52-2
Beatty, Michael, 29 Apr. 1851, Mary O'Masterson   5/ 1/51-2
Beatty, Wm. Hamilton, 11 July 1855, Amelia Ann Slater, dau.
    of Henry   7/12/55-2
Beaty, John T., 8 July 1856, Sarah E. Stevens   7/15/56-2
Beaty, William, 19 Aug. 1857, Susan Quinne   8/22/57-2
Beauchamp, Robert S., 6 June 1854, Elenora C. Mulliken   6/10/54-2
Beaumont, Elias, 31 Oct. 1854, (Mrs.) Martha M. Holland, dau.
    of Thomas Ford   11/ 2/54-2
Beaumont, John A., 7 Oct. 1851, Ann E. Stelle   10/ 9/51-2
Bechtol, Samuel; no date given, Mary P. Wickes, dau. of
    (Rev.) Wm.   10/ 7/52-2
Beck, Francis, 13 Feb. 1859, Martha W. Laverty   3/ 9/59-2
Beck, Frederick, 30 Jan. 1859, Anna M. Doll; corrected copy 2/10/59-2
Beck, Frederick, 30 Jan. 1859, Ella Mary Doll   2/ 9/59-2
Beck, Frederick W., 22 Feb. 1854, Emma Frances Munroe, dau. of
    Nathaniel   2/23/54-2
Beck, John, 12 July 1854, Lizzie M. Trimble   7/13/54-2
Beckenbaugh, G. W., 23 Oct. 1860, Mollie A. Kline, dau. of
    Andrew   10/26/60-2
Beckert, George M., 13 June 1854, Mary Elenora Hustew   6/20/54-2
Beckhaus, Joseph, 19 Apr. 1860, (Mrs.) Annie G. Snyder   4/25/60-2
Beckley, Daniel, 27 Jan. 1852, Mary Ann C. Zouck   1/29/52-2
Beckwith, David G., 24 Nov. 1853, Mary A. Edgarton   11/29/53-2
Beckwith, John (Rev.), 29 Sept. 1857, Ella Brockenbrough,
    dau. of John F.   10/ 7/57-2
Bedford, Charles Henry D., 27 Feb. 1855, Margaret Greewood 2/28/55-2
Bee, Jas., 24 July 1860, S. R. Badger   7/28/60-2
Beefelt, Edward, 24 Nov. 1858, Rosa T. Schinkel   12/ 8/58-2
Beeler, L. F., 3 Feb. 1851, Amanda Fillus   2/ 6/51-2
Beeman, T. J., 11 Apr. 1854, Mary L. Bolton   4/17/54-2
Begnell, John H., 21 Mar. 1859, Emma D. Mannar   4/ 5/59-2
Behrens, Wm. H., 17 May 1852, Eliza Jane McCann   5/19/52-2
Beichell, Philip P., 19 Oct. 1852, Margaret Ann Murray   10/29/52-2
Beird, Henry W., 15 Nov. 1853, Georgeanna E. B. Cate, dau. of
    Amon   11/16/53-2

Belknap, Edward, 19 Oct. 1857, Ellen C. Soran, dau. of
    Charles   11/16/57-2
Bell, Alexander, 20 Dec. 1856, Margaret Boyd   12/29/56-2
Bell, Edward, 2 July 1855, Martha Ann Pindell, dau. of
    (Col.) Thomas   7/ 6/55-2
Bell, Geo. W. C., 20 Oct. 1859, Mary E. A. Maguire   10/21/59-2
Bell, George, 25 Nov. 1852, Emeline Cunningham   11/27/52-2
Bell, H., 8 Apr. 1857, Lizzie A. Small, dau. of (Capt.) Wm.   4/10/57-2
Bell, Hamilton, 6 Dec. 1853, Mary E. Greenwood, dau. of Wm. S.   12/ 8/53-2
Bell, Henry G., 19 Jan. 1860, Leonora Harris   1/23/60-2
Bell, James J., 3 July 1853, Fanny Marshall   7/ 9/53-2
Bell, John, 21 June 1860, Jane Stewart   6/23/60-2
Bell, John H., 6 Sept. 1857, Harriet A. Stembler   9/ 7/57-2
Bell, John W., 24 Jan. 1860, (Mrs.) Elizabeth A. Burford   1/27/60-2
Bell, John W., 18 Oct. 1860, Annie M. Scott   10/20/60-2
Bell, McHenry, 26 May 1853, Ellen Mitchell   5/28/53-2
Bell, Seneca P., 9 Sept. 1852, Susannah W. Seymour   9/11/52-2
Bell, Thomas H.; no date given, Julia A. Hubbard   2/12/53-2
Bell, William, 8 Dec. 1853, Nannie Thomas, dau. of William G.   12/13/53-2
Bell, William W., 24 Sept. 1855, Carie Bandell; corrected copy   10/ 3/55-2
Bell, Winfield Scott, 26 Aug. 1852, Estelle Hewitt, dau. of
    (Prof.) J. H.   8/27/52-2
Belt, John T., 4 Nov. 1860, Mary E. Ayers   11/ 6/60-2
Belt, Solomon, 10 Feb. 1853, Maria Fowler   2/11/53-2
Belt, William H., 3 Apr. 1860, Mary A. C. Brown, dau. of James   4/ 6/60-2
Bembury, James H., 16 Jan. 1855, Anna E. Lloyd, dau. of Wilson   1/19/55-2
Bender, Samuel, 3 May 1853, Mary Elizabeth Bechler   5/ 5/53-2
Benjamin, Geo. A., 13 May 1856, Elizabeth J. Kilmond   5/23/56-2
Benjamin, Solomon, 3 Feb. 1852, Rosa Myers, dau. of Aaron   2/10/52-2
Benn, Jacob, 7 July 1853, Alice Jeffries   7/ 8/53-2
Bennect, Thomas, 29 June 1854, Elizabeth C. Abrahams   7/ 3/54-2
Benner, Ferdinand C., 1 June 1856, Emma Sterling   6/14/56-2
Benner, Thaddeus S., 9 May 1854, Elizabeth A. McCain   5/13/54-2
Benner, Thaddeus S., 27 Aug. 1857, Margaret Walker   10/ 2/57-2
Bennert, Robert, 15 May 1860, Caroline Braun   5/18/60-2
Bennet, Adolphus, 13 July 1854, Fannie Barker   7/20/54-2
Bennet, Joshua V., 16 June 1859, Anna Smith   6/18/59-2
Bennet, P. Henry, 27 May 1851, Sophia Farnham, dau. of
    William   7/19/51-2
Bennett, Alexander, 21 Apr. 1857, Annie Coram   4/24/57-2
Bennett, Alfred, 14 Sept. 1852, Marianna Thompson, dau. of
    John   9/17/52-2
Bennett, B. C. S., 23 June 1853, Elizabeth A. Anderson   6/30/53-2
Bennett, D. Custis, 27 June 1853, Blanche E. Richardson   7/ 2/53-2
Bennett, Elisha H., 14 Feb. 1854, Mary Ellen Bennett, dau. of
    Wesley   2/17/54-2
Bennett, Enoch, 24 Nov. 1853, Willie C. Wedebauch   11/26/53-2
Bennett, Geo. W., 13 Feb. 1855, Annie L. Biddle, dau. of
    Noble   2/17/55-2
Bennett, George J., 14 Feb. 1854, Agnes Mary De Beet   2/16/54-2
Bennett, J. Irving, 29 Oct. 1860, Annie E. Joynes   11/ 7/60-2
Bennett, J. R., 22 Nov. 1855, Letitia E. Solomon   11/27/55-2
Bennett, Jesse Lee, 10 Apr. 1851, Naomi Baseman, dau. of
    John   4/21/51-2
Bennett, John H., 28 Nov. 1860, Helen A. Shannon, dau. of
    Samuel   12/ 5/60-2
Bennett, Joshua, 1 May 1853, Licinia Scofield   5/20/53-2
Bennett, Livingston M., 7 June 1853, Mary A. Lewin   6/10/53-2
Bennett, R. A. (Capt.), 5 July 1860, Lizzie Bates   7/12/60-2
Bennett, Robert H., 28 Jan. 1851, Matilda D. Norris   1/30/51-2
Bennett, Thomas S., 10 Sept. 1856, Mary E. Creamer, dau. of
    David   9/12/56-2
Bennett, William, 22 Oct. 1857, Catherine Carter   10/27/57-2
Bennett, William, 7 July 1858, Mary Elizabeth Bogle   7/10/58-2

Benny, John, 6 Jan. 1851, Laura L. Webb, dau. of John and
    Ann   1/ 8/51-2
Benny, Wm. O., 30 Apr. 1856, Rose Ann Thomas   5/ 5/56-2
Benoid, George W., 10 Aug. 1851, Isabella Magraw   8/13/51-2
Benson, B. F. (Rev.), 8 Mar. 1860, Mittie E. Thomas, dau. of
    John B.   3/16/60-2
Benson, Frank A., 10 Jan. 1856, Ada A. Skinner, dau. of
    William C.   3/20/56-2
Benson, Geo. W. (Dr.), 30 Aug. 1855, Susie E. Dexter   9/ 1/55-2
Benson, George C., 2 Apr. 1858, Margaret A. Harrison   4/ 7/58-2
Benson, John P., 30 Oct. 1856, Sarah L. Gorsuch   11/ 4/56-2
Benson, Joshua, 30 Oct. 1856, Hannah A. Miller   11/ 4/56-2
Benson, Robert P., 12 July 1853, Margaret O. Carter, dau. of
    Jesse   7/14/53-2
Benson, Rufus, 30 Oct. 1851, Catharine S. Harman   11/ 1/51-2
Benson, Samuel B., 13 Nov. 1853, Mary A. Hibble   11/15/53-2
Benson, Samuel M., 12 Dec. 1855, Louisa W. Dorsey   12/18/55-2
Benson, William, 11 Nov. 1851, Mary Amelia Rinzidore   11/12/51-2
Benson, William P., 23 Apr. 1858, Kate J. Ford   9/ 9/58-2
Benthall, Thos. W., 20 Mar. 1859, Amelia J. McCormick   10/17/59-2
Benthall, Wm. McR., 2 Apr. 1857, Sophia F. Mitchell   4/ 3/57-2
Bentley, John T., 10 Apr. 1851, Catherine Mills   4/12/51-2
Bentley, Joseph, 20 Oct. 1857, (Mrs.) Julia A. Miller   11/ 5/57-2
Benton, Francis, 7 Apr. 1857, Charlotte Williams   4/10/57-2
Bentz, Andrew, 22 Mar. 1853, Eliza Jane O'Neal   3/26/53-2
Bentz, Andrew, 24 Sept. 1856, Kate Kerner   9/26/56-2
Bentz, J. Henderson, 8 June 1853, Harriet B. Beckett, dau. of
    (Dr.) E. M.   6/26/53-2
Benzell, Henry J., 15 Dec. 1857, Rebecca Bruen   12/16/57-2
Benzinger, Fredk. F., 16 Jan. 1854, Rose C. Finknaur   1/17/54-2
Beown, William A., 17 Feb. 1853, Emily B. Pearce   3/ 7/53-2
Bergee, John, 13 Sept. 1860, Maggie Miller   9/21/60-2
Berger, Alexander, J., 2 May 1854, Mary Anne Allport   5/ 5/54-2
Berger, John, 12 May 1857, Maria McIlvain   5/13/57-2
Berger, Joseph B., 26 Feb. 1852, Aney Riley   3/ 1/52-2
Berkley, Chas. W., 25 Sept. 1853, Mary Ann Shannon   9/28/53-2
Bernard, William, 30 Aug. 1855, Sallie E. Phoebus   9/21/55-2
Berrell, Samuel, 27 Dec. 1855, Clara A. Vernetson, dau. of
    William   1/ 2/56-2
Berry, Charles C., 18 Mar. 1856, Sarah E. Prather   3/25/56-2
Berry, Charles W., 23 Nov. 1856, Mary A. McComas   11/24/56-2
Berry, Edward, 3 Nov. 1859, Fannie Mullen   11/ 5/59-2
Berry, Henry O., 6 Nov. 1855, Susan Brady   11/24/55-2
Berry, J. Thomas, 20 Apr. 1854, Belle C. Burns, dau. of
    Francis   4/22/54-2
Berry, Jasper M., 13 Feb. 1854, Lydia W. Emory   2/15/54-2
Berry, Peter, 29 Apr. 1851, Rosa Bradley   5/ 5/51-2
Berry, Richard, 21 Mar. 1858, Lucretia Ann Bond   3/22/58-2
Berry, Thomas S., 4 Oct. 1855, Elizabeth Haner, dau. of
    Charles and Sarah   10/ 6/55-2
Berry, William, 1 July 1857, Lydia Matthews   8/ 4/57-2
Berthy, Patrick, 28 Sept. 1853, Catharine Branan   9/30/53-2
Best, John Henry, 19 Aug. 1851, Mary Ann Rittenhouse   8/21/51-2
Bestor, Norman L., 10 Jan. 1854, Willie J. Childs   1/11/54-2
Betton, Wm. T., 23 Sept. 1852, Sophia Horsey, dau. of
    Thomas H.   9/25/52-2
Betts, John H., 31 July 1851, Ellenora Thomas   8/ 7/51-2
Betts, Thos. J., 18 Nov. 1858, Mary H. Duvall   11/19/58-2
Betts, William, 10 June 1853, Annie E. Ballentine   6/16/53-2
Beufort, Melville P., 30 Jan. 1851, Margaretta A. Townsend,
    dau. of Thos. B.   2/ 1/51-2
Bevan, John S., 27 Jan. 1857, Jane M. Fitzpatrick   3/11/57-2
Bevan, Samuel, 3 May 1859, Jane Eliza Roche   5/ 5/59-2
Bevan, Thomas H., 1 Mar. 1858, (Mrs.) Ann Lawson   3/10/58-2
Bevan, William J., 10 July 1851, Fanny Fuss   7/14/51-2

```
Bevans, John T., 1 Jan. 1852, Mary Jane Hunter                  1/ 5/52-2
Bevans, Reuben A. L., 5 Feb. 1852, Mariette Hall                2/ 7/52-2
Bevans, William, 3 Apr. 1860, Kate Wilsey                       4/ 5/60-2
Bevard, Wakeman, 24 Feb. 1853, Elizabeth Street                 2/25/53-2
Bever, James W., 16 Nov. 1851, Sarah Jane Goughf               11/18/51-2
Beveridge, Daniel W., 26 May 1859, Rebecca C. Sheeler, dau.
    of John                                                     5/28/59-2
Beveridge, John, 5 Sept. 1855, Lizzie Williamson, dau. of
    Andrew                                                      9/18/55-2
Beyer, Charles A.; no date given, Mary A. Carter               10/ 1/55-2
Beyer, Frederick A., 16 Nov. 1856, (Mrs.) Catherine E. Roeder  11/25/56-2
Beyer, Samuel B., 8 May 1851, Sarah A. Reeside, dau. of James   5/12/51-2
Biass, John W., 30 Jan. 1851, Mary Frances Sherman        •     2/ 3/51-2
Bibby, Edward A., 22 May 1860, Eliza Aldridge, dau. of
    Andrew S.                                                   5/25/60-2
Bibby, J. Monroe, 27 Oct. 1856, Elizabeth K. Heiskell          10/30/56-2
Bicketts, David F., 30 Nov. 1854, Mary A. Billmyer             12/ 2/54-2
Biddison, Samuel J., 15 Nov. 1855, Kate Thearle               11/17/55-2
Biddle, Joseph, 2 Jan. 1851, Mary Elizabeth Keys                1/ 4/51-2
Biddle, William H., 13 Oct. 1857, Rebecca J. Richardson        11/18/57-2
Biden, Joseph, 23 Dec. 1852, Lydia Ann Randel                 12/25/52-2
Biden, Joseph J., 23 Dec. 1852, Lydia A. Randle, dau. of
    Thomas H.; corrected copy                                 12/30/52-2
Biede, Adolphus H., 24 June 1852, Charlotte Mund                6/25/52-2
Bier, George H., 1 July 1857, Josephine V. Stone, dau. of
    (Lt.) John P. R.                                            7/ 3/57-2
Biggs, James, 11 Jan. 1853, Sarah Louisa Hasson                 1/12/53-2
Biggs, James, 22 Oct. 1855, Josephine Smith                   10/26/55-2
Billmard, Michael J., 16 Oct. 1859, Sarah J. Nagle             4/11/60-2
Billups, Joseph R., 12 Apr. 1853, Rebecca L. Richardson        4/13/53-2
Binnix, Geo. W., 20 Apr. 1851, Lavenia A. High                 4/22/51-2
Binnix, Louis D., 17 July 1859, Ellen R. Stitcher              8/25/59-2
Binnix, Samuel George, 8 July 1852, Julia A. Walmbsly          7/10/52-2
Birchett, Robert D., 23 Sept. 1858, Mary E. Ha-(?)-f, dau. of
    Lewis L. and Barbery                                       9/30/58-2
Birckhead, Rich'd. S. W., 6 Apr. 1852, Margaret J. Smith       4/13/52-2
Birckhead, Samuel, 20 Aug. 1857, Elizabeth A. Swormstede       8/21/57-2
Birckhead, William H., 14 Dec. 1859, Elizabeth E. Dowell      12/17/59-2
Bird, Jacob W., Jr., 12 Nov. 1851, Sally Annabella Ditty       11/13/51-2
Bird, John W. C., 25 Nov. 1852, Mary Elizabeth Sanders         11/29/52-2
Bird, Joseph A., 9 Nov. 1858, Judith E. Eubank                 11/11/58-2
Bird, Odeon J., 13 Aug. 1853, Mary H. Blandel                  8/17/53-2
Bird, Samuel R., 5 June 1851, Mary E. Law, dau. of Smith        6/ 7/51-2
Bird, Stephen, 5 Nov. 1851, Mary Scrivener                     11/ 6/51-2
Bird, Thos., 25 Nov. 1852, Fanny Smith                         11/27/52-2
Bird, William, 27 Oct. 1855, Susan Bird                        10/31/55-2
Birely, George K., 13 Dec. 1859, Annie Schley, dau. of
    (Col.) Edwd.                                               12/14/59-2
Birely, John Thomas, 10 Jan. 1856, Eliza Jane Gaylord          1/15/56-2
Birely, John Thos., 14 Oct. 1860, Ann Eliza Fee               10/22/60-2
Birmingham, Cain, 17 Jan. 1854, Mary O'Tool                    1/20/54-2
Birmingham, Jas. E., 10 July 1856, Laura V. Richter;
    corrected copy                                            11/ 8/56-2
Birmingham, Jas. E., 10 July 1856, Laura Y. Richter           11/ 5/56-2
Birmingham, Wm. Totten, 8 Mar. 1859, Sarah H. Sheeler          3/ 9/59-2
Birthistle, Patrick, 25 Apr. 1852, Maria Byrne                 5/ 6/52-2
Biscoe, James A., 15 June 1858, Caroline E. Smith              6/17/58-2
Biscoe, John W., 18 Sept. 1853, Henrietta V. Blackiston        9/19/53-2
Bishop, Charles R., 8 Nov. 1860, Lizzie A. Bird               11/19/60-2
Bishop, Geo. W., Jr., 25 Nov. 1857, Anne Gaskins              11/28/57-2
Bishop, Nicholas, 1 May 1856, Eliza Clark                      5/ 3/56-2
Bishop, Nicholas, 12 June 1860, Mary Nichols                   6/14/60-2
Bishop, Robert F., 7 Sept. 1854, Ann Domaly                    9/12/54-2
Bishop, W. T., 4 July 1860, Sarah E. German                    7/10/60-2
Bitzel, Martin, 20 Oct. 1856, Elizabeth Baker                 10/23/56-2
```

Bitzel, William, 24 Mar. 1854, Ernestine Bloomer   3/25/54-2
Bitzer, Franklan, 28 Dec. 1858, Lydia Howard   12/30/58-2
Bixby, John C., 16 Oct. 1854, Elizabeth E. Worthington;
   10/17/54-2   10/18/54-2
Black, Emanuel, 24 Apr. 1853, Rebecca Lippy   4/26/53-2
Black, H. J., 21 Sept. 1858, Lethe F. Hawkins   10/ 1/58-2
Black, Henry, 11 Nov. 1852, Margaret Curll   11/15/52-2
Black, J. N., 1 Jan. 1856, Lizzie C. Ewing   1/19/56-2
Black, James Henry, 11 Oct. 1855, Henrietta Gates   10/18/55-2
Black, John F., 7 June 1857, (Mrs.) Sarah A. Q. Mask   6/ 9/57-2
Black, Lewis H., 5 July 1860, Anna Maria Downes   7/ 7/60-2
Black, Lewis W., 31 July 1859, Nora E. Peregoy   9/29/59-2
Black, William D., 5 July 1855, Adeline Virginia Wellslager   7/ 9/55-2
Black, William K., 27 May 1851, Catharine Thompson   5/30/51-2
Blackburn, John W., 8 May 1860, Nancy Jane Barnes   5/ 9/60-2
Blacklar, Charles R., 12 Jan. 1853, Mary Alice Miller   1/14/53-2
Blackston, Wm., 28 Apr. 1859, Jane Hamer   5/ 5/59-2
Blackwell, Wm. H., 18 June 1856, J. Pinckney Noel   6/19/56-2
Blair, C. E.; no date given, F. J. Mitchell, dau. of James;
   corrected copy   9/26/60-2
Blair, Chas. E., 16 Nov. 1855, Lizzie A. Adams   11/28/55-2
Blair, E. E.; no date given, F. J. Mitchell, dau. of James   9/25/60-2
Blake, George A., 26 May 1856, Harriet Griggs, dau. of Wm.   7/ 3/56-2
Blake, John C., 5 Nov. 1858, Mary E. Tilghman   11/ 6/58-2
Blake, Joseph, 24 Nov. 1853, Maria Smith, dau. of John K.   11/26/53-2
Blake, Solomon, 14 Dec. 1857, Mary Ann Brown   1/16/58-2
Blake, Thomas, 27 Dec. 1860, Mary Matilda Tyler   12/29/60-2
Blakemore, George B., 28 Dec. 1852, Clara A. Gist   12/30/52-2
Blakeslee, Abram, 9 Sept. 1856, (Mrs.) M. Virginia Lovett   9/11/56-2
Blamire, John E., 9 Nov. 1857, Sarah Ann McElwee   11/11/57-2
Blanch, James, 24 July 1854, Ann Appleby   7/25/54-2
Blanch, James C., 30 Oct. 1851, Susan Underwood   11/ 3/51-2
Blaney, Charles E., 1 Oct. 1860, Martha F. Loane   10/ 6/60-2
Blaney, John T., 9 May 1853, Amanda Mumma, dau. of Saml.   5/11/53-2
Blatchley, Peter, 13 Dec. 1855, Priscilla Dogged   12/15/55-2
Blessing, G. W., 16 Sept. 1851, Minerva Homrick   9/18/51-2
Blessings, Daniel, 8 May 1851, Mary Ann Egleston   5/10/51-2
Blick, Jas. C., 7 Oct. 1852, Elizabeth Marcella Bowen, dau. of
   Wilkes   10/ 9/52-2
Blick, William, 12 May 1851, Elizabeth Ann Curtian   5/13/51-2
Blinsinger, George F., 6 Sept. 1851, Mary Ann Daugherty, dau.
   of James   9/ 9/51-2
Blizzard, John, 18 May 1857, Eliza Sheppard   11/20/57-2
Blizzard, John R., 25 June 1860, Laura J. Chambers   6/28/60-2
Blogg, Edw. N. S., 3 Aug. 1853, Charlotte C. Thayer, dau.
   of C.   8/12/53-2
Blom, M. G. (Dr.), 1 Nov. 1852, Rosina Eytinge, dau. of Simon   11/ 3/52-2
Blondhaem, Henry, 27 Jan. 1856, Olevia Anker   1/29/56-2
Blondhaem, Samuel, 23 Mar. 1856, Caroline Weinman, dau. of
   Emanuel   3/26/56-2
Bloomenour, Henry, 21 Apr. 1859, Anna M. Smith, dau. of James   4/26/59-2
Bloomer, Frederick, 29 July 1858, Eliza H. Solomon   8/ 1/58-2
Bloomer, John W., Jr., 10 Jan. 1860, Cordelia Howard   3/10/60-2
Blottenberger, George W., 22 Sept. 1853, Temperance Rebecca
   Jones   9/29/53-2
Bloxham, William P., 10 June 1858, Mary Ellen Mitchell   6/12/58-2
Bloxom, George W., 20 May 1856, Sarah E. Andrews   5/22/56-2
Blum, G., 7 June 1860, Anny Hechinger   6/ 9/60-2
Blundon, Wm. H., 1 May 1851, Harriet E. D. David   5/ 3/51-2
Boardley, John, 28 Oct. 1858, Mary Jane Tasco   10/30/58-2
Boardman, Sidney R., 10 Nov. 1852, Margaret J. Morrow   11/17/52-2
Boarman, Robt., 16 Jan. 1854, Rebecca Askey, dau. of James   1/17/54-2
Boarman, Wm. Alfred, 16 June 1858, Amanda Deacon   7/10/58-2
Bobart, Wm. H., 6 June 1855, Mary L. Mears, dau. of William   6/20/55-2

Bockmiller, William P., 9 July 1857, Mary Emily Bunting   7/14/57-2
Bocrie, Charles, 26 Dec. 1850, Georgie James, dau. of John   1/ 1/51-2
Boden, Wm., 16 May 1852, Margaret Jane Boden, dau. of Frances   7/23/52-2
Bodensick, Chas. F., 8 Jan. 1856, Lucy A. Lippey   1/12/56-2
Bodensick, David A., 21 Dec. 1857, Mary E. Jones   12/24/57-2
Bodensick, George H., 7 Aug. 1853, Mary Ann Woodward   8/23/53-2
Bodin, Edwd. L., 18 Dec. 1860, Harriet B. Porter   12/20/60-2
Boehm, John L., 18 May 1857, Catharine Geddes   5/20/57-2
Boernstein, August S., 12 Jan. 1854, Frederika Behlen   1/14/54-2
Boesche, Herman Louis, 21 Oct. 1860, (Mrs.) Johanna Emily
     Augusta Schaefer   10/23/60-2
Boettinger, Christian, 1 Jan. 1857, Antonia Doll   1/ 3/57-2
Boggs, John W., 2 May 1854, Hester A. Wilson   5/ 5/54-2
Boggs, Wm., 11 Nov. 1851, Henrietta Sewel   11/13/51-2
Bogue, John J., 20 Jan. 1853, E. R. Donnelly   1/22/53-2
Bohen, George T., 17 July 1852, Josephine Lyon   2/ 2/53-2
Bohmer, Henry, 4 Oct. 1859, Helene Hesselbein   10/ 5/59-2
Bohs, John, 15 Mar. 1858, Agnes Dettling   3/16/58-2
Bokee, Geo. M., 16 Oct. 1860, Jennie E. Campbell   10/20/60-2
Bokee, William F., 4 Feb. 1857, Mary A. McGrane   2/ 6/57-2
Bokee, Wm. H., 10 Sept. 1860, Mary Amelia Parker   9/18/60-2
Boland, James, 2 May 1858, Rose Fitzpatrick, dau. of Andrew   6/ 7/58-2
Boldeman, Theodore, 22 Sept. 1851, Bertha Sondheimer   9/26/51-2
Bolgiano, John C., 9 Sept. 1858, Sarah A. Bockmiller; corrected
     copy   9/16/58-2
Bolgiano, John C., 9 Sept. 1858, Sarah A. Rockmiller   9/15/58-2
Bolgiano, Joseph A., 3 May 1859, Laura Virginia Hamelin   5/10/59-2
Bolley, George, 9 Aug. 1860, Alice Simms   8/11/60-2
Bollman, Edw'd. H., 2-(?) Aug. 1852, Eliza Jane Smith   8/31/52-2
Bollman, James B., 18 Nov. 1858, Sarah R. Geddes   11/20/58-2
Bollman, James Henry *, 22 Feb. 1857, Sarah Geddes   3/10/57-2
Bolt, Edward L., 19 May 1853, Hannah Townend   5/20/53-2
Bolton, Robert (Rev.), 16 Nov. 1858, Mary A. Allender   11/22/58-2
Bomberger, John H., 3 Mar. 1852, Mary Ann Richards   3/ 9/52-2
Bomberger, John H., 9 Aug. 1859, Catherine Ann Albert   8/16/59-2
Bond, Alexander, 10 Feb. 1853, Mary Bullack   2/11/53-2
Bond, Alexander J., 30 Aug. 1860, Matilda Hindel   9/ 4/60-2
Bond, Alfred, 9 June 1853, Lydia Welsh   6/14/53-2
Bond, Benjamin A., 15 July 1859, Elizabeth McIlvain   8/ 9/59-2
Bond, Charles (Dr.), 13 July 1857, Mary Rodham   1/ 9/58-2
Bond, Elijah, 28 July 1853, Martha Frisby   7/30/53-2
Bond, Emery, 18 Mar. 1851, Ann Elizabeth Gipson   3/20/51-2
Bond, Frank A., 26 Oct. 1859, Landie Webster, dau. of (Capt.)
     John A.   10/31/59-2
Bond, Geo., 13 Jan. 1853, Julia Goodin   1/15/53-2
Bond, Geo. T., 7 Oct. 1852, Margaret Johnston   10/ 9/52-2
Bond, George L., 12 Jan. 1854, Ann E. Livingston, dau. of
     John H.   1/18/54-2
Bond, Hugh Lennox, 16 Jan. 1855, Annie G. Penniman, dau. of
     Wm.   1/20/55-2
Bond, James H., 25 Jan. 1853, Sarah J. George, dau. of
     James B.   1/27/53-2
Bond, John, 11 Sept. 1855, Mary Elizabeth Shaney   9/17/55-2
Bond, John R., 26 June 1855, Virginia D. Morgan, dau. of
     Thos. W.   6/28/55-2
Bond, John W., 16 July 1852, Josephine W. Noyes   9/13/52-2
Bond, Joseph H., 29 May 1855, Melissa A. Fletcher   6/ 6/55-2
Bond, Josiah, 7 Aug. 1853, Catherine Wells   8/10/53-2
Bond, Lorenzo, 15 Jan. 1856, Anne Elizabeth Zorgabble   1/18/56-2
Bond, Michael, 18 Jan. 1855, Mary E. Lane   3/ 6/55-2
Bond, N. J., 22 Sept. 1859, Eliza J. Kimberly   9/24/59-2
Bond, Thomas C., 2 June 1857, M. Virginia Anderson   6/ 5/57-2
Bond, Thomas D., 1 May 1853, Caroline E. Burge   5/ 3/53-2
Bond, Thos., 25 Nov. 1852, Arianna Rankin Tipton, dau. of
     William   12/ 2/52-2

```
Bond, William Lee, 5 June 1851, Margaret Moody                  6/11/51-2
Bond, Wm., 16 Sept. 1852, Mary E. Ellingsworth                  9/23/52-2
Bond, Wm., 22 Dec. 1853, Mary E. Smallwood                      12/28/53-2
Bond, Wm. R., 6 Sept. 1859, Catherine Pearce                    9/ 7/59-2
Bone, Wm., 5 Jan. 1858, (Mrs.) A. L. Brian                      1/11/58-2
Bonine, Thomas W., 12 May 1857, Maria L. Hallar                 5/13/57-2
Bonitz, G. W. Henry, 10 Apr. 1860, Lisette A. Stegner           4/13/60-2
Bonn, Anthony, 14 Sept. 1857, Eliza Dell                        9/19/57-2
Bonn, Daniel W., 5 May 1857, Susan H. Addison                   5/ 7/57-2
Bonn, George W., 28 May 1853, Sarah J. Anderson                 6/15/53-2
Bonner, Elijah, 1 May 1854, Judith A. George                    5/ 3/54-2
Bonney, Elias, 9 Oct. 1851, Mary Elizabeth Miles                10/10/51-2
Bookman, Joseph, 11 Nov. 1855, Catharine Mulligan               11/12/55-2
Boon, John A., 26 Mar. 1857, Ariel Tipton                       3/28/57-2
Boon, Jos. H., 5 Aug. 1852, Martha Ann Morgan, dau. of
    Ephram                                                      8/14/52-2
Boon, Joshua, 2 Nov. 1857, Mary Elizabeth Lee                   11/ 4/57-2
Boon, Robert Wesley, 12 Nov. 1856, Mary Ann Brooks              12/11/56-2
Boon, Thomas H., 23 Sept. 1860, Ann E. Kennedy                  9/25/60-2
Boon, William H., 27 May 1856, Sarah R. Young                   5/31/56-2
Boone, Charles, 13 Dec. 1860, Mary Alverda Johnson              12/22/60-2
Boone, James H. (Dr.), 9 June 1859, Lizzie Gault, dau. of
    Cyrus                                                       6/11/59-2
Boone, Wm., 6 May 1852, Elizabeth Rattle                        7/30/52-2
Boone, Wm. M., 22 Sept. 1858, Harriet A. Galloway               9/24/58-2
Booth, George, 25 Aug. 1853, Lydia Ewing                        9/ 1/53-2
Booth, John C., 22 Sept. 1851, Margaret E. Bartol               9/23/51-2
Booth, William H., 27 Nov. 1856, Mary A. Pinkney                11/28/56-2
Booz, Charles W., 1 Nov. 1855, Harriet Shinnick                 11/ 5/55-3
Booz, Daniel W., 29 May 1860, Zeziah W. Ball                    6/12/60-2
Booze, James W., 24 Sept. 1851, Mary E. Delcher                 9/26/51-2
Booze, Jos. (Capt.), 22 Apr. 1858, Mary E. Mereines             4/24/58-2
Booze, William F. (Capt.), 20 Jan. 1859, Susan M. Harrington    1/25/59-2
Bordley, James, 3 Nov. 1853, Ellen Johnson                      11/ 5/53-2
Bordley, Perry, 23 Dec. 1860, Julia Roberts                     12/25/60-2
Borgman, C. J. (Dr.), 30 Dec. 1851, Mary Dickson                12/31/51-2
Borland, William P., 22 July 1856, Lizzie Hassan, dau. of
    John                                                        7/26/56-2
Bortle, John E., 1 Oct. 1857, Eliza Jane Hadley                 10/19/57-2
Bosday, James, 19 Oct. 1852, (Mrs.) Kate M. Brennan             10/21/52-2
Bosley, Charles H., 17 Oct. 1860, Mary A. Rogers                11/14/60-2
Bosley, George, 13 Sept. 1857, Elizabeth M. M-(?)-ser, dau. of
    Charles                                                     9/18/57-2
Bosley, Grafton (Dr.), 5 May 1857, Margaretta M. Nicholson,
    dau. of Isaac L.                                            5/ 7/57-2
Bosley, John, 11 Dec. 1851, Mary Pearce                         12/25/51-2
Bosley, Nicholas M., 25 Sept. 1860, Emily A. Hooper             9/26/60-2
Bostick, Joseph, 8 Jan. 1857, Hester A. Neal                    1/19/57-2
Boston, Antony, 28 Sept. 1852, Harriet Ennis                    9/29/52-2
Boston, James, 15 Nov. 1860, Mary J. Dorsey                     11/17/60-2
Boston, John E. H., 8 June 1852, Cecilia Guyton                 6/11/52-2
Boswell, Allan T., 3 Mar. 1855, Ellen J. Collier                4/ 6/55-2
Boswell, M. F. S., 31 Jan. 1860, Mittie Williams                2/ 3/60-2
Boswell, Marriott, 8 Mar. 1859, Emily J. Tuttle, dau. of
    Wm. N.                                                      3/ 9/59-2
Boswell, Otho., 19 Oct. 1853, Sallie Katurah Simpson, dau.
    of Rezin B.                                                 10/28/53-2
Bosworth, Jeremiah, 14 June 1860, Ann Maria L. Bennett          6/18/60-2
Boteler, J. W., 12 May 1857, Fannie M. Miller, dau. of J. C.    5/13/57-2
Botterill, Francis, 20 Apr. 1852, Eliza Jane Knight             4/27/52-2
Botterill, Francis, 7 June 1860, Susan Brooks                   6/ 8/60-2
Botterill, John, 17 Jan. 1856, Mary A. Brown                    2/ 6/56-2
Bottiger, John G., 26 Oct. 1857, Mary L. Fegabeth               10/28/57-2
Bottiger, John G., 26 Oct. 1857, Mary L. Hegabeth; corrected
    copy                                                        10/29/57-2
```

Bottomore, Uriah J., 21 Oct. 1858, Mary L. Troxler   11/25/58-2
Botts, Ishmael Herman, 11 June 1857, Metilda Ann Russell   6/16/57-2
Bouchet, Joseph A., 22 Nov. 1860, Elizabeth A. Brown   12/ 8/60-2
Boudar, Joseph G., 23 Nov. 1859, Nannie H. Piet, dau. of
   John   11/29/59-2
Boughan, J. H., 21 Apr. 1858, Ella S. Atkinson, dau. of
   (Hon.) Archibald   4/24/58-2
Bouis, Robt. H. G., 17 July 1854, Eliza Jane Simpson   7/19/54-2
Boulden, James E. P. (Dr.), 6 Apr. 1852, Mary France, dau. of
   (Capt.) Richard   4/ 7/52-2
Boulden, Wm. Jas., 17 July 1856, Martha E. Cathell   7/21/56-2
Bourke, James M., 9 Oct. 1855, Mary Ann Lucas   10/10/55-2
Bowdel, Thomas, 20 Feb. 1855, Louisa Slater, dau. of John   2/21/55-2
Bowdle, Alexander, 2 Sept. 1851, Emily C. Kirby, dau. of
   Edward   9/ 3/51-2
Bowdle, Thomas, 20 Feb. 1854, Mary Louisa Slater, dau. of
   John; corrected copy   2/24/55-2
Bowen, G. A., 7 Aug. 1857, (Mrs.) E. J. Ginevan   8/11/57-2
Bowen, George W., 4 Oct. 1859, Charlotte Wilk   10/13/59-2
Bowen, Granville, 2 Nov. 1854, M. E. Miller   11/30/54-2
Bowen, James D., 13 Sept. 1855, Marietta Chenoweth, dau. of
   John B.   9/19/55-2
Bowen, John A., 6 Aug. 1857, Nellie C. Morant   8/ 7/57-2
Bowen, John M. C., 5 Apr. 1859, Esta B. Foley, dau. of
   (Maj.) S. Jas.   5/ 3/59-2
Bowen, John S., 26 Feb. 1852, Eliza A. Treadaway   3/ 3/52-2
Bowen, John W., 9 Oct. 1851, Laura A. Fox   10/16/51-2
Bowen, Joseph L., 4 Dec. 1856, Susan Bailey   12/ 6/56-2
Bowen, Josiah S., 17 Apr. 1860, Martha J. Slack   4/18/60-2
Bowen, Josiah W., 18 Jan. 1854, Mary J. Mince   1/20/54-2
Bowen, Levi, 21 Oct. 1851, Henrietta L. Trust, dau. of
   Harmon   10/23/51-2
Bowen, Nathaniel C., 15 June 1858, Frances C. Mudge   6/16/58-2
Bowen, Samuel, 11 Aug. 1858, Sarah Akehurst   8/20/58-2
Bowen, Solomon, 4 Dec. 1860, (Mrs.) M. A. Stewart, dau. of
   George Kraft   12/ 7/60-2
Bowen, Sylvester, 15 Aug. 1859, Mary A. E. Langeley   8/17/59-2
Bowen, Talbot, 16 June 1857, Rhoda E. League   7/ 2/57-2
Bowen, Thomas E., 2 Dec. 1860, Elizabeth A. Blucher   12/ 4/60-2
Bowen, William H., 3 July 1855, Mary Augusta Parker   7/ 7/55-2
Bowen, Wm. P. E., 16 June 1859, L. Gosnell   6/20/59-2
Bower, George W., 22 June 1853, Isabella Peck   6/25/53-2
Bower, Henry C., 27 June 1852, Mary Catharine Stump   7/ 1/52-2
Bowerman, Neville, 3 Jan. 1854, Eliza Hammond, dau. of Henry 1/ 5/54-2
Bowers, Abraham, 26 Oct. 1852, Kate M. Sheetz, dau. of Jacob 10/27/52-2
Bowers, Charles W., 26 Feb. 1854, Catharine Quail   2/28/54-2
Bowers, Chas. W., 15 Apr. 1858, Mary Elizabeth Wiseman   4/19/58-2
Bowers, Frederick J., 10 May 1853, Sarah Ann Peacock   5/13/53-2
Bowers, Gotleib, 1 July 1856, Savilla C. Robinson   7/12/56-2
Bowers, James W., 17 Feb. 1857, Emily J. Newman   2/19/57-2
Bowers, Martin H., 4 Dec. 1855, Margaret Ann Gruber   12/11/55-2
Bowers, Nathan L., 27 Feb. 1853, (Mrs.) Ann Carlton, dau. of
   John Ebb   3/ 1/53-2
Bowers, Pierce, 19 Mar. 1857, Mary Margaret Lawrence, dau. of
   Hammond D. and Louisa   3/31/57-2
Bowers, Rufus K., 8 Nov. 1853, Penelope Plowman   11/17/53-2
Bowers, Wm. H., 27 Dec. 1859, Rose Ann McMullin   12/30/59-2
Bowers, Wm. T., 16 Aug. 1859, George Ann Gerbriek   8/18/59-2
Bowersox, Theodore K., 24 Apr. 1854, Mary Jane Small, dau. of
   J. W.   4/25/54-2
Bowhan, Jno. W., 25 May 1859, Ella J. Carter   6/ 3/59-2
Bowie, Benjamin P., 20 Oct. 1858, Charity E. Sinclair   10/26/58-2
Bowie, J. Orlando, 8 Nov. 1859, Martha E. Barnes, dau. of
   James   11/11/59-2

Bowles, B. F., 22 Oct. 1857, Mary E. Bailey, dau. of James G.   10/26/57-2
Bowman, Aaron L., 26 Apr. 1859, Mary Louisa Stine, dau. of
    Frederick   5/ 9/60-2
Bowman, Henry C., 26 May 1852, Mary Ann Swarts   5/27/52-2
Bowman, James H., 1 July 1860, Mary R. Wiles   7/ 4/60-2
Bowser, Isaac B., 16 Apr. 1859, Louisa Taylor   5/14/59-2
Bowser, Jacob W., 10 Aug. 1851, Susannah Clark   8/12/51-2
Bowyer, John Wesley, 14 May 1857, Ann Jane Boardley   5/18/57-2
Boxwell, William F., 20 Aug. 1857, Elizabeth J. Wright   8/24/57-2
Boyce, Edward, 10 June 1852, Margaret Pease   6/12/52-2
Boyce, Robert, 7 Apr. 1858, Mary E. Mulligan   4/10/58-2
Boyce, Thos., 24 Nov. 1852, Mary J. Wylie   11/27/52-2
Boyd, Andrew, 18 Mar. 1857, Eliza Fullerton   3/21/57-2
Boyd, Andrew J., 14 Aug. 1860, Sarah A. Foster   8/20/60-2
Boyd, De Witt Clinton, 20 May 1851, Harriet G. Elliott,
    adopted dau. of T. Jefferson Rusk   5/21/51-2
Boyd, George S., 27 Feb. 1855, Margaret Ann Reese   3/ 1/55-2
Boyd, Hugh S., 25 Apr. 1854, (Mrs.) Elizabeth Ferguson;
    corrected copy   4/29/54-2
Boyd, Hugh S., 25 Apr. 1854, (Mrs.) Elizabeth Furguson   4/27/54-2
Boyd, John C., 6 July 1852, Mary Lizzie Jones, dau. of David   7/ 7/52-2
Boyd, John D., 27 Oct. 1853, Susanna W. Botter   11/ 4/53-2
Boyd, John R., 6 May 1852, Mary E. Johnson, dau. of (Capt.)
    Thos.   5/ 7/52-2
Boyd, Jos. D., 10 Feb. 1853, Malgaret Hyland   2/11/53-2
Boyd, Louis J. M., 9 Apr. 1860, Martha J. Hersch   8/ 4/60-2
Boyd, Robert, 5 Oct. 1854, Ann Elizabeth Birner, dau. of W. G. 10/11/54-2
Boyd, Stephen D., 15 Feb. 1859, Maggie A. Northcraft   2/19/59-2
Boyd, William H., 1 Jan. 1860, Sarah E. Jackson   2/ 8/60-2
Boyd, Wilson R., 6 Mar. 1860, Lizzie H. Roche   3/ 7/60-2
Boyd, Wm. A., Jr., 29 Dec. 1857, Lydia Cumming, dau. of Chas. 1/ 8/58-2
Boyer, Charles H., 9 Sept. 1858, Maggie V. Waldman   9/11/58-2
Boyer, Stephen, 20 Apr. 1852, Agnes Adh-(?)   4/22/52-2
Boyest, Henry, 15 Nov. 1858, Margaret Ann Reynolds   11/16/58-2
Boyle, James, 11 Apr. 1858, Louisa Loney   4/14/58-2
Boyle, James, 11 Apr. 1858, Louisa Long; corrected copy   4/16/58-2
Boyle, Lawrence, 27 Jan. 1856, Elizabeth Holton   2/ 2/56-2
Boyle, William H., 20 Feb. 1856, (Mrs.) Harriet H. Taylor   2/28/56-2
Boylen, James, 1 Nov. 1858, C. McCoy   11/ 4/58-2
Boylen, James, 1 Nov. 1858, Catherine McCoy; corrected copy   11/ 5/58-2
Bozman, Alexander, 22 Oct. 1851, Anna R. Sherlock, dau. of
    William and Susan   1/21/52-2
Bozman, John T., 14 Oct. 1858, Fannie Core   10/16/58-2
Brace, R. (Dr.), 15 Dec. 1851, Helen Darling, dau. of (Hon.)
    Noyes   12/17/51-2
Brackston, Richard, 10 Dec. 1857, Laura J. Warner   12/12/57-2
Brackston, William Dent, 3 June 1856, Rebecca J. Jones   6/ 5/56-2
Bradenbaugh, Charles, 20 Sept. 1859, Sidney E. Williams   9/26/59-2
Bradens, Robert J., 14 Apr. 1853, Mary V. Souder   4/16/53-2
Bradford, Henry, 13 Dec. 1856, Margaret Wilson   12/16/56-2
Bradford, J. D., 20 Feb. 1855, Emily K. Pierson   2/22/55-2
Bradford, Joseph T., 11 Oct. 1860, Annie E. Chamberlain   10/16/60-2
Bradley, Alexander H., 29 Oct. 1857, (Mrs.) Mary Ann G. Ring-
    gold   11/ 4/57-2
Bradley, Phillip, 21 Aug. 1854, (Mrs.) (?) McElroy   10/ 3/54-2
Bradley, Robert, 7 Jan. 1854, (Mrs.) Isabella Ryen   1/17/54-2
Bradley, Saml. L., 26 Dec. 1854, Lucinda Ann Greener   12/28/54-2
Brady, Chas. H., 3 June 1851, Mary A. Heard   12/ 3/51-2
Brady, George C., 18 Nov. 1857, Margaretta E. Hill, dau. of
    (Capt.) R. M.   11/20/57-2
Brady, George W., 23 Dec. 1858, Mary C. McBride   12/28/58-2
Brady, James H., 5 June 1856, Rose Ann Golden   6/ 9/56-2
Brady, James W., 25 Dec. 1850, Martha W. Mason, dau. of
    Richard C.   2/24/51-2
Brady, John, 3 Sept. 1852, Rosanna Neill   9/17/52-2

```
Brady, John, 13 Sept. 1860, Emily Bowen                       9/15/60-2
Brady, John W., 24 Nov. 1856, Annie M. Revell                11/26/56-2
Brady, Lawrence E., 25 June 1851, Sarah V. Caufield           6/27/51-2
Brady, Robert H., 24 July 1853, Ann Rebecca Nugent            8/ 1/53-2
Brady, Thomas F., 23 Nov. 1853, Lizzie A. Dicus              11/29/53-2
Brafman, A., 20 May 1855, Susan Weylein, dau. of A.           5/21/55-2
Bragdon, J. B., 3 June 1852, M. Virginia Higgins, dau. of
   (Capt.) A.                                                 6/ 4/52-2
Brager, Joseph, 28 Sept. 1856, Isabella Weinman               9/30/56-2
Braidwood, John, 31 Dec. 1850, Precilla J. Addams             1/ 2/51-2
Bramble, Charles H.; no date given, Catherine Derr            5/29/56-2
Bramble, Henry T., 18 Sept. 1853, Sarah J. D. Kelley          9/20/53-2
Bramwell, Tyson, 8 Dec. 1852, Henrietta Yenrick Chamberlin,
   dau. of Reuben                                            12/10/52-2
Brand, Charles A., 11 Jan. 1853, Mary A. Wheatley             1/14/53-2
Brannan, E. J., 8 June 1852, A. Leddon                        6/15/52-2
Brannan, Thos., 17 Jan. 1853, Eliza Jane Kennedy              1/27/53-2
Brannan, Wm., 6 Sept. 1857, Sarah Jane Key, dau. of Gabriel P. 9/ 9/57-2
Brannon, John, 10 Dec. 1854, Rosan Waters                    12/18/54-2
Bransby, John C., 2 July 1854, Jane Ager; corrected copy      7/ 6/54-2
Bransby, John C., 2 July 1854, Jane Ayer                      7/ 4/54-2
Branscombe, Robert B., 15 Apr. 1858, (Mrs.) Sarah A.
   Harrison                                                   6/ 9/58-2
Branson, Charles H. S., 13 Feb. 1851, Isabel Geddes           6/14/51-2
Brant, Craton W., 31 Dec. 1850, Martha Anna Riall, dau. of
   Absalom                                                    1/ 2/51-2
Brant, Erastus, 21 Aug. 1853, Margaret A. Miller, dau. of
   Henry                                                      8/23/53-2
Bratt, John, Jr., 21 Aug. 1852, Henrietta M. Bratt            8/31/52-2
Bratzel, William H., 12 Apr. 1857, Elizabeth J. Kelty         4/29/57-2
Brawner, Andrew H., 10 Jan. 1856, Kate V. McEvoy              1/14/56-2
Brawner, George A., 13 Feb. 1854, Elizabeth Ann Green, dau.
   of Alexious                                                2/27/54-2
Brawner, J. Campbell, 26 July 1859, Carrie S. Ould, dau. of
   Henry                                                      7/30/59-2
Brawner, James H., 16 July 1860, Mary E. Elliott              7/25/60-2
Bray, Alfred W., 1 Feb. 1855, Catharine Merken                2/ 3/55-2
Bready, John, 20 July 1851, Catherine Kenan                   7/22/51-2
Breeden, John W. (Capt.), 25 Dec. 1860, Laura V. Buckless, dau.
   of H.                                                     12/29/60-2
Breese, Samuel Livingston, 27 July 1853, Rosa Lee, dau. of
   Thomas                                                     8/17/53-2
Bregel, Joseph F., 7 Oct. 1852, Mary A. Hemmel               10/13/52-2
Bregel, William G., 3 Jan. 1854, Ellen E. Deal, dau. of John  1/ 6/54-2
Breidwieser, Jacob, 28 Feb. 1856, Elizabeth Merrill           3/ 4/56-2
Brenan, L. Oliver, 17 Oct. 1854, Harriet Bennett, dau. of
   Matthew                                                   10/27/54-2
Brendel, John G., 31 July 1853, Susanah M. Canoles            8/26/53-2
Brennan, Edmund, 20 Sept. 1857, Mary Elizabeth Wrightson     10/12/57-2
Brent, Frances N., 18 Nov. 1858, J. A. Magill, dau. of James 11/24/58-2
Brent, Vivian, 10 Nov. 1857, Josephine Merrick, dau. of
   (Hon.) Wm. D.                                             11/14/58-2
Brenton, Alfred, 21 Sept. 1852, Mary Shakespeare              9/25/52-2
Brewer, John, 14 July 1857, Ann Elizabeth West                8/29/57-2
Brewer, Joseph W., 3 Nov. 1853, Martha Bell                  11/ 5/53-2
Brfhme, Ottomar, 5 Nov. 1860, Mary Hall, dau. of Thos. J.    11/ 7/60-2
Brian, Edward N., 27 July 1859, Eleanora Stewart              8/16/59-2
Brian, Garret, 20 Nov. 1859, Margaret Nash                   11/26/59-2
Brian, James N., 13 Sept. 1855, Lina Roche, dau. of Geo. J.   9/17/55-2
Brian, John O., 10 July 1854, Ann L. Steady                   7/19/54-2
Brian, Martin P., 18 May 1856, Jane A. Orr                    5/22/56-2
Brian, Wm. H., 23 Mar. 1857, Justina Hubbard                  3/25/57-2
Brice, Lewis, 23 Dec. 1851, Georgeanna Johnson               12/25/51-2
Bridge, Stephen, 10 June 1860, (Mrs.) Margaret F. Linville    6/15/60-2
Bridges, Joseph H. (Capt.), 17 Feb. 1859, Margaret F. Anderson 3/ 7/59-2
```

Bridges, W. J., 20 Aug. 1857, J. S. Johnson   8/25/57-2
Bridges, William, 2 Oct. 1860, Angeline Howith   10/ 4/60-2
Briding, E. W., 12 Aug. 1858, Anna Maria Stewart   8/24/58-2
Briel, Christian, 20 Nov. 1853, Elizabeth Hartman, dau. of
    John   11/21/53-2
Brien, Patrick, 16 Aug. 1855, Catherine Mallooly   8/21/55-2
Briggs, A. G., 6 Dec. 1853, Rebecca Sewell, dau. of Thomas, Sr. 12/ 7/53-2
Bright, Henry, 10 July 1856, Martha Jane Hales   7/12/56-2
Bright, Henry J., 2 June 1859, Mary Ellen Carrol   6/ 8/59-2
Bright, James, 26 July 1855, Leonora Dixon Welch, dau. of
    Benjamin   7/27/55-2
Bright, John W., 13 Jan. 1853, Mira Ann Allen   1/19/53-2
Bright,an, W. P. (Capt.), 21 May 1857, Mary E. Stewart   5/23/57-2
Brigsam, Elijah W., 4 Dec. 1860, Elia R. Lefferman, dau. of Wm. 12/ 6/60-2
Brill, Charles, 9 Oct. 1855, Elizabeth Netter   10/27/55-3
Brink, Henry A. D., 16 June 1858, Louisa Wild   6/17/58-2
Brinkman, Charles, 4 Mar. 1855, Sophia Uphman   3/24/55-2
Briscoe, Andrew J., 29 Dec. 1856, Eliza Ann Coleman   12/31/56-2
Briscoe, Gabriel, 9 Jan. 1860, Susan C. Toomey   1/20/60-2
Briscoe, James, Jr., 8 Oct. 1851, Ellen S. Anderson, dau. of
    (Col.) Theodore   10/24/51-2
Briscoe, James T., 11 Dec. 1851, Anna M. Parran, dau. of
    (Hon.) John   12/19/51-2
Briscoe, John Augustine, 1 May 1854, Elizabeth S. Mettee,
    dau. of Philip   5/19/54-2
Briscoe, Lucelius H., 25 Feb. 1857, Arreana Polk, dau. of
    (Col.) James   2/27/57-2
Briscoe, Saml. N., 29 Feb. 1860, Virginia V. Hooper   3/ 6/60-2
Briscoe, William D., 24 Nov. 1855, Mary Gregory Coleman   1/ 1/56-2
Briscoe, William D., 19 Nov. 1860, Sallie J. B. Carrow, dau.
    of William   11/24/60-2
Bristow, John B., 12 Nov. 1856, Eliza A. Gadd   11/20/56-2
Bristow, Thomas M., 8 May 1855, Catharine Grove   5/10/55-2
Brito, Joseph, 19 June 1851, Eliza Scimons   6/23/51-2
Britt, Geo. R. P., 2 Apr. 1851, Georgianna Mitchell   4/ 4/51-2
Britton, Francis, 25 Dec. 1852, Martha Chester   12/29/52-2
Broaders, Henry R., 15 Apr. 1851, Margaret E. Mason   4/17/51-2
Broadfoot, J. O., 3 Apr. 1860, M. Louisa Sanner, dau. of
    (Capt.) J. S.   4/ 5/60-2
Brock, Perry B., 4 Nov. 1852, Charlotte Chew   11/ 5/52-2
Broderick, Dennis, 15 May 1857, Alice E. Walsh   5/25/57-2
Broderick, William E., 8 Sept. 1859, Ellen Jane Mullen   9/ 9/59-2
Brodrick, Thomas, 2 Dec. 1852, Jane Blair   12/ 9/52-2
Brogden, Richard L., 30 May 1856, Mary J. Brogden   6/18/56-2
Brognard, Ferdinand F., 28 Aug. 1851, Martha E. Carman   8/30/51-2
Bromley, John L., 15 Dec. 1851, Ann Levering   12/30/51-2
Bromwell, John E., 27 Nov. 1854, Hester A. Tall   12/ 9/54-2
Bromwell, Josiah R., 11 Dec. 1851, Margaret Woolford Apple-
    garth   12/15/51-2
Bromwell, R. E. (Dr.), 17 Oct. 1860, Josephine Evans, dau. of
    Levi H.   10/23/60-2
Bronzo, Edward, 1 Nov. 1853, Henrietta Wallace   11/ 5/53-2
Brook, John L.; no date given, Cecillia Birmingham   9/17/51-2
Brook, Robert S., 24 Jan. 1854, Sarah E. Gordon   1/26/54-2
Brooke, Thomas S., 14 Apr. 1853, S. Annette Harvey, dau. of
    James   4/15/53-2
Brooke, Wm. H., 7 Mar. 1855, Hester M. Lawton   4/ 7/55-2
Brooks, And'w., 21 Nov. 1852, Elizabeth Antony   11/23/52-2
Brooks, Dan'l. M., 25 Nov. 1851, Emily M. Gasaway   11/27/51-2
Brooks, Edwin F., 15 Sept. 1858, Emma C. Cooper, dau. of
    Thomas A.   9/18/58-2
Brooks, Elijah, 19 Nov. 1854, (Mrs.) Hester Bell   11/28/54-2
Brooks, George Washington, 12 Nov. 1857, Henrietta Ray   11/17/57-2
Brooks, James, 21 Apr. 1855, Ellenora C. Squires   4/18/55-2

```
Brooks, James, 16 Apr. 1857, (Mrs.) Mary Ann Bowen, dau. of
    Henry Freenan                                            4/21/57-2
Brooks, James H., 15 Nov. 1860, Rebecca Turner              11/16/60-2
Brooks, James W., 13 July 1856, Mary Susanna Morrison        8/ 6/56-2
Brooks, Jesse, 28 July 1859, Mary C. Richards                8/ 1/59-2
Brooks, John C., 13 May 1856, Armenia M. Ives                5/19/56-2
Brooks, John T., 15 Sept. 1853, Mary Buckingham              9/22/53-2
Brooks, Jonathan, 6 Apr. 1854, Sarah E. Booz, dau. of
    Benjamin                                                 4/10/54-2
Brooks, Nathaniel C., 12 Feb. 1851, Mary Ann Radcliff        2/14/51-2
Brooks, Rezin H., 17 Dec. 1853, Sarah Jane Moore            12/26/53-2
Brooks, Robert F., 27 June 1852, Lizzie A. Smith, dau. of
    Griffin                                                  6/29/52-2
Brooks, Samuel, 4 Nov. 1858, Comfort Conley                 11/ 8/58-2
Brooks, Samuel M., 1 Oct. 1857, Laura V. King, dau. of Henry 10/ 2/57-2
Brooks, Samuel R., (?) May 1851, Elizabeth Ann Haupt         5/20/51-2
Brooks, William H., 4 July 1858, Rachel Hobbs               7/ 7/58-2
Brooks, William J., 29 May 1860, Elizabeth Harris            6/ 1/60-2
Brooks, Wm. B., 2 July 1851, Susanna V. Baldwin              7/ 9/51-2
Brooks, Wm. H., 9 Aug. 1852, Ellen C. Gray                   8/17/52-2
Broshell, James W., 20 Nov. 1855, Henrietta Skinner         11/26/55-2
Brothers, Rufus S. (Dr.), 8 May 1860, Mattie J. White        5/11/60-2
Brotherton, William E., 2 May 1854, Jane Wyatt               5/ 9/54-2
Brotsell, Jacob, 20 Mar. 1853, Sarah J. Voyce                3/28/53-2
Broughton, James, 5 June 1856, Sarah J. Gibbons, dau. of James 6/ 7/56-2
Broughton, John, 12 July 1853, Sarah Ann Blain               7/19/53-2
Broughton, W. H., 1 Mar. 1859, Bettie Nickerson              3/ 3/59-2
Brow, B. Franklin, 2 Nov. 1852, Dorcas H. Reich, dau. of
    Philip                                                  11/ 4/52-2
Brower, Abraham, 5 Apr. 1859, Achsa Virginia Stover          4/12/59-2
Brower, John J., 1 Jan. 1853, Sarah J. Holmes, dau. of Wm.   1/ 3/54-2
Brown, Abraham (Rev.), 15 Sept. 1859, Mary J. Carroll        9/27/59-2
Brown, Alexander, 1 July 1851, Sarah Rebecca Freburger       7/ 3/51-2
Brown, Amon, 3 Nov. 1853, Bridget Burns                     11/19/53-2
Brown, Augustus, 1 Dec. 1853, Rosetta Fletcher              12/ 3/53-2
Brown, B. Peyton, 12 Jan. 1859, Henrietta H. Dorsey, dau. of
    Noah                                                     1/13/59-2
Brown, Benjamin, 27 May 1858, Mary J. Spires                 5/29/58-2
Brown, Charles, 12 Nov. 1856, (Mrs.) Ann Madix              11/17/56-2
Brown, Chas., 22 Oct. 1860, Cecilia Jane Lee                10/24/60-2
Brown, Cicero, 28 Jan. 1857, Mary Murry                      1/30/57-2
Brown, Edward, 26 May 1856, Margaret Ann Tasker              5/28/56-2
Brown, Edward W., 2 Feb. 1858, Almira Perkins                3/ 4/58-2
Brown, Elias, Jr., 9 Dec. 1852, Catharine E. P. Barnett     12/11/52-2
Brown, Felix, 13 Jan. 1859, Mary Ann McGruder                1/15/59-2
Brown, Franklin, 27 Sept. 1859, Amanda A. Greentree         10/13/59-2
Brown, Geo. W., 18 Dec. 1851, Mary Jane Gross               12/20/51-2
Brown, George, 17 Nov. 1853, Sarah C. Sharp, dau. of (Rev.)
    Daniel                                                  11/26/53-2
Brown, George H., 24 Dec. 1859, Mary Ginn                   12/26/59-2
Brown, George L., 29 Oct. 1854, Harriet Ann Wilson          10/30/54-2
Brown, George S., 18 Sept. 1856, Emily E. Ridgely            9/22/56-2
Brown, George S., 15 Oct. 1857, Hattie Eaton, dau. of D. C. 10/20/57-2
Brown, George Thomas, 19 June 1856, Anne Solenback           8/ 4/56-2
Brown, George W., 14 Oct. 1852, Mary Jane Scott             12/24/52-2
Brown, George W., 11 Dec. 1855, Sarah Rebecca Frederick      6/13/55-2
Brown, George W., 29 Sept. 1857, Sarah Ann Grey, dau. of James 10/ 2/57-2
Brown, George W., 14 Apr. 1859, Mary A. Lee                  4/19/59-2
Brown, Henry A., 15 Sept. 1853, Mary R. Carter               9/23/53-2
Brown, Henry C., 28 Mar. 1854, Mary Ann Patterson, dau. of
    John                                                     3/30/54-2
Brown, J. A., 17 Oct. 1851, M. A. O'Farrell                 10/18/51-2
Brown, J. A., 30 Aug. 1853, Rosena S. White                  9/ 7/53-2
Brown, J. Frank, 8 Apr. 1856, Fannie M. Davis, dau. of (Dr.)
    Charles W.                                               4/10/56-2
```

```
Brown, James, 3 Jan. 1858, (Mrs.) Josephine Montgomery;
     corrected copy                                          1/ 7/58-2
Brown, James, 21 Nov. 1859, Margaret Williams               11/23/59-2
Brown, James E., 23 Nov. 1859, Annie Riley                  11/28/59-2
Brown, James H., 4 Oct. 1860, Juliet B. Hall                10/11/60-2
Brown, James M., 21 Mar. 1860, Elizabeth A. Henson           3/23/60-2
Brown, James S., 27 Apr. 1858, Mary Tistle                   4/30/58-2
Brown, Jas. W., 1 May 1852, E. C. Maong                      5/22/52-2
Brown, Jasper, 4 May 1852, Eliza Seabrook                    5/10/52-2
Brown, John, 20 Nov. 1853, Catharine R. Longley             11/22/53-2
Brown, John, 23 Oct. 1858, Margaret L. Callender            11/ 1/58-2
Brown, John, 4 Nov. 1858, Margaret A. Brook                 11/11/58-2
Brown, John F., 21 Nov. 1860, Margaret A. Harfield          11/24/60-2
Brown, John J. L., 4 Nov. 1852, Louisa Smith                11/ 5/52-2
Brown, John L., 9 Mar. 1857, Margaret Gibson                 3/11/57-2
Brown, John T., 21 Nov. 1860, Margaret A. Warfield          11/26/60-2
Brown, John W., 25 Sept. 1851, Sarah Wild                    9/27/51-2
Brown, John W., Jr., 6 May 1860, Mary R. Crook               5/10/60-2
Brown, John Wilson, 6 Sept. 1860, Elizabeth Shellman Baer,
     dau. of (Dr.) M. S.; 9/10/60-2                          9/11/60-2
Brown, Joseph; no date given, Margaret McQuillin             3/31/59-2
Brown, Joseph, 17 Jan. 1860, Susan Malter                    1/19/60-2
Brown, Joshua, 29 Apr. 1852, Mary Light                      4/30/52-2
Brown, Joshua, 5 May 1859, (Mrs.) Anna Ross                  5/ 7/59-2
Brown, L., 24 June 1856, Charlotte A. Edwards                6/27/56-2
Brown, Levi, 25 June 1857, Anna Marton, dau. of Isaac        6/26/57-2
Brown, Louis Charles, 23 Aug. 1860, Elizabeth Dorsey         8/25/60-2
Brown, Louis M., 3 Jan. 1858, (Mrs.) Josephine Montgomery    1/ 5/58-2
Brown, Louis M., 6 July 1858, (Mrs.) Josephine Montgomery;
     corrected copy                                          7/ 8/58-2
Brown, Matthew J., 26 May 1855, Lizzie M. Pentland           5/26/55-2
Brown, Mercer, 23 June 1858, Annie M. E. Sappington          6/26/58-2
Brown, Napoleon, 31 May 1855, Elizabeth Roke                 6/ 4/55-2
Brown, Perry, 15 Apr. 1860, (Mrs.) Margaret Pratt            4/17/60-2
Brown, Peter, 3 May 1857, Catharine Shaffer                  5/ 6/57-2
Brown, R. Watson (Dr.), 21 Oct. 1856, Laura Younger, dau. of
     Richard                                                10/22/56-2
Brown, Richard, 21 Jan. 1851, Elizabeth W. Duvall; 1/25/51-2 1/29/51-2
Brown, Richard W., 20 Aug. 1851, Louise E. Montgomery, dau. of
     (Dr.) J.                                                8/22/51-2
Brown, Robert, 14 Mar. 1854, Araminta Hall, dau. of Cuthbert 3/16/54-2
Brown, Robert, 24 Dec. 1854, Laura Edwards                  12/28/54-2
Brown, Saml. L., 26 Oct. 1857, Ellen A. Harbaugh, dau. of
     (Dr.) Joseph                                           11/28/57-2
Brown, Samuel, Jr., 26 July 1854, Emma T. Deaver, dau. of
     Amos and Eliza                                          7/28/54-2
Brown, Samuel J., 26 Feb. 1855, Caroline Evans, dau. of
     Frederick and Ann                                       2/28/55-2
Brown, Samuel M., 30 July 1854, Sarah H. Hurst               8/ 1/54-2
Brown, Thomas, 15 Feb. 1853, Mary A. Comegys                 2/18/53-2
Brown, Thomas, 17 June 1857, Mary Jane Roloson               7/22/57-2
Brown, Thomas C., 21 Jan. 1857, Margaret C. Miller, dau. of
     John                                                    1/30/57-2
Brown, Thomas C., 31 Mar. 1859, Mary J. Dudley               4/ 2/59-2
Brown, Thomas E., 11 Feb. 1858, Eliza A. Chambers            2/16/58-2
Brown, Thomas W., 1 Dec. 1856, Margaretta R. Riall          12/18/56-2
Brown, Thos. H., 15 Sept. 1859, Martha Robb                  9/16/59-2
Brown, Thos. W., 11 Nov. 1852, Mary Jane Couley             11/13/52-2
Brown, Vachael J., 27 Oct. 1853, Mary A. Cook               10/29/53-2
Brown, W. Roberts, 30 Sept. 1858, Virginia E. Sangston      10/ 2/58-2
Brown, William, 2 Dec. 1858, Hester Ann Sadler             12/ 4/58-2
Brown, William A., 20 Nov. 1855, Mary M. Gifford, adopted dau.
     of Thomas and Maria                                    11/22/55-2
Brown, William H., 23 Dec. 1852, Martha A. Ritter, dau. of
     Jos.                                                   12/25/52-2
```

```
Brown, William H., 14 June 1853, Sarah E. Stretehoff            6/24/53-2
Brown, William H., 28 Aug. 1853, Mary F. Seymour                9/13/53-2
Brown, William H., 1 Feb. 1854, Eliza Ann Dorsey                2/ 7/55-2
Brown, William H., 15 Nov. 1859, Margaret A. Watson            11/17/59-2
Brown, William M., 20 Oct. 1853, Mary E. Tippett               11/ 8/53-2
Brown, William W., 7 May 1857, Sarah Gertrude Brinkly           5/23/57-2
Brown, Wilson E., 29 May 1851, Eliza Hibbs, dau. of Charles     6/ 5/51-2
Brown, Wm., 13 Feb. 1851, Rosanna Clayton, dau. of (Rev.) M. C.;
    2/19/51-2                                                   2/21/51-2
Brown, Wm., 8 Sept. 1851, Mary Jane Ondutch                     9/10/51-2
Brown, Wm., 19 Apr. 1858, Augusta Bruening                      4/21/58-2
Brown, Wm. H., 30 Mar. 1854, Emily J. Handy, dau. of Ishmael    4/ 1/54-2
Brown, Wm. W., 23 Oct. 1856, Harriet Steward                   10/25/56-2
Browne, Alfred, 31 Dec. 1857, Mary L. Silence                   1/ 5/58-2
Browne, Wm. B., 1 Sept. 1856, Rose Smyth                        9/ 3/56-2
Browning, Edward, 27 Jan. 1853, Margaret King                   1/28/53-2
Browning, Rufus A., 23 Dec. 1856, Mary A. Moore                12/24/56-2
Browning, Warfield T., 31 Mar. 1859, Carolyn M. Cinnamond, dau.
    of George R.                                                4/ 4/59-2
Browning, William Wirt, 10 Dec. 1857, Priscilla V. Hardy       12/15/57-2
Brownley, Hiram L., 25 Mar. 1850, Mary Ann Zerweck, dau. of
    Daniel                                                      4/ 1/51-2
Brownley, Jesse J., 7 May 1853, Elizabeth L. Hawes              5/10/53-2
Brownley, Joseph, 14 Oct. 1853, Mahitabel C. Sorter            10/18/53-2
Bron, George Ambrose, 17 Sept. 1856, Eliza Mattingly            9/20/56-2
Bruce, Charles, 27 Sept. 1860, M. Posey                         9/29/60-2
Bruce, David, 8 Nov. 1860, Ellen E. V. Frasier, dau. of David  11/13/60-2
Bruce, Robert, 20 Aug. 1860, Ella Hoey                         12/12/60-2
Bruce, Robert J., 13 Mar. 1856, Mary Finney                     4/ 5/56-2
Bruck, Henry M., 4 May 1852, Anna Maria Lindenmann, dau. of C.  5/ 7/52-2
Bruehl, William H., 26 Sept. 1858, Sarah F. Keltner            10/ 1/58-2
Bruff, John K., 3 Mar. 1851, Susan Jane Bevans, dau. of John
    and Priscilia                                               3/ 5/51-2
Bruff, Joseph D., 28 Oct. 1852, Ann Maria Carroll, dau. of
    Edward                                                     11/ 2/52-2
Bruff, Richard W., 30 May 1853, Jane C. Fry                     6/ 1/53-2
Brugess, Sam'l. C., 15 Mar. 1851, Fanny A. Cole                 3/26/51-2
Bruggy, Martin, 25 Oct. 1859, Ann Jane Cunningham              11/ 8/59-2
Brummell, Albert, 10 Apr. 1851, Mary Jane Hunt                  4/14/51-2
Brummer, Carsten, 9 July 1851, Mary Dapner                      7/11/51-2
Brunck, Julius A., 24 Feb. 1859, Mariana Reed, dau. of Charles
    W.                                                          2/28/59-2
Brundidge, William H., 1 Nov. 1855, Mary E. Laughler           11/12/55-2
Brundige, Chas. H. W., 24 Dec. 1860, Hannah S. Parker          12/27/60-2
Brungart, Francis, 29 Mar. 1853, Olivia Davis, dau. of (Capt.)
    John                                                        4/ 1/53-2
Brunner, Andrew B., 4 Oct. 1854, Susan W. Y. Taylor, dau. of
    John M.                                                    10/ 6/54-2
Brunner, Andrew B., Jr., 6 Nov. 1855, Mary E. Crockard         11/ 8/55-2
Bruscup, Thomas, Jr., 20 Sept. 1856, Nicey Ann Nield, dau. of
    Hugh                                                        9/24/56-2
Bryan, Arthur, 7 Jan. 1854, (Mrs.) Eleanor Butler               1/ 9/54-2
Bryan, Bernard M., 16 Apr. 1857, Sarah P. Howee                4/19/57-2
Bryan, C. Carroll, 2 Mar. 1859, Marianna G. Kemp                3/ 3/59-2
Bryan, James L. (Dr.), 7 Dec. 1852, Aurelia Pattison, dau. of
    Jas. M.                                                    12/13/52-2
Bryan, James Z., 9 Nov. 1858, Susan G. Steward                 11/19/58-2
Bryan, Lewis P., 3 Aug. 1858, Amanda Hughes                     8/ 5/58-2
Bryan, Samuel L., 14 Jan. 1851, Eliza G. Johnstone              1/15/51-2
Bryan, Thos. E., 19 Mar. 1857, Bennette Earlougher              3/25/57-2
Bryan, William A., 25 Jan. 1859, Mary R. Milov                  1/26/59-2
Bryan, William C., 22 Feb. 1853, Zebiah Pearce, dau. of Obed    2/24/53-2
Bryan, William H., 9 Oct. 1851, Mary Ann Wilkinson             10/10/51-2
Bryan, William Shepard, 1 Oct. 1857, Lizzie Edmondson
    Hayward, dau. of William H.                                10/ 2/57-2
```

Caldwell, Alonzo, 28 Sept. 1854, Mary Dunning, dau. of George   10/ 3/54-2
Caldwell, D. C., 13 Dec. 1860, Sarah Jane Blundin   12/15/60-2
Caldwell, Henry L., 21 Apr. 1853, Eliza A. Byrne, dau. of
    Kavin   5/ 3/53-2
Caldwell, John A., 9 Aug. 1860, Virginia C. Williams, dau. of
    Z. H.   8/16/60-2
Caldwell, John J., 4 Dec. 1856, Ellen E. Hubbard   12/ 5/56-2
Caldwell, John T., 4 Dec. 1856, Elim E. Hubbard; corrected
    copy   12/ 6/56-2
Caldwell, William McGill, 7 May 1857, Eliza Robinson   5/ 8/57-2
Caldwell, Wm. Q., Jr., 30 Apr. 1860, Mattie A. Manner, dau. of
    J. B.   9/29/60-2
Calfor, Nicholas, 10 Jan. 1856, Margaret A. Swain   1/12/56-2
Calhoun, Charles, 23 Oct. 1855, Charlotte E. Strider, dau.
    of August F. Hamner   10/24/55-2   *
Calhoun, Frank, 20 Dec. 1859, Susie H. Fairbank   12/26/59-2
Callaghan, R. C. C. Chas., 24 July 1852, Mary Bourke   7/28/52-2
Callahan, Daniel, 18 Apr. 1853, Margaret Fryer   5/ 3/53-2
Callahan, Thomas, 9 June 1853, Harriet Amanda Delcher   6/11/53-2
Callaway, Joseph, 27 June 1857, Emma Harvy   6/29/57-2
Calleta, Joseph, 27 Apr. 1853, Louisa Marshall   5/25/53-2
Calliman, Thomas, 15 Aug. 1860, Catherine Freaser   11/19/60-2
Callinan, Thomas, 15 Aug. 1860, Catherine Fraser; corrected
    copy   11/22/60-2
Callow, Samuel, 11 Sept. 1860, Susanna V. Duke   10/24/60-2
Callow, William, 29 Mar. 1857, Sarah Jane Brown   4/22/57-2
Camber, John Henry, 21 May 1857, Rebecca Ann Carroll   5/23/57-2
Cameberon, C. C., 1 Mar. 1859, Mary C. Wrinn, grandau. of
    Jeremiah Berry   3/ 8/59-2
Cameron, Chas. C., 18 Jan. 1858, Ella Weast   1/22/58-2
Cameron, Henry A., 7 Sept. 1859, Martha A. Butler   9/19/59-2
Cameron, James, 12 May 1853, Julia Mabee   5/16/53-2
Cameron, P. A., 18 Apr. 1854, Eliza M'Intire, dau. of (Dr.)
    Jas.   4/19/54-2
Camman, Charles, 21 Oct. 1858, Mary Ashton, dau. of W. R.   10/22/58-2
Camp, James J., 11 Dec. 1856, Elizabeth Ann Holbrook   2/ 4/57-2
Campbell, Edward S., 20 Oct. 1853, Mary W. Corse, dau. of
    William   11/ 3/53-2
Campbell, Geo., 15 Jan. 1851, Ann King   1/17/51-2
Campbell, George L., 8 Mar. 1858, Henrietta E. P. Sroud   3/11/58-2
Campbell, James, 25 July 1853, Elizabeth (?), dau. of James   7/27/53-2
Campbell, James E., 7 Oct. 1856, Julia A. Bussey   10/14/56-2
Campbell, James J., 25 Apr. 1854, Martha A. Coale   5/ 1/54-2
Campbell, John, 5 May 1857, Charlotte A. Calhouer   5/ 8/57-2
Campbell, John, 29 Sept. 1860, C. M. Crowle   9/24/60-2
Campbell, John F., 13 Sept. 1857, Annie E. Hess   9/22/57-2
Campbell, John G., 2 Mar. 1852, Matilda Ellison   3/ 9/52-2
Campbell, John R., 2 Mar. 1852, (Mrs.) Mary A. Waltemeyer   3/ 8/52-2
Campbell, M. H., 4 Mar. 1851, Eliza C. Townsind   3/20/51-2
Campbell, Rachel, 10 Jan. 1859, Henry Gayto   1/11/59-2
Campbell, Robert, Jr., 28 July 1859, Georgie McDowell   8/ 3/59-2
Campbell, S. K. J., 28 Feb. 1860, Clara M. Noble, dau. of H.   3/ 3/60-2
Campbell, Sam'l., 14 Oct. 1851, Eliza Fendall   10/15/51-2
Campbell, Thomas; no date given, Mary O'Neil   2/10/59-2
Campbell, Thos. C., 4 May 1851, Ruth Clements   5/ 7/51-2
Campbell, William, 4 Dec. 1853, Sally Diehl, dau. of (Capt.)
    Jacob   12/16/53-2
Camper, John A., 23 June 1859, Lizzie C. Daughaday   6/24/59-2
Camphor, Daniel, 16 Feb. 1860, Hester Ann Wright   2/23/60-2
Canaway, John S., 4 Oct. 1860, Leah E. Taylor   10/ 5/60-2
Canby, Edward L., 1 Feb. 1857, Louisa H. Mohler, dau. of
    Jacob T.   2/ 2/57-2
Canby, William, 5 Nov. 1856, Emily Baily, dau. of George   11/11/56-2
Candy, John, 18 July 1854, Hannah Vickers   7/20/54-2
Cane, George, 14 Nov. 1853, Anna Smith   11/17/53-2

```
Cane, John, 2 Dec. 1856, Ann Rebecca Robbinson                    12/27/56-2
Cane, Thomas, 2-(?) June 1857, Elizabeth A. Burnett               6/30/57-2
Cann, Edward R., 11 June 1857, Mary A. Fardwell                   6/18/57-2
Cann, John James, 12 Apr. 1855, Frances A. Patrick, dau. of
    L. D.                                                         4/16/55-2
Cann, Michael, 7 Feb. 1858, Ann Turner                           2/10/58-2
Cannoles, Oliver, 16 Sept. 1860, Mary Shealy                     10/ 6/60-2
Cannon, Richard B., 26 Dec. 1852, Ann E. Travers                 12/29/52-2
Cannon, Thomas, 1 Sept. 1853, Anna J. Wiggers                     9/ 6/53-2
Cannon, Wm. W., 19 Nov. 1853, Sarah Jane Burrington              11/22/53-2
Canole, Charles, 24 June 1856, Martha King                        7/ 4/56-2
Canoles, James H., 24 Dec. 1857, Susan L. Jackson                 1/ 9/58-2
Caples, Wm. M., 16 Feb. 1858, Ann B. Hampton                     2/23/58-2
Cappeaau, Jabez W., 10 May 1860, Mary E. Hannagan                5/14/60-2
Capron, Francis B., 23 Feb. 1859, Olivia E. Royston              2/26/59-2
Carback, David, 5 Apr. 1854, Mary Wells; corrected copy          4/22/54-2
Carback, David S., 6 Apr. 1854, Mary Wells                       4/ 8/54-2
Carback, Elisha, 8 June 1851, Sarah Jane Fox                     6/17/51-2
Carback, John Wesley, 25 Nov. 1856, Sarah H. Bevans             11/28/56-2
Carcaud, Thomas, 20 Jan. 1859, Lizzie A. Jones, dau. of
    James                                                        1/22/59-2
Carcaud, Wm. M., 27 Sept. 1857, Mary A. T. Paul                 10/16/57-2
Carey, Francis, 22 Oct. 1851, Mary Ann Hogan                    10/29/51-2
Carey, George G., 10 Apr. 1860, Josephine C. Poe, dau. of
    Neilson                                                      4/16/60-2
Carey, Gill A., 23 Sept. 1856, Jennie L. A. Smith               9/24/56-2
Carey, Hugh, 3 May 1855, Mary E. Marshall                       5/24/55-2
Carey, John, 25 Oct. 1853, Ann Skelly                           11/ 9/53-2
Carey, Michael, 8 July 1857, Margaret McLaughlin                7/13/57-2
Carey, Nathan; no date given, Mary Ann Frost                    4/18/51-2
Carey, Thos. J., 1 Oct. 1851, Margaret A. Kerner                10/ 3/51-2
Carey, William, 7 Aug. 1856, Lucy Ennis                         8/11/56-2
Carlan, James *, 1 Jan. 1851, Mary F. Keenan, dau. of William   1/ 7/51-2
Carland, James H., 24 July 1853, Ellen M. Ring                  7/26/53-2
Carlin, John, 23 Dec. 1856, Anne D. Lyeth                       1/10/57-2
Carlisle, J. H. (Capt.), 24 May 1860, Sallie S. Murray          5/28/60-2
Carlisle, Joseph, 6 June 1860, Martha Nash                      6/21/60-2
Carlisle, Joseph, 18 Sept. 1860, Elizabeth A. Meredith          9/21/60-2
Carlisle, Wm. H., 14 May 1857, Matilda A. Lawder, dau. of
    Samuel                                                       5/18/57-2
Carlton, Arthur, 28 Nov. 1860, Susan A. Chanceaulme             12/ 4/60-2
Carlton, C. H., 24 Oct. 1853, America Wright                    10/27/53-2
Carlton, Oliver, 18 Mar. 1859, Sarah C. McCaulley               3/24/59-2
Carmac, Hosea Francis, 15 July 1855, Priscilla Gilbea           7/19/55-2
Carmack, John, 25 Mar. 1851, Elizabeth Shipley, dau. of Henry   3/27/51-2
Carman, Caleb, 19 Apr. 1854, Ann Todd                           4/20/54-2
Carman, Elijah A., 7 Dec. 1859, Elizabeth Karr                  12/ 9/59-2
Carman, William H., 13 Apr. 1860, Annie Brown                   4/23/60-2
Carmichael, James, 12 Nov. 1851, Caroline Chadwick, dau. of
    Radcliffe                                                   11/22/51-2
Carmine, Thomas H., 2 Oct. 1860, Mary V. Lennox                 10/ 5/60-2
Carnan, Johnson, 11 Dec. 1853, Mary Ann McLain                 12/13/53-2
Carnan, Robert N., 4 June 1857, Elizabeth Byerley               6/18/57-2
Carney, Raphel, 25 Dec. 1855, Margaret Tucker                   1/ 4/56-2
Carns, Alex. G. W., 24 Aug. 1856, Emeline Fisher                8/28/56-2
Carpenter, Alva L., 7 Feb. 1856, Emily J. Cook, dau. of C. E.   2/ 9/56-2
Carpenter, F. D., 3 July 1856, Jemima Peddicord, dau. of John   7/ 4/56-2
Carr, Benjamin R., 13 May 1858, Mary C. Thompson                5/18/58-2
Carr, Chas., 20 July 1851, Mary Ellen Duvall                    7/23/51-2
Carr, Edward N., 13 Jan. 1851, Sophie N. Carvalho, dau. of
    D. N.                                                        1/16/51-2
Carr, Francis A., 14 May 1857, Rosena W. Johnston, dau. of
    Wm.                                                          5/15/57-2
Carr, George McNathaniel, 5 July 1855, Maria Jane Carroll, dau.
    of James M.                                                  7/ 7/55-2
```

Carr, George W., 15 Apr. 1856, Sophia Miller   4/17/56-2
Carr, James, 4 Oct. 1853, Eliza McClintock   10/ 7/53-2
Carr, James, 6 July 1854, Elizabeth A. Colton   7/ 8/54-2
Carr, James, 13 Dec. 1855, Ann Maria Dorsey   12/15/55-2
Carr, Jas., 23 July 1857, Margaret Timmons   7/28/57-2
Carr, John, 14 Dec. 1854, Elizabeth Frances Batty   12/19/54-2
Carr, Marshall H., 23 Nov. 1859, Anna Eliza Childs   11/28/59-2
Carr, Richard, 1 July 1851, Mary E. Bennett   7/ 4/51-2
Carr, Roseby T., 4 May 1854, Mary L. Moon, dau. of Edward   5/ 5/54-2
Carr, Samuel T., 22 Feb. 1859, Catherine G. Walters   3/11/59-2
Carr, Wilson (Dr.), 7 Apr. 1857, Susan E. Johnson   4/ 9/57-2
Carrere, John Merven, 1 July 1857, Donna Anna Louisa Maxwell,
    dau. of Joseph   8/20/57-2
Carrick, Thomas J., 29 May 1856, Sarah L. Bray   6/ 5/56-2
Carrico, Wm. H., 8 Apr. 1851, Emily A. G. Cox   5/ 7/51-2
Carrigan, Charles W., 23 Oct. 1857, Lizzie C. R. Seymour   10/27/57-2
Carroll, Albert H., 4 May 1858, Mary Cornelia Read, dau. of
    Wm. Geo.   5/ 6/58-2
Carroll, Andrew, 2 Oct. 1856, Jane Sheffield   10/ 7/56-2
Carroll, Charles, Jr., 24 June 1857, Caroline Thompson, dau.
    of (Hon.) Lucas P.   7/ 2/57-2
Carroll, George; no date given, Alice McKittrick   1/24/53-2
Carroll, George W., 21 May 1855, Fannie E. Dadds   5/23/55-2
Carroll, James, 23 Aug. 1852, Sarah S. Gibson   8/24/52-2
Carroll, James, 6 Nov. 1859, Margaret Kane   11/15/59-2
Carroll, James J., 22 Mar. 1858, Adaline R. Hamilton, dau. of
    (Rev.) George D.   3/27/58-2
Carroll, John, 2 Sept. 1856, Catherine Carr   9/ 3/56-2
Carroll, John, 1 Jan. 1857, Elizabeth A. Cottrell   1/ 6/57-2
Carroll, John, 10 June 1858, Mary M. Carland   6/12/58-2
Carroll, Michael, 8 May 1856, Ellen F. Watts   5/15/56-2
Carroll, Robert B., 24 Dec. 1854, Polly Powers   12/27/54-2
Carroll, Sinclair S., 12 June 1856, Emily White   6/20/56-2
Carroll, Stephen Charles, 12 Dec. 1854, Elizabeth Jane
    Campbell   1/ 1/54-2
Carroll, Thomas B., 25 Dec. 1856, Mary C. Grieffith, dau. of
    Elisha R.; corrected copy   12/29/56-2
Carroll, Thomas C., 22 Sept. 1858, Margaret E. Orem   9/30/58-2
Carroll, Thomas G., 16 Nov. 1859, Carrie G. Judik   11/19/59-2
Carroll, Thomas P., 21 Dec. 1852, Charlotte Kettler   12/25/52-2
Carroll, Thomas W., 25 Dec. 1856, Mary C. Griffith, dau. of
    Elisha R.   12/30/56-2
Carroll, William H., 27 Jan. 1859, Cyntha Schofield   1/29/59-2
Carroll, Wm. H., 12 Sept. 1854, Cinthia Schofield   10/ 2/54-2
Carron, Robert, 8 Mar. 1860, Mary Morrow   3/ 9/60-2
Carson, Carvill H., 24 May 1855, Sarah F. Gere, dau. of (Rev.)
    John A.   5/25/55-2
Carson, Geo. M., 8 June 1854, Ellen Rimby   6/24/54-2
Carson, John H., 14 Nov. 1859, Mary P. Brown   11/16/59-2
Carson, Joseph, 27 Oct. 1857, Matilda G. Moore, dau. of
    William   10/30/57-2
Carson, Samuel Rowland, 17 Nov. 1857, Virginia Edwards Ran-
    dolph, dau. of John W.   11/20/57-2
Carson, Theodore M., 3 July 1860, V. E. Allison   7/13/60-2
Carter, Arther, 23 Oct. 1855, Mary L. Conser, dau. of M.   11/ 3/55-3
Carter, D. J., 29 Nov. 1855, Elizabeth Pearce   12/ 1/55-2
Carter, David, 17 Nov. 1857, Sarah Jane Stokes   12/19/57-2
Carter, George F., 12 Nov. 1854, Margaret A. Seibert   8/22/55-2
Carter, H. C., 5 June 1852, Martha B. Kelso   6/ 7/52-2
Carter, H. Clay; no date given, Edith Dawson, dau. of Thos. H. 5/17/59-2
Carter, Israel D., 4 Oct. 1854, Eliza Ann Levis; corrected
    copy   10/ 6/54-2
Carter, Israel D., 4 Oct. 1854, Eliza Ann Lewis   10/ 5/54-2
Carter, James, 11 Aug. 1853, Elizabeth F. Maffett   8/13/53-2
Carter, James, 20 Oct. 1860, Rebecca Powell   10/23/60-2

Carter, John Calvin, 28 Oct. 1858, Emma Irene Ratcliffe, dau.
   of Luther   11/ 5/58-2
Carter, Josiah T., 27 Oct. 1857, Isabel Brien Wilson, dau. of
   Benjamin H.   10/ 3/57-2
Carter, Richard T. (Dr.), 9 Sept. 1852, (Mrs.) Eliza A.
   Dudley   9/11/52-2
Carter, William B., 6 Jan. 1859, Mary Greenwood   1/ 8/59-2
Carter, William H., 21 Mar. 1858, Annie Tottle   3/23/58-2
Carter, William M., 7 Nov. 1854, Elizabeth Jane M. Hale   11/13/54-2
Cartey, William, 4 Oct. 1858, (Mrs.) Tabitha H. Foxwell   10/23/58-2
Carver, George W., 2 June 1853, Sarah A. Peters   6/ 3/53-2
Carver, John H., 14 Jan. 1858, Nancy Cox   1/16/58-2
Carver, John W., 30 July 1857, Kate C. Wells, dau. of Benj. 8/ 1/57-2
Case, S. H., Jr., 9 Apr. 1859, Sallie J. Case   12/15/59-2
Casey, Abraham S., 30 Nov. 1852, Elizabeth A. Plummer   12/ 7/52-2
Casey, Francis W., 29 May 1855, Margaret H. Gibbs   6/14/55-2
Casey, John, 5 Sept. 1858, Julia Shockrue   9/ 9/58-2
Cashimire, Augustus P., 4 June 1854, Rosanna Werneth; corrected
   copy   6/10/54-2
Cashmier, Philip, 20 May 1852, Margaret Ann Mullan, dau. of
   (Capt.) James   5/22/52-2
Cashmyer, Augustus, 4 June 1854, Rosanna Werneth   6/ 9/54-2
Caspari, John, 2-(?) Oct. 1851, Rose Ellen Geary   11/ 5/51-2
Caspart, John, 29 Nov. 1853, Martha A. Burk, dau. of Robert 12/ 2/53-2
Cassady, Thomas J., 17 Aug. 1856, Ann Maria Whaley, dau. of
   Jas., grandau. of Jos. Hussey   9/29/56-2
Cassard, Frank W., 16 June 1858, Almira A. Stonebraker, dau.
   of Samuel   6/17/58-2
Cassard, Gilbert H., 6 June 1858, Mary M. Rust, dau. of
   Joseph G.   7/10/58-2
Cassard, John, 29 May 1856, Amanda Lippincott, dau. of Wm.   6/ 4/56-2
Cassard, Lewis A., 20 Jan. 1859, Emily G. McCurley   1/21/59-2
Cassell, Thomas D., 24 Nov. 1857, Esther L. Burk   11/26/57-2
Cassell, Wm. H., 23 Sept. 1851, Mary A. Forrest, dau. of John 9/25/51-2
Cassidy, Francis, 14 Oct. 1858, Kate A. Callan   10/16/58-2
Cassidy, John P., 14 Feb. 1852, Elizabeth Rogers   2/21/52-2
Cassidy, Owen, 18 Oct. 1858, Mary Clark   10/20/58-2
Castari, John, 29 Nov. 1853, Martha A. Buck, dau. of Robert;
   corrected copy   12/ 3/53-2
Castine, E. M., 3 Jan. 1856, Laura Batchelor   1/ 5/56-2
Castle, Charles, 11 Feb. 1858, Lavinia Boston   2/13/58-2
Castor, J. N., 18 Apr. 1856, Frances R. Pierce   4/23/56-2
Castor, Noel F., 23 Aug. 1857, Ann Elizabeth Bower   8/25/57-2
Cathcart, George H., 30 Dec. 1852, Mary A. Shmuck   1/ 1/53-2
Cathell, Platt M., 4 July 1858, Sarah Williams   7/ 7/58-2
Cather, Jas. R., 17 May 1859, Josephine Elder   5/18/59-2
Catlin, William, 17 Dec. 1852, (Mrs.) Priscilla E. Wright   12/20/52-2
Caton, William G., 14 Sept. 1860, Annie L. Turner, dau. of
   J. Mabury   9/18/60-2
Cator, Benjamin F., 16 Dec. 1851, Sallie McNamara   12/18/51-2
Cator, Wm. E., 5 Jan. 1860, Roxanna Marines   1/ 7/60-2
Cator, Wm. W., (Capt.), 25 Nov. 1856, Mary A. Travers, dau. of
   Thos. B.   12/ 4/56-2
Caufman, E. Gray, 12 May 1859, Sue V. Gore, dau. of (Capt.)
   Tilghman   5/14/59-2
Caughy, Noah W., 16 Nov. 1852, Mary J. Tormey, dau. of Patrick 11/18/52-2
Caulfield, J. P., 28 July 1856, F. Estelle Carusi, dau. of
   Samuel   8/ 1/56-2
Caulk, Alonzo, 29 Dec. 1852, Sarah Cameron, dau. of Squire   1/26/53-2
Caulk, James T., 18 Mar. 1855, Annie M. Donahue   3/22/55-2
Caulk, William H., 23 May 1860, Mary S. Buckner   6/12/60-2
Caulk, William J., 25 Nov. 1852, Margaret E. Waring   12/21/52-2
Causey, Uriah F., 21 Dec. 1858, Angeline Rawlings   12/22/58-2
Cavana, John, 26 Apr. 1859, Kate Crangle   4/27/59-2
Cayton, John, 22 Dec. 1851, Mary Yates   12/27/51-2

Cazier, Robert W., 10 Apr. 1856, Sarah M. Jackson, dau. of
    Jonathan   4/15/56-2
Cecil, Elias Edward, 7 Mar. 1860, Lizzie Thomas   3/ 9/60-2
Cecil, Rudolph, 11 Nov. 1860, Eliz. M. Gosnell, dau. of L. W.   12/18/60-2
Cecil, William, Sr., 16 Aug. 1853, Amelia Coffield   8/18/53-2
Cephas, John W., 18 Jan. 1855, Mary Jane Booth   1/20/55-2
Cerns, Joseph, 31 Mar. 1853, Sarah Ann Brown   4/ 6/53-2
Cessar, John H., 10 Aug. 1851, Louisa W. Marmelstein   8/12/51-2
Chaffin, George M., 25 Aug. 1859, Susan Crabson   8/30/59-2
Chaffinch, Samuel E., 11 May 1858, Elizabeth A. Bostwick   5/15/58-2
Chaffinch, William W., 14 Feb. 1854, (Mrs.) Cecelia E. Barrett,
    dau. of (Rev.) Saml. Sparklin   2/16/54-2
Chafman, Chas., 18 May 1856, (Mrs.) Matilda Meads   5/20/56-2
Chaillow, Augustus, 8 Jan. 1860, Eliza Cummings   1/16/60-2
Chaimberlain, John R., 21 Dec. 1851, Annie E. Hewitt   12/23/51-2
Chairs, Franklin, 13 Nov. 1855, Maria Priscilla Walker, dau.
    of Samuel   11/19/55-2
Chalk, James A., 16 Jan. 1853, Sophia Beck   1/26/53-2
Chalk, Joseph A., 20 July 1859, Sarah E. Cox, dau. of Amos A.   7/29/59-2
Chalk, Zenos, 25 Dec. 1854, Sarah Ann Guyton   12/27/54-2
Chamberlain, Edward, 23 Mar. 1852, Isabella M. Cassell, dau.
    of Sam'l. C.   3/29/52-2
Chamberlin, T. Warren, 17 July 1853, Virginia Young, dau. of
    Lawrence   7/26/53-2
Chambers, Alfred S., 26 Feb. 1857, Margaret Maria Fisher   2/28/57-2
Chambers, Anthony S., 2 Oct. 1860, Mary E. Middelkauff   10/ 5/60-2
Chambers, Benjamin; no date given, Helen Burnett, dau. of
    J. H.   8/23/53-2
Chambers, James B., 21 Jan. 1858, Mary Haslett   2/ 2/58-2
Chambers, James Z., 22 Dec. 1859, Mary E. Giles, dau. of
    George B.   12/30/59-2
Chambers, Perry, 10 July 1856, Emily Lane   7/14/56-2
Chambers, Robert B., 15 May 1857, E. Williams   7/15/57-2
Chambers, Robert M., 26 July 1859, Sarah E. Carter   7/28/59-2
Chambers, William, ly Aug. 1854, Margaret Stark   8/31/54-2
Champayne, Henry R., 21 June 1859, Area E. Wirt   6/24/59-2
Champayne, John R., 28 Feb. 1854, Ell Maria Beall   3/ 4/54-2
Champier, Robert, 2 June 1859, Eliza A. Wilson   6/ 4/59-2
Chana, Thomas, 28 Oct. 1855, Meliza Ann Dickerson   10/30/55-2
Chance, James R., 26 Nov. 1857, Mary Jane Muth   11/28/57-2
Chance, Tilghman N., 6 May 1852, Sarah E. Turner   5/10/52-2
Chanceaulme, R. P., 22 June 1852, Olivia R. Lusby, dau. of
    Wm.   6/24/52-2
Chandlee, Edwin, 8 May 1851, Cassandra Turner, dau. of
    Joseph, Jr.   5/14/51-2
Chandlee, H. P., 6 Dec. 1854, Kate M. Beattie   12/11/54-2
Chandlee, Wm. E., 13 Dec. 1858, Martha E. Sutton   12/16/58-2
Chandler, D. T., 9 May 1860, Louisa Golder, dau. of
    Arch'd.   5/14/60-2
Chandler, David M., 20 May 1857, Henrietta Conradt, dau. of
    P. E.   5/21/57-2
Chandler, William, 8 Sept. 1853, Susanna Grahame   9/12/53-2
Chaney, A. W., 27 Sept. 1857, Imogen Riley   10/ 1/57-2
Chaney, Andrew W., 17 Aug. 1851, Catherine Barber   8/18/51-2
Chaney, Christopher C., 25 Aug. 1851, Laura Shope   8/27/51-2
Chaney, James T., 2 Aug. 1860, Mary A. Sefton   8/ 4/60-2
Chaney, R. G. (Rev.), 10 Apr. 1851, Sallie E. Koontz, dau. of
    Godfrey   4/11/51-2
Channel, Allen A., 1 Nov. 1853, Sarah Rebecca Medcalf   11/30/53-2
Chanslum, Charles H., 3 July 1853, Martha P. Baker   7/22/53-2
Chaplin, Wilson E., 11 July 1854, Esther Dashiell   7/13/54-2
Chapling, Daniel, 21 Sept. 1854, Mary Lawrence   9/23/54-2
Chapman, George R., 24 Sept. 1857, Caroline M. Duvall   9/26/57-2
Chapman, Greenbury, 2 Sept. 1855, Catharine J. Zigler   9/17/55-2
Chapman, Jacob, 11 Nov. 1858, Sarah Gilbert   11/13/58-2

Chapman, James E., 20 May 1859, Laura W. Worthington   9/29/59-2
Chapman, N. P., 25 Mar. 1851, Emily V. Gawthrope   3/26/51-2
Chapman, Thomas H., 2 Jan. 1855, Maria F. Leary, dau. of
    James E.   1/ 4/55-2
Chapman, Thomas H., 2 Jan. 1855, Maria F. Searley, dau. of
    James E.; corrected copy   1/ 5/55-2
Chapman, William H. (Rev.), 6 Nov. 1851, Cornelia B. Hall,
    dau. of Edward   11/ 8/51-2
Chappell, P. Stockton, 22 Nov. 1853, Allie M. Baltzell, dau.
    of Thomas   11/23/53-2
Chappell, Saml. M., 13 Feb. 1855, Louisa Ophelia Emmart   2/14/55-2
Charles, David, 27 Oct. 1858, Mary Jankins   10/29/58-2
Charles, R. King, 22 Nov. 1859, Nellie R. Greenwell   12/ 3/59-2
Charles, Thos. J., 8 Mar. 1860, (Mrs.) Mary E. Linhard   3/10/60-2
Charr, Robert, 6 July 1851, Mary Jane Andrew   8/ 8/51-2
Chase, Benjamin F., son of (Capt.) John, 6 Sept. 1859,
    Adeline Mullin, dau. of James   9/ 8/59-2
Chase, Charles F., 1 Aug. 1854, Julietta Essex, dau. of
    James F.   8/ 2/54-2
Chase, Charles W., 15 Aug. 1859, Alice A. Tillery   8/17/59-2
Chase, Daniel, 23 Nov. 1854, Caroline Sampson, dau. of Jacob
    and Lilley   11/25/54-2
Chase, Darius, 20 Oct. 1857, Sarah Ann Merryman   10/21/57-2
Chase, George B., 21 Oct. 1858, Mary A. W. Mason, dau. of R.   10/22/58-2
Chase, Henry, 4 Mar. 1857, Ann Louisa McCubbin   3/ 6/57-2
Chase, James, 26 Dec. 1857, Jane Mitchel   1/ 1/58-2
Chase, James, 8 Oct. 1860, Julia Ann Baldwin   10/10/60-2
Chase, S. W. (Rev.), 17 May 1855, Winey Graham   5/22/55-2
Chase, Wm., 1 Jan. 1857, M. E. Linkins   1/ 3/57-2
Chason, Peter A., 1 Jan. 1856, Mary Jane Doyle   1/ 3/56-2
Chasteau, Thos. E., 3 May 1857, Sallie A. Holmes, adopted
    by John H. W. Hawkins   5/ 6/57-2
Chauncey, Joseph R., 11 Oct. 1854, Mary Ann Leonard E. Natton   10/27/54-2
Cheagh, Henry A., 4 May 1853, Mary Catharine Vaige, dau. of
    Edward   5/ 7/53-2
Chenoweth, Geo. E., 18 Dec. 1854, Joanna Pearce   2/20/55-2
Chenoweth, John, 26 Feb. 1852, Sarah Jane Beary, dau. of John
    and Ellen   4/29/52-2
Chenoweth, Mary A., 11 Jan. 1855, Charles Hillyard   1/13/55-2
Chenoweth, Richard, 29 Apr. 1852, Mary J. B. Bell   5/22/52-2
Chenoweth, William, 11 Nov. 1852, Eliza Jane Cromwell, dau.
    of Jacob G.   11/13/52-2
Cheris, Henry, 8 July 1852, Rachel Williams   7/12/52-2
Cherry, M. J. (Dr.), 22 May 1851, Laura J. Welsh, dau. of
    Thomas   5/24/51-2
Chersgreen, William J., 7 Sept. 1854, Eliza Emily Harrison   9/11/54-2
Chesley, N. D., 7 July 1859, Sallie J. Rieman   7/ 9/59-2
Chesney, Benjamin H., 12 Aug. 1856, Kate Lipels   8/15/56-2
Chesney, James R., 23 Jan. 1855, Sarah R. Thompson   1/25/55-2
Chesney, Jesse T., 22 Oct. 1857, Josephine Dukehart, dau. of
    Joseph   10/23/57-2
Chesney, Samuel, 4 May 1854, Caroline F. Stein   5/ 8/54-2
Chesney, William Franklin, 25 Jan. 1853, Almira Morgiana Griggs,
    dau. of (Capt.) Geo.   1/27/53-2
Chester, William, 13 Oct. 1855, Bridget Goff   11/ 1/55-2
Chester, William, 30 Oct. 1855, Bridget Goff; corrected copy   11/ 2/55-2
Chew, John, 11 Sept. 1851, Isabella E. Stewart   9/25/51-2
Chew, Philemon I., 17 May 1855, Laura F. Pattison   5/21/55-2
Chichester, Washington B., 17 Jan. 1854, Lydia H. Brown, dau.
    of Amos P.   1/25/54-2
Chilcoat, George, 3 Oct. 1854, E. Josephine Griffith   10/ 4/54-2
Childs, Benj. E., 2 Dec. 1858, Mary E. Leeke   12/ 4/58-2
Childs, Charles A., 16 Sept. 1851, Catherine A. Kirkpatrick   9/18/51-2
Childs, J. H., 14 May 1851, Mary R. Owens   5/16/51-2
Childs, Samuel, 10 July 1851, Susan Baker   7/12/51-2

Childs, William H., 13 May 1857, Mary Klinedinst   5/15/57-2
Childs, William W., 15 Dec. 1859, Barbara A. Sunderland   1/ 4/60-2
Chillcoatt, Elijah, 15 Dec. 1853, Mary Jane Pearce, dau. of
     Joseph   12/23/53-2
Chisham, John (Capt.), 14 May 1857, Ellen Kenney   5/18/57-2
Choupin, A., 6 May 1856, Elizabeth A. Courtney   5/13/56-2
Chowley, Philip, 12 June 1858, Rebecca Morgan   6/15/58-2
Chrismer, H. W., 1 July 1857, Susan Alice Frazer, dau. of
     Alexander   7/ 2/57-2
Christian, Thos., 4 June 1860, Jane Dewey   6/ 6/60-2
Christie, Edward Giles, 16 Dec. 1851, Eliza Harris, dau. of
     Samuel   12/18/51-2
Christie, G. John, 7 Feb. 1855, M. Catharine Snow, dau. of
     (Capt.) Freeman   2/10/55-2
Christie, Wm., 29 Aug. 1858, Mary Ann Nugent; 6/ 7/59-2   6/ 8/59-2
Christopher, Aquila B., 22 Mar. 1855, Sarah E. Turner   3/23/55-2
Christopher, Elisha, 16 Sept. 1852, Mary Louisa Erdman   9/20/52-2
Christopher, James Francis, 19 Aug. 1860, Laura V. Anderson   9/25/60-2
Christopher, Milton, 20 Sept. 1855, Kate Lynch   9/25/55-2
Christopher, Olive H., 9 Apr. 1860, Martha Ashburn   4/23/60-2
Christopher, Robert W., 16 Apr. 1857, Emma A. M. Waldin, dau.
     of F. A.   5/14/57-2
Christopher, Thomas J., 6 Nov. 1856, Mary Catherine Ramsdell,
     dau. of (Mrs.) Caroline Andrews   11/12/56-2
Christopher, William, 13 May 1857, Matilda Law   6/ 1/57-2
Christopher, Z. Woolen, 18 June 1856, S. M. Welch   6/23/56-2
Chronister, J. B., 28 Feb. 1858, Mary E. Coulson; corrected
     copy   3/ 5/58-2
Chronister, J. R., 28 Feb. 1858, Mary E. Coulson   3/ 4/58-2
Chrystal, John, 8 Feb. 1853, Anna Victoria Clark   2/10/53-2
Church, Jas. A., 8 June 1851, Caroline R. Ennis   6/28/51-2
Church, John, 19 Apr. 1860, Ann Matilda Harris   4/21/60-2
Churchill, A. B., 6 Jan. 1857, Almira Sutton   1/ 7/57-2
Cinnamond, Edward, 24 Aug. 1858, Mary Wilkinson   9/11/58-2
Ciscoe, Edward L., 12 Apr. 1860, Josephine Day   5/14/60-2
Clabaugh, George H., 9 Aug. 1855, Ellen Evans   8/11/55-2
Clabaugh, J. Addison, 6 Nov. 1855, Ella Rider   11/10/55-2
Clackner, G. F., 15 Feb. 1853, M. A. Zitzman   2/19/53-2
Clackner, James G. B., 5 Feb. 1857, Elizabeth Kiplinger   3/ 3/57-2
Clagett, Lewis H., 27 June 1857, Carrie F. Alcock, dau. of
     Wm. H. D.; corrected copy   7/ 1/57-2
Clagett, O. H. W. (Capt.), 17 Aug. 1853, Julia S. Oliver   11/15/53-2
Clagett, William (Gen.), 18 Oct. 1860, Romonia G. W. Prince   10/20/60-2
Claggett, Louis H., 27 June 1857, Caroline F. Alcock   6/30/57-2
Claggett, William T., 26 Dec. 1855, Elizabeth Ann Tudor   2/ 6/56-2
Clapham, J. Henry, 11 Dec. 1859, Lydia E. Grubb, dau. of
     Ebenezer   12/13/59-2
Clapham, John, 11 Feb. 1851, Ann M. Barber   2/12/51-2
Clapp, C. Clinton, 22 Nov. 1860, Annie Amelia Gibson, dau. of
     James Keennan   11/23/60-2
Clapsaddele, Francis M., 4 Nov. 1852, Elizabeth Logan   11/ 6/52-2
Claridge, Henry R., 30 Aug. 1859, Henrietta E. Bombarger   9/ 1/59-2
Clark, Bernhard, 22 Feb. 1859, Hester Ann Mitchel   2/23/59-2
Clark, Charles H., 26 Aug. 1858, Martha Ellen Jenkins   8/28/58-2
Clark, Edward C., 31 Dec. 1857, Delilah Parker   1/ 2/58-2
Clark, Geo. W., 7 Dec. 1851, Susan A. Stephenson   12/11/51-2
Clark, George, 30 Sept. 1860, Laura Virginia Parlett   11/ 5/60-2
Clark, George A., 16 Oct. 1860, Matilda E. Kirby   10/22/60-2
Clark, Henry, 27 Jan. 1857, Ann Virginia Colmary, dau. of
     (Capt.) A. L.   1/30/58-2
Clark, James, 16 Mar. 1857, Mary E. Keyworth, dau. of (Rev.)
     Charles B.   3/19/57-2
Clark, James, 29 Dec. 1859, Nancy McHenry   12/31/59-2
Clark, James R., 25 Oct. 1859, Martha E. Logue, dau. of James 11/ 1/59-2
Clark, John, 24 Nov. 1855, Maria Brown   11/27/55-2

Clark, John, 19 Nov. 1857, Mary Levina Sliner   11/23/57-2
Clark, John D., 26 Nov. 1855, Henrietta T. Frazier, dau. of
    Elihu   11/28/55-2
Clark, John P., 7 Oct. 1851, Sarah Jane Buckley   10/ 8/51-2
Clark, John P., 3 May 1860, Mary Johnson   5/ 4/60-2
Clark, John S., 13 Dec. 1853, Martha Jane Shipley   12/16/53-2
Clark, John W., 18 July 1858, Elennora S. Glass   7/21/58-2
Clark, John Wheeler, 20 May 1852, Elizabeth Aler   5/22/52-2
Clark, Joseph, 9 Jan. 1853, Harriet A. Kidwell   1/18/53-2
Clark, Joseph Alex., 12 Dec. 1854, Margaret Moore   12/19/54-2
Clark, Josiah Quincy, 31 Aug. 1852, Elizabeth Cohee, dau. of
    (Capt.) James   9/ 2/52-2
Clark, Levi Henry, 12 May 1853, Carrie G. Smith   5/13/53-2
Clark, Richard T., 28 Sept. 1854, Mary Coutenay Nimmo, dau. of
    Sidney E.   10/ 3/54-2
Clark, Robert B., 22 Apr. 1855, Margaret Hickman   4/27/55-2
Clark, Robert B., 12 Jan. 1858, S. Jane Gaither, dau. of
    Stuart   1/14/58-2
Clark, Robert R., 10 Oct. 1859, Henrietta Brown   11/26/59-2
Clark, Robert T., 30 July 1855, Olevia M. Allbright, dau. of
    Jesee P.   8/ 1/55-2
Clark, Samuel G., 15 Sept. 1859, Virginia A. Poole   2/22/60-2
Clark, Thomas F., 12 Feb. 1855, Margaret Primrose   2/16/55-2
Clark, Thomas W., 4 Jan. 1859, Sarah E. Powers   1/13/59-2
Clark, Thos., 26 June 1859, Mary A. Barron   6/28/59-2
Clark, William A., 18 Dec. 1856, Mary Matilda Crew   12/25/56-2
Clark, William H., 17 Sept. 1851, Caroline Porter   7/22/52-2
Clark, William H., 8 Mar. 1859, Carrie M. Eckman   3/12/59-2
Clark, William R., 23 May 1860, Mary E. Milburn   5/24/60-2
Clarke, Edward L., 15 Apr. 1857, Mary A. Carson   4/17/57-2
Clarke, J. Lyle; no date given, Martha M. Clark, dau. of Wm. H. 11/25/56-2
Clarke, John F., 27 Jan. 1859, (Mrs.) Harriet Clarke   1/28/59-2
Clarke, John S., 21 Aug. 1853, Emily J. Norvill   8/23/53-2
Clarke, John Thomas, 3 Aug. 1857, Mary Tennison   8/ 5/57-2
Clarke, R. King, 22 Nov. 1859, Nellie R. Greenwell; corrected
    copy   12/ 5/59-2
Clarke, Ray S. (Capt.), 2 June 1852, Susan Gardner   6/ 3/52-2
Clarke, Robert T., 16 June 1857, Sarah A. Clarke, dau. of
    James H. and Elizabeth F.   6/18/57-2
Clarke, Samuel T., 1 May 1860, Delia J. Pierce, dau. of
    Stephen A.   5/ 5/60-2
Clarke, Stephen N., 1 Dec. 1858, Emmagene C. Huckless, dau. of
    Henry   12/ 3/58-2
Clarke, Thos., 27 Aug. 1851, Catherine Maguire   9/ 2/51-2
Clarke, W. W., 21 Jan. 1857, Alice E. Argier, dau. of (Rev.)
    Aaron   2/14/57-2
Clary, Joseph M., 1 July 1855, Louisa Wilson   7/ 3/55-2
Claude, Dennis, 26 Feb. 1856, Mary Steele, dau. of Henry M.   2/28/56-2
Clautice, George J., 14 Oct. 1857, Ellen Quinn   10/17/57-2
Clautice, Henry C., 25 Dec. 1856, Magdelena C. Brunham   12/27/56-2
Clautice, Henry Clay, 1 Apr. 1858, Georgeanna Vincente   4/ 3/58-2
Clautice, John W., 22 Oct. 1854, Laura A. Farring   10/25/54-2
Clawson, H. (Dr.), 17 Sept. 1855, Mary Elizabeth Lyne   9/28/55-2
Clayton, A. R., 21 Feb. 1860, Maggie N. McCeney; 2/23/60-2   2/24/60-2
Clayton, Alfred S., 21 Aug. 1860, Sarah Ann Coulbourn   9/19/60-2
Clayton, R. Vinton, 14 July 1853, Elizabeth A. Saussar   7/16/53-2
Clazy, William, 28 Dec. 1852, Mary Hughes   4/27/53-2
Clement, Jas. H., 21 Oct. 1852, Mary Ann Pagan   10/23/52-2
Clements, John W., 14 May 1851, Emma J. Phillips   5/16/51-2
Clements, Stephen C., 24 Nov. 1857, Isabella M. Boyle, dau.
    of John F.   12/ 3/57-2
Clemson, John, Jr., 15 May 1855, Louisa Cross, dau. of (Maj.)
    Osborn   5/18/55-2
Cleney, John, 5 May 1853, Eliza Jane Carter   5/ 9/53-2
Clevenger, John, 21 Nov. 1858, Rebecca Aler   11/23/58-2

Clickner, Samuel A., 6 Nov. 1853, Jane Eliza Reed   11/17/53-2
Cliffe, Robert W., 24 May 1853, Augusta Middleton, dau. of
    Richard   5/25/53-2
Clifford, J., 29 Mar. 1860, Mary Bond   4/ 2/60-2
Clifton, Junius A., 5 Mar. 1856, (Mrs.) Mary S. MacArthur, dau.
    of (Com.) J. J. Young   3/ 6/56-2
Clifton, Louis Deloul, 3 Jan. 1859, L. Bodman   1/ 6/59-2
Clifton, Theodore E., 12 Nov. 1860, Rebecca J. Moore   11/15/60-2
Clindest, John, 3 Nov. 1857, Margaret D. Brady   11/11/57-2
Cline, Anthony, 12 Sept. 1860, Elizabeth Sweeney   9/17/60-2
Cline, George H., 8 Sept. 1857, Margaret H. C. Long   9/10/57-2
Cline, James P., 10 Sept. 1855, Margaret P. Miller   9/21/55-2
Cline, Joseph C., 4 Oct. 1857, Elizabeth V. Plant   10/ 6/57-2
Cline, William E., 13 Mar. 1860, Millie E. Olwine   3/14/60-2
Clinton, H. De Witt, 4 May 1857, Mary L. Courts   5/ 6/57-2
Clipper, William, 2 Aug. 1860, Maggie Dorathea Eilbacher,
    dau. of John V.   8/ 7/60-2
Clocker, George R., 1 Oct. 1860, (Mrs.) Mary E. Henning   10/ 3/60-2
Clogg, Geo. S., 30 Mar. 1851, Catharine C. Ritz   4/ 1/51-2
Clogg, Geo. S., 23 Oct. 1860, Olevia A. Marden, dau. of
    Jesse   10/24/60-2
Clokey, Wm. N., 8 Nov. 1860, Mary H. King   11/16/60-2
Cloony, John, 19 Apr. 1853, Rosanna McLoghlin   4/20/53-2
Clotworthy, Wm., 11 Dec. 1851, Sarah Ann Akers   12/13/51-2
Clotworthy, Wm. P., 27 May 1858, Kate Mattingly, dau. of
    Francis   6/ 1/58-2
Cloud, John J., 25 Mar. 1856, Mary Elmira Cloud, dau. of
    Charles F.   3/28/56-2
Clough, John J., 14 Aug. 1855, Catherine E. Cole   8/17/55-2
Clough, Martin T. B., 13 Aug. 1855, Ann Elizabeth Thompson 8/15/55-2
Clouse, Edward C., 6 Oct. 1856, Rose M. Feig   10/ 8/56-2
Coale, Chas., 3 May 1854, Mary Anna Walton, dau. of Thornton 5/ 5/54-2
Coale, George Buchanan, 9 Oct. 1855, Caroline Donaldson Dorsey,
    dau. of (Dr.) Robert E.   10/11/55-2
Coale, John B., 16 Sept. 1858, Emily Woolford   9/18/58-2
Coale, Joseph M., 29 Nov. 1855, Louisa E. Greble   12/ 4/55-2
Coale, Louis P., 22 Sept. 1853, Henrietta Gwin   9/24/53-2
Coale, S. Robinson, 10 May 1859, Hetty J. Sutton, dau. of Jas.
    L.   5/14/59-2
Coale, Thomas E., 18 Jan. 1855, Cecelia Harvey   1/20/55-2
Coale, William Edward, 17 May 1860, Elizabeth T. Bell, dau.
    of Joseph   5/23/60-2
Coale, Wm. Ellis, Jr., 9 Oct. 1858, Louisa Schmidt, dau. of
    L. V.   10/13/58-2
Coates, Israel B., 6 Jan. 1852, Wilminia E. Harman   1/13/52-2
Coates, J. Pennock, 24 July 1858, Susie T. Ellison, dau. of
    Lewis   9/16/58-2
Coates, Leonard, 10 Apr. 1860, Mary A. Jake   4/12/60-2
Coats, J. S., 7 Jan. 1858, Louise Graham   1/ 8/58-2
Cobb, A. D. (Capt.), 4 May 1854, Margaret A. Chisholm, dau.
    of (Capt.) James   5/ 6/54-2
Cobb, Edward D., 4 Nov. 1852, Tillie Stuart, dau. of David 11/ 6/52-2
Cobb, Gardner A., 23 Mar. 1856, Anne E. Israel, dau. of
    William   4/ 1/56-2
Cobb, George F., 16 June 1857, Mary A. Poulson, dau. of
    Alexander W.   6/17/57-2
Coblentz, Joseph (Dr.), 20 Dec. 1852, Annie R. Coblentz, dau.
    of (Dr.) Jacob   12/28/52-2
Coburn, George Cornelius *, 26 Dec. 1858, Anna Cabbuel   10/28/59-2
Coburn, Thomas H., 26 Aug. 1852, Adelia Kirby   8/30/52-2
Cochran, Andrew, 5 Apr. 1860, Isabella E. Watson   4/10/60-2
Cochran, Francis P., 11 Oct. 1852, Mary Ann Barick   10/14/52-2
Cochran, Stephen L., 8 Sept. 1853, Albertine Frost, dau. of
    William   9/ 9/53-2

Cochran, Wm. J., 29 July 1852, Sarah Elizabeth Ainey, dau.
   of Samuel and Mary Ann   8/ 4/52-2
Cockey, Charles Thomas, 18 Mar. 1852, Susannah D. Brown, dau.
   of Wm.   3/22/52-2
Cockey, Chas. E., 29 Oct. 1856, Fanny A. Eareckson   10/30/56-2
Cockey, Covington W., 24 Jan. 1854, Clara Hall, dau. of
   John Thomas   1/25/54-2
Cockey, Thomas Beal, 30 Oct. 1851, Margaret Amelia Shipley   11/ 8/51-2
Cockrill, Lyttleton, 10 Mar. 1858, A. B. C. Harcum   5/ 3/58-2
Codd, Edward J., 12 July 1855, Avarilla E. Hooper   7/17/55-2
Codling, James J., 3 Oct. 1859, Mary J. Emmart   10/ 5/59-2
Codling, John, 4 Oct. 1854, Jane Wilson, dau. of Philip   10/24/54-2
Coe, C. H., 30 May 1860, Ruth A. Deaver   6/ 2/60-2
Coe, C. H. P., 30 May 1860, Ruth A. Deaver; corrected copy   6/ 4/60-2
Coe, James S., 6 Oct. 1859, Tacy Fox   10/13/59-2
Coe, W. Gwynn, 4 May 1853, Annie M. Armstrong   5/ 6/53-2
Coffee, Michael, 11 Apr. 1853, Catharine Reynolds   4/14/53-2
Coffield, G. C. H., 16 Nov. 1853, Constance Keppler   11/17/53-2
Coge, Simon, 18 Feb. 1855, Gracy Ann Johnson   2/20/55-2
Coggins, Charles H., 30 Mar. 1858, Martha A. Denny, dau. of
   James E.   4/ 5/58-2
Coggins, James, 1 Oct. 1857, Caroline Medora Frederick, dau.
   of William A.   10/ 3/57-2
Coggins, John *, son of (Rev.) Thos., 7 Oct. 1858, Richard
   Ann Wilkison, dau. of William and Ann   10/ 9/58-2
Coggins, John W., 23 Dec. 1858, Angeline E. Mead, dau. of
   (Capt.) William J.   12/25/58-2
Coggins, Robert, 22 Dec. 1859, Mary Amanda Cox, dau. of
   William F.   12/24/59-2
Coghill, J. Henry, 9 Mar. 1854, Mary Mulford, dau. of James
   H.; corrected copy   3/13/54-2
Coghill, J. Henry, 9 Mar. 1854, Mary Mulford, dau. of James W.   3/11/54-2
Cogswell, Geo. A., 25 Oct. 1855, Kate Kerney   11/10/55-2
Colberth, Lloyd, 11 Apr. 1854, Willimena Crockett   4/14/54-2
Colburn, Edward A., 28 Apr. 1859, Annie Rogers   4/29/59-2
Colclazer, Henry (Rev.), 3 Dec. 1851, Sallie Hicks, dau. of
   Thos. H.   12/ 5/51-2
Cole, A. Cornelius, 22 May 1856, Sarah E. Gorsuch, dau. of
   Wm. G.   5/23/56-2
Cole, B. F.; no date given, Martha N. Beasley   4/ 6/53-2
Cole, Benjamin, 8 Sept. 1853, Susan Ann Lucas   9/12/53-2
Cole, Benjamin F., 31 Jan. 1859, Jane K. Littig   2/ 3/59-2
Cole, Conrad, 15 Apr. 1858, Elizabeth Horn   4/22/58-2
Cole, Edward, 12 Nov. 1858, Mary Frances (?), step-dau. of
   Robert Hanna, grandau. of (Rev.) John Cornelius   11/24/58-2
Cole, Edward H., 2 Feb. 1860, Gillie Watts   2/ 4/60-2
Cole, James W., 3 Feb. 1857, Mary Jane Young   2/ 4/57-2
Cole, Jno. R., 29 Mar. 1855, Mary A. Ross   4/ 3/55-2
Cole, John B., 7 Mar. 1858, Margaret Ann Patterson, dau. of
   William   3/ 9/58-2
Cole, John E., 12 Jan. 1857, Elmira A. Fisher   1/14/57-2
Cole, John R., 29 Mar. 1855, Mary Ann Ross; corrected copy   4/ 4/55-2
Cole, Joseph, 1 Dec. 1859, Catharine J. Hopkins   12/ 3/59-2
Cole, Lewis H., 2 July 1856, Fannie E. Williams, dau. of Levi   7/ 4/56-2
Cole, Lewis Hiram, 10 Jan. 1860, Tamzon Weatherby, dau. of J.   1/11/60-2
Cole, Luther, 15 Jan. 1856, Mary Jane Maddox   2/ 7/56-2
Cole, Maran, 18 June 1854, Elizabeth Foster   6/20/54-2
Cole, Robert C., 10 Feb. 1857, Ellen L. Wise   2/16/57-2
Cole, Stephen, 28 Feb. 1858, Mary Jane Holland   3/ 4/58-2
Cole, Taylor, 15 June 1854, Sarah Louisa Kemble   6/16/54-2
Cole, William, 22 Nov. 1860, Frances Isaacs   11/24/60-2
Cole, William H., 16 May 1853, Hannah W. Hawkins, dau. of
   John H. W.   5/21/53-2
Cole, William H., 15 Oct. 1857, Emma C. Cooke, dau. of
   Samuel   10/16/57-2

```
Cole, William L., 21 Oct. 1852, Casandra Lynch                   11/ 9/52-2
Cole, Wm. H., 28 Oct. 1852, Virginia D. Hiss, dau. of
    Jacob, Jr.                                                   10/29/52-2
Cole, Wm. V., 21 May 1851, Mary Ann O'Neal                        5/23/51-2
Colegate, Wm. H., 15 Jan. 1852, Eleanor Thomas                    2/ 3/52-2
Colehower, Frederick A., 20 Dec. 1860, Rutha A. Skipper          12/22/60-2
Colein, John, 3 Jan. 1854, Sarah E. Maguire                       1/ 5/54-2
Coleman, Charles C., 24 Apr. 1859, Mary Frances Taylor            6/20/59-2
Coleman, Henshaw, 15 Dec. 1857, Elizabeth Sherman, dau. of
    Geo. W.                                                      12/16/57-2
Coleman, James, 4 Jan. 1855, Ann Baker                            1/ 8/55-2
Coleman, Jno. A., 4 Dec. 1854, Williamene Georgetta Queen, dau.
    of Eliza, grandau. of William Wikerson                       12/ 7/54-2
Coleman, John, 20 Nov. 1851, Martha A. Wagner                    11/22/51-2
Coleman, John Wood, 8 June 1859, Amelia F. Miles, dau. of
    George                                                       11/28/59-2
Coleman, Joseph, 24 Dec. 1854, Rosabella Cooper                  12/27/54-2
Coleman, Morgan, 5 Apr. 1853, Elizabeth A. Ness                   4/ 7/53-2
Coleman, Robert B., 21 Nov. 1860, Emeline Angevine               11/26/60-2
Coleman, Thomas, 9 Oct. 1859, Ellen Murphy                       11/30/59-2
Coleman, Zebulan S., 27 July 1857, Mary E. Hayden                 7/29/57-2
Coles, Wm. Oscar, 26 Aug. 1851, Martha A. Jay                     9/10/51-2
Colfer, John, 19 Jan. 1852, Cecelia Patterson, dau. of James     6/ 7/52-2
Colineau, Lawrence G., 12 Dec. 1854, Mary L. Phipps; corrected
    copy                                                         12/19/54-2
Colineau, Lawrence G., 13 Dec. 1854, Mary L. Phipps              12/18/54-2
Colison, Wm. H., 14 Dec. 1852, Martha H. Glenn, dau. of
    Michael                                                      12/16/52-2
Colladay, Joseph M., 3 May 1860, Lizzie Freshour, dau. of
    Wm. H.                                                        4/ 5/60-2
Colley, John W., 4 Jan. 1852, Elizabeth J. Brown                  1/ 9/52-2
Colley, William H., son of John W., 20 Jan. 1857, Lizzie A.
    Hesser, dau. of George N.                                     1/22/57-2
Collier, Chas. E., 19 Feb. 1857, Eliza Carland                    2/25/57-2
Collier, Henry, 13 Jan. 1856, Mary Ann B. V. Johnston             1/15/56-2
Collier, John, 16 Mar. 1851, Rebecca S. Vink                      3/22/51-2
Collins, Charles H., 25 Dec. 1856, Elizabeth Ann Kelly            1/ 1/57-2
Collins, Daniel, 26 May 1853, Emeline McKinley                    6/14/53-2
Collins, Geo. C., 24 Dec. 1851, Martha A. Purdy                  12/29/51-2
Collins, Geo. Francis, 27 May 1856, Sarah Elizabeth Williams      5/30/56-2
Collins, Geo. T.; no date given, Elizabeth Eschbach              11/16/52-2
Collins, Geo. W., 13 Feb. 1853, Ann Rebecca Vickers               2/26/53-2
Collins, George H., 13 Apr. 1852, Lisette Jeckel                  4/16/52-2
Collins, George W., 21 Apr. 1856, Miranda Holland                 4/23/56-2
Collins, H. J. L., 26 Apr. 1857, Annie M. Silk                    4/28/57-2
Collins, Henry, 4 Aug. 1859, Adaline H. Switzer                   8/ 9/59-2
Collins, J. Henry, 2 Nov. 1852, Susannah Compton, dau. of
    Samuel Carr                                                  11/ 4/52-2
Collins, J. J., 9 June 1852, Mary Hughes                          6/25/52-2
Collins, James F., 8 May 1855, Naomia C. L. Hoffman               5/ 9/55-2
Collins, Jas., 13 Jan. 1853, Margaret Harper                      1/26/53-2
Collins, Jas., 10 July 1856, Bridget Irwin                        7/16/56-2
Collins, John, 7 July 1853, Bridget Trilley                       8/ 5/53-2
Collins, John Nicholas, 4 Jan. 1857, Margaret Jane Trumbo         1/ 9/57-2
Collins, Jos. H., 14 Mar. 1854, Sallie R. Betton, dau. of
    Thos.                                                         3/17/54-2
Collins, Julius W., 24 May 1852, Ann Rebecca Kirby                5/26/52-2
Collins, Michael, 3 May 1851, Mary Jane Kennedy                   5/ 8/51-2
Collins, Noah, 29 Mar. 1860, Mary Sophia Jones                    4/ 2/60-2
Collins, Wm., 8 Nov. 1852, Margaret Quinn                        11/29/52-2
Collins, Wm. A. (Capt.), 7 Jan. 1858, Elizabeth Phillips          1/30/58-2
Collins, Wm. H., 30 Jan. 1853, Ann M. Johnson                     2/ 3/53-2
Collison, Benjamin F., 11 Jan. 1858, Sarah A. Finley              1/16/58-2
Collison, Charles W., 10 May 1854, Ann E. Andrew                  5/13/54-2
```

Collmus, Solomon, 19 Feb. 1860, Martha Ann Fish   2/21/60-2
Collom, James *, 5 Feb. 1859, (Mrs.) Sarah McCollum   3/10/59-2
Colman, William, 12 Jan. 1851, Susan Conn   1/16/51-2
Colmary, Alexander, 28 Nov. 1859, Mary Ann Conery   12/17/59-2
Colson, Joseph, 9 Nov. 1856, Sarah L. Jones   11/11/56-2
Colston, J. Harrison, 3 Jan. 1856, Mary C. Watson   1/ 5/56-2
Coltart, John Andrew, 23 Feb. 1857, Mary Teresa Pollard   3/24/57-2
Colton, Frederick, 19 Dec. 1855, Janet Carr   4/17/56-2
Colton, Henry Holmes, son of Wm. H., 18 Dec. 1851, Mary E.
    Stout, dau. of Francis   12/20/51-2
Colton, John W., 24 May 1855, Lizzie Jane Colwell   5/28/55-2
Coltrider, George, 13 Feb. 1855, Margaret J. Wooden   2/21/55-2
Comeger, William, 17 Jan. 1858, Mary E. Edenton   1/23/58-2
Comegeys, Edward, 10 July 1853, Catharine Vink   7/12/53-2
Compton, Barnes, 27 Oct. 1858, Margaret Holliday Sothoron,
    dau. of (Col.) John H.   11/ 4/58-2
Compton, John A., 3 June 1856, B. O. Lawrence; 6/12/56-2   6/13/56-2
Conaway, Francis A., 11 Sept. 1859, Georgeanna Ilgenfrutz   9/23/59-2
Conaway, George Thomas, 1 May 1853, Julia Ann Stockstell   5/ 3/53-2
Conaway, George W., 14 May 1860, Hester A. Brooks   5/22/60-2
Conaway, James C., 4 June 1857, Eliza J. McAllister   6/ 5/57-2
Conden, Henry S., 3 May 1854, Martha B. Levering   5/ 5/54-2
Conerey, Bedtom, 11 Nov. 1860, (Mrs.) Peggy Markham   11/12/60-2
Conklin, Joseph, 16 Nov. 1852, Mary A. Kirby   11/19/52-2
Conklin, Thomas, 7 Feb. 1853, Josephine M. Schaefer, dau. of
    C. A.   2/ 8/53-2
Conley, Thomas E., 13 Oct. 1856, Rebecca Pitcher   10/18/56-2
Conly, Patrick, 15 July 1851, Margaret Quinn   7/18/51-2
Conn, Malcom, 24 Apr. 1860, Sallie E. Stevenson; 5/ 9/60-2   5/11/60-2
Conn, William, 19 Nov. 1857, Lida R. Moran, dau. of Gabriel   11/25/57-2
Connelly, Edward, 29 May 1859, Bridget Coen   6/ 8/59-2
Connelly, John, 11 Dec. 1853, Mary McAleer   12/15/53-2
Connelly, John D., 17 Jan. 1854, Mag. A. Will   1/19/54-2
Connelly, Martin W. A., 24 May 1854, Susan Virginia Taylor   6/28/54-2
Conner, Constantine O., 17 June 1858, Sarah C. Miller, dau. of
    John and Catherine   6/19/58-2
Conner, John T., 11 Oct. 1858, Amanda E. Elder   2/21/59-2
Conner, Jos. G., 28 Apr. 1853, Mary Lee Beard   5/ 2/53-2
Conner, Maxwell, 31 Mar. 1859, Rebecca Gourly   4/ 4/59-2
Conner, Richard R., 18 Dec. 1855, Eliza J. Bryan, dau. of C.   12/25/55-2
Conner, Richard T., 17 Oct. 1860, Lizzie Franklin   10/20/60-2
Connolly, Edw'd., 25 Nov. 1851, Eliza Ennis   12/ 2/51-2
Connolly, John B., 18 Aug. 1857, Mary M. Mullin   8/20/57-2
Connoly, Michael, 24 Dec. 1854, Mary Young   1/ 6/55-2
Connolly, Patrick, 6 Apr. 1858, Elizabeth Gray   4/29/58-2
Connolly, Thomas F., 29 Oct. 1856, Emma H. Pryor, dau. of
    G. W.   10/31/56-2
Connor, John S., 15 Nov. 1854, Susan P. Miles   11/16/54-2
Connor, Michael J., 17 Nov. 1859, Mary J. Monk   11/19/59-2
Connor, Patrick, 29 July 1856, Mary Cash   7/31/56-2
Connor, Paul D., 12 Jan. 1860, Elizabeth J. Harveycutter   1/21/60-2
Connor, William A., 21 Jan. 1857, Mary Anne Seers, dau. of
    Thomas   1/29/57-2
Conolly, James, 11 Apr. 1852, Bridget Stokes   4/14/52-2
Conolly, Jas., 3 Nov. 1851, Ellen C. Quinn   11/ 5/51-2
Conolly, Martin, 2-(?) Apr. 1852, Margaret Dougher   4/28/52-2
Conoway, Wildiam E., 1 Feb. 1859, Elizabeth A. Johnson   2/ 3/59-2
Conrad, F. M., 28 Aug. 1855, Bettie H. Young   9/ 4/55-2
Conradt, George F., 1 Mar. 1855, Ann Eastwood, dau. of Joseph   3/ 9/55-2
Conrey, Henry S., 20 Nov. 1860, Angeline Tripolett   11/23/60-2
Conroy, Thomas, 11 Nov. 1860, Margaret Markham   11/14/60-2
Constable, Stevenson, 27 Nov. 1860, Alice A. Riley   12/ 5/60-2
Constable, Wm. R., 1 July 1852, Fannie H. Hodges   7/ 5/52-2
Constance, George, 9 Apr. 1860, Ida Sherwood   4/12/60-2
Constancer, Theodore, 1 Mar. 1860, Anna Neely   3/ 3/60-2

Constantine, J. W. (Dr.), 5 Mar. 1852, Margaret A. Solomon,
   dau. of Wm.   3/ 9/52-2
Constantine, Richard, Jr., 5 June 1859, Martha Cooper   6/ 9/59-2
Constantine, Thomas, 15 Jan. 1853, Mary Kennedy   1/27/53-2
Conway, Charles L., 27 Dec. 1853, (Mrs.) Margaret Key   1/20/54-2
Conway, James, 21 May 1856, Anne Louisa Derring, dau. of Henry 5/24/56-2
Conway, M. F., 19 June 1851, Emily Frances Dykes   6/21/51-2
Conway, R. Joseph, 22 Aug. 1853, Lucinda E. A. Smyth   8/25/53-2
Conway, Richard H., 14 June 1855, Jennie Stockton Scott, dau.
   of Townsend   6/18/55-2
Conway, William, 28 Nov. 1860, Sarah J. Cook   12/27/60-2
Coogins, Edwin R., 24 Oct. 1860, Mary A. Rowe   10/31/60-2
Cook, A. G., 13 June 1854, Mary Ella Trainor   6/15/54-2
Cook, Albert, 14 Sept. 1854, Anna Maria Kirby   9/19/54-2
Cook, Alexander, 1 June 1855, Catherine Keough   6/ 4/55-2
Cook, Allen, 28 Apr. 1859, Mary Jane Lawder   5/ 5/59-2
Cook, Archibald L., 21 Oct. 1851, Margaret Elizabeth Turner,
   dau. of (Col.) J. Maybury   10/22/51-2
Cook, Charles Addison, 19 Aug. 1860, Georgianna Plummer, dau.
   of John and Hannah   10/19/60-2
Cook, David, 23 Sept. 1859, Mary E. Bright   10/14/59-2
Cook, E., 24 Feb. 1859, Willy Ann Davis   2/25/59-2
Cook, Edward B., 3 Nov. 1859, J. Bellmena Fell, dau. of
   Philip S.   11/ 5/59-2
Cook, Frederick, 25 Apr. 1854, Mary A. M. Carkell   4/29/54-2
Cook, Frederick, 17 May 1859, Lizzie Bruce, dau. of James A. 5/23/59-2
Cook, George, 17 Apr. 1851, Ellenor A. Hurst, dau. of Jacob   4/18/51-2
Cook, George L., 22 Aug. 1858, Margaret A. Hamilton   9/14/58-2
Cook, Henry, 29 Aug. 1853, Catharine Kinder   9/13/53-2
Cook, Henry, 26 Feb. 1857, Martha E. Woodrow   2/28/57-2
Cook, Henry, 21 Feb. 1858, Henrietta Allen, dau. of Joseph and
   Amelia   2/23/58-2
Cook, Jacob, 16 Aug. 1852, Clarissa Ann Ritter   8/25/52-2
Cook, James, 24 Feb. 1859, Martha Coggins   3/ 1/59-2
Cook, John Adam, 7 Nov. 1855, Wilheminea Sadler   11/ 7/55-3
Cook, Jonathan W., 8 Feb. 1856, Cary Ann Bartin   2/ 9/56-2
Cook, Joseph B., 4 July 1860, Medora S. Roelkey   7/17/60-2
Cook, N. P. (Col.), 9 Feb. 1859, Artridge R. Waters   2/11/59-2
Cook, Robert A., 2 Sept. 1858, Olevia L. S. Shreck   9/ 6/58-2
Cook, Septimus J. (Dr.), 16 Mar. 1852, (Mrs.) Mary A. Wilson,
   dau. of James A. D. Dairymple   3/18/52-2
Cook, Silas, 6 Apr. 1859, Catherine Sexton   4/ 9/59-2
Cook, Thomas, 6 Sept. 1853, Julia Rice   9/ 8/53-2
Cook, William, 25 Dec. 1853, Emma Lant   12/30/53-2
Cook, William (Rev.), 13 Apr. 1856, M. Elizabeth Simson   5/ 2/56-2
Cook, William, 22 Dec. 1857, Margaret Ann Baldner   12/31/57-2
Cook, William, 11 July 1859, Julia Lawless   8/ 3/59-2
Cook, Wm., 29 Sept. 1853, Matilda Becket   10/ 3/53-2
Cook, Wm. W., 17 Jan. 1853, Emily F. Wright   1/19/53-2
Cooke, Andrew J., 26 May 1851, Frances Reynolds   5/29/51-2
Cooke, Benjamin D., 19 Sept. 1860, E. Zuleika Dorsey, dau. of
   John W.   10/ 4/60-2
Cooke, Charles W. S., 18 Oct. 1859, Anna G. Rowe   10/20/59-2
Cooke, Isaac McKim (Capt.), 13 Feb. 1853, Carmen Arrosemena,
   dau. of Diego   2/23/53-2
Cooke, J. P., 16 Dec. 1857, E. M. Lennor   12/25/57-2
Cooke, John, 2 June 1856, Rosanna Donelly   8/ 1/56-2
Cooke, Wm., 4 Oct. 1855, (Mrs.) Margaret Thomas, dau. of
   David T. McKim   10/10/55-2
Cookson, John C., 10 Dec. 1856, Emma Howard, dau. of Edward 12/12/56-2
Cooley, Edward, 18 Sept. 1854, Elizabeth Eural   9/20/54-2
Cooling, William T., 2 Oct. 1853, Mary E. Lowrey, dau. of
   William   10/22/53-2
Coon, John W., 29 Dec. 1859, Emma S. Gosnell   1/ 5/60-2
Cooney, Geo. A., 1 Feb. 1855, Sarah A. Thurlow   2/ 3/55-2

```
Cooney, James L., 24 Dec. 1854, Ellen F. Mooney              12/28/54-2
Cooney, Michael, 9 Sept. 1860, M. E. McCroden; corrected
     copy                                                    10/13/60-2
Cooney, P. H., 30 Oct. 1855, Arabella V. Thompson, dau. of
     Richard                                                 11/ 1/55-2
Cooney, Richard, 9 Oct. 1860, M. E. McCroden                 10/12/60-2
Cooper, Benj. F., 2 Aug. 1859, Martha McGee                   8/ 4/59-2
Cooper, Bishop, 28 Oct. 1858, Sarah Ellen Babb               11/ 3/58-2
Cooper, Daniel, 19 Apr. 1853, Elizabeth Horsford              4/26/53-2
Cooper, Edward K., 26 Apr. 1859, Mary R. Golibart, dau. of
     Joseph                                                   4/30/59-2
Cooper, George W. (Rev.), 17 Feb. 1852, Levinia R. Beckwith   2/20/52-2
Cooper, George W., 12 Apr. 1855, Eliza S. Clarke              4/16/55-2
Cooper, George W., 3 Apr. 1856, (Mrs.) Mary Jane Ambrose      4/ 7/56-2
Cooper, Henry, 17 Apr. 1853, Chesteaner Merryman              4/23/53-2
Cooper, Horace, 22 Feb. 1857, Mary Jane Saunders              2/24/57-2
Cooper, James, 16 Oct. 1856, Nancy A. Johnson                10/23/56-2
Cooper, Jas. C., 8 Dec. 1851, (Mrs.) Elizabeth Kennedy       12/10/51-2
Cooper, John W., 28 Oct. 1858, Rachel Ann Hodgers            10/30/58-2
Cooper, John W. F., 25 July 1853, Julia A. E. Foster          7/30/53-2
Cooper, John Wesley, 16 July 1853, Louisa F. Mosher           7/20/53-2
Cooper, Joseph, 13 Feb. 1851, (Mrs.) Sarah Jerome             2/28/51-2
Cooper, Joseph M., 7 Jan. 1857, Mary M. Noel                  6/12/57-2
Cooper, Joshua T., 13 Feb. 1851, Elizabeth A. Cassell         2/28/51-2
Cooper, Richard Allen, 25 July 1855, Martha Garner            7/26/55-2
Cooper, Teigo, 15 Jan. 1852, Mary Williams                    1/19/52-2
Cooper, William, 22 Aug. 1853, Barbary Hemer                  8/31/53-2
Cooper, William, 20 Nov. 1856, Mary E. Brown                 11/22/56-2
Cooper, William H., 16 Mar. 1851, Henrietta Jarvis            3/24/51-2
Cooper, William O., 16 Jan. 1855, (Mrs.) Margaret Spedden     1/17/55-2
Cootee, George S., 12 Apr. 1854, Sarah C. Mowell, dau. of
     Peter                                                    4/14/54-2
Coots, G. A., 6 May 1855, Ellen Stuart                        5/ 8/55-2
Cope, Charles, 17 Nov. 1857, Frances Martin, dau. of William;
     corrected copy                                          11/25/57-2
Coppage, Thomas, 3 Aug. 1852, Mary Jane Beane                 8/ 4/52-2
Copper, Cyrus, 14 Dec. 1858, Drucilla Shearlock, dau. of
     John                                                    12/18/58-2
Copper, Joseph, 13 Feb. 1851, (Mrs.) Sarah Jerome; corrected
     copy                                                     3/ 1/51-2
Copper, Joshua T., 13 Feb. 1851, Elizabeth A. Cassell, dau. of
     Samuel C.; corrected copy                                3/ 1/51-2
Cora, John T., 23 Sept. 1858, Sarah J. Crusen                10/19/58-2
Corbett, Timothy, 19 Feb. 1852, Margaret Rickards             2/24/52-2
Cord, Wm. S., 28 Oct. 1852, Matilda Dimmitt                  11/ 3/52-2
Cordray, William, 31 July 1855, Mary Harrington               8/ 2/55-2
Core, John, 11 Oct. 1855, Ann E. Warrik                      10/13/55-2
Corey, M. Frederick, 1 Sept. 1853, Rebecca W. Young           9/ 6/53-2
Cork, John H., 18 Aug. 1853, Elizabeth Gossage                8/25/53-2
Cork, William Henry, 28 Dec. 1853, Mary A. Dearm             12/31/53-2
Corkran, Benjamin W., 4 May 1854, Augusta B. Hiss, dau. of
     Benjamin                                                 5/ 5/54-2
Corkrin, Nathan J., 11 Dec. 1856, Margaret M. Wilson         12/13/56-2
Cornelius, Hezekiah B., son of (Rev.) John, 4 Sept. 1851,
     Rebecca Frances Burn, dau. of James                      9/ 6/51-2
Corner, Benjamin, 30 Sept. 1857, Elizabeth Morrow            10/ 2/57-2
Corner, Thomas, 31 Mar. 1857, Sallie Cromwell, dau. of Richard 4/ 6/57-2
Cornish, Harmon, 22 Jan. 1852, Nancy Laws, dau. of Daniel and
     Margaret                                                 1/24/52-2
Cornish, James, 19 July 1860, (Mrs.) Elizabeth Williams       7/21/60-2
Cornish, John, 17 Dec. 1857, Elizabeth Queen                 12/19/57-2
Cornish, Liberia, 26 Dec. 1852, Ellen Hanes                  12/30/52-2
Cornthwait, James H. (Capt.), 16 July 1857, Mary J. Melcher   7/21/57-2
Cornthwait, Thomas, 11 Oct. 1860, Eliza Griffin              10/17/60-2
Correa, Matthew O., 21 Aug. 1856, Sarah Ann Treadway         10/20/56-2
```

Correa, Wm. J., 29 Sept. 1857, Sarah E. Patterson   11/25/57-2
Correll, Jacob, 1 Sept. 1853, (Mrs.) Eliza Moore   9/ 3/53-2
Corrie, Jas. (Dr.), 6 July 1858, Elizabeth A. Thomson   7/ 7/58-2
Corson, John T., 25 May 1854, Henrietta M. Dorman   5/26/54-2
Corson, Robt., 28 Nov. 1854, Mary A. Haskell   12/ 1/54-2
Cortney, Edmond, 30 Mar. 1856, Catherine Hoban   4/ 2/56-2
Corwin, James C., 10 Nov. 1859, Sallie E. Clark   11/12/59-2
Cosens, Charles Sidney, 1 Nov. 1855, Hortensia Monroe Rogers,
    dau. of Lloyd N.   11/ 3/55-3
Cosgrove, Michael, 14 July 1853, Mary A. Whelan   7/22/53-2
Cost, Henry, 20 Sept. 1859, Mary A. S. Shipley   9/30/59-2
Coster, Joseph, 28 Oct. 1852, Mary A. Beck   11/ 1/52-2
Coster, Wm. F., 16 Dec. 1858, Mary J. Burup   12/18/58-2
Costin, Robt. S., 7 Dec. 1853, Kate P. Parker, dau. of
    (Gen.) S. E.   12/ 9/53-2
Costolay, P. J., 18 Oct. 1858, Margaret C. McCann   10/20/58-2
Cotter, John, 19 May 1859, (Mrs.) Mary McAuliffe   5/24/59-2
Cottman, Geo. S., 20 Apr. 1852, Telitha Marker   4/22/52-2
Cotton, William Henry, 26 Oct. 1857, Rachel Ann Simms   11/28/57-2
Cottrell, Daniel G., 10 Dec. 1856, Maquada Ann Cathell   12/15/56-2
Cottrell, Henry W. (Capt.), 18 Oct. 1852, Rosanna Sumwalt 10/22/52-2
Cottrell, Jeremiah (Capt.), 1 Sept. 1855, Ellen Layfield   9/ 4/55-2
Couchman, David, 3 Dec. 1857, Mary Ann McLorney   12/ 5/57-2
Coudon, Henry S., 3 May 1854, Martha B. Levering   5/ 6/54-2
Cougle, Thomas W., 5 Mar. 1860, Sarah E. Withers   11/19/60-2
Coulson, Andrew J., 25 Jan. 1860, Cora Ann E. Hudgins, dau.
    of Wm. T.   1/28/60-2
Coulson, Thomas F., 6 Feb. 1853, Amelia C. Chambers   2/11/53-2
Coulter, Alexander M., 5 July 1856, M. Jane McKinley   7/21/56-2
Coulter, James J., 25 Nov. 1857, Harriet E. Halfpenny   12/ 7/57-2
Coulter, John, 30 Mar. 1854, A. Eliza Smith   4/ 4/54-2
Coulter, Leonidus L., 8 July 1852, Martha E. Boone   7/10/52-2
Coulter, Samuel, 25 Jan. 1853, Jane Adams   2/ 1/53-2
Councell, Joel P., 9 June 1853, Sarah Sparks   6/11/53-2
Courtney, James A., 16 Jan. 1856, Mary A. W. Mann, dau. of
    Wm. H.   1/19/56-2
Courts, George W., 19 Mar. 1857, Sarah Jane Wolfenden   4/ 7/57-2
Covell, John T. J., 3 July 1860, Ann R. Buckey   7/ 6/60-2
Covell, William H., 7 Aug. 1855, Geneva Tracey, dau. of John 8/14/55-2
Covey, James H., 15 Aug. 1859, Sallie S. S. Seth   9/ 3/59-2
Cowan, David, 13 Aug. 1857, Eliza J. Baker   8/14/57-2
Cowles, Henry M., 1 Aug. 1854, Matilda C. Forrester, dau. of
    Joseph   8/ 3/54-2
Cowley, Joel, 2 Jan. 1851, Ann M. Harris   1/ 4/51-2
Cowley, William D., 2-(?) Apr. 1853, Alice M. Morford   5/ 6/53-2
Cowman, J. Henry, 25 Feb. 1857, Emily A. Stammers, dau. of
    Shepard   2/26/57-2
Cowman, Samuel S., 15 Oct. 1859, Harriet A. Hopkins   11/18/59-2
Cox, Amos A., 18 Nov. 1851, Sarah Jane Cullison   11/20/51-2
Cox, Edwin J., 3 May 1856, Mary Elizabeth Donley, dau. of
    Thomas B.   5/ 7/56-2
Cox, George, 21 Dec. 1857, (Mrs.) Elizabeth Paul   1/ 1/58-2
Cox, J. Thomas, 6 May 1856, Lydia S. Forrester   6/ 3/58-2
Cox, Jas. H., Jr., 13 Sept. 1860, Mary R. Shields, dau. of
    R. D.   9/15/60-2
Cox, John A., 6 Dec. 1860, Mary E. Harrison   12/ 8/60-2
Cox, Luther J., Jr., 21 Nov. 1854, Marie L. Lee, dau. of
    James H.   11/25/54-2
Cox, Perry, 1 Nov. 1851, Caroline Hurtt   3/ 3/52-2
Cox, William A., 7 Apr. 1856, Eliza C. Emerick   4/ 9/56-2
Coyle, Charles, 11 Jan. 1853, (Mrs.) Margaret Norton   1/13/53-2
Coyle, W. Francis, 7 July 1859, Maggie E. Rhodes, dau. of
    John R.   7/14/59-2
Coyne, John, 23 Nov. 1858, Julia Carroll   11/29/58-2
Cozine, James W., 2 July 1857, Sarah A. Rider   7/ 6/57-2

```
Cozine, John T., 14 Oct. 1852, Ursula Cross                    10/18/52-2
Crabbe, J. E. R., 20 Jan. 1852, Annie C. Biscoe, dau. of
     James; corrected copy                                      1/22/52-2
Crabbe, J. E. R., 20 Jan. 1852, Annie C. Briscoe, dau. of
     James                                                      1/21/52-2
Crabbs, F., 24 July 1856, M. Emilie Morris                      8/ 8/56-2
Craddock, J. T., 27 Apr. 1854, Lizzie Selvage                   4/28/54-2
Craft, Chas. H., 23 Apr. 1850, Sarah E. Merritt                 9/25/51-2
Cragg, Henry, 13 May 1852, Mary E. Graff, dau. of (Capt.)
     Richard Edwards                                            5/14/52-2
Craig, James, 10 Feb. 1852, Margaret Shorts                     2/14/52-2
Craig, John, 20 May 1852, Elizabeth Jamison                     6/15/52-2
Craig, Robert, 19 July 1859, Jane Denny                         7/22/59-2
Craige, Albert B.; no date given, Maria Virginia Hill, dau. of
     David                                                      9/ 5/53-2
Cramblitt, Geo. H., 12 June 1860, Anna Gerns                    6/20/60-2
Cramblitt, Henry, 12 Mar. 1860, Emma V. Corwine, dau. of Wm. R. 3/21/60-2
Crampton, S. W., 2 Feb. 1858, Isabella Perryman, dau. of
     George H.                                                  2/ 3/58-2
Crandal, Hiram, 18 July 1853, Margaret A. McDaniel; corrected
     copy                                                      10/21/53-2
Crandal, Hiram, 18 Oct. 1853, Margaret A. McDaniel             10/20/53-2
Crane, John W., 7 Oct. 1856, Eliza Augusta Brooks, dau. of
     N. C.                                                     10/ 9/56-2
Crane, Thomas R., 24 Aug. 1853, Ann R. Leche, dau. of David     8/25/53-2
Crant, James A., 21 June 1852, Johannah Murphy                  2/27/54-2
Crawford, Daniel J., 9 June 1859, Emma M. Simonson              6/15/59-2
Crawford, Elisha R., 20 Aug. 1853, Elizabeth E. Hutchings      10/21/53-2
Crawford, Fell E., 27 Nov. 1860, Lizzie Lawrence               12/18/60-2
Crawford, Free E., 27 Nov. 1860, Lizzie Lawrence; corrected
     copy                                                      12/20/60-2
Crawford, James, 1 June 1854, Anna Wheeler                      6/ 8/54-2
Crawford, Richard J., 13 Nov. 1856, Mary E. Dodson             11/22/56-2
Crawford, Saml. T., 25 Nov. 1856, Malinda Virginia Brooks      11/29/56-2
Crawford, W. A., 2 Apr. 1857, (Mrs.) Elizabeth E. Graham,
     dau. of David Leche                                        4/ 3/57-2
Crawford, William H., 6 Nov. 1851, Eliza J. Smith              11/ 7/51-2
Crawford, Wm., 11 Apr. 1854, Mary E. Trimble                    4/13/54-2
Crawford, Wm. R., 26 Aug. 1857, Annie A. Masterton             3/30/58-2
Crawl, Henry, 5 Nov. 1856, Agnes Murray                        11/ 7/56-2
Creamer, Christian, 30 Aug. 1859, Shealoty J. Scroggs           9/ 1/59-2
Creamer, J. F., 1 May 1852, Mary L. Clare, dau. of Thos. J.     5/ 3/52-2
Creamer, John, 6 July 1852, Caroline Regina Schiable, dau. of
     Charles F. and Regina                                      7/20/52-2
Creamer, Thomas H., 25 Jan. 1859, Annie Gardner                 6/23/59-2
Creamer, William, 21 Oct. 1851, Catharine Green, dau. of
     (Col.) Joshua                                             10/28/51-2
Creamer, William, 21 Oct. 1851, Catharine Green, dau. of
     (Col.) Josiah; corrected copy                             10/29/51-2
Creamer, William, 9 Dec. 1858, Elleanor Ledley                 12/11/58-2
Creenly, Wm., 9 Feb. 1858, Emeline C. Burley                    2/12/58-2
Creery, William R., 18 May 1852, Annie C. Thornton, dau. of
     Stephen                                                    5/21/52-2
Creighton, Augustus W., 18 Apr. 1854, Mary A. Patterson         4/19/54-2
Creighton, Francis, 26 July 1860, (Mrs.) Julia Cameron          7/31/60-2
Creighton, George, 1 Jan. 1856, Mary Catharine Hopwood          1/ 3/56-2
Creighton, John H. (Capt.), 10 May 1852, Maria Green            5/18/52-2
Creighton, William (Capt.); no date given, Rosetta Patterson
     Mitchell, dau. of James and Jane, grandau. of (Sir)
     Robert                                                     4/ 4/55-2
Creighton, William, 20 Jan. 1853, Elizabeth H. Gist             1/26/53-2
Creny, Thos. C., 17 Sept. 1857, (Mrs.) Catherine Cusick         9/19/57-2
Cressy, Geo. N., 5 June 1860, Mary L. Bayley                    6/ 7/60-2
Crever, F. E. (Rev.), 26 Feb. 1857, Rachel A. Hendrix, dau. of
     Isaac                                                      3/ 5/57-2
```

Crew, Richard L., 25 Apr. 1852, Maria J. Anster   5/ 3/52-2
Crider, Charles A., 2 Oct. 1856, Ann Rebecca Smith   10/ 7/56-2
Crimmen, W. T., 18 Oct. 1853, Mary Jane Muliem, dau. of Peter 10/19/53-2
Crippen, L. C., 6 Mar. 1855, Ann Elizabeth Ringold   3/16/55-2
Cripper, John F., 27 Feb. 1855, Mary C. Carter   3/ 7/55-2
Cripps, John T., 17 Oct. 1852, Julia Ann Hudchins; 10/30/52-2 11/ 1/52-2
Cripps, William W. L., 3 July 1855, Henrietta M. Forsyth,
     dau. of Francis, grandau. of (Capt.) Wm. Bryden   7/ 4/55-2
Crisp, F. Grafton, 12 May 1859, Alvirda J. Shipley   5/18/59-2
Crisp, Joseph, 22 Feb. 1852, Fredericka Snyder   2/24/52-2
Crisp, Richard O., 13 Nov. 1856, Annie E. Slater, dau. of Jas. 11/17/56-2
Criss, James Edwin, 6 June 1854, Elizabeth Ann L. Donaldson   6/ 8/54-2
Criswell, James, 10 Apr. 1856, Mary Ann Sowers   4/18/56-2
Criswell, James, 15 June 1856, Mary Ann Sowers   6/19/56-2
Crocker, Abram, 14 Sept. 1851, Lydia L. Mellin   9/15/51-2
Crocker, Francis P., 17 Sept. 1860, Louisa Taylor, dau. of
     Mordecai   9/25/60-2
Crockett, Alison, 12 June 1860, Lizzie J. Bennett, dau. of
     (Col.) A. B.   6/28/60-2
Crockett, John B., 31 Jan. 1853, Emily B. Robinson   2/17/53-2
Crockett, Josiah (Capt.), 11 Sept. 1855, Mary Elizabeth Harris 9/18/55-2
Crohen, Patrick, 8 May 1859, Mary Longan   5/10/59-2
Crole, Joseph S., 8 May 1851, Mary F. Wiegard   5/ 6/51-2
Cromelien, James Monroe, 29 Feb. 1860, Sarah Heilbrun, dau. of
     Michael; corrected copy   3/ 5/60-2
Cromelier, James Monroe, 29 Feb. 1860, Sarah Heilbrun   3/ 3/60-2
Crommer, John, 3 July 1856, Sophia Anderson   7/ 8/56-2
Crompton, Jehu, 13 Feb. 1855, Mary F. Moore   2/20/55-2
Cromweld, Jacob G., 27 May 1851, Catharine Agnes Peirson   6/ 3/51-2
Cromwell, Geo. H., 2 Oct. 1853, Sarah Jane Russel   10/ 5/53-2
Cromwell, John E., 19 Feb. 1857, Eliza Ann Vain   2/24/57-2
Cromwell, John G., 17 Feb. 1853, Amanda Hammond   2/21/53-2
Cromwell, Levi, 5 Dec. 1857, Esther Ann Myers, dau. of (Capt.)
     Daniel   1/ 6/58-2
Cromwell, Oliver H., 9 Mar. 1857, Emma Frances Miller   3/24/57-2
Cromwell, Oliver H., 29 Sept. 1859, Sarah E. Somerville   10/ 1/59-2
Cromwell, Samuel, 5 Apr. 1860, Maria T. Wilson   4/ 7/60-2
Cromwell, Thomas, 1 Feb. 1859, E. Serena Lauck   2/ 3/59-2
Cromwell, William T., 27 Apr. 1859, Mary Ann Fay   11/29/59-2
Cronan, Charles P., 24 July 1854, Eliza H. Evans   7/26/54-2
Cronen, Wm. T., 6 Jan. 1857, Elizabeth Hoopman   1/12/57-2
Croney, Philip H., 9 Feb. 1858, Margaret B. Harryman   2/11/58-2
Cronin, Patrick M., 28 Jan. 1851, Ann Cain   2/27/51-2
Cronmiller, Thos. LePage (Dr.), 13 Nov. 1860, Joshwaine
     Gardner   11/22/60-2
Crook, Charles, Jr., 24 Apr. 1851, Charlotte S. Gardner, dau.
     of Wm.   5/ 8/51-2
Crook, Geo. W., 12 Jan. 1860, Mary Manion   1/16/60-2
Crook, George W. L., 15 Sept. 1853, Jane D. Eitonhead, dau. of
     Thomas   9/19/53-2
Crook, Henry, 5 Nov. 1851, Amelia J. Crooke   11/29/51-2
Crook, James, Jr., 20 Sept. 1853, Emma Crooks, dau. of James
Crook, Victor V., 9 Feb. 1854, Georgiana Eltonhead   2/14/54-2
Crook, W. Musgrave, 15 May 1860, Hannah M. Lewis, dau. of
     Jacob   6/ 1/60-2
Crook, William S., 8 Dec. 1853, Esther E. Huflington, dau. of
     (Capt.) W. W.   12/10/53-2
Crooks, Saml. W., 13 Apr. 1854, Ann R. Walters   4/14/54-2
Crookshanks, Chas. S., 20 Dec. 1853, Ann Elizabeth Washington,
     dau. of James H.   12/22/53-2
Cropper, Stephen, 15 Dec. 1853, Martha Fenall   12/21/53-2
Cropper, Thos. J., 14 Mar. 1855, Mary E. Campbell, dau. of
     John   3/21/55-2
Crosby, Frank J., 7 May 1860, Ella Watson   5/ 9/60-2
Crosby, Louis, 21 Aug. 1853, Mary Jane Bryson   8/23/53-2

```
Cross, Alexander, 25 Apr. 1855, Cordelia A. Simpson              4/27/55-2
Cross, Caleb, 27 Oct. 1853, Mary E. Merryman, dau. of Benj. B.  12/13/53-2
Cross, Cyril, 5 May 1854, Elizabeth White, dau. of Nicholas
    and Ann J.                                                   5/ 9/54-2
Cross, David H., 15 Apr. 1858, Margaret Hughes                   4/17/58-2
Cross, George, 26 Mar. 1854, (Mrs.) Elizabeth Eleanor Cretin     3/28/54-2
Cross, John H., 3 Apr. 1855, Sarah Jane Allen                    4/ 5/55-2
Cross, John Henry, 25 Nov. 1858, Rachel Adams                   12/ 2/58-2
Cross, John L., 30 Mar. 1852, Mary Lowe, dau. of John            4/ 1/52-2
Cross, John W. P., 12 Aug. 1858, Elizabeth A. R. Fairbank, dau.
    of Noah                                                      8/16/58-2
Cross, Stephen, 28 Jan. 1855, Elizape H. Belry                   2/ 2/55-2
Cross, William R., 27 Sept. 1860, Neppie A. Jameson             10/ 6/60-2
Crossan, Thomas M. (Lieut.), 11 July 1854, Rebecca Brehon,
    dau. of (Dr.) James G.                                       7/14/54-2
Crossley, J. P., 11 Jan. 1858, Mary C. Hewitt                    2/17/58-2
Crother, John (Capt.), 25 Dec. 1855, Susan M. Johnson           12/29/55-2
Crotty, David, 12 Aug. 1860, Margaret A. Welsh                   8/30/60-2
Crouch, Alexander, 24 Aug. 1854, Elizabeth Noel                  9/ 4/54-2
Crouch, Hugh B., 8 Apr. 1852, Ann E. Blundon                     4/10/52-2
Crouch, Thomas Davis, 25 June 1855, Ann Lavinia Sumwalt;
    7/10/55-2                                                    7/11/55-2
Crouch, Wm. T., 16 Jan. 1851, Maria L. Williams, dau. of A. M.   1/20/51-2
Croucher, George E., 5 Jan. 1860, Margaret Dumphy               1/10/60-2
Crouse, Edwin H., 30 Dec. 1856, S. C. Ensor, dau. of Charles     1/ 1/57-2
Crouse, John, 24 Jan. 1854, Olevia L. McIlvan                    1/30/54-2
Crow, John, 11 Oct. 1857, Charlotte Onditch                     10/23/57-2
Crow, John T., 3 Aug. 1853, Mary E. Owens                        8/ 4/53-2
Crow, Sheldon, 12 May 1851, Ann Catharine C. Hildreth            5/14/51-2
Crowder, A. N.; no date given, Debbie J. Warfield               12/13/60-2
Crowell, John (Capt.), 4 Nov. 1858, Fanny H. Bennett, dau. of
    (Capt.) Richard                                             11/ 5/58-2
Crowl, Andrew S., 12 Oct. 1852, Isabella Battee, dau. of
    Samuel; corrected copy                                      10/19/52-2
Crowl, David H., 29 Sept. 1857, Caroline Greble, dau. of
    Benjamin                                                     9/30/57-2
Crowl, Edward W., 8 Apr. 1852, Josephine Greble, dau. of
    Benjamin                                                     4/10/52-2
Crowley, John, 18 Nov. 1858, Sophia E. Mason                    11/20/58-2
Crowley, William, 10 Aug. 1851, Mary Ann Watts                   8/12/51-2
Crownfield, Herman F., 7 Aug. 1860, Sophia H. Ring               8/10/60-2
Crowt, John E., 1 Jan. 1855, Sarah F. Brown, dau. of James M.    3/12/55-2
Crowther, James, 25 Oct. 1860, Eliza Ann Baughman               10/29/60-2
Crowther, John, Jr., 29 Sept. 1853, Fannie Bosley, dau. of
    Wm., grandau. of Jno.                                       10/ 1/53-2
Crowther, Joshua, 9 Mar. 1859, Althea M. Redden                  3/11/59-2
Cruickshank, George, 17 Nov. 1858, Septma Howell, dau. of
    Thomas                                                      11/22/58-2
Crumbaugh, John, 24 Oct. 1853, Catherine Virginia King          10/31/53-2
Crummer, Daniel, 13 Mar. 1856, Mary E. Claiborne                 3/18/56-2
Crummer, Nathan J., 31 May 1853, (Mrs.) Rose Anna Talbott        6/ 2/53-2
Cruse, Edward, 20 Sept. 1859, Hester Ann Gray Collins, dau. of
    Samuel; 9/24/59-2                                            9/26/59-2
Cruse, Elias T., 15 Mar. 1858, Elizabeth Smith                   3/16/58-2
Cruse, George W., 16 May 1859, Mary L. Mann; corrected copy      5/19/59-2
Cruse, John H., 18 Dec. 1856, Susan E. Mann, dau. of W. P.      12/20/56-2
Crutchley, John L., 30 Nov. 1857, Sallie Ford                   12/ 4/57-2
Cruzen, Edward, 27 Oct. 1859, (Mrs.) Julia Vanhorn              10/31/59-2
Cruzen, George Z., 29 Apr. 1855, Mary C. McCrea                  5/ 2/55-2
Cudbirth, Benjamin, 15 Dec. 1856, Caroline Tinker               12/19/56-2
Cuddy, Thomas, 28 Apr. 1859, Annie M. Gardner                    5/ 5/59-2
Cuff, Thomas, 15 Nov. 1860, (Mrs.) Rachel Ann Tascoe            11/17/60-2
Culbertson, Isaac G., 6 Jan. 1857, Sarah E. Barbour              4/23/57-2
Cullen, Charles M., 4 May 1853, C. Virginia Waugh                5/ 5/53-2
Cullen, James, 20 Jan. 1856, (Mrs.) Anne Madden                  1/23/56-2
```

Culley, Wesley P., 6 Jan. 1852, Lucy Street, dau. of Wm.   3/12/52-2
Culley, Wm., 30 Dec. 1852, (Mrs.) Elizabeth Lighton   1/ 1/53-2
Cullimore, John T., 26 Oct. 1852, Esther E. Nelson   11/22/52-2
Cullin, Patrick, 28 Apr. 1853, Mary Malany   5/10/53-2
Cullison, James M., 2 Dec. 1856, Alexine Turner   12/ 6/56-2
Cullum, George W., 6 Apr. 1854, Mary J. Whiteley   4/ 8/54-2
Cully, Robert, 16 June 1859, (Mrs.) Margaret Jane Jacobs   6/17/59-2
Culp, Michael Sisler, 1 July 1857, Elender Ann Holland   7/ 4/57-2
Culp, Wm., 27 Sept. 1853, Salome Sheads   10/14/53-2
Culver, Charles H., 29 May 1856, Adeline J. Chanceaulme   7/ 8/56-2
Culver, Charles P., 29 Dec. 1859, Emie A. Scrivener   1/11/60-2
Culverwell, William, 1 Nov. 1854, Elizabeth A. McDonall   11/ 7/54-2
Cuming, James, 12 Apr. 1855, Ellen McCormick   4/14/55-2
Cumings, John, 2 Mar. 1854, Ellen E. Gorman   3/ 4/54-2
Cummings, John Lewis, 27 Feb. 1853, Caroline Routzel   3/ 3/53-2
Cummings, Lewis H., 11 Dec. 1851, Amanda King   12/13/51-2
Cummings, Wm. F., 6 Dec. 1860, Mary E. Gardner   12/ 8/60-2
Cummins, D. James, 14 May 1855, Emma Basset   5/22/55-2
Cummins, John Lewis, 27 Feb. 1853, Caroline Routson; corrected
     copy   3/ 4/53-2
Cuningham, John D., 21 July 1857, Sarah Ann Stewart   9/21/57-2
Cunnane, Michael, 15 Apr. 1852, Eliza Onthank   5/14/52-2
Cunningham, Charles S., 20 Oct. 1857, Lucy V. Dameron, dau. of
     Wm.   10/22/57-2
Cunningham, G. W. (Capt.), 12 Oct. 1860, Annie Clautice   11/ 1/60-2
Cunningham, George, 22 Nov. 1859, Mary Jane Hooper   12/29/59-2
Cunningham, George A., 26 Apr. 1859, Rosanna Fisher   4/27/59-2
Cunningham, John, 6 Sept. 1860, Jane Little   9/18/60-2
Cunningham, John C., 28 May 1855, Eliza J. Freling   6/ 4/55-2
Cunningham, John E. A., 13 Sept. 1860, Isabella E. Brunner   9/14/60-2
Cunningham, William, 14 Apr. 1853, Isabella C. Leckey   4/27/53-2
Cunningham, William R., 18 Dec. 1851, Jane Clark, dau. of
     Samuel   12/20/51-2
Cunningham, Wm. Amos, 4 Oct. 1855, Mary Louisa Horn, dau. of
     Jacob   10/ 5/55-2
Cunningham, Wm. H., 27 Dec. 1852, Rachel Ann Nicholson   1/ 3/53-2
Cunningham, Wm. Wesley, 27 Mar. 1856, Eleanora V. Harrison,
     dau. of Jeremiah   4/ 1/56-2
Curlett, Lewis G., 16 Nov. 1859, Mollie Allen, dau. of Solomon   11/17/59-2
Curlett, William, 13 July 1852, Annie Dungan, dau. of
     Francis D.   7/14/52-2
Curlett, William, 13 May 1857, Georgeanna Spicer, dau. of
     Thomas   5/18/57-2
Curmene, John, 12 May 1859, (Mrs.) Sarah Tull   5/30/59-2
Curran, John F., 27 Sept. 1858, Mary Haight   10/ 7/58-2
Curran, John H., 14 Nov. 1850, Mary A. Donohoe   1/24/51-2
Curran, William, 15 Apr. 1855, Mary E. Andrews, dau. of (Capt.)
     Elijah   5/ 1/55-2
Curry, John, 5 Feb. 1857, Sarah Elizabeth Piersol   9/29/57-2
Curry, Robt., 23 Aug. 1860, Christianna Owens   8/25/60-2
Curtain, Samuel; no date given, Julia Stout   1/17/55-2
Curtis, Geo. W., 7 Oct. 1852, Eliza Jane Thompson   10/14/52-2
Curtis, George W., 15 June 1856, Ann Maria Bell   6/19/56-2
Curtis, John, 29 Nov. 1852, Rose Carroll   11/30/52-2
Curtis, Joseph, 4 Sept. 1853, Ann Elizabeth Hilton; 9/10/53-2;
     9/13/53-2   9/14/53-2
Curtis, Joseph W., 26 Aug. 1856, Sarah A. Proctor   8/28/56-2
Curtis, Wm. H., 31 Aug. 1859, Marthella Dobbins   9/12/59-2
Curville, William, 30 Sept. 1857, Eliza Jane Beacham   10/14/57-2
Cushan, John, 16 Mar. 1859, Caroline Pease   3/18/59-2
Cushaw, Edward L. *, 5 Dec. 1855, Mary A. McCleand   12/ 7/55-2
Cushman, Wm., 11 Nov. 1859, Martha Jane Horseman   11/22/59-2
Cushman, Wm. H., 19 May 1851, Marcelina W. Younker   5/21/51-2
Cusick, Laughlin, 28 Mar. 1853, Mary Quinn   3/30/53-2
Cutts, Thos. W., 20 May 1852, Mary E. Barnes   7/31/52-2

Dahm, Peter, 14 Dec. 1854, Hester A. Madden   12/20/54-2
Daiger, Charles H., 2 May 1859, Amelia M. DeBow   5/ 9/59-2
Daiger, Edward, 10 Nov. 1860, Susie Meeks   5/ 3/60-2
Daiger, Jospeh, Jr., 21 Apr. 1857, Catharine V. Stine   4/25/57-2
Daiger, Joseph F., 7 Nov. 1860, Amelia Jane McNeal   11/14/60-2
Daily, Ephraim V., 16 Sept. 1852, Julia A. Herring   9/18/52-2
Daily, Patrick, 4 Sept. 1854, Mary Ellen Kerr, dau. of John   9/14/54-2
Daily, Thomas, 23 Dec. 1856, Josephine Satterfield   12/25/56-2
Dale, Saml., Jr., 25 Apr. 1854, Margaret A. Saville   4/27/54-2
Dales, Robert, 25 Nov. 1858, Margaret A. Miller   11/27/58-2
Daley, John, 2 July 1854, Sarah Ann Corr; 7/ 4/54-2   7/ 6/54-2
Daley, Wm. J., 23 Jan. 1856, Sophia Olivia Hore, dau. of
    Benjamin   1/26/56-2
Dallam, Joseph W., 31 Jan. 1855, Octavia A. Gough, dau. of
    Harry D.   2/ 1/55-2
Dallam, M. Clay, 16 Dec. 1856, Pettie Braxton   12/25/56-2
Dallett, Henry C., Jr., 12 Dec. 1860, Laura A. Herring, dau.
    of J. L.   12/31/60-2
Dalrymple, A. J. (Dr.), 29 June 1858, Naomi Passmore, dau. of
    John L.   7/ 1/58-2
Dalrymple, George, 21 May 1853, Elvira Steever, dau. of (Capt.)
    George   6/ 8/53-2
Dalrymple, George, 31 Mar. 1859, Lavinia Benson, dau. of
    Robt. W.; 4/ 2/59-2   4/ 4/59-2
Dalton, James M., 2 May 1859, (Mrs.) Mary J. Shields; 5/ 4/59-2   5/ 9/59-2
Daly, Charles R., 15 Jan. 1856, Harriet Ann Wright   1/17/56-2
Daly, Patrick, 7 May 1854, Catharine Jane Hughes   5/22/54-2
Dameron, Jas. A., 9 Dec. 1858, Mary A. Courtney   12/11/58-2
Dames, Augustus, 5 Jan. 1860, Elizabeth Pos-(?)-ffe   1/30/60-2
Damuth, Simon P., 6 Oct. 1860, Rebecca J. Sutton   11/ 8/60-2
Daneker, Charles W., 12 May 1856, Joana E. Yewell   5/20/56-2
Daneker, David H., 18 July 1860, Elizabeth G. Meekings   9/ 4/60-2
Daneker, George H., 7 Oct. 1852, Kate Sechrist   10/11/52-2
Danels, Bolivar D., 6 Nov. 1856, Marie Louise Repplier, dau.
    of Charles A.   11/10/56-2
Danels, Joseph D., 5 Nov. 1857, Julia Carroll Paca, dau. of
    John P.   11/ 7/57-2
Dange, Alexander; no date given, Rachel C. Ensor   12/19/59-2
Daniel, J. W., 27 Mar. 1854, Mira Ann Bristow, dau. of
    Larkin S.   3/29/54-2
Daniel, William, 5 June 1860, Ella Y. Guiteau, dau. of (Rev.)
    Sheridan   6/ 9/60-2
Daniels, Wm. H. (Capt.), 21 June 1854, Julia A. Dutton, dau. of
    (Col.) John   6/22/54-2
Dann, Conrad, 5 Aug. 1855, Mary Swartz   8/10/55-2
Dannels, Geiels, 7 Apr. 1859, Mary Elizabeth Hennen   4/11/59-2
Danner, Joseph B., 27 Aug. 1860, Mary E. Armstrong   9/ 1/60-2
Danner, Putnam, 21 July 1859, Elizabeth L. Willar   7/25/59-2
Dannettel, Henry L., 16 Jan. 1851, Mary F. C. Brokering   1/18/51-2
Danskin, Washington Aloysius, Jr., 9 May 1857, Rosalia Cahill,
    dau. of John   6/ 2/57-2
Dant, Chas. H., 12 Sept. 1851, Margaret Worrel, dau. of James
    Dull   1/27/52-2
Dant, William E., 4 Dec. 1851, Sarah J. Berdsley   12/ 8/51-2
Darbaugh, Robert J., 10 May 1859, Jane A. Dougherty, dau. of
    Thomas   5/12/59-2
Darby, Benj., 14 Nov. 1855, Carrie Marston Collier, dau. of
    Charles   11/15/55-2
Darby, Montilion, 22 Mar. 1857, Jane Ewing   3/26/57-2
Darden, Stephen H., 10 Aug. 1858, Lena C. Stewart   8/11/58-2
Dare, Wm. H., 23 Nov. 1853, Caroline Cowman   2/ 4/54-2
Darley, John W., 1 Nov. 1860, Louisa E. Hall   11/ 3/60-2
Darling, F. Taylor, 21 Sept. 1858, Hanna B. Boloneaux   9/25/58-2
Darling, Lewis, 15 Mar. 1855, Adeline Eldridge   3/17/55-2
Darlington, Abraham, 17 July 1860, Emma C. Spalding   7/23/60-2

```
Darrell, Stewart, 24 Jan. 1856, Lydia H. Winder, dau. of
    Wm. Sydney                                                  1/29/56-2
Dart, John R., 26 May 1859, Rebecca Andrews                     5/30/59-2
Dasheri, Thomas H. (Rev.), 5 Apr. 1852, (Mrs.) Mary A. Gosnell,
    dau. of E. L. Crawford                                      4/ 7/52-2
Dashields, Henry; no date given, Marg. Dixon                    11/29/56-2
Dashiell, Charles F., 12 Nov. 1856, Emily G. E. Rose, dau. of
    Wm. H.                                                      11/15/56-2
Dashiell, Nicholas L., 20 Dec. 1855, Louisa T. Wright           12/27/55-2
Dashiell, R. L., 4 May 1854, Mary Jane Hanly                    5/ 5/54-2
Dashiell, William R., 4 June 1857, Mary C. Smith                6/ 6/57-2
Daughaday, J. S., 22 Dec. 1859, S. J. Daughaday                 3/24/60-2
Daughaday, Joseph, 13 Apr. 1856, Henrietta Chard                5/23/56-2
Daugherty, Thomas (Rev. Dr.), 27 Feb. 1854, Mary Jane Trout,
    dau. of Isaac                                               3/ 7/54-2
Daugherty, William H. (Capt.), 9 Mar. 1856, Virginia Anne
    Bowie; 3/11/56-2
                                                                3/13/56-2
Daughton, Joseph L., 14 Sept. 1857, Ruth H. Hull                9/18/57-2
Daughty, William (Col.), 18 July 1854, Sarah McConnell          7/19/54-2
Daulby, Rich'd., 15 June 1852, Caroline Sarah Small             6/17/52-2
Davidson, Clark Y., 19 Nov. 1854, E. R. Kernan, dau. of James
    and Mary                                                    11/25/54-2
Davidson, Hunter, (?) July 1852, Mary Ray, dau. of (Dr.) Hyde   7/27/52-2
Davidson, James W., 3 July 1853, Zugia Knight, dau. of Jacob    7/ 6/53-2
Davidson, Joseph, 12 Apr. 1853, Eliza Sedwick                   4/14/53-2
Davies, Solomon B., 17 Nov. 1853, Elizabeth Munroe, dau. of
    James                                                       11/22/53-2
Davis, A., 26 Sept. 1858, Elenora Bosley, dau. of Wm. and
    Elizabeth                                                   10/ 8/58-2
Davis, A. B., 14 Sept. 1851, Margaret England                   9/18/51-2
Davis, A. B., 27 Jan. 1859, Janie P. Whitlock                   2/14/59-2
Davis, Archibald T., 28 Oct. 1852, Catharine M. Foos            11/ 4/52-2
Davis, Charles E., 1 Nov. 1853, Caroline L. Fritz, dau. of
    George                                                      11/ 5/53-2
Davis, Chas. A. P., 22 July 1858, Susan M. Shenton, dau. of
    John                                                        7/26/58-2
Davis, Chas. D., 6 Mar. 1851, (Mrs.) Elizabeth Dey              3/ 8/51-2
Davis, Chas. W., 1 Sept. 1852, Rebecca Salter                   9/ 6/52-2
Davis, Christopher C. B., 30 Sept. 1856, Sarah Frances Shipley  10/ 4/56-2
Davis, David, 25 Nov. 1855, (Mrs.) Rebecca S. Casey             11/27/55-2
Davis, Edward, 21 Mar. 1854, (Mrs.) Amelia Beown                3/28/54-2
Davis, Edward, 1 Apr. 1855, Susan Kraft                         12/13/55-2
Davis, Enos, 20 May 1858, Elizabeth A. Amoss                    5/22/58-2
Davis, Geo. H., 1 June 1852, Margaret E. Waters                 6/ 4/52-2
Davis, George J., 3 Oct. 1858, Mary Catharine Cochran           10/ 5/58-2
Davis, George M., 1 Apr. 1859, Abbie L. Porter                  4/ 4/59-2
Davis, Hamilton James, Jr., 7 Feb. 1858, Louisa Smith           2/15/58-2
Davis, Henry, 16 Sept. 1858, Sophia Williams                    9/18/58-2
Davis, Henry, 13 Jan. 1859, Elizabeth S. Stinchcomb, dau. of
    Beal C.                                                     1/18/59-2
Davis, Henry, 31 May 1859, Alice B. Mettam                      6/ 6/59-2
Davis, Henry G., 22 Feb. 1853, Kate Bantz, dau. of Gideon       2/28/53-2
Davis, Hugh, 27 Aug. 1857, Sarah Catherine Groves               8/28/57-2
Davis, James E., 6 Nov. 1860, Mary A. J. Hardesty               11/ 9/60-2
Davis, James M., 21 Mar. 1853, Ellenor Waddell                  3/31/53-2
Davis, James R., 10 May 1853, Elizabeth Shorter, dau. of
    Charles and Charity                                         5/12/53-2
Davis, Jesse, 13 Feb. 1860, Elizabeth Crawford                  9/ 1/50-2
Davis, John, 14 Dec. 1856, Delia Howard                         12/18/56-2
Davis, John D., 13 Feb. 1851, Susan Batchelor                   2/17/51-2
Davis, John H., 3 Feb. 1857, Cornelia Mitchell, dau. of
    Solomon H.                                                  2/ 4/57-2
Davis, John Robert, 8 Jan. 1855, Nancy Maxwell Coleman, dau. of
    Daniel and Mary Naff                                        8/11/55-2
Davis, John T., 21 Mar. 1852, Sarah Blundon                     3/23/52-2
```

Davis, John T., 15 May 1854, Melicent N. Wamsley		5/17/54-2
Davis, John T., 1 July 1858, Susan Calloway		7/ 7/58-2
Davis, John W., 27 Apr. 1856, Sarah Virginia Moxley		5/ 5/56-2
Davis, Joseph, 31 May 1853, Mary Jane Rhodes		6/ 2/53-2
Davis, Joseph, 1 Oct. 1853, (Mrs.) Grace A. Francis		10/ 7/53-2
Davis, Joseph, 3 May 1855, Sophia J. Binnix		5/ 5/55-2
Davis, Joseph Henry, 30 Oct. 1851, Mary A. Grooms		11/ 5/51-2
Davis, Joshua B., 30 Mar. 1852, Catharine A. Davis		5/ 4/52-2
Davis, Josiah, 26 Apr. 1854, Martha Hoyt		5/16/54-2
Davis, Levi, 23 Aug. 1860, Laura Waters		8/25/60-2
Davis, Louis D., 7 Oct. 1858, Fannie P. Conrad, dau. of James M.		10/13/58-2
Davis, Mansfield Vinton, 21 Jan. 1857, Mary Ann Johnson		1/25/58-2
Davis, Owen R., 9 Sept. 1851, Rachel Bell		9/13/51-2
Davis, Richard L., 28 June 1860, Amelia R. Barnes		6/30/60-2
Davis, Robert, 4 Oct. 1857, Elizabeth Kelly		10/19/57-2
Davis, Robert, 4 Jan. 1858, Henrietta Jones		2/ 6/58-2
Davis, Robert H., 17 Apr. 1860, Clara R. Hoover, dau. of Francis		4/23/60-2
Davis, Robert P., 8 Feb. 1853, Elizabeth A. Brenton		2/10/53-2
Davis, Samuel L., 16 July 1857, Sarah C. Derr		7/24/57-2
Davis, Thos. B., 1 Sept. 1853, Mary Ann Alan		9/ 3/53-2
Davis, Thos. H., 24 Aug. 1858, Mary Hammond		9/11/58-2
Davis, William, 17 Sept. 1857, Ellen Bregle		9/19/57-2
Davis, William H., 23 Dec. 1856, Georgeanna Deuhay		12/30/56-2
Davis, William T., 5 Mar. 1857, Martha A. Rodgers		3/ 7/57-2
Davis, Willson, 8 Jan. 1855, Mary Anderson		1/19/55-2
Davis, Wilson, 30 Oct. 1856, Hannah M. Wilson		11/ 3/56-2
Davis, Wm., 11 May 1857, Mary J. Williams		5/12/57-2
Davis, Wm. Henry, 31 Mar. 1851, Caroline Landon		4/ 2/51-2
Davis, Wm. R., (?) May 1851, Susan J. Gray		5/20/51-2
Davison, Henry J., 1 Dec. 1858, Helen M. Jones, dau. of Saml., Jr.		12/ 3/58-2
Davison, John A., 31 May 1859, Agnes A. Ramsay		6/15/59-2
Davison, William J., 25 Jan. 1860, Jennie D. Hopkins		1/27/60-2
Davolt, Jacob, 4 Dec. 1851, (Mrs.) Clara Richardson		12/ 6/51-2
Dawes, Francis, 4 Sept. 1856, Nancy Millar		9/ 9/56-2
Dawes, George R. (Capt.), 27 Jan. 1859, Sarah A. Parker, dau. of Samuel and Jane		1/31/59-2
Dawes, Henry, 16 Sept. 1852, Elizabeth R. Philips		9/17/52-2
Dawes, John S., 27 Jan. 1859, Clementine C. Taylor		1/29/59-2
Daws, George R., 26 Feb. 1857, Mary R. Black		2/27/57-2
Dawson, Hugh, 20 Aug. 1857, Mary Ann Smith		9/ 4/57-2
Dawson, J. M.; no date given, Jenny Ashmore, dau. of Thomas		6/10/58-2
Dawson, Nelson; no date given, A. E. Meese		11/22/53-2
Dawson, Philip T., 19 Oct. 1852, Sarah Bell, dau. of Thomas Frotton		10/22/52-2
Dawson, Wm. K., 15 Nov. 1859, Margaret R. Simmons		11/21/59-2
Dawson, Wm. P., 20 Nov. 1856, Mary Jane Matthews, dau. of Thomas R.		11/22/56-2
Day, Edward Horatio, 4 Apr. 1854, Jenette Frances Morrison		4/ 7/54-2
Day, George A., 25 Apr. 1858, Eliza Jane Peacock		5/ 4/58-2
Dayhoff, Christian L., 29 Jan. 1852, Sarah Ann Mallonee		1/31/52-2
Dayton, Charles W., 3 Jan. 1858, Susan S. Doyle		1/ 5/58-2
Deal, John Thomas, 30 Apr. 1857, Rebecca J. Wilcox		5/ 4/57-2
Deale, John S. (Rev.), 16 Dec. 1851, Sallie Buckmaster, dau. of N.		12/19/51-2
Deale, Lemuel, 12 Jan. 1851, Caroline E. Norris		1/21/51-2
Dean, James, 27 June 1857, Julia A. Richardson		6/30/57-2
Dean, Nathan, Jr., 3 Jan. 1854, Rachel L. Robinson		1/18/54-2
Dean, Robert S., 14 July 1853, Mary Julia Baltzell, dau. of Charles		7/15/53-2
Dean, William, 1 Jan. 1856, Keturah Longly		1/16/56-2
Dean, William A., 3 Jan. 1856, Cornelia A. Gordon		1/14/56-2

Dean, Wm. F., 18 May 1852, Eudora L. Eareeson, dau. of
    Joseph   5/20/52-2
Dean, Wm. F., 18 May 1852, Eudora L. Eaverson, dau. of
    Joseph; corrected copy   5/21/52-2
Dean, Wm. H., 24 Dec. 1853, Laura S. Keilholtz   12/28/53-2
Dear, John T., 29 Apr. 1860, Margaret A. Merryman   5/ 4/60-2
Dearing, Robert M., 29 July 1860, Martha A. Wickens   8/29/60-2
Deaver, Geo. R., 11 Apr. 1860, Sophia Lancaster   4/14/60-2
Deaver, James C., 20 May 1858, Emily A. Oliver   5/22/58-2
Deaver, John N., 7 Feb. 1854, (Mrs.) Julia M. Billups   2/28/54-2
Deboise, Larmea, 15 Jan. 1857, Josephine Myers   1/20/57-2
Debow, Nicholas G., 26 June 1856, Mary E. Robinson, dau. of
    Jas. A.   7/ 1/56-2
Debring, Frederick, 5 May 1857, Louisa Getcha   6/ 9/57-2
De Courcey, James, 30 Mar. 1854, Jane Gordon   3/31/54-2
De Coursey, Christopher, 11 Jan. 1855, Ellen H. Pindall   1/13/55-2
De Coursey, Christopher, 11 Jan. 1855, Ellen H. Tindall;
    corrected copy   1/15/55-2
Dee, Richard, 28 June 1855, Hanora Supple   7/ 3/55-2
Deems, Geo. W., 10 Apr. 1851, Ann B. B. Kauffman   4/12/51-2
Deems, Jacob, 29 May 1857, Eliza Jane Yealdhall   7/ 1/57-2
Deems, James, 7 June 1857, Ellen O'Connor   6/17/57-2
Deems, John H., 29 Aug. 1854, Laura V. Martin, dau. of
    George M.   9/ 4/54-2
Deer, Samuel B., 11 Dec. 1856, Sarah A. Ruark   12/23/56-2
De Ford, Richard S., 14 Oct. 1858, Eliza J. Brown, dau. of
    Jas.   10/19/58-2
De Ford, Sam. T., Jr., 5 Oct. 1854, Kate M. Wright   10/19/54-2
De Goey, John M., Jr., 13 Dec. 1855, Isabella A. Magness   5/ 8/58-2
Deibel, Jacob, 12 May 1857, Margaret Wilson   5/18/57-2
Deidel, Adolph, 28 Dec. 1858, Caroline M. Gluck   12/31/58-2
Deilman, Louis, 20 Apr. 1854, Theodora Mueller   4/22/54-2
Deitch, Jacob, 25 Sept. 1851, Catharine L. Ness   9/30/51-2
Deitz, Francis, 26 Sept. 1859, Margaret Wode   10/12/59-2
Deitz, Henry, 26 Dec. 1859, Sarah R. Miller   1/27/60-2
Delahay, Jacob B., 22 July 1856, Annie E. Alloway   7/24/56-2
Delahay, Jesse S., 11 Nov. 1856, Mary M. Taylor   11/13/56-2
Delano, William H., 8 Jan. 1857, Anna Maria Johnson   1/14/57-2
Delany, John, 19 Dec. 1858, Eliza King   12/20/58-2
Delaplane, Thos. H., 12 Aug. 1851, Sarah Mildred Utterback,
    dau. of Armistead   8/22/51-2
Delashmentt, Andrew J., 18 May 1851, Phebe R. Reich   6/ 3/51-2
Delcher, Ed. W., 4 Dec. 1855, Mary Elizabeth Amos   12/ 7/55-2
Delcher, George B., 3 July 1854, Georgianna Wilderman   8/ 4/54-2
Delcher, John S., 25 Mar. 1858, Louisa A. Watts   5/22/58-2
Delcher, W. J., 24 Jan. 1860, Barbara Peirce   2/21/60-2
Dell, David B., 30 Nov. 1858, Georgeann V. Bikler   12/ 2/58-2
Dell, David B., 30 Nov. 1858, Georgeann V. Bitler; corrected
    copy   12/ 4/58-2
Dell, George W., 23 May 1858, Ann L. Martin   5/25/58-2
Della, George W., 5 July 1853, Elizabeth A. Miles   8/ 1/53-2
Della, Peter D., 12 July 1854, Emily A. Ross   7/19/54-2
Demuth, John, 24 Nov. 1859, Sarah A. McKee   11/28/59-2
Deloach, Francis R., 14 Aug. 1856, Elizabeth A. Nairne   8/15/56-2
Deloney, Charles M., 15 June 1858, Rose Ann Wills   8/17/58-2
Deloste, Joseph, 3 Mar. 1851, Josephine M. Arquit   3/ 5/51-2
Demby, Thos., 9 June 1859, Julia Ann Cooper   6/13/59-2
Deming, Edward A., 13 Dec. 1854, Anne R. Owens   12/16/54-2
Demmon, Francis H., 20 Apr. 1854, Elizabeth Gay   5/10/54-2
Dempsey, John M., 27 Dec. 1852, Sarah Elizabeth Rae   12/30/52-2
Dempster, John, 2 Dec. 1852, (Mrs.) Ann Waterton   12/ 4/52-2
Denbow, John, 20 May 1852, Mary Scott   5/22/52-2
Denbow, Thomas, 2 Mar. 1852, Catharine Stritehoof   3/ 3/52-2
Denighy, John, 15 June 1857, Julia Leanard   6/16/57-2
Denio, Asa, 4 Feb. 1855, Catherine Lappierre   2/10/55-2

Denison, John M., 12 June 1855, Sophia J. Williams, dau. of James; corrected copy	6/14/55-2
Denison, John M., 12 June 1855, Sophia J. Wilson, dau. of James	6/13/55-2
Denison, Thomas H., 30 Oct. 1856, Sarah E. Plummer	11/10/56-2
Denison, Thos. H., 30 Oct. 1856, Sarah E. Plummer; corrected copy	11/29/56-2
Denmead, Edward, Jr., 29 May 1856, Henrietta M. Sanders	6/ 2/56-2
Denmead, Francis, 13 Nov. 1854, Rosalin V. Labby, dau. of Pleasant	11/22/54-2
Dennis, Andrew T., 3 May 1855, Mary Jane R. Kline	5/ 5/55-2
Dennis, Andrew T., 11 Nov. 1858, Mary A. Martin	11/13/58-2
Dennis, Benjamin N., 24 Dec. 1857, Annie M. Smith	12/25/57-2
Dennis, Edward, 29 Nov. 1859, Mary Jones	12/ 2/59-2
Dennis, Francis H., 1 Apr. 1858, Mary J. Cromwell	4/ 3/58-2
Dennis, George (Dr.), 16 Apr. 1856, Ellen R. Johnston, dau. of William	5/10/56-2
Dennis, John M., 4 Dec. 1853, Clarissa Houck	1/ 6/53-2
Dennis, Louis, 30 Nov. 1851, (Mrs.) Margaret Bush	12/ 2/51-2
Dennis, William, Jr., 4 July 1855, Lydia J. Emory	7/ 6/55-2
Dennison, Francis, 29 Aug. 1852, Eliza Stone	8/31/52-2
Denny, B. F. Eugene, 21 Dec. 1854, Sarah J. K. Newman	12/27/54-2
Denny, Francis M., 28 Jan. 1858, Henrietta K. Hughes	1/30/58-2
Denny, George, 5 Apr. 1858, Elizabeth McManus	4/13/58-2
Denny, J. Addison, 19 Aug. 1851, Rebekah Bonham, dau. of (Hon.) Samuel C.	8/25/51-2
Denny, Jacob T. (Capt.), 4 Aug. 1853, Hennie Mawbray	8/10/53-2
Denny, John, 24 Oct. 1854, Anna Pohlen	11/ 1/54-2
Denson, Wm. I. E., 4 Nov. 1858, Lizzie Young, dau. of Frederick	11/ 6/58-2
Dent, James H., 13 Dec. 1859, Mary E. Pembroke	1/28/60-2
Depar, Frederick, 6 July 1851, Mary C. Cudlipp	7/10/51-2
Deppish, Edward C., 11 July 1852, Sarah Emeline Deuhurst	7/13/52-2
Deppre, Augustus F., 27 Oct. 1858, Martha Fenix	10/30/58-2
Derenberger, George, 29 Sept. 1857, Elizabeth Treasey Clautice	10/14/57-2
Derenberger, Jacob, Jr., 8 Feb. 1855, Jane Finigan	2/28/55-2
De Roncery, Charles, 11 Feb. 1858, H. Rosalie Crosson, dau. of (Dr.) H. J.	2/16/58-2
Derr, Daniel J., 17 May 1860, Rachel A. C. Albaugh	5/23/60-2
Derr, John P., 5 Oct. 1859, Annie C. N. Warner, dau. of Michael	10/ 8/59-2
Derry, John, 10 Nov. 1859, Margaret A. Hipsley	11/14/59-2
De Saules, Julius, 19 Feb. 1852, Sarah Susan Speaks, dau. of Edward	2/21/52-2
Des Forges, John P., 25 Dec. 1854, Mary Jane Ogle, dau. of A. S.	12/27/54-2
Deshiell, G. M., 9 Nov. 1858, Rachel M. Hudson; corrected copy	11/17/58-2
Deshiell, J. M., 9 Nov. 1858, Rachel M. Hudson	11/16/58-2
Devenny, Robert John, 20 Oct. 1859, Susan Courtney	10/25/59-2
Dever, Wm. K., 11 May 1853, Maria L. Carlett, dau. of George	5/25/53-2
Devereux, Joseph, 22 Apr. 1854, (Mrs.) Sarah A. Sullivan	4/25/54-2
Devine, James, 13 Sept. 1855, Elizabeth Brogan	9/19/55-2
Devoe, William H., 28 Oct. 1855, Martha Bannister	10/30/55-2
Devries, Robert T., 6 Apr. 1858, Josephine Haase	4/ 7/58-2
Dew, William James, 23 Dec. 1854, Kezia Perry	1/ 6/55-2
Dewalt, William H., 2 Apr. 1860, Rebecca Boswell	4/ 7/60-2
Dewees, Joseph, 2 Feb. 1852, Susannah Daugherty	2/10/52-2
Dexter, Levy, 6 Jan. 1858, Henrietta Lemon	1/ 9/58-2
Day, Daniel, 24 June 1858, (Mrs.) Louisa Hammond	6/25/58-2
Deyer, Jesse Columbus, 17 Oct. 1852, Louisa Young	10/23/52-2
De Young, Thomas, 4 Sept. 1853, Mary R. Willcox	9/ 7/53-2
Diamond, George H., 16 Oct. 1856, Sarah M. Jones	10/20/56-2

Diamond, Wm. C., 25 October 1853, Josephine Jenkins, dau.
   of Oswald   10/31/53-2
Dibb, James, 22 Jan. 1860, Ann Eliza Hubbart
Dibb, John, 23 Nov. 1852, Sarah Elizabeth Sutton   11/30/52-2
Dice, John C. (Rev.), 25 Nov. 1857, Sallie A. A. Roszel, dau.
   of S. C.   12/ 1/57-2
Dicges, Dudley, 18 Oct. 1860, H. M. Manro, dau. of (Dr.) J. 10/23/60-2
Dickel, Henry, 22 Mar. 1859, Susanna Limley   3/24/59-2
Dickerson, Alfred A., 7 Oct. 1858, Caroline V. Matherson 10/ 9/58-2
Dickerson, George W., 24 Aug. 1859, Mary A. Duff   7/17/60-2
Dickerson, Silas, 12 July 1860, Susan C. Rice; 7/20/60-2   7/21/60-2
Dickerson, William H., 5 June 1856, Ellen Brady   6/12/56-2
Dickey, Charles E., 28 Nov. 1854, Lizzie Sadtler, dau. of
   P. B.   12/ 2/54-2
Dickey, George S., 13 Dec. 1855, Anna Eliza Ridgely, dau. of
   Wm. A.   12/22/55-2
Dickey, Robt. L., 1 July 1857, Mary Josephine Croxall, dau.
   of Thos.   7/ 7/57-2
Dickinson, Abel T., 25 Aug. 1851, Sarah Jane Grice   8/26/51-2
Dickinson, James A., 7 Feb. 1858, Lizzie A. Wheeler   4/ 3/58-2
Dickson, James, 12 Dec. 1852, Margaret Brown   12/20/52-2
Dickson, John, 27 Nov. 1855, Rebecca C. Flint   11/28/55-2
Dickson, John C., 26 Apr. 1853, Mary Ann Cain   4/30/53-2
Didenhover, William W., 5 Jan. 1858, Martha Baldwin   5/ 5/58-2
Didier, Henry, 7 Oct. 1851, Lucy F. Alderson, dau. of G. N. 10/17/51-2
Dieter, Vallentine, 4 Sept. 1851, Margaret Dielman   9/ 6/51-2
Dieterly, Christopher F., 27 Dec. 1857, Mary A. Waltjens 5/ 8/58-2
Dietrich, Adam, 16 July 1856, Mary Logan   9/24/56-2
Dietz, William H., 13 Oct. 1857, Marie Reed   10/16/57-2
Diffee, Owen, 2 July 1855, Margaret Collins   7/19/55-2
Diffenderffer, James P., 4 Nov. 1852, Mary B. Armstrong, dau.
   of Henry   11/ 9/52-2
Diffenderffer, John F., 27 Dec. 1851, Georgia E. Cowan, dau.
   of Thos.   12/29/51-2
Diffenderffer, Octavus, 24 June 1857, Annie R. Crown   6/25/57-2
Diffenderffer, Wm. H., 15 Nov. 1858, Rebbie Rich Kelso, dau.
   of George Y.   11/23/58-2
Diffley, Michael, 22 Sept. 1857, Elizabeth Melley   9/23/57-2
Diggs, Daniel E., 23 Sept. 1856, Eliza Jane Bayless;
   10/28/56-2   10/29/56-2
Diggs, Samuel J., 6 Dec. 1859, Fannie E. Rochester, dau. of
   Francis and Ellen   12/12/59-2
Diggs, William J., 20 Nov. 1855, Catharine E. Warren   11/23/55-2
Diggs, Wm. J., 31 July 1859, Mary Blanche Griffith, dau. of
   Levi P.   8/ 2/59-2
Digs, Aaron, 26 Jan. 1857, Susan Enis   1/28/57-2
Digs, Beverly, 27 Feb. 1860, Louisa Goodisson   4/28/60-2
Dikes, William, 27 July 1858, Catherine Primrose   7/29/58-2
Dill, John, 4 June 1857, Margaret A. Baurtscheer   6/ 8/57-2
Dill, John, 4 June 1857, Margaret A. Bwartscheer, dau. of
   Christopher M.; corrected copy   6/ 9/57-2
Dillahay, Francis, 26 Nov. 1856, Jane C. Morgan   12/ 3/56-2
Dillahay, James, 21 Oct. 1856, (Mrs.) Eliza Sheppard 10/23/56-2
Dillahay, John, 30 July 1857, Anna C. Morgan   8/ 1/57-2
Dillaway, Wm. Dorithee, 15 June 1851, Anna M. Watson   6/19/51-2
Dillehunt, John G., 1 Aug. 1860, Mary E. Kinsey   9/ 3/60-2
Dillehunt, John T., 5 May 1857, Sarah J. Botterill   5/ 7/57-2
Dillenburg, David, 19 Aug. 1860, Fannie Rosenfeld, dau. of
   Simon   8/23/60-2
Diller, Cyrus, 17 June 1852, Mary E. Garrettson   7/ 5/52-2
Dillis, Henry, 8 Aug. 1854, Rachel Ann Mezdorf, dau. of
   Henry   9/ 2/54-2
Diltrow, John S., 1 June 1854, Harriet A. Quaill   6/ 2/54-2
Dilworth, Oliver, 4 Oct. 1859, Caroline Isabella Meeks, dau.
   of Wm. P.   •   10/12/59-2

Dilworth, Robert, 1 Nov. 1859, Mary E. Ramsey   11/ 5/59-2
Dimmet, Joshua, 4 Sept. 1851, (Mrs.) Ann Eliza Hartshorn   10/ 1/51-2
Dimmett, Joshua, 6 Dec. 1856, Martha Nunlee   12/ 8/56-2
Dimmitt, Charles E., 8 Mar. 1858, Mary E. Walter, dau. of
     Esma M.   3/15/58-2
Dimmock, Charles H., 12 May 1857, Emily Louisa Moale, dau.
     of John C.   5/16/57-2
Dimon, Robert, 30 Dec. 1856, Charlotte Ann Fershee   1/ 1/57-2
Dingle, Jacob R., 3 Feb. 1851, Rosana Herbert   2/ 5/51-2
Dinsmore, James, 21 Oct. 1855, (Mrs.) Mary Mettee   10/25/55-2
Dinsmore, Jas., 2 Nov. 1852, Elizabeth Rebecca Woollin   1/ 8/53-2
Dinsmore, John T., 4 June 1853, Emma Burt; corrected copy   6/ 7/53-2
Dinsmore, John T., 4 June 1853, Emma Hurt   6/ 6/53-2
Disney, John W., 15 Jan. 1856, Hannah Ann Jones   1/17/56-2
Disney, John Wesley; no date given, Susanna C. Harrison   3/26/57-2
Disney, Lemuel, 27 Jan. 1853, Mary Harman, dau. of John   1/29/53-2
Disney, Leonard, 14 Feb. 1854, Mary V. Dunn   2/20/54-2
Disney, Oliver H., 3 June 1851, Eliza A. Wheat   6/11/51-2
Disney, Owen A., 15 Dec. 1853, Sarah Ann Boyer, dau. of Rezin   12/17/53-2
Disney, Philip, 20 Oct. 1853, Louisa A. Harman   10/21/53-2
Disney, Richard E., 28 Oct. 1852, Sarah E. Wheeler   11/ 1/52-2
Disney, Samuel, 24 Jan. 1854, Ellen R. Goodwin   2/ 1/54-2
Disney, Snowden, 30 Jan. 1851, Margaret Ann Gawthrop   2/ 6/51-2
Disney, Theodore, 11 Mar. 1851, Mary Ann Clagett   3/15/51-2
Dissoway, Mark (Capt.), 8 Apr. 1852, Matilda Eugenia Zorne   4/10/52-2
Ditman, John J., 28 Oct. 1851, Susanna R. Gregory, dau. of
     Wm.   10/30/51-2
Ditman, William H., 20 Mar. 1860, Martha J. Reinicker   3/22/60-2
Divine, John, 7 Aug. 1851, Bridget Reily   8/ 9/51-2
Dix, J. Franklin, 2 June 1853, Fannie R. Jenks, dau. of
     Alfred   6/ 4/53-2
Dix, J. H., 11 Sept. 1856, (Mrs.) S. D. Lamb   9/29/56-2
Dixon, John, 23 Aug. 1859, Annie E. Trine   8/30/59-2
Dixon, Nehemiah M., 13 Jan. 1853, Alverda Anderson   1/20/53-2
Dixon, Robert R., 27 July 1854, Isabella Travers   8/ 1/54-2
Dixon, Thomas, 16 June 1859, Susan M. Measell   6/25/59-2
Dixon, Wm. J. T., 20 Oct. 1856, Josephine C. Holmes, dau. of
     William   10/22/56-2
Dobbyn, George W., 4 Mar. 1852, (Mrs.) Martha Dowling   3/10/52-2
Dobler, John, 6 May 1851, Mary E. Jenkins, dau. of Thomas   5/21/51-2
Dobson, Abraham, 28 Nov. 1853, (Mrs.) Amelia Henson   12/ 3/53-2
Dobson, George H., 5 Sept. 1860, Martha L. Cazier, dau. of
     John   9/ 7/60-2
Dobson, James T., 16 May 1859, Ellen A. Mathison   5/18/59-2
Dobson, John A., 22 Mar. 1857, Mary Agnes Williams   4/ 6/57-2
Dobson, Thomas H., 9 Nov. 1855, Angeline E. Elmore   12/11/55-2
Dobson, Thomas J., 8 Mar. 1860, Mary Ellen Tracey   3/12/60-2
Dobson, Wm. H., 3 Aug. 1854, Jane McCroden   8/ 5/54-2
Docwra, E. H., 2 Dec. 1852, Marion F. Griswold   12/ 6/52-2
Dodd, George E., 28 July 1859, Amanda L. Chalk   7/30/59-2
Dodson, Eugene (Dr.), 21 June 1859, Celeste A. Bromwell, dau.
     of Josiah R.   6/23/59-2
Dodson, John W., 22 Nov. 1855, Ann M. Walter   11/27/55-2
Dodson, Rich'd. S., 20 Sept. 1859, Maria F. Pfeltz, dau. of
     G. A.   9/24/59-2
Dodson, Robert, 20 Dec. 1860, Elizabeth H. Carter   12/22/60-2
Dodson, Wm. K., 2 Dec. 1856, Sallie A. Cropper   12/30/56-2
Doell, Christopher, 24 May 1858, Agnes Emma Zimetsch, dau. of
     William   5/26/58-2
Doerschel, Wm., 16 Nov. 1851, Margaret Anna Wallace   11/20/51-2
Doft, George, 25 Apr. 1852, Mary E. J. Booth   5/ 6/52-2
Doft, John V., 13 June 1854, Mary C. Howser   6/15/54-2
Doherty, James, 4 Mar. 1854, Mary A. V. Holton, dau. of David   4/24/54-2
Dolan, Kierans, 20 Sept. 1855, Martha Ann McLevey   10/ 5/55-2
Donal, M., 27 May 1860, Julia Mayher   6/ 6/60-2

Donaldson, Francis (Dr.), 19 Jan. 1853, Elizabeth Wimbester,
    dau. of Wm.   1/20/53-2
Donaldson, James, 1 Sept. 1856, Mary Goodacre, dau. of
    Daniel   9/ 4/56-2
Donegan, Thomas, 13 Nov. 1851, Rosa White   11/15/51-2
Donley, John, 27 June 1855, Martha E. Martin   7/ 3/55-2
Donnell, William, 29 Mar. 1859, Mary E. Sprigg, dau. of D.   3/30/59-2
Donnelly, Daniel, 31 Jan. 1856, Mary H. Milholland   2/ 6/56-2
Donnley, Joseph F., 30 May 1852, Alexina Clautice   5/31/52-2
Donnolson, Moses P., 19 Apr. 1858, Elizabeth A. Sansbury   4/26/58-2
Donohue, George W., 10 May 1853, Amanda L. Fox   5/19/53-2
Donohue, Jas. D., 11 Nov. 1856, Charlotte Ann Wright   11/25/56-2
Donohue, M. Lafayette, 4 Mar. 1856, H. E. Spencer, dau. of
    T. H.   4/ 7/56-2
Donohue, Thomas H., 13 Sept. 1853, Alice Hester Gaskins   9/15/53-2
Donovan, Owen, Jr., 1 Feb. 1855, Maranda Shearman   2/23/55-2
Dority, George, 14 Feb. 1856, Elizabeth Jackson   2/16/56-2
Dorman, Geo. T., 7 Oct. 1852, Mary E. Miles   10/ 9/52-2
Dorman, William, 14 June 1856, Sarah Henry   6/17/56-2
Dorman, William, 28 Oct. 1858, Matilda Ellen Taylor   11/ 1/58-2
Dormandy, John, 20 Apr. 1851, Margaret Ann Gallagher   4/22/51-2
Dorritee, Charles W., 17 June 1857, Harriet Bergesheimer   6/19/57-2
Dorsett, John F., 10 Oct. 1860, Annie M. Warner, dau. of
    George K.   10/11/60-2
Dorsey, Allen, 15 May 1856, (Mrs.) Annie E. Holt   5/16/56-2
Dorsey, Andrew, 12 June 1859, Mary A. Thompson   6/14/59-2
Dorsey, C. C., 1 May 1860, Susan C. Hutchins   5/ 2/60-2
Dorsey, C. R., 2 July 1857, Nancy Ann Wood   7/ 3/57-2
Dorsey, Caleb, 16 Mar. 1858, Esther M. Nabb   3/19/58-2
Dorsey, Edward, 12 Oct. 1857, Kate Goldsmith   10/19/57-2
Dorsey, Edwin S., 28 Feb. 1855, Anna H. Harding   3/ 2/55-2
Dorsey, H. W. (Dr.), 13 Oct. 1859, A. P. Waters   10/14/59-2
Dorsey, James, 1 Jan. 1857, Anne Robinson   1/ 5/57-2
Dorsey, James B.; no date given, Rachel Shipley   1/28/51-2
Dorsey, John R., 6 Dec. 1860, Margaret F. Harveylutter   12/14/60-2
Dorsey, John W., 17 Jan. 1854, Amanda Warfield Stevens   1/19/54-2
Dorsey, Joseph S., 13 Nov. 1854, Amanda F. Mitchell, dau. of
    (Rev.) Richard H.   11/17/54-2
Dorsey, Lloyd, 6 Apr. 1858, Caroline Howard   4/ 8/58-2
Dorsey, Nimrod B., 24 Mar. 1853, Manelia Forythe   3/25/53-2
Dorsey, R. W., 13 Sept. 1860, Mary E. Wilson   9/14/60-2
Dorsey, Reuben, 20 Jan. 1857, Mary E. Krafft   1/24/57-2
Dorsey, W. B. G., 9 Nov. 1853, Comfort W. Dorsey, dau. of
    C. S. W.   11/15/53-2
Dorsey, Washington L., 27 Nov. 1851, (Mrs.) Mary Logan   12/ 3/51-2
Dorsey, Wm. H., 13 July 1858, Maggie Miller   7/21/58-2
Dossa, Samuel, 25 Nov. 1860, Martha Stand   11/29/60-2
Dos Santos, Filippe Simoens, 4 Oct. 1855, Mary A. Murray,
    dau. of James C.; corrected copy   10/ 8/55-2
Dos Santos, Simoens, 4 Oct. 1855, Mary A. Murray, dau. of
    James C.   10/ 6/55-2
Dotterweih, Frederick, 24 June 1860, Susannah Krager   6/28/60-2
Doud, Francis A., 31 July 1853, Margaret S-(?)-rgeon   8/ 2/53-2
Doud, John M., 16 Mar. 1854, Mary Russel   3/20/54-2
Dougheney, Thos., 18 Sept. 1860, Ellen Gorman   9/19/60-2
Dougherty, B. J. (Dr.), 17 Apr. 1860, Eliza F. Mathaws   4/21/60-2
Dougherty, Chas. M., 21 Jan. 1858, Agnes Kelly, dau. of
    Timothy   1/22/58-2
Dougherty, Edward, 12 Apr. 1852, Sally Edmunds   4/17/52-2
Dougherty, J. J. C., 5 June 1855, Mary E. Stapleton   6/ 6/55-2
Dougherty, John, 14 Sept. 1854, Virginia Martiacq   9/18/54-2
Dougherty, William, 4 Oct. 1852, (Mrs.) Elizabeth Wilson   10/ 8/52-2
Doughty, William (Col.), 21 Apr. 1857, Mary A. Bangs   4/29/57-2
Douglas, Jackson, 23 Mar. 1858, S. Olevia Whitehill, dau. of
    John C.   3/25/58-2

Douglas, James H. B., 22 May 1859, Mary Ann Toder   6/ 3/59-2
Douglas, James S., 7 Dec. 1854, Harriet F. Whittington   12/12/54-2
Douglass, Albert P., 9 Feb. 1858, Laura V. Pitcher   2/10/58-2
Douglass, James H. B., 22 May 1859, Margaret A. Tudor;
    corrected copy   6/ 4/59-2
Douglass, Jeremiah (Capt.), 11 June 1857, Portia B. Richardson 6/15/57-2
Douglass, Robert, 1 May 1855, Frances Heeble   5/ 7/55-2
Douglass, William R. F., 14 June 1858, Emma Pohlen   9/20/58-2
Douns, Jas. H., 13 Jan. 1853, Sallie E. Howard   1/17/53-2
Dove, Elijah, Jr., 9 Dec. 1851, Sarah Ellen Miller   12/11/51-2
Dove, Milton C., 17 June 1857, Mary F. Lawrenson, dau. of
    James   6/18/57-2
Dowden, Philip, 28 June 1852, Meranda Sancks   6/29/52-2
Dowell, Henry, 16 Dec. 1852, Anna Louisa Nixdorn, dau. of
    Tobias   12/20/52-2
Dowling, Edward, 28 Apr. 1853, Ann Elizabeth Turner   4/29/53-2
Dowling, James, 20 Nov. 1856, Carolina Smith, dau. of Richd.
    W.   11/24/56-2
Dowling, Jas., 17 Dec. 1851, Mary Jane Martin   2/24/52-2
Dowling, Thomas, 29 June 1858, Amanda Ellen Wioney   7/ 1/58-2
Downes, Jos. B., 12 Feb. 1851, Elizabeth Adams   2/14/51-2
Downey, Edward, 19 Mar. 1854, Mary Anne Sullivan, dau. of
    Eliza   4/21/54-2
Downing, Francis P., 21 Sept. 1854, Alice Ann Ireland   9/22/54-2
Downing, Howel, 18 Jan. 1855, Lizzie Lefferman, dau. of
    William   2/17/55-2
Downing, Sam'l. W., 6 Oct. 1852, Caroline Lavenia Flynn   10/ 7/52-2
Downing, Thomas, 15 Apr. 1860, Elizabeth F. Meads, dau. of
    Zackariah H.   4/24/60-2
Downing, William H., 24 June 1851, Margaret A. Miller, dau. of
    Augustine   6/28/51-2
Downing, William H., 3 June 1856, Susan J. Pritchett   6/10/56-2
Downing, William T., 28 Nov. 1854, Mary A. Osler   12/14/54-2
Downs, John, 21 July 1853, Hester J. Hartley   7/23/53-2
Downs, Robert F., 2 Nov. 1856, Selina Gust   12/ 4/56-2
Downs, Saml. F., 14 May 1857, Mary Megarvy   5/19/57-2
Downs, Steward D., 23 May 1855, Mary E. Huggins   5/28/55-2
Downs, Wm. H., 26 Jan. 1854, Elizabeth Wellham   2/ 2/54-2
Doxzen, Jacob, 22 Dec. 1859, Susan P. Maddox   1/ 2/60-2
Doyle, Augustus J., 3 Aug. 1854, Isabella J. Wilderman   8/ 4/54-2
Doyle, Samuel B., 2 Oct. 1851, Mary E. Madden   10/ 9/51-2
Drake, Addison C., 28 Nov. 1852, (Mrs.) Ann Jefferson   11/30/52-2
Drake, William H., 24 Dec. 1857, Mary Ann Kenley   1/ 2/58-2
Draper, Edward G., 29 Oct. 1857, Jane R. Jordan, dau. of
    (Rev.) John   10/31/57-2
Drayer, John, 21 Sept. 1851, Caroline Cross   10/11/51-2
Dresel, Warner, 30 Sept. 1852, Louisa Brauns, dau. of F. L.   10/ 2/52-2
Drew, Arthur, 24 June 1860, Margaret O'Brien   7/13/60-2
Drew, S. S., 4 Aug. 1852, Amanda Lucia Williams   8/ 5/52-2
Drill, Henry C., 22 Oct. 1857, Harriet Virginia Keefer   10/24/57-2
Drill, James M., 21 Mar. 1860, Sallie T. Bosee   3/24/60-2
Driscoll, Dennis C., 29 July 1851, Caroline K. Hiss   7/30/51-2
Droham, David, 9 July 1857, Mary Amelia Roche, dau. of Wm. H. 9/17/57-2
Drost, G. A., 12 Apr. 1854, Laura Sutro   4/13/54-2
Drury, C. Augustus, 15 Oct. 1853, Susan E. Welch, dau. of
    Henry C.   10/18/53-2
Drury, C. Augustus, 2 Nov. 1854, Susan E. Welch; corrected
    copy   11/ 4/54-2
Drury, William, 30 Sept. 1860, Sarah E. Keys   10/19/60-2
Dryden, John L. H., 6 Oct. 1859, Fannie B. Massie   11/26/59-2
Dryden, Joshua (Maj.), 26 Feb. 1856, (Mrs.) Catharine Appold   2/27/56-2
Dryden, Robt. H., 21 Dec. 1854, Rosalie Ritchie, dau. of Wm.   2/26/55-2
Dryden, Samuel J., 21 June 1860, Rebecca Dwyer   6/23/60-2
Dryden, Samuel T., 26 Feb. 1857, Mary McCulley   3/16/57-2

Dryden, William H., 22 Feb. 1859, Mollie E. Hanway, dau. of Washington	2/23/59-2
Dubel, James A. (Capt.), 27 Nov. 1856, Rosina Witman	11/29/56-2
Dudley, Henry C., 7 Nov. 1854, Caroline Gildner	11/ 9/54-2
Dudley, John, 14 Feb. 1860, Julia Linch	2/16/60-2
Dudley, R. E., 19 May 1859, Sarah A. Carter	5/23/59-2
Duff, J. J., 25 Jan. 1860, Mary J. Stevens	4/11/60-2
Duff, John W., 3 July 1860, Sallie R. Hennick	7/ 6/60-2
Duff, Patrick, 10 Sept. 1857, Almira Forman	10/ 5/57-2
Duff, Patrick, 13 Sept. 1860, Joanna Grady	9/26/60-2
Duffey, Edward, 27 Aug. 1857, Kates Linthicum	8/29/57-2
Duffy, Edward, 6 Mar. 1851, Mary Jane McKewen, dau. of John	3/17/51-2
Duffy, John, 14 Sept. 1851, Elizabeth McGlone	9/22/51-2
Duffy, Michael, 11 Mar. 1855, Mary Parran	3/14/55-2
Duffy, Owen Eugene, 14 Apr. 1857, Margaret Sarah Callan, dau. of Peter	4/21/57-2
Duffy, Peter, 19 Nov. 1856, Mary McGowan	11/29/56-2
Dugan, Cumberland, 16 Sept. 1856, Harriet Buchanan, dau. of (Dr.) James A.	9/19/56-2
Dugan, Hammond, 14 June 1859, Lucy A. Tabb, dau. of John H.	6/21/59-2
Dugan, J. Osborn, 5 Dec. 1859, Jennie A. Chaille	12/12/59-2
Dugas, Lewis C., 8 Nov. 1853, Margaretta D. Alcock	11/11/53-2
Duggan, Thomas, 24 Feb. 1852, Jane Mullen, dau. of Thos.	2/27/52-2
Du Hamel, W. J. C. (Dr.), 3 Apr. 1853, (Mrs.) Bettie H. Agate	5/ 3/53-2
Duke, Augustin W., 10 Aug. 1852, Josephine Victoria Rosensteel	8/11/52-2
Dukehart, Balderson, 11 May 1854, Isabella Lynch	5/13/54-2
Dukehart, John P., 28 Apr. 1857, J. Ada Bantz	4/30/57-2
Dukehart, Samuel L., 7 Mar. 1859, Lydia A. Bull	5/10/59-2
Dukehart, William H. B., 18 Apr. 1854, Susan E. Taylor	4/20/54-2
Duker, Geo. E., 25 May 1858, Annie K. Sanders	6/ 1/58-2
Duker, Otto, 16 June 1857, Anna Catherine Radecke, dau. of D. H.	6/19/57-2
Dull, Casper, 27 July 1852, Catharine Joyce	8/10/52-2
Dull, James M., 21 Mar. 1860, Sallie T. Bosee	3/23/60-2
Dumpfries, Edward, 19 Jan. 1851, Jane Taylor	1/23/51-2
Dumphy, John, 27 Aug. 1860, Ellen Moan	9/ 3/60-2
Dunahue, James H. (Dr.), 24 May 1853, Lizzie E. Nicholls	5/27/53-2
Dunahue, John, 27 Feb. 1859, Sarah Kelly	3/ 7/59-2
Dunavon, John, 17 July 1851, Elizabeth Murry	7/22/51-2
Duncan, Charles, 25 June 1860, Prudence Eckerts, dau. of George M. and Teresa	7/ 2/60-2
Duncan, John, 20 Oct. 1856, Mary Brockmun	10/28/56-2
Duncan, John Fletcher, 14 Mar. 1853, Virginia Morgan	3/22/53-2
Duncan, John P., 1 May 1853, Mary Hubbard, dau. of John	5/ 5/53-2
Duncan, Lucias Campbell, 12 Sept. 1854, Mary Rebecca Smith, dau. of Dennis A.	9/13/54-2
Duncan, Richard McKim, 12 Apr. 1851, Rosella Lafitte, dau. of Jno. S.	4/14/51-2
Duncan, Thomas M., 7 June 1853, Sarah Elizabeth Leonard	6/17/53-2
Dundon, Michael, 18 Dec. 1854, Susan A. M. Rose	12/20/54-2
Dundore, Henry, 10 Jan. 1856, Lavinia Cunningham	1/11/56-2
Dungan, Abel S., 16 June 1853, Lizzie L. Vondersmith	6/18/53-2
Dungan, Lewis, 22 June 1852, Margaret L. Mason, dau. of R.	6/24/52-2
Dungan, S. Henry, 27 Sept. 1860, Annie S. Brown, dau. of Robt.	10/ 1/60-2
Dunigan, Jas. C. A., 26 July 1853, Mary C. E. Knipe, dau. of Jacob	12/30/53-2
Dunigan, Thomas, 15 Jan. 1857, Emma Virginia Thomas	1/26/57-2
Dunkerly, Geo. L., 3 June 1857, Elmira D. Thompson	6/ 5/57-2
Dunkerly, George W., 7 Mar. 1853, Minerva Ann Lee	3/ 8/53-2
Dunkerly, Richard, 22 Dec. 1857, Margaret Thomas	12/24/57-2
Dunkerly, Richard B., 24 Dec. 1857, Margaret J. Thomas; corrected copy	12/25/57-2
Dunlap, C. Lewis, 21 Jan. 1860, Carrie M. Bloomer	1/23/60-2
Dunlap, Hugh, 27 Jan. 1857, Rachel Ann Neill	3/ 9/57-2

Dunlap, Silas G. (Rev.), 5 June 1860, Jennie L. Goodrich   6/19/60-2
Dunlevy, Andrew F., 18 May 1859, Louise F. Placide   5/21/59-2
Dunn, Ballard S., 19 May 1860, Lizzie Stansbury   5/26/60-2
Dunn, Charles (Rev.), 30 Sept. 1856, (Mrs.) Ann Maria Dorsey   10/ 2/56-2
Dunn, Edward, 4 Sept. 1854, Virginia Hughes   9/ 6/54-2
Dunn, George W., 3 Apr. 1851, Catherine Nash   4/ 7/51-2
Dunn, James J., 4 July 1855, Mary Jane Winters   7/25/55-2
Dunn, Michael, 1 Sept. 1853, Susan Coulter   9/ 3/53-2
Dunn, Peter, 1 Jan. 1852, Bridget Colwell   1/ 3/52-2
Dunn, Robert, 9 Jan. 1854, Christiana Abell   1/16/54-2
Dunn, Robert W., 2 Aug. 1859, Matilda Sneed   8/10/59-2
Dunnigan, Edw. J., 2 Jan. 1859, Susan A. Fitzpatrick   1/18/59-2
Dunning, Chas. H., 30 Nov. 1853, Ella J. Karsner   12/ 3/53-2
Dunning, Thomas B., 21 Feb. 1858, Lenora Broughton   3/ 3/58-2
Dunnock, Samuel R., 20 Apr. 1858, (Mrs.) E. R. Pattison   5/21/58-2
Duns, John S., 5 Sept. 1854, Louisa Stier, dau. of John;
     corrected copy   11/29/54-2
Duns, John V., 5 Nov. 1854, Louisa Stier, dau. of John   11/28/54-2
Durand, Thomas W., 15 June 1858, Ann Elizabeth Langley, dau.
     of Edward   6/17/58-2
Durbin, Jesse (Rev.), 16 Mar. 1852, Lucy A. Cain, dau. of
     Levi   3/18/52-2
Durkee, Henry H., 2 Sept. 1851, Julia Ann Marfield, dau. of
     Wm. Henry   9/10/51-2
Durst, Felix V., 7 Mar. 1854, Cordelia F. LeCompte, dau. of
     Charles L.   3/11/54-2
Dusenberry, Constantine, 17 Sept. 1856, Virginia Hills Wilson   9/20/56-2
Dushane, J. Alex., 12 Nov. 1857, E. Marion Duke, dau. of (Dr.)
     James; corrected copy   12/ 1/57-2
Dushane, J. Alexander, 12 Nov. 1857, E. Marion Duke, dau. of
     (Dr.) James   11/20/57-2
Dushane, John T., 1 Apr. 1858, Mary F. Caldwell, dau. of Wm.   4/ 3/58-2
Dutrow, Curtin F., 9 Sept. 1856, Maria Shepard   9/13/56-2
Dutrow, David E., 10 Sept. 1857, Emma V. Wherritt   9/15/57-2
Dutton, George W., 4 June 1856, Susan M. Harrison   6/11/56-2
Dutton, John R., 18 Oct. 1858, Anna M. Letournau   10/21/58-2
Dutton, N. P. (Capt.), 2 Apr. 1851, Elizabeth A. Mitchell,
     dau. of Robert   4/ 4/51-2
Dutton, Thos. H., 23 Dec. 1851, Ellenor Jane Lane, dau. of
     Jos.   12/24/51-2
Duval, Geo. W., 7 Apr. 1856, Martha A. Bennett, dau. of
     Asher D.   4/10/56-2
Duval, H. Sheffield, 1 Nov. 1860, Louisa Roszel, dau. of
     (Rev.) S. Asbury   11/15/60-2
Du Val, H. Sheffield, 1 Nov. 1860, Mary Louisa Roszel, dau.
     of (Rev.) S. Asbury; corrected copy   11/16/60-2
Duval, Jacob S., 4 Oct. 1859, Mary E. Brashears   10/10/59-2
Duval, James S., 14 July 1858, Clay Royston   7/21/58-2
Duvall, Alexander, 25 Oct. 1859, Mary Emily Ray   10/26/59-2
Duvall, Andrew J., 6 May 1852, Mary J. Jordan   5/ 8/52-2
Duvall, Frederick, 12 Oct. 1858, Caroline Riddle   10/15/58-2
Duvall, Jacob, 12 May 1859, Mary Ann Lennox   5/19/59-2
Duvall, Leonidas, 14 Aug. 1857, Mary Abby Pickens   8/15/57-2
Duvall, Luther, 1 May 1860, Mary A. Hilton   5/ 2/60-2
Duvall, Richard, 19 Dec. 1858, (Mrs.) Hester Ann Jones   12/21/58-2
Duvall, Ridgely, 4 June 1858, Sophia H. Post   4/13/60-2
Dwinelle, James E. (Dr.), 21 Nov. 1860, Mary E. Bowditch   11/28/60-2
Dwyer, Daniel O., 21 Oct. 1852, Maria Macgill   10/26/52-2
Dwyer, Michael, 6 June 1853, Rebecca Costello   6/ 8/53-2
Dyer, Joseph A., 3 July 1853, Elizabeth W. Powell   7/ 7/53-2
Dyser, Jacob, 4 Nov. 1860, Mary Virginia Mockebee, dau. of
     John B.   11/15/60-2
Dyson, George T., 24 Mar. 1857, Susan A. Boyer   3/25/57-2
Dyson, Rob't., 28 Oct. 1852, Agnes E. A. Healy   11/ 3/52-2

E-(?)-igleha-(?)-t, Charles D., 18 Oct. 1853, E. A. Haslup   10/28/53-2
E-(?)-lton, Edward, 31 May 1858, Kate R. Willis   6/ 1/58-2
Eachus, Edwin, 3 May 1853, Eliza Jane Cunningham   5/ 5/53-2
Eagan, John, 16 Sept. 1854, Marietta M. Taylor, dau. of
     Wm. M.   9/29/54-2
Eames, John, 3 June 1856, Mary E. Crabson   6/ 4/58-2
Eareckson, Vincent O., 21 Dec. 1854, Matilda A. Pierce   12/23/54-2
Earl, John R., 2 Dec. 1855, (Mrs.) Susan Syford   1/ 4/56-2
Earley, William H., 25 Oct. 1860, Matilda M. Sippley   11/20/60-2
Earlougher, John M., 16 Jan. 1860, Louisa D. Charles   1/18/60-2
Early, Joseph Ignatius, 2 June 1857, Ella V. Mowell   6/ 5/57-2
Earp, Benjamin P., 28 June 1855, Ann E. Perry   6/29/55-2
Earp, James, 5 Feb. 1857, Lydia A. Litchfield   2/ 6/57-2
Easley, John T., 26 Mar. 1855, Emily A. Spicer, dau. of
     Samuel G.   3/31/55-2
East, Caleb J., 2 Nov. 1855, Mary A. Ware   11/ 7/55-3
Easter, James W., 3 Feb. 1859, Maggie E. Miller   2/ 5/59-2
Easter, Jas. H., 6 Mar. 1851, Susan Cookley, dau. of P. H.   3/ 8/51-2
Easter, John, son of Jno., 13 June 1854, Mary Sharpley, dau.
     of (Rev.) John   6/14/54-2
Easter, John, Jr., 22 Jan. 1852, Mary Augusta Fitzharris, dau.
     of Lawrence   1/31/52-2
Easter, Robert A., 17 Dec. 1857, S. Elizabeth Miller   1/13/58-2
Eastman, Henry Wm., 15 Jan. 1856, Anna M. Wentz   1/16/56-2
Eastwood, Geo. H., 8 Jan. 1856, Sarah T. Stephenson   1/10/56-2
Eaton, John T., 19 Dec. 1858, Sophia Slager   12/23/58-2
Eaton, John T., 24 Feb. 1859, Margaret Ann Elizabeth
     Greenwood   3/ 8/59-2
Ebaugh, David F., 26 Jan. 1858, Lizzie Ball   2/ 1/58-2
Ebbets, Arthur M., 31 Jan. 1854, Lottie W. Penniman, dau. of
     Thomas   3/ 9/54-2
Eben, Henry D., 9 July 1860, Amanda Scott   7/11/60-2
Eberahrt, Francis Henry, 31 May 1853, Mary Jane Dorr   6/ 2/53-2
Eberman, George R., 8 Feb. 1859, Joanna Clifford   3/26/59-2
Eborall, John G., 23 May 1853, Sarah Ann Bedford   5/28/53-2
Echman, John H., 28 June 1859, Ann E. Kraft   7/ 1/59-2
Eckardt, Henry, 28 Nov. 1852, Ellen Falconer   12/ 1/52-2
Eckert, Adam, 17 May 1855, Adeline Deal   5/29/55-2
Eckert, John C., 11 Nov. 1851, Mary Isabella Davis, dau. of
     John   11/18/51-2
Eckman, Jacob A., 25 Sept. 1856, Anne Maria Marsh   9/27/56-2
Eckman, John Henry, 19 Aug. 1856, Mary Ann Virginia Love   8/21/56-2
Edel, John W., 3 Apr. 1851, Elizabeth M. Richardson, dau.
     of Sam'l. M.   4/ 5/51-2
Edelen, Jacob, 25 Sept. 1859, Laura Frifrogle   9/27/59-2
Edger, Thos. J., 18 Dec. 1856, Mary E. Dobson   12/31/56-2
Edmonds, William E., 28 Apr. 1859, Maggie R. Shannon   4/30/59-2
Edmondson, Jeremiah H., 1 May 1855, Emily F. Crowle   5/ 4/55-2
Edwards, Charles, 5 Dec. 1858, Susan Waters   12/ 7/58-2
Edwards, David, 20 Apr. 1854, Margaret McCleary, dau. of
     James Hastings   4/22/54-2
Edwards, E. W. (Dr.), 7 Aug. 1851, C. R. Diffenderffer   8/ 8/51-2
Edwards, Elkanah, 25 Apr. 1859, Elizabeth Ellen Byrd   4/26/59-2
Edwards, Henry, 8 Nov. 1854, Ann M. Chinn   1/16/55-2
Edwards, Joseph W., 6 Dec. 1860, Amanda M. Usilton   12/ 7/60-2
Edwards, William, 10 June 1851, Elizabeth A. Mattingly   6/12/51-2
Edwards, William H., 3 May 1854, Anna M. King   5/ 5/54-2
Edwards, William M., 6 May 1851, Clara C. Smith   5/ 8/51-2
Edwards, Wilson, 9 Jan. 1851, (Mrs.) Julia Ann France   1/17/51-2
Egan, Martin, 9 Feb. 1858, Kate Cannon   2/11/58-2
Ege, A. Galbraith (Col.), 8 Dec. 1852, Matilda H. Craig, dau.
     of William   12/11/52-2
Egerton, A. Dubois, 21 Oct. 1852, Adeline L. P. McRea   10/22/52-2
Eggert, Geo. D., 20 Mar. 1851, Helene L. Rimby   3/26/51-2
Egle, George C. (Dr.), 12 Oct. 1853, Annie M. Cooke   10/20/53-2

Ehlers, Bernard D., 3 Sept. 1860, Annie G. Linville	9/ 8/60-2
Ehlers, John D., 14 June 1860, Mary Cassandra Linville	6/16/60-2
Ehrman, Chas. H., 27 Mar. 1851, Sarah Emily Dorman, dau. of William	3/29/51-2
Eichelberger, Albert G., 31 Jan. 1860, Martha Snyder, dau. of W. C.	2/10/60-2
Eichelberger, Charles F., 10 May 1859, Lottie E. Sperry	5/11/59-2
Eichelberger, J. Dix, 27 Nov. 1851, Maria H. Cloud, dau. of Jesse	12/ 1/51-2
Eichelberger, Joseph N., 7 July 1857, Olevia F. Gray	7/22/57-2
Eichelberger, William, 29 Apr. 1857, Maria Louisa Burdick, dau. of Henry	5/ 5/57-2
Eichhorn, Rudolph, 6 Jan. 1853, Ann Elizabeth Conlan	1/12/53-2
Eichler, Charles C. F., 19 Jan. 1857, Elizabeth Frey	1/27/57-2
Eichner, John, 31 May 1859, S. C. Leib	6/ 8/59-2
Eichorn, Chas. F., 13 Mar. 1860, Ann Maria Miller	3/20/60-2
Eickel, H. L., 12 June 1859, Mary R. Manstead	6/14/59-2
Eigleburner, Thomas F., 19 June 1860, C. Victorine Stidham	6/21/60-2
Eigus, Henry, 8 Oct. 1857, Ellen Neale	10/ 9/57-2
Einbrod, C., 24 Aug. 1851, Elizabeth Stumpf	8/26/51-2
Eisenbrandt, Henry W. R., 2 Feb. 1860, Jeannette C. Wild	2/ 9/60-2
Eisenhart, J. G., 12 Mar. 1851, Mary Emma Richardson, dau. of Ebuz	3/14/51-2
Elbert, Jno. W., 21 June 1860, (Mrs.) Eliza Jane Cornish, widow of James	6/23/60-2
Elder, Fras. W., 24 Jan. 1856, Matilda M. Doering, dau. of B. Winchester; 2/13/56-2	2/14/56-2
Elder, James Armitage, 11 Sept. 1855, Susannah Catharine Bilson	9/14/55-2
Elder, John, 6 Feb. 1859, Eliza Jones	2/ 8/59-2
Eldred, Henry, 11 Sept. 1851, Hettie A. Cooper	9/15/51-2
Elfing, William, 23 Aug. 1858, Anne Elizabeth Swiggette	8/25/58-2
Eli, William, 23 Mar. 1854, Margaret Smith	4/ 1/54-2
Eliason, James M., 20 July 1853, Rachel Ann Freeberger	7/25/53-2
Eline, Jacob A., 11 July 1854, Mary F. Brooks, dau. of Joseph E.	7/14/54-2
Eliott, Daniel S., 14 Mar. 1853, Virginia Sophia Essex	3/15/53-2
Elles, John, 12 Sept. 1854, Mary A. Rowbotham	9/25/54-2
Ellicott, John, Jr., 5 Nov. 1856, Jennie Gordon, dau. of William	11/13/56-2
Ellicott, Thomas P., 19 Sept. 1855, Caroline M. Allen, dau. of Francis P.	9/24/55-2
Elliot, Robert O., 12 Jan. 1854, (Mrs.) Mary E. Hardy	1/16/54-2
Elliot, Thomas M., 30 Dec. 1850, Elizabeth Hunter	3/ 9/53-2
Elliott, Benjamin S., 28 Jan. 1858, Letitia E. McCausland	2/ 1/58-2
Elliott, Curtis E., 15 Nov. 1859, Margaret Wheeler	11/17/59-2
Elliott, Edward, 19 Oct. 1860, Annie Smith	10/25/60-2
Elliott, Francis A., 4 July 1851, Amanda M. Brown	7/ 7/51-2
Elliott, Henry A., 21 June 1855, Eliza M. Heagy	6/22/55-2
Elliott, Isaac, 13 June 1860, Louisa Queen	6/15/60-2
Elliott, James B., 12 Oct. 1855, Mary Jane Hall	10/15/55-2
Elliott, Joseph, 26 Dec. 1850, Catharine Clayton	1/ 4/51-2
Elliott, Samuel, 3 May 1853, Virginia Proctor	5/ 6/53-2
Elliott, William H., 16 Dec. 1856, Elizabeth A. Gilbert, dau. of Aquilla	12/18/56-2
Elliott, Wm. H., 24 Jan. 1851, Matilda Frances Allworth	3/13/51-2
Ellis, James W., 16 June 1856, Sarah C. Nicolas	6/30/56-2
Ellis, John T., 21 Oct. 1860, Anna Hays	11/ 6/60-2
Ellis, William H., 9 Nov. 1856, Elizabeth Jane Dixon	11/19/56-2
Ellis, Wm. H., 12 Sept. 1855, Elizabeth Ann Watkins	9/13/55-2
Elliss, John C. H., 25 July 1853, Maria Pine	7/27/53-2
Ellwig, Charles, 13 Nov. 1860, Susan W. Burnes	11/14/60-2
Elmore, Charles A., 2 July 1855, Sallie A. Caskey, dau. of Joseph	7/ 3/55-2
Elster, Frederick, 17 Apr. 1854, Margaret Allen	5/ 9/54-2

Elston, Isaac N., 26 July 1859, Sarah E. Lednum   7/29/59-2
Ely, Albert Welles (Dr.), 15 Jan. 1856, Susan B. Triplett   1/16/56-2
Ely, James, 25 Feb. 1855, Catherine Patner   2/27/55-2
Ely, John W., 15 Nov. 1860, Carrie E. Barton   11/21/60-2
Ely, Samuel, 14 May 1857, Catherine Riley   5/18/57-2
Ely, William P., 9 Oct. 1851, Elizabeth M. Moke, dau. of
     George   10/11/51-2
Ely, Wm. T., 3 Nov. 1856, Maria Eugenia Meades   11/ 5/56-2
Emerick, Wm. H., 25 Jan. 1854, Kate V. Lambden   1/27/54-2
Emerson, G. F., 23 Apr. 1851, Augusta A. Whittier   5/ 3/51-2
Emerson, Samuel, 18 Aug. 1859, Marion L. Harrison   8/19/59-2
Emery, M. G., 3 Apr. 1854, Mary K. Hasltine, dau. of Wm.   4/ 8/54-2
Emich, Columbus V., 21 June 1859, Ann E. Snyder   6/23/59-2
Emich, Daniel J., 19 Jan. 1854, Martha Jane Warner, dau. of
     Andrew E.   1/25/54-2
Emich, Wesley D., 29 July 1855, Susan Rebecca Forman   8/ 9/55-2
Emick, Henry F., 15 Nov. 1860, Mary S. Hiser   11/20/60-2
Emmart, John M., 28 June 1860, Laura Woodcock, dau. of Wm.   7/19/60-2
Emmart, Neilson S., 2 July 1856, Alvinia Wonn   7/ 3/56-2
Emmett, William Wirt, 6 Nov. 1856, Sarah J. Hartzell   8/25/57-2
Emory, A. Walsh (Dr.), 16 May 1854, Juliet O'Donnell   5/18/54-2
Emory, J. K. B., 28 Apr. 1859, S. Amanda Williams   4/29/59-2
Emory, Jesse, 4 July 1860, Agnes Linton   8/23/60-2
Emory, John W., 16 Mar. 1854, Ellenora W. Gosnell   3/17/54-2
Emory, Robert S., 9 Jan. 1860, Juliana Wilkins, dau. of
     (Col.) Edwd.   1/13/60-2
Endley, Francis H., 29 Mar. 1857, Frances Virginia Meekens   4/ 1/57-2
Eney, Jeremiah, 26 Dec. 1859, Maggie V. Kirby   12/30/59-2
Eney, Oliver N., 7 June 1852, Anna G. Denyer, dau. of Peter   6/ 9/52-2
Eney, Thomas, 30 May 1853, Susan F. C. Stickel   6/ 2/53-2
England, John, 12 Feb. 1852, Hannah Tucker   2/13/52-2
Englar, John, 17 Feb. 1852, Sarah E. Cornelius, dau. of
     (Rev.) Samuel   2/25/52-2
Engler, Adolph, 4 Nov. 1858, Julia E. Spilcker, dau. of C. W. 11/ 8/58-2
English, John R., 30 Sept. 1858, Mary Ann McCoy   12/ 1/58-2
Enis, Wm., 28 Dec. 1854, Mary Newell   1/ 5/55-2
Ennels, Stephen, 17 Sept. 1857, Margaret Gaines   9/19/57-2
Ennis, John, 22 June 1854, Mary Murphy   6/24/54-2
Ennis, John, 9 Feb. 1860, Rebecca Jimison   2/11/60-2
Ennis, Solomon, 10 July 1854, (Mrs.) Sarah Ann Crismas   7/13/54-2
Enright, Charles J., 15 Aug. 1860, Louisa S. March   8/17/60-2
Ensey, Augustus W., 24 May 1855, Catherine V. Wright   8/ 6/57-2
Ensey, Richard F., 6 May 1852, Jinnie J. Richardson, dau. of
     (Dr.) Charles   5/ 7/52-2
Ensey, Richard L., 1 Sept. 1853, Mary J. Gosnell, dau. of
     John   9/ 3/53-2
Ensor, Hiram, 7 July 1852, Eliza A. Oakley   7/13/52-2
Ensor, Isaac, 10 Mar. 1852, Mary Jane Naylor   3/16/52-2
Ensor, James W., 11 Nov. 1860, Esther J. Cole   11/13/60-2
Ensor, Jesse, 4 July 1860, Agnes Linton; corrected copy   8/24/60-2
Ensor, John H., 22 Nov. 1853, Isabella Griffith, dau. of
     (Capt.) David   11/24/53-2
Entz, Andrew, 25 July 1854, Mary L. Mister, dau. of Abram   7/27/54-2
Epparts, Sylvester, 5 Dec. 1856, Ann Maria Conley   12/ 6/56-2
Epron, Francis H., 14 Jan. 1851, Roxanna Devaughn   1/16/51-2
Erdman, Frederick, (?) June 1857, Grace Reid, dau. of Peter   7/ 9/57-2
Erdman, Frederick, 6 July 1857, Grace Reid, dau. of Peter;
     corrected copy   7/16/57-2
Erdman, Gotleib H., 26 Mar. 1860, Dorothy C. Loamley   4/ 2/60-2
Erdman, John, 17 Nov. 1853, Sarah E. Bamberger   11/21/53-2
Erdman, Peter G., 9 Oct. 1851, Letitia Waddell   10/10/51-2
Erek, Daniel F., 27 Oct. 1853, Catherine A. Clarkson, dau. of
     G. L.   10/29/53-2
Erek, Henry, 28 Nov. 1860, Sarah E. Pierce   12/ 1/60-2
Ergood, Gabriel S., 14 May 1856, (Mrs.) Caroline Miller   5/17/56-2

Erie, John H., 29 July 1855, Mary E. Mead   7/30/55-2
Erles, Perry, 5 Jan. 1858, Susan Ann Brooks   1/ 8/58-2
Ernest, Wm. H., 3 Jan. 1860, Louisa L. Phillips   1/10/60-2
Erney, R. V. L., 13 Feb. 1851, Catharine Matilda Smith   2/20/51-2
Ervin, Charles T., 20 Jan. 1859, Letitia B. Clark   1/24/59-2
Erving, Elwyn, 30 Apr. 1860, Lydia E. H. Adams   5/ 1/60-2
Erving, Langdon, 18 Dec. 1860, Sophia C. Pennington   12/21/60-2
Erwin, George, 13 Mar. 1851, Elizabeth R. Frazer   3/14/51-2
Escavaille, Jos. B., 14 Oct. 1852, Susannah B. Shock, dau. of
    George E. and Marsha B.   10/19/52-2
Eschbach, Frederick Alphonsus, 18 Sept. 1851, Rebecca Virginia
    Lupton, dau. of Syrus C., step-dau. of George A. Megee   9/22/51-2
Eschbach, Jos. A. (Dr.), 11 June 1855, Annie M. Bryan   6/12/55-2
Esherick, Thomas, 27 Jan. 1858, Sarah Tippit   2/ 3/58-2
Eskridge, A. A. (Rev.), 18 Nov. 1858, (Mrs.) Eliza Weems, sister
    of (Rev.) Richard Brown   11/23/58-2
Espey, John J., 1 Oct. 1857, E. A. Espey   10/ 3/51-2
Espey, William P., 25 Sept. 1853, Mary Lucinda Smith   9/29/53-2
Estabrook, E., 17 May 1853, Kate E. Allen, dau. of Solomon   5/18/53-2
Estep, John C., 30 Oct. 1855, E. Emilie Wiley, dau. of (Rev.)
    John   11/ 2/55-2
Esterline, Geo. K.; no date given, Lizzie V. Holter, dau. of
    Lewis and Mary A.   10/ 4/60-2
Etchison, E. Dorsey, 14 Aug. 1851, Rachel Ann Stevens   8/19/51-2
Etter, P. L., 14 Dec. 1859, Cecelia Green   1/ 4/60-2
Euker, Edward J., 2 Nov. 1858, Leonore Kracke   11/ 4/58-2
Evans, Abel, 18 May 1852, Catharine Potter Bell, dau. of
    Benjamin Theodore   5/28/52-2
Evans, Amos, 18 Nov. 1852, Ann E. Mitchell   11/22/52-2
Evans, Arthur Charles, 14 July 1857, (Mrs.) Frances Rogers   7/16/57-2
Evans, Charles W., 28 Dec. 1858, Maria J. Wilcox, dau. of
    Thomas S.   12/31/58-2
Evans, Daniel, 2 July 1854, Susanna B. Hugh   7/ 4/54-2
Evans, Daniel, 2 July 1854, Susanna R. High; corrected copy   7/ 6/54-2
Evans, Geo. P., 6 Aug. 1852, Catharine A. Blackburn   8/10/52-2
Evans, Henry, Jr., 10 July 1856, Hester A. King, dau. of
    John and Hester   7/11/56-2
Evans, Henry C., 4 Oct. 1860, Mary E. Garretson   10/ 5/60-2
Evans, Henry M., 12 Sept. 1854, Caroline Amanda Raisin, dau.
    of McCan   9/13/54-2
Evans, James, 12 Dec. 1854, Cevila Price   12/14/54-2
Evans, James, 19 Aug. 1859, (Mrs.) Jane Jacobi   8/22/59-2
Evans, James M., 11 Dec. 1851, Mary Mitchell, dau. of A. D.   12/20/51-2
Evans, James M., 18 June 1855, Julia Ryon   12/ 3/55-2
Evans, John, 26 Jan. 1854, Virginia Joyes, dau. of Jesse   1/27/54-2
Evans, John B., 13 Sept. 1853, Mary Jane Joye   9/20/53-2
Evans, John E., son of (Rev.) French S., 26 Jan. 1854, Sophia
    Smiley Lawrence, dau. of James   1/27/54-2
Evans, Joseph, 21 Dec. 1851, Margaret Ann Clarige   1/10/52-2
Evans, Joseph, 4 Sept. 1856, Sarah A. Hites   9/ 6/56-2
Evans, Joseph V., 11 Nov. 1858, Emilie Goodison   4/16/59-2
Evans, Joshua, 18 Dec. 1853, Adaline R. Cullen   12/22/53-2
Evans, Joshua J., 26 Feb. 1854, Margaret A. Purcelle   2/28/54-2
Evans, Maybury, 9 Jan. 1851, Mary Blanche Bond, dau. of
    Zacheus O.   1/11/51-2
Evans, Nathan W. (Capt.), 10 Dec. 1851, Rebecca M. Ayres   12/11/51-2
Evans, Randolph, 14 Feb. 1856, Laura Jane Bramble   2/25/56-2
Evans, Richard A., 2 Apr. 1860, Zipporah M. Davis   4/ 9/60-2
Evans, Samuel, 10 Aug. 1851, Mary Kidd   8/15/51-2
Evans, Samuel M., 13 Nov. 1854, Anna M. Bryan, dau. of
    William   1/26/55-2
Evans, Thomas A., 17 Nov. 1852, Mary Ann Crisp   11/19/52-2
Evans, Thomas J., 27 Mar. 1859, Sarah C. Bowen   3/30/59-2
Evans, William, 15 Apr. 1858, Mary E. Trott   4/17/58-2
Evans, William H., 27 Dec. 1859, Mary A. Bate   3/28/60-2

Evans, William Hooper, 10 Mar. 1857, Mary Jane Wolf   3/12/57-2
Evatt, Edward J., 14 Oct. 1852, Sarah E. Reckitt   10/16/52-2
Evatt, William, 14 Oct. 1856, Lydia M. Arthur, dau. of John 10/17/56-2
Eveans, John C., 2 June 1853, Kate Brown   6/ 4/53-2
Evens, William A. J., 12 June 1856, Catharine R. Willson   6/17/56-2
Everding, Henry D., 7 Apr. 1851, Sarah J. Cramer   4/11/51-2
Everett, James, 6 May 1855, Elizabeth Domman   5/ 9/55-2
Everett, John, 21 Apr. 1853, Julia Ann Carr   5/ 7/53-2
Everhart, O. T. (Dr.), 26 Apr. 1859, Sallie Kister, dau. of
     (Rev.) Jacob G.   4/28/59-2
Everhart, William H., 29 Nov. 1859, Tryphena A. Smardon   12/ 1/59-2
Everheart, George W., 8 May 1860, Martha Moore   5/10/60-2
Everist, Ephraim, 18 Nov. 1857, Rachel E. Hoopman   11/23/57-2
Everist, Joseph J., 3 July 1854, Susan O. Thompson   7/10/54-2
Everitt, John H., 4 July 1852, Margaret J. Kohler   7/ 7/52-2
Eversman, John F., 12 Dec. 1857, Elmira Nelson   12/14/57-2
Evitt, Robert, 7 Oct. 1856, Amelia Burdett, dau. of Aaron   10/ 8/56-2
Ewalt, Sam'l. A., 13 Mar. 1852, Mary F. Miller   3/20/52-2
Ewen, Jeremiah E., 18 Oct. 1853, Sarah Gill   10/22/53-2
Ewing, William, 23 Feb. 1851, Ann Elizabeth Coursey   2/25/51-2
Ewing, William, 2 Sept. 1858, (Mrs.) Elizabeth Brickley   9/ 3/58-2
Eyanson, John E., 18 Oct. 1860, Annie C. Knipe   10/19/60-2
Faber, John C., 10 May 1852, Ellen Minor   5/13/52-2
Fagan, Nicholas, 24 Apr. 1851, Ellenora J. Ginevan   4/28/51-2
Faherty, John P., 21 Jan. 1852, Eliza J. Caton   1/22/52-2
Faherty, Thomas M., 13 Feb. 1855, Annie Median   2/21/55-2
Fahey, Chas. J., 26 May 1856, Mary Ann Tinken   6/ 5/56-2
Fahnestock, Arthur A., 2 Aug. 1853, Sue Davis, dau. of Geo. W. 8/ 3/53-2
Fahnestock, Edward, 15 Oct. 1856, Martha Davis   10/17/56-2
Fahnestock, G. Washington, 14 Dec. 1858, Phebe A. B. Peirce 12/18/58-2
Fahnestock, Joseph D., 28 Apr. 1857, Helen Grafton, dau. of
     Mark   4/29/57-2
Fairall, Thomas L., 27 Apr. 1854, Maria A. Baldwin   5/ 4/54-2
Fairbank, George W., 18 Jan. 1859, Louisa R. Harman   1/21/59-2
Fairbanks, Andrew Jackson, 13 July 1854, Julia Ann Bann   7/19/54-2
Fairbanks, George K., 19 Aug. 1858, Mary R. Benton   8/24/58-2
Fairbanks, William J., 5 May 1859, Sarah A. Armeger   5/ 7/59-2
Fairbanss, Charles, 10 July 1854, Catharine E. Whitten   7/27/54-2
Fairncross, John M., 4 Sept. 1855, Amanda F. Carter, step-dau.
     of John Wall   9/12/55-2
Faithful, William T., 10 Mar. 1858, (Mrs.) Kitty A. Hood   3/17/58-2
Faithful, William Thomas, Jr., 28 Oct. 1852, Lydia E. Grimes,
     dau. of Josiah D.   10/30/52-2
Falconar, John H., 24 June 1851, Angelina M. Griffith, dau.
     of Richard H.   6/26/51-2
Fales, Edward, 28 Dec. 1850, Imogene C. Francicus   1/18/51-2
Fales, Nathan G., 16 Dec. 1851, Mary E. O'Connor   12/18/51-2
Fallen, Wm. (Capt.), 10 Feb. 1859, Mary Thomas, dau. of John 2/14/59-2
Fallon, Edward, 12 June 1860, Sarah Ward   6/18/60-2
Fallows, W. J., 4 Sept. 1853, Martha Grime   9/17/53-2
Falls, Robert Wilson, 21 Nov. 1855, Mary Johnson Furlong   11/23/55-2
Falvey, Michael, 13 Oct. 1852, Catharine Connelly   10/19/52-2
Fames, Henry E., 5 July 1860, Fannie R. Alexander   7/ 6/60-2
Fanan, James, 16 July 1853, Ellen Craighton   7/20/53-2
Fanning, John, 25 Nov. 1858, Maria Flaherty   11/27/58-2
Fanning, Michael, 15 Apr. 1858, Bridget Noughton   5/ 8/58-2
Fant, Hamilton G., 16 May 1853, Josephine Helen, dau. of
     Johnson   5/18/53-2
Farber, Henry J., 2 Oct. 1855, Annie Stalport, dau. of F.   10/ 3/55-2
Fardwell, Isaac, Jr., 15 May 1851, Charlotte C. Myers   5/17/51-2
Fardwell, William A., 16 Nov. 1851, Sarah Frances Mister, dau.
     of Levin R.   12/ 4/51-2
Fardy, John T., 27 May 1851, Emily J. Kone   6/ 2/51-2
Fardy, Matthew James, 21 Apr. 1857, Louisa C. Huffman   4/22/57-2

Faringer, John J., 17 Sept. 1857, Carrie M. Smyser, dau.
   of Adam   9/21/57-2
Farinhalt, William H., 12 Oct. 1854, Sarah E. Tupman   11/16/54-2
Farlow, John T., 5 Sept. 1855, Sophia Augusta Hancock, dau.
   of A.   9/10/55-2
Farnandis, Henry D., 1 Mar. 1853, Hannah T. Poultney   3/ 3/53-2
Farnandis, William, 15 May 1856, Fanny Tilghman   5/17/56-2
Farquarson, Charles, 24 July 1851, Ann Bell   7/28/51-2
Farr, William, 20 June 1852, Charity Lowe   6/24/52-2
Farrar, S. C. (Dr.), 9 July 1857, (Mrs.) Ann Sherrod   7/10/57-2
Farrel, Mathew, 17 Nov. 1853, Eliza Ryan   1/23/54-2
Farson, John S., 22 Nov. 1860, Sarah R. Phillips, dau. of
   C. C.   11/24/60-2
Farson, Samuel F., 30 Sept. 1852, Indiana T. Grant, dau. of
   William   10/ 2/52-2
Faulk, Andrew, 28 Feb. 1858, Anna M. Schevenn   4/ 3/58-2
Faxon, Eben, 21 July 1853, Ambrosia M. Jenkins   7/22/53-2
Fay, James, 18 Nov. 1856, Elizabeth Cecelia McMahon   11/24/56-2
Faye, James R., 21 Nov. 1854, Rosina C. Passano, dau. of
   Joseph, Sr.   11/22/54-2
Feast, John, 18 Aug. 1857, Sarah Uppercue   8/22/57-2
Feast, John E., 12 Apr. 1860, Mary J. Neely   4/13/60-2
Feast, Samuel, 22 Apr. 1858, Sarah Neely   4/26/58-2
Featherson, Edward M., 10 Aug. 1853, Mary Ann Navy, dau. of
   (Capt.) Moses   8/11/53-2
Fectig, George F., 14 Sept. 1854, Mary Elizabeth Berger   9/16/54-2
Fedricks, Nelson, 2 Mar. 1854, (Mrs.) Sarah A. Locke   3/ 4/54-2
Fee, Joseph H., 15 Nov. 1855, Mary Jane Smith   11/17/55-2
Feehan, John, 4 Sept. 1851, Martha E. McAleese   9/11/51-2
Feelmyer, Geo. W., 23 May 1854, Christiania Copper   6/24/54-2
Fefel, Joseph, Jr., 20 July 1854, Amanda Thompson   8/ 3/54-2
Feige, August Henry, 6 July 1852, Henrietta Amelia Wagen-
   schwarz   7/ 7/52-2
Feige, Frederick, 2 Nov. 1858, Mary A. E. Roden   11/ 9/58-2
Feilds, John Harman, 16 Aug. 1852, Mary Caroline Brant   8/17/52-2
Feldhaus, Joseph A., 13 Dec. 1855, Mary Jane Willey   12/20/55-2
Fellows, R. T., 29 Nov. 1855, Carrie K. Dameron, dau. of Wm.   12/ 8/55-2
Fells, George, 23 Nov. 1853, Sarah Foster   11/28/53-2
Fells, Samuel L., 11 Dec. 1855, Laura Virginia League, dau.
   of Luke   12/13/55-2
Felthouse, W. H., 23 Oct. 1853, Susan Kirkwood   10/25/53-2
Felton, James, 21 Oct. 1853, R. Elizabeth Peregoy   10/24/53-2
Fenby, William, 15 Jan. 1852, Anna Mary Jones, dau. of
   Thomas S.   1/20/52-2
Fendrich, Joseph, 12 Dec. 1860, Elizabeth Wilson   12/15/60-2
Fenhagen, James C., 29 Sept. 1853, Mary E. Cath-(?), dau. of
   (Col.) Levi   10/ 3/53-2
Fenner, George, 25 Apr. 1859, Annie Gerber   4/27/59-2
Fenner, Henry, 31 Dec. 1853, Mary Lutz   2/ 3/53-2
Fenran, John, 2-(?) June 1857, Margaret Divine   7/ 2/57-2
Fensley, William, 13 Dec. 1854, Louisa B. Baker   12/18/54-2
Fenton, Samuel, 17 Feb. 1853, Anna Jane Barnett, dau. of
   William   2/19/53-2
Fentress, George D., 21 Jan. 1858, Josephine Davis   1/27/58-2
Fenwock, Henry A., 8 July 1852, Helen C. Tiernan, dau. of
   Chas.   7/12/52-2
Ferguson, Colin B., 13 Jan. 1859, Mary Elinor Leman, dau. of
   Walter Moore   1/15/59-2
Ferguson, George H., 1 Aug. 1859, Annie L. Mettee, dau. of
   Philip   8/11/59-2
Ferguson, John, 23 Jan. 1855, Elizabeth McCormack   2/15/55-2
Ferguson, Robert, 15 Oct. 1857, Margaret Wilson   10/19/57-2
Ferrell, Elisha, 23 Dec. 1851, Julia Ann Amos   1/ 1/52-2
Ferry, Daniel, 26 Jan. 1854, Mary Jane Scott   2/ 2/54-2

Fetterman, George W., 4 Sept. 1856, Louise E. Moone, dau.	
of Thomas	9/ 8/56-2
Fheim, Josiah G., 30 Nov. 1852, Ellen C. Johnson	12/ 6/52-2
Fhrenpfort, Wm., 6 Oct. 1860, Marie Christine Dietrich	10/18/60-2
Ficher, Albert, 30 Jan. 1859, Sarah Jane Curry	2/ 1/59-2
Fickey, Andrew J., 14 July 1859, Mattie Iglehart Fairall,	
dau. of Truman	7/16/59-2
Field, Philip S. (Dr.), 26 Oct. 1854, Rosalind Bulkley	10/28/54-2
Fields, John A., 7 Sept. 1854, Mary E. Phillips	9/ 9/54-2
Fields, Stephen B. *, 10 May 1855, Caroline Jarrette	5/12/55-2
Fields, Thompson, 3 Dec. 1855, Cecelia Virginia Gibson, dau.	
of John R.	12/10/55-2
Filbert, John A., 30 Apr. 1856, Mary B. Beltzhoover, dau. of	
John G.	5/ 6/56-2
Fillinger, John M., 17 Oct. 1854, Catherine Ann Smith, dau.	
of Martin; 10/19/54-2	10/20/54-2
Fink, Martin L., 8 Apr. 1856, Lizzie C. Keyser, dau. of Jas.	4/10/56-2
Finlay, James, 28 Mar. 1853, Henrietta A. Shephard, dau. of	
James	4/ 5/53-2
Finley, Francis, 14 May 1855, Willamina Boyd, dau. of H. S.	8/10/55-2
Finley, Geo., 14 Dec. 1852, Joanna Rochester	12/25/52-2
Finley, William, 9 May 1859, Eleanora Jennings, dau. of	
Samuel	5/12/59-2
Finnaran, Hugh, 13 Feb. 1851, Anne Caughlin	2/21/51-2
Finnegaen, Charles, 22 Jan. 1856, Mary Ann Ball	1/25/56-2
Finnell, Hanson (Dr.), 17 Aug. 1852, Mary Finnell	8/26/52-2
Firor, Ephraim A., 14 Sept. 1852, Elizabeth Beggett	9/18/52-2
Fischach, John, Jr., 7 Oct. 1858, Amanda E. Horner	10/13/58-2
Fischer, F. H. G., 27 Jan. 1856, Catherine Maring	1/28/56-2
Fish, Allen C., 6 Apr. 1857, Sarah A. Williams	4/13/57-2
Fisher, Alfred H., 7 June 1853, Mary Hodges	6/11/53-2
Fisher, George W., 11 Sept. 1851, Emily J. Holtzman, dau. of	
Thos.	9/13/51-2
Fisher, George W., 10 Dec. 1857, Mary Lizzie Emerick	12/16/57-2
Fisher, George W., 29 Dec. 1857, Meriam C. Little	12/30/57-2
Fisher, Henry N., 19 Aug. 1858, Elizabeth Nichols	8/21/58-2
Fisher, J. Harmanus, 17 June 1857, Sallie R. Beatty, dau. of	
Cornelius	6/19/57-2
Fisher, James M., 19 May 1859, Sallie O. Pierce	6/29/59-2
Fisher, Jesse, 1 Nov. 1860, Elspeth Boberson	11/ 6/60-2
Fisher, John, 13 Nov. 1856, Annie E. Mothland, dau. of	
Robert	11/17/56-2
Fisher, John C., 7 May 1857, Emma Borgelt, dau. of George	6/ 1/57-2
Fisher, John L., 9 Aug. 1860, Ann Maria Sherlock	8/10/60-2
Fisher, John S., 24 July 1855, Kate M. Mackelfresh	7/27/55-2
Fisher, Josiah, 25 Dec. 1856, Mary E. Bowen	12/29/56-2
Fisher, Lemuel, 19 Sept. 1858, Jesse Ann Shafer	9/22/58-2
Fisher, Thomas A., 16 Oct. 1860, Mary C. Hartlove	10/23/60-2
Fisher, William, 4 Jan. 1859, Elenora Weyl, dau. of (Rev.)	
Chas. G.	1/ 5/59-2
Fisher, William H., 31 May 1853, Ann A. Wright	6/11/53-2
Fisher, William H., 18 Jan. 1858, Frances A. Lamy	3/ 1/58-2
Fisher, William H. G., 6 Apr. 1851, Jane Stubbins	4/15/51-2
Fisher, Wm. L., 15 Dec. 1857, Lizzie A. Carback, dau. of	
Elisha	12/19/57-2
Fishpaugh, John L., 11 Oct. 1857, Rebecca J. Price	10/13/57-2
Fitch, John C., 6 July 1854, Margaret Dehaven, dau. of	
Joseph	7/17/54-2
Fitzgerald, David, 12 Dec. 1855, Ann Cotter, dau. of Richard	2/12/56-2
Fitzgerald, Edmund H., 14 June 1852, Anna Augusta Gatch	6/16/52-2
Fitzgerald, Hugh, 3 Mar. 1853, Sarah Elizabeth Evans	3/ 5/53-2
Fitzgerald, James, 16 Apr. 1854, Mary Nolan	4/19/54-2
Fitzgerald, John (Capt.), 5 June 1851, Sophie Fitzgerald	6/10/51-2
Fitzgerald, Patrick, 23 June 1853, Mary Smith	6/29/53-2
Fitzgerald, Thos. H., 27 Feb. 1855, Mary Ann Newman	3/ 1/55-2

```
Fitzhugh, Henry W., 21 Sept. 1852, (Mrs.) Augusta J. Grundy      9/24/52-2
Fitzmaurice, William, 6 Sept. 1855, Anne Kelly                    9/ 9/55-2
Fitzmorris, Michael, 15 Dec. 1851, Ann Garvin                    12/17/51-2
Fitzmorris, Patrick, 22 Dec. 1851, Mary Fitzmorris               12/25/51-2
Fitzpatrick, T., 3 Sept. 1857, M. F. Ball                        10/ 6/57-2
Fitzpatrick, Thomas, 25 Nov. 1852, Mary E. Hall                  11/27/52-2
Fitzsimmonds, James, 10 Sept. 1855, Amanda Brittainham            9/22/55-2
Flack, Jas. W., 4 May 1858, Mary E. Baker                         5/ 6/58-2
Flack, William M., 4 Feb. 1852, Susan M. Perkins, dau. of
     (Rev.) John D.; 2/ 5/52-2                                    2/ 6/52-2
Flaharty, Thomas, 2 Dec. 1856, Margaret Phoebus                  12/ 4/56-2
Flaherty, Edward, 8 Feb. 1857, Ann Hagan; 2/10/57-2               2/11/57-2
Flaherty, John A., 18 Oct. 1857, Euphemia M. A. Dillaway         10/27/57-2
Flaherty, Michael; no date given, Rachel Minzey                  12/23/57-2
Flaherty, Patrick, 31 Aug. 1853, Mary Hughes                      8/19/53-2
Flanagan, Charles L., 26 Sept. 1854, Martha W. Campbell, dau.
     of Geo. R.                                                   9/28/54-2
Flanagan, Jas., 5 Oct. 1851, Esther Flanagan                     12/13/51-2
Flanigan, Andrew Mc. E., 17 May 1855, Sarah F. McDaniel           5/24/55-2
Flather, Edwin, 13 Aug. 1854, Eliza T. Evans, dau. of
     Henry F.                                                     8/17/54-2
Flather, John H., 16 Mar. 1860, Martha V. Webster                3/21/60-2
Flaxcomb, Charles, 24 Feb. 1856, Elizabeth Jeffries              2/26/56-2
Flayharty, William E., 28 Oct. 1856, Emma Pool                   10/30/56-2
Fledderman, Henry Garrett, son of H. P., 6 Oct. 1859, Catherine
     Augustine Stolpp, dau. of J. L.; 10/11/59-2                 10/12/59-2
Fleisheld, Joseph H., 2 Sept. 1860, Josephine Kamara             9/ 4/60-2
Fleishman, Henry, 17 Feb. 1858, R. J. Gentry                      3/16/58-2
Fleming, J. Perkins (Dr.), 19 Oct. 1858, Lizzie R. Smith, dau.
     of (Col.) Alex.                                             10/20/58-2
Fleming, William S., 4 Dec. 1860, Ginnie L. Miller, dau. of
     Jacob B.                                                    12/ 6/60-2
Fletcher, Spencer D., 18 Oct. 1855, Roberta Lee, dau. of
     Richard D.                                                  10/22/55-2
Flick, William N., 31 May 1860, Mary A. Johnston                  6/ 2/60-2
Flinn, Michael, 6 June 1858, Mary Clark                           6/ 8/58-2
Flint, James, 26 June 1851, Anna Maria Allan                      7/ 1/51-2
Flint, John W., 28 Sept. 1852, Caroline Fanwell                   9/30/52-2
Flitt, Charles, 1 Nov. 1853, Laura Hilbert                       11/ 3/53-2
Flood, James, 7 Jan. 1852, Anna Corkcoran                         1/15/52-2
Flood, James, 29 Dec. 1857, Mary Ann Gailer                       1/ 1/58-2
Floury, Elias G., 20 Mar. 1851, Julia Ann Bryan                   3/22/51-2
Floyd, William, 27 Oct. 1858, E. Adaline Dobson                  10/29/58-2
Floyd, William T., 25 Nov. 1855, Sarah A. Larkin                 12/11/55-2
Floyd, Wm. Jas., 10 July 1851, Elizabeth McCleary                 8/12/51-2
Fluhart, George W., 11 May 1851, Mary Ann Smith                   5/12/51-2
Fluharty, Wm. R., 5 Aug. 1859, Mary E. R. Toms, dau. of
     Anderson C.                                                  8/19/59-2
Flynn, John, 20 Aug. 1855, Margaret Ward                          8/22/55-2
Flynn, Laurence, 26 Oct. 1853, Margaret Ann Carr                 11/ 8/53-2
Flynn, Michael, 27 Nov. 1851, Mary Hughes                        12/ 4/51-2
Flynn, Patrick, 6 Dec. 1857, Catherine McConell                  12/10/57-2
Foard, Addison Kemp, 5 June 1851, Mary Parker, dau. of John
     Jones                                                        6/ 7/51-2
Foard, Chas. D., 3 Feb. 1857, Kate E. Showacre, dau. of John      2/ 7/57-2
Foertsch, John G., 2 July 1859, Sophia W. Giffhorn               7/ 6/59-2
Fogelson, Lewis, 3 May 1855, Emily Burgan                         5/ 9/55-2
Fogg, Josiah, 16 Feb. 1858, Josephine L. Brooks, dau. of
     Meritt                                                       2/22/58-2
Fogle, Henry H., 20 Sept. 1860, Lottie J. Rowe                    9/26/60-2
Foley, John, 6 May 1858, Mary Louisa Chorter                      5/12/58-2
Foley, John, 1 Jan. 1859, Martha V. Reay                          1/ 5/59-2
Foley, Matthew J., 15 June 1858, Mary W. A. Roper                 6/16/58-2
Foley, Patrick, 27 Nov. 1851, Anna Flynn                         12/ 2/51-2
```

Follansbee, Lambertt, 26 Feb. 1857, Emily J. Stevens, dau. of
    Isaac   3/17/57-2
Folanshee, Joseph Vinton, 2 Dec. 1852, Henrietta S. Webb,
    dau. of James   12/ 4/52-2
Fooks, Albert G., 9 Jan. 1854, Juliet V. Silk, dau. of
    Thomas R.   1/28/54-2
Foos, James, 14 Aug. 1859, Ann Scarf   8/17/59-2
Foos, John A., 3 July 1855, Martha Ann Young   7/16/55-2
Foos, John S., 18 Sept. 1851, Sarah E. Daves   9/20/51-2
Foos, Thomas B., 25 Sept. 1854, Charity Almira Foos   9/28/54-2
Foos, William A., 14 Oct. 1860, Kate Askins   10/22/60-2
Foos, Wm. C., 14 Sept. 1858, Anne M. Peregoy   9/16/58-2
Foose, Charles S., 17 Feb. 1859, Freddy H. Rousselot   2/19/59-2
Foote, Benjamin, 15 Mar. 1855, Ellen N. Jefferson   3/17/55-2
Foote, Jno. P., 26 Nov. 1856, Elmira G. Parsons, dau. of
    Joseph   11/28/56-2
Forbes, William H., 5 Nov. 1859, Mary Ann Garrison   11/10/59-2
Ford, Benjamin, 26 July 1855, Margaret E. Cashour, dau. of
    Jacob   7/27/55-2
Ford, Edward C., 10 Jan. 1859, Laura V. Mettee   1/18/59-2
Ford, Gustavus, 6 Apr. 1854, Pleashia A. Frizzell, dau. of
    Beale   4/ 7/54-2
Ford, John F., 9 Jan. 1856, Adalaide Chasteau, dau. of
    (Capt.) Louis A.   1/11/56-2
Ford, John S., 28 Feb. 1860, Mary Frances Lambert   3/ 2/60-2
Ford, Lewis Marion, 2 Nov. 1853, Alice Elizabeth Wheedon   6/ 7/54-2
Ford, S. Calvert, Jr., 28 Nov. 1860, Anna C. LeCompte, dau. of
    Jas. L.   12/ 5/60-2
Ford, Thomas, 29 Oct. 1857, Sarah A. Nickles   10/31/57-2
Ford, Thomas James, 26 Apr. 1855, Elizabeth Ellen Cloarity   5/16/55-2
Ford, William F., 9 Mar. 1854, Henrietta B. Story   3/10/54-2
Ford, William Henry, 15 Apr. 1851, Mary Catherine Spence   4/16/51-2
Forde, Joseph M., 20 Oct. 1860, Sarah Rebecca Yundt   10/26/60-2
Foreman, Chas., 2 Jan. 1853, (Mrs.) Julia Ann Reasin   1/ 8/53-2
Foreman, Joshua, 10 Mar. 1851, Sarah E. Boyd   7/15/51-2
Foreman, Wm. K., 9 Nov. 1855, Ellen Dempsey, dau. of B. H.   11/14/55-2
Forester, James, 29 Nov. 1855, Hester Ann Butler; 12/ 1/55-2 12/ 4/55-2
Forman, Alfred R., 4 Oct. 1859, Britannia A. Brown   10/ 5/59-2
Forman, Geo. Washington, 13 Dec. 1859, Elizabeth Ann
    Eagleston   12/24/59-2
Forney, C. W. (Dr.), 20 Nov. 1851, Emily R. Cassell   11/24/51-2
Forney, George M., 27 Apr. 1854, Ellen K. Bayley   4/29/54-2
Fornshill, Columbus C., 1 Oct. 1857, Margaret E. Ballard;
    corrected copy   11/18/57-2
Fornshill, Columbus C., 1 Nov. 1857, Margaret E. Ballard   11/17/57-2
Forrest, George W., 21 June 1860, Mary W. Lankford   6/23/60-2
Forrest, John, 25 Sept. 1856, Sarah E. Ray   9/27/56-2
Forrest, John, 11 Mar. 1860, L. Jackson   3/26/60-2
Forrest, Joshua, 24 Dec. 1854, (Mrs.) Ann Rebecca Cropper   12/28/57-2
Forrest, Leonard, 9 Sept. 1856, Mary Catharine Brown   2/18/56-2
Forrest, Matthias, 5 July 1852, Mary E. Richardson   7/ 7/52-2
Forrester, A. *, 13 June 1853, Mary A. Barrenger   6/16/53-2
Forrester, Alexander, 9 Aug. 1857, Mary Ann Baringer   8/13/57-2
Forrester, Allen E., 5 July 1852, Caroline K. Orrick   7/ 9/52-2
Forrester, Benjamin F., Jr., 14 Apr. 1857, Margaret A.
    Faithful, dau. of Wm.   4/16/57-2
Forrester, G. L., 13 Nov. 1851, M. A. McComas   11/22/51-2
Forrester, Elex. *, 23 Oct. 1855, Elizabeth Warfield   10/25/55-2
Forrester, George L., 4 Oct. 1858, Lucrecia C. Coulter   11/23/58-2
Forrester, Perry, 10 June 1852, Matilda Higgins   6/12/52-2
Forrester, William H., 4 Nov. 1852, Julia A. Armstrong, dau.
    of Henry   11/ 9/52-2
Forrster, John, 16 Feb. 1857, Amanda Ellen Ramsay   2/18/57-2
Forster, Donaldson K., 13 Mar. 1851, Annie Marie Baltzell,
    dau. of Alexander   3/19/51-2

```
Forsyth, John A., 10 Aug. 1852, Eliza Laurrison                      8/12/52-2
Forsyth, Joseph James, 27 May 1858, Elizabeth Brooks                 6/10/58-2
Forsythe, David, 12 June 1856, Josephine Geese                       6/19/56-2
Forsythe, Edward S., 18 Nov. 1856, Charlotte E. Baron               12/19/56-2
Forsythe, Franklin J., 30 Dec. 1857, Amelia Frances Patterson        1/ 7/58-2
Forsythe, Jas., 18 Sept. 1851, Lillie Young                          9/22/51-2
Forsythe, Louis E., 16 Oct. 1856, Elizabeth F. Hunt, dau. of
   Stephen                                                          12/ 5/56-2
Forsythe, Robert T., 15 Mar. 1855, Harriet A. Smith                  3/17/55-2
Fort, Allen T., 26 Dec. 1855, Cordelia Clarke, dau. of Horace        1/12/56-2
Fortie, John C., 2 Apr. 1858, Georgeanna Robinson                    5/ 4/58-2
Fortie, Lou. Roz., 8 Apr. 1858, Ellen E. Davis Hacon, dau. of
   Wm.                                                               6/ 9/58-2
Fortling, John H., 12 Feb. 1852, Sarah A. Gettier                    2/16/52-2
Fortune, John A., 1 Apr. 1856, Susan Morrison                        4/ 3/56-2
Forwood, H. S., 24 July 1855, Virginia C. Mauhl, dau. of
   (Capt.) Winheld                                                   7/28/55-2
Forwood, Robert B., 17 June 1856, Mary E. Hendon                     6/25/56-2
Foss, John H., 7 July 1853, Margaret Ann Jones                       7/19/53-2
Foss, Wm. J. C., 25 May 1854, Theresea E. East                       6/ 3/54-2
Fossett, James H., 10 Oct. 1854, Ann Maria Wooden                   10/17/54-2
Foster, Charles F., 15 May 1860, Ella Marshall                       5/23/60-2
Foster, D. Hall, 31 Aug. 1859, Mary E. Griffith, dau. of
   (Capt.) John                                                      9/21/59-2
Foster, Franklin, 7 Apr. 1858, Sarah F. Davis                        4/14/58-2
Foster, George E., 2 June 1859, Anna E. Courtneay                    6/ 6/59-2
Foster, George S., 9 Dec. 1855, Mary C. Poole                       12/11/55-2
Foster, James K., 1 May 1851, Amelia Jarvis                          5/ 6/51-2
Foster, John C., 19 Nov. 1856, Ellenora C. Krems                    11/22/56-2
Foster, Sam'l. W., 14 Nov. 1852, Elizabeth M. Coburn, dau.
   of Henry                                                         11/16/52-2
Foster, W. C., 17 May 1857, Indie M. Beall                           5/19/57-2
Foster, William, 6 May 1858, Sarah Johns                             5/ 8/58-2
Foster, William J., 8 Sept. 1859, Mary F. Cambel                     9/13/59-2
Foster, Wm. H., 12 Oct. 1853, Mary Rountree                         10/20/53-2
Foster, Wm. Swift, 14 Oct. 1850, Maria Agnes English, dau. of
   W. M.                                                             1/ 8/51-2
Fountain, J. A. J., 3 Jan. 1854, Malvina V. Mopps                    1/ 5/54-2
Fountain, George W., 1 July 1856, Pauline Sands                      7/11/56-2
Fountain, John T., 2 June 1853, Mary Amanda Pearce                   6/ 4/53-2
Fowble, Stephen M., 13 Jan. 1853, Charlotte C. Fowble                1/15/53-2
Fowler, E. H., 17 Oct. 1854, Adeline C. Fisher                      10/18/54-2
Fowler, Isaac J., 9 Oct. 1853, Anne M. Hughlett                      1/10/54-2
Fowler, John L., 14 Oct. 1851, Hannah K. Wentz                      10/16/51-2
Fowler, John R., 15 Jan. 1856, Amanda C. Parson                      1/19/56-2
Fowler, John W., 7 Nov. 1854, Jane R. Taylor                        11/ 8/54-2
Fowler, Saml. L., 25 Oct. 1859, Olevia M. C. Larkin, dau. of
   (Rev.) James                                                     12/ 7/59-2
Fowler, T. Walter, 4 June 1857, Virginia Griffin Wall, dau.
   of Daniel                                                         6/ 6/57-2
Fowler, Thomas, 22 Mar. 1859, Sarah Cole, dau. of Frederick          3/25/59-2
Fowler, William, 4 June 1857, Sarah Jane Gilchrist                   6/ 6/57-2
Fowler, William H., 9 Aug. 1855, Ann Jane Hogarth                    3/11/55-2
Fowler, Wm. B., 19 May 1857, Lydia F. Morgan                         5/23/57-2
Fowner, Augustus, 25 Dec. 1859, Mary Ann Lewin                      12/31/59-2
Fox, Jesse T., 29 Oct. 1857, Eliza J. Schmuck                       10/31/57-2
Fox, Joseph E., 27 Sept. 1852, Mary Matilda Cooksey                 10/ 7/52-2
Fox, William, 16 July 1855, Margaret Rody                            7/20/55-2
Foxwell, C. Layton, 16 Oct. 1860, Frankie A. Mason; corrected
   copy                                                             10/19/60-2
Foxwell, Charles L., 16 Oct. 1860, Frances A. Mason, dau. of
   Richard                                                          10/18/60-2
Foy, James H., 1 Nov. 1860, Eliza A. Vining                         11/ 3/60-2
Foy, James H., 1 Nov. 1860, Eliza A. Wining; corrected copy         11/ 5/60-2
Foy, James W., 25 Oct. 1855, Mary A. Lowery                          2/ 9/56-2
```

Foy, John F., 6 Apr. 1854, Sarah Ann Michael   4/14/54-2
Foy, Phillip Chas. H., 30 June 1853, Sarah J. F. Aburn   7/ 2/53-2
Frames, George A., 5 Feb. 1856, Emma F. Hamelin   4/21/56-2
Frampton, Henry, 15 Oct. 1857, Susan E. James   10/20/57-2
Frampton, Thomas H., 15 June 1859, Josephine K. Dillehunt,
    dau. of William T.   7/18/59-2
France, G. W. (Dr.), 16 Nov. 1853, Mary J. Glass   11/22/53-2
France, Thomas A., 20 Oct. 1859, Sarah Jane Stine, dau. of
    Christopher   10/28/59-2
Frances, Wm. P., 17 May 1854, S. Lavinia Cowart   5/23/54-2
Francis, Elias, 19 Feb. 1852, Ellen Eddicks   2/20/52-2
Francis, James, 8 Jan. 1854, Elizabeth Marsh   1/19/54-2
Francis, Richard, 9 Dec. 1852, Ellen Toreffer   12/11/52-2
Francis, Thomas, 28 Nov. 1852, Eliza Jane Hall McKeown, dau. of
    H. Marrion   12/ 3/52-2
Francis, William J., 27 July 1858, Kate A. Lorman   7/29/58-2
Francis, William P., 2 Oct. 1851, Mary Gulie Mathiot, dau. of
    Augustus   10/ 4/51-2
Frank, John P., 20 Oct. 1857, Sarah Louisa Carey   10/26/57-2
Frank, John T., 5 Dec. 1852, Lucy F. Adams   12/ 7/52-2
Frankand, G. W. 10 Dec. 1856, Sarah E. Ager   12/11/56-2
Frankland, Henry, 3 Aug. 1858, Mary Jane Morrison   9/30/58-2
Franklin, Edward C., 2 July 1856, Mary Ann Monteith   7/ 4/56-2
Franklin, Joseph F., 5 June 1860, Melissa Skillman   6/ 8/60-2
Franklin, Robert, 14 Nov. 1860, Mary S. W. Gantt, dau. of
    B. F.   11/16/60-2
Franklin, Saml. D., 1 July 1855, Frances A. Wroten   7/ 4/55-2
Franklin, Thomas J. (Dr.), 30 Dec. 1856, Mary A. Fitzhugh,
    dau. of Daniel D.   12/31/56-2
Frantom, William T., 5 July 1853, Jane E. Humes   7/20/53-2
Fraser, Frank S., 4 Dec. 1859, Mary M. Stigerwald   12/ 7/59-2
Frasher, Bazeil, 7 Apr. 1859, Mary E. Williams   4/ 8/59-2
Frazer, William, 24 Aug. 1854, Julia A. M. E. S. Worster   8/26/54-2
Frazier, Charles W., 15 Mar. 1855, (Mrs.) Elizabeth A. Brown   3/17/55-2
Frazier, Chas. H., 30 Sept. 1856, Ellen Rollins, dau. of
    James   10/ 3/56-2
Frazier, Elihu Hinton, 20 Jan. 1853, Margaret Augusta Johnson   1/26/53-2
Frazier, F. C., 4 Dec. 1859, Mary M. Stigerwald   12/ 6/59-2
Frazier, John L., 19 July 1859, Sarah Jane Mann, dau. of
    Geo.   7/21/59-2
Frazier, John M., 14 Mar. 1859, Mattie L. Grafton, dau. of
    Mark   3/16/59-2
Frazier, John W., 26 June 1851, Catherine A. Evritt   7/11/51-2
Frazier, John W., 13 Sept. 1857, Sarah Foots   9/26/57-2
Frazier, Joseph E., 17 May 1860, Susannah Fryfogle   5/21/60-2
Freberger, James H., 7 Dec. 1856, Emily Jane Richter   12/ 9/56-2
Freburger, Henry J., 6 Jan. 1853, Lydia Huffnagel   1/ 8/53-2
Freburger, Wm., 17 June 1853, Jane Ann Rudgate   6/22/53-2
Fred, William, 3 Apr. 1851, Mary Catherine Schwartz   4/ 5/51-2
Frederick, George, 3 Oct. 1858, Caroline Kilhelmine Stahl,
    dau. of Charles G. and Louisa   10/ 5/58-2
Frederick, George Alocks, 11 July 1860, Carrie Berger   7/13/60-2
Frederick, Henry, 13 Oct. 1856, Henrietta Norwood   10/17/56-2
Frederick, William R., 17 Sept. 1853, Rebecca Armstrong   9/19/53-2
Fredericks, Levy, 20 Apr. 1852, Henrietta Rosenberg, dau. of
    Moses   4/24/52-2
Free, Adam, 10 Mar. 1857, Emily Kirby   3/12/57-2
Free, E. W. (Dr.), 25 Dec. 1855, Virginia A. Michael, dau. of
    John   1/ 5/56-2
Free, John L. (Dr.), 1 Jan. 1852, Martha Jane Jordan   1/26/52-2
Free, Peter, Jr., 9 Jan. 1851, Margaret A. Hooey   1/13/51-2
Freeburger, Andrew J., 22 May 1853, Martha Ann Earles   5/24/53-2
Freeburger, Andrew J., 22 Feb. 1855, Mary Ann Wirts   2/24/55-2
Freeburger, Francis M., 21 Apr. 1851, Julianna M. Spriggs   4/28/51-2
Freeburger, Geo. A., 29 June 1852, Teresa Brown   7/ 7/52-2

Freeburger, Peter; no date given, Sarah Ann Deames   7/20/58-2
Freeland, George T., 6 Dec. 1860, Wilhelmina Lyles   12/11/60-2
Freeland, John Henry, 18 July 1855, Mary Hall   7/24/55-2
Freeland, Robert, 18 June 1856, Maria W. Franklin   6/19/56-2
Freeman, James, 24 Dec. 1857, Mary E. Lee   12/25/57-2
Freeman, John, 28 Nov. 1855, Sarah E. Hammond   12/ 4/55-2
Freeman, Levin, 23 Jan. 1851, Sarah Jane Hamilton   1/25/51-2
Freeman, W. H., Jr., 13 Jan. 1857, Mary Ellen Smith, dau. of
    Abraham   1/21/57-2
Freeman, William, 7 Feb. 1853, Mary Ann Freeman   2/ 8/53-2
Freeman, William, 5 Sept. 1854, Frances E. Simmons   9/ 7/54-2
Freeston, Hezekiah, 6 May 1856, Ann Eliza Channell, dau. of
    Abel and Jane   6/ 7/56-2
Frence, Wm. H., 1-(?) Mar. 1852, Elizabeth A. Faulkner   3/17/52-2
French, Andrew Jackson, 9 Nov. 1854, Elizabeth Lee   11/16/54-2
French, Charles D., 5 July 1859, Matilda Jackel; 7/ 8/59-2   7/11/59-2
French, Charles S., 22 May 1856, Clementina Albertson, dau. of
    John   5/27/56-2
French, Cornelius, 21 Aug. 1859, Alice Ohler   9/23/59-2
French, Edward, 30 Mar. 1856, Bridget Callan   4/ 4/56-2
French, George W., 18 Aug. 1853, Mary A. Green   8/20/53-2
French, John Henry, 4 Jan. 1853, Mary Ann Hamilton   1/ 5/53-2
French, Martin V. B., 2 Mar. 1857, Mary C. Todd   3/ 9/58-2
French, Richard, 5 Mar. 1854, Marietta Stanley   3/ 7/54-2
French, William, 15 Nov. 1854, Rebecca Liddell   11/14/54-2
Fretwell, George M., 21 Mar. 1853, Margaret J. Lilley   3/23/53-2
Frey, Jacob, 12 Oct. 1858, Eliza J. Armstrong   10/18/58-2
Frey, Jas. L., 23 Dec. 1856, Charletta S. Bruce   12/27/56-2
Frey, John J., 20 Aug. 1854, Maria Broughton   8/23/54-2
Frick, Charles (Dr.), 12 Oct. 1853, Achsah C. Sargent   10/15/53-2
Frick, E. Arnold, 24 Nov. 1859, Cecelia J. Shower, dau. of
    Geo.   12/ 3/59-2
Friedenthal, Isaac, 10 Mar. 1856, Sarah Lobenstein   3/29/56-2
Friedenwald, Jos., 14 Feb. 1852, Rosina Roswald, dau. of
    Juca   2/19/52-2
Friedrich, J. Louis, 14 Dec. 1854, Minna Schadetebeck   12/16/54-2
Friel, James B., 5 Oct. 1856, Ellen L. Lennan, dau. of B.   10/ 7/56-2
Friend, Alfred, 6 Mar. 1860, Ella D. Quincy   3/ 8/60-2
Fries, John, 6 July 1852, Eva Roman   7/15/52-2
Fries, John H., 16 Aug. 1852, (Mrs.) Johanna Meusel   8/23/52-2
Friese, James F., 15 Apr. 1856, Elizabeth Jane Bradford   4/16/56-2
Friese, John, 17 Apr. 1856, Mary M. Prinz   4/19/56-2
Friese, Philip C., 7 Aug. 1851, Harriet C. Yater   8/ 9/51-2
Frieze, J. Thompson (Col.), 11 Nov. 1858, Lizzie Green   11/13/58-2
Frink, Joseph, Jr., 14 Nov. 1853, Rose Mary Hand   11/15/53-2
Frior, Uriah S., 12 Oct. 1854, Leonora C. Grim   10/14/54-2
Frisbey, Andrew, 15 Nov. 1860, Emily Jane Marsh   11/20/60-2
Frisby, Andrew, 23 Dec. 1855, Mary E. Abell   12/31/55-2
Frisby, Samuel, 22 Mar. 1855, Julian Talbort   4/ 4/55-2
Fritz, Marcellus S. Ilgen, 6 Oct. 1857, Lizzie J. Chamberlain   10/ 9/57-2
Fritz, William, 28 Apr. 1851, Caroline Clark   5/13/51-2
Fritz, William J., 4 Sept. 1853, Dorathy Whittington   9/ 6/53-2
Frizill, Richard T., 16 Mar. 1859, Sarah E. Sheppard, dau. of
    James   3/18/59-2
Frizzell, D. W., 7 Apr. 1857, Harriet B. Stull   5/ 8/57-2
Frost, George W., 24 Feb. 1852, Anna E. Frost   9/25/52-2
Frost, James A., 11 Feb. 1851, Caroline B. Moore   2/14/51-2
Frost, John, 12 July 1855, Mary E. Kirby   7/16/55-2
Frost, John W., 26 May 1859, Julia M. Richards, dau. of (Rev.)
    Amon   5/30/59-2
Frost, Nathan S., 24 Feb. 1853, Sophia B. Williar, dau. of
    Andrew   2/25/53-2
Frost, William E., 12 Jan. 1853, Henrietta Bailey, dau. of
    Chas.   1/18/53-2
Fry, Geo., 17 May 1857, (Mrs.) Isabella McDade   5/19/57-2

Fry, S. Gross, son of (Hon.) J., Jr., 25 May 1858,
    Josephine Cassaday, dau. of Wm. H.   5/27/58-2
Fry, Thomas W. G., 3 July 1858, Fanny E. Brooks, dau. of
    Samuel R.   7/13/58-2
Fry, Wm. W., 13 Aug. 1856, Mary M. Hook   9/26/56-2
Fryer, James, 7 Oct. 1857, Sue H. Dutton, dau. of (Gen.) Robt.   10/12/57-2
Fryeugle, Henry, 25 June 1858, Mary Jane Owings   6/29/58-2
Fryfogle, David, 27 Feb. 1851, Ann Eliza Porter   2/28/51-2
Fryfogle, Thomas, 25 Dec. 1850, Elizabeth Ann Hook   1/14/51-2
Fugitt, Benjamin, 31 July 1855, Hattie A. Clark   8/ 2/55-2
Fugitt, J. Preston, 15 Sept. 1859, Mary H. Williams, dau. of
    (Capt.) John Ruffin   9/22/59-2
Fuller, Charles, 10 Sept. 1856, Indiana Owings, dau. of Levi   11/15/56-2
Fuller, Charles F., 19 Nov. 1857, Lizzie W. Newman   11/21/57-2
Fuller, Edmond B., 12 Jan. 1854, Sarah L. Watts   1/14/54-2
Fuller, Edwin T., 11 Sept. 1860, Maggie A. Davis   9/25/60-2
Fuller, Joseph H., 6 Jan. 1856, Mary Jane Clark, dau. of
    Benj. C.   1/ 9/56-2
Fuller, Wilson N., 2 Aug. 1855, Sudie M. McDermott, dau. of
    John   8/ 3/55-2
Fulmer, Thos., 1 Mar. 1853, Susannah Miller   3/10/53-2
Fulton, David, 24 Feb. 1853, Mary E. Mercer   2/25/53-2
Fulton, Thos. H., 28 Sept. 1854, Emma F. Hough, dau. of (Col.)
    John   9/30/54-2
Funk, John W., 17 June 1858, Eliza A. McMechen   7/ 1/58-2
Furney, Jackson, 20 Oct. 1852, Elizabeth Ryland   10/22/52-2
Furniss, Thomas J., 25 Apr. 1855, Anne Fletcher, dau. of
    Edward   4/27/55-2
Furgerson, Wm. H., 15 May 1860, (Mrs.) Mary A. Riley   5/26/60-2
Furze, James, 5 June 1856, Regina Gates, dau. of (Capt.)
    Lemuel   6/ 9/56-2
Fusselbaugh, John S., 15 Sept. 1853, Amanda M. Riley, dau. of
    David   9/19/53-2
Fusselbaugh, Wm. H. B., 1 Oct. 1856, Sarah R. Hall, dau. of
    Robt.   10/ 3/56-2
Fussell, Joseph B., 31 Oct. 1855, Lydia M. Gorden   11/19/55-2
Gacht, Edward, 19 Sept. 1852, Marina Young   9/21/52-2
Gaddess, Thomas A., 27 Dec. 1853, Sydney Hepburn, dau. of
    Peter   1/ 3/54-2
Gaddis, Lemuel, 19 May 1859, M. Leonora Speiser, dau. of
    Frederick   5/21/59-2
Gaehle, Henry F., 29 June 1858, Alma Graeser   7/ 1/58-2
Gafford, Samuel D., 30 Sept. 1851, Jane Matterson   10/ 9/51-2
Gafney, James, 26 Aug. 1860, Sidney Lee   8/31/60-2
Gager, Edwin V. (Capt.), 11 May 1857, Rose Morley   5/13/57-2
Gail, G. W., 12 Sept. 1854, Maria S. Felgney, dau. of G. W.   9/13/54-2
Gain, Philip H., 2 Feb. 1854, Mary C. Staddings   2/ 4/54-2
Gain, Thomas, 26 July 1855, Frances Davis   8/11/55-2
Gaines, Benjamin, 24 June 1852, Catharine Owney   6/28/52-2
Gaines, Causman H.; no date given, Mary R. Jackson   11/ 3/60-2
Gaines, Henry, 14 Nov. 1854, Margaretta Baum   11/21/54-2
Gaines, Robt. O., 8 Mar. 1855, (Mrs.) Mary J. Ford   3/ 9/55-2
Gaither, Geo. R., Jr., 7 Aug. 1851, Rebecca Hanson, dau. of
    C. S. W. Dorsey   8/15/51-2
Gaither, George, 16 Dec. 1857, Kate Poole, niece of Jesse Sling-
    luff   12/18/57-2
Gaither, Richard, 21 May 1857, Anna Miller   5/23/57-2
Gaither, Samuel C., 2 June 1859, Mary H. Brown   6/ 3/59-2
Gaither, Thos. G., 10 Mar. 1853, Mary E. Rider   3/11/53-2
Gaither, William H., 25 Sept. 1860, Susan F. Warfield   9/26/60-2
Galaway, James, 24 Apr. 1856, Harret Elizabeth Hall   4/26/56-2
Galaway, William A., 29 May 1856, Jemima Porter   5/31/56-2
Gale, George, 7 Jan. 1856, Susan Matilda Mathiot, dau. of Aug.   1/ 8/56-2
Gale, George, 18 Aug. 1856, Hester Ann Jones   8/20/56-2

Gale, Henry C., 24 Aug. 1852, Laura Anne E. Dixon, dau. of
    James B.   8/28/52-2
Gale, James, 4 Nov. 1852, Harriet A. Miller   11/ 6/52-2
Gales, Joseph H., 12 July 1855, Laura V. Frush   7/14/55-2
Gale, Levin, 14 Oct. 1856, Sallie W. Dorsey, dau. of John W.   10/22/56-2
Gale, Littelton, 10 Oct. 1855, (Mrs.) Charlotte Ann Brown   10/11/55-2
Gale, Samuel C., 24 July 1856, Elizabeth Jenkins Morton, dau.
    of J. H. B.   7/25/56-2
Gale, Wm. H., 2-(?) Sept. 1858, Anna L. Walker   9/30/58-2
Galer, George, 13 Mar. 1856, Rosa Ann Ambrose   3/18/56-2
Gallagher, Alexander, 10 Nov. 1857, Isabel Foreman   11/12/57-2
Gallagher, Francis T., 19 May 1859, Mary Clarke McElroy   5/23/59-2
Gallagher, James, 2 Oct. 1853, H. McNail   10/ 6/53-2
Gallagher, James, 20 Sept. 1855, Rose Carbury   9/25/55-2
Gallagher, John, 21 Sept. 1855, Rosy A. Lawn   9/25/55-2
Gallagher, Michael, 18 Nov. 1851, Catherine Lafever Meloney   11/21/51-2
Gallagher, Michael, 12 Sept. 1858, Margaret O'Neill   9/14/58-2
Gallagher, Patrick, 24 May 1855, Elizabeth Bians   5/29/55-2
Gallagher, Patrick, 15 Nov. 1857, Margaret Cunningham   11/17/57-2
Gallaher, B. Frank, 13 May 1857, Eliza A. Buckner, dau. of
    Richard Bernard   5/14/57-2
Gallaher, Edward, 20 Oct. 1852, (Mrs.) Margaret Leahey   11/ 6/52-2
Gallant, Peter, 2 Aug. 1860, Mary E. Murray   8/ 4/60-2
Gallaway, Goldsmith D., 8 Jan. 1854, Mary E. Green   1/12/54-2
Gallaway, James H., 25 July 1860, Mary A. Lloyd   7/28/60-2
Gallaway, Jesse F., 3 Sept. 1857, Sarah Ann E. Ledley   9/ 7/57-2
Gallaway, Thos., 14 Aug. 1856, Elizabeth C. Welch   8/16/56-2
Gallet, John, 9 Dec. 1857, Margaret Ganley   12/11/57-2
Galligher, John, 5 May 1856, Jane Connahan   5/ 7/56-2
Galligher, Phil., 10 Apr. 1855, Imogen M. Baugher, dau. of
    Joseph   4/12/55-2
Galling, James, 7 Oct. 1858, Mary A. Riely   11/12/58-2
Gallion, Garrett G., 5 May 1857, Susan O. Stockham   5/ 7/57-2
Galloway, John, 11 June 1853, Margaret Bucey, dau. of Joseph   6/15/53-2
Galloway, Moses G., 11 Dec. 1851, Isabella Hulse   12/13/51-2
Galloway, Thomas, 15 Dec. 1853, Martha Reder   12/19/53-2
Galloway, Thomas, 15 Dec. 1853, Martha Rider; corrected copy   12/20/53-2
Galvin, Joseph T., 5 Apr. 1860, Harriet A. Holland   4/ 7/60-2
Gambel, Geo. S., 13 Dec. 1860, Margaret A. Baker   12/18/60-2
Gambel, Thomas Buchanan, 15 July 1855, Julia Adler   7/18/55-2
Gambril, Joseph J., 27 Nov. 1856, Mary J. Young   11/29/56-2
Gambrill, George E., 24 Dec. 1854, Georgietta W. Brown   12/27/54-2
Gambrill, Henry W., 21 June 1855, Mary C. Mecaslen   6/27/55-2
Gambrill, James H., 26 July 1860, Antionette Staley   7/27/60-2
Gambrill, James P., 24 Dec. 1852, Mary A. Hill   12/29/52-2
Gammie, Geo. L., 26 Feb. 1851, Rebecca A. McGreevy   2/28/51-2
Gandy, John, 26 Oct. 1859, (Mrs.) Ann Jenett Bailey   10/31/59-2
Gant, Otho T., 13 Nov. 1855, Margaret A. Moore   11/14/55-2
Ganthrop, Wm. H., 22 June 1851, Arianna Hissey   6/30/51-2
Gantt, Benj. E., 26 Jan. 1854, Maria E. Baldwin, dau. of Wm. H.
    and Jane M.   1/31/54-2
Gantt, James, 6 Dec. 1860, Adeline Johnson   12/ 8/60-2
Gantt, James M., 21 May 1856, (Mrs.) Margaret B. Creekmore   5/26/56-2
Gardiner, Isaac, 11 Feb. 1851, Julia Miller, dau. of Enoch   2/13/51-2
Gardiner, John T., 31 Aug. 1854, Elizabeth C. Dietz   9/ 9/54-2
Gardner, Benjamin H., 14 May 1856, Sarah C. Martin, dau. of
    John B.   6/ 3/56-2
Gardner, Eli H., 24 Oct. 1854, Caroline M. Thomas   10/28/54-2
Gardner, Isaac, 1 Jan. 1852, Mary Smith   1/ 3/52-2
Gardner, James, 12 Nov. 1852, Nancy Taylor, dau. of Yardly   11/16/52-2
Gardner, James F., 8 Aug. 1860, Emma J. Wells   8/11/60-2
Gardner, John M., 15 Nov. 1855, Mary Emma Tennant, dau. of
    Thomas   11/17/55-2
Gardner, Joseph L., 25 Nov. 1860, Sarah J. Johnson   11/27/60-2
Gardner, Thos. H., 3 May 1855, Marcella C. Tongue   5/ 8/55-2

Gardner, William, 23 July 1856, Amma Omphries	7/25/56-2
Gardnes, Geo., Jr., 28 Apr. 1857, Annie E. Knox	5/12/57-2
Garey, Basil, 27 June 1859, Sarah A. Wilkinson	7/ 2/59-2
Garey, Thomas H., 22 July 1856, Margera J. Boswell	7/24/56-2
Garhard, Valintine, 2 July 1852, Manday Hickman	7/ 9/52-2
Garing, William H., 22 June 1851, Anna Kimble	6/27/51-2
Garland, James G., 4 Dec. 1854, Elizabeth Howland	12/18/54-2
Garner, Robert, 24 Dec. 1858, Wye Lyles	12/28/58-2
Garrell, Jas. C., 29 Jan. 1857, Elizabeth M. Fitzgerald	1/31/57-2
Garrett, James, 26 Nov. 1860, Bany Corns	11/28/60-2
Garrett, James H., 1 Nov. 1860, Catharine Davis	11/ 5/60-2
Garrett, John H., 12 Sept. 1853, Ann E. Bean	9/17/53-2
Garrett, Levi, 29 May 1851, Rachel Ann Thornton	6/ 4/51-2
Garrett, Unit A. C., 8 Mar. 1855, Mary E. Apsley	3/24/55-2
Garrett, William, 15 Nov. 1852, (Mrs.) Julia Ann McClenald	11/24/52-2
Garrettson, Geo. W., 17 Feb. 1858, Maggie Webbert, dau. of George	2/19/58-2
Garrettson, Richard F., 5 June 1860, Rebecca Jane Mackenzie, dau. of (Dr.) Colin	6/ 6/60-2
Garrish, William, 4 Oct. 1857, Margaretta Lamy, dau. of John	10/ 6/57-2
Garrison, Jesse, 15 Nov. 1859, Laura Galway	11/30/59-2
Garrison, Vincent, 11 Mar. 1858, Sarah A. Miller, dau. of Joseph	3/13/58-2
Garrison, William Henry, 15 Dec. 1852, Anne Rebecca Holroyd	12/18/52-2
Garthe, August, 13 Jan. 1859, Christine M. Pielert	1/18/59-2
Garto, Domingo, 28 Oct. 1855, Rachael Gotena	10/29/55-2
Garvy, Patrick Henry, 21 Oct. 1858, Jane Mundy	10/27/58-2
Gary, James A., 27 Nov. 1856, Lovinia W. Corrie	11/29/56-2
Gassaway, Edwin, 13 Sept. 1860, Alice S. Taylor	9/14/60-2
Gassaway, Nicholas, 11 Oct. 1855, Maria Ravey	10/16/55-2
Gatch, Joseph A. R., 5 Oct. 1854, Maria Louisa S. Hopkins	10/ 7/54-2
Gately, Michael A., 12 May 1856, Mary Jane Cavanaugh	5/13/56-2
Gates, Francis, 20 July 1857, Mary A. Hartzell; 9/25/57-2	9/26/57-2
Gates, George H. C., 23 Oct. 1851, Margaret E. H. Wall, dau. of Daniel	10/25/51-2
Gates, Lemuel, 9 Mar. 1854, Rebecca Morgan; corrected copy	3/14/54-2
Gates, Samuel, 9 Mar. 1854, Rebecca Morgan	3/13/54-2
Gates, Sylvester F., 12 Mar. 1851, Mary Jane Holroyd	3/14/51-2
Gathell, Joseph, 1 May 1855, Catharine Claig	5/ 9/55-2
Gauline, Jas. R., 22 Apr. 1852, Amanda M. Mace	6/21/52-2
Gauline, Joseph C., 21 Apr. 1854, (Mrs.) Ann E. Chandler	4/29/54-2
Gault, Albert, 6 Mar. 1860, Sarah E. Harrison	4/18/60-2
Gaunt, Richard, 18 Dec. 1856, Angelina Clarke	12/18/56-2
Gavet, James, 16 Feb. 1860, Lizzie Smith, dau. of (Dr.) Gideon B.	2/17/60-2
Gavin, Matthew, 25 Apr. 1852, Anna McLoughlin	4/30/52-2
Gaw, Alex'r. F., 28 Oct. 1851, Susan H. Wright	11/12/51-2
Gawthrop, William H., 22 June 1851, Arianna Hissey; corrected copy	7/ 1/51-2
Gayle, Benjamin R., (Capt.), 29 July 1854, Charlotte Lipton	8/ 3/54-2
Gayle, Robt. E., 28 June 1855, Sarah R. Neill, dau. of George S.	6/30/55-2
Gayley, Samuel A., 26 Feb. 1852, Agnes Malcom	3/ 1/52-2
Gaynor, John, 29 Jan. 1856, Ellen McDonald, dau. of (Capt.) Michael	2/ 1/56-2
Gazaway, Thomas, 28 July 1853, Mary A. Augusta Key	7/30/53-2
Geagan, Michael, 24 Aug. 1857, Julia A. Reilly, dau. of Jos.	9/ 5/57-2
Geal, George McK., 11 Nov. 1851, Mary A. Clark	4/12/52-2
Gear, H. H. (Capt.), 10 Oct. 1851, Francenia Trego; corrected copy	11/10/51-2
Gear, H. H. (Capt.), 10 Oct. 1851, Franconia Trego	11/ 8/51-2
Gearhart, Miles, 7 Mar. 1859, Elizabeth Albert	3/12/59-2
Gebb, Henry, 12 Aug. 1851, Mary B. Read	10/ 2/51-2
Geddess, T. Stockton, 13 May 1853, Bettie C. Revely	5/13/53-2
Gee, Henry Simon, 15 Feb. 1859, Kate Doublebaggs	4/28/59-2

```
Geer, Emanuel, 29 Apr. 1856, Mary Owens                          5/ 7/56-2
Gees, B. Franklin, 21 Oct. 1851, Mary Chase                      10/23/51-2
Gehring, J. George, 15 Oct. 1857, Mary C. Sickel                 10/17/57-2
Geiger, Charles, 17 Sept. 1856, Clara Barcher                    9/18/56-2
Geiger, Conrad, 27 Nov. 1860, Emily Jane Phillips                12/ 1/60-2
Geiger, Frederick E., 31 Dec. 1851, Jane Meager, dau. of Jno.    1/ 1/52-2
Geiger, Theodore S., 24 Nov. 1859, J. Virginia Beltz, dau.
   of (Dr.) Henry E.                                             12/13/59-2
Geiger, William, 26 Aug. 1860, Catherine M. T. Mitchell          8/27/60-2
Geis, Sebastian, 17 Aug. 1852, Matilda Bradford                  8/25/52-2
Geist, John W., 16 June 1856, Maria M. Kirby                     6/23/56-2
Gemeny, John, 9 Aug. 1858, Amelia Summers Ballenger              8/26/58-2
Gemmil, John B., 21 Nov. 1860, Agnes M. Workman                  11/23/60-2
Gemmill, Joseph B., 21 Apr. 1857, Lucinda B. West                4/25/57-2
Gemundt, Charles, 26 Apr. 1855, Maria Louisa Stauffer            4/30/55-2
George, Alfred, 4 Nov. 1852, Ellen M. Shriver                    11/ 6/52-2
George, Charles W., 2 May 1854, Mary A. Pennington, dau. of
   Thomas                                                        5/ 3/54-2
George, James B., Jr., 29 Aug. 1853, Eliza J. Papp               8/31/53-2
George, Jas. S., 31 Aug. 1859, Charlotte J. Skinner, dau. of
   Philamon                                                      9/ 2/59-2
George, John B., 20 Dec. 1852, Clara S. Chnculum                 12/24/52-2
George, Parker, 2 June 1853, Ellen Reese, dau. of Daniel M.      6/ 7/53-2
George, William H. W., 15 May 1853, Nancy Parks                  5/17/53-2
Gerber, O. P., 10 June 1858, Louisa D. Waidner, dau. of J. M.    6/12/58-2
Gerke, Carl, 23 June 1859, Elizabeth B. Lisle                    7/ 4/59-2
German, Howell P., 20 May 1852, Nancy Hickman                    5/22/52-2
German, Joseph S., 6 Nov. 1851, Lucretia L. D. Norwood           11/11/51-2
German, Joshua E., 15 Nov. 1855, Julia A. Fowler                 12/ 7/55-2
German, Thomas Rozell, 27 Nov. 1851, Josephine Scott             11/29/51-2
Gernand, Edwin K., 18 Apr. 1860, Frances H. Parke                4/20/60-2
Gerry, N. R. (Dr.), 8 Sept. 1858, Margaret E. Fusting            9/10/58-2
Gessford, Charles, 5 Oct. 1852, Elizabeth Evans, dau. of Wm.     10/12/52-2
Gessford, G. W., 18 Nov. 1857, Mary Parr                         3/22/58-2
Gessford, James W., 26 Mar. 1854, Margaret M. Keer               5/ 2/54-2
Gest, John W., 17 Dec. 1856, Ann Downs                           12/19/56-2
Gettier, Augustus J., 5 June 1851, Ellizabeth Fincher            6/ 7/51-2
Gettier, Charles A., 12 Apr. 1854, Fannie Steever                4/14/54-2
Gettier, Cornelius E., 18 May 1852, Sarah Eliza Harrison         5/20/52-2
Gettier, Edmund P., 21 Apr. 1858, Sallie R. Robinson             6/14/58-2
Gettier, Edward, 14 July 1859, Kate Shipley                      7/16/59-2
Gettier, George W., 28 Apr. 1853, Ann Maria Shultz, dau. of
   Henry                                                         4/30/53-2
Gettier, John, 21 Apr. 1853, Angelina Maxfield, dau. of Levi     4/23/53-2
Gettier, John, 8 July 1860, Elizabeth A. Kreager                 8/22/60-2
Gettier, John T., 25 Dec. 1853, Sarah A. Briggs                  12/28/53-2
Gettier, Wm. P., 24 Mar. 1859, Jemima V. Cross                   4/25/59-2
Getty, David A., 1 Nov. 1853, Catharine Fields, dau. of James    11/11/53-2
Getz, Chas. B., 20 Feb. 1860, Rosa Steigerwald, dau. of Meyer    2/22/60-2
Getz, W. Louis, 10 May 1857, George Ann Endley                   5/12/57-2
Gevan, Thomas, 26 May 1851, Maria Kennedy                        5/30/51-2
Ghent, Thomas D., 29 Apr. 1855, Mary Louisa Turner               5/12/55-2
Ghequiere, Louis J., 28 July 1853, Sarah Long, dau. of Robert
   Carey                                                         8/ 1/53-2
Gibb, William W. (Capt.), 17 Dec. 1851, Sarah E. Solomon, dau.
   of Wm.                                                        12/20/51-2
Gibbon, John, 16 Oct. 1855, Fannie N. Mo-(?)-te, dau. of
   (Col.) Samuel                                                 10/20/55-2
Gibbons, Alexander S. (Rev.), 30 Mar. 1852, Sarah E. Cloud,
   dau. of Mordecai                                              4/ 5/52-2
Gibbons, John, 3 Jan. 1852, Catharine Ward                       1/12/52-2
Gibbons, Wm. J., 27 Aug. 1857, Elizabeth A. Whayland             9/ 8/57-2
Gibbs, John G., 12 Oct. 1856, Eliza A. Dryden                    11/ 4/56-2
Gibbs, N. Heyward (Dr.), 15 June 1858, Henrietta E. Croxall,
   dau. of Richard                                               6/24/58-2
```

Gibbs, Robert, 7 Dec. 1854, Lucy Ann Smith	12/11/54-2
Gibney, George J., 4 Mar. 1851, Mary A. Bunting, dau. of	
Wm. J.	3/ 6/51-2
Gibney, Thos. S., 27 July 1854, Ann Maria King, dau. of John	8/ 3/54-2
Gibson, Andrew, 26 June 1853, Susanna F. Atchison	6/28/53-2
Gibson, Charles T., 15 May 1855, Mary A. Botterill	5/16/55-2
Gibson, David, 11 June 1857, Sarah Ann Neely	6/22/57-2
Gibson, John, 29 June 1852, Mary J. Walton	7/ 1/52-2
Gibson, John, 15 Mar. 1856, Elizabeth Kennedy	3/17/56-2
Gibson, Joseph, 14 Aug. 1854, Sarah D. Price	8/16/54-2
Gibson, Joseph, Jr., 25 Oct. 1859, Margaret A. Fusselbaugh	10/27/59-2
Gibson, Nathaniel, 12 June 1860, Matilda Matthews	6/22/60-2
Gibson, Robert, 23 Mar. 1852, Nancy Cochrane, dau. of David	3/29/52-2
Gibson, Robt. F., 13 Sept. 1855, Annie E. Welch, dau. of J. B.	9/15/55-2
Gibson, Thomas T.; no date given, Mary Ann Kerr	11/ 1/59-2
Gibson, William, 18 Sept. 1855, Rosabel Allen, dau. of Henry	9/20/55-2
Gibson, Wm. H., 27 Oct. 1859, E. Augusta Carlile, dau. of	
(Capt.) W. W.	10/31/59-2
Giddens, Edw'd., 7 Oct. 1852, (Mrs.) Elizabeth Vickers	10/14/52-2
Giddings, Marshall, 7 Feb. 1856, Louisa A. Powell	4/ 4/56-2
Gies, James W., 5 June 1853, Mary Ann Bush	6/ 9/53-2
Giese, Albert L., 4 Nov. 1857, Kate L. Knapp	11/18/57-2
Giese, J. Henry, 2 Sept. 1852, Kate Guiger, dau. of (Maj.) J.	
H. Huling	9/ 7/52-2
Gilbert, George E., 13 Nov. 1856, Gracy Ann E. Smith, dau. of	
Sarah Young	11/15/56-2
Gilbert, Jacob, 5 Feb. 1856, Sarah A. Merryman	2/16/56-2
Gilbert, Nicholas B., 20 Mar. 1854, Kate Wills	4/ 4/54-2
Gilbert, William H., 2 Jan. 1855, Ruth A. Cromwell	1/ 4/55-2
Gildea, John H., 6 May 1852, Rachel Hunter	5/10/52-2
Gilder, Wm. H., 21 Sept. 1856, Mary G. Howard, dau. of Wm.	
Govane; 10/23/56-2	10/24/56-2
Gilds, Urias H., 9 June 1853, Barbara Ann Thomas	6/15/53-2
Giles, Aquila P., 25 Sept. 1856, Lucretia Poole	9/29/56-2
Giles, H. M., 15 May 1856, Lizzie Mason, dau. of Richard	5/16/56-2
Giles, John W., 1 Feb. 1859, Harriet A. Griffith, dau. of	
Allan	2/ 7/59-2
Giles, Joseph, 16 July 1854, (Mrs.) Mary Ann Shriver	7/19/54-2
Giles, Joseph E., 26 Apr. 1860, Louisa Ann Griffith	5/ 4/60-2
Gill, Asher B., 15 May 1856, Margaret Fisher Thompson	5/30/56-2
Gill, Bryson, Sr., 14 Aug. 1860, (Mrs.) Mary E. Hunichenn	8/20/60-2
Gill, Bryson Jerome, 15 Aug. 1860, Jane Miller Perry	8/20/60-2
Gill, Chas. M., 5 Nov. 1860, Kate M. Hunichenn	11/ 7/60-2
Gill, Elisha H., 26 Sept. 1852, Malinda Jane Cannon	10/ 6/52-2
Gill, John C., 15 Nov. 1859, Rebecca Jones	12/ 6/59-2
Gill, John G., 26 Nov. 1851, Amanda Baily, dau. of Thos.	12/ 9/51-2
Gill, Lewis R., 24 May 1855, Mary A. McMahon	5/29/55-2
Gill, Samuel H., 12 Oct. 1858, Helen M. Leffler, dau. of	
George R. H.	1/14/58-2
Gill, Stephen, 5 Oct. 1852, Margaret Robinson	10/11/52-2
Gill, Thomas E., 21 Nov. 1860, Etherlinda R. Evans, dau. of	
(Col.) John	11/26/60-2
Gill, William F., 4 July 1852, Maria Louisa Popp	8/ 2/52-2
Gill, William S., 7 Oct. 1856, Estell Madora Spurry	10/ 9/56-2
Gillan, Patrick, 11 Apr. 1858, Ellen Ryan	4/15/58-2
Gillen, Robert, 10 Apr. 1855, Emma Moffitt	4/12/55-2
Gillespie, Jonathan, 13 May 1855, Ann McCauley	5/19/55-2
Gillespie, William, 7 Oct. 1852, Annie Maria Warfield, dau. of	
(Dr.) B. Hanson	10/ 8/52-2
Gillespie, Wm., 3 Mar. 1853, Elizabeth Ann Hughes	3/ 4/53-2
Gillett, George M., 23 Dec. 1857, Antionette J. Jacobsen	12/29/57-2
Gillispie, Charles A., 26 May 1857, Virginia De Roncerny, dau.	
of Charles	6/ 2/57-2
Gillot, John G., 20 Apr. 1854, Elizabeth Jane Jones, dau. of	
Bennett	4/27/54-2

Gilman, J. S.; no date given, Ellen A. Abbott, dau. of H.   10/ 5/54-2
Gilman, John S., 4 Oct. 1860, Eliza Weyl   10/ 5/60-2
Gilman, William P., 9 Mar. 1855, Mary Maguire   9/ 6/55-2
Gilmer, Bernard, 1 Dec. 1859, Elizabeth A. Riley   12/ 9/59-2
Gilmore, James, 31 Aug. 1852, (Mrs.) Nancy C. Dorry, dau. of
    John Campbell   9/ 3/52-2
Gilpin, Edward C., 23 Feb. 1854, Annie Feast   3/ 1/54-2
Gilpin, John W., 28 Oct. 1853, Mary Jane Gilpin   10/31/53-2
Gilpin, Joseph B., 16 Oct. 1852, Mary A. Cleaves   10/29/52-2
Gilson, Wm. J., 25 Dec. 1855, Harriet E. Crapster   12/29/55-2
Ginn, Edward Y., 12 Mar. 1857, Lucy Ginn   3/16/57-2
Ginn, Samuel B., 8 Mar. 1860, Laura V. Adkisson   3/13/60-2
Ginnamon, George W., 2 Jan. 1859, Sarah E. Stiner   1/11/59-2
Ginter, Francis, 25 Dec. 1853, Sarah Jane Stigers   12/28/53-2
Girvin, Samuel S., 5 Oct. 1857, Zuleika Smith, dau. of (Capt.)
    John W.   10/13/57-2
Gist, George, 21 Feb. 1854, Sarah L. Crofford   2/24/54-2
Gist, Mordecai W., 23 Sept. 1852, Barbara Storm, dau. of
    George   9/27/52-2
Gist, William, 28 Aug. 1856, Lizzie A. Dukehart, dau. of
    R. W.   8/29/56-2
Gittings, David S., Jr., 16 June 1859, Varina S. Brandon, dau.
    of Girard C.   6/21/59-2
Gittings, Isaiah, 31 Mar. 1853, Lucretia Ann Lee, dau. of
    Philip, Jr.   4/ 2/53-2
Gittings, John S., 29 Nov. 1853, Charlotte Carter Ritchie,
    dau. of Thomas   12/ 3/53-2
Gittings, Richard J., 5 June 1855, Victoria Sellman, dau. of
    (Col.) Alfred   6/ 7/55-2
Giurovich, Jacob, 19 Dec. 1859, (Mrs.) Julia Willey   12/21/59-2
Given, John C., 5 Feb. 1859, Ellen W. Thompson   2/ 7/59-2
Gladfelter, Reuben, 21 Nov. 1852, Elizabeth J. Roles   11/23/52-2
Glading, Thos., 16 Feb. 1852, Frances A. Commerell   2/25/52-2
Gladson, Charles A., 16 July 1855, Mary A. C. Douglass   12/27/55-2
Glaen, Anthony J., 7 Sept. 1858, Elizabeth Kloke   9/24/58-2
Glandin, Alexander B., 3 Dec. 1857, Maria Mosher   12/ 7/57-2
Glanville, Thomas, 9 Sept. 1852, Mary Ann Fairbank   9/11/52-2
Glascow, John S., 12 Apr. 1860, Margaret A. Smith   4/16/60-2
Glass, Isaac, 17 Nov. 1858, Mary Ann Brown   11/22/58-2
Glass, James A., 29 July 1852, Sarah V. Gault, dau. of (Capt.)
    Henry   7/31/52-2
Glass, Rob't. J., 21 Dec. 1852, Sophia F. Bowers, dau. of
    Martin, Jr.   12/25/52-2
Glass, Thomas, 5 Nov. 1853, Averella Wilson, dau. of
    Saml. A.   11/ 8/53-2
Gleeson, John; no date given, Isabel M. Longley, dau. of
    Samuel   5/ 5/58-2
Glen, Alexander, 17 Nov. 1854, Isabella McNeely   11/21/54-2
Glen, Wm. M., 29 Jan. 1858, Sarah L. Ashton   3/ 3/58-2
Glenn, Benjamin, 17 Jan. 1856, Catharine Waggner, dau. of
    George J.; corrected copy   1/29/56-2
Glenn, Benjamin, 17 Jan. 1856, Kitty Waggner, dau. of
    George J.   1/28/56-2
Glenn, Sam'l. B., 22 Feb. 1859, Rachel J. Givvines   2/25/59-2
Glenn, Samuel M., 18 Sept. 1854, Rebecca Caroline Kirtz   9/20/54-2
Glenn, Wm. W., 29 Oct. 1857, Ellen M. Smith   11/ 5/57-2
Glisan, Samuel, 24 Feb. 1852, Margaret Ann Harding   2/27/52-2
Gloninger, John R., 21 June 1859, Mary Ledley, dau. of James   6/23/59-2
Glover, John, 1 Mar. 1859, Marian L. Thursby   3/ 4/59-2
Glover, John, 1 Mar. 1859, Marian L. Thursby, dau. of William
    T.; corrected copy   3/ 8/59-2
Gminder, Jacob, 15 Dec. 1859, Eliza Bruebach   12/29/59-2
Godfrey, Edward A., 18 Mar. 1851, Isabella J. Kennedy, dau. of
    John H.   3/22/51-2
Godfrey, George, 27 Mar. 1859, Martha E. Conley; 4/ 7/59-2   4/ 8/59-2

Godman, John D., 4 Oct. 1855, Sarah A. Funk, dau. of Jacob   10/ 6/55-2
Godman, John Thomas, 20 Oct. 1859, Mary Jane Swain   11/ 1/59-2
Godman, Thos. S., 2 Jan. 1854, Emma A. Bell, dau. of Geo.   1/ 4/54-2
Godwin, Benjamin F., 7 Aug. 1851, Anna F. Hancock   8/ 8/51-2
Godwin, John C., 8 Jan. 1856, Adelia Jane Kyler   1/12/56-2
Godwin, Littleton S., 22 Oct. 1857, Mary E. Fields   10/24/57-2
Goehegan, John P., 24 Apr. 1856, Susan Ford   5/14/56-2
Goettmann, John, 17 May 1855, Mary C. Snyder   5/18/55-2
Goertz, Hugo H., 2 Oct. 1860, Fredericka Scheck   10/16/60-2
Gold, William A., 20 Oct. 1857, Emily C. Mott, dau. of James   10/21/57-2
Golden, John, 14 Nov. 1859, Maria Louisa Felthouse   11/28/59-2
Golden, Lucas, 11 June 1856, Sarah Jane Hany   7/28/56-2
Goldin, John, 15 Sept. 1852, Cordelia Stevens   9/20/52-2
Goldsborough, John T., 16 Sept. 1860, Caroline V. Topman   9/19/60-2
Goldsborough, Robert, 21 June 1854, A. Sidney Winder, dau.
    of W. S.   6/23/54-2
Goldsborough, Thos., 5 Mar. 1853, Mary Ann Todd   3/ 8/53-2
Goldsmith, R. H., 7 Aug. 1855, Hannah C. Lewis, dau. of
    John N.   11/17/55-2
Goldsmith, Samuel, 20 Nov. 1853, Mary Jane Rose   11/24/53-2
Golibart, Joseph R., 9 Oct. 1855, Mary O. Walter   10/10/55-2
Golibart, Joseph R., 9 Oct. 1855, Mary O. Walter, dau. of
    Francis S.; corrected copy   10/26/55-2
Gomez, Edward, 2 Oct. 1856, Georgeanna Chew   10/15/56-2
Gonder, Jacob A., 22 Sept. 1853, Rachel E. Houck   9/24/53-2
Gonder, William, 19 Dec. 1858, Martha J. Davis   1/28/59-2
Gone, Enos, 24 Dec. 1851, Julia A. Gist   12/25/51-2
Gontrum, Conrad, 9 Feb. 1854, Christianna Cramer   2/15/54-2
Good, Wm., 4 Sept. 1856, Elizabeth Steward   9/ 9/56-2
Goodman, John Thomas, 20 Oct. 1859, Mary Jane Swain   10/29/59-2
Goodmann, Aaron, 25 Jan. 1852, Rosaly Behrend, dau. of B.   1/27/52-2
Goodwin, E. C., 10 Jan. 1854, Mary Kennard   1/12/54-2
Goodwin, Thomas, 11 Oct. 1859, Julia Agnes Barret   10/18/59-2
Goodwin Wm. J. R., 28 Oct. 1852, Elizabeth A. Norton   11/ 3/52-2
Gordin, Jerry, 26 Apr. 1855, Elizabeth Butler   4/28/55-2
Gordon, George W., 6 Mar. 1851, Isabel F. Smith, dau. of Jno.   3/ 7/51-2
Gordon, J. W., 3 June 1856, Lizzie H. Fulton   6/ 4/56-2
Gordon, James, 14 July 1851, Sarah E. Brown, dau. of Elijah   7/22/51-2
Gordon, John, 25 Sept. 1855, Jennie Cunningham   9/28/55-2
Gordon, John, 10 Apr. 1859, (Mrs.) Mary A. Bartholomew   4/19/59-2
Gordon, John, 18 Apr. 1860, Inez Routh Ellis, dau. of Thos. G.   5/ 2/60-2
Gordon, John T., 12 Oct. 1854, Alverda Jeffers   10/14/54-2
Gordon, Josias W., 13 Jan. 1852, Catharine A. Sibreet   1/19/52-2
Gordon, Patrick, 1 Nov. 1859, Mary Williamson   11/22/59-2
Gordshell, George W., 4 July 1853, Fanny Ford   7/12/53-2
Gore, Chas., 30 Dec. 1852, Caroline Wilhelm   1/ 1/53-2
Gore, Geo. W., 21 Oct. 1852, Lydia Shipley   10/25/52-2
Gore, John W., 13 Jan. 1853, Sarah Jane Askew, dau. of
    Thos. W.   1/18/53-2
Gore, Michael, 7 Dec. 1854, Mary Jane Hardin   12/ 9/54-2
Gore, Michael, 8 Nov. 1859, Rebecca T. Snyder, dau. of
    William C.   11/17/59-2
Gore, Philip M., 3 Feb. 1856, Margaret Caples   2/ 9/56-2
Gorges, John A. S., 21 Sept. 1859, Leonora S. Schumacher   9/22/59-2
Gorman, Arnold T., 23 Nov. 1859, Jane Marchbanks   11/26/59-2
Gorman, John, 29 July 1856, Ann E. Roberts   10/20/56-2
Gorman, Nicholas L., 23 Sept. 1852, Hannah E. Minzey   9/25/52-2
Gorman, William H., 1 Feb. 1857, Margaret Bradley   2/ 3/57-2
Gormley, Thomas, 18 July 1859, Maggie R. Hargrove   7/26/59-2
Gorrell, Joseph, 20 Dec. 1855, Sarah J. Ward   12/25/55-2
Gorrell, Joseph B., 25 Nov. 1856, Mary E. Norris   11/29/56-2
Gorsuch, Dickson, 13 Jan. 1853, Rebecca Frances Matthews, dau.
    of Benj.   1/15/53-2
Gorsuch, George Washington, 2 Dec. 1852, Mary Gosnell   12/25/52-2
Gorsuch, J. T., 18 May 1856, Elizabeth Durring   5/24/56-2

Gorsuch, John T., 14 Oct. 1858, Sarah R. Griffin, dau. of Levi	10/16/58-2
Gorsuch, John W., 29 Nov. 1859, Carrie V. Beaver	11/30/59-2
Gorsuch, Joseph H., 11 Jan. 1860, Margaret E. Quinlin	1/18/60-2
Gorsuch, Joshua, 3 Apr. 1853, Cassandra Fisher	4/ 5/53-2
Gorsuch, Stephen, 14 July 1857, Elizabeth Franklin	7/21/57-2
Gorsuch, Thomas J., 17 Nov. 1859, Ellen Wells	11/21/59-2
Gorsuch, William, 31 Jan. 1856, Pleasants C. Stover	2/ 2/56-2
Gorton, Wm. S., 19 Feb. 1854, Mary A. Marshall	4/20/54-2
Gosage, Thompson, 26 Aug. 1851, Amanda Shockney, dau. of Samuel	8/28/51-2
Gosnell, Francis M., 19 Jan. 1854, Louisa Underwood	1/23/54-2
Gosnell, James L. B., 14 Apr. 1851, Addie Gosnell	4/16/57-2
Gosnell, Richard, 4 Jan. 1853, Ann Rebecca Harryman	6/16/53-2
Gosnell, Upton S., 7 Dec. 1859, (Mrs.) Julia Ledley	12/12/59-2
Gosnell, Wm. A., 15 May 1851, H. E. Brown	5/16/51-2
Gosnell, Zebediah, 9 Jan. 1851, Susan Ann Ward	1/10/51-2
Goss, Job, 16 Dec. 1855, Anna C. Barnett	4/ 8/56-2
Goss, John A., 20 July 1854, Mary E. Austen	8/ 3/54-2
Gossage, John, 17 Mar. 1853, Sarah Longwell	3/30/53-2
Gossage, Samuel, 19 Oct. 1854, (Mrs.) Lydia Bloodgood	10/27/54-2
Gossom, Thos. S., 7 Jan. 1858, Mary E. Duvall	1/ 9/58-2
Goudy, Alfred, 11 Jan. 1860, Clara A. Ingalls	1/18/60-2
Gough, Dixon (Dr.), 8 May 1851, Lizie J. Williams, dau. of James R.	5/ 9/51-2
Gough, Wm. Thomas, 29 Oct. 1857, Elizabeth F. Mallery	1/13/58-2
Gould, Edmund G., 1 Aug. 1858, Sarah J. Wilkinson, dau. of Hezekiah	8/ 4/58-2
Gould, James A., 28 Aug. 1856, Mary A. Wilson	9/ 1/56-2
Gould, John H., 20 June 1854, Mary F. Keever	6/26/54-2
Gould, John R., 21 Jan. 1851, Adele Huet de La Chelle, dau. of Achilles	1/22/51-2
Gould, John R., 21 Dec. 1859, Rose Jordan	12/23/59-2
Gourly, James, 30 June 1855, Mary F. Weaver	7/ 7/55-2
Gover, George W., 18 Oct. 1853, Ann E. Robinson	10/21/53-2
Gover, Robert; no date given, Electa E. Cooper	9/17/60-2
Gowan, Michael A., 10 Sept. 1857, Eleanora E. Slate, dau. of George A.	9/17/57-2
Grabau, Wm. F., 7 July 1853, Adeline A. Walker, dau. of Joshua	7/ 9/53-2
Grace, James H., 31 May 1860, Frances R. Mercer	6/ 2/60-2
Grace, Redmond J., 7 Feb. 1860, Alice E. Gloninger	2/ 9/60-2
Gracey, Hugh, 3 July 1855, Elenora Ball, dau. of John	7/ 7/55-2
Gracey, William C., 2 Sept. 1860, Lizzie A. Hewett	9/10/60-2
Grady, Michael J., 1 May 1855, Mary E. S. McGrath	5/ 9/55-2
Graff, Readwood Vande, 17 Sept. 1856, (Mrs.) Eliza Hartzell	9/18/56-2
Graff, William S., 26 Aug. 1852, Rebecca Turner	8/27/52-2
Grafflin, Christopher L., 15 Oct. 1856, Mary E. S. Lowe, dau. of O. G.	10/24/56-2
Grafflin, Joseph, 6 May 1855, Sidney A. N. Lynch, dau. of Benjamin A.	11/23/55-2
Grafflin, Wm. H., 18 May 1853, Sarah S. Mason, dau. of Peter	5/23/53-2
Grafs, Thomas R., 29 Dec. 1850, Elizabeth A. Conaway	1/ 4/51-2
Grafton, Nathan, 26 Dec. 1850, Barbara Hartman	1/ 1/51-2
Graham, Benjamin, 1 Apr. 1851, Persusia A. Bradley	4/ 3/51-2
Graham, Benjamin, 22 Feb. 1858, Mary E. B. Adams	2/24/58-2
Graham, Daniel, 25 June 1857, Mary Oswald	6/27/57-2
Graham, Edward, 21 Apr. 1851, Susan Brady	5/10/51-2
Graham, James, 20 Nov. 1855, Adelaide Hoffman	11/30/55-2
Graham, John, 9 Jan. 1856, Mary M. Creager	1/15/56-2
Graham, John, 11 Mar. 1856, Mary Margaret Davidson	3/14/56-2
Graham, John T., 29 Apr. 1858, Elizabeth Turner, dau. of John C.	5/ 1/58-2
Graham, Joseph F., 31 Jan. 1856, Bridget L. Plunkett	2/ 6/56-2
Graham, Michael, 21 Sept. 1852, Anne Maria Healey	9/24/52-2

```
Graham, Robert, 21 Apr. 1853, Jane Ross                          4/26/53-2
Graham, W. M., 4 Sept. 1860, Mary B. Ricketts, dau. of (Capt.)
    Jas. B.                                                      9/ 7/60-2
Graham, W. S. F. (Rev.) 10 June 1852, Elizabeth E. Leche, dau.
    of David                                                    6/11/52-2
Graham, Wm., 11 Jan. 1858, Ellen Barnes                         3/23/58-2
Graham, Wm. J., 12 Mar. 1860, Alice A. Jones                    3/17/60-4
Grain, John M., 2 Nov. 1851, Eliza Jane Emory                   11/ 7/51-2
Grainger, Wm. H., 8 May 1854, (Mrs.) Harriet E. Blundon         5/10/54-2
Grammer, Fred'k. Louis, 5 Feb. 1857, Cornelia A. Reynolds       2/ 7/57-2
Grammer, George S., 26 Jan. 1860, (Mrs.) Susan A. Bogardus      1/30/60-2
Grammer, William H., 10 Feb. 1851, Julia A. Baumgardner, dau. of
    Samuel                                                      2/11/51-2
Granger, Geo. R., 20 Mar. 1858, Imogen S. Raynor                3/23/58-2
Granger, James, 22 July 1858, Martha A. Hopkins                 7/24/58-2
Granger, Nathan James, 15 Nov. 1859, Sarah Jane Warwick         11/26/59-2
Grant, Alpheus C., 23 Feb. 1858, Heppie B. Jackson, dau. of
    (Rev.) William                                              4/ 3/58-2
Grant, Edward H., 19 Apt. 1855, Cornelia Duval                  4/30/55-2
Grant, Henry, 17 Mar. 1853, (Mrs.) Julian Cook                  3/18/53-2
Grant, Jas. B., 10 June 1856, Amelia Schwartz, dau. of G.       6/12/56-2
Grape, John T., 15 Dec. 1857, Sophia F. MacCubbin, dau. of
    Samuel                                                      12/22/57-2
Graphin, Julien, 25 Aug. 1856, Mary Mills                       9/ 9/56-2
Graves, Frances E., 8 Dec. 1858, Mary P. Hamilton, dau. of
    Saml. H.                                                    12/25/58-2
Graves, Thos. S., 30 Sept. 1852, Anna M. Moore, dau. of
    Stephen H.                                                  10/ 2/52-2
Gray, E., Jr., 30 May 1855, Rosa A. Ross                        6/ 2/55-2
Gray, Francis E., 21 July 1853, Charlotte F. Eggerton           8/ 1/53-2
Gray, George, 25 Dec. 1851, Margaret Tauto                      3/ 2/52-2
Gray, Henry C., 1 Jan. 1860, Catherine B. Barley, dau. of
    Thos.                                                       1/14/60-2
Gray, Hugh, 22 May 1853, Rosanna Mallen; corrected copy         5/27/53-2
Gray, Hugh, 22 May 1853, Rosanna Mallers                        5/26/53-2
Gray, Isaac D., 15 Feb. 1855, Maria Louisa Ohareo              8/13/55-2
Gray, James, 9 Jan. 1851, Frances Smith                         1/14/51-2
Gray, James, 8 Oct. 1851, Kate S. Rust, dau. of Paul            10/29/51-2
Gray, Jas. E., 12 June 1851, Louisa S. Tindle                   6/17/51-2
Gray, John F., 31 Jan. 1860, Laura E. Claggett                  2/ 4/60-2
Gray, John M., 16 Feb. 1860, Ellen Dudley                       2/21/60-2
Gray, Joseph, 29 July 1852, Mary Ann N. Ely                     8/ 4/52-2
Gray, Leonard W., 30 July 1857, Mary C. Ryan                    8/ 3/57-2
Gray, Nelson, 18 July 1857, Emily Jane Tittle                   7/21/57-2
Gray, Wesley, 25 Dec. 1851, Hester A. Collins, dau. of
    Samuel                                                      12/30/51-2
Gray, William, 26 May 1853, Charlotte Fisher; corrected copy    5/28/53-2
Gray, William, 26 May 1853, Isabella Lewis                      5/28/53-2
Gray, William, 13 Aug. 1857, Maria Steward                      8/17/57-2
Gray, William, 15 Sept. 1859, Eliza J. Bower                    9/19/59-2
Gray, William M., 3 Oct. 1854, Mary Dickson                     10/14/54-2
Gray, Wm. J., 9 Sept. 1858, Serena H. Scott                     9/10/58-2
Graybill, Samuel, 21 July 1855, Emma Jane Butler                7/28/55-2
Graydon, Thomas, 3 July 1857, Margaret F. Teldan                7/ 8/57-2
Greason, Robert M., 18 Oct. 1855, Margaret Ann King             10/20/55-2
Greble, William, 20 May 1852, Julia C. W. Mason, dau. of
    Edward and Lorana                                           5/24/52-2
Green, Andrew O., 17 May 1853, Amelia A. Hewell, dau. of
    Lewis                                                       5/19/53-2
Green, Archibald H., 19 May 1853, Henrietta Peters              5/26/53-2
Green, Charles, 29 June 1854, Mary E. Mills, dau. of Robert     7/ 1/54-2
Green, Charles, 18 Jan. 1860, Catherine Butler                  1/19/60-2
Green, Charles A., 23 Sept. 1852, Mary Elizabeth Brown          9/25/52-2
Green, Edw'd. (Capt.), 18 Sept. 1851, Magdalene Crist           9/19/51-2
Green, Edw'd. J., 29 Apr. 1852, Sophia A. Peddicord             4/30/52-2
```

Green, George, 12 Feb. 1855, Caroline Wilson   2/14/55-2
Green, Henry, 13 Sept. 1851, Ellen Elizabeth League, dau. of
     Luke   9/23/51-2
Green, Henry, 3 Aug. 1853, Amanda J. Ray   12/ 6/53-2
Green, Henry, Jr., 5 Mar. 1857, Mary Brown   4/13/57-2
Green, Hugh T., 18 Sept. 1856, Mary L. Glass, dau. of David W.   9/29/56-2
Green, Jacob, 22 Mar. 1857, Elizabeth Cooper   3/24/57-2
Green, James B., 18 Oct. 1853, Christina Ann Fisher, dau. of
     William   10/22/53-2
Green, James H., 16 Sept. 1860, (Mrs.) Mary A. Fields   11/17/60-2
Green, John, 11 May 1851, Sarah Matilda Marsh   5/20/51-2
Green, John E., 11 Mar. 1858, (Mrs.) Maria Juricks   3/15/58-2
Green, John H., 16 Sept. 1852, Martha Cook   9/17/52-2
Green, John N., 22 Dec. 1859, Matilda E. Moore   12/24/59-2
Green, Joseph N., 20 Aug. 1857, Elizabeth Stallings   9/21/57-2
Green, Joseph Wesley, 25 Aug. 1856, Elizabeth Amanda Carroll   8/27/56-2
Green, M., 18 Apr. 1860, S. K. Deitz   4/20/60-2
Green, Michael, 29 Jan. 1852, Mary F. Gannon   2/ 2/52-2
Green, Philander, 20 Aug. 1856, Mary E. Eliason   8/23/56-2
Green, Robert, 31 May 1857, Eliza Bryen   6/ 4/57-2
Green, Rob't. T., 8 Feb. 1853, Sallie R. Fresh   2/ 9/53-2
Green, Saml. F., 27 Dec. 1859, Lizzie R. Wright, dau. of John R. 1/ 3/60-2
Green, Samuel, 12 Sept. 1859, Eliza Ellen Haines   9/15/59-2
Green, Samuel F., 27 Dec. 1859, Lizzie R. Wright   12/31/59-2
Green, Stephen A., 31 May 1859, Margaret Pamelia Mayger, dau.
     of Richard   6/ 2/59-2
Green, Thomas, 25 Feb. 1858, Martha Ann Green   3/ 2/58-2
Green, Thomas M., 8 Aug. 1854, Sarah A. Hooper, dau. of
     William   8/10/54-2
Green, William, 14 June 1853, Rosanna M. Ozier   6/15/53-2
Green, William, 21 Jan. 1855, Amanda Gettier, dau. of Michael
     and Elizabeth   1/24/55-2
Green, William, 11 Nov. 1858, Rosannah Brown   11/13/58-2
Green, Wm. H. (Capt.), 2 June 1854, Eleanora Marshall, dau. of
     James B.   6/26/54-2
Green, Wm. H. (Dr.), 12 Sept. 1855, Mary Berry   9/18/55-2
Greenage, Asbury, 3 May 1856, Phebe Jones   5/ 5/56-2
Greenfield, Aquila H., 14 Sept. 1858, Laura V. Blades, niece of
     Nicholas Oram   9/16/58-2
Greenfield, Wm. Edwin, 31 Oct. 1858, Clara B. Sullivan   11/ 3/58-2
Greentree, H. (Dr.), 20 Oct. 1857, E. M. A. Meyer   10/27/57-2
Greenway, Clarence E., 17 June 1856, Sallie B. Hoke, dau. of
     Jacob   6/26/56-2
Greenwell, James C., 6 Sept. 1859, Mary A. Slater, dau. of
     George   9/ 7/59-2
Greenwell, Thos. F., 7 Dec. 1858, Cornelia Robb   12/15/58-2
Greenwell, Wm. F., 23 Oct. 1860, Sarah M. Floyd   10/24/60-2
Greenwood, Chas. S., 7 May 1857, Elizabeth A. Bolen, dau. of
     John T.   5/15/57-2
Greenwood, Wm. D., 16 Oct. 1855, Matilda E. Betts   10/18/55-2
Greer, David, 21 July 1851, Ellen Greer   7/22/51-2
Greer, H. C., 24 Sept. 1857, M. A. Culbertson   10/ 2/57-2
Greer, Matthew, 5 Jan. 1857, Letitia Griffin   3/ 9/57-2
Greet, William, 2 June 1853, Ann Crew   6/ 7/53-2
Gregg, Andrew A., 5 June 1860, Rose Morris, dau. of Geo. W.   6/ 7/60-2
Gregory, J. Henry, 29 Oct. 1857, Caroline Williams   10/31/57-2
Gregory, John, 29 Sept. 1851, (Mrs.) Mary Wilcox   9/30/51-2
Greham, J. Thompson, 2 Feb. 1852, Rebecca H. Campbell, dau. of
     David S.   2/ 7/52-2
Grell, John F., 16 May 1859, Catharine Lay   5/20/59-2
Grenier, Edouard L., 1 Jan. 1857, (Mrs.) Jane M. Ferguson   1/10/57-2
Greshoff, Francis A., 29 Apr. 1858, Julie Koechling, dau. of
     H. M.   5/ 1/58-2
Greves, David, 11 Apr. 1858, (Mrs.) Matilda West   4/24/58-2

```
Greves, Garrett David R., 25 Aug. 1859, Catherine F. Hall        9/ 2/59-2
Grey, Richard W., 1 Nov. 1855, Anna P. Hunt                     11/ 6/55-2
Grice, E. L., 30 Jan. 1851, Elizabeth Kehlenbeck                 1/31/51-2
Grice, George W., 16 Oct. 1856, (Mrs.) Elizabeth Cripps         11/25/56-2
Grieves, H. G. (Dr.), 27 Apr. 1859, Mary M. Kirby               4/28/59-2
Griffin, A. P., 6 Sept. 1855, Mary Marrow                       9/20/55-2
Griffin, Columbus, 23 June 1859, Melvina Isabel Sheppard, dau.
    of George                                                    7/11/59-2
Griffin, George, 2 Oct. 1854, Mary Cropper                      10/ 4/54-2
Griffin, Henry C., 8 Sept. 1857, Virginia Daw                    9/16/57-2
Griffin, Henry J., 10 June 1852, Sarah Knight                    6/14/52-2
Griffin, Jacob, 18 Nov. 1852, Abbe Colbert                      11/20/52-2
Griffin, John Thomas, 29 Apr. 1858, E. Virginia Henson, dau.
    of (Mrs.) L. A. Prattis                                      5/ 1/58-2
Griffin, Joshua, 30 June 1853, Mary A. Long                      7/27/53-2
Griffin, Luke, 25 June 1853, (Mrs.) Mary A. Waller               7/ 6/53-2
Griffin, Michael, 12 Apr. 1860, Mary Jane Halpin                 4/14/60-2
Griffin, Robert J., 4 Oct. 1855, Eliza Dawes, dau. of Ed. B.    10/ 8/55-2
Griffin, T. D., 20 Oct. 1855, Dollie Boyd                       10/22/55-2
Griffin, William H., 24 Mar. 1856, Eliza J. White                3/25/56-2
Griffith, Abraham, 12 July 1859, Ellen M. Gent, dau. of Wm. C.   7/15/59-2
Griffith, Charles G., 17 May 1851, Frances Knowles, dau. of
    Hazard                                                       5/24/51-2
Griffith, Charles G., 14 Dec. 1859, Mary E. Burnes              12/31/59-2
Griffith, Daniel Greenberry, 19 July 1853, Julia Beacham         7/28/53-2
Griffith, Daniel M., 7 Apr. 1853, Mary S. Eaton                  4/22/53-2
Griffith, Edward (Dr.), 9 Mar. 1859, Eleanor Griffith;
    3/11/59-2                                                    3/12/59-2
Griffith, Edwin R., 9 Jan. 1851, Penelope Parks, dau. of John    1/21/51-2
Griffith, F. Louis, 9 Dec. 1851, Mary E. Allen                  12/10/51-2
Griffith, H. L., 12 Sept. 1853, Susanna Greaff                   9/26/53-2
Griffith, Mortimer C., 15 Nov. 1859, Mary J. B. Cassell, dau.
    of Saml.                                                    11/18/59-2
Griffith, Robt. Henry, 14 Aug. 1860, Margaret Jane LeCompte      8/18/60-2
Griffith, Romulus Roggs, Jr., 9 Dec. 1852, Alverda Griffith,
    dau. of Israel                                              12/13/52-2
Griffith, Saml. K., 22 Feb. 1859, (Mrs.) Kate Daneker            3/ 1/59-2
Griffith, Thomas W., 15 Jan. 1856, Mary L. Cook                  1/16/56-2
Griffith, William, 10 May 1854, Martha L. Horan                  5/17/54-2
Griffith, William, 10 May 1854, Martha L. Moran; corrected
    copy                                                         5/18/54-2
Griffith, William M., 26 Nov. 1856, Laura V. Duvall             12/ 1/56-2
Griffith, Wm. Ridgely, 1 Feb. 1859, Mary Brewer, dau. of
    Geo. G.                                                      2/ 2/59-2
Griggs, George, 14 Jan. 1855, Mary V. Norman                     1/16/55-2
Griggs, James E., 23 Nov. 1858, Sarah J. Wherrett               11/27/58-2
Griggs, John J., 9 Nov. 1857, Mary Virginia Williams            11/25/57-2
Grimes, Larkin, 5 May 1858, Ellen Barry                          5/15/58-2
Grindall, Joseph J., 2 Oct. 1851, Mary E. Campbell              10/ 4/51-2
Grinder, Adam, 16 Nov. 1854, (Mrs.) Maria E. Kirby              11/18/54-2
Grinett, William, 29 Jan. 1857, Martha Furgerson                 1/31/57-2
Grinsfelder, Joseph, 30 Nov. 1851, Hannah Ridger, dau. of
    Aaron                                                       12/ 3/51-2
Griswold, F. A. (Rev.), 11 May 1858, Anna Jane Patterson         5/13/58-2
Groeninger, George, 21 Jan. 1851, Margaret Kreis, dau. of
    Peter                                                        2/11/51-2
Gronewall, John H., 15 Sept. 1851, Margaret C. Heslen            9/18/51-2
Groninger, Frederick, 9 May 1854, Veronica Wissel                5/10/54-2
Groom, George T., 19 Aug. 1851, Margaret Silver                  8/21/51-2
Groome, Charles O., 24 Nov. 1858, Virginia Daingerfield         11/25/58-2
Groome, Isaac J., 23 June 1853, Elizabeth Collett                6/30/53-2
Groomes, William H., 27 Oct. 1857, Elizabeth Wilmer Harris,
    dau. of James B.                                            10/30/57-2
Grooms, James, 26 Sept. 1860, Elizabeth A. Turner               10/ 1/60-2
Grooms, John E., 9 Dec. 1851, Jane L. Grayson                   12/11/51-2
```

Grooscoks, Herman H., 30 Nov. 1854, Mary C. Poor, dau. of
    Dudley   12/ 4/54-2
Grosh, Eugene, 1 Jan. 1855, Maria L. Watts, dau. of (Capt.)
    William J.   10/31/55-2
Gross, Benjamin, 7 Sept. 1854, (Mrs.) Lydia Leonard   9/ 9/54-2
Gross, Geo. R., 4 May 1858, Fanny Gettier, adopted dau. of
    Henry and Ellen   5/11/58-2
Gross, Howerton, 1 Feb. 1853, Elizabeth Baldwin   2/ 2/53-2
Gross, Jacob, 3 Aug. 1854, Eliza Jane White   8/ 5/54-2
Gross, Jacob, 25 Dec. 1860, Kate Stieff   12/27/60-2
Gross, John, 20 Jan. 1851, Catharine Gluck   1/25/51-2
Gross, Richard, 27 Sept. 1855, Harriet Ann Dickerson, dau. of
    James   9/29/55-2
Grove, David, 5 Oct. 1856, Rachel Amelia High   10/13/56-2
Grove, James H., 1 June 1858, Sarah Louisa Berry, dau. of
    (Mrs.) Mary R.   6/14/58-2
Grove, James J., 1 Nov. 1853, Carrie Randall Dorsey, dau. of
    Henry K.   11/ 3/53-2
Grove, L. Jewett (Dr.), 25 Sept. 1856, Frances A. Gaskins   9/30/56-2
Grove, Solomon, 3 May 1860, Nancy Biggerstaff   5/ 5/60-2
Grove, T. A. (Rev.), 31 Mar. 1857, Lizzie Stewart   4/ 1/57-2
Grover, Grafton, 6 Feb. 1851, Hannah Stover   2/ 8/51-2
Grover, Leonard B., 22 July 1857, Laura Sinn   7/23/57-2
Grow, Andrew S., 12 Oct. 1852, Isabella Battee, dau. of Samuel   10/18/52-2
Grubb, George, 7 July 1851, (Mrs.) Mary Ann E. Mann   7/10/51-2
Grubb, George W., 28 Apr. 1852, Anna Eliza McGinnis   4/30/52-2
Gruby, George, 7 May 1851, Jane Simons   5/14/41-2
Grymes, Benjamin R., 8 May 1860, Rebecca Johnson, dau. of
    A. Livingston   5/11/60-2
Grymes, James M. (Dr.), 23 Dec. 1858, Mary E. Peyton Torbert,
    dau. of James M.   12/25/58-2
Gude, Frederick W., 20 Dec. 1860, Amelia M. Medinger   12/22/60-2
Gudewill, Hermann, 31 Aug. 1854, Emma J. Brauns   9/ 4/54-2
Guest, George H., 11 Nov. 1856, Eliza Jane Wheatley, dau. of
    (Capt.) Levin and Ann Eliza   12/30/56-2
Guest, J. Wesley, 27 Oct. 1853, Emily R. Mulley, dau. of John
    M.   10/29/53-2
Guest, Richard S., 27 Jan. 1857, Ella Guyton   1/29/57-2
Guiselin, Henry, 25 Jan. 1855, Matilda E. Ellis   1/27/55-2
Gulp, Michael S., 9 Aug. 1851, Mary Ann Cross   8/11/51-2
Gumbine, William H., 7 Oct. 1855, Mary Elizabeth Burk   10/18/55-2
Gunn, Bernard, 17 July 1859, Ellen Flynn   7/22/59-2
Gunn, Jno. P. (Dr.); no date given, Sallie Wright, dau. of
    (Dr.) T. G.   10/28/57-2
Gunn, John P. (Dr.), 27 Oct. 1857, Sallie Wright, dau. of
    (Dr.) Thomas H.; corrected copy   10/29/57-2
Gunning, John, 4 June 1855, Catherine Carroll   6/ 6/55-2
Gunst, John, 30 Dec. 1857, Mary Elizabeth Thompson, dau. of
    Edward   1/ 5/57-2
Gunter, Ludolph W., 4 Jan. 1855, Martha Ann Cecil   1/13/55-2
Gurney, James, 29 Apr. 1855, (Mrs.) Amelia Burk   5/ 3/55-2
Gurney, Nathan G., 3 Jan. 1858, Margaret Seipler   1/ 5/58-2
Gutman, E., 16 May 1854, Sarah Gazan, dau. of Jacob   5/17/54-2
Gutman, Emanuel, 22 Aug. 1857, Caroline Meyers   8/24/57-2
Gutmann, Joel, 15 Aug. 1852, Elizabeth Katton, dau. of Lewis   8/21/52-2
Guy, John, 1 Apr. 1859, Sarah Corbin   4/ 4/59-2
Guy, Robert J., 17 Mar. 1857, Lizzie Algers, dau. of Charles   3/20/57-2
Guy, William, 3 Sept. 1851, Sarah Ann Guy   9/ 5/51-2
Guyton, Archibald M., 6 May 1856, Hannah Elizabeth Scarf   5/10/56-2
Guyton, John H., 31 July 1856, Mary E. Sappington   8/ 7/56-2
Guyton, William Asbury, 26 Apr. 1860, Cecilia Shearman   5/ 2/60-2
Gwin, L. N., 29 Dec. 1859, Emily E. Stine   1/ 3/60-2
Gwinn, Charles H., 17 Feb. 1859, Mary Ann Rhodes, dau. of
    Jno. R.   2/19/59-2
Gwinner, Henry W., 29 Mar. 1851, Louisa J. Flynn   3/31/51-2

Gwynn, Charles J. M., 26 Jan. 1858, Matilda E. Johnson,
    dau. of (Hon.) Reverdy   1/27/58-2
Habbersett, John, 11 Dec. 1853, Ellen A. Hardester   12/13/53-2
Habbersett, Wm., 29 Jan. 1852, Ellen R. Nickson   2/ 3/52-2
Habliston, Frederick H., 26 Nov. 1857, Kate V. Barham   11/28/51-2
Hackett, Zachariah, 12 Nov. 1857, Mary Hackett   11/14/57-2
Hadaway, James Henry, 1 Apr. 1852, Sarah Ann Hammond   4/ 3/52-2
Hadaway, William H., 29 Nov. 1857, Louisa Mieeks; 12/ 1/57-2 12/ 2/57-2
Hadley, John Wesley, 6 Feb. 1855, Margaret Ann Chaney   2/ 9/55-2
Hafner, Charles, 19 Feb. 1855, (Mrs.) Mary Ann Funk   2/27/55-2
Hagan, Arthur L., 7 Sept. 1859, Cornelia Ridgely   9/ 9/59-2
Hagan, Charles, 22 Apr. 1858, Mary Lizzie Moltz   4/27/58-2
Hagan, George, 3 Apr. 1851, Mary McNulty   4/ 7/51-2
Hagan, James P., 12 Apr. 1855, Mary Welsh   4/26/55-2
Hagan, John, 31 July 1853, Martha Vanhorn   8/ 2/53-2
Hagan, John W., 30 Jan. 1855, Mary E. Gungan   2/ 1/55-2
Hagan, William Thomas, 9 Oct. 1856, Mary Ann Corrick   10/11/56-2
Hagemaier, Gustav, 12 Aug. 1856, Catharine Reinhard   8/21/56-2
Hagen, H. G., 13 Nov. 1859, Clara S. Griffith   11/17/59-2
Hagen, Levi, 9 Nov. 1851, Ann R. Conrad   11/12/51-2
Hagger, Chas. E., 15 May 1858, Mary F. Mattingly   7/19/58-2
Hagner, Fred'k., 18 Jan. 1852, Mary Ann Wesley; corrected copy 1/22/52-2
Hagner, John, 13 Jan. 1859, Julia M. Seirs   1/15/59-2
Hagner, Patrick, 18 Jan. 1852, Mary Ann Wesley   1/21/52-2
Hahn, William, 27 Apr. 1853, Mary Olevia Dorsey   4/30/53-2
Haig, Geo. B. (Capt.), 11 Oct. 1853, Kate Proudfoot, dau. of
    Wells   10/19/53-2
Haig, James M., 9 Oct. 1856, (Mrs.) Sallie E. Noel   10/15/56-2
Haighs, George M., 13 July 1851, Sabina E. Lewis, dau. of
    Wilson   7/25/51-2
Haill, Jonathan, 10 July 1860, Sarah Simmons   7/12/60-2
Haines, C. R. (Rev.), 5 Oct. 1858, C. G. Hall   10/16/58-2
Haines, De Wilton, son of (Hon.) Towsend, 10 June 1851, R.
    Ellen Duvall, dau. of Benjamin   6/12/51-2
Haines, Joseph, 15 July 1851, (Mrs.) Louisa Wilhelm   7/16/51-2
Haines, Mordecai, 12 Apr. 1855, Ann M. Babylon   4/14/55-2
Haines, William F., 15 May 1860, Sarah J. Sunderland   5/18/60-2
Haislop, Walter A. (Col.), 22 June 1857, Ann H. Hall   7/24/57-2
Hakesley, Chas., 25 June 1851, Sarah Jane Taylor   6/27/51-2
Hakesley, George W., 25 Oct. 1859, Mary E. Bandel, dau. of
    Andrew J.   10/26/59-2
Halbert, Wm. E., 7 Dec. 1852, Sarah R. Burnett   12/11/52-2
Hale, E. Wesley, 19 Jan. 1860, Hennie E. Konze, dau. of Lewis 1/23/60-2
Hale, Nicholas H., 1 June 1852, Sarah E. Merryman   6/ 4/52-2
Halitt, (?), 3 June 1860, Mary H. Ortlip   4/ 4/60-2
Hall, Aaron, 23 Dec. 1852, Jane W. Manifold   1/ 1/52-2
Hall, Alexander, 19 Oct. 1854, Sarah Ann Hunter   10/24/54-2
Hall, Ambrose E., 7 Dec. 1854, Anna Eliza Vickers   12/ 9/54-2
Hall, Andrew, 8 Sept. 1859, Rachel A. Fisher   9/10/59-2
Hall, Charles L., 2 June 1853, Margaret E. Riggin   1/ 8/53-2
Hall, E. G. W., 17 Aug. 1858, Isabel Scott, dau. of H. C.   8/24/58-2
Hall, Elbridge G., 20 May 1858, Amanda Bosley   5/21/58-2
Hall, Elijah, 9 Nov. 1852, Caroline Smith   11/12/52-2
Hall, Eugene, 4 Nov. 1855, Mary Ann Kerr   11/20/55-2
Hall, Francis J., 12 Feb. 1852, Mary C. Foard   2/14/52-2
Hall, Geo. Henry M., 27 Mar. 1851, Annie M. Kemp   3/31/51-2
Hall, Horace, 28 June 1854, Harriet A. Ruste   7/14/54-2
Hall, Isaac C., 29 Mar. 1856, (Mrs.) Ann Eliza Dorman   4/ 1/56-2
Hall, J. Thomas, 22 June 1854, Harriet Barker, dau. of John 6/28/54-2
Hall, James, 26 May 1853, Sallie J. Quincy   5/27/53-2
Hall, James, 29 Sept. 1859, Sarah Trott   10/ 4/59-2
Hall, James P.; no date given, Mary Linthicum, dau. of O. M. 5/15/58-2
Hall, Job H., 24 Mar. 1856, Mary E. Marsh   4/16/56-2
Hall, John, Jr., 9 Feb. 1853, Ann Maria Williams   2/10/53-2

Hall, John H., Jr., 21 Mar. 1854, Margaret Brooks, dau. of
    Joseph   3/23/54-2
Hall, John P., 29 Aug. 1859, Almedia J. Woody   9/23/59-2
Hall, John Q. A., 10 July 1853, Susan Brown   7/12/53-2
Hall, John T., 17 May 1859, Mary D. Fusselbaugh   11/19/59-2
Hall, John W., 7 Dec. 1851, Caroline G. Cox   12/ 9/51-2
Hall, John W., 23 Nov. 1852, Rebecca D. Jones   11/25/52-2
Hall, Levin J., 10 June 1856, Margaret A. Brannan; corrected
    copy   6/14/56-2
Hall, Levin J., 10 June 1856, Margaret Brennan   6/12/56-2
Hall, Nathaniel, 29 Apr. 1856, Mary E. McPherson   5/ 7/56-2
Hall, Richard, 2 Dec. 1852, Margaret R. Armstrong   12/ 7/52-2
Hall, Rich'd. C., 24 Nov. 1859, Mary C. Gibson, dau. of John 11/26/59-2
Hall, Robert, Jr., 11 Aug. 1857, Eleanora R. C. Cook, dau. of
    Wm. B.   9/ 8/57-2
Hall, Robert C., 2 Oct. 1855, Mary R. Cunningham, dau. of B. A. 10/ 4/55-2
Hall, Robert H., 13 Sept. 1855, Annie E. Holton   11/ 6/55-2
Hall, Washington, 10 June 1853, Blanche Bujac, dau. of
    (Madame) A. T.   6/11/53-2
Hall, William, 11 Feb. 1858, (Mrs.) Julia Colbert   2/17/58-2
Hall, William, 15 Nov. 1860, Adeline Patterson   11/17/60-2
Hall, William H., 27 Nov. 1851, Mary Ann Price   12/ 1/51-2
Hall, William H., 3 Apr. 1855, Adelia A. Peterson, dau. of
    (Capt.) E.   4/ 9/55-2
Hall, William H., 3 May 1860, Ellennore Barnett   5/ 5/60-2
Hall, William J., 8 June 1852, Maria Jones   6/11/52-2
Hall, William Kent, 22 Sept. 1851, Mary Jane Brannon   9/23/51-2
Hall, William P., 19 June 1860, Martha A. Mullen   6/21/60-2
Hall, Wm. E., 6 Oct. 1859, Margaret E. Wallace   10/10/59-2
Hall, Wm. W., 18 Feb. 1857, Elizabeth H. Rittenhouse   2/20/57-2
Hallar, Abner, 27 Nov. 1856, Mary A. Wilson   11/29/56-2
Haller, David E., 27 Dec. 1855, Mary Catherine Fultz   1/ 4/56-2
Hallett, John T., 25 Mar. 1851, Mary Snyder   3/27/51-2
Ham, John H.; no date given, Ellen A. Badger, dau. of Albert J. 2/16/55-2
Hambleton, Alfred H., 28 Sept. 1851, Margaret E. Sheeler   10/ 4/51-2
Hambleton, John A., 5 June 1855, Mary E. Woollen   6/ 6/55-2
Hambleton, Thos. B., 20 Oct. 1853, Sallie W. Albright, dau. of
    John W.   10/25/53-2
Hamil, P., 5 Nov. 1857, Margaret Ann Hughes   11/ 7/57-2
Hamill, Alexander, 26 Feb. 1857, Mary E. Bokee   3/ 2/57-2
Hamill, James H., 3 May 1855, Annie Woods, dau. of James   5/ 5/55-2
Hamill, Wm. J., 10 Dec. 1851, Sylvia C. Hunt   12/20/51-2
Hamilton, Caleb B., 14 June 1859, Annie E. Hadaway   6/25/59-2
Hamilton, Charles R., 27 Mar. 1853, Catharine Noble   5/ 4/53-2
Hamilton, Chas., 24 Oct. 1856, Margaret Barnhill   10/28/56-2
Hamilton, Geo. B., 27 Feb. 1855, (Mrs.) Mary Clayland Jacobs 3/ 1/55-2
Hamilton, Geo. W., 16 May 1851, Mary Ann Milroy   5/17/51-2
Hamilton, Henry, 7 Nov. 1854, Elizabeth Ann Rhinehart, dau. of
    Philip   11/ 9/54-2
Hamilton, James, 15 Mar. 1853, Anna Maria Boyer, dau. of
    Jacob   3/17/53-2
Hamilton, James, 21 Nov. 1855, Mary Batchlor   11/28/55-2
Hamilton, James, 9 Oct. 1860, Lydia A. Renshaw   10/10/60-2
Hamilton, James B., 31 May 1859, Mary J. Riley   6/ 2/59-2
Hamilton, James p., 5 Aug. 1858, Sallie E. Newman, dau. of
    Joseph J.   8/ 7/58-2
Hamilton, James W., 20 Oct. 1854, Virginia C. Coiner   10/23/54-2
Hamilton, Jas. H., 19 June 1851, Ann Jane Hughes, dau. of
    Richard   6/21/51-2
Hamilton, John, 1 Jan. 1851, Mary T. Stevenson, dau. of
    Stephen   1/27/51-2
Hamilton, John, 18 May 1856, Catherine Ann McElroy   5/31/56-2
Hamilton, John, 10 May 1860, Mary C. Ehlers   5/17/60-2
Hamilton, John W. D., 1 Sept. 1857, Gabrella M. C. Shaffelter,
    dau. of Peter   9/ 3/57-2

Hamilton, Joseph E., 27 Oct. 1853, Mary J. Parlett   10/29/53-2
Hamilton, Joseph E., 23 Oct. 1855, Elizabeth Fleeharty   10/29/55-2
Hamilton, Robt., 27 May 1856, Frances M. O'Reilley   6/ 3/56-2
Hamilton, Samuel, 1 Apr. 1857, Hannah E. Ford, dau. of John B.   4/17/57-2
Hamilton, Thomas, 7 Nov. 1851, Caroline McMurray   11/14/51-2
Hamilton, William, 18 Jan. 1853, Elizabeth Shay   1/22/53-2
Hamilton, William E., 24 Nov. 1857, Nannie M. Willson, dau. of
     Geo. H.   11/28/57-2
Hamilton, William H., 17 Aug. 1851, Catharine Cole   8/22/51-2
Hamilton, Wm., 6 Dec. 1859, Henrietta Frisby   1/20/60-2
Hamilton, Wm. L., 22 Dec. 1857, Lavinia Hobbs   12/25/57-2
Hamman, John A., 31 May 1859, Margaret Ostendorf, dau. of A.   6/ 4/59-2
Hammel, Jacob, Jr., 27 Apr. 1858, Margaret Ann Meredith   5/ 4/58-2
Hammer, Peter, 17 Mar. 1857, Sarah C. Shoemaker   3/23/57-2
Hammer, Peter G., 8 Nov. 1853, Mary A. Chew, dau. of H. M.   11/11/53-2
Hammerslough, S., 2 Sept. 1855, Louisa Sommers, dau. of
     Anthony   9/11/55-2
Hammett, John R., 13 Sept. 1855, A. B. Zachary, dau. of Wm.   9/17/55-2
Hammett, W. S., 8 Apr. 1856, Susan A. Birch   4/ 9/56-2
Hammill, John, 23 Dec. 1858, (Mrs.) Elizabeth Skipper, dau. of
     John Cockey   12/24/58-2
Hammill, William J., 1 June 1854, Emily Louisa Caprilla   6/ 3/54-2
Hammond, Augustus, 2 Oct. 1855, Mary Virginia Hammond   10/ 8/55-2
Hammond, Geo. W., 26 July 1852, Sarah J. Clark   7/28/52-2
Hammond, Harry, 12 Oct. 1859, Adele C. Burke Moore, dau. of
     William   10/14/59-2
Hammond, John, 4 Apr. 1853, Harriet Elberd   4/ 6/53-2
Hammond, John D., 10 July 1856, Mary A. Kemp   7/14/56-2
Hammond, John S., 12 Sept. 1855, Keturah S. Horney   9/17/55-2
Hammond, Joseph, 19 Dec. 1852, Mary Ann Deems   12/23/52-2
Hammond, Mathias (Capt.), 20 Apr. 1854, Achsa S. Warfield, dau.
     of George   4/22/54-2
Hammond, Milton (Dr.), 15 Feb. 1853, Mary Dungan, dau. of
     F. D.   2/16/53-2
Hammond, Milton (Dr.), 15 Apr. 1858, Lizzie Hubball, dau. of
     Ebenezer   4/16/58-2
Hammond, Nicholas W., 14 Oct. 1856, Mary E. Wood   10/15/56-2
Hammond, Thos. W. (Dr.), 28 Jan. 1852, Mildred E. Gambrill   2/ 3/52-2
Hamon, James, 14 July 1853, Elizabeth Gourlay   7/16/53-2
Hampson, Joseph, 21 Mar. 1851, Margaret A. L. Harvey   3/22/51-2
Hampton, Jesse B., 16 July 1855, Lydia Ann Rhoads   7/24/55-2
Hampton, Wm. Wilberforce, 10 Jan. 1860, Caroline L. Limberry   1/13/60-2
Hanah, Samuel, 29 Sept. 1859, Sarah Gamble   10/ 1/59-2
Hanan, George, 13 Jan. 1856, Sarah E. Mallon   1/29/56-2
Hance, B. O. (Dr.), 10 Dec. 1857, Anna E. Wilson, dau. of
     (Rev.) Wm. T.   12/18/57-2
Hancock, William, 1 Jan. 1859, Mary A. Reay   1/ 5/59-2
Hand, John H., 25 July 1859, Margaret C. Scott   7/28/59-2
Hanister, Joseph, 14 Dec. 1852, Mary E. Selby   12/15/52-2
Hank, A. Summerfield, 13 Mar. 1858, Mary E. Vandiver, dau. of
     John   3/25/58-2
Hank, J. Wm. T. (Dr.), 30 June 1853, Anna M. Keener   7/ 2/53-2
Hanly, Michael, 18 Nov. 1858, Kate Ward   11/27/58-2
Hanlon, Patrick H., 1 Aug. 1859, Ellen Welty   9/ 3/59-2
Hanna, J. Wesley, 26 Nov. 1857, Anna Maria Hanna, dau. of
     William, Jr.   11/28/57-2
Hanna, John H., 10 June 1852, Sarah Heaney   6/12/52-2
Hanna, Robert, 13 Sept. 1857, (Mrs.) Elizabeth Brown, dau. of
     John Cornelius   9/17/57-2
Hanna, William Charles, 15 Oct. 1860, Rebecca L. Lawn   12/17/60-2
Hannam, Uriah Geo., 3 Dec. 1851, Sarah Ann Miller, dau. of
     Thos.   12/ 9/51-2
Hannan, Edward, 23 Aug. 1852, Cecelia Long   8/30/52-2
Hanshaw, John G., 21 Dec. 1854, E. Jennie Clark, dau. of
     John A.   12/27/54-2

Hanson, Elias, 21 Nov. 1854, Laura V. Mooney   11/22/54-2
Hanson, Enoch F., 14 June 1855, Caroline A. Pennington   6/16/55-2
Hanson, Ford B., 22 Apr. 1856, Ann Eliza Greenland   4/23/56-2
Hanson, George A., 23 Sept. 1857, Courtney C. Barraud   9/29/57-2
Hanson, J. P., 14 Nov. 1855, M. Louisa Scrivener   11/17/55-2
Hanson, John B., 4 Mar. 1858, Anna M. Carey, dau. of John F.   3/15/58-2
Hanson, Thos. H., 9 Mar. 1852, Anna Rebecca Hynes, dau. of Thos. 3/20/52-2
Hanzsche, Edward, 27 Nov. 1856, Kate Delano   12/ 1/56-2
Hanzsche, Frederick A., 29 Dec. 1853, Lizzie James   12/31/53-2
Hanzsche, Harry, 29 Feb. 1860, Lizzie A. Richardson, dau. of
     E. H.   3/13/60-2
Happersett, John B., 17 Dec. 1857, Sarah A. Sheeler, dau. of
     George   12/19/57-2
Harb, John, 25 Apr. 1859, Amelia Waise   8/ 9/59-2
Harb, John, 25 Apr. 1859, Amelia Weise; corrected copy   8/18/59-2
Harbaugh, Thomas, 1 Apr. 1851, Louisa Miller   4/ 2/51-2
Harbeson, Wm., 24 Dec. 1852, Margaret Wilson   1/18/53-2
Harbuck, Samuel, 25 Dec. 1859, Martha Allen   1/ 3/60-2
Harday, Samuel, 19 Aug. 1858, Mary Ann Harris; 8/25/58-2   8/26/58-2
Hardcastle, Edmund L. F., 28 Sept. 1853, Sallie D. Hughlett,
     dau. of (Col.) Wm.   10/ 1/53-2
Hardeeng, James, 20 Dec. 1859, Barbara Jane Williams   12/28/59-2
Harden, Joseph E., 13 Feb. 1855, Emily E. Leach   2/19/55-2
Harden, William, 7 June 1853, Lizzie S. Slicer, dau. of (Rev.)
     Henry   6/10/53-2
Harden, William, 20 Aug. 1857, Mary Winbourne, dau. of
     Philip   8/25/57-2
Hardenwerder, Louis, 1 Dec. 1858, Georgine Hayeulew   12/14/58-2
Hardester, David, Jr., 12 Jan. 1858, Rachael Ann Adams   1/25/58-2
Hardester, Thomas, 15 Jan. 1856, Josephine Zimmerman   1/17/56-2
Hardesty, George W., 28 Nov. 1855, Mary S. Nutwell, dau. of
     John S.   12/ 1/55-2
Hardesty, J. H., 25 July 1859, Fannie A. Gantt, dau. of
     Thomas P.   7/28/59-2
Hardesty, John W., 27 July 1858, Mary Jane Cadd   7/29/58-2
Hardesty, Joseph; no date given, Elizabeth J. Cox   1/25/60-2
Hardesty, Samuel W., 23 Oct. 1856, Lizzie A. Welsh, dau. of
     (Mrs.) Sarah A.   10/31/56-2
Harding, Charles H., 18 Feb. 1858, Ann E. Dorsey   2/23/58-2
Harding, James, 12 Nov. 1851, Henrietta M. Ridgaway   11/14/51-2
Harding, John H., Jr., 29 Oct. 1857, Louisa Willis   10/31/57-2
Harding, Joseph, Jr., 14 Dec. 1858, Mary E. Edelen   12/18/58-2
Harding, Richard A., 17 July 1859, Sarah Alice Woodall   7/19/59-2
Harding, William A., 17 Jan. 1854, (Mrs.) Rosanna E. Stokes   2/ 8/54-2
Harding, William H., 26 Apr. 1859, Susie R. House, dau. of
     William A.   4/27/59-2
Hardisty, John E., 15 Dec. 1852, Cornelia Ann Montague   12/18/52-2
Hardt, George, 22 Apr. 1852, Mary Ann Hissey   4/24/52-2
Hardwick, W., 1 Nov. 1855, Anne Keys; 11/ 3/55-3   11/ 5/55-3
Hardy, Benjamin R., 24 Mar. 1859, Annie F. Charles   3/26/59-2
Hardy, Geo. L., 1 May 1852, Catharine Batty   5/ 8/52-2
Hardy, George T., 15 Nov. 1860, J. A. Linegar   11/23/60-2
Hardy, Henry, 25 Jan. 1859, Susan A. Feenhagen, dau. of
     (Capt.) Thos. H.   1/27/59-2
Hardy, John M., 11 Sept. 1859, Mary A. Coleman   9/13/59-2
Hardy, John T., 13 Sept. 1859, Sarah E. Charles   9/14/59-2
Hardy, William H., 13 Feb. 1851, Mary Ellen Bean, dau. of
     Richard   2/22/51-2
Hardy, Wm. H., 7 Feb. 1859, Mary Ann Burk   2/14/59-2
Hare, Henry F., 22 July 1856, Catharine Bollinger   7/24/56-2
Hare, John L., 12 Feb. 1852, Mary E. Bull   2/13/52-2
Hare, William B., 27 May 1852, Ellender Kane   5/29/52-2
Hargrove, Kindred, 27 Oct. 1859, Louisa Ashton   10/29/59-2
Harig, Bernard L., 5 May 1856, Mary A. Wonn   4/ 4/57-2

```
Harig, John Joseph, 2-(?) Apr. 1852, Mary Anna A-(?)-ndschoen    4/28/52-2
Harington, Samuel (Capt.), 21 Nov. 1854, Susan E. Keene          11/22/54-2
Harker, Andrew J., 9 Oct. 1851, Frances A. Gladson, dau. of
     Michael                                                     10/15/51-2
Harker, Charles C., 23 Sept. 1858, (Mrs.) Rachel A. Brooks       9/25/58-2
Harker, John V., 16 Dec. 1852, Elizabeth Johaning                12/29/52-2
Harkins, John H., 3 Mar. 1859, Lizzie K. Toy                     3/ 4/59-2
Harkins, Stephen W., 23 Dec. 1859, Sarah E. Michael              12/29/59-2
Harkness, Thomas, 2 Aug. 1858, Agnes McCoy                       8/10/58-2
Harlan, Louisa G., 15 Feb. 1853, Isabella Grant                  2/18/53-2
Harley, James K., 21 Dec. 1857, Josephine E. Baker               12/23/57-2
Harman, A. R., 27 Nov. 1856, Fannie Eveline Ijams, dau. of
     J. Plummer                                                  12/ 3/56-2
Harman, Berzilla W., 19 Jan. 1860, Louisa Ann Shipley            1/26/60-2
Harman, Charles W., 1 June 1852, Henrietta Simmons               3/28/53-2
Harman, J. M., 4 June 1856, Ann R. Link                          6/ 7/56-2
Harman, Philip G., 8 May 1855, Eliza J. Buckingham               5/10/55-2
Harman, W. H. B., 28 Feb. 1857, Louise A. B. Larkin, dau. of
     (Rev.) J.                                                   10/21/57-2
Harmer, Saml. M., 9 Oct. 1855, Hannah L. Brown                   10/11/55-2
Harp, Chas., 6 Mar. 1853, Mary Woodfield                         3/19/53-2
Harp, Edward, 1 July 1851, Mary E. Shaw                          7/31/51-2
Harper, John C., 23 Nov. 1858, Rowie H. Auld                     11/27/58-2
Harper, Levi A., 1 July 1856, Sophia E. Merker, dau. of
     Andrew                                                      7/ 4/56-2
Harper, Samuel, 20 Jan. 1859, Martha Mc Elroy                    1/21/59-2
Harper, Thomas J., 31 May 1853, Mary A. Lafferty                 6/ 6/53-2
Harper, Washington, 14 Nov. 1855, Dianna Susannah Herlinger      11/20/55-2
Harper, William A., 27 July 1854, Sarah Martha Cripp             7/29/54-2
Harper, Wm., 17 Jan. 1853, Mary Angeline Norton                  1/21/53-2
Harper, Wm. W., 14 Oct. 1852, Isabella Stall                     10/26/52-2
Harr, George, 15 Nov. 1855, Elizabeth Whistler                   11/17/55-2
Harread, Wm. T., 24 June 1852, Mary C. Spence, dau. of
     Elijah and Mary                                             6/29/52-2
Harrigan, Andrew F. A., 21 Apr. 1853, Ann Matilda Petis          4/23/53-2
Harrimon, (?) (Dr.), 19 Oct. 1854, Mary Ellen Howard             10/27/54-2
Harrington, George W., 28 Apr. 1853, Mary M. Callaghan           5/ 3/53-2
Harrington, Henry L., 16 Nov. 1859, Maria Root                   11/19/59-2
Harrington, Joshua S., 6 Mar. 1851, Eliza Busch                  3/10/51-2
Harrington, Milton C., 4 July 1853, Eliza Ann Smith, dau. of
     (Hon.) P. F.                                                7/29/53-2
Harrington, Samuel, 15 Nov. 1858, Margaret Bradford              11/18/58-2
Harrington, Samuel, 9 June 1859, Susan Geoghgan                  6/17/59-2
Harrington, Stewart, 1 July 1851, Mary Amelia Lee, dau. of
     James H.                                                    7/ 4/51-2
Harris, Benj. G., 2 May 1854, Nellie A. Neale                    5/ 4/54-2
Harris, Benjamin, 1 Jan. 1855, Virginia Elizabeth Armstrong      1/ 8/55-2
Harris, David, 10 Apr. 1856, Harriet Williams                    4/14/56-2
Harris, Frederick, 18 Jan. 1859, Rosina Toy                      1/19/59-2
Harris, George, 10 Oct. 1856, Rebecca Craig                      10/14/56-2
Harris, Henry C., 25 May 1858, Eliza Smith; corrected copy       5/28/59-2
Harris, Henry C., 25 May 1859, Eliza Smith                       5/27/59-2
Harris, James, 13 Jan. 1853, Catharine Kelly                     1/17/53-2
Harris, James H., 29 May 1853, Ellen Bradford                    5/31/53-2
Harris, John P., 17 June 1855, Louisa Cooper                     6/23/55-2
Harris, John W., 31 Aug. 1851, Margaret Corbit, dau. of Isaac    9/ 2/51-2
Harris, John W., 1 Apr. 1858, Caroline M. Friedhofer             4/28/58-2
Harris, Nicholas, 30 Nov. 1853, Susan Thomas                     12/ 2/53-2
Harris, Robert, 30 July 1857, Mary E. Mead                       8/ 3/57-2
Harris, Robert W., 3 Oct. 1853, Mary Lizzie Tarring, dau. of
     Henry                                                       10/ 4/53-2
Harris, Theodore, 12 Apr. 1860, (Mrs.) Priscilla Thomas          4/16/60-2
Harris, Thomas J., 10 Sept. 1851, Emily J. Howell                9/12/51-2
Harris, William, 20 Dec. 1853, Sara A. Smith                     12/24/53-2
Harris, William A., 24 Dec. 1855, Sarah Ann Collier              12/31/55-2
```

Harris, William Henry, 11 Oct. 1855, Susan Johnson   10/12/55-2
Harris, Wm. H., 16 June 1857, Henrietta Gould   6/18/57-2
Harrison, Charles E., 29 Nov. 1860, Georgeanna Price   12/11/60-2
Harrison, Clement, 11 Nov. 1858, Martha Cramblett   11/13/58-2
Harrison, E. H., 25 Nov. 1858, Juliet Gardner, dau. of Geo. F. 7/19/59-2
Harrison, George, 5 Jan. 1854, Barbara E. Knapp   2/ 8/54-2
Harrison, George L., 20 Nov. 1855, Helen Davidge   11/24/55-2
Harrison, George W., 8 Feb. 1853, Virginia Smith   2/11/53-2
Harrison, Henry E., 17 July 1856, Emily H. Denison   7/25/56-2
Harrison, J. W., 13 Feb. 1851, Mary A. Medcalf   2/17/51-2
Harrison, James C., 13 Sept. 1855, (Mrs.) Sarah J. Trogler;
   9/15/55-2   9/18/55-2
Harrison, John O., 25 June 1852, Catharine Herling, dau. of
   George   6/29/52-2
Harrison, Mark, 26 June 1852, Margaret Davis   7/ 1/52-2
Harrison, Phil. L., 23 Jan. 1851, Kate M. Wright   1/25/51-2
Harrison, Robert G., 14 July 1859, Mary E. Hughes   7/16/59-2
Harrison, Samuel, 27 Oct. 1857, Olivia Smith, dau. of
   Griffin   10/31/57-2
Harrison, T. Justin, 22 Nov. 1855, Fannie Browning, dau. of R. 11/26/55-2
Harrison, Thomas H., 30 Oct. 1855, Mary L. Beauchamp, dau. of
   Jesse   11/ 6/55-2
Harrison, W. H., 8 June 1854, Margaret Walker   6/12/54-2
Harrison, William, 18 Mar. 1852, Catherine S. Brayfield   3/24/52-2
Harrison, William, 27 Sept. 1860, Annie Carlisle   10/ 2/60-2
Harrison, William, 1 Nov. 1860, Mary Reed   11/ 3/60-2
Harrison, William H., 8 Dec. 1853, Mary J. McConkey   12/10/53-2
Harrison, William H., 30 Oct. 1855, Mary Ann Williams   11/ 1/55-2
Harrison, William J., 21 Nov. 1855, Mary E. Thomas   11/30/55-2
Harrison, William T., Jr., 7 Dec. 1854, Sarah Wilburn   12/ 9/54-2
Harrison, Wm. Thomas, 25 Oct. 1859, Margaret Jane Price   4/ 5/60-2
Harriss, Mathias, 18 Oct. 1853, Rebecca V. Sherwood   11/ 3/53-2
Harrmon, Marton, 26 Apr. 1853, Rose Weser   5/ 3/53-2
Harrow, Jacob, 25 Jan. 1859, Mary V. Ensey   1/26/59-2
Harryman, Walter, 17 Nov. 1856, Rebecca Boone, dau. of
   Stephen and Eliza   11/19/56-2
Harryman, William, 17 July 1851, Martha Ann Newcom   7/19/51-2
Harryman, William George, 19 Aug. 1855, Margaret Long   9/ 3/55-2
Harsh, John Martin, 18 Aug. 1859, Elizabeth Jane Lowe   9/14/59-2
Harshbarger, William H., 16 Dec. 1858, Rebecca A. Tracy   12/25/58-2
Hart, Francis, 21 May 1857, (Mrs.) Mary Montgomery; 5/23/57-2 5/25/57-2
Hart, George, 20 Nov. 1858, (Mrs.) Amelia M. White, dau. of
   (Capt.) Thomas Clark   11/29/58-2
Hart, James T., 1 Sept. 1851, (Mrs.) Jane McElwee   9/11/51-2
Hart, Wm. James, 11 Nov. 1851, Mary C. Miller   11/13/51-2
Harten, Francis V., 1 Oct. 1857, Barbara Caldwell, dau. of
   Wm.   10/ 3/57-2
Hartland, Maurice G., 25 Apr. 1858, Susie L. Timmans, dau.
   of E. W.   6/15/58-2
Hartley, Charles, 20 Apr. 1851, Hester Ann Court   4/22/51-2
Hartley, Elias P., 10 May 1860, Martha Paxson   5/16/60-2
Hartlove, Enoch, 27 Nov. 1853, Amanda Smith   12/ 2/53-2
Hartly, John L., 31 Mar. 1853, Margaret Funk   4/ 2/53-2
Hartman, Nicholas, 30 Dec. 1852, Matilda Leigg   1/19/53-2
Hartmann, John P. F., 18 Nov. 1858, Ellen Swann   11/22/58-2
Hartner, John L., 2 Oct. 1856, Elizabeth Charick   10/11/56-2
Hartwell, Geo., 30 Oct. 1854, Rosina E. Bannerman   11/ 2/54-2
Hartzel, John, 12 Dec. 1854, (Mrs.) Eliza Hammet   12/14/54-2
Hartzell, Edwin H., 27 Sept. 1859, Mary F. Bullen   9/30/59-2
Hartzell, J. Franklin, 14 May 1855, M. E. Switzer   5/29/55-2
Hartzell, Jacob, 8 Feb. 1859, (Mrs.) Julia Burney; corrected
   copy   2/23/59-2
Hartzell, Jacob, 8 Feb. 1859, (Mrs.) Lulia Burney   2/22/59-2
Hartzell, John A. L., 10 May 1860, Mary A. Relnicker   5/14/60-2
Hartzell, John T., 2 Aug. 1858, Martha A. Collins   8/24/58-2

Hartzell, William H., 6 Sept. 1852, Elizabeth Longwell   9/10/52-2
Harvey, A. J., 4 July 1853, Sarah Ann Bratt   8/ 1/53-2
Harvey, Andrew, 23 Nov. 1853, Catharine Latchford   11/26/53-2
Harvey, George W., 14 Feb. 1860, Mary A. Evans, dau. of
    Benjamin   2/22/60-2
Harvey, Harrison, 21 Nov. 1856, (Mrs.) Caroline Trukenborg   11/24/56-2
Harvey, J. George, 11 Nov. 1852, Emily E. Burns, dau. of
    Francis   11/15/52-2
Harvey, Jno. F., 21 Sept. 1853, Lavinia C. Horn, dau. of
    Jacob   9/23/53-2
Harvey, Jos., Jr. (Capt.), 3 Oct. 1853, Catharine Dye   10/11/53-2
Harvey, Joshua, Jr., 24 Jan. 1860, Rebecca Bryan, dau. of C.   1/28/60-2
Harvey, Moses, 7 June 1859, Rebecca Jane White   6/10/59-2
Harvey, Robert J., 20 May 1851, Pamela Walus, dau. of Wm. T.   5/22/51-2
Harvey, Samuel F., 26 Jan. 1860, Jane Gibson   1/31/60-2
Harvey, Thomas F., 20 Sept. 1855, Amelia E. Jacobs   9/21/55-2
Harvey, William C., 29 Dec. 1858, Selina Timanus   1/18/59-2
Harvey, William Washington, 12 Jan. 1858, Elizabeth Ann Belt,
    adopted dau. of Humphrey and Ann G.   1/15/58-2
Harvey, Wm. H., 13 Dec. 1859, Sarah M. League   12/15/59-2
Harvey, Wm. H., 13 Dec. 1859, Sarah M. League, dau. of
    (Capt.) L.; corrected copy   12/17/59-2
Harward, Walter S., 3 Jan. 1854, Annie E. Clapman   2/ 1/54-2
Harwood, Edward O., 5 Mar. 1857, Margarette Anna Mask   3/10/57-2
Haryy, Llewellyn F., 14 Oct. 1858, Annie Harrison, dau. of
    Joseph, Jr.   10/18/58-2
Hashall, David, 26 Mar. 1857, Ann H. Free, dau. of Peter   4/ 1/57-2
Haslem, Thomas, 3 Oct. 1851, Charlotte Townsend   10/ 4/51-2
Haslett, James, 7 Oct. 1859, Mary McDermot   12/ 6/59-2
Haslup, Geo. H., 17 Apr. 1860, Georgianna E. Spurrier   4/20/60-2
Haslup, John, 5 July 1860, Catherine Baron   7/ 9/60-2
Haslup, Jonathan W., 22 Jan. 1852, Susan Harrison   2/ 3/52-2
Haslup, Lloyd J., 28 Apr. 1857, Margaret Frankland   5/ 5/57-2
Haslup, Marion J., 15 May 1856, Laura A. Hewett, dau. of
    John H.   5/16/56-2
Hasselberger, Louis J., 6 Aug. 1857, Catherine Reperger   8/10/57-2
Hasson, Hugh, 23 Dec. 1855, Ann Stein Back; corrected copy   1/11/56-2
Hasson, Hugh, 23 Dec. 1855, Ann S. Beck   1/10/56-2
Hasson, James, Jr., 6 July 1851, Elizabeth McLaughlin   9/10/51-2
Hasson, John M., 22 Dec. 1853, Sallie J. Glass   12/28/53-2
Hatch, Saml. T., 11 Feb. 1858, Lavenia C. Rhinehart   2/13/58-2
Hatcheson, Benjamin N., 10 July 1853, Sophia N. Letts   12/15/53-2
Hatheway, Albion L., 1 Mar. 1852, Annie E. Earley   3/20/52-2
Hatheway, Albion L., 1 Mar. 1852, Annie E. Easley; corrected
    copy   3/23/52-2
Hatton, Thomas E., 9 Apr. 1857, Ellen F. Hatton, dau. of
    George   4/15/57-2
Haubert, Adam, 8 Sept. 1856, Matilda Graham   10/22/56-2
Haubert, Harman Y., 29 July 1851, Mary Elizabeth McDonald, dau.
    of Martin Smith   8/ 1/51-2
Haugh, Solomon, 14 Sept. 1852, Catharine V. Colegate   9/16/52-2
Haupt, Charles M., 15 Nov. 1858, Elizabeth A. Miles   11/18/58-2
Haupt, John, 20 Feb. 1859, Margaret Ann Constable   3/ 5/59-2
Haupt, Joseph, 13 Nov. 1853, Sarah Ruckle   11/15/53-2
Haupt, Joseph, 13 Nov. 1853, Sarah Elizabeth Ruckle; corrected
    copy   11/16/53-2
Haupt, Joseph, 15 Aug. 1858, Mary Ann Clark   8/17/58-2
Haupt, Mathias, 6 June 1853, (Mrs.) Elizabeth Freeland   6/ 9/53-2
Haurand, William, 19 Oct. 1857, Carrie McDonald, dau. of
    Daniel   1/ 4/58-2
Hause, Benjamin F., 27 Oct. 1855, Mary A. Pouder   10/29/55-2
Hause, Geo. W., 29 Aug. 1853, Maggie C. Stauber   9/ 2/53-2
Haustaffer, Jno., 23 May 1858, Christina Gatchfelter   5/31/58-2
Haw, John F., 4 July 1851, Ann C. Shedrick   7/ 7/51-2
Hawk, David C., 24 Mar. 1856, Marcella Bell   3/27/56-2

Hawkins, Edward, 6 Sept. 1858, Rachel A. Watts   9/ 9/58-2
Hawkins, George P., 29 Nov. 1857, Mary E. McPherson, dau. of
     John T.   12/ 1/57-2
Hawkins, James H., 11 Oct. 1857, Ann M. Butler   10/13/57-2
Hawkins, Joshua, 15 Apr. 1858, Ann Elizabeth Smith, dau. of
     Cephas   4/17/58-2
Hawkins, Luther, 18 Dec. 1857, Margaret Ellen Macktimore   12/19/57-2
Hawkins, Robert S., 28 Dec. 1856, Susan Rider   12/29/56-2
Hawkins, William N., 17 Dec. 1850, Sarah J. Wood, dau. of
     (Capt.) John   6/ 6/51-2
Hawley, Charles C., 16 Feb. 1852, Eliza Jane Chace   2/21/52-2
Hawly, Chas. C., 16 Feb. 1852, Eliza Jane Chase, dau. of
     (Capt.) John, Jr.; corrected copy   2/23/52-2
Hax, John P., 10 Jan. 1855, Anna C. Hiltz   1/15/55-2
Hay, F. Marion, 27 Nov. 1855, Catherine Gwynn   11/29/55-2
Hay, John (Dr.), 11 Jan. 1853, Mary J. Dawson   1/13/53-2
Hay, John C., 17 Oct. 1859, Sallie H. Keyser   10/22/59-2
Hayden, Aloysius, 6 Sept. 1855, Eliza Jane Green, dau. of
     Richard C.   9/ 9/55-2
Hayden, H. Mozart (Dr.), 14 May 1857, Sallie A. Foard   5/20/57-2
Hayden, Henry (Capt.), 14 Dec. 1853, Maria Louisa Andrews,
     dau. of James   12/17/53-2
Hayden, John F., 23 Apr. 1855, Harriet A. Ogle   4/25/55-2
Haydon, JOhn H., 21 July 1852, Matilda Peterson, dau. of
     (Capt.) F.   7/26/52-2
Haydon, John H., 13 May 1858, Eliza P. Chapman   4/15/58-2
Hayes, Edward, 14 Jan. 1855, Mary Hesler   1/17/55-2
Hayes, Edward, 13 May 1855, Emily Chase   5/15/55-2
Hayes, Edward F., 6 Feb. 1860, Maggie C. Staylor   4/ 3/60-2
Hayes, Henry K., 10 Apr. 1855, Margaret J. Armstrong   4/12/55-2
Hayes, James, 30 May 1855, Margaret McHenry   6/ 1/55-2
Hayes, Thomas, 29 Nov. 1851, Maria Henderson   12/ 2/51-2
Hayman, John, 15 Apr. 1860, (Mrs.) Mary Jane Thompson   4/28/60-2
Haymon, Addison, 13 Jan. 1853, Leah Jane Adams   1/14/53-2
Hayne, Geo. W., 9 Feb. 1854, Sarah A. Bowen   2/11/54-2
Hayne, John F. (Capt.), 12 Aug. 1856, Kate Walker, dau. of
     Francis   8/15/56-2
Hayne, William, 13 Mar. 1851, (Mrs.) Ellen Jones   3/14/51-2
Haynes, Andrew Jackson, 27 Sept. 1857, (Mrs.) Elizabeth
     Henson   9/30/57-2
Hays, Archer, 15 Dec. 1857, Louise De Broux   12/25/57-2
Hays, Charles F., 7 Sept. 1857, Cordelia T. Gray   9/ 9/57-2
Hays, Charles F., 7 Sept. 1857, Cordelia T. Gray, dau. of
     George; corrected copy   9/10/57-2
Hays, Geo. Thomas (Dr.), 25 June 1851, Susan Hays, dau. of
     (Dr.) J. G.   6/30/51-2
Hays, Geo. W., 15 Oct. 1851, Amanda F. Mitton, dau. of
     John P.   11/ 4/51-2
Hays, James H., 26 Feb. 1857, Priscilla S. Bosley   2/28/57-2
Hays, Nathaniel W. S., 13 Apr. 1858, Maria C. Fulford, dau.
     of Alexander Mitchell   4/14/58-2
Hayward, Ely B., 4 Nov. 1857, Sarah W. Kelly, dau. of Eli and
     Lydia R.   11/14/57-2
Haywood, William, 15 Apr. 1857, Anna Rebecca Vincent   4/17/57-2
Hayworth, George, 1 Nov. 1860, Emily Berry   11/ 3/60-2
Hazard, Josiah, 28 Sept. 1852, Sarah Jane Sloan   9/30/52-2
Hazard, Robert A., 3 July 1851, Mary E. Dillehunt   7/ 8/51-2
Hazelip, Benjamin M., 14 May 1852, Mary E. Whitlock, dau. of
     John W.   5/19/52-2
Hazelton, Edward, 7 July 1858, Carriet C. Bennett   7/ 8/58-2
Hazlehurst, Henry R., 4 Oct. 1853, Lizzie McKim, dau. of
     David   10/ 5/53-2
Hazlitt, James, 30 Sept. 1852, Amanda M. Sears   10/ 9/52-2
Hazzard, Geo. W., 30 Sept. 1856, Mary E. Elder, dau. of
     Francis W.   10/ 2/56-2

```
Hazzard, Solomon W., 9 Sept. 1855, Harriet Ann Thomas            9/12/55-2
Heacock, Israel R., 14 Sept. 1852, Caroline Wheary              10/ 6/52-2
Heagy, William H., 9 Feb. 1860, Amelia C. Harris                 2/11/60-2
Heald, John, 21 Mar. 1854, Georgeanna E. Smith, dau. of
    John J.                                                      3/22/54-2
Healey, Owen, 17 June 1852, Kate Doyle, dau. of John Murphy      6/19/52-2
Healy, J. Oscar, 8 Mar. 1860, Rose M. Funk                       3/10/60-2
Healy, James, 1 Sept. 1852, Johanna Stack                        9/21/52-2
Healy, Thomas, 5 Sept. 1852, Anne McLaughlin                     9/ 8/52-2
Heany, James, 20 Oct. 1857, Kate Baker                           7/ 8/58-2
Heany, William, 9 Sept. 1852, Mary G. Osborn                     9/10/52-2
Heap, Robert, 23 Dec. 1852, Mary Ann Murphy                      1/ 1/52-2
Heape, David H., 29 Dec. 1853, Susan Thomas                     12/30/53-2
Heapes, William A., 11 Mar. 1852, Araminta E. Channell, dau. of
    Abel and Jane                                                3/27/52-2
Heard, William, 29 May 1857, Margaret Ann Jones                 11/20/57-2
Heaton, V. B. (Dr.), 9 Oct. 1857, Mary E. Clark                 12/ 1/57-2
Heatzman, Mathias, 5 July 1860, Margaret A. Poole                7/ 7/60-2
Heavel, Ross, 17 Sept. 1851, Anna Thompson                       9/19/51-2
Hebb, John S., 28 Aug. 1851, Sarah C. Thomas                     8/30/51-2
Hebbard, John, 21 Oct. 1852, Drucilla Gibbs                     10/26/52-2
Heberton, James, 2 Sept. 1858, Louisa Hinton                     9/ 7/58-2
Hechenthall, Louis M., 20 Mar. 1855, Laura V. White              8/26/55-2
Hecht, Lewis, 6 Apr. 1856, Caroline Himmelreich; corrected
    copy                                                         4/ 9/56-2
Hecht, Lewis, 6 Apr. 1856, Cerleim Himmelreich                   4/ 8/56-2
Heck, Frederick W., 15 May 1856, Sarah Jane Neely                6/ 6/56-2
Heck, Geo. C. L., 25 Dec. 1852, Julia Ann C. Waltjen            12/27/52-2
Heckrotte, Charles J., 26 July 1854, Mary Jane Brown             6/ 2/55-2
Heckrotte, William, 3 Sept. 1851, Ruth Ann Thomson               9/ 8/51-2
Hedian, Martin, 2 Oct. 1854, Mary Emma Leach, dau. of William   10/13/54-2
Hedian, P. Z., 20 Dec. 1853, Mary A. Maffey, dau. of A.         12/21/53-2
Hedinger, James H., 16 Feb. 1852, Mary E. Burgess                2/19/52-2
Hedington, Jas., 15 Nov. 1859, Caroline V. Davis                11/18/59-2
Hedley, Anthony, 8 Sept. 1859, Mary E. Baker                     9/10/59-2
Hedrick, Antone, 26 Jan. 1854, Susanna Roupp                     1/31/54-2
Hedrick, William, 21 May 1857, Julia Potter                      5/25/57-2
Hedrick, William, 21 May 1857, (Mrs.) Julia L. Potter;
    corrected copy                                               5/26/57-2
Hedrick, William, 18 Sept. 1860, Mary Funk                       9/22/60-2
Heffner, John, 24 Oct. 1852, Mary Shilling                      10/25/52-2
Hegeley, John A., 7 Mar. 1859, Susey Bishop                      3/15/59-2
Heilbrun, Joseph, 13 Jan. 1858, Lizzie L. Sommers, dau. of E.    1/22/58-2
Heinecker, Theodore, 18 Mar. 1855, (Mrs.) A. E. Barbes           3/26/55-2
Heir, Christian, 13 June 1852, (Mrs.) Susannah Young             6/17/52-2
Heiss, J. F., 14 Feb. 1860, Kate Fisher                          2/29/60-2
Heiss, Wm. H., 21 Jan. 1851, R. Harriet Whaley, dau. of Thos.    1/28/51-2
Hellen, Luke W., 31 Aug. 1852, Mary Appelton                     9/ 3/52-2
Helm, Erasmus, 12 July 1853, Mary Ann Goodwin, dau. of Robt.
    Hart                                                         7/14/53-2
Helm, Jos. H., 27 Sept. 1852, Margaret P. Crowly                 9/29/52-2
Helm, Leonard A., 11 Mar. 1852, Eleanor Martha Haney, dau. of
    Daniel                                                       3/22/52-2
Helmling, Charles A., 13 Jan. 1860, Sophia V. Stewart            2/ 8/60-2
Helmling, George R., 18 Oct. 1858, Eliza A. Fennell             10/20/58-2
Helms, John B., 23 Jan. 1853, Sarah Jane Sindall                 1/25/53-2
Helmuth, Wm. T., 10 Feb. 1859, Fannie Ida Pritchard, dau. of
    John N.                                                      2/18/59-2
Helvestine, Lewis B., 1 Apr. 1852, Elizabeth Ann Boden           4/ 3/52-2
Hemenway, Appleton S., 5 Feb. 1856, Mary E. Patton               2/ 6/56-2
Hemmick, Jacob, Sr., 26 Oct. 1853, Eliza Stockett, dau. of
    Benjamin Williams                                           11/14/53-2
Henck, Frederick W., 2 June 1853, Sarah Andrews, dau. of
    Robert                                                       6/ 7/53-2
Henck, J. H., 1 June 1858, Louisa Roussell Meade                 6/ 5/58-2
```

Henderson, Benjamin F. (Capt.), 8 Nov. 1853, Elizabeth Ellen
    Jones, dau. of (Capt.) Alexander   11/10/53-2
Henderson, Gustavus A., 29 Nov. 1853, Mary Cecilia Mayger,
    dau. of Richard   12/ 1/53-2
Henderson, Henry C., 11 Jan. 1853, Sarah E. Start   11/14/53-2
Henderson, John F., 18 July 1859, Emma Bayzand   7/29/59-2
Henderson, John W., 26 June 1860, Georgeanna Russell, dau. of
    Henry   6/28/60-2
Henderson, Nicholas R., 20 Jan. 1859, Hettie M. Warfield   1/21/59-2
Henderson, William, 20 Nov. 1851, Sarah Jane Faucett   11/24/51-2
Henderson, William, 7 Oct. 1852, Susan E. Grant   10/ 9/52-2
Henderson, William, 12 Oct. 1852, Amelia Mann   10/15/52-2
Henderson, William M., 19 Nov. 1856, Jennie R. Tagart, dau. of
    Hugh   12/ 3/56-2
Henderson, Wm. B. (Dr.), 23 Dec. 1858, Fannie L. Thomas   12/25/58-2
Hendren, Hardy, 23 Mar. 1852, Emily Jane Rowe, dau. of
    William   3/25/52-2
Hendren, Judson, 11 Oct. 1860, Sallie B. Barroll, dau. of
    Wm. H.   10/13/60-2
Hendrix, J. W. (Dr.), 9 Nov. 1852, Helen Hines, dau. of
    (Col.) George   11/11/52-2
Henkelman, Frederick, 24 Aug. 1852, Julia Ann Lindenman   8/26/52-2
Henneberger, D. Clinton, 13 Oct. 1852, Margaret Ann Cole   10/14/52-2
Hennick, Christopher, 13 May 1852, Mary Ann Kelly   5/15/52-2
Hennick, John M. P., 1 Nov. 1859, Mary E. Jones, dau. of
    Wm. C.   11/ 4/59-2
Hennicks, James F., 22 Sept. 1859, Anna E. Reifsnider, dau. of
    Wm. and Mary   9/26/59-2
Henrix, Edward G.; no date given, Ann Mason   2/15/56-2
Henry, Edward J., 31 Dec. 1855, Annie Israel   1/ 1/56-2
Henry, James, 4 Mar. 1852, Rachel Amelia Clements, dau. of
    John S.   3/ 5/52-2
Henry, James Buchanan, 9 Aug. 1859, Mary H. Nicholson, dau. of
    (Col.) Joseph H.   8/13/59-2
Henry, John, 4 May 1853, Sarah Pumphrey   5/20/53-2
Henry, John B., 3 Mar. 1853, Mary G. Whitaker   3/26/53-2
Henry, John J., 28 Jan. 1851, Martha A. Wheary, dau. of John   1/31/51-2
Henry, John S., 14 Sept. 1851, Ann Penn   9/16/51-2
Henry, Patrick, 2 Nov. 1854, Ann Rebecca Smith   11/ 4/54-2
Henry, Phadas, 16 Apr. 1856, Mary Ann Scott   4/19/56-2
Henry, Richard, 19 Oct. 1852, Elizabeth B. Levick   10/22/52-2
Henry, T. Walton, 16 Aug. 1850, M. Ann Coleman, dau. of Thos.   2/ 1/51-2
Henry, William L., 11 Oct. 1853, (Mrs.) Ann Wharry   10/13/53-2
Henry, Wm., 14 Sept. 1853, Ann M. Clements   9/20/53-2
Henry, Wm. P., 12 June 1856, Matilda J. Baker   6/21/56-2
Hensel, Philip, 13 Nov. 1854, Sarah Gormly   2/20/54-2
Henson, James D., 10 Aug. 1858, Lucretia Cooper   8/11/58-2
Henson, Jeremiah, 28 May 1854, Clara Vannekle   6/ 1/54-2
Henson, Oliver, 23 July 1857, (Mrs.) Indiana Young   7/25/57-2
Henson, William H., 17 Jan. 1855, Amelia E. Dore   1/18/55-2
Henthorn, James, 2 May 1854, Margaret Christopher   5/ 8/54-2
Heppela, Henry, 17 Nov. 1858, Mary L. Cole   11/22/58-2
Herbert, Alexander J., 3 Mar. 1859, Milcah Smith, dau. of
    John K.   3/ 4/59-2
Herbert, Charles; no date given, Margaretta M. A. De Vinsse   11/ 8/53-2
Herbert, Geo. L., 5 June 1860, Lizzie Hance   6/ 9/60-2
Herbert, John H., 12 June 1851, Sallie A. Sawyer   6/14/51-2
Herbert, Joseph B., 16 Oct. 1858, Mary Ann Dobbins   10/18/58-2
Herbert, L. Nelson, 19 May 1857, Leah E. Hoffman   5/21/57-2
Herbert, William, 25 June 1851, Elizabeth A. Herbert   7/ 7/51-2
Herbert, William B., 5 May 1858, Susan Barnes   5/ 6/58-2
Hergersheimer, Joseph, 29 July 1857, Margaret A. Sly   8/11/57-2
Hering, J. W. (Dr.), 17 Oct. 1855, Hettie Trumbo, dau. of
    Lewis   10/18/55-2
Herington, Francis P., 6 Oct. 1852, Agnes Clementine Pittenger 10/18/52-2

Herlin, Stephen, 7 Feb. 1860, (Mrs.) (?) Schuster   2/10/60-2
Herling, George, Jr., 24 Mar. 1859, Joanna Louisa A. Siegmann   3/26/59-2
Herman, Martin, 30 May 1854, Mary C. Thomason   6/ 2/54-2
Herman, William, 20 Sept. 1860, Hannah Eliza Holland   10/ 5/60-2
Hern, John F., 27 May 1850, Margaret Josepha Tucker   5/30/51-2
Hern, Jonathan, 20 Oct. 1851, Sarah Elizabeth Lerman   10/21/51-2
Herring, Benjamin W., 5 May 1857, Ellen Slaven   5/ 9/57-2
Herring, David, 22 Nov. 1853, Mary Jane McNeal, dau. of James   11/24/53-2
Herring, Lewis, 22 Dec. 1853, Matilda Brunner, dau. of
    Andrew   12/24/53-2
Herron, Levin D. (Rev.), 11 Jan. 1859, Sallie G. Belt   1/13/59-2
Hersch, Augustus, 5 May 1859, Mary Foster   5/10/59-2
Hersh, Frank, 20 June 1860, Eliza A. McClellan   6/23/60-2
Hershfeld, John A., 7 Dec. 1858, Sarah Johnson   12/24/48-2
Herten, Francis Y., 1 Oct. 1857, Barbara Caldwell, dau. of
    Wm.   10/ 2/57-2
Herzberg, Philip, 13 Feb. 1859, Bertha Thanhauser   2/15/59-2
Herzog, John, 7 Oct. 1851, Josephine Shiek   10/ 9/51-2
Hess, Emanuel, 18 Dec. 1853, Rebecca Rosenstock, dau. of
    Lewis   12/20/53-2
Hess, M. S., 18 Jan. 1857, Marian Arnold, dau. of Abm.   1/20/57-2
Hess, William O., 23 Nov. 1858, Lizzie Kehoe   11/29/58-2
Hessey, Richard A., 17 Mar. 1852, Ann S. Wise   3/18/52-2
Hessler, Chas. F., 9 June 1859, Sophia Caroline Knox   6/21/59-2
Heston, William D., 20 Dec. 1853, Laura M. Riley   1/19/54-2
Hetzler, Wm. E., 30 July 1860, Mary C. Murphy   8/20/60-2
Heuisler, Joseph S., 29 Mar. 1853, Kate McCann   4/ 1/53-2
Heuser, Chas. F., 26 Feb. 1856, Delia H. Colburn, dau. of E.   3/10/56-2
Hewett, Asahel H., 14 Oct. 1851, Catherine Jane Hartman   10/24/51-2
Hewett, Thomas H., 22 Jan. 1856, Henrietta Scoon   2/12/56-2
Hewitt, Geo. H., 25 Sept. 1855, (Mrs.) Sarah Frances
    Petherbridge   9/28/55-2
Hewitt, George W., 30 June 1859, Sarah E. Willis   7/ 1/59-2
Hewitt, Horatio D., 23 Aug. 1853, Maria Louisa Gade, dau. of
    John   8/25/53-2
Hewlett, James W., 21 Oct. 1856, E. Augusta Kempton, dau. of
    Samuel, Jr.   10/23/56-2
Hewley, William C., 16 Nov. 1858, (Mrs.) Lizzie D. Brown, dau.
    of James DuHamel   11/18/58-2
Hexter, Geo., 31 Jan. 1858, Amanda Kann, dau. of Julius   2/ 2/58-2
Heyse, George, 16 Sept. 1857, Eliza Balls, dau. of John   9/17/57-2
Heyward, James F. (Dr.), 4 Nov. 1851, Maria T. Presstman   11/ 6/51-2
Heyward, James F. (Dr.), 4 Nov. 1851, Maria T. Presstman, dau.
    of (Rev.) S. W.; corrected copy   11/ 7/51-2
Hibbs, Charles, 2 Aug. 1853, (Mrs.) Sophia Blakeney   10/10/53-2
Hibener, William H. Frederick, 23 Oct. 1853, Margaret Jane
    Hubbert   11/14/53-2
Hich, Marselas, 4 Feb. 1855, Elizabeth Taylor   2/ 9/55-2
Hichcock, Daniel, 31 Oct. 1852, Margaret Ann Sigler   11/17/52-2
Hichcock, James B., 6 Feb. 1856, (Mrs.) Mary S. Beasley   2/12/56-2
Hickman, Isaac L., 11 June 1851, Margaret Ann Taylor   6/17/51-2
Hickman, John T., 10 Dec. 1860, Sarah Pruitt   12/11/60-2
Hickman, Nathaniel (Gen.), 22 Apr. 1851, Margaret S. Floyd   4/25/51-2
Hickman, Wm. H., 10 Mar. 1853, Laura J. Hooper   3/21/53-2
Hickman, Wm. H., 22 Feb. 1860, Sarah Brooks, dau. of Joseph   3/ 6/60-2
Hicks, George A., 14 Dec. 1860, Mary E. Clark   3/21/60-2
Hicks, John, 2 Sept. 1855, Amanda E. Mitchell   9/ 5/55-2
Hicks, William G., 17 Aug. 1852, Sarah E. Waddell   5/ 9/53-2
Hieller, John, Jr., 29 Dec. 1859, Margaretha Heinlein   12/30/59-2
Higdon, Alexander, 5 June 1856, Ann Eliza Allison   6/ 7/56-2
Higdon, Andrew F., 6 June 1852, Elizabeth Ann Thomas   6/ 7/52-2
Higgens, Walter J., 27 Sept. 1857, Joseph M. Langley   10/ 3/57-2
Higgins, Joseph O., 4 Feb. 1858, Elizabeth A. Brown   2/ 6/58-2
High, David Henry, 15 Oct. 1860, Margaret Jane Preston   10/23/60-2
High, John, 25 Dec. 1853, Isabella Disney   12/29/53-2

```
High, John, 29 June 1858, Ann Eliza Neal                      7/ 7/58-2
High, Joseph H., 18 Nov. 1856, Mary A. M. Martin, dau. of
    (Capt.) Wm. C.                                           11/20/56-2
High, Samuel E., 30 July 1860, Mary A. Humes                 12/14/60-2
High, Thomas, 2 Mar. 1856, Ann Louisa Fishpaw                 5/ 6/56-2
Hightman, H., 19 Oct. 1851, Jane Martin                      10/22/51-2
Hilbert, Henry, 9 Aug. 1860, Georgianna Stone                 8/11/60-2
Hilbert, John, 2 Sept. 1851, Elizabeth Hilbert               9/ 4/51-2
Hild, Jacob F., 1 Sept. 1855, Susan Andrews                   9/ 4/55-2
Hildebrandt, Harmann, 19 Apr. 1853, Mary Catherine Wehn       4/21/53-2
Hile, Thomas, 14 June 1855, Christiana Farall                 6/18/55-2
Hill, Charles, 30 Sept. 1855, Mary E. Foxwell                10/ 6/55-2
Hill, Chas., 8 May 1851, Eliza Jane McCollam                  5/10/51-2
Hill, Edward, 29 Oct. 1856, (Mrs.) Elizabeth Hill            10/31/56-2
Hill, George H., 2 Oct. 1851, Jane J. Stevens                10/ 8/51-2
Hill, James, 19 Aug. 1858, (Mrs.) Sarah J. McGuffin           8/23/58-2
Hill, James Henry, 14 Feb. 1860, Eliza Ann Virginia Sorel     2/16/60-2
Hill, John, 12 Dec. 1859, Elizabeth C. Davis, dau. of
    Benjamin                                                 12/14/59-2
Hill, Nathaniel, 28 May 1857, Mary Amanda Myers               5/30/57-2
Hill, Nicholas S., 19 Jan. 1854, Ann Rebecca Anderson, dau. of
    Joseph C. and Eliza                                       2/15/54-2
Hill, Samuel C., 9 Oct. 1856, Kate Dunn                      10/11/56-2
Hill, W. G., 23 June 1857, Millie J. Burke                    6/30/57-2
Hill, W. S., 23 June 1857, Nellie J. Burke; corrected copy    7/ 1/57-2
Hill, William, 19 Mar. 1851, Jane Woodside                    3/24/51-2
Hill, Wm. B., 20 Nov. 1851, Sarah R. Creamer, dau. of
    Jeshua                                                   11/22/51-2
Hill, Wm. E., 14 June 1853, Mary V. Walter                    6/16/53-2
Hillard, Frank, 18 Mar. 1852, Amelia Ramsay, dau. of Robert
    Barry                                                     3/22/52-2
Hilleary, W. T., 22 July 1857, Margaret A. Ware               9/30/57-2
Hillery, O. W., 19 Oct. 1858, Maria L. Beall                 10/29/58-2
Hillyard, Charles, 11 Jan. 1855, Mary A. Chenoweth            1/16/55-2
Hilton, George, 2 Sept. 1855, Catharine McIntyre             9/ 4/55-2
Hilton, James, 19 June 1859, Laura Hilton                     6/21/59-2
Hilton, John T., 7 Nov. 1856, Marian E. Rutter               11/11/56-2
Hilton, William M., 10 June 1856, Catharine M. Bohanan, dau.
    of John                                                   6/11/56-2
Hilton, William M., 10 June 1856, Kate M. Bohanan, dau. of
    John; corrected copy                                      6/14/56-2
Hiltz, Charles W., 15 Mar. 1853, Sarah A. Towson, dau. of
    Thomas                                                    3/24/53-2
Himes, Wm. H., 20 Jan. 1859, Ella S. Whitter                  1/22/59-2
Hindes, Jos. F., 16 June 1859, Mary A. Seccombe, dau. of
    Thomas                                                    6/20/59-2
Hindes, Moses G., 14 Nov. 1854, Rachel Ann Wilson, dau. of
    J. M.                                                    11/21/54-2
Hindes, Thos., Jr., 2 Apr. 1857, Olevia J. Goodwin            4/ 4/57-2
Hinds, William S., 6 Jan. 1853, Emilie M. Barrow, dau. of
    Denwood H.                                                1/12/53-2
Hineker, Fred'k., 13 May 1852, Sarah J. James                 5/21/52-2
Hiner, Samuel, 17 July 1856, (Mrs.) Sarah Jane Jones          7/22/56-2
Hines, Edward, 17 May 1853, Mary E. Jones                     5/24/53-2
Hines, John C., 3 Feb. 1852, Isabella Weeks                   2/ 6/52-2
Hinkel, Adam, 21 May 1854, Christina Scheefer                 6/ 8/54-2
Hinkle, Jacob, 15 May 1853, Catharine Wallerweine             5/17/53-2
Hinkle, Richard (Rev.), 10 Feb. 1859, Lizzie H. Purvis, dau. of
    James F.                                                  2/12/59-2
Hinkley, George, 29 Oct. 1856, Elting Mary Loder             10/31/56-2
Hinkley, Willard H., 14 June 1855, Rebecca B. Robb, dau. of
    John A.; corrected copy                                   6/18/55-2
Hinkley, William H., 14 June 1855, Rebecca H. Robb, dau. of
    John A.                                                   6/16/55-2
Hinman, Louis A., 1 Aug. 1857, Mary L. Hyland                 8/ 3/57-2
```

```
Hintear, Monroe, 24 Dec. 1853, Julia Ann Fray                    12/28/53-2
Hinton, James E., 10 Sept. 1857, Margaret A. Maddin               9/12/57-2
Hinton, John T., 15 Oct. 1854, Virginia Gudgeon, dau. of Jesse    7/11/55-2
Hinton, William, 14 Jan. 1851, Anna R. Hunt                       1/28/51-2
Hipkins, Charles D., 18 Dec. 1853, Mary Ann Clarke, dau. of
    Daniel                                                       12/23/53-2
Hipner, Conrad, 8 July 1860, Rosetta B. Thamerd; corrected
    copy                                                          7/11/60-2
Hipner, Conrad, 8 July 1860, Rosetta B. Tharnerd                  7/10/60-2
Hirschfeld, H. M., 25 Nov. 1857, Harriet Phillips, dau. of
    Jacob                                                        12/ 2/57-2
Hiser, Jas. H. F., 20 Sept. 1859, E. Carrie Littig                9/22/59-2
Hishly, Cecelia, 19 Nov. 1857, James McFall                      11/20/57-2
Hiss, Benjamin S., 23 June 1853, Sarah E. Spears                  7/ 2/53-2
Hiss, C. J., 23 Dec. 1852, Mary E. Brown                         12/29/52-2
Hiss, Emory, 9 Feb. 1860, Amelia E. Hudders                       2/14/60-2
Hiss, George H. C., 13 Nov. 1857, Catharine Weaver               11/17/59-2
Hiss, Jesse, Jr., 24 Feb. 1853, Ellen Parks                       2/25/53-2
Hiss, P. Hanson, 5 Oct. 1852, Susan Shirk, dau. of Henry         10/ 7/52-2
Hiss, William J., 20 May 1856, Annie Ames, dau. of (Rev.) E. R.   5/22/56-2
Hitchcock, Alexander W., 25 Dec. 1854, Mary Whitworth            12/27/54-2
Hitchcock, Wm. H., 16 June 1859, Mary A. Nelson                   6/17/59-2
Hite, William Edward, 9 Oct. 1860, Mary E. Choate, dau. of
    Richard                                                      10/13/60-2
Hiteshue, Wm., 18 Feb. 1851, Luciana Sweigart                     2/27/51-2
Hitselberger, John A., 29 Oct. 1855, Laura J. Morgan             11/ 2/55-2
Hitz, Florin, 28 Nov. 1857, Susana Dolf                          11/30/57-2
Hitz, Geo. W., 28 Nov. 1857, Lucy Wetzel                         11/30/57-2
Hitz, John, Jr., 5 Aug. 1856, Kate Shanks                         8/ 6/56-2
Hitzelberger, Charles H., 21 Mar. 1859, Fannie A. Stoutsberger    2/ 6/60-2
Hitzelberger, John A., 23 Mar. 1851, Mary Ann Meekins             3/25/51-2
Hobbs, Alexander W., 9 June 1852, Sarah E. Moore                  6/11/52-2
Hobbs, Andrew J., 7 Apr. 1859, Anna Mathilda Hunt                 4/12/59-2
Hobbs, Brice H., 13 Apr. 1854, Mary Ann White                     4/15/54-2
Hobbs, Charles Labaren, 21 Dec. 1859, (Mrs.) Annie McDaniel
    Rice                                                         12/24/59-2
Hobbs, Evan N., 3 July 1860, Letitia E. Winbigler                 7/18/60-2
Hobbs, Hamilton, 6 Apr. 1858, Jane Loud                           4/ 8/58-2
Hobbs, J. F., 6 Aug. 1859, Isabella C. Gosnell                    9/16/59-2
Hobbs, James H. (Rev.), 5 May 1859, Sophy E. Hobbs, dau. of
    George W.                                                     5/ 7/59-2
Hobbs, John H., 14 July 1851, Mary Ann Leach                      7/24/51-2
Hobbs, L. Lorenzo, 29 Aug. 1858, Martha Vinyard                  11/29/58-2
Hobbs, Nathan C., 29 May 1856, (Mrs.) Lydia Gosnell               6/ 7/56-2
Hobbs, Samuel A., 10 June 1858, Ann L. Smith                      6/12/58-2
Hobbs, William, 6 Oct. 1859, Lucinda Thompson, dau. of
    Lucinda S.                                                   10/ 8/59-2
Hobbs, William Z., 5 June 1859, Elizabeth Ann Bullin             10/19/59-2
Hobbs, Yelverton T., 28 June 1855, Josephine Fox                  7/ 6/55-2
Hobson, R. N., 24 Feb. 1857, T. J. Bosley                         2/26/57-2
Hobson, Richard V., 24 Feb. 1857, Laura Bosley, dau. of
    John A.; corrected copy                                       2/28/57-2
Hoburg, Wm. H., 4 Oct. 1859, Sallie Ann Johnson                  10/ 6/59-2
Hockel, Conrad, 21 Feb. 1856, (Mrs.) Catharine Kendall;
    corrected copy                                                2/26/56-2
Hoddinott, James W., 25 Dec. 1852, Mary Woods                    12/31/52-2
Hodge, James, 4 Mar. 1856, Amanda E. Hewett                       3/ 8/56-2
Hodges, John T., 18 Oct. 1860, Mary A. Davis                     10/23/60-2
Hodges, Jos., 23 Nov. 1852, Anne Hunt, dau. of John W.          11/25/52-2
Hodges, William R., 19 Apr. 1860, Matilda Phillips, dau. of
    S. H.                                                         4/23/60-2
Hodgister, Charles, 18 Aug. 1857, Mary McDowel                    8/21/57-2
Hodson, Eugene (Dr.), 21 June 1859, Celeste A. Bromwell, dau.
    of Josiah R.; corrected copy                                  6/24/59-2
Hoen, Ernest, 9 Nov. 1854, Fannie E. Nixdorff                    11/10/54-2
```

Hoey, James W., 13 Feb. 1855, Rachel Ebaugh   3/31/55-2
Hoff, John M., 14 Apr. 1859, Sarah E. Gardner   4/20/59-2
Hoffman, Anderson, 27 July 1854, Mary Jane Woodrow   7/29/54-2
Hoffman, Anderson, 31 Mar. 1857, Sarah Elizabeth Smallwood   4/ 4/57-2
Hoffman, Charles E., 1 Feb. 1855, Mary E. Myers   7/26/55-2
Hoffman, Daniel V., 13 Apr. 1858, Barbara A. Cline   4/19/58-2
Hoffman, George W. (Capt.), 5 May 1853, Mary E. Marynes   5/ 6/53-2
Hoffman, Harry, 7 Apr. 1857, Kate Hush, dau. of Henry   4/15/57-2
Hoffman, J. R., 12 Oct. 1859, Elizabeth Stitz   10/18/59-2
Hoffman, John, 28 June 1857, Elizabeth R. Robinson   6/30/57-2
Hoffman, John George, 11 Mar. 1856, Mary Elizabeth Adwood   3/18/56-2
Hoffman, John H., 26 Apr. 1854, Ann Maria Adams   4/28/54-2
Hoffman, Joseph, 27 June 1854, Mary Magdelena Lerch   7/20/54-2
Hoffman, Samuel, 15 Jan. 1852, Sarah Louisa Johnson, dau. of
     Ezekiel C.   1/20/52-2
Hofheimer, Zacharias, 24 Mar. 1857, Margaret Friedenrich   3/28/57-2
Hogarth, James A., 9 Oct. 1860, Ann P. Layman   10/18/60-2
Hogg, James D., 21 Sept. 1859, Etta C. Ruff, dau. of John   9/22/59-2
Hogg, James H., 30 June 1856, Margaret C. Raborg   7/10/56-2
Hogg, John S., 2 Aug. 1852, Julia Letitia Maxwell   8/ 4/52-2
Hogg, John W., 15 July 1852, Susannah Frances Goodwin, dau.
     of Lyde   7/16/52-2
Hogg, Samuel R., 29 May 1860, Sarah Jane Magniss   5/31/60-2
Hohlbein, Jacob, 30 Nov. 1853, Sarah A. Nock   12/14/53-2
Hohn, David, 1 Oct. 1855, Margaret Ramsey   10/ 2/55-2
Holbrook, George W., 25 May 1856, Kate M. Griffin   5/27/56-2
Holbrook, Henry, 24 Mar. 1852, Sarah Ann Grigley   3/27/52-2
Holbrook, Joseph T., 1 Nov. 1855, R. Amelia Stevens   11/ 3/55-3
Holbrook, Nicholas W., 23 Jan. 1859, Maggie A. J. McElroy   2/ 1/59-2
Holdcraf, Elisha, 7 June 1855, Bridget Smith   6/ 8/55-2
Holladay, Henry, 12 Feb. 1854, Jane Brown   2/14/54-2
Hollan, Jonas, 12 July 1860, Ann Mills   7/14/60-2
Holland, Andrew Jackson, 9 Oct. 1856, Mary Catherine Skinner   10/10/56-2
Holland, Bernard, 8 Feb. 1853, Catharine McTaige   2/24/53-2
Holland, Charles G., 5 Aug. 1852, Sarah A. Lyddan   8/ 7/52-2
Holland, Daniel A., 20 Mar. 1851, Mary J. Fuller   3/26/51-2
Holland, Edward S., 20 May 1858, Amanda Stuart   5/22/58-2
Holland, George M., 16 Aug. 1853, Bridget Devine   8/19/53-2
Holland, James, 1 May 1856, (Mrs.) Elizabeth Hahn   5/ 3/56-2
Holland, John C., 24 Mar. 1853, Eleanor Myers, dau. of (Capt.)
     John   3/26/53-2
Holland, John G., 24 Feb. 1859, Sarah Malvina Hipsley   2/26/59-2
Holland, Nicholas B., 29 Nov. 1854, M. Amanda Bouldin, dau. of
     Charles D.   11/30/54-2
Holland, Oliver P.; no date given, Saloma M. Stum   2/21/60-2
Holland, Oliver P., 16 Feb. 1860, Salome M. Sturm; corrected
     copy   2/22/60-2
Holland, Robert, 8 June 1859, Catherine Young   6/ 9/59-2
Holland, Samuel, 21 Mar. 1854, Christian Cladfelter   3/23/54-2
Hollansbee, J. M. (Rev. Dr.), 24 Nov. 1852, Eliza G. Stevens,
     dau. of Isaac   12/ 4/52-2
Hollenstein, John C., 28 May 1857, Emma Harman, dau. of
     Samuel   5/30/57-2
Holley, George, 15 July 1858, Mary Lanzell   7/20/58-2
Holliday, Daniel, 5 Feb. 1852, Fannie M. Rutherford   2/10/52-2
Holliday, Robert B., 18 Feb. 1851, Susan McHenry   2/19/51-2
Holliday, Wm. H., 11 Aug. 1858, Matilda E. Maynard   8/13/58-2
Hollin, Alexander, 12 Mar. 1857, Ann Sophia Simms   3/13/57-2
Hollingshead, D. A., 27 Dec. 1859, Ellenor Sullivan   12/28/59-2
Hollingsworth, Zebulon, 17 Sept. 1855, Kate F. Beam, dau. of
     Jacob   9/19/55-2
Hollins, C. Dugan, 26 May 1857, Mary Jane Wilson, dau. of
     (Com.) J. P.; 5/27/57-2   5/28/57-2
Hollinshead, William, 9 June 1859, Margaret Ann Brown   7/29/59-2
Hollis, William B., 3 Dec. 1856, Anna B. Clarke   12/16/56-2

Hollis, Wm. B., 1 Dec. 1856, Anna R. Clark, dau. of (Capt.)
    John S.   12/10/56-2
Hollitt, Joseph A., 24 Dec. 1854, Ann Rebecca Johnson   1/ 2/55-2
Holloway, Charles T., 12 Oct. 1854, Anna H. Ross, dau. of
    Reuben   10/13/54-2
Holloway, John M., 7 Sept. 1852, Fannie Bayley, dau. of
    William   9/ 8/52-2
Holloway, John Q. A., 21 Oct. 1854, Susannah P. McKew   11/ 1/54-2
Holly, Isaiah, 23 Oct. 1860, Elizabeth Dudley   10/30/60-2
Hollyday, Wm. M., 6 Jan. 1852, R. Louisa Powell, dau. of
    (Col.) H. B.   1/13/52-2
Holmes, Henry (Capt.), 23 June 1859, (Mrs.) Catherine Jones 7/ 4/59-2
Holmes, Henry C., 5 Aug. 1852, Mary Virginia Woods   8/ 9/52-2
Holmes, John, 3 Nov. 1859, Anne P. Pattison   11/ 7/59-2
Holmes, John J., 6 Dec. 1859, Virginia J. Hanney   12/ 9/59-2
Holmes, Solomon, 3 Feb. 1859, Mary Louisa Davis   11/12/59-2
Holmes, William Wesley, 20 Feb. 1853, Mary M. Fanwell   2/22/53-2
Holms, Samuel, 13 July 1854, Mary Elizabeth Baurgelt   7/15/54-2
Holt, Charles, 8 May 1853, Cassandra A-(?)-rey, dau. of James 5/16/53-2
Holt, Enoch T., 28 Sept. 1854, Sarah Ann Winders   10/ 7/54-2
Holt, Harrison (Dr.), 1 July 1856, Marion Ellen Boteler, dau.
    of Joseph J. and Ellen W.   7/ 4/56-2
Holt, Isaac P., 28 Apr. 1859, Catherine Harkens   5/ 3/59-2
Holt, John T., 9 Apr. 1860, Marion V. Horney   4/17/60-2
Holt, Wm. H., 30 Mar. 1851, Marcelleaner Personette   4/ 2/51-2
Holt, Wm. O., 28 June 1853, Sarah F. Brashears   7/13/53-2
Holthaus, John Henry, 14 Mar. 1859, Elizabeth Schwartzhaupt,
    dau. of Conrad   2/25/60-2
Holthaus, John Henry, 4 June 1859, Elizabeth Schwartzhaupt,
    dau. of Conrad; corrected copy   2/27/60-2
Holton, Charles A., 29 July 1860, Sarah A. Heath   8/25/60-2
Holton, Francis H., 20 Apr. 1854, Mary L. Higgins, dau. of
    (Capt.) Jacob   4/22/54-2
Holtz, Alexander, 25 Feb. 1859, Mary E. Fowler   2/28/59-2
Holtz, Charles C., 5 July 1859, Olevia C. Coleman   7/11/59-2
Holtz, David A., 3 May 1860, Josephine Beauchamp, dau. of
    Thomas   5/ 5/60-2
Holtzinger, E., 60 Oct. 1853, Zette Feldenheimer   10/ 7/53-2
Holtzman, William F., 6 Apr. 1854, Mary M. Patten, dau. of
    Richard   4/10/54-2
Homans, Benjamin, Jr., 15 Aug. 1854, Fanny Ellen Williams, dau.
    of Nathaniel F., Sr.   8/17/54-2
Homans, Benjamin, Jr., 16 Aug. 1854, Frances Ellen Williams, dau.
    of Nathl. F., Jr.; corrected copy   8/18/54-2
Home, John W., 17 May 1860, Sarah Elizabeth Hughes   5/22/60-2
Homes, Levi, 11 July 1860, Mary E. Cullison   8/21/60-2
Homrich, Jas. H., 5 May 1859, Elizabeth V. Marks   5/ 7/59-2
Hood, Francis B., 30 Dec. 1858, Josephine Lidard   1/ 1/59-2
Hood, John, 16 Nov. 1854, Alverda McAlster, dau. of James 11/18/54-2
Hood, John W., 2 Oct. 1856, G. P. Chaney   10/10/56-2
Hood, Reason, 29 Mar. 1853, Margaret T. Anderson   3/31/53-2
Hood, Richard, 16 Oct. 1851, Rachel Ann Whitman   10/21/51-2
Hood, Thomas John, 7 Apr. 1851, Julia A. Perkins, dau. of
    Thatcher   4/15/51-2
Hooff, John L., 15 Jan. 1855, Clara S. Bennett   1/16/55-2
Hoofnagle, Andrew J., 6 Dec. 1853, Elizabeth Donahue   12/ 9/53-2
Hoofnagle, Jno. G., 22 Nov. 1860, Eleanor C. Mitchell   11/28/60-2
Hook, Wm. W., 1 July 1858, Sarah Jane Sands   7/ 8/58-2
Hooker, Edward G., 8 Mar. 1859, Lizzie Horney   3/14/59-2
Hooker, George, 9 Jan. 1856, Martha M. Howard   1/11/56-2
Hooper, Charles H., 20 Apr. 1854, Eugenia Heckrotte, dau. of
    William   4/21/54-2
Hooper, Charles V., 14 Feb. 1856, Frances J. Watts   2/19/56-2
Hooper, Edward, 30 Mar. 1857, Sarah Ann Dunnig   3/31/57-2
Hooper, Frederick, 20 Jan. 1851, Martha Ann Collins   1/21/51-2

Hooper, George W., 8 Jan. 1857, Arietta Matthews, dau. of
  Wm.   1/12/57-2
Hooper, Iremich P., , 13 Sept. 1860, Alice E. Drake   9/14/60-2
Hooper, James, 25 May 1854, Mary E. Vernetson, dau. of Wm.   7/11/54-2
Hooper, James B., 26 May 1859, Marietta Greenwell   5/27/59-2
Hooper, Jeremiah P., 13 Sept. 1860, Alice E. Drake; corrected
  copy   9/18/60-2
Hooper, Theodore, 27 Sept. 1859, Margaret E. McWilliams   9/29/59-2
Hooper, Thomas H., 2 Dec. 1851, Mary Maria Young, dau. of
  Wm. G.   12/ 4/51-2
Hooper, Thomas J., 13 Dec. 1855, Eliza A. Codd, dau. of
  Pilkington   12/20/55-2
Hooper, William, 30 Sept. 1856, Mary S. Prout   11/ 1/56-2
Hooper, William J., 7 Oct. 1856, Emily Gladding; 10/10/56-2   10/11/56-2
Hooper, William R., 24 Dec. 1856, Elizabeth V. Williamson   12/27/56-2
Hooper, Wm. (Capt.), 31 Jan. 1854, Eliza A. Wells, dau. of
  Wm.   2/17/54-2
Hoopes, Charles, 11 Jan. 1854, Emma Hoopes, dau. of Caleb and
  Sarah   1/28/53-2
Hoopes, William P., 12 Oct. 1858, Elizabeth Cowman, dau. of
  Samuel S.   10/13/58-2
Hoopes, Wm. H. (Dr.), 23 June 1857, Georgiana Wilhelm   6/25/57-2
Hoopper, Aug. D., 9 Nov. 1855, Mary A. L. Pattison, sister of
  (Rev.) Rob. H.   11/15/55-2
Hoose, Will. S., 12 June 1856, Lucy Murray   6/17/56-2
Hoover, Chas. A., 21 Nov. 1858, Georgiana Brown   11/23/58-2
Hover, David R., 1 June 1857, Elizabeth Jane Thomas   6/10/57-2
Hoover, Francis W., 7 Apr. 1858, Louisa Turner, dau. of Lewis 4/16/58-2
Hoover, George R., 28 Sept. 1851, Anne E. Bishop   9/30/51-2
Hoover, J. W. (Rev.), 17 Feb. 1852, Emily Sanford Brown, dau.
  of Thomas   2/19/52-2
Hoover, Jacob, 6 May 1851, Caroline Heidler   5/ 9/51-2
Hope, James Barrow, 10 June 1857, Annie Boush Whiting, dau. of
  Kennon   6/15/57-2
Hopkins, David M., 2 Dec. 1856, Amanda P. Lea   12/11/56-2
Hopkins, Edward A., 8 Jan. 1851, Martha Harris   1/ 9/51-2
Hopkins, George, 30 June 1858, Martha A. Bolins   7/ 2/58-2
Hopkins, Gideon P., 4 May 1854, Mary E. McClellan, dau. of
  Andrew   5/ 5/54-2
Hopkins, James H., 7 Sept. 1854, Mary E. Stewart   9/ 9/54-2
Hopkins, Jas. W., 26 Aug. 1858, Maria L. Anderson, dau. of
  F. D.; corrected copy   8/30/58-2
Hopkins, Jas. W., 26 Aug. 1858, Maria L. Anderson, dau. of
  J. D.   8/28/58-2
Hopkins, John, 10 June 1851, Sarah G. Harrison, dau. of J. W. 6/17/51-2
Hopkins, John T., 5 Jan. 1854, Mary Sophia Boone   1/ 7/54-2
Hopkins, Louis, 24 June 1855, Ann Elizabeth Wilson   6/27/55-2
Hopkins, Samuel B., Jr., 11 Aug. 1858, Lucy Andrews, dau. of
  John   8/12/58-2
Hopkins, Thomas, Jr., 24 Aug. 1858, Martha Ellen McCeney   8/28/58-2
Hopkins, William H., 1 Apr. 1855, Virginia Dashiell; 4/ 5/55-2 4/ 6/55-2
Hopkins, William M. S., 5 Jan. 1854, Sarah E. Fickey, dau. of
  Frederick   1/ 6/54-2
Hopkins, William S., 27 Feb. 1860, Ellen C. Robb   3/12/60-2
Hopkins, Wm. L., 12 Oct. 1858, Annie E. Reese   10/14/58-2
Hopkinson, M. A. (Dr.), 5 Oct. 1853, Lizzie Frailey, dau. of
  L.   10/ 7/53-2
Hoppe, J. L., 23 Aug. 1854, Hannah Reese   8/25/54-2
Hoppe, Wm., 1 July 1855, Margaret Bruning   7/ 2/55-2
Hopper, Thomas W., 29 Nov. 1855, M. Fannie Tolson   12/ 1/55-2
Hopps, Joseph, 21 Oct. 1856, Annie Henderson   10/29/56-2
Horan, James, 18 Feb. 1851, Margaret Jane Sparklin   2/20/51-2
Horan, William S., 30 July 1857, Sophia E. Wiles   8/ 3/57-2
Horigan, Cornelious, 20 May 1852, Mary Dunworth   6/ 1/53-2
Horn, Henry, 10 May 1860, Elizabeth Elliott   5/12/60-2

Horn, John W., 22 Feb. 1860, Elizabeth A. Wilkins   2/25/60-2
Horn, William, 27 Dec. 1858, Ann E. Green   2/10/59-2
Horne, George, 11 Sept. 1856, Amanda Hamilton, dau. of Wm.   9/23/56-2
Horne, Henry, 31 Oct. 1850, Ellen Gross   1/25/51-2
Horner, Jas. R., 6 Nov. 1860, Agnes V. P. Blacklar   11/ 8/60-2
Horner, John A., 15 Nov. 1853, Kate E. Forrester, dau. of
    Benj. F.   11/17/53-2
Horner, Levan H., 23 Feb. 1853, Emily D. Jackson   3/ 1/53-2
Horner, Wilson G., 7 Dec. 1858, Annie M. Bowers   12/10/58-2
Horney, Charles, 1 June 1856, Elizabeth Jane Joy   6/23/56-2
Horney, James W., 3 Sept. 1854, Mary Josephine Robelet   9/ 5/54-2
Horney, Samuel C., 23 Dec. 1857, Margaret A. Wells   12/25/57-2
Horney, Thomas, 24 Aug. 1852, Jane Score   11/ 9/52-2
Hornley, Thomas, 20 Feb. 1851, Martha E. McComb   2/22/51-2
Horny, Benjamin F., 12 Dec. 1859, Eliza Rebecca Dunning, dau.
    of Samuel   4/ 2/60-2
Horstman, John E., 17 Feb. 1852, Margaret P. Parrish   2/25/52-2
Horwitz, P. J. (Dr.), 2 Nov. 1854, Carrie Norris, dau. of
    Joseph Parker   11/ 6/54-2
Horwitz, Theophilus B., 9 Oct. 1860, Mary Barroll, dau. of
    James E.   10/15/60-2
Horze, John A., 21 Mar. 1852, Ann Maria Carter, dau. of Wm.
    and Sarah   3/23/52-2
Hosbach, Frederick, 10 July 1860, (Mrs.) H. L. Eggert   7/14/60-2
Hosefrose, Francis, 29 Apr. 1851, Mary A. Cassidy   5/13/51-2
Hoshall, David, 26 Mar. 1857, Ann H. Free, dau. of Peter   4/ 2/57-2
Hoshall, Jesse, Jr., 19 Apr. 1855, Sarah Ann Kroh   4/20/55-2
Hoshall, Nelson, 22 Oct. 1857, Joanna Hameshire   12/ 1/57-2
Hoskins, James, 19 Nov. 1857, Sarah J. Maire   11/21/57-2
Hosmer, Horace B., 2 Dec. 1853, Margaretta V. Tagart; corrected
    copy   12/ 6/53-2
Hosmer, James R., 21 Dec. 1858, Jeannie Albert, dau. of
    Augustus J.   12/23/58-2
Hoster, Wm. W., 10 May 1859, Martha P. Bacon   5/21/59-2
Hottes, George, 23 Nov. 1857, Mary Pfeiffer   12/ 2/57-2
Hotz, Charles, 12 Apr. 1860, Mary J. Appold   4/13/60-2
Houck, Alphonza T., 11 May 1859, Emma V. Netre, dau. of G. R.   5/14/59-2
Houck, Charles, 7 Oct. 1858, Mary A. Stockett   10/16/58-2
Houck, Charles A., 1 Apr. 1851, Frances J. Weaver   4/ 3/51-2
Houck, Geo. A., 26 July 1860, Emma R. Fryer   7/28/60-2
Houck, J. W. (Dr.), 15 Nov. 1852, Sudie F. Porter, dau. of
    Jas.   11/18/52-2
Houck, Jacob W., 12 June 1859, Mary E. Thomson   6/15/59-2
Houck, Samuel G., 16 Apr. 1857, Lydia A. Watkins   4/22/57-2
Hough, Benjamin B., 10 Oct. 1854, Jennet Marshall   11/29/55-2
Hough, Charles B., 12 Apr. 1860, Regina A. M. Horwell   4/13/60-2
Hough, R. R. S. (Rev.), 29 Mar. 1859, Virginia Baer, dau. of
    (Rev.) John   3/30/59-2
Hough, William M., 5 Jan. 1854, Frances V. Smith   1/12/54-2
Houghton, Charles E., 5 Oct. 1858, Carrie S. McMurray   10/ 6/58-2
Houlton, Thomas T., 26 Sept. 1854, Franciner D. Hill, dau. of
    John E.   3/ 5/55-2
Houlton, William, Jr., 1 Nov. 1859, Laura A. Punderson   11/ 3/59-2
House, Geo. W., 8 Feb. 1852, Mary E. Peregoy   7/28/52-2
House, John Q. A., 15 July 1852, Jane Thorpe   7/20/52-2
House, Wm. H., 26 May 1858, Margaret A. Determan   6/ 5/58-2
Houston, Andrew, 13 Sept. 1853, Agnes Bruce   9/16/53-2
Houston, James F., 27 Nov. 1859, Mary E. Anderson   12/ 6/59-2
How, Wesley, 20 Oct. 1857, Ellen S. Boardman, dau. of Lyman   10/21/57-2
Howard, Bernardo, 20 May 1851, Sarah Ann Folder   5/21/51-2
Howard, Charles, 5 Mar. 1854, Elizabeth Ann Holliday   3/ 7/54-2
Howard, Charles, 14 Jan. 1858, Susan Beho   1/18/58-2
Howard, Charles, 5 Jan. 1860, Mary Ann Carrell   1/ 7/60-2
Howard, Charles, Jr., 11 July 1855, Mary C. Winder, dau. of
    N. J.   7/24/55-2

Howard, Dennis, 3 May 1860, Phillis Ann Earl; corrected copy   5/ 7/60-2
Howard, Dennis, 3 May 1860, Phllis Ann Earl   5/ 5/60-2
Howard, George, 26 Dec. 1860, Julia Garrett   12/28/60-2
Howard, Henry, 22 May 1856, Ann Eliza Brown   5/23/56-2
Howard, Henry, 20 Sept. 1860, Elizabeth Jordan   9/24/60-2
Howard, Jarrett, 2 Feb. 1854, Susan Cahoon   2/ 3/54-2
Howard, John S., 7 Feb. 1860, Augusta H. Richardson, dau. of
     B. H.   2/15/60-2
Howard, John T., 24 Dec. 1857, Rose Anna Reed   12/28/57-2
Howard, Joseph, 14 Aug. 1856, (Mrs.) Rebecca Coleman   9/ 6/56-2
Howard, Joseph, 18 Oct. 1858, Amanda Evans, dau. of Thomas   10/30/58-2
Howard, Joseph, 2 Aug. 1859, Emily Jane Dickerson, dau. of
     James R. and Sophia   8/ 6/59-2
Howard, Joseph C., 3 Sept. 1857, Mary E. Mullen   9/ 5/57-2
Howard, Joseph J., 12 Sept. 1854, Henrietta E. Holding   9/14/54-2
Howard, Joshua, 25 Nov. 1852, Julia A. Bowen   12/ 6/52-2
Howard, Leonard P., 11 Mar. 1852, Sarah Ann Magness   3/13/52-2
Howard, Mathias, 26 June 1858, Anna Maria Lyons   6/28/58-2
Howard, Moses, 27 July 1854, Amelia Williams   7/28/54-2
Howard, Robert, 11 June 1854, Mary A. K. North   7/12/54-2
Howard, Thomas E., 25 Dec. 1860, Eugenia M. Brigham   12/27/60-2
Howard, Walter S., 3 Jan. 1854, Annie E. Clapman   1/31/54-2
Howard, William, 12 Nov. 1856, Elizabeth Williams   11/13/56-2
Howard, William P., 15 Jan. 1856, Mary E. Boulden   1/17/56-2
Howard, William Z., 19 Dec. 1859, Ann Elizabeth Ward   12/23/59-2
Howard, Wm., 13 July 1852, Octavia Duvall, dau. of J. H.   7/16/52-2
Howarth, James, 5 Apr. 1853, Mary Ann Howarth   4/12/53-2
Howe, Walter, 2 June 1857, Mary E. Biscoe   6/ 3/57-2
Howell, E. Milton, 21 Aug. 1856, Cammille Warfield   8/25/56-2
Howell, John H., 6 Feb. 1860, Georgeanna Crouch   2/10/60-2
Howes, Ezea C., 25 Nov. 1860, Maggie A. Reed, dau. of
     Charles W.   11/27/60-2
Howes, McCleney, 22 Dec. 1859, Elizabeth Ann Lovelis   12/29/59-2
Howes, William L., 16 Sept. 1858, Henrietta J. Foard, dau. of
     John B.   9/18/58-2
Howle, Peter Caze-(?)-ave, 20 Jan. 1859, Mary Louisa
     Ki-(?)-ckhoefer, dau. of A. J.   1/22/59-2
Hozter, Thomas G., 1 Sept. 1859, Mary A. Taylor   9/24/59-2
Hoyle, George A., 7 July 1851, Eliza Jane Lutts, dau. of
     John F.   8/ 8/51-2
Hoyt, Henry F., 16 Jan. 1860, Maggie C. Beard   1/25/60-2
Hubbard, Alex. J., 13 June 1855, Mary E. Brown   6/19/55-2
Hubbard, Andrew J., 4 July 1855, Dorothy E. Murphy   7/16/55-2
Hubbard, Daniel, 13 Jan. 1852, Mary A. E. Cook   1/15/52-2
Hubbard, Edw'd., 13 May 1851, (Mrs.) Allice Stanton   5/16/51-2
Hubbard, Edwin O., 12 Oct. 1854, Sarah B. Bowen   10/14/54-2
Hubbard, James N., 4 Aug. 1857, Elizabeth C. Watson   8/13/57-2
Hubbard, James W., 10 Jan. 1859, Elizabeth Croose   1/25/59-2
Hubbard, Samuel, 24 Aug. 1851, B. McElhaney   8/26/51-2
Hubbard, Willam (Capt.), 6 Apr. 1852, Sarah Mace   4/ 8/52-2
Hubbel, Benedict, 10 Nov. 1859, Anna Amelia Cross   11/11/59-2
Hubbell, J. S., 9 Aug. 1859, Carrie V. Wentz, dau. of
     Saml. H.   8/10/59-2
Huber, Casper, 5 Oct. 1856, (Mrs.) Dorothea Welder   10/ 6/56-2
Huber, Henry, 8 May 1851, Mary M. Burgess   5/12/51-2
Hudgin, Washington, 22 July 1857, Ann Jenario Cannon   7/25/57-2
Hudgins, Richard, 21 Sept. 1852, Ann Dudley   9/22/52-2
Hudnall, Milo E., 16 July 1859, H. Rebecca Davidson   8/19/59-2
Hudson, D. R., 13 Apr. 1854, Harriet Ann Bond   4/14/54-2
Hudson, Jas. H., 16 June 1857, Jemima Ledley   6/17/57-2
Hudson, John Henry, 2 Aug. 1857, Martha Alexina Smith   8/14/57-2
Hudson, John L., 3 Nov. 1851, Mary Dear   11/ 5/51-2
Hudson, William H., 9 June 1852, Nancy Allen   6/12/52-2
Hugg, James M., 25 July 1853, Sarah Thomas   8/ 3/53-2
Huggins, Henry S., 14 Dec. 1852, Margaret A. Myers   12/16/52-2

Huggins, Thos. J., 29 Mar. 1859, Jane E. Magraw	4/ 6/59-2
Hughes, Alexander, 25 Oct. 1859, Martha Buly	10/28/59-2
Hughes, Arthur (Capt.), 3 May 1855, Louisa Lewis	5/ 7/55-2
Hughes, Edward, 2 Dec. 1851, Margaret A. Collins	12/12/51-2
Hughes, George W., 24 July 1855, Laura C. Decker	7/25/55-2
Hughes, James, 11 July 1854, Mary C. Wiest	7/13/54-2
Hughes, John, 26 July 1853, Margaret Therese Faherty	8/ 4/53-2
Hughes, John S., 28 Feb. 1854, Mary A. Gray	3/ 6/54-2
Hughes, Joseph R., 12 July 1853, Rachel E. Lewis	7/20/53-2
Hughes, Levi, 1 Sept. 1857, Emily Glassco	9/ 3/57-2
Hughes, Michael; no date given, Julia Lynskey	7/17/55-2
Hughes, Peter, 16 May 1858, Sarah O'Neal	5/26/58-2
Hughes, Thos. J. (Dr.), 5 Oct. 1854, Sarah Fort	10/10/54-2
Hughes, William, 9 Jan. 1851, Catherine Murray	1/11/51-2
Hughes, William H., 6 July 1858, Emily Campher	8/21/58-2
Hughes, William J., 3 Sept. 1851, Margaret Burney	9/ 5/51-2
Hugo, George T., 20 July 1851, Theresa McCabe	7/22/51-2
Huhn, Wm. P., 5 Oct. 1852, Grace A. Hardesty	10/ 7/52-2
Hull, Robert, 7 July 1852, Susan R. Thompson, dau. of (Hon.) Lucas P.	7/13/52-2
Hull, William, 29 Dec. 1859, Carrie R. Sanks, dau. of H. C.	1/ 3/60-2
Hull, William, 26 May 1860, Catharine A. Mace	5/31/60-2
Hull, Wm. E. V., 25 July 1854, Henrietta Hugg, dau. of (Capt.) John	8/ 7/54-2
Hulme, William H., 28 Apr. 1853, Mary F. Melhorn, dau. of Jacob	5/ 4/53-2
Hultz, Samuel, 19 Oct. 1860, (Mrs.) Elizabeth Cassidy	10/26/60-2
Humes, Wm. J., 11 Feb. 1852, Mary S. Scanlan	2/13/52-2
Humrichouse, John R., 24 Aug. 1857, Virginia L. Hammond	9/ 2/57-2
Hunckel, Otto, 25 Aug. 1856, Kate Voneiff	8/26/56-2
Hungerford, Wm. L. (Dr.), 15 Sept. 1857, (Mrs.) Fanny A. Worthington	9/26/57-2
Hunichenn, August, 27 May 1851, Catherine Baker	6/ 5/51-2
Hunt, Benjamin F., 5 June 1859, Ida Simpson	2/27/60-2
Hunt, David B., 25 Oct. 1853, Mollie A. H. Gorrell, dau. of (Mrs.) J. J.	10/28/53-2
Hunt, German H., 16 Dec. 1856, Louisa Hiser	12/17/56-2
Hunt, German H., 16 Dec. 1856, M. Louisa Hiser; corrected copy	12/18/56-2
Hunt, Henry A., 2 Jan. 1851, Ann Rebecca Ford	1/ 6/51-2
Hunt, Jesse John, 17 June 1851, Mary C. Roszel, dau. of S. C.	6/18/51-2
Hunt, Joshua, 23 Dec. 1852, Margaret R. Keys	12/30/52-2
Hunt, Judson W., 6 July 1852, Margaret Ann Brown	7/10/52-2
Hunt, Montgomery, 14 Jan. 1858, S. Rebecca Bennett	1/15/58-2
Hunt, Thomas James, 13 Mar. 1851, Bedelia Drew	3/29/51-2
Hunt, Thos. J., 1 Apr. 1856, Margaret Murray	5/26/56-2
Hunt, William, 7 June 1860, Charlotte W. Merryman	6/12/60-2
Hunt, Wm. H., 26 Dec. 1855, Evelyn H. Morrow	12/28/55-2
Huntemuller, Herman F. D., Jr., 24 Apr. 1855, Helen F. Brodemeyer, dau. of Fred'k.	4/25/55-2
Hunter, A. B., 16 Jan. 1857, Mary McCollum	1/21/57-2
Hunter, A. E. (Capt.), 17 Jan. 1856, Ellen Olivia Taylor, dau. of (Capt.) William S.	1/21/56-2
Hunter, Adam M., 3 Sept. 1852, Jane Gallagher	9/18/52-2
Hunter, Andrew, 15 June 1859, Margaret J. Scott	6/20/59-2
Hunter, George, 1 Aug. 1857, Kate Staphens	8/ 3/57-2
Hunter, J. Harrison (Dr.), 23 Apr. 1857, Sophie Summers	4/25/57-2
Hunter, James (Rev.), 30 Mar. 1852, Elizabeth A. Lowe, dau. of John	4/ 1/52-2
Hunter, John F., 30 Apr. 1860, Mary R. Watson	5/ 1/60-2
Hunter, John T., 26 June 1860, Martha Jane Wroten	8/ 7/60-2
Hunter, P. G., 30 Mar. 1857, Cephronia Watts	4/10/57-2
Hunter, Richard, 29 Sept. 1856, Catherine Coburn	4/ 2/57-2
Hunter, Thomas V., 9 Mar. 1854, Mary Cameron	3/10/54-2
Hunter, Walter P., 5 June 1856, Mary C. Laub	6/10/56-2

Hunter, Wm. T., 2 July 1856, Frances Ann Brison   7/ 7/56-2
Hurd, Wilson, 5 Sept. 1854, (Mrs.) Emily Clark   9/ 9/54-2
Hurdle, Geo. W., 1 Apr. 1851, Elizabeth Moorhead   4/ 4/51-2
Hurley, George B., 11 Apr. 1860, Margaret Ellen Wiles   5/ 8/60-2
Hurley, John H., 2 May 1855, Mary E. Downs   5/ 4/55-2
Hurst, John, 19 Jan. 1860, Eleanora Gray   2/ 4/60-2
Hurst, John E., 25 May 1858, Mary R. Bell, dau. of (Dr.) Ephraim   5/26/58-2
Hurst, John M., 15 Nov. 1860, Amelia Cross   11/21/60-2
Hurst, Leonard C., 1 May 1860, Margaret Walters   5/ 5/60-2
Hurst, Leonard C., 1 May 1860, Margaret Watkins; corrected
     copy   5/ 7/60-2
Hurst, Thos. A., 3 Oct. 1854, Barbara Nagengast   10/10/54-2
Hurst, William R., 22 Dec. 1856, Annie E. Fooks   12/24/56-2
Hurt, Lloyd B., 5 May 1854, Clara E. Chappell   5/ 6/54-2
Huster, James G., 9 July 1857, Jane E. Lemmon   7/21/57-2
Hutchings, John T., 27 Apr. 1859, Sarah E. Anderson, dau. of
     James   4/28/59-2
Hutchins, Alonzo, 28 Apr. 1851, Mary A. Kennedy, dau. of N. R.   5/ 7/51-2
Hutchins, Joseph J., 17 Oct. 1860, Mary L. Hutchins   10/19/60-2
Hutchins, L. Harman, 27 Dec. 1859, Kate Kennard   12/30/59-2
Hutchins, Robert H., 9 Dec. 1858, Cynthia A. Nichols, dau. of
     Samuel   1/14/58-2
Hutchins, Samuel B.; no date given, Ann M. Frazier   4/ 5/56-2
Hutchins, Wm. Henry, 10 Feb. 1854, Emily Jane Matthews   6/26/54-2
Hutchinson, Hayward M., 7 Sept. 1859, Eliza C. Abbott   9/ 9/59-2
Hutchinson, James H., 11 Nov. 1856, Susan J. Kendall   11/13/56-2
Hutchinson, William E., 27 Jan. 1851, Ann Catharine Harrison   1/30/51-2
Hutton, George Nicholas, 3 Jan. 1859, Rebecca Ann Townsend   3/10/59-2
Hutton, Henry H., 15 Apr. 1851, Rachel M. Watkins   4/17/52-2
Hutton, John J., 8 Aug. 1859, Mary Brady   8/18/59-2
Hutton, N. H., 1 Nov. 1859, Meta M. Van Ness, dau. of
     (Lt. Col.) E.   11/10/59-2
Hutton, William, 25 Oct. 1860, Catharine Smith   10/27/60-2
Huzza, Albert J., 11 Sept. 1851, Charlotte Ann Miller, dau.
     of William   9/15/51-2
Huzza, Henry C., 8 July 1852, Elizabeth Snyder   11/17/52-2
Hyams, Solomon M., 20 Oct. 1858, Clara M. Carvalho, dau. of
     D. N.   10/26/58-2
Hyatt, Charles, 24 Mar. 1852, Bridget Murry   4/ 1/52-2
Hyatt, Edward, 1 June 1858, Margaret A. Wright   6/ 4/58-2
Hyde, George W., 1 Apr. 1851, Mary Bird, dau. of Francis   4/ 3/51-2
Hyde, James, 27 Nov. 1855, Charlotte Mitchel   11/29/55-2
Hyde, S. Gridley, Jr., 1 Oct. 1852, Mary A. Hall Ridgley   10/27/52-2
Hyland, James, 20 Jan. 1853, Elizabeth A. Adison   1/24/53-2
Hyman, William C., 15 Oct. 1854, Ann C. Bartlett   11/ 7/54-2
Hyman, Wm. C., 29 May 1853, Margaret A. Collins, dau. of
     Hugh   7/ 7/53-2
Hymer, Anthony, 6 Mar. 1854, Catharine Weeks; 3/25/54-2   3/27/54-2
Hymes, Alexander, 28 June 1855, Sarah A. Sturgeon   7/ 2/55-2
Hynes, C. W., 18 Dec. 1860, S. Lizzie Smith, dau. of
     Ferdinand   12/19/60-2
Hynson, Benjamin T., 4 Apr. 1854, Ann R. Simpson   4/ 8/54-2
Hyson, Augustus, 12 Aug. 1860, Eliza Ann Hughes   8/27/60-2
Hyson, Charles F., 22 June 1856, Mary Anderson   12/15/56-2
Iglehart, Richard H., 20 Nov. 1853, Mary A. Delay   12/ 1/53-2
Iglehart, W. H., 29 July 1852, Adelphine Hubert   7/30/52-2
Ijams, Alfred, 1 May 1856, Priscilla A. Meekins   5/ 5/56-2
Ijams, Gassaway W., 1 Dec. 1853, Mary Jane Clark, dau. of
     Wheeler   12/ 2/53-2
Ijams, John J., 12 June 1853, Rebecca A. Clay   6/13/53-2
Ijams, Van Buren, 29 Mar. 1853, Flavilla Spears, dau. of John   4/ 4/53-2
Ijams, Van Buren, 31 Mar. 1853, Flavilla Spears; corrected
     copy   4/15/53-2
Ijams, William H., 6 Oct. 1853, Isabella King   10/10/53-2

Ijems, Jacob W., 23 Dec. 1858, Annie M. Howard, dau. of John C.	12/27/58-2
Ilgenfritz, Marcellus S., 6 Oct. 1857, Lizzie J. Chamberlain; corrected copy	10/12/57-2
Ilginfritz, Oliver C., 24 Dec. 1854, Sarah E. Robinson	12/29/54-2
Ing, William, 13 Sept. 1860, Mattie E. White	9/18/60-2
Ingle, William P., 22 Sept. 1857, Eliza Crummer, dau. of Edward A.	9/24/57-2
Ingleson, Charles, 18 June 1857, Louisa Burgan	6/19/57-2
Ingleson, John C., 20 July 1851, Mary Wellbeorn	7/22/51-2
Inman, Barton, 24 June 1857, Martha E. Gadd	7/ 7/57-2
Innes, W. Melville, 2 Nov. 1852, Elizabeth A. Larrabee, dau. of Ephraim	11/ 5/52-2
Irelan, C. Davis, 29 Nov. 1860, Ellen Morris	12/ 6/60-2
Ireland, Hans, 15 Apr. 1851, Margaret Ann Hart	4/17/51-2
Ireland, Hans, 14 Sept. 1858, Martha A. Mackenzie	9/16/58-2
Ireland, J. Thomas, 27 June 1857, Sarah E. C. Alcock; corrected copy	7/ 1/57-2
Ireland, James G., 5 June 1851, Margaret Ann Humphreys, dau. of James	6/ 9/51-2
Ireland, John T., 27 June 1857, Sarah E. Alcock	6/30/57-2
Ireland, Robert, 28 June 1860, Joanna McDonough	7/ 3/60-2
Ireland, William, 28 June 1860, Virginia Richardson, dau. of Thomas J.	7/11/60-2
Ironmonger, Chas. B. G., 27 June 1858, Ellenor V. S. White	7/ 2/58-2
Irons, Edw'd. P., 20 Mar. 1851, Annie R. Sewell, dau. of Thomas H.	3/21/51-2
Irvin, J. W., 26 Aug. 1856, Ann Maria Sullivan	8/29/56-2
Irvin, James, 7 Aug. 1855, Kate Jakes	8/10/55-2
Irvin, James H., 3 Oct. 1853, Kate G. Schimp, dau. of J. A.	10/ 6/53-2
Irvin, John A., 3 June 1856, Emily Clautice	6/ 5/56-2
Irvines, A. Marshall *, 25 Aug. 1855, Beckie J. Mullen	12/18/55-2
Irving, John, 22 Feb. 1853, Matilda Ellen Taylor	2/24/53-2
Irving, Levin H. H., 27 July 1858, Mary J. George	7/29/58-2
Irving, Thomas J., 19 Oct. 1857, F. Amelia Delmas, dau. of Alexis A.	10/21/57-2
Irving, Thomas W., son of Leving G., 18 Dec. 1853, Mary E. Rowe, dau. of Thomas	1/ 5/54-2
Irwin, Alex'r., 8 Mar. 1852, Eliza Brewer	8/19/52-2
Irwin, Francis, 29 Mar. 1859, Catharine A. Coles	3/31/59-2
Irwin, William, 1 Jan. 1855, Sarah McAllester	1/ 2/55-2
Isaac, William M., 19 Sept. 1859, Ella Phillips, dau. of Thomas	10/ 3/59-2
Isaacs, C. C., 20 May 1858, Ama B. Rogers	6/ 2/58-2
Isaacs, Daniel, 16 Sept. 1860, (Mrs.) Anna Gasbury	9/18/60-2
Isaacs, George W., 24 Dec. 1858, Ann S. Askey	1/ 5/59-2
Isaacs, John W., 13 Feb. 1856, Julia A. White	2/26/56-2
Isaacs, T.; no date given, Isabella Jane Jones	11/ 5/56-2
Isaacs, Wm. W., 3 Jan. 1854, Sarah Jane Chew, dau. of Henry M.	1/13/54-2
Ison, William H.; no date given, Mary A. E. Gaither; 10/13/53-2	10/14/53-2
Israel, Dewitt C., 13 June 1854, Marie E. Cliffe	6/14/54-2
Jackel, John Jacob, 25 Dec. 1859, \Mary Stofel	12/28/59-2
Jackson, Albert W., 16 Aug. 1859, Adela V. Young	8/20/59-2
Jackson, Andrew, 13 July 1851, Catherine Wagner	7/15/51-2
Jackson, Andrew C., 24 Aug. 1856, Elizabeth E. Cape, dau. of John C.	8/28/56-2
Jackson, Charles, Jr., 14 Feb. 1854, Julia F. Brannan; 2/27/54-2	3/ 1/54-2
Jackson, Charles H., 3 Jan. 1854, Sarah F. Numbers, dau. of James	1/ 5/54-2
Jackson, Hugh, 22 Jan. 1852, Nancy Brown	1/26/52-2
Jackson, Jacob, 29 Sept. 1859, (Mrs.) Mary Emory	10/12/59-2
Jackson, James, 6 Jan. 1852, Adele Martin, dau. of Henry W.	1/ 8/52-2
Jackson, James, 8 Jan. 1857, Mary Ann Ball	1/13/57-2

Jackson, James, 14 Oct. 1858, Litham Pinkett	10/16/58-2
Jackson, James F., 23 Jan. 1855, Mary Ella Worthington	2/ 2/55-2
Jackson, James Thomas, 24 Apr. 1855, Lucinda Carroll Ford	4/28/55-2
Jackson, John, 8 Sept. 1859, Sarah Carrigan	9/23/59-2
Jackson, John D., 5 Dec. 1853, Mary Jane Cook	12/ 7/53-2
Jackson, John H., 8 Dec. 1853, Sarah W. Wilson	12/10/53-2
Jackson, Peter, 9 Oct. 1851, Malvina Johnson	10/11/51-2
Jackson, Philip, 26 Oct. 1857, Mary E. Lysinger	10/28/57-2
Jackson, Richard P., 29 May 1856, Mary Sophia Ward, dau. of William	5/31/56-2
Jackson, Samuel, 16 May 1854, Annetta Jones	5/17/54-2
Jackson, Samuel, 15 Feb. 1860, Mary E. Cooper	2/18/60-2
Jackson, Samuel, 19 Apr. 1860, Bell Bullin	4/23/60-2
Jackson, Samuel J., 14 Mar. 1853, Maria E. L. Parks; corrected copy	3/16/53-2
Jackson, Samuel J., 14 Mar. 1853, E. L. M. Sparks	3/15/53-2
Jackson, T. H. (Dr.), 5 May 1857, C. B. Eaton, dau. of William A.	5/ 8/57-2
Jackson, William, 13 Sept. 1860, Sarah Jones	9/18/60-2
Jackson, William G. (Rev.), 28 July 1852, Lydia E. Hollings- worth, dau. of (Col.) Jacob	7/29/52-2
Jackson, William R., 3 Feb. 1852, Annie Maria Patrick, dau. of John	2/ 6/52-2
Jackson, Wm., 16 Nov. 1852, Catharine Henson Jakes, dau. of Frederick	11/18/52-2
Jackson, Wm., 11 Nov. 1858, Mary E. Tucker	11/29/58-2
Jacob, B., 4 Oct. 1857, J. Raab	10/ 7/57-2
Jacob, James A., 3 Nov. 1853, Miranda Disney	12/ 1/53-2
Jacobs, James E., 25 May 1852, Isabella McDonald	6/12/52-2
Jacobs, John, 3 May 1853, Martha A. Manning	5/ 5/53-2
Jacobs, Samuel F., 1 June 1858, Lucy G. Owen, dau. of William	6/ 5/58-2
James, Daniel, 27 Mar. 1854, Louisa M. Lineberger	3/29/54-2
James, Geo. W. R., 6 Jan. 1856, Sarah A. Willson	1/14/56-2
James, George, 12 Apr. 1855, Annabella Little	4/16/55-2
James, Gilbert C., 15 Nov. 1860, Elizabeth Baum	11/17/60-2
James, Henry, 20 Feb. 1851, Amelia B. Cate	2/28/51-2
James, Henry, 5 Aug. 1860, Sarah Ann Parker	8/25/60-2
James, James, 15 Dec. 1857, Annie M. Evans, dau. of Thomas	12/21/57-2
James, John Harris, 8 Apr. 1856, Sarah Ann Magee	4/16/56-2
James, John R., 19 Jan. 1856, Mary A. Donaldson	1/21/56-2
James, Joseph, Jr., 2 July 1851, Sarah Emily Murray, dau. of Edward	7/ 4/51-2
James, Joseph, Jr., 10 Nov. 1853, Mary E. King; 11/12/53-2	11/14/53-2
James, Levi, Jr., 13 Dec. 1855, Lizzie F. Sanner, dau. of Isaac S.	12/15/55-2
James, Levi, Jr., 12 July 1860, A. L. Broadfoot	7/14/60-2
James, Richard, 23 Dec. 1853, Susanah James	12/30/53-2
James, Thomas J., 3 Jan. 1854, Sarah J. Fossett	1/ 4/54-2
James, William H., 4 July 1858, Mary J. Scarff	7/24/58-2
Jameson, Charles M., 10 June 1856, Harriet Josephine Canon, dau. of (Capt.) Thomas	6/12/56-2
Jameson, Horatio Gates, Sr. (Dr.), 14 Oct. 1851, Hannah Jane Dashiell Fearson	10/18/51-2
James, William Thomas, 2 June 1857, Ellen Adelaide Selway	6/17/57-2
Jamison, Archibald, 11 Sept. 1856, Henrietta E. Weber	9/13/56-2
Jamison, Daniel, 21 Oct. 1852, Mary Ann Preston	10/26/52-2
Jamison, Jos., 13 Aug. 1857, Sarah C. Barnett	8/15/57-2
Jamison, William S., 23 Dec. 1852, Rachel A. Reynolds	12/29/52-2
Janney, Wm. W., 12 June 1855, Marion E. Dean, dau. of Wm.	6/14/55-2
January, Charles, 7 Feb. 1860, Selima C. Leishear	2/14/60-2
Janvier, Edwin P., 24 Oct. 1855, Maggie S. Neuman	10/31/55-2
Jarboe, John A., 15 Oct. 1860, Maggie A. Bunting	12/ 6/60-2
Jarrett, Gideon, 7 July 1858, Sarah J. Quigley	7/10/58-2

Jarrett, William B., 8 Jan. 1857, Mary V. Caimes   1/12/57-2
Jason, William, 16 Dec. 1858, Mary E. Wing, dau. of (Rev.)
    Charles   12/16/58-2
Javens, Charles, 13 Sept. 1860, Isabella Lutts, dau. of
    John F.   9/14/60-2
Jay, Charles E., 16 Sept. 1851, Lucind Baylor, dau. of Jacob 9/18/51-2
Jay, Stephen, 28 Apr. 1856, Elizabeth A. Wellslager   7/16/56-2
Jeanes, George W., 30 Oct. 1856, Cassandra M. Walter   11/ 4/56-2
Jeanes, Nicholas, 4 Oct. 1855, Mary Elizabeth Gosnell   10/ 8/55-2
Jeckel, Julius, 13 Mar. 1859, Lena Graf   3/18/59-2
Jefferson, Nathaniel, 12 Aug. 1856, Margaret Young   8/20/56-2
Jefferson, Noah, Jr., 26 July 1859, Mary E. Gardner   7/27/59-2
Jefferson, Stephen, 20 Oct. 1853, Martha Davis   10/26/53-2
Jefferson, Thomas E., 5 June 1853, Susannah Fowler   6/ 9/53-2
Jefferson, Zachariah, 2 Aug. 1860, Averick P. Fleetwood   8/10/60-2
Jeffery, Enos, 8 Mar. 1852, Caroline Shipley   3/13/52-2
Jeffries, Granville S., 26 Oct. 1852, Phebe A. Nowland   10/27/52-2
Jeffry, James H., 24 May 1855, Sarah E. Ridgely   5/25/55-2
Jelly, Henry, 22 July 1851, Mary Ann Tracey   7/30/51-2
Jenkins, Albert, 4 Jan. 1854, Kate E. Ingeham   1/15/55-2
Jenkins, Augustus, 24 July 1851, Harriet Rainer   7/30/51-2
Jenkins, Busiris, 13 Dec. 1859, Diana Rich   12/15/59-2
Jenkins, C. D., 15 Jan. 1852, Mary F. J. Melville   1/17/52-2
Jenkins, Charles L., 23 Jan. 1854, Elizabeth Carter   1/25/54-2
Jenkins, Clement, 14 July 1857, Mary Trueman   7/16/57-2
Jenkins, Enoch Fenwock, 18 Apr. 1853, Martha A. Coleman, dau.
    of Jas.   4/20/53-2
Jenkins, George W., 18 Apr. 1854, Catharine T. Mansteadt   5/ 4/54-2
Jenkins, Henry, 13 Dec. 1855, Amanda J. Gettier   12/25/55-2
Jenkins, James H., 7 Sept. 1854, Rachel Webb   9/ 9/54-2
Jenkins, John, 6 Jan. 1859, Arra Ann Webb   1/ 8/59-2
Jenkins, John H., 22 Oct. 1857, Mary E. Erdman, dau. of G.   10/31/57-2
Jenkins, John W., 20 Oct. 1853, Margaret J. Palmer   10/25/53-2
Jenkins, John W., 21 Nov. 1854, Alice J. Shaw, dau. of T. P. 11/22/54-2
Jenkins, Joseph, 28 Oct. 1852, Ann Rayner   10/29/52-2
Jenkins, Josiah, 5 Jan. 1858, Augusta Wilson   1/ 8/58-2
Jenkins, Josias, 5 Jan. 1858, L. Augusta Wilson; corrected
    copy   1/12/58-2
Jenkins, Mark W., Jr., 16 Dec. 1851, Mary A. George, dau. of
    Wm. E.   12/17/51-2
Jenkins, Richard L., 23 Oct. 1856, Ellen Maloney   10/24/56-2
Jenkins, William, 5 Jan. 1858, Addie E. Webb   1/14/58-2
Jennings, John W., 31 Mar. 1853, Almira Gregory   4/ 4/53-2
Jennings, Joshua, Jr., 8 Apr. 1851, Louiza Siple   4/12/51-2
Jennings, N. Hynson, 16 Oct. 1856, Mary L. Sauerwein, dau.
    of Peter   10/21/56-2
Jennings, Samuel T., 11 Mar. 1856, Kate Kerner   5/ 7/56-2
Jennings, Stephen, 7 Aug. 1856, Jane Dillaha   8/ 8/56-2
Jennings, Wm., 27 Mar. 1856, Susan Newton   4/ 5/56-2
Jenson, Nicolay, 13 Nov. 1860, Ellen L. Hawkins, dau. of
    (Dr.) John L.   11/21/60-2
Jessop, George W., 21 Apr. 1859, Hannah E. Haile   4/27/59-2
Jester, B. Edward, 16 May 1860, Sallie K. Royston, dau. of
    Thomas   5/21/60-2
Jester, John W. *, 6 Jan. 1857, Marian Woodford   1/10/57-2
Jester, Joseph R., 4 Nov. 1855, Emeline L. King   1/29/56-2
Jewell, V. D., 9 Sept. 1856, Laura Thompson, dau. of Charles 9/12/56-2
Jewett, Isaac W., 11 Oct. 1853, Elizabeth O. Page   10/12/53-2
Jirdinston, James A. N., 27 Sept. 1853, Mary E. Brashears   9/30/53-2
Jisop, Samuel, 14 July 1851, Mary Myers   8/ 6/51-2
Jo-(?)-kel, Conrad, 21 Feb. 1856, (Mrs.) Catharine Fendall   2/25/56-2
Jobes, Jeremiah, 15 Nov. 1860, Mary Fnances Waters   11/19/60-2
Johannes, Edward, 22 Nov. 1859, Adeline Williams   11/24/59-2
Johannes, Martin J., 4 Dec. 1856, Sallie Brewington   12/ 8/56-2
Johns, Asbury F., 12 Nov. 1854, Sarah Caroline Giles   12/14/54-2

```
Johns, E. W. (Dr.), 13 Dec. 1854, Sarah A. Lovell              12/18/54-2
Johns, George W., 17 June 1858, Mary Skinner                    6/19/58-2
Johns, John A., 1 Oct. 1851, Laura J. Mainster                 10/ 7/51-2
Johns, Joseph, Jr., 3 May 1859, Susie A. Waring, dau. of
    Spencer M.                                                  5/ 6/59-2
Johns, Thomas, 31 Jan. 1856, Mary Ann Baison                    2/ 9/56-2
Johns, W. B. (Capt.), 11 Dec. 1856, Leonora R. De La Roche     12/13/56-2
Johns, Wm. A., 27 Jan. 1853, Eliza A. Franklin                  1/28/53-2
Johnson, Abraham, 25 Dec. 1856, Mary Ann Hile                   1/ 2/57-2
Johnson, Abraham G., 3 June 1856, Rebecca Frances Merryman      6/ 7/56-2
Johnson, Abram, 22 July 1858, Kate C. White; 7/23/58-2          7/26/58-2
Johnson, Alexander W., 11 Oct. 1857, Mary A. Gafney            12/ 8/59-2
Johnson, Aquilla, 6 May 1860, (Mrs.) Mary A. Waters             5/ 8/60-2
Johnson, Augustus F., 24 May 1852, Sarah Ann Thomas             5/27/52-2
Johnson, Benjamin F., 21 Oct. 1858, Susan A. Watts             10/23/58-2
Johnson, Charles, 5 Mar. 1856, Julia A. Wernwag                 3/ 6/56-2
Johnson, Charles, 15 June 1859, Kate Barns                      6/18/59-2
Johnson, Charles C., 16 June 1853, Martha Ann Griffin           6/18/53-2
Johnson, Charles R., 20 Jan. 1852, Charlotte M. Frazier, dau.
    of (Capt.) James                                            1/23/52-2
Johnson, Charles W., 21 Oct. 1858, Cecelia P. Jessop, dau. of
    Joshua                                                     10/22/58-2
Johnson, Chas., 28 Mar. 1852, Catharine Carey                   3/31/52-2
Johnson, Chas., 13 Jan. 1853, (Mrs.) Frances Pratt              1/15/53-2
Johnson, Chas., 5 June 1856, Hannah Barrett                     6/ 7/56-2
Johnson, Chas. W., 3 Oct. 1852, Mary Louisa Howser             10/11/52-2
Johnson, Chauncy G., 11 Oct. 1853, Miranda Davis, dau. of
    Thomas                                                     10/18/53-2
Johnson, Columbus, 2 July 1860, Emeline Grinage                7/ 6/60-2
Johnson, Dewitt C., 16 Sept. 1856, Lydia B. Ball, dau. of
    John R.                                                     9/20/56-2
Johnson, Edward, 30 Dec. 1852, Mary Ann Johnson                 1/ 1/53-2
Johnson, Francis M., 20 Aug. 1856, Anna Lockhart                8/23/56-2
Johnson, Franklin, 1 Dec. 1859, Harriet Martin                 12/ 3/59-2
Johnson, Freeman K., 14 Apr. 1856, Sarah Ann Overman, dau. of
    John, Jr.                                                   4/15/56-2
Johnson, George, 19 Dec. 1858, Sarah Hazleton                 12/27/58-2
Johnson, George H., 29 Apr. 1855, Josephine Ennis              5/ 1/55-2
Johnson, George M., 29 Apr. 1860, Lizzie H. Chaille            5/ 7/60-2
Johnson, George R., 10 Mar. 1852, Annie Chadwick, dau. of
    Radcliffe                                                   3/12/52-2
Johnson, George W., 22 Oct. 1851, Sarah E. Thomas             11/ 1/51-2
Johnson, George W., 6 Aug. 1857, Julia Ann Taylor              8/ 8/57-2
Johnson, George W., 20 Oct. 1858, Maggy McMullen, dau. of
    Richard                                                     1/22/59-2
Johnson, Grafton, 14 Nov. 1855, Elizabeth T. Carterwall, dau. of
    John                                                       11/20/55-2
Johnson, Henry, Jr., 26 Mar. 1855, Elizabeth Frantom           3/28/55-2
Johnson, Isaac, 23 Aug. 1855, Martha Nichols, dau. of
    William                                                     8/27/55-2
Johnson, Isaiah, 27 Nov. 1855, Ann Barnes                     12/ 3/55-2
Johnson, Jacob, 8 Sept. 1853, Ann Maria Hooper                 9/10/53-2
Johnson, James, 5 Mar. 1851, Agnes Bryson                      3/ 6/51-2
Johnson, James, 24 Nov. 1853, (Mrs.) M. A. Fultz              11/30/53-2
Johnson, James, 8 Dec. 1859, Elizabeth Johnson                12/10/59-2
Johnson, James D., 26 Apr. 1860, Mary E. Wherrett              4/28/60-2
Johnson, James H. A., 1 June 1858, Ellen Carr                  6/ 3/58-2
Johnson, James W., 17 June 1855, Hannah J. Debruler            6/19/55-2
Johnson, James W., 23 Jan. 1858, Hannah Michael                2/ 2/58-2
Johnson, James W., 13 Oct. 1859, Susanna Chambers             10/17/59-2
Johnson, Jas., Jr., 1 Oct. 1857, Frances A. Harris, dau. of
    Samuel R.                                                  10/ 5/57-2
Johnson, Jas. D. (Capt.), 3 Mar. 1853, Mary A. Sultzer, dau.
    of Sebastian                                                3/ 5/53-2
Johnson, Jas. H., 20 June 1860, Sarah Sims                     6/30/60-2
```

Johnson, Jas. W., 24 Feb. 1853, E. A. Stockham   2/26/53-2
Johnson, John, 25 Mar. 1852, Susan McClelland   4/ 2/52-2
Johnson, John, 28 July 1852, Julia Maden   7/31/52-2
Johnson, John, 16 Oct. 1860, Ann Johnson   10/23/60-2
Johnson, John G., 2 May 1859, Marrion M. Minton   5/ 5/59-2
Johnson, John R., 26 Dec. 1854, Elizabeth Shaw   12/30/54-2
Johnson, John S., 4 Dec. 1856, Harriet Holley   12/ 8/56-2
Johnson, John W., 22 Nov. 1855, Elizabeth E. Hebbern   11/24/55-2
Johnson, Joseph, 17 June 1856, Emeline Stafford   6/19/56-2
Johnson, Joseph M., 9 Oct. 1851, Caroline Costello   10/10/51-2
Johnson, Josiah, 25 Dec. 1856, Mary E. Boing   12/27/56-2
Johnson, Leonard H., 11 June 1851, Henrietta Jones   7/ 3/57-2
Johnson, M., 24 Oct. 1855, Sophia Hill   10/25/55-2
Johnson, Philip, 15 Sept. 1859, Sophia Wilson; 9/17/59-2   9/19/59-2
Johnson, Phillip, 15 June 1853, Julia Ann Ledsinger   6/17/53-2
Johnson, Reverdy, Jr., 6 Jan. 1853, Caroline Patterson   1/10/53-2
Johnson, Richard, 26 May 1854, Mary Jane Claughley   5/27/54-2
Johnson, Richard, 19 July 1858, Jane Dorsey   7/21/58-2
Johnson, Robert, 29 May 1860, Susan Jane Chew   6/ 1/60-2
Johnson, Samuel P., 6 Feb. 1851, Martha Jane Dixon   2/ 8/51-2
Johnson, Stephen, 27 Jan. 1859, Emily Ann Benson   2/ 5/59-2
Johnson, Stephen B., 27 May 1851, Gracey Ann Phillips   5/29/51-2
Johnson, Stephen H., 20 June 1860, Phiebe A. Spencer   6/23/60-2
Johnson, Thomas, 9 Jan. 1856, (Mrs.) M. J. Burgan   4/26/56-2
Johnson, Thomas J., 3 Nov. 1860, Margaret A. Stuck   12/25/60-2
Johnson, Thomas M., 23 Jan. 1851, Fanny Spedden   1/28/51-2
Johnson, Thos. W., 28 Oct. 1852, Martha Ann Gray   10/30/52-2
Johnson, W. R., 5 June 1855, Julia A. Adams, dau. of J. C.   6/ 8/55-2
Johnson, Walter, 12 Dec. 1858, Julia Donaldson   12/16/58-2
Johnson, Walter L., 22 Dec. 1853, Catharine A. Deaver   12/28/53-2
Johnson, William Milton, 3 July 1854, Mary Ann Bracken   7/ 4/54-2
Johnson, William Y., 1 Nov. 1854, Huldah M. Howard   11/ 3/54-2
Johnson, Wilmot, 24 Apr. 1851, Margaret Schuyler, dau. of
     Stephen Van Renseeiner   4/26/51-2
Johnson, Wm., 17 Aug. 1851, Lorrenna Mills   8/22/51-2
Johnson, Wm., 16 Aug. 1856, Rosa Worthington   8/23/56-2
Johnson, Wm. H., 17 Apr. 1853, Mary Ann Franklin   4/19/53-2
Johnson, Wm. M., 30 Apr. 1854, Mary A. Richardson   5/ 2/54-2
Johnston, Alexander, 3 May 1855, Margaret McPherson Owens,
     dau. of Isaac   5/ 9/55-2
Johnston, Arthur T., 19 July 1852, Ann Virginia Collins   7/21/52-2
Johnston, Christopher (Dr.), 26 Sept. 1855, Sally Smith, dau.
     of (Col.) B. P.   9/28/55-2
Johnston, Clement, 28 July 1853, Ellen McFaul   7/29/53-2
Johnston, George F., 26 Feb. 1856, Annie R. Waters, dau. of
     Thos. L.   2/28/56-2
Johnston, John, 14 July 1853, Rebecca Metz   7/16/53-2
Johnston, John H., 21 Aug. 1854, Caroline Dawson   8/24/54-2
Johnston, John T., 19 July 1855, Mary Jane Reese, dau. of
     Samuel   7/21/55-2
Johnston, Thomas Jefferson, 25 Dec. 1850, Charlotte Penn, dau.
     of Jacob and Elizabeth   1/ 3/51-2
Johnston, William A., 9 Aug. 1859, Fannie E. Courts   8/25/59-2
Johnston, William R., 11 Sept. 1858, Catherine R. Meekins   9/14/58-2
Johnston, Wm. (Rev.), 17 Aug. 1854, Virginia Lee Neill, dau.
     of Lewis   8/18/54-2
Johnston, Wm. J., 2 June 1853, Julia Henry   6/ 9/53-2
Joice, George W., 17 Apr. 1856, Mary E. Dill   4/22/56-2
Joines, Joseph L., 21 Sept. 1856, Jane R. Duvall   9/23/56-2
Jolly, William H., 16 Apr. 1857, Margaret E. McComas   4/20/57-2
Jonathan, (?), 16 Sept. 1852, Virginia R. Latham   9/17/52-2
Jones, (?) H.; no date given, Sarah Lavenia Henning, dau. of
     David and Mary A.   6/20/60-2
Jones, A. Jackson, 6 Dec. 1859, Sallie J. Cissel, dau. of Wm.   12/ 9/59-2

Jones, Adrain, 4 Mar. 1852, Mary Ann Moore	3/12/52-2
Jones, Alonzo V., 13 Feb. 1851, Eliza Ducatel	2/15/51-2
Jones, Andrew D., 11 Nov. 1851, Frances Moore; 11/13/51-2	11/15/51-2
Jones, Buckler (Dr.), 5 May 1852, Priscilla Agnes Myers, dau. of Jacob	5/ 6/52-2
Jones, Charles, 12 Jan. 1852, Margaret Ann McClana	2/23/57-2
Jones, Charles, 27 Feb. 1860, (Mrs.) Sarah Blottenberger	3/ 1/60-2
Jones, Charles H.; no date given, Mary Elizabeth Wheeler	2/27/57-2
Jones, Charles H. (Dr.), 14 June 1860, Mary E. Norris	6/18/60-2
Jones, Charles R., 28 Apr. 1853, (Mrs.) Rebecca G. Huffman	5/ 4/53-2
Jones, Christopher, 22 May 1851, Elizabeth Smardon	5/26/51-2
Jones, D. R. (Lieut.), 15 Feb. 1853, Rebecca Taylor, dau. of J. P.	2/17/53-2
Jones, David H., 22 July 1852, Agnes Read	7/24/52-2
Jones, Edward, 31 July 1855, Virginia Geoghegan	8/ 9/55-2
Jones, Eli V., 1 Nov. 1853, Hannah M. Bottrell	11/12/53-2
Jones, Elijah, 1 June 1852, Catharine Hays	6/ 9/52-2
Jones, Elijah A., 27 Sept. 1857, Josephine S. Smith	10/25/59-2
Jones, Francis W., 7 Aug. 1859, Mary A. Scott	12/29/59-2
Jones, G. M. C., 14 Sept. 1858, Angie B. Patterson	9/15/58-2
Jones, G. W., 29 July 1856, Evelyn S. Speights	8/19/56-2
Jones, Geo. W. R., 29 Jan. 1852, Louisa Rush	2/ 2/52-2
Jones, George, 14 Apr. 1851, Elizabeth Edmundson	4/15/51-2
Jones, George, 22 Dec. 1853, Mary A. Diggs	12/24/53-2
Jones, George, 13 Dec. 1860, Susanna Rush	12/14/60-2
Jones, George T., 14 Sept. 1859, Janet C. Rae	9/21/59-2
Jones, George W., 29 July 1856, Evelyn S. Speights, dau. of (Capt.) Jeremiah T.	8/21/56-2
Jones, Henry, 2 Aug. 1859, Sarah E. Rogers	11/ 4/59-2
Jones, Henry C., 2 Oct. 1856, Mary E. Fisher	10/ 6/56-2
Jones, Henry E., 15 Feb. 1855, Ann Sophia Tuck	2/21/55-2
Jones, Isaac, 7 Apr. 1853, Martha Ann Jordan	4/12/53-2
Jones, Isaacs S., 20 Oct. 1857, Mary A. Hampson, dau. of A. J.	10/22/57-2
Jones, Israel, 3 May 1857, Susan Nichols	5/12/57-2
Jones, J. R., 22 May 1855, S. L. Brashear	5/28/55-2
Jones, Jacob, 4 Sept. 1858, (Mrs.) Sophia Kirwan	10/ 2/58-2
Jones, Jacob G., 14 Sept. 1858, Sarah J. Baker	9/24/58-2
Jones, James, 1 July 1852, Eliza Almira Brownley	7/16/52-2
Jones, James, 31 May 1855, Elizabeth Swan	6/ 2/55-2
Jones, James, 19 July 1860, Eliza Ann Roads	7/21/60-2
Jones, James, 29 Nov. 1860, Ellen Maria Brown	12/ 1/60-2
Jones, James H., 17 Dec. 1857, Elizabeth Curtis	12/19/57-2
Jones, James H., 24 Dec. 1857, Mary S. Gogel	1/ 2/57-2
Jones, James M., son of (Capt.) James and Mary, 14 Jan. 1858, Mary A. Holebein	1/18/58-2
Jones, James R., 25 Oct. 1860, Julia A. Robinson	10/30/60-2
Jones, John, 7 Dec. 1852, Emily Drury, dau. of H. C. and Mary	12/ 8/52-2
Jones, John, 30 Oct. 1856, Ann R. Jubb	11/ 1/56-2
Jones, John H., 15 May 1854, Ellen A. Sterling, dau. of Thomas	5/17/54-2
Jones, John R., 15 May 1853, Lavinia Anderson, dau. of Aden	5/17/53-2
Jones, John R., 3 May 1859, Mary F. Keenan	12/29/59-2
Jones, John S., 22 Sept. 1856, Mary J. Tolbart	10/25/56-2
Jones, John T., 18 Apr. 1852, Hannah Jones	4/20/52-2
Jones, John Wesley, 31 Aug. 1856, Elizabeth A. Glaspie	9/12/56-2
Jones, Joseph T., 16 Nov. 1851, Mahaley Pead	11/22/51-2
Jones, Josiah M., 20 Dec. 1860, Alphonsa Lampley, dau. of Oliver E.	12/24/60-2
Jones, L. R., 1 Oct. 1860, E. S. Webster	12/24/60-2
Jones, Littleton, 14 May 1855, Sophia Watts	5/16/55-2
Jones, Martin L., 8 May 1860, Sarah Lavinia Kirwan	5/11/60-2
Jones, Nat. C., 8 Oct. 1854, Jane McSpadden	10/23/54-2

Jones, Oliver B., 7 Jan. 1854, Matilda F. Goldsborough,
   dau. of Wm. J.   1/10/54-2
Jones, Oliver B., 6 Jan. 1858, Mary Jane Godman, dau. of
   Thos. W.; 1/13/58-2   1/14/58-2
Jones, Reuben, 20 Dec. 1853, Julia W. Thomas   12/22/53-2
Jones, Richard, 11 Nov. 1858, Violet Reed   11/19/58-2
Jones, Richard H., 6 May 1858, Mary R. Hunter, dau. of Wm.   5/ 8/58-2
Jones, Richard P., 1 Jan. 1854, Sarah Jane Boldin   1/ 3/54-2
Jones, Robert H., 12 June 1856, Laura J. Jones, dau. of
   James C.   6/17/56-2
Jones, Rodger D. (Capt.), 9 Sept. 1852, Sarah Ann Stone   9/15/52-2
Jones, Samuel E., 7 Aug. 1856, Catherine Manion   8/ 8/56-2
Jones, Samuel R. (Dr.), 27 Oct. 1853, Mary E. Edmondson 10/29/53-2
Jones, Simon L., 8 Nov. 1855, Eliza Williams   11/10/55-2
Jones, Talbot, 14 June 1855, Margaret Ann Carson   6/16/55-2
Jones, Thomas J., 25 Oct. 1854, Angeline Slacum, dau. of
   Barzillai   10/26/54-2
Jones, Thomas S., 14 Oct. 1856, Angelina Sellers   10/16/56-2
Jones, Thomas W., 6 Sept. 1858, (Mrs.) Emma Stanley   10/30/58-2
Jones, Thos. W. (Capt.), 21 June 1857, Catherine Bunting,
   dau. of Smith R.   6/23/57-2
Jones, Uriah, Jr., 17 May 1854, Williamanna Pawley   5/19/54-2
Jones, Uriah, Jr., 20 Nov. 1859, Mary A. Butler   10/29/60-2
Jones, W. H., 3 Jan. 1860, Isabella Cariss, dau. of Samson   1/ 9/60-2
Jones, Washington, 11 Aug. 1851, Ann Eliza Barnet   8/12/51-2
Jones, William, 13 Apr. 1852, Marian J. Baum   4/15/52-2
Jones, William, 7 Dec. 1852, Mary Matthews   12/ 9/52-2
Jones, William, 12 Jan. 1856, Seville Ann Thompson   2/19/56-2
Jones, William, 14 Nov. 1858, Isabel Jackson   11/17/58-2
Jones, Willian, 8 Mar. 1860, Ellen J. Crow   3/12/60-2
Jones, William H., 15 Nov. 1855, Martha Snowden   11/17/55-2
Jones, William H., 1 July 1857, Henrietta Booker   7/ 9/57-2
Jones, William H., 3 Dec. 1860, Caroline V. Scarf   12/12/60-2
Jones, William T., 9 May 1854, Margaretta Roche   5/12/54-2
Jones, William T., 14 Jan. 1857, Mary G. Thompson   1/22/57-2
Jones, Wm. B., 20 June 1852, Mary S. Brown   6/22/52-2
Jones, Wm. H., 16 June 1852, Caroline A. Hague   6/29/52-2
Jones, Wm. H., 27 Jan. 1853, Emma Beatson   1/29/53-2
Jones, Wm. Horace, 29 Nov. 1859, Julia A. Demby   11/30/59-2
Jones, Wm. P., 17 May 1851, Louisa Brambell   5/27/51-2
Jonse, Isaac, 28 June 1860, Rebecca Pinar   6/30/60-2
Jordan, Edward, 12 July 1852, Julia Sutro   7/14/52-2
Jordan, Francis, 1 Jan. 1857, Isabella Virginia Shreck, dau. of
   Jacob N.   1/ 3/57-2
Jordan, Henry, 2 June 1859, Ann Eliza Jordan   6/10/59-2
Jordan, John, 16 Jan. 1851, Mary Elizabeth Levingston   1/23/51-2
Jordan, John, Jr., 25 May 1854, Mary F. Woods   5/26/54-2
Jordan, Marshall P., 1 Apr. 1858, Ellen F. Doland, dau. of
   Jas.   4/ 3/58-2
Jordan, R. M. (Dr.), 22 Dec. 1859, Emilih Alexander, dau. of
   B. W.   1/10/60-2
Jordan, Thos., 25 Sept. 1856, Frances High   9/29/56-2
Jordan, Wm. H., 8 Apr. 1858, Sallie E. Austin   4/10/58-2
Jorden, Samuel, 7 Nov. 1860, Amelia Jane Breaton, dau. of
   (Capt.) Samuel K.   11/ 8/60-2
Jorden, Thomas, 8 June 1860, Margaret McCaddam   11/ 1/60-2
Jory, Lewis W., 12 July 1857, Anne E. Colwell   7/18/57-2
Joseph, James, 18 Mar. 1851, Mary Ann Humphries   3/26/51-2
Joseph, John, 25 Feb. 1852, Margaret Jane Humphreys   2/27/52-2
Joseph, Wm., 8 Nov. 1852, Jane Johanna Brown   6/21/53-2
Josephs, John, 18 Nov. 1851, Mary Jane Wilson   11/20/51-2
Jouett, James E., 14 Aug. 1852, Galena Stockett   8/17/52-2
Joyce, Eugene T., 29 Jan. 1860, Margaret C. Gronewell   3/ 1/60-2
Joyce, John, 12 Sept. 1852, Mary Ann Peacock   9/16/52-2
Joyce, John B., 25 Feb. 1855, Josephine Anderson   3/13/55-2

Joyner, Thomas A., 22 Dec. 1859, Julia Gately, dau. of John   1/17/60-2
Joynes, Daniel, 21 Oct. 1852, Margaret Oler   10/22/52-2
Joynes, Daniel, 16 July 1860, Annie E. Rokess   7/18/60-2
Joynes, Levin S. (Dr.), 12 Dec. 1854, Rosa F. Bayly, dau. of
  (Hon.) Thomas M.   12/20/54-2
Joynes, Oliver, 22 July 1856, Mary Jane Hutchinson   7/26/56-2
Jubb, Lloyd, 11 May 1856, Sarah Smith   6/11/56-2
Jubb, Thomas J., 6 Sept. 1854, Charlotte Huberd   9/ 8/54-2
Jubb, William (Capt.), 6 Feb. 1853, Ellen Frances Watkins, dau.
  of Noble G. and Ann   2/11/53-2
Jubilee, Shepherd, 17 June 1860, Tisha Maiden   6/19/60-2
Judd, William H., 3 Nov. 1853, Amanda M. Stearns, dau. of
  John L. and Mary Ann   11/12/53-2
Judge, Arthur J., 12 Oct. 1859, Kate M. Clarke   10/13/59-2
Judge, John M., 30 Oct. 1855, Ellen A. McDermott, dau. of
  William   11/ 1/55-2
Judge, John M., 3 May 1859, Fannie M. Hubbard   5/18/59-2
Juhn, Isaac, 8 Jan. 1860, Caroline Delevie   1/ 9/60-2
Julian, Thomas, 8 May 1851, 8 May 1851, Margaret Ann Clark   5/10/51-2
Jury, Joseph Henry, 23 Feb. 1860, Eliza Jane Moore   3/20/60-2
Jury, Stephen, 17 Aug. 1859, Elizabeth Yeager   8/19/59-2
Juvenal, Abraham W., 1 Feb. 1853, Anna D. Reese, dau. of
  G. Daniel   2/ 3/53-2
Kahlert, Ernest J., 1 July 1858, Olivia A. Wilson   7/ 9/58-2
Kahn, Moses, 25 Jan. 1859, Rebecca Hess   1/28/59-2
Kain, Rufus K., 13 Sept. 1853, (Mrs.) Camilla Donelson Bohen   9/19/53-2
Kain, Wm., 2 Mar. 1854, Alsinda H. Nelson, dau. of Robt.   3/ 8/54-2
Kalkman, Henry F., 9 Aug. 1852, Mary J. Herbert   8/24/52-2
Kalmey, Jeremiah W., 23 Aug. 1860, Mary E. Davis, dau. of
  (Capt.) John   8/31/60-2
Kamp, Henry, 2 Aug. 1857, Emily V. Hays   8/ 8/57-2
Kane, James, 9 Aug. 1857, Ellen Curtis   3/24/58-2
Kann, J., 12 Nov. 1851, (Mrs.) Arnoldine Cohen   11/15/51-2
Kaudever, Andrew J., 10 Nov. 1857, Margaret F. Davidson   11/18/57-2
Kauffman, Geo., 8 Feb. 1853, Mary Elizabeth Rowe   2/10/53-2
Kauffman, Jesse A. D., 24 May 1859, Emma Virginia Lindsay   5/26/59-2
Kaufman, A., 4 Sept. 1859, H. Kaufman   9/ 7/59-2
Kaufman, Augustus, 11 July 1860, Lizzie A. Donaldson   8/27/60-2
Kaufman, John T., 22 Apr. 1856, Mary A. Bond, dau. of J. W.   4/26/56-2
Kavanaugh, Patrick J., 30 Dec. 1860, Kate R. Luber   12/31/60-2
Kaylor, John, 7 Sept. 1858, Mary Jane Hennaman   9/ 9/58-2
Kean, James (Capt.), 9 Nov. 1859, Helen M. P. Levering, dau.
  of Decatur E.   11/11/59-2
Keane, Michael K., 31 Jan. 1856, Mary A. Parks, dau. of
  P., Sr.   2/15/56-2
Keane, Michael L., 31 Jan. 1856, Mary A. Parks, dau. of P., Sr.;
  corrected copy   2/16/56-2
Kearfott, Robert W., 5 June 1855, Annie E. Dunham, dau. of
  T. C.   6/ 8/55-2
Kearney, Edward, 8 July 1856, Rose H. M. Hughes, dau. of
  (Capt.) Hugh C.   7/12/56-2
Kearns, James, 20 May 1855, Mary Byrne   5/26/55-2
Keasbey, Charles A., 30 Oct. 1851, Emma Hazlehurst, dau. of
  Andrew   10/31/51-2
Keating, John P., 10 July 1855, Sarah Jane Hammond   7/12/55-2
Keating, Laurence, 16 July 1852, Mary Wight   7/30/52-2
Keck, Albert, 10 May 1860, Christian Litchfield   6/29/60-2
Keech, Henry H., 25 Jan. 1860, Hattie B. Pigman   1/26/60-2
Keech, Thos. A. R. (Dr.), 7 Apr. 1859, Virginia M. Keech,
  dau. of Alexander   4/ 9/59-2
Keech, Wm. S. (Dr.), 14 July 1857, O. T. Wiley   7/17/57-2
Keefer, Charles H., 19 Oct. 1858, Anna M. Bentz   10/21/58-2
Keeffe, Wm. D., 1 Mar. 1859, Sallie E. Hugo, dau. of S. B.   3/14/59-2
Keelen, Edward, 19 July 1857, Sarah Frances Eager   8/ 5/57-2
Keeler, Edward, 4 Aug. 1856, (Mrs.) Emily Harris   9/10/56-2

Keen, Charles H., 10 Apr. 1860, Louisa J. Weigan	4/24/60-2
Keen, Eberhard, 24 June 1858, Anne Elizabeth Wehn	6/26/58-2
Keen, Wm. R., 17 Feb. 1857, Mary C. Hammar, dau. of Andrew	2/19/58-2
Keenan, John, 17 Sept. 1856, Ellen Noonan	9/24/56-2
Keenan, Joseph Daniel, 8 Mar. 1859, Mary J. Derry	4/ 6/59-2
Keenan, Thomas, 27 Mar. 1853, Ellen Hughes	4/ 1/53-2
Keene, Ben. Hall, 26 June 1855, Mary C. Michael, dau. of Ethan	6/27/55-2
Keene, Benj. R., 29 Oct. 1859, Virginia W. Ricketts	10/31/59-2
Keene, Henry, 16 Dec. 1851, (Mrs.) Charlotte Gouley	12/20/51-2
Keene, M. L., 7 Dec. 1852, Sophia S. Travers, dau. of L. D.	12/13/52-2
Keene, Saml. R., 1 Nov. 1855, Anne E. Bourke	11/ 2/55-2
Keene, Thos. H., 13 May 1856, Eliza E. Travers	5/21/56-2
Keene, Wesley, 23 Aug. 1860, Mary Dixon	8/25/60-2
Keene, Wm. W., 10 July 1856, Laura Dean	7/30/56-2
Keener, Augustus D., 21 Aug. 1855, Lizzie C. Williams	9/18/55-2
Keener, J. Harry, 20 June 1858, Celeste P. Thompson, dau. of David	6/24/58-2
Keener, J. Harry, 29 Apr. 1860, Mattie J. Morse	5/ 1/60-2
Keenright, James M., son of Nicholas and Catharine, 27 Sept. 1859, Mary E. Bayley	11/ 7/59-2
Keenwright, John A., 23 Nov. 1854, Amelia A. Logan, dau. of Jos.	11/25/54-2
Keerl, Thomas M., 28 Jan. 1858, Spaight Donhell, dau. of (Hon.) John R.	2/ 1/58-2
Kees, John B., 31 May 1860, Bettie A. Conn; 6/ 5/60-2	6/ 6/60-2
Kehn, William H., 4 Sept. 1860, (Mrs.) Caroline A. Storch	9/ 7/60-2
Kehoe, Thomas, 20 July 1856, Louisa A. Brooks	7/23/56-2
Keiberneigel, Hermann, 22 Feb. 1852, Susan Elizabeth Mustermann	2/24/52-2
Keilholtz, Charles, 24 Mar. 1853, Sophia Wheeler	5/17/53-2
Keilholtz, Otis, 20 Oct. 1860, Emily Shannessy, dau. of Jas.; 11/21/60-2	11/22/60-2
Keilhultz, William, 25 Oct. 1859, (Mrs.) Mary Ann Harrington	10/27/59-2
Keirby, Joseph, 11 Apr. 1853, Sophia Hutton	4/19/53-2
Keirle, H. Clay, son of Matthew, 19 Nov. 1856, Emilie Taylor, dau. of Matthew	11/22/56-2
Keister, Richard, 30 Sept. 1853, Catherine Leffler; 11/ 1/53-2	11/ 7/53-2
Keister, Richard, 30 Sept. 1853, Catherine Lesfler; corrected copy	11/ 5/53-2
Keith, George, 20 Nov. 1860, Mary Calligan	11/23/60-2
Keithley, James M., 21 Dec. 1858, Mary C. Cullum, dau. of George	1/22/59-2
Keithley, Richard, 8 Feb. 1853, Jane Desmond	2/14/53-2
Keithley, Thomas, 5 Jan. 1854, Matilda A. Pensons, dau. of Nicholas	1/ 9/54-2
Kelbaugh, Jeho, 6 Apr. 1858, Servania Gormley	6/15/58-2
Kellam, Arthur, 26 Feb. 1853, Mary Ann Warrington	3/ 1/53-2
Kellenberger, James W., 8 Nov. 1853, Mary E. Colhour	11/21/53-2
Keller, Andrew J., 21 June 1855, Margaret Q. Ryan	6/27/55-2
Keller, Conrad, 22 Sept. 1852, (Mrs.) Amelia Ingram	9/23/52-2
Keller, William, 28 Jan. 1855, Christina Bach	1/31/55-2
Kelley, Benjamin, 28 Jan. 1857, Hannah Ann Fitssegalbaugh	1/31/57-2
Kelley, Edward, 12 June 1859, (Mrs.) Mary S. Bogue	6/15/59-2
Kelley, John, 25 Jan. 1857, Kate M. Gorman, dau. of Nicholas	4/ 4/57-2
Kelley, John T., 13 Jan. 1853, Susan Appleby	1/15/53-2
Kelley, Lewis, 2 Nov. 1859, Mary V. Scott	3/27/60-2
Kelley, Patrick, 29 Dec. 1857, Ellen Hayes	1/ 1/58-2
Kellinger, Wm. J. (Maj.), 6 Dec. 1860, Lizzie B. Rogers, dau. of Geo.	12/ 7/60-2
Kelly, Andrew J., 29 May 1851, Ann L. Rothrock	6/ 3/51-2
Kelly, Daniel, 3 Nov. 1859, Clara Babbesson	11/ 5/59-2
Kelly, Daniel, 3 Nov. 1859, Clara Rabbeson; corrected copy	11/ 7/59-2
Kelly, Francis, 8 May 1860, Fanny Kelly	5/17/60-2

Kelly, Henry, 14 Nov. 1860, Fannie S. Forry, dau. of
    Edward G.   11/16/60-2
Kelly, Henry H., 2 Feb. 1860, Laura L. B. Hutchings   2/ 4/60-2
Kelly, James, 22 Dec. 1859, M. A. Byrne   12/30/59-2
Kelly, John, 18 Dec. 1853, Mary A. Cunningham   12/21/53-2
Kelly, John, 6 Aug. 1854, Mary Murphy   8/ 8/54-2
Kelly, John, 1 July 1860, Elizabeth C. Ellis   7/ 9/60-2
Kelly, John F., 6 Apr. 1854, Elizabeth A. Nixon   4/19/54-2
Kelly, John T., 2 Oct. 1859, (Mrs.) Eliza A. McFaul   10/ 6/59-2
Kelly, John W., 8 Dec. 1859, Julia Tall   12/10/59-2
Kelly, Joseph D., 2 May 1859, Margaret Jane Hastings   5/ 5/59-2
Kelly, Joseph M., 1 Oct. 1860, Mary Ann Bishop   10/ 3/60-2
Kelly, Lewis S., 30 Nov. 1851, Mary Pumpherey   12/ 2/51-2
Kelly, Oscar F., 2 July 1860, Anna McGraw   9/ 4/60-2
Kelly, Patrick, 8 Jan. 1854, Eliza Moore   1/10/54-2
Kelly, Peter A., 11 Jan. 1854, Mary Jane Russell, dau. of
    John, grandau. of Dennis Kelly   1/13/54-2
Kelly, Philip, 26 Aug. 1860, Catharine Connor   8/28/60-2
Kelly, Sebastian, 13 June 1852, Elizabeth Miller   6/15/52-2
Kelly, Sylvester R., 17 Mar. 1851, Catharine J. Spence   3/19/51-2
Kelly, Thomas E., 13 Jan. 1859, (Mrs.) Julia Welch   1/29/59-2
Kelly, Thomas G., 27 Jan. 1856, Anne Corkran   1/29/56-2
Kelly, Uriah H., 28 Jan. 1858, Lydia A. Curry   1/30/58-2
Kelly, Washington, 3 Nov. 1857, Mary A. Robinson, dau. of
    Joseph D.   11/ 7/57-2
Kelly, William, 4 Feb. 1858, Elizabeth Cole   2/ 5/58-2
Kelly, William H., 8 Feb. 1858, Agnes Stewart   2/ 9/58-2
Kelly, William H., 26 June 1860, Rebecca J. McCauley   6/27/60-2
Kelly, Wm. R., 13 Sept. 1854, (Mrs.) Elizabeth Hall   9/14/54-2
Kelsey, Benjamin, 20 July 1852, Mary A. Gray, dau. of (Capt.)
    Adams   7/23/52-2
Kelso, John, 7 Jan. 1851, Harriet Evans   1/17/51-2
Kemble, Geo., 29 Mar. 1859, Martha Sproul   4/ 2/59-2
Kemp, George M., 5 Jan. 1854, Indiana Arthur   1/11/54-2
Kemp, Joseph F., 14 May 1853, Alice Caroline Kemp   5/16/53-2
Kemp, Richard C., 20 Nov. 1856, Mary J. Adams, dau. of (Capt.)
    W. F.   11/25/56-2
Kemp, Thomas H., 25 Nov. 1858, Sarah E. Turner, dau. of
    (Dr.) John   11/27/58-2
Kemper, Moses, 19 Sept. 1858, Fanny Gump   9/22/58-2
Kendall, Henry Lee *, 15 Feb. 1853, Alice MacCart   2/17/53-2
Kendall, John M., 6 May 1852, Mary A. Hamilton   5/ 7/52-2
Kendall, William T., 8 Apr. 1858, Carrie Meredith Appold,
    dau. of George   4/10/58-2
Kenely, Lewis, 28 Feb. 1860, Lydia Ann Wilson   2/29/60-2
Kenhall, Stephen M., 6 Jan. 1858, Sarah Jane Scott   1/26/59-2
Kenly, Benjamin F., 23 June 1857, Mary J. Murphy   6/24/57-2
Kenly, James B., 24 Oct. 1854, Phebe T. Cook   10/26/54-2
Kennan, Patrick, 16 Oct. 1856, Julia G. McComas, dau. of
    Geo. A. and Elizabeth   10/17/56-2
Kennard, Baltis H., 24 Oct. 1854, Annie R. Carson, dau. of
    David   10/26/54-2
Kennard, Joseph, 16 Dec. 1852, Ann Robinson   12/21/52-2
Kennard, Joseph E., 8 Dec. 1853, Sarah Ann Shirlock   12/21/53-2
Kennard, Joseph M. (Dr.), 1 June 1857, Virginia Newman, dau.
    of Henry   6/ 6/57-2
Kennard, Perry, 15 Jan. 1857, Mary A. V. Kelsor   1/21/57-2
Kennard, Thomas A., 4 July 1854, Maria A. Jacobs   7/11/54-2
Kennedy, Anthony, 8 July 1851, Margaret Smith, dau. of (Hon.)
    Christopher Hughes   7/ 9/51-2
Kennedy, Charles G., 17 July 1855, Mary Jane Hilleary, dau. of
    Wm.   7/18/55-2
Kennedy, Isaac, 20 June 1860, Mary Eliza Wells   6/25/60-2
Kennedy, John, 10 May 1854, Hortensia Massicot, dau. of
    (Capt.) Wm.   5/18/54-2

Kennedy, Michael, 20 Jan. 1853, Catharine Jane Stahl   1/27/53-2
Kennedy, Peter F., 12 Oct. 1853, Caroline Burnett, dau. of
   (Capt.) Joseph J.; corrected copy   10/15/53-2
Kennedy, Peter F., 12 Oct. 1853, Caroline P. Burnett   10/14/53-2
Kennedy, Wm. W., 11 June 1856, Annie T. Shane   6/16/56-2
Kenney, Robert; no date given, Margaret Dinn   10/12/52-2
Kenney, William A. (Capt.), 26 May 1856, Mary A. Getty   5/28/56-2
Kenny, George, 9 June 1851, Ellen Doyle   6/11/57-2
Kenny, Thomas, 30 Apr. 1854, Ellen S. McMahon   5/ 2/54-2
Kenny, William J., 5 Sept. 1860, Lydia R. Hill, dau. of John   9/ 7/60-2
Kent, John W., 3 May 1855, Louisa E. Kent   8/ 1/55-2
Kent, Thomas Hl, 22 Sept. 1852, Mary E. Hunter, dau. of
   Andrew   9/24/52-2
Keplinger, John W., 27 Mar. 1859, Lucy Wells   4/15/59-2
Kerby, Benjamin Franklin, 14 July 1853, Mary E. McCoy   10/ 1/53-2
Kerby, Dennis, 2 Nov. 1854, Anna Travers, dau. of Charles   11/ 8/54-2
Kerchner, Adolph, 12 July 1860, Mary Hubbel   7/16/60-2
Kerchner, Ferdinand, 2 May 1858, Fredericka Hubel   5/ 4/58-2
Kerchner, Francis Wm., 22 Dec. 1857, Lydia Catharine Hatch   1/23/57-2
Kerchner, Frederick A., 8 June 1854, Ann C. Berger   6/ 9/54-2
Kerlinger, Geo. A., 25 Jan. 1854, Elizabeth McDonald   1/31/54-2
Kermode, John, 18 Aug. 1859, Margaret P. O'Bryon, dau. of
   Solomon   8/19/59-2
Kern, Emil Eugene Davoust, 8 Sept. 1852, Jeannette Ludovicke
   Christine Hoerster   9/ 9/52-2
Kernan, Edward, 31 Oct. 1854, Ellen Gleason   11/ 2/54-2
Kernan, John, 4 Oct. 1860, Emma D. Klockgether   10/ 5/60-2
Kernan, John, 4 Oct. 1860, Emma S. Klockgether, dau. of D.;
   corrected copy   10/ 6/60-2
Kerns, Bernard J., 14 Aug. 1856, Sarah Smith   8/16/56-2
Kerr, John, 23 Dec. 1851, Jane Coburn   12/29/51-2
Kerr, John, 5 Feb. 1856, Mary Bawden   2/14/56-2
Kerr, John, 8 Nov. 1859, Ann Maria Hamilton   11/15/59-2
Kerr, John L., 5 Mar. 1857, Mary E. Chaney   3/10/57-2
Kerr, Joseph H., 6 Sept. 1860, Harrietta T. Finigan   9/ 8/60-2
Kerr, Michael, 4 Feb. 1858, (Mrs.) Margaret Brady   2/16/58-2
Kerr, W. Robert, Jr., 6 Nov. 1851, Mary Ann Forsyth   11/12/51-2
Kersey, James F., 18 Nov. 1852, Mary Jane Thompson   11/27/52-2
Kershaw, James L., 27 Oct. 1857, Eliza A. Theban   11/14/57-2
Kershner, Benjamin F., 20 Nov. 1853, Margaret Costello   11/26/53-2
Kertner, William, 21 Oct. 1858, Caroline Geldmacher   10/23/58-2
Kerwan, George W. (Capt.), 4 Feb. 1854, Louisa Vardel   2/11/54-2
Keseling, George, 25 Feb. 1858, Mary Lawton   3/ 4/58-2
Kesler, Fred'k., 1 Feb. 1853, Elizabeth A. Chandlee, dau. of
   George and Nancy   2/ 4/53-2
Kesmodel, M., 16 Aug. 1852, E. Dahle   8/18/52-2
Kess, Washington, 13 Nov. 1856, Mary Ann Hill   11/15/56-2
Kessler, Andrew, 5 Dec. 1857, Mary B. Neuffer   1/ 6/57-2
Kesterson, William, 8 May 1853, Winefred T. Fulham, dau. of
   Thomas and Catherine   5/12/53-2
Kettler, Frederick Augustus, 8 Feb. 1852, Wilhelmina Charlotte
   Fredricka Genthner   2/10/52-2
Key, Chas. H., 30 Nov. 1852, Elizabeth Lloyd, dau. of (Col.)
   Edward   12/ 4/52-2
Keys, George, 18 Dec. 1851, Mary Jane Cox   12/20/51-2
Keys, Hugh, 16 Nov. 1859, Caroline V. Fickey, dau. of
   Fred'k.   11/18/59-2
Keys, James, 23 May 1854, Eliza Jane Owings   5/30/54-2
Keys, James, 5 Sept. 1854, Mary J. Edgin   9/ 7/54-2
Keys, Robert T., 21 Dec. 1854, Rebecca S. Norris, dau. of
   Edward S.   12/22/54-2
Keys, Walter, 17 Jan. 1856, Elizabeth Montgomery   1/18/56-2
Keyworth, Charles E., 28 Dec. 1858, Philipine Stansbury   2/19/59-2
Keyworth, Thomas, 15 Oct. 1856, Christina Hipperly   10/16/56-2
Kibler, Frederick, 30 May 1855, Mary Ann Livesey   6/ 1/55-2

Kibler, J. S., 15 Nov. 1852, Belinda Mathews   11/29/52-2
Kidd, Benjamin, 24 Feb. 1853, Mary Dowling   2/28/53-2
Kidd, Charles, 23 Nov. 1853, Rebecca Deets   11/26/53-2
Kidd, Charles H., 27 July 1859, Eliza M. Weeks   7/28/59-2
Kidd, Robert, 29 Oct. 1857, Ann Maria Higgins   10/31/57-2
Kidd, James R., 12 Apr. 1855, Amelia Mege   4/14/55-2
Kidd, Larred D., 21 Sept. 1852, Jane Akehurst   9/23/52-2
Kidd, William G. (Dr.), 27 Feb. 1856, Mary E. Hall, dau. of
     (Hon.) Samuel   2/29/56-2
Kier, Conrad, 28 July 1859, Caroline Albrecht   8/ 4/59-2
Kilgore, Alderman B., 16 Jan. 1858, Hannah McRown, dau. of
     (Capt.) Samuel and Grace   1/18/58-2
Kilgore, James R., 16 Dec. 1856, (Mrs.) Lizzie A. Wheeler   12/27/56-2
Kilman, William P., 9 Mar. 1855, Mary Maguire   9/ 7/55-2
Kilpatrick, John H., 29 Sept. 1853, Tabitha Halbert   10/ 3/53-2
Kimball, Wm. P., 15 Feb. 1854, Mary Ann Daughaday   2/20/54-2
Kimble, Hiram, 26 Feb. 1852, Maria Wells   3/ 3/52-2
Kimble, Lewis Henson, 19 July 1860, (Mrs.) Amelia Kimble   7/24/60-2
Kime, Geo., 24 Feb. 1853, Sarah B. Shepherd   3/ 9/53-2
Kimmel, S., 23 June 1853, Mary Lizzie Lambert   6/25/53-2
Kimmel, William, 26 Nov. 1857, Elizabeth Garrett King   11/28/57-2
Kincade, James R., 25 Nov. 1852, Anne Cave   12/ 7/52-2
Kincheloe, Elias W., 17 Jan. 1854, Hannah A. Catts;
     1/20/54-2   1/24/54-2
Kines, John G., 25 Nov. 1858, Susan M. Robinson   11/30/58-2
King, Albert H., 17 Apr. 1854, Mary R. Peters   4/27/54-2
King, Charles T., 30 Mar. 1859, Annie R. Bean, dau. of
     Joseph H.   3/31/59-2
King, Firmadge, 25 May 1854, Lucy Adell   5/27/54-2
King, Firmadge, 1 Dec. 1857, Mary Ellen Conaway   1/ 5/57-2
King, Francis, 8 Dec. 1853, (Mrs.) Ellen Smith   12/10/53-2
King, G. Morrison, 15 Dec. 1859, Nettie M. Hopkins   12/11/59-2
King, Geo. R., 16 Apr. 1860, Emma A. Soran   5/ 7/60-2
King, George, 8 Apr. 1858, Anna Clarkson   4/15/58-2
King, George B., 9 May 1855, Kissih Gallaway   5/12/55-2
King, George S., 9 Sept. 1856, M. Josephine Campbell   9/11/56-2
King, George S., 9 Sept. 1856, M. Josephine Campbell, dau.
     of (Col.) B. U.; corrected copy   9/12/56-2
King, George W., 15 Apr. 1851, Mary A. A. Jones, dau. of
     William   4/17/51-2
King, H., 21 Apr. 1851, Elizabeth Rutherford   5/ 3/51-2
King, Henry S., 5 June 1860, Louisa P. Smith, dau. of
     Job, Jr.   6/ 9/60-2
King, J. W., 26 Apr. 1855, Clara A. St. A. Straub, dau. of
     (Hon.) C. M.   4/28/55-2
King, James Andrew, 13 June 1854, Margaret Virginia Peck   6/14/54-2
King, James B., 2 Dec. 1856, Anna Austin   12/ 4/56-2
King, James H., 23 Sept. 1856, Lottie R. Ely, dau. of
     Mahlon S.   9/24/56-2
King, John, 30 Oct. 1853, Rachel Ann Smith   10/31/53-2
King, John, Jr., 16 Apr. 1857, Hattie J. Jackson, dau. of
     Stephen M.   4/18/57-2
King, John F., 22 Mar. 1853, Catharine Zerweck, dau. of
     Daniel   3/24/53-2
King, John H., 11 Jan. 1860, Annie Lovell   1/13/60-2
King, John T.; no date given, Eliza May May; dau. of (Capt.)
     James   7/30/57-2
King, John T., 3 July 1856, Ellen Murphy   8/ 4/56-2
King, Patrick H., 12 June 1855, Mary Elizabeth Heuisler, dau.
     of George A.   6/14/55-2
King, Peter, 21 Oct. 1855, Mary Ann McAvoy   11/ 3/55-3
King, R. F., 10 Feb. 1855, Alice Peet   2/13/55-2
King, Robert G., 20 Apr. 1853, Lizzie D. Pindle, dau. of Thos.   4/22/53-2
King, Thomas, 28 Apr. 1854, Martha Ann Bosworth; 4/29/54-2;
     5/ 3/54-2   5/ 4/54-2

King, Thomas H., 8 Apr. 1858, Ann Rebecca Booz   4/12/58-2
King, W. Albert, 17 May 1853, Mary E. O. Neal   5/18/53-2
King, William H., 1 June 1851, Eleanor A. Scrivener   6/ 3/51-2
King, Wm. H., 14 Apr. 1853, Adeline E. Stevens   4/26/53-2
Kinnally, Martin, 8 Apr. 1858, Johana Maher   4/10/58-2
Kinnear, Geo. A., 15 Nov. 1853, Margaret Ann Fullerton   11/17/53-2
Kinnear, Robert K., 28 Jan. 1854, Theresa Parkes   2/ 1/54-2
Kinnemon, Thomas, 13 Dec. 1860, Emma Turner   12/15/60-2
Kinnersley, William T., 15 Aug. 1858, Alabama V. Moore   9/ 2/58-2
Kinsey, Edward (Rev.), 30 Oct. 1860, Mattie C. Wells, dau. of
    J. Wesley   10/31/60-2
Kinsey, Joseph, 1-(?) June 1852, Rachel Pettett   6/23/52-2
Kinsler, Charles, 2 May 1854, Charlotte Pohlen   5/ 5/54-2
Kinsler, Charles, 26 Jan. 1860, Sabina Hayes   2/ 1/60-2
Kinsley, Herbert M., 31 Mar. 1853, Angie M. Gilman, dau. of
    Jno.   4/ 4/53-2
Kinstensdorf, Charles A., 11 Apr. 1853, Caroline H. Cook   4/15/53-2
Kinzel, Henry, 17 Sept. 1851, Lucy C. Hardy   9/22/51-2
Kinzer, Saml. Gore, 19 Oct. 1858, Maria Louise Shorb, dau. of
    (Dr.) Joseph A.   10/20/58-2
Kinzly, Josiah, 20 Apr. 1852, Emma H. Smyrk   4/23/52-2
Kirby, Geo. J., 9 Mar. 1857, Eliza Busick   3/17/57-2
Kirby, Gilman, 23 Oct. 1852, Virginia B. Little   5/13/53-2
Kirby, J. E., 20 July 1854, Kate McCormick   7/24/54-2
Kirby, James, 11 July 1852, Maria Todd   7/12/52-2
Kirby, James A., 28 Apr. 1857, Joanna Lippey   5/ 1/57-2
Kirby, James H., 15 Mar. 1859, Sarah E. Mahare   3/23/59-2
Kirby, James W., 13 Feb. 1859, Eleanora Brice   2/21/59-2
Kirby, John E., 24 Sept. 1857, Mary Ellen Richardson   9/26/57-2
Kirby, Nathan C., 28 May 1857, Kate C. Hill, dau. of John E. 5/30/57-2
Kirby, William H., 5 Oct. 1851, Rosanna Wherritt   10/ 7/51-2
Kirby, William N., 9 Nov. 1858, Mahala Brian   11/11/58-2
Kirch, Wm. H., 29 July 1860, Kate L. Sewell   7/31/60-2
Kirby, Wm. N., 1 May 1856, Catherine E. Herald   5/ 5/56-2
Kirk, Allen, 15 Apr. 1851, Deborah Slicer   4/22/51-2
Kirk, Samuel E., 11 June 1857, Harriet J. Waters   6/13/57-2
Kirk, Samuel, 21 June 1860, (Mrs.) Eleanor Ann Hager   6/22/60-2
Kirk, W. A., 22 Dec. 1857, M. E. Corcoran   12/31/57-2
Kirker, John, 13 Jan. 1853, Matilda Gaston   1/19/53-2
Kirkland, O. A., 19 Nov. 1857, Sarah W. Adreon, dau. of Wm. 11/23/57-2
Kirkman, John W., 30 Sept. 1851, Sallie Emmart   10/ 2/51-2
Kirkpatrick, Samuel, 14 Oct. 1859, Rachel M. Young   10/15/59-2
Kirkwood, Philip, 31 Oct. 1851, Margery C. Stewart   11/ 1/51-2
Kirwan, Jacob (Capt.), 19 Jan. 1854, (Mrs.) Susan E. Griffith 1/28/54-2
Kitson, John E., 17 Nov. 1859, Emily V. Goodacre, dau. of
    Daniel   11/22/59-2
Kitts, John, 6 Oct. 1851, (Mrs.) Mary M. M-(?)-llion   10/13/51-2
Klages, Frederick, 6 Aug. 1860, Jane Houston   8/16/60-2
Klein, Emanuel, 13 May 1860, Elizabeth Vollandt   5/17/60-2
Kleindienst, Joseph, 18 Nov. 1852, Mary E. Dellzell, dau. of
    Benj. Fowler   11/24/52-2
Klem, Joseph, 28 Sept. 1857, Catherine Weaver   10/ 5/57-2
Kline, Francis M., 3 July 1854, Ruth Ann Colflesh   7/11/54-2
Klinedinst, Andrew, 28 Apr. 1853, Isabel Price   5/ 3/53-2
Klinefelter, Charles, 25 Dec. 1856, Mary Holmes   12/31/56-2
Klinefelter, Gartman, 15 Nov. 1860, Olivia Rodenmayer, dau.
    of John   11/19/60-2
Klinefelter, Geo. W., 20 Dec. 1856, Elizabeth Wilson, dau. of
    Robert   12/22/56-2
Klinefelter, Jesse, 15 Nov. 1855, Kate Lippincott   11/17/55-2
Klinefelter, V. V., 15 Oct. 1857, Sarah Hooper   10/19/57-2
Kloman, Lewis, 9 June 1852, Maria Thomas   6/15/52-2
Kloman, W. C. (Dr.), 23 Apr. 1857, Miriam C. Hunt, dau. of
    Jesse   4/25/57-2

Klugh, John, 27 July 1859, Mary A. Hogg, dau. of John A.	8/ 2/59-2
Klunk, Charles C., 12 Apr. 1852, Elizabeth A. Swem	4/13/52-2
Klunk, Francis A., 1 Jan. 1854, (Mrs.) Louisa Wilson	1/ 3/54-2
Knapp, Daniel, 19 Oct. 1852, Mary O. Thomas	11/ 1/52-2
Knawer, George, 3 Oct. 1858, Mary Louisa Stahl, dau. of	
Charles G. and Louisa S., corrected copy	10/ 5/58-2
Knichols, William, 16 Oct. 1856, Ellen Jobs	10/18/56-2
Knight, Albert, 20 Jan. 1859, Letitia Moulton, dau. of J. T.	1/22/59-2
Knight, Charles, 13 Sept. 1860, Wilhelmina Hutchins Smith	9/18/60-2
Knight, Edwin R., 1 Nov. 1860, Annie Easton	11/ 3/60-2
Knight, George, 21 Mar. 1854, Mary Eliza Ahern, dau. of	
Timothy J.	3/23/55-2
Knight, George M., 10 May 1859, Sarah V. Cutlipp	5/14/59-2
Knight, George W. H., 15 May 1860, Elizabeth L. Colester	6/23/60-2
Knight, Humphrey B. (Capt.), 16 Aug. 1855, Elizabeth A.	
Lecompt	8/20/55-2
Knight, James, 12 Jan. 1858, Elizabeth Virginia Lanahan	1/16/58-2
Knight, John T., 12 May 1859, Mary J. Watkins	6/ 4/59-2
Knight, Robert, 1 Oct. 1860, Mary Ann Bradley	10/ 6/60-2
Knight, Samuel T., 2 Sept. 1852, (Mrs.) Mary Hopkins, dau.	
of Wm. McConkey	9/ 7/52-2
Knight, Thomas, 28 May 1854, Frances A. Foss	5/30/54-2
Knight, William H., 23 Mar. 1856, Sarah A. Fulington Watson	3/26/56-2
Knipp, Jacob, Jr., 13 Sept. 1855, Mary E. Bitzel	9/15/55-2
Knoblock, John C., 28 Dec. 1858, (Mrs.) Eliza J. Bates	12/29/58-2
Knodel, Christian F., 19 Sept. 1858, Elizabeth Kroft	9/22/58-2
Knorr, Edward W., 1 Jan. 1855, Mary E. Moore	1/30/55-2
Knorr, Henry, 18 July 1858, Caroline Leech	10/13/58-2
Knorr, John, 7 Aug. 1853, Marianna Gulnare Aiken; corrected copy	8/26/53-2
Knott, C. Edward, 10 July 1854, Emily A. Smith, dau. of	
Samuel	7/26/54-2
Knott, Cornelius L., 17 June 1856, Roselia Borroughs	6/23/56-2
Knott, J. H., 5 Oct. 1858, Sallie V. Pic	10/15/58-2
Knotts, Edwin, 1 May 1856, Emily Jane Tipton	5/ 2/56-2
Knotts, John W., 27 Nov. 1860, Susan P. Loker	12/ 1/60-2
Knouer, George, 3 Oct. 1858, Mary Louisa Stahl	10/ 5/58-2
Know, John, 7 Aug. 1853, Marianna Gulnare Aiken	8/25/53-2
Knowles, James W., 26 Mar. 1851, Martha A. Burgess, dau. of	
C. W.	3/28/51-2
Knox, David, 19 Sept. 1859, Julia A. Norris	9/20/59-2
Knox, James, 23 Mar. 1859, Josephine G. Kernan, dau. of Peter	3/25/59-2
Knox, S. Bolivar, 29 Jan. 1852, Mary F. Selden, dau. of	
Jas. M.	1/31/52-2
Knox, William, 1 Sept. 1852, Martha Ann Stone	9/ 3/52-2
Kohler, Augustus, 6 Nov. 1855, Leocadia Deville, dau. of	
Francis	11/ 7/55-3
Kohlhepp, Valentine, 1 Feb. 1858, Margaret Krauss	2/ 3/58-2
Kolbort, Mathias, 29 Mar. 1853, Anne O. Rourk	4/27/53-2
Koller, Andrew J., 29 Mar. 1860, Elizabeth A. Garrett	5/19/60-2
Koller, George W., 27 Nov. 1860, Susan Prosser	12/ 1/60-2
Kone, Andrew J., 28 Aug. 1851, Sarah M. Collings	8/30/51-2
Konig, Fred'k., 23 Feb. 1853, Mary A. Burk	2/25/53-2
Koo-(?), Daniel, 21 Dec. 1857, Mollie Stuart, dau. of (Dr.)	
Ridgley	1/15/58-2
Koockogey, Samuel, 7 Sept. 1856, Susan M. Megraw	10/11/56-2
Kook, Christian, 29 Nov. 1857, Margaret Stockhaus	12/ 3/57-2
Kookogey, Samuel, 18 Dec. 1851, Mary E. Love	1/14/52-2
Koon, Charles L., 31 Dec. 1854, Eliza Detmar	1/ 2/55-2
Koonig, William, 14 Feb. 1853, Mary B. C. Magers, dau. of	
P. A.	2/16/53-2
Koontz, Charles F., 19 Feb. 1854, Rose Callahan	2/21/54-2
Koontz, George S., 18 Oct. 1853, Jane Gaston	11/21/53-2
Koors, William, 12 Oct. 1856, Lizzie Friedrich, dau. of John	10/20/56-2
Kosmer, Horace B., 2 Dec. 1853, Margaretta V. Tagart	12/ 5/53-2
Koster, Albert J., 25 Feb. 1851, Caroline Crouch	2/27/51-2

Kouch, Andrew, 2 Feb. 1851, Martha Ann Wellslager   2/ 4/51-2
Kraft, Charles O., 1 Jan. 1855, Mary Elizabeth Adams   6/12/55-2
Kraft, George, Jr., 24 Sept. 1852, Elizabeth A. Eagleston, dau.
  of (Mrs.) Andrews   10/ 5/52-2
Kraft, George W., 8 Aug. 1854, Catharine J. W. Chambers   9/25/54-2
Kraft, J. Christian, 30 Nov. 1852, Charlotte E. Diffenderffer,
  dau. of Henry T.   12/ 7/52-2
Kraft, James, 17 Dec. 1857, Mary Meriken   12/24/57-2
Kraft, Joseph A., 6 May 1860, Julia A. Shingel   5/25/60-2
Kraft, Lewis, 26 Aug. 1851, Marion Wigart Cook, dau. of
  (Capt.) Bernard H., grandau. of Geo. Wigart   8/28/51-2
Kraft, Thomas, 11 Apr. 1858, Elizabeth Croft   5/ 1/58-2
Krager, Henry, 3 Jan. 1851, Virginia Holland   2/ 6/51-2
Krager, John L., 16 Dec. 1852, Sarah G. Hemling   12/18/52-2
Krager, Joseph H., 18 Jan. 1857, Sarah A. Bentley   1/20/57-2
Kramer, James (Rev.), 18 July 1859, Harriet Ann Barriere;
  corrected copy   7/26/59-2
Kramer, James, 18 July 1859, Harriet Bevere   7/20/59-2
Kramer, Jas. Sewell, 22 Apr. 1858, Emily Olivia Hagger   4/26/58-2
Kramer, Samuel (Rev.), 14 Nov. 1852, Mary A. Weaver   11/25/52-2
Krantz, George, 25 Mar. 1860, Margaretha Buchheimer   4/10/60-2
Kratt, Carl Gottlob, 9 May 1852, Eliza J. Ebenwein   5/17/52-2
Kratz, John, 10 Dec. 1854, Catharine Schwartz   12/12/54-2
Kraus, John F., 13 Jan. 1859, Amelia Fisher   1/15/59-2
Krauss, Charles L. P., 21 Sept. 1851, Amelia Dreyer   9/23/51-2
Krauss, Wm. H., 16 Dec. 1852, Eleanor H. Rundle, dau. of Wm.
  and Sarah   12/28/52-2
Kreamer, John, 16 June 1856, Margaret Long   6/19/56-2
Kreber, Christian, 24 May 1859, Susan C. Burrier   5/27/59-2
Krebs, George M., 14 June 1853, Mary Jane Norris   6/16/53-2
Krebs, John J., 1 June 1854, Adeline Kriel, dau. of John G.   6/ 5/54-2
Krebs, M. W., 5 Dec. 1853, E. S. Balderston   12/14/53-2
Krebs, William Geo., 25 Nov. 1851, Susan Warner, dau. of
  Michael   11/27/51-2
Kreis, Geo. W., 10 Feb. 1853, Mary Elizabeth Irelan, dau. of
  David   2/12/53-2
Kreiss, Wm. J., 8 May 1860, Flavilla A. Shaw   5/12/60-2
Kreitman, Philip, 21 Apr. 1857, Christiann Hartman   5/13/57-2
Kremelberg, John D., 13 Nov. 1851, Elizabeth Deford, dau. of
  Benjamin   11/14/51-2
Kremer, John T., 27 Oct. 1859, Lizzie Ruff   11/ 2/59-2
Kriel, Charles G., 25 Dec. 1856, Hannah E. Scaumacher, dau. of
  Henry C. and Elizabeth   12/30/56-2
Kriese, James F., 15 Apr. 1856, Elizabeth Jane Bradford   4/17/56-2
Kriete, Edward W., 23 Oct. 1856, Lusendy Bodd   10/29/56-2
Kroehl, Julius H., 25 Nov. 1858, Sophie Lueber, dau. of
  Francis   12/ 1/58-2
Kroh, Philip H., 25 Mar. 1852, Slender Kidd   3/30/52-2
Kronad, Henry, 5 Aug. 1856, Mary C. Moran   8/ 6/56-2
Kroner, George, 2 Apr. 1857, (Mrs.) Amelia S. Devalin, dau. of
  C. H. Olhaber   4/24/57-2
Kruse, George W., 16 May 1859, Mary L. Mann   5/18/59-2
Kugler, Thos., 5 June 1860, Elizabeth Brooks   6/ 7/60-2
Kuhl, Henry, 6 Jan. 1852, Caroline T. Erney, dau. of Edw'd.   1/ 9/52-2
Kuhl, John Henry, 5 June 1860, Alverta Virginia Rickter   6/ 8/60-2
Kuhn, John; no date given, Mary Jane McQuinan   3/15/59-2
Kuhn, Napoleon B., 5 May 1856, Mary A. Rimby   5/10/56-2
Kuhn, Sylvester J., 26 Oct. 1856, Louisa E. Lipp   2/11/57-2
Kulp, Henry Hackman, 9 Dec. 1852, Anna Mary O'Connor   12/11/52-2
Kunsman, William H., 2 Jan. 1855, Sarah T. Hardesty   1/ 5/55-2
Kunz, Alexander, 12 Aug. 1855, Mary Bineman   8/14/55-2
Kunzen, Carl F. A., 4 Apr. 1851, (Mrs.) Catharine Friend   5/ 6/51-2
Kurtz, J. F. (Dr.), 31 Oct. 1854, Sallie L. Hurst, dau. of
  Elijah   11/ 1/54-2
Kyer, John, 22 Aug. 1858, Frances Ann Isaacs   8/24/58-2

Kyle, Wm., 5 May 1856, Mary Anders   5/ 8/56-2
Kyper, John W., 10 July 1853, Ann Louisa Schaffer, dau. of
    Jacob   7/14/53-2
Labar, Michael, 29 Sept. 1851, Caroline Ball   9/30/51-2
Ladd, Rufus M., 2 Apr. 1860, Abbie C. Perry   4/ 3/60-2
Laddie, John Henry, 21 Jan. 1858, Mary Dorsey   1/26/58-2
Ladkins, James T., 15 Nov. 1852, Maria T. Caufield   11/18/52-2
Ladson, William Henry, 18 Sept. 1851, Isabel Ann Brien, dau. of
    John McPherson   9/20/51-2
Laessig, John Henry, 3 Jan. 1858, Johannah Wilstorf   2/15/58-2
Laferty, Patrick, 27 June 1852, Rose Ann T. Murray   6/29/52-2
Laferty, Robert, 21 Nov. 1858, Ellen L. McLeavy, dau. of James   5/ 7/59-2
Lafferty, Marty, 13 Oct. 1856, Ellen Gartland   10/17/56-2
Lafferty, Robert, 21 Nov. 1858, Ellen L. McLevy, dau. of
    James; corrected copy   5/10/59-2
Laffey, Daniel, 6 July 1854, Bridget Ann Elizabeth Costolay   8/ 8/54-2
Lamar, Israel, 27 May 1851, Catherine Ann Seward   6/ 4/51-2
Lamb, Francis F., 18 Apr. 1853, Mary Riddell   4/25/53-2
Lamb, George D., 24 June 1860, Emma G. Bigelow   6/29/60-2
Lamb, James A., 15 Jan. 1857, Mary Jane Conway   1/31/57-2
Lamb, John H., 27 Nov. 1853, Margaret A. Steighleman   11/29/53-2
Lamb, Lyman H., 7 Apr. 1859, Margaret C. Wright   10/15/59-2
Lamb, Thos. J., 15 Apr. 1854, Kate A. Jennings, dau. of
    Wm. H.   4/20/54-2
Lamb, Thos. P., 8 July 1858, Rebecca Wills   7/24/58-2
Lamb, William, 5 Apr. 1853, (Mrs.) Jane Young   4/ 8/53-2
Lambden, James D., 27 Jan. 1853, Annie E. Welsh, dau. of
    Warren   1/29/53-2
Lambdin, Joseph H., 18 Jan. 1854, Margaret Johnson   1/23/54-2
Lambdin, Thomas H., 14 Sept. 1853, Sarah Adams   9/16/53-2
Lambdin, W. Wallace (Dr.), 24 Mar. 1859, Lizzie Olive Pettit   3/25/59-2
Lambert, John P., 29 May 1853, Mary Frances Umphries   5/31/53-2
Lambeth, J. Wesley, 6 Mar. 1853, Jane Shemell   3/ 9/53-2
Lambie, William C., 7 Oct. 1851, Olevia Augusta Phillips, dau.
    of Wm. B.   1/22/52-2
Lambright, John, 1 Aug. 1855, Barbara Ann Shalbarger, dau. of
    John   8/ 8/55-2
Lambright, John W., 5 Aug. 1856, Ann Virginia Harris   8/12/56-2
Lamdin, Edward S., 2 Dec. 1852, Sarah Lizzie Muller, dau. of
    James N.   12/ 3/52-2
Lamdin, Edward S., 16 Oct. 1856, Eliza Peters, dau. of
    William   10/20/56-2
Lamdin, John H., 28 Apr. 1859, Sarah A. Hilditch   4/30/59-2
Lamdin, Robert P., 4 Oct. 1855, Fanny P. Dungan, dau. of
    (Capt.) Abel S.   10/ 8/55-2
Lamdin, Wm. J., 24 Jan. 1860, Laura V. Gist, dau. of Wm.   1/25/60-2
Lampley, Nathaniel Lewis, son of Oliver Evans, 20 Sept. 1853,
    Ann Maria Herrison, dau. of William Nelson   9/23/53-2
Lanahan, John, 24 Dec. 1850, Catharine Britt   1/ 3/51-2
Lanan, Patrick, 31 July 1853, Susan McDonald, dau. of Paddy   8/ 9/53-2
Lancaster, Benjamin B., 13 Jan. 1852, Catharine Schmucks   1/17/52-2
Landen, John W., 17 May 1854, Zipporah Cropper   5/31/54-2
Landey, Thomas, 21 June 1860, Cornelia Green   6/25/60-2
Landon, George H., 30 Nov. 1853, Sophronia E. Rives   12/ 2/53-2
Landstreet, Jno., Jr. (Rev.), 17 Aug. 1852, Mary Frances
    Swisk, dau. of William   8/25/52-2
Lane, Henry C., 9 Feb. 1860, Mary Connor   2/15/60-2
Lane, William H., 15 Aug. 1859, Roxanna C. Langley   8/17/59-2
Lang, John G., 30 Dec. 1852, Ann E. Wimpsett, dau. of Robert   1/12/53-2
Lang, John J., 12 Jan. 1857, Clarissa W. Turner   1/14/57-2
Langan, Patrick, 16 Sept. 1860, Catherine Cox   9/19/60-2
Langdon, Charles H., 16 Feb. 1860, M. Rebecca Wright, dau. of
    W. E. and Margaret   2/25/60-2
Langdon, James E., 3 Nov. 1853, Mary Ann Garritee   11/ 5/53-2
Lange, J. P., 22 July 1858, (Mrs.) Virginia Ann Loring   7/28/58-2

```
Langenin, Andrew, 5 July 1852, Margaret Shehan                7/ 8/52-2
Langheld, G. F., 8 Apr. 1858, Mary Kate Cooper                4/13/58-2
Langley, James R., 11 Oct. 1853, Indiana Milburn             10/12/53-2
Langley, Lewis J., 16 Aug. 1853, Margaret Jane Decorsey;
   corrected copy                                             8/22/53-2
Langley, Lewis James, 16 Aug. 1853, (Mrs.) Margaret Jane
   De Corsey                                                  8/18/53-2
Langley, William Robert, 16 Dec. 1851, Catharine Olevia Taylor 12/18/51-2
Langvill, John T., 23 June 1859, Sarah A. McClaskey           6/28/59-2
Langville, John Nathaniel, 24 Sept. 1860, Ruth Jane Smith     9/27/60-2
Lankford, Henry S., 23 Sept. 1851, Martha A. Riggin           9/26/51-2
Lankford, Henry S., 31 July 1854, Mary D. Pinckard, dau. of
   (Rev.) Robert                                              8/ 2/54-2
Lankford, William, 1 Apr. 1852, (Mrs.) Mary O. Hagen          4/12/52-2
Lankford, William, 4 June 1857, Josephine Adams               6/11/57-2
Lansdale, Francis A., 1 Nov. 1859, Hattie A. Morrow, dau. of
   John                                                      11/ 4/59-2
Lansdale, Robert V., 10 Dec. 1857, Lizzie A. Tucker, dau. of
   Joseph                                                    12/15/57-2
Lantz, John George, 17 Aug. 1852, Mary Rieger                 8/18/52-2
Lantz, Oliver F., 4 Dec. 1855, Cassie R. Appold              12/ 6/55-2
Lapourelie, Alfred P., 29 May 1855, Mary B. Gross             5/31/55-2
Lappe, Martin, 16 May 1859, Mary Elilabeth Hax, dau. of
   John B.                                                    6/17/59-2
Laprade, Lewis, 5 June 1855, Caroline A. Holly, dau. of
   George and Martha                                          6/ 7/55-2
Lare, David W., 6 May 1858, Ellisene B. Lockwood              5/ 8/58-2
Lare, George H., 20 Jan. 1859, Mary J. Ingalls               1/22/59-2
Larence, Henry, 30 Dec. 1857, Jane Steward                    1/ 2/58-2
Larfield, George W., 7 June 1853, Matilda Ann Semour          6/ 9/53-2
Large, J. L. (Dr.), 20 May 1851, Olivia Towson, dau. of O. W. 5/23/51-2
Largent, Joseph J. (Rev.), 19 Oct. 1854, Mary Jane Tinges,
   dau. of Lewis                                             10/20/54-2
Larkin, Hugh C., 24 Apr. 1859, Virginia Slasman              5/ 3/59-2
Larkin, J. Milton, 20 July 1858, Charlotte A. Gordon, dau. of
   John H.                                                    8/13/58-2
Larkin, J. Milton A., 8 Apr. 1851, Almira Gordon, dau. of
   J. H.                                                      4/10/51-2
Larkin, Patrick, 5 Sept. 1857, Cecelia Fenerty               10/ 7/57-2
Larkin, William, 24 Apr. 1860, Malvina Watson                4/26/60-2
Larkins, Augustus L. H., 14 Sept. 1857, Gennie S. Daughton,
   dau. of Joshua                                             9/18/57-2
Larmour, Wm. B., 13 Nov. 1855, Mary A. H. Moffett            11/15/55-2
Larned, Frank H., 9 Nov. 1858, Helen Murray, dau. of John    11/15/58-2
Larsh, James C., 13 Oct. 1857, Maggie E. Haughey             10/14/57-2
Larus, John R., (?) Mar. 1852, Theresa Tucker, dau. of
   William A.                                                 3/17/52-2
Laski, John Thomas, 3 Feb. 1860, Anna E. Booze                2/ 6/60-2
Lassiter, Thomas J., 1 May 1859, B. V. M. Barry               5/ 5/59-2
Laudeman, Fred'k., 29 July 1852, Barbetta E. Kuhn            7/31/52-2
Lauder, Wm. S., 26 Nov. 1851, Elizabeth King; corrected copy 12/18/51-2
Lauderman, Edward J., 9 June 1859, Mary E. Collins            6/11/59-2
Lauffer, Samuel B., 11 Mar. 1851, Eliza E. Buchanan, dau. of
   J. M.; corrected copy                                      3/17/51-2
Laughlin, J. McHenry, 6 Jan. 1857, Mary E. King              1/14/57-2
Laughten, Jeremiah A., 12 Feb. 1854, Mary Ann Marshall        3/11/54-2
Laughton, John W., 6 Dec. 1860, Martha A. Pearson, dau. of
   Levi                                                      12/11/60-2
Lauhheimer, Henry, 4 Jan. 1852, Baubet Aishberg               1/ 6/52-2
Laurence, George R., 4 May 1856, Virginia Jordon             5/12/56-2
Laurence, Thomas W., 17 June 1858, Ellen Brewer              6/19/58-2
Lauster, Charles Wm., 2 Oct. 1859, Henrietta Echardt         10/ 4/59-2
Lavinder, Fleming J., 12 May 1857, Lizzie T. O'Dell          5/14/57-2
Lavine, John Wm., 8 Nov. 1858, Amanda V. Webster             11/ 9/58-2
Law, William, 21 Nov. 1859, Annie Fehely; 11/26/59-2         11/28/59-2
```

Lawder, John, 23 Feb. 1857, Arabella Ruley   2/25/57-2
Lawder, Samuel M., Jr., 23 Dec. 1853, Dorcas Amanda Willey,
    dau. of William   12/24/53-2
Lawder, Wm. S., 26 Nov. 1851, Elizabeth King   12/17/51-2
Lawless, John, 15 Mar. 1858, Ann McDermot   4/22/58-2
Lawn, R. S., 14 Aug. 1851, E. B. Grove   8/16/51-2
Lawrence, Francis, 3 Nov. 1859, Ann M. Lawrence   11/ 5/59-2
Lawrence, Jacob, 25 Jan. 1855, Caroline Monroe   1/30/55-2
Lawrence, Richard, 15 June 1851, Lizzie F. Stalens   6/16/51-2
Laws, David O., 23 Apr. 1851, Emily Ricketts   4/26/51-2
Laws, J. Newton, 2 June 1859, Sallie A. Ferry   6/ 4/59-2
Laws, J. Thomson, 24 June 1852, Elizabeth M. Cariss, dau. of
    Samuel   6/26/52-2
Laws, Robert H., 6 Sept. 1854, Louisa Pierce   9/ 8/54-2
Laws, William, 7 July 1857, Charity Ferry   7/11/57-2
Lawson, H. S., 13 Jan. 1851, (Mrs.) Virginia S. Kennard, dau.
    of (Capt.) Jacob Lauderman   1/20/51-2
Lawton, Charles H., Jr., 8 Sept. 1859, Margaret J. Walton   9/13/59-2
Lawton, Elbridge, 10 Aug. 1852, Matilda E. Durham   8/12/52-2
Lawton, John, 10 Feb. 1851, Rebecca Sykes Beaumont   2/14/51-2
Lawton, William H., 4 Aug. 1853, Harriet Waters   8/12/53-2
Layfield, James T., 1-(?) Jan. 1853, Sarah E. Jefferson   2/ 3/53-2
Layman, Jacob, 15 Apr. 1858, Margaret Kelly   4/16/58-2
Layman, James, 9 Feb. 1853, Ann Madderson   3/ 5/53-2
Layton, Albert S., 11 Feb. 1853, Martha Agnes Rogers   2/12/53-2
Lea, J. N., 6 Oct. 1858, (Mrs.) M. R. Duncan, dau. of Dennis
    S. Smith   10/12/58-2
Lea, Samuel T., 6 Oct. 1845, Elizabeth Busch; 6/ 6/56-2   6/ 7/56-2
Leabay, Thomas, 26 Oct. 1853, Emily Hush   10/29/53-2
League, Albert H. (Capt.), 19 June 1856, Permelia Clark   6/23/56-2
League, George W., 16 Dec. 1851, Lizzie A. Gorsuch, dau. of
    Thomas   12/18/51-2
League, John J., 17 Oct. 1853, Annie Amelia Rose   12/13/53-2
League, John S., 26 Sept. 1859, Lucy E. Bradshaw   9/29/59-2
League, Leander C., 11 Aug. 1855, Sallie A. Merriken   2/12/56-2
Lealend, John W., 14 Apr. 1852, Elizabeth F. A. Lee   4/26/52-2
Leamy, James C., 23 Sept. 1858, Sarah E. Bayley   10/ 5/58-2
Leary, Jeremiah, 6 Sept. 1860, Margaret E. Burneston   9/ 7/60-2
Leary, John, 16 Nov. 1858, Lydia F. Howard   11/17/58-2
Leary, Thomas, 6 Sept. 1852, Margaret McSweney   9/ 9/52-2
Leas, Chas. A. (Dr.), 14 Feb. 1852, Lizzie Swigart Frush, dau.
    of William   2/17/52-2
Lease, Jacob Frederick, 3 July 1856, Phebe Elizabeth Benton   7/ 7/56-2
Leathe, Henry A., 17 May 1856, Matilda A. Venabels   7/30/56-2
Leatherberry, Chas. P., 19 Dec. 1860, Rachel A. F. Deale   12/20/60-2
Leatherwood, John H., 21 Sept. 1851, Ellen Grimes   10/ 1/51-2
Leber, J. H., 2 Oct. 1860, Emma L. Tilyear, dau. of (Dr.)
    H. W.   10/ 8/60-2
Lechmere, H. E., 24 July 1856, F. O. Nelson   8/ 1/56-2
Lecompte, Chas. I., 24 Nov. 1852, Harriet A. Rawleigh   11/27/52-2
Lecompte, Francis A., 20 May 1858, Eveline B. Foxwell   5/21/58-2
Lecompte, Thomas, 10 Oct. 1854, Mary Boston   10/13/54-2
Lecoumpt, Thomas, 9 Apr. 1852, Catharine Mills   4/13/52-2
Le Count, James, 24 Feb. 1853, Harriet Ann Clark   2/26/53-2
Ledley, George W., 20 Dec. 1855, Olivia A. Steuart   12/24/55-2
Ledwell, David F. Wall, 18 Oct. 1855, Margaret Peckchok   10/20/55-2
Lee, Andrew G., 16 Aug. 1860, (Mrs.) C. M. McLean   8/20/60-2
Lee, Benjamin, 15 Feb. 1859, Lizzie M. Taylor   2/19/59-2
Lee, Charles C., 23 Nov. 1858, Mary Ella Grant, dau. of
    Joseph P.   11/29/58-2
Lee, Columbus W., 7 Sept. 1853, Lizzie E. Timmons   9/ 9/53-2
Lee, Edmond, 16 June 1852, Mary Ann Cullimore   6/29/52-2
Lee, Edward, 5 Jan. 1858, Mary J. Grinage   1/ 7/58-2
Lee, George A. (Rev.), 24 Sept. 1857, Ann Kent   10/ 8/57-2
Lee, Henry W., 31 May 1855, Mary Ann Elizabeth Dade   6/ 4/55-2

Lee, Hezekiah, 14 May 1857, Mary E. Kirby   5/16/57-2
Lee, Isaiah, 4 Nov. 1860, Mary Hynea   11/ 5/60-2
Lee, J. Oliver, 15 Mar. 1860, Marian W. Woodall   3/19/60-2
Lee, John Wesley, 9 Dec. 1852, Emily Blatchley   12/14/52-2
Lee, Joseph, 16 Jan. 1851, Rosanna Towson   2/ 1/51-2
Lee, Levi, 26 May 1859, Martha Ann Brown   6/10/59-2
Lee, Levin (Rev.), 26 Oct. 1854, (Mrs.) Henrietta Williams   10/28/54-2
Lee, Lycurgus, 4 Feb. 1851, Mary E. Hall   2/ 5/51-2
Lee, Thomas D., 22 July 1859, Rebecca J. Purdy   7/28/59-2
Lee, William D., 1 June 1859, Isabella V. Keene, dau. of
     (Capt.) Samuel   7/ 1/59-2
Lee, William G., 11 Feb. 1856, Rebecca Grant, dau. of Charles
     and Mary   3/13/56-2
Lee, Wm. Collinson, 30 Sept. 1852, Sarah Jane Terry, dau. of
     Thomas   10/ 2/52-2
Lee, Wm. W., 13 May 1851, Frances P. Costin, dau. of William   5/15/51-2
Leebbehesen, Clemens, 19 Jan. 1851, Jane E. Lurty; corrected
     copy   1/29/51-2
Leebbehesen, Clemens, 19 Jan. 1851, Jane E. Twety   1/28/51-2
Leeke, Arthur W., 11 Sept. 1860, Lizzie R. Merriken, dau. of
     (Rev.) Joseph   9/21/60-2
Leeke, James Adgate, 18 Aug. 1853, Anna M. Webb   8/29/53-2
Leeke, William H., 14 May 1857, Maggie J. McCauley   5/16/57-2
Leemer, John W., 3 Oct. 1860, Victorine S. Henry   10/ 9/60-2
Leerenon, Michael McG., 2 June 1857, Catherine E. Fullerton   6/10/57-2
Lees, Robert T. N., 2 Sept. 1855, Mary Jane Shaw   9/18/55-2
Lees, Simeon, 16 Aug. 1854, Ann Maria Culimere, dau. of John   8/24/54-2
Leeson, Maurice C., 24 May 1855, Rachel L. Ridge   5/25/55-2
Leet, J. D., 22 June 1852, Mary J. Sanders   6/24/52-2
Lefevre, J. A., 19 Oct. 1858, Kate L. Sauerwein   10/20/58-2
Lefevre, Wm. H., 29 Mar. 1860, Mary E. Anderson   4/ 3/60-2
Lefsver, William, 8 Feb. 1854, Sally Ann Windoes   2/10/54-2
Legg, John T., 25 Sept. 1854, Elizabeth D. Bowen   9/28/54-2
Le Gourde, Lawrence L., 15 May 1856, Sallie C. Small   5/16/56-2
Lehes, John, 9 Nov. 1854, Sarah Helena McAvoy   11/11/54-2
Lehmayer, Simon, 28 Aug. 1860, Henrietta Deiievie, dau. of
     Samuel; corrected copy   8/30/60-2
Lehmayer, Simon, 28 Aug. 1860, Henrietta Pe-(?)-levil, dau.
     of Samuel   8/29/60-2
Lehr, Philip, 25 May 1852, Augusta Caroline Wiedner   5/27/52-2
Leicht, John J., 17 Apr. 1856, Caroline Fry, dau. of Michael   4/19/56-2
Leishear, Albert Fairfax, 18 May 1856, Jane P. Gibbs   5/20/56-2
Leishear, Richard J., 30 July 1856, Elizabeth Norris   7/31/56-2
Leishear, William M., 20 Jan. 1852, Mary M. Moore   1/22/52-2
Leist, Frederick, 7 June 1859, Isabella Horn   6/ 9/59-2
Leitz, James H. B., 26 Jan. 1860, Aliceanna Poole   2/ 8/60-2
Leman, John, 23 July 1857, Ann M. Shipley   7/25/57-2
Lemcke, Morritz H., 8 Oct. 1859, Elleanor G. Thompson   10/11/59-2
Lemmon, Andrew H.; no date given, (Mrs.) Susannah Tyson   8/ 6/57-2
Lemmon, James, 6 Nov. 1856, Anna Ross   11/ 8/56-2
Lemmon, John Washington, 8 Mar. 1855, Ann Rebecca McLean   5/ 7/55-2
Lemmon, Robert, Jr., 14 Nov. 1854, Fannie C. Hall, dau. of
     Henry A.   11/20/54-2
Lemon, Joshua, 7 Apr. 1853, Elizabeth Darr   4/ 8/53-2
Lempkin, R. G., 22 July 1856, Lusie H. Ferry, dau. of Edward   7/26/56-2
Lennan, Samuel C., 25 Mar. 1852, Sarah Ann Kennard, dau. of
     Kennard   4/ 3/52-2
Lennou, Joseph G., 21 Oct. 1852, Isabella R. Rudd   10/30/52-2
Lennox, George T., 26 Apr. 1859, Susanna Rankin, dau. of
     Samuel   5/ 2/59-2
Lenzner, Christian, 19 June 1851, Susanna Stone   7/ 7/51-2
Leobold, Joseph, 23 Sept. 1860, Rosa Weiller   9/24/60-2
Leonard, John, 8 Apr. 1856, Angeline L. Healey   5/ 7/56-2
Leonard, John W. R., 29 Feb. 1860, Annie P. Greekley   3/21/60-2
Leonard, Patrick, 12 Jan. 1853, Bridget Ford   1/20/53-2

Leonard, Thos. P. Stran, 7 June 1857, Sarah Virginia Vain	6/30/57-2
Lepson, William H., 20 Oct. 1859, Matilda Ann Owings	3/25/59-2
Lerew, M., 28 Feb. 1858, Barbara M. Herr	3/ 5/58-2
Le Roy, Joseph, 23 June 1857, Ann Bernard	7/13/57-2
Lerp, Theodore, 3 May 1858, Ann Catharine Henkell	5/14/58-2
Lester, Samuel T., 11 Aug. 1859, Rosina W. Saumenig, dau. of Conrad	8/17/59-2
Lester, Thomas, 12 Jan. 1854, Sophia L. Wiley	1/14/54-2
Lester, William W., 9 Feb. 1858, Elizabeth J. Walker	2/11/58-2
Letournau, Peter G., 8 Dec. 1859, Susan Harvey	12/13/59-2
Letsinger, James, 18 May 1857, (Mrs.) Elenor White	5/21/57-2
Leucht, Joseph, 9 Aug. 1860, Caroline Rice	8/10/60-2
Levering, Samuel S., 22 May 1854, Victoria L. Wright, dau. of W. H. D. C.	5/23/54-2
Levy, Andrew J., 29 June 1856, Susan Ann Sloffer	7/ 1/56-2
Levy, Charles, 20 Jan. 1857, Clarina Scott	1/24/57-2
Lewin, Thomas, 2 Mar. 1858, Elizabeth J. Fee	3/ 4/58-2
Lewis, Abraham L., 14 June 1853, Caroline J. Clark	6/21/53-2
Lewis, Antonia, 16 July 1857, Caroline Koburn	7/18/57-2
Lewis, Archibald S., 11 Jan. 1852, (Mrs.) Catharine J. Bagwell	1/13/52-2
Lewis, Benjamin L., 14 June 1853, Caroline J. Clarke	6/18/53-2
Lewis, Elijah, 28 Sept. 1851, Nancy Richardson	9/30/51-2
Lewis, George F., 18 Jan. 1859, Julia A. Morford, dau. of James C.	1/22/59-2
Lewis, George Washington, 25 Mar. 1852, Emily Contee, dau. of (Hon.) Reverdy Johnson	3/29/52-2
Lewis, Henry, 12 Mar. 1853, Elizabeth Harding	3/14/53-2
Lewis, Henry, 6 Apr. 1853, Julia A. Baker	4/ 8/53-2
Lewis, Henry B., 5 Aug. 1852, Elizabeth Ann Pell	8/10/52-2
Lewis, Hester Jane, 12 Dec. 1854, Hiram Washington	1/ 1/55-2
Lewis, Homer C., 21 Dec. 1852, Editha Williams	12/23/52-2
Lewis, Jacob S., 5 Oct. 1852, Elizabeth D. Perry	10/ 9/52-2
Lewis, James, 12 June 1851, Ellen Elizabeth Dubant	6/17/51-2
Lewis, John, 3 July 1852, Ann Winks	7/19/52-2
Lewis, John B., 21 Sept. 1851, Caroline B. Dorritie	9/22/51-2
Lewis, John T. K., 28 Feb. 1860, E. Whistler	4/21/60-2
Lewis, Joseph N., 6 Sept. 1860, Sallie C. Little	9/10/60-2
Lewis, Mathew, 16 Aug. 1853, Ann C. Slocum, dau. of George	8/17/53-2
Lewis, Stephen, 7 Dec. 1853, Mary C. Starr	12/ 9/53-2
Lewis, Thomas, 23 Jan. 1851, Mary E. Beal	1/25/51-2
Lewis, Thomas, 19 June 1856, Maria E. Clark	6/23/56-2
Lewis, Thomas Browne, 11 Feb. 1851, Mary Lizzie Innes	2/13/51-2
Lewis, William P., 31 Dec. 1855, (Mrs.) Nancy A. Simms; 3/14/56-2	3/15/56-2
Lewis, William Penn, 24 June 1852, Isabel Jane MacFerran, dau. of Wm.	6/25/52-2
Lewis, William W., 8 Mar. 1855, Ann Whitney	3/12/55-2
Lewis, Wm. H., 23 Nov. 1859, Rebecca W. Stuard	11/26/59-2
Leydecker, Theodore, 20 Mar. 1853, (Mrs.) Margaret Ann Reh	3/21/53-2
Lidard, John, 16 Oct. 1856, Laura A. McAfee	10/18/56-2
Lidard, Moses, 7 Mar. 1855, Delia A. Mason	3/16/55-2
Liebig, G. A. (Dr.), 15 Oct. 1860, Lizzie Holland	10/16/60-2
Lightner, Isaac N., 14 Sept. 1858, Kate Arthur	9/17/58-2
Lightner, John M., 26 Oct. 1852, Mary Ann Woolen	1/31/53-2
Lightner, William H., 27 Feb. 1851, Margaret A. Pascon	3/ 4/51-2
Ligoe, L. (Capt.), 26 Apr. 1854, Elizabeth Jane Prichard	4/27/54-2
Lilly, A. W. (Rev.), 4 Dec. 1851, Margery A. Herman, dau. of Martin	12/25/51-2
Lilly, Edwin, 21 Apr. 1853, Anna Josephine Ridgely, dau. of James L.	4/22/53-2
Lilly, John, 17 June 1856, Sarah E. Fortnet	6/19/56-2
Lilly, Richard, Jr., 6 Dec. 1855, Josephine Chamberlin	12/ 7/55-2
Lillybridge, Octavius C., 20 Mar. 1856, Martha A. Young, dau. of A. L. Hanson	3/24/56-2

Linaweaver, John N., 2 Jan. 1853, Catharine Cropp   3/ 1/53-2
Lincoln, Jonah S., 6 Mar. 1855, Elizabeth Pollock
Linden, Clarence M., 1 Nov. 1854, (Mrs.) Elizabeth Hammock   11/ 3/54-2
Lindenman, John F., 24 Aug. 1852, Mary Louisa Gillingham   8/26/52-2
Lindley, Jacob, 19 Aug. 1856, Sallie A. Ellicott   8/31/58-2
Lindsay, James M., 20 Dec. 1860, Sarah Frances Jarrett   12/24/60-2
Lindsay, John; no date given, (Mrs.) Amelia Archer   10/26/52-2
Lindsay, Wm. R., 15 Oct. 1856, Mary D. Thompson, dau. of
    John A.   10/20/56-2
Line, Thomas, 24 Feb. 1859, Anne E. Briscoe, dau. of H. T. M.   2/26/59-2
Lineaweaver, George W., 16 Feb. 1857, Sarah A. Emerick   2/19/57-2
Lingenfelter, James D., 2 May 1852, Frances Gilliena   5/ 3/52-2
Linhard, John, 17 June 1858, Jennie H. Brawner, dau. of
    Andrew   10/19/58-2
Linhard, Michael A., 16 July 1857, Annie M. Bishop   7/20/57-2
Linstead, Charles *, 27 June 1858, Mary C. Brady   3/ 5/59-2
Linthicum, A. S. (Dr.), 30 June 1858, Eleanor R. Conaway   7/ 7/58-2
Linthicum, Charles, 6 Mar. 1860, Louisiana C. Linthicum, dau.
    of Richard   3/ 9/60-2
Linthicum, Charles G., 12 Oct. 1854, Mary Jane Miller   10/14/54-2
Linthicum, Frederick, 11 Feb. 1851, Hannah P. A. Garrott   2/15/51-2
Linthicum, G. Washington, 26 May 1859, Mary Louisa Clark, dau.
    of (Hon.) T. S.   6/ 9/59-2
Linthicum, Harman R., 18 Oct. 1854, Mary Catharine Hill   10/25/54-2
Linthicum, J. G. (Dr.), 16 Oct. 1860, Marie R. Wilson, dau.
    of Jno. W.   10/18/60-2
Linthicum, J. Solon S., 22 Feb. 1855, Sarah C. Carr, dau. of
    Roscay   2/27/55-2
Linthicum, James A., 6 June 1855, Leah Frances Davis   6/ 8/55-2
Linthicum, L. S., 23 Oct. 1855, Mary A. Walker, dau. of
    Richard   10/30/55-2
Linthicum, Stephen L., 25 Sept. 1851, Ella M. Hause   10/ 2/51-2
Linthicum, Stephen L., 8 May 1855, Sarah E. Sherbert   5/11/55-2
Linthicum, Thales A., 22 Aug. 1860, Emma S. Alexander, dau. of
    J. S.   8/24/60-2
Linthicum, Thomas J., 19 Jan. 1858, Mary D. Smith   1/23/58-2
Linthicum, Wm. A., 8 Feb. 1853, Sarah E. Mullikin, dau. of
    M. H.   2/12/53-2
Lintner, John A., 28 Dec. 1857, Margaret Connell   12/31/57-2
Linton, John, 6 Mar. 1851, Kezia S. Webster   3/ 8/51-2
Linton, Samuel, 31 Aug. 1851, Matilda Ballauf   9/27/51-2
Linzey, John H.; no date given, (Mrs.) Olevia Ann Kelley   5/21/53-2
Lipp, Francis X., 29 Nov. 1860, Laura C. Getty   12/ 1/60-2
Liscom, Jehial, 12 Apr. 1857, Margaret S. Allen   4/14/57-2
Litsinger, Jos. A., 14 Feb. 1853, Mary J. Pool, dau. of John   2/22/53-2
Littig, A. Ward, 3 Nov. 1858, Kate Ritchie   11/23/58-2
Little, Henry (Capt.), 3 Apr. 1855, Martha Morrison, dau. of
    (Col.) P.   4/20/55-2
Little, Joseph, 12 Aug. 1851, Sarah E. Fairall   8/15/51-2
Little, Joseph D. A., 6 Aug. 1855, Sarah E. Gallaway, dau. of
    William   8/ 9/55-2
Little, Wm. H., 21 Nov. 1852, Christina Ellen Spear   11/25/52-2
Littrell, James W., 4 Jan. 1858, (Mrs.) Mary E. Shrive   2/18/58-2
Lively, James, 19 Apr. 1857, Charlotte Hutchins   4/21/57-2
Lively, Statia, 5 Apr. 1860, Ellen Fields   4/ 9/60-2
Livingston, Wm., 1 Mar. 1853, Margaret C. Hall   3/ 4/53-2
Livingston, James, 1 Jan. 1860, Georgeann Martin   4/11/60-2
Livsey, Jas., 12 Dec. 1858, S. J. Carmine   12/16/58-2
Llowe, Thos. J., 16 Dec. 1856, Annie E. Pindell, dau. of
    R. G.   12/23/56-2
Lloyd, George, 27 Dec. 1853, Ann Maria Thomas   12/31/53-2
Lloyd, James T., 18 Nov. 1855, Louisa R. Locke, dau. of
    Andrew R.   12/ 7/55-2
Lloyd, John H., 21 Dec. 1854, Eugenia D. McDonald   12/23/54-2
Lloyd, Rush, 25 May 1858, Adelaide House   5/26/58-2

Lloyd, William, 2 May 1855, Emily V. Johnston   5/ 4/55-2
Loage, Samuel W., 26 Aug. 1855, Virginia Ann Galloway   8/27/55-2
Loan, John, 3 July 1851, Sarah Hughes   7/ 9/51-2
Loane, Edwin D., 28 Nov. 1855, Mary E. Solomon   11/29/55-2
Loane, Geo. B., 23 Dec. 1855, Mary Ann Morrison   12/24/55-2
Loane, Jos. G., 30 Jan. 1853, Lizzie Fitzpatrick   2/ 3/53-2
Lock, John M., 17 Feb. 1853, Bettie C. Riley   2/18/53-2
Lockard, John, 26 Aug. 1858, Elizabeth E. Souders   8/30/58-2
Lockard, Samuel H., 29 Apr. 1852, Maggie Boyd, dau. of James   5/ 3/52-2
Lockie, John, 4 July 1852, Matilda Catharine Clark   7/ 7/52-2
Lockman, Benjamin, 12 Nov. 1857, Harriet Cooper   11/14/57-2
Lockner, Chas. F., 20 Dec. 1855, Rebecca Jones   12/28/55-2
Locks, John W., 4 Feb. 1858, (Mrs.) Mary Ann Ford   3/ 6/58-2
Lockwood, Charles; no date given, Mary B. Mathiot, dau. of
     John B.   1/19/53-2
Lockwood, Wm. F., 10 Apr. 1856, Maggie Bayley   4/21/56-2
Loeffler, Constantine, 11 Jan. 1859, Margaret Reinig   1/19/59-2
Loewenstein, J. M., 6 June 1854, Dina J. Loebenstein   6/30/54-2
Loftus, James, 10 Nov. 1857, Susan Lainhart   11/18/57-2
Logan, Charles W., 5 Oct. 1852, Maria T. Wall, dau. of George   10/ 9/52-2
Logan, James, 1 Nov. 1859, Eliza Emory   12/ 6/59-2
Logan, James H., 21 Sept. 1859, Mary Louise League   9/23/59-2
Logan, Joseph T., 24 May 1859, Sallie A. Maguire   5/28/59-2
Logan, Samuel L., 1 Apr. 1851, Lucy Milburn   4/24/51-2
Logan, William C., 20 Aug. 1857, Josephine Zinkand   8/22/57-2
Logsdon, Wm. H., 9 Jan. 1854, Mary Algie   1/10/54-2
Logue, A. J., 28 Sept. 1853, Susanna Flinchem   10/ 1/53-2
Logue, David, 27 Dec. 1858, Elizabeth Mulligan   1/ 6/59-2
Logue, W. J., 28 Aug. 1858, Armina E. Donaldson   8/31/58-2
Lohman, Frederick, 7 May 1854, Caroline Preistrejahn   5/10/54-2
Lohmeyer, H. H., 14 Feb. 1860, Eliza Moelich   2/23/60-2
Loker, James B., 10 Dec. 1857, Elizabeth Warner, dau. of
     Maehael   12/12/57-2
Lomack, Thomas, 6 Sept. 1860, Emma Armstrong   9/ 8/60-2
Loman, Denton, 29 May 1857, Mary Ann Larrance   5/30/57-2
Loney, Robert W., 18 Apr. 1854, Margaret Jane Wilson   4/25/54-2
Long, Andrew, 15 July 1858, Mary B. Richardson   7/20/58-2
Long, Cornelius B., 11 June 1859, Louisa Bellows   6/28/59-2
Long, David; no date given, Elizabeth Hook   4/ 6/55-2
Long, John, 13 Feb. 1854, Malinda Owens   2/24/54-2
Long, John, 23 Dec. 1858, Anna M. Bond   12/24/58-2
Long, John F., 25 June 1851, Anna S. Crop   8/ 2/51-2
Long, John M., 6 June 1855, Modeste V. Affayroux   6/11/55-2
Long, Littleton B. (Capt.), 11 July 1854, Kate Tucker   7/15/54-2
Long, Louis L., 2 May 1854, Annie E. Storm, dau. of James   5/ 8/54-2
Long, Peter, 3 June 1855, Ann Grimes   6/ 9/55-2
Long, Richard D., 14 Nov. 1855, Catherine Craddick   11/17/55-2
Long, Stephen B., 30 Sept. 1856, Emily E. Byrne   10/ 2/56-2
Long, William, 24 Apr. 1851, Catherine Ann Smith   4/26/51-2
Long, Wm. J.; no date given, Mary M. Taylor   5/25/53-2
Longley, Samuel T., 7 June 1855, Mary A. Peastor, dau. of
     J. C.   6/13/55-2
Longsill, John Nathaniel, 24 Sept. 1860, Ruth Jane Smith   9/26/60-2
Longstreth, Charles, Jr., 6 Dec. 1853, Virginia L. Dunham, dau.
     of T. C.   12/10/53-2
Longwell, David, 29 May 1851, Mary Ann Maddux   6/17/51-2
Lookingland, John, 1 June 1852, Lydia M. Davis   6/ 3/52-2
Loper, John H., son of Henry G., 14 Feb. 1854, Annie Pierce,
     dau. of Peter P.; corrected copy   2/17/54-2
Loram, Wm., 6 Oct. 1859, Ellen T. Mullen, dau. of John   10/11/59-2
Lorando, Bartholomew; no date given, Laura Taylor Shaw   8/ 9/58-2
Lord, Charles W., 19 Nov. 1856, Laura G. Robbins, dau. of
     Rowland A.   11/22/56-2
Lord, Daniel S., 16 July 1854, Theresa H. Mendon   7/20/54-2
Lord, Edward K., 23 May 1853, Narcissa C. Ferguson   5/24/53-2

```
Lord, Geo. W., 10 Nov. 1859, Matilda A. Solomon              11/18/59-2
Loscom, James, 23 Dec. 1857, Elizabeth Magaw                  4/ 1/58-2
Lotz, Edward F., 2 Nov. 1853, Catherine Hughes               11/ 4/53-2
Loucks, Jacob, 1 Jan. 1856, Catherine E. Slagle               1/ 3/56-2
Loudenslager, John W., 13 Dec. 1851, Eliza Mabyn             12/16/51-2
Louderman, Frederick R., 16 May 1855, Eliza J. Fardwell       5/18/55-2
Lougherty, Michael, 3 Feb. 1856, Mary Ann Gillson             2/ 6/56-2
Lougston, Wm., 5 Mar. 1853, Ellen Miller                      3/10/53-2
Love, Geo. B., 18 June 1860, Carrie J. Starr; 7/17/60-2       7/18/60-2
Love, James E., 19 Nov. 1857, Susan Ledley                   11/21/57-2
Love, James M., 12 June 1851, Ruth M. Cullison, dau. of
     Micajha                                                  6/24/51-2
Love, John A., 10 July 1851, Amy Elizabeth Brown              7/23/51-2
Loveday, Thomas S., 15 Jan. 1851, Susan A. Silence            2/11/51-2
Lovejoy, Amos, 3 Aug. 1858, Kate Virginia Monoreiff, dau. of
     (Capt.) James                                            8/ 4/58-2
Lovet, Samuel, 25 Dec. 1853, Mary Ann Jeanes                 12/29/53-2
Lovet, William, 7 Jan. 1855, Tabitha Jenes                    1/10/55-2
Lovett, Josiah (Capt.), 8 Jan. 1853, Mary Virginia Masslcot, dau.
     of (Capt.) Wm.                                           1/10/53-2
Low, Franklin, 21 Apr. 1853, Julia F. Munroe, dau. of
     Nathaniel                                                4/29/53-2
Lowe, Alexander, 29 Sept. 1858, Ellen McQuail                10/ 2/58-2
Lowe, Daniel W., 24 Sept. 1854, Isabel Yackel                 9/30/54-2
Lowe, David J., 13 Sept. 1857, Urilla A. Slayback            12/ 4/57-2
Lowe, Henry, 16 Dec. 1851, Kate Mentzel                      12/19/51-2
Lowe, James P.; no date given, Nannie E. Bowers               6/ 8/54-2
Lowe, John, 4 Jan. 1853, Elizabeth A. Pilkington              1/10/53-2
Lowe, John V., 31 Mar. 1853, Mary Clendenin                   4/ 5/53-2
Lowe, Joseph, 14 Oct. 1852, Margaret Dean                    10/18/52-2
Lowe, Yelverton M., (?) June 1857, Mary A. Slayback          12/ 4/57-2
Lowenthal, Charles H., 17 Aug. 1856, Julia Marcum             8/19/56-2
Lowman, John Randolph, 26 June 1859, Julia Kilman             6/28/59-2
Lowman, Lewis, 10 Dec. 1854, Nanny Baner, dau. of Henry      12/13/54-2
Lowman, Mathias, 5 June 1851, Harriet Preston, dau. of
     Thomas                                                   6/ 6/51-2
Lowman, William, 29 June 1851, Martha Ann Wingate             7/ 1/51-2
Lownds, Calvin G., 12 Oct. 1858, Cecilla C. Smith, dau. of
     John L.                                                 10/15/58-2
Lowrey, Elijah A., 20 May 1852, Elizabeth E. Floyd            5/21/52-2
Lowrey, William, 7 Aug. 1855, Martha E. Hook, dau. of
     Joseph and Hannah                                        8/10/55-2
Lowry, Alexander Francis, 1 Oct. 1857, Mary Frances Watts,
     dau. of P. A.                                           10/ 5/57-2
Lowry, John, 9 Feb. 1859, (Mrs.) Sophia Kenan                 2/15/59-2
Lowry, Robert J., 10 July 1851, Mary E. Keighler, dau. of
     John                                                     7/14/51-2
Loyd, Reuben, 29 Aug. 1852, (Mrs.) Susan Rouse                8/30/52-2
Lubbehusen, Clement, 9 Oct. 1853, Ann Maria Lurty            10/22/53-2
Lubee, Thos., 16 Oct. 1851, Rosa Ann O'Reilly                10/28/51-2
Lucas, John W., 15 Feb. 1852, Hannah R. Warwick               2/21/52-2
Lucas, Richard James, 1 Aug. 1855, Margaret Jane Fisher       8/ 3/55-2
Lucas, Saml., 13 Nov. 1855, Mary R. Rourke                   11/15/55-2
Lucas, Sylvanus H., 16 Mar. 1859, Esther E. White            3/22/59-2
Lucas, Thos., 24 July 1860, Rosanna Jones                     7/26/60-2
Lucas, William B., 31 Oct. 1855, Maggie J. Knox, dau. of
     Alexander                                               11/ 3/55-3
Lucas, William F., 13 July 1853, Mary B. Roberts              7/13/53-2
Lumley, Dowling T., 7 May 1856, Emma De Baufre                5/ 8/56-2
Lusby, Charles A., 21 Oct. 1856, Sarah F. Thompson           10/25/56-2
Lusby, Henry W., 21 Mar. 1851, Elizabeth Jane Clarke          4/ 2/51-2
Lushbaugh, B. Franklin, 13 Aug. 1851, Sallie R. Fitzpatrick   8/15/51-2
Luttgerding, Charles H., 8 Nov. 1857, Mary A. Peacock        11/10/57-2
Lutts, Charles G., 1 May 1855, Mary B. Statamen, dau. of
     U. B.                                                    5/ 3/55-2
```

Lutts, John, Jr., 13 Feb. 1851, Cecilia Pendergast   2/26/51-2
Lutz, Cornelius F., 15 June 1853, Isabella Huffington   6/17/53-2
Lutz, Henry, 26 July 1860, Elizabeth A. Bugen   8/ 1/60-2
Lycett, Geo., 7 May 1857, Eliza A. Flint, dau. of Thos.   5/ 8/57-2
Lyddane, John L., 6 Apr. 1853, Emily Moxley   4/11/53-2
Lyeth, Andrew H., 3 May 1859, Ann Frances Warner, dau. of
    (Dr.) Alfred L.   5/10/59-2
Lyman, Charles, 29 Oct. 1857, Mary Flynn   10/31/57-2
Lynch, Dixon S., 15 Dec. 1859, Elizabeth Brown   12/23/59-2
Lynch, Edward H., 5 Sept. 1853, Margaret A. White   9/20/53-2
Lynch, J., 22 Nov. 1853, Caroline M. Tucker   12/ 2/53-2
Lynch, J. G. (Dr.), 29 Apr. 1858, Emma V. Clarke, dau. of
    (Dr.) L. B.   5/ 3/58-2
Lynch, James W., 13 May 1854, Lydia Pumphrey   5/15/54-2
Lynch, John H., 21 May 1851, Frances R. Ensor   5/22/51-2
Lynch, John S. (Dr.), 8 Dec. 1857, M. Louise Sutton   12/10/57-2
Lynch, Joseph S., 31 Mar. 1857, A. Rebecca Ensor   4/ 7/57-2
Lynch, Joshua, 26 Nov. 1852, Susan Jones, dau. of John   11/29/52-2
Lynch, Lewis, 29 Mar. 1859, Cornelia E. Ensor   7/30/59-2
Lynch, Michael, 6 Feb. 1853, Julia Fahey   2/ 7/53-2
Lynch, Patrick, 19 Oct. 1857, Mary McWilliams   10/24/57-2
Lynch, Thos. A. (Dr.), 31 May 1860, Mary M. Hooper   6/ 1/60-2
Lynch, Thos. E., 4 Nov. 1852, Sarah F. Gayle, dau. of
    Edward T.   11/ 6/52-2
Lynch, William, 30 Dec. 1851, Catharine C. R. Buck, dau. of
    Benjamin   1/10/52-2
Lynde, R. D. (Dr.), 29 Dec. 1853, Carrie R. Wigart, dau. of
    Henry   1/ 7/54-2
Lyne, Leonard H., 16 Nov. 1854, Marie B. Ferguson, dau. of
    Thomas   11/23/54-2
Lyon, Charles H., 10 May 1854, Tamazine Parker   5/18/54-2
Lyon, Ira C., 2 Aug. 1854, Martha Rebecca Myer, dau. of Jno. J. 8/ 5/54-2
Lyon, John T., 6 May 1858, B. D. Kane   5/ 8/58-2
Lyon, Robert, 21 Aug. 1853, Elizabeth Jane Duncan   8/23/53-2
Lyon, William J., 14 June 1852, Mary A. Thompson, dau. of
    Wm. A.   6/17/52-2
Lyon, Wm. L., 18 Oct. 1853, Garafilia C. Berryman, dau. of
    John   10/21/53-2
Lyons, John, 26 Sept. 1852, Mary Machale   9/30/52-2
Lyons, John C., 1 Oct. 1857, Kate Lloyd   10/12/57-2
Lyons, John H., 30 Sept. 1856, Margaret A. Seymour   10/22/56-2
Lyons, Wm. B., 4 Oct. 1855, Mary I. Burley   10/ 6/55-2
Lyttle, James S., 22 Dec. 1859, Mary Ann Michael   12/29/59-2
Mabbitt, A. Joseph, 1 Oct. 1857, Annie S. Whitaker   10/ 5/57-2
Macartney, John E., 22 Dec. 1857, Susan H. Brown   12/31/57-2
Macartney, Robert, 5 Aug. 1852, Sarah A. Lanhart   8/ 7/52-2
Maccabe, Solomon, 4 Aug. 1859, Agnes Johnson, dau. of G. W.   8/ 8/59-2
Macclayland, R. Welss, 30 Nov. 1852, Sophia Josephine Jones   12/ 1/52-2
Maccubbin, Chas. T., 1 June 1857, Margaret Ann Kirk   6/ 3/57-2
Maccubbin, William M., 10 June 1860, Annie Gorman   6/26/60-2
MacDonald, P. M., 23 Nov. 1852, Leonora Spear, dau. of (Capt.)
    Wm.   11/24/52-2
Mace, George A., 6 June 1860, Ellen Brooks   6/18/60-2
Mace, Stephen T., 5 July 1853, Ann D. Cullum, dau. of Sutton   7/ 7/53-2
Mace, Theodore M., 25 Sept. 1860, Eliza Brooks   10/ 8/60-2
Mace, W. H. (Dr.), 22 Nov. 1853, Henrietta M. F. Johnson   11/24/53-2
Mace, William, 21 Sept. 1851, (Mrs.) Susan Adkerson   9/23/51-2
Macfarlan, C., 4 Nov. 1852, Clemenia E. Holley, dau. of
    John M. and Clemenia   11/20/52-2
Macgill, Wm. A., 21 Aug. 1851, Maria E. Gambrill, dau. of
    (Dr.) S.   8/23/51-2
Machmi, Joseph, 27 May 1859, Sarah A. Petticord   5/30/59-2
Mackenzie, John C. (Dr.), 26 Oct. 1852, Ella Nolard, dau. of
    (Col.) Lloyd   10/29/52-2

Mackey, Alexander H., 6 Apr. 1853, (Mrs.) S. A. Bradford,
    dau. of Wm. H. Crawford   4/16/53-2
Mackey, Haslett C., 26 Jan. 1852, Williamina H. Crawford,
    dau. of Wm. H.; 1/28/52-2   1/29/52-2
Mackin, Michael J., 10 July 1851, Mary Annie Timmins   7/12/51-2
Mackingham, Richard, 27 Nov. 1851, Permelia Lyeth   12/ 4/51-2
Macklin, John J., 6 May 1851, Jane Cecilia McCaffrey   5/ 7/51-2
Macknew, Chas., 4 Oct. 1852, Elizabeth Boom   10/12/52-2
MacKubin, James, 9 Nov. 1854, Comfort Augusta Worthington
    Dorsey, dau. of (Col.) Charles   11/11/54-2
Macky, Samuel, 22 Nov. 1854, Maggie Ewing, dau. of Samuel   11/28/54-2
Mac Lea, William H., 12 Mar. 1860, Hester Ann Ledard   3/16/60-2
Maclellan, Arthur R., 5 July 1859, Louisa J. Talbott   7/ 6/59-2
MacReady, John H. (Capt.), 25 Oct. 1855, Mary Frances Shelton 11/ 3/55-3
Mactavish, Alexander S., 10 Nov. 1856, Ellen Gilmor, dau. of
    Robert   11/14/56-2
Maculey, David H., 2 June 1853, Elizabeth Richardson   6/ 6/53-2
Macutuheans, Jas., 13 Apr. 1852, Mary Christina Sebeh   10/21/52-2
Macy, Chas. H., 19 Feb. 1856, Helen M. Hall, dau. of James   3/ 6/56-2
Madden, Israel, 9 Feb. 1858, Eliza Jane Emerson   2/12/58-2
Madden, John W., 13 Aug. 1857, Rachel A. R. Dorsey   8/15/57-2
Madden, Patrick, 31 Dec. 1857, Mary Barry   1/ 2/58-2
Madden, Samuel W., 29 Apr. 1858, Phebe Banks   5/ 1/58-2
Madden, Thos., 1 June 1852, Ann McNulty   6/ 9/52-2
Madeiry, Nicholas B., 10 May 1859, Mary R. Thomas, dau. of
    Saml.   5/21/59-2
Maffitt, John T., 1 May 1851, Rachel S. Helming, dau. of
    William   5/ 5/51-2
Mage, Oscar A., 5 June 1853, Virginia Wright   6/ 9/53-2
Magee, George E., 26 May 1853, Ann L. Davis   5/30/53-2
Magee, Paterson, 12 Feb. 1853, May Jane Boyd   2/16/53-2
Magers, Elias, 15 Jan. 1852, Mary R. T. Russell, dau. of Wm.   1/21/52-2
Magill, John M., 28 Sept. 1853, Ann Rebecca Dorney   10/ 1/53-2
Magill, Thomas (Dr.), 5 Jan. 1852, Lucinda S. King   1/ 6/52-2
Magness, George R., 20 Sept. 1860, Ann Maria Morgan   9/22/60-2
Magness, Jerome C., 5 June 1856, Josephine Debrow   7/ 7/56-2
Magness, Lee A., 13 Nov. 1860, Mary E. Price   11/15/60-2
Magness, Parker, 14 Jan. 1856, Mary Ann Martin   1/16/56-2
Magness, Stephen P., 22 Apr. 1858, Julia A. Treadwell   4/24/58-2
Magrath, John T. (Dr.), 10 Aug. 1854, Margaret E. Smiley   8/18/54-2
Magraw, Edward, 18 Jan. 1852, Eliza McCollam   1/28/52-2
Magrudder, John, 6 Feb. 1853, Mary Smith   2/15/53-2
Magruder, Aquilla, 27 Jan. 1853, Elizabeth Harris   1/29/53-2
Magruder, Fielder M., 17 Feb. 1853, Mary A. Cummins   2/26/53-2
Magruder, James E., 9 Oct. 1856, Sarah E. Moran   11/15/56-2
Magruder, Jesse H., 20 Apr. 1853, Kate Floyd   4/30/53-2
Magruder, John F. D., 27 Apr. 1854, Deborah Jane Gaither;
    corrected copy   5/12/54-2
Magruder, John F. D., 27 Apr. 1854, Jane Gaither   5/11/54-2
Magruder, Joseph, 4 Aug. 1851, Louisa Johnson   8/ 7/51-2
Magruder, Robert B., 11 Aug. 1859, Mary M. Wise   10/ 7/59-2
Magruder, Wm. T., 12 July 1860, Mary C. Hamilton, dau. of Wm. 7/13/60-2
Maguire, J. Ferguson, 11 June 1854, Martha M. Reeves   6/16/54-2
Maguire, James C., 31 Aug. 1854, Louisa Fahs   9/ 1/54-2
Maguire, Michael, 3 June 1855, Ellen Jane Mills   7/ 3/55-2
Maguire, Patrick, 23 Sept. 1855, Susan Quinn   10/16/55-2
Maguire, Robert, 29 Apr. 1859, Bridget Redden   5/ 2/59-2
Maguire, Wm. H. A., 5 Sept. 1855, Susannah Rooney   9/12/55-2
Maheny, Garret, 1 Dec. 1859, Elizabeth Stork   12/ 9/59-2
Mahon, O. S. (Dr.), 5 Oct. 1858, Theodosia Barriere   10/ 6/58-2
Mahorny, John T., 10 May 1860, Sarah J. Dixon   5/12/60-2
Mahorney, Woodford, 17 Apr. 1859, (Mrs.) Mary Ann Phipps   4/19/59-2
Maines, James, 1 Jan. 1852, Anna McMahon   1/10/52-2
Mainley, Samuel, 10 Mar. 1853, Elizabeth Ayres   3/14/53-2
Mainster, Jacob, 23 Dec. 1858, Mary A. Hipkins   1/ 4/59-2

Mainster, Samuel, 12 Mar. 1857, Josephine Turner   3/24/57-2
Maitland, Benjamin, 9 Aug. 1860, Estelle Deshon, dau. of C. M. 8/11/60-2
Maize, Andrew, 10 June 1858, Anna Maria Gleaves; 6/12/58-2   6/14/58-2
Makee, Hugh, 29 Aug. 1855, Anne G. Rutherdale   9/ 5/55-2
Makinson, Daniel, 9 Mar. 1854, Caroline Johannes   3/14/54-2
Male, Ezekiel A., 20 Oct. 1856, Eliza Page   12/30/56-2
Mallalieu, Franklin S., 17 June 1856, Martha E. Tredway   6/19/56-2
Mallen, Thomas F., 4 Jan. 1859, Maggie H. Devilbriss   1/ 6/59-2
Mallon, Patrick, 1 Nov. 1860, Rose A. McGearey   11/20/60-2
Mallonee, Wm. L., 6 Jan. 1859, Camilla E. Robinson, dau. of
     (Capt.) Wm.   2/10/59-2
Malloy, John, 2 Oct. 1856, Fannie A. Sollers, dau. of Thos. O. 10/ 4/56-2
Maloney, Andrew J., 11 Nov. 1855, Maria Ann Duncan   3/24/56-2
Maloney, James M., 16 Jan. 1859, Anna A. Beuhler   1/22/59-2
Maloney, P. J., 23 Dec. 1851, Jeanette Primrose   12/25/51-2
Maloney, Thomas, 6 May 1860, Mary Dugan   5/11/60-2
Malooly, Thomas, 8 Dec. 1851, Eliza Summers   12/13/51-2
Manger, Martin M., 1 May 1860, Margaret C. Hieatzman   5/ 8/60-2
Manifold, Andrew, 21 July 1856, Rebecca Chamberlian   8/18/56-2
Manion, James, 13 Apr. 1853, (Mrs.) (?) Monohon   4/16/53-2
Manlee, William, 13 Nov. 1855, Sarah E. P. Santmyer   11/17/55-2
Manley, Wm., 2 Oct. 1853, Ann Maria Owings, dau. of Richard   10/ 4/53-2
Manly, R. G., 29 June 1851, Elizabeth A. Parrish   7/ 3/51-2
Mann, Griffin A., 30 Sept. 1855, Priscilla Pinkney   10/ 2/55-2
Mann, James O., 23 July 1851, Eliza E. Brown   7/24/51-2
Mann, John Fletcher, 7 Jan. 1858, Maggie Newton, dau. of Wm.   1/16/58-2
Mann, John M., 16 Nov. 1851, Mary J. Croney   11/18/51-2
Mann, Joseph L. P., 4 Jan. 1858, Annie F. Bond   1/11/58-2
Mann, William Howard, 21 June 1859, Mary Frances Durham   6/22/59-2
Mannahan, J. F., 5 June 1855, Sarah A. Reese, dau. of
     John E.   6/ 6/55-2
Manning, Hugh, 17 Aug. 1854, Catharine Kennedy   8/22/54-2
Manning, James, 7 Dec. 1853, Catherine Golden   12/ 9/53-2
Manning, Patrick, 2 Feb. 1858, Margaret Keary   2/ 4/58-2
Manning, Valentine, 13 Feb. 1857, Mary Frances Hickman, dau. of
     Laurence   2/24/57-2
Manning, Wm. S., 12 Jan. 1858, Maria E. Fahnestock, dau. of
     Jesse   1/14/58-2
Manro, Wm. E., 26 Apr. 1859, Carrie M. Tucker, dau. of Joseph 4/28/59-2
Mansfield, James, 27 May 1858, Sarah E. Wehn, dau. of Philip
     and Elizabeth   5/29/58-2
Mansfield, James D., 11 Nov. 1851, Margaret Price, dau. of
     David   11/17/51-2
Mansfield, John F., 4 Dec. 1860, Laura J. Newnam   12/ 6/60-2
Mansfield, Nathan, 15 Apr. 1852, Matilda D. Wever   5/ 4/52-2
Mantz, D. Allen, 16 June 1859, Julia A. Miller   6/20/59-2
Mantz, Peter, 13 Aug. 1857, Elizabeth Buzzard   8/19/57-2
Maples, Cornelius, 25 Mar. 1856, Louisa Matilda Maples   5/14/56-2
Mapp, Richard A., 14 Apr. 1859, Mary Virginia Ashby   4/18/59-2
Marceron, Peter T.; no date given, Elizabeth F. X. Gartland,
     dau. of Francis   9/17/51-2
March, Wm. G., 31 Mar. 1851, Margaret P. Stiltz   4/ 3/51-2
Marchand, John B., 11 Nov. 1856, Margaret D. Thornton, dau.
     of Francis A.   11/14/56-2
Marden, William, Jr., 20 Jan. 1857, Lillie L. Cantor   1/28/57-2
Marfield, Samuel, 1 Jan. 1851, Margaret A. Short   1/ 4/51-2
Marie, Eugene, 1 Jan. 1856, Catherine Killen   1/ 1/56-2
Marion, Peter, 26 Nov. 1856, Isabella V. Quinn   11/29/56-2
Maris, Edward A. (Dr.), 12 Dec. 1853, Ellen A. Peterkin, dau.
     of George W.   12/14/53-2
Markell, Francis, 11 Dec. 1856, Caroline M. Delaplaine   2/ 7/56-2
Markriter, John, 12 Oct. 1858, Mary J. Larmour   10/15/58-2
Marks, John, 14 Feb. 1859, Jane Taylor   2/19/59-2
Marks, Oscar M., 24 Aug. 1858, Harriet A. Hanson   8/26/58-2

Marks, Thomas Hammond, 8 Feb. 1853, Mary Jane Clarke, dau.
   of Austen S.   2/10/53-2
Marlain, David, 18 Sept. 1860, Emily Watts; corrected copy   9/21/60-2
Marley, John, 10 Mar. 1859, Ellen Gardner   3/14/59-2
Marony, James, 20 Apr. 1855, Margaret McCarthy   5/ 3/55-2
Marr, William, 8 Apr. 1856, Louisa Bentley   4/10/56-2
Marren, John, 30 Oct. 1855, Mary Jane Carrigan   11/14/55-2
Marriott, B. W., 13 Dec. 1859, Lucinda Mitchell   12/19/59-2
Marriott, George H. M., 6 June 1860, Mary J. Grim   8/ 9/60-2
Marriott, William H., 23 Apr. 1856, Sophia E. Boyd   4/26/56-2
Marriott, Wm. H.; no date given, Lucy Spencer   12/20/60-2
Marrow, Isaac H., 3 Feb. 1851, Clara Allen   2/ 5/51-2
Marsden, Isaiah, 1 May 1854, Jane M. Gant   5/ 8/54-2
Marsden, John H., 16 Oct. 1851, Eliza Elton   10/18/51-2
Marsel, John, 17 Oct. 1855, Amelia Reed   10/19/55-2
Marselas, Charles, 28 Feb. 1854, Eliza J. Ferrell   3/ 2/54-2
Marselas, John J., 10 Aug. 1854, Mary P. Ward, dau. of Joseph
   C. and Elizabeth   8/17/54-2
Marsh, Geo. H., 29 Apr. 1852, Sarah H. Fergusson   5/ 1/52-2
Marsh, Henry C., 5 Jan. 1851, Sarah Ann Hodges   1/25/51-2
Marsh, Richard, 12 Sept. 1855, Mary Ellen Armstrong   9/21/55-2
Marsh, William, 30 Apr. 1851, Margaret Ann Thatcher   5/ 6/51-2
Marshall, Albert N., 23 Mar. 1859, Marietta Sands   4/18/59-2
Marshall, Charles, 11 Nov. 1855, Elizabeth Mecaslin   11/15/55-2
Marshall, Francis E., 24 Oct. 1854, Sarah Jane Lee   10/30/54-2
Marshall, Henry, 22 Oct. 1857, Amanda C. Jessop, dau. of
   Joshua   10/24/57-2
Marshall, Jas. C., 22 Jan. 1852, Catherine A. Grooms, dau.
   of William   3/ 1/52-2
Marshall, Jesse, 13 July 1854, Martha A. Hull   1/16/55-2
Marshall, John, 7 Oct. 1852, Margaret Dunn   10/18/52-2
Marshall, John E., 28 Oct. 1851, Susan Ann Dorritee, dau. of
   William   10/30/51-2
Marshall, John T., 9 Dec. 1852, Lydia Morrow   12/31/52-2
Marshall, Nathan S. (Dr.), 24 Apr. 1860, A. Maria Price   5/ 3/60-2
Marshall, Robt. W., 26 May 1856, Maria Farea   9/12/57-2
Marshall, Samuel V., 10 Feb. 1859, Mary J. Ogier   7/14/59-2
Marshall, Thomas, 13 July 1851, Henrietta M. Bull   7/15/51-2
Marshall, Thomas J., 27 Mar. 1859, Mahala Ann League   3/30/59-2
Marshall, Thos., 10 Mar. 1853, Sarah A. W. Turner   3/15/53-2
Marshall, William L., 12 Feb. 1854, Margaret R. Mitchell   2/16/54-2
Marshall, William M. L., 6 Oct. 1853, Mary Josephine Stafford   10/ 7/53-2
Marshall, Wm. L., 2 Dec. 1856, Mary W. Williams   12/ 5/56-2
Marshall, Wm. T., 13 May 1859, Sallie A. King   6/ 3/59-2
Marston, H. A., 13 May 1856, M. A. Fillinger   5/15/56-2
Martan, Charles H., 16 Nov. 1858, Sarah L. Schultz   11/27/58-2
Martenet, G. W., 7 Jan. 1857, Maria A. Conway, dau. of (Dr.)
   Wm. D.; corrected copy   2/ 7/57-2
Martenet, Leman, 16 Aug. 1853, Philena L. Pussel   8/19/53-2
Martenet, Simon, 18 Aug. 1853, Philena L. Fussell; corrected
   copy   8/20/53-2
Martey, Gulius, 23 Apr. 1860, Lizzie A. McCoy   4/25/60-2
Martien, Geo., 4 Mar. 1851, Narcissa Fields   3/ 6/51-2
Martin, Charles W., 21 Feb. 1852, Annie M. Debow, dau. of John   2/27/52-2
Martin, D., 7 June 1860, Lucie Henshall, dau. of (Dr.) J. G.   6/11/60-2
Martin, Daniel, 10 Nov. 1852, Martha Ann Morgan   11/12/52-2
Martin, Francis, 1 Nov. 1858, Catherine Ann Rodewald   11/10/58-2
Martin, George (Capt.), 12 Feb. 1852, Kesiah G. Pitt, dau. of
   Thos.   2/13/52-2
Martin, George Jefferson, 14 May 1853, Sarah Elizabeth Chat-
   burn   5/14/53-2
Martin, Isaac W., 11 Sept. 1851, Mary S. Walstrum, dau. of
   Samuel S.   9/12/51-2
Martin, J. Jos., 6 Sept. 1858, Virginia Hisky   1/ 1/59-2

Martin, J. S. (Dr.), 18 June 1857, Lucretia G. Warfield, dau.
    of Philemon   6/20/57-2
Martin, James, 27 Feb. 1853, Margaret Nicolai   2/28/53-2
Martin, James, 27 Mar. 1855, Helen M. Simpson, dau. of
    Rezin B.   3/30/55-2
Martin, James H., 28 Apr. 1859, Kate A. Lee, dau. of William   5/11/59-2
Martin, James J., 22 Oct. 1857, Josephine Vernetson, dau. of
    Wm.   10/29/57-2
Martin, James L., 19 Aug. 1855, Sarah Jane Marfield, dau. of
    Wm.   9/14/55-2
Martin, James V., 13 Nov. 1853, (Mrs.) Mary E. J. Hopkins   8/14/56-2
Martin, Jesse *, 11 June 1853, Sarah J. Garvey   6/15/53-2
Martin, John, 4 May 1854, Catherine M. Himmell   5/ 6/54-2
Martin, John Monroe, 27 Jan. 1856, Kate Keiser, dau. of
    Nicholas and Frances   4/15/56-2
Martin, John W., 20 Oct. 1853, M. E. Baar   10/27/53-2
Martin, Joseph Samuel, 13 Mar. 1851, Sarah Anna P. Frazier   3/17/51-2
Martin, Joshua, 6 Nov. 1856, Mary Ann Sewell   11/ 7/56-2
Martin, Lawson L., 27 Dec. 1858, Jane R. Henning, dau. of
    David and Mary A.   12/31/58-2
Martin, Luther, 8 Mar. 1859, Ellen Stokeley   3/10/59-2
Martin, O. R. (Capt.), 27 Apr. 1852, Sarah J. Swiggette   4/29/52-2
Martin, Samuel J. (Capt.), 28 June 1855, Emma H. Wheden   7/ 4/55-2
Martin, W. Pinkney, 6 Oct. 1859, Mary Georgia Merritt   10/24/59-2
Martin, Walter, 9 Apr. 1857, P. L. Pocock   4/30/57-2
Martin, William H., 28 July 1853, Barbara Shuck, dau. of Adam   7/29/53-2
Martin, Wm. H., 8 Mar. 1854, Mary C. Hoin   4/21/54-2
Martin, Wm. N. (Dr.), 30 Dec. 1856, Penelope Mering, dau. of
    George   1/ 1/57-2
Martines, Antonio, 26 Sept. 1851, Ellen Jane Marshall   10/13/51-2
Martinet, G. W., 7 Jan. 1857, Maria A. Conway, dau. of (Dr.)
    Wm. D.   2/ 2/57-2
Martinet, Morris T., 14 Nov. 1860, Mattie B. Morrison   11/16/60-2
Martz, Joseph, 24 Nov. 1853, Johanna Ann Braudwick   11/26/53-2
Masingo, John H., 13 July 1860, Amanda Hudson   7/17/60-2
Mask, Edward T., 27 Feb. 1855, Rebecca A. Keith   3/ 3/55-2
Mask, Isaac M., 5 Mar. 1851, Mary C. Nigh   3/20/51-2
Mask, Jacob J., 23 Jan. 1851, Jessie L. Contstable   1/25/51-2
Mask, John M., 16 Jan. 1854, Sarah A. J. Selby   1/19/54-2
Mask, Wm. A., 9 Oct. 1860, Martha E. Kenney   10/11/60-2
Maskall, William, 24 July 1856, Sarah C. Chatk   7/26/56-2
Maslin, Philip T., 26 June 1851, Susan Harvey   7/ 1/51-2
Maslin, Thos. J., 15 Dec. 1858, Hannah M. Johnson   12/28/58-2
Mason, David, 4 Jan. 1853, Sarah A. Gatewood, dau. of
    Thomas   1/ 7/53-2
Mason, Frederick, 27 Oct. 1853, Alice Norton   10/29/53-2
Mason, Geo. A., 25 Sept. 1851, Margaret J. Button   9/30/51-2
Mason, George E., 14 June 1859, Lizzie Garrett, dau. of
    Robert W.   6/17/59-2
Mason, James D., 26 Aug. 1851, Mary Cooke, dau. of Samuel   9/ 3/51-2
Mason, John C., 14 Jan. 1858, Emma Woodland   1/16/58-2
Mason, John H., 20 June 1857, Louisa Phelps   6/24/57-2
Mason, Randolph B., 8 Nov. 1853, Augusta E. Remmey, dau. of
    Edward   12/ 1/53-2
Mason, Richard O., Jr., 1 Feb. 1853, Louisa Chaytor   2/ 3/53-2
Mason, Richard R., 14 Apr. 1858, Nannie Van Dyke Johns   4/17/58-2
Mason, Samuel M., 29 Dec. 1856, Isabella C. Waddell, dau. of
    (Capt.) Henry M.   12/30/56-2
Mason, Thomas, 28 Dec. 1854, Ann R. Spalding   12/30/54-2
Mason, Thomas M., 11 Aug. 1857, Hellen F. Huntemuller   8/12/57-2
Mason, Thomas W., 9 Oct. 1860, Eliza Gooseberry   10/12/60-2
Mason, Wesley, 29 Sept. 1853, (Mrs.) Maria A. E. Hartlove   10/ 1/53-2
Mason, Wm. A., 11 Nov. 1858, Carrie C. Boulden   11/13/58-2
Mass, Edmund A., 14 July 1857, Adelaide L. McKnight   7/21/57-2

Mass, Frank (Fr.), 23 Sept. 1858, Marceline Virginia Cappeau,
    dau. of Joseph, Sr.   9/30/58-2
Massey, George (Capt.), 20 Feb. 1851, Mary F. Tarr, dau. of
    Edwin S.   2/21/51-2
Massey, John R., 3 Oct. 1854, Fannie Harrison, dau. of John   10/ 4/54-2
Massey, Theodore H., 12 Dec. 1860, Emma C. Gillard, dau. of
    William   3/23/60-2
Massicott, Robert, 14 Sept. 1852, Sarah Ann Smyrk   9/16/52-2
Masson, William E., 4 Nov. 1851, Elizabeth J. Wilson   11/ 6/51-2
Mathaus, John H., 8 Nov. 1860, Eliza Carpenter   11/10/60-2
Mathers, James, 3 Sept. 1857, Eliza A. Randall   9/ 9/57-2
Mathews, Charles J., 14 Jan. 1854, Sarah Galloway   2/16/54-2
Mathews, Emanuel R. (Capt.), 27 Oct. 1851, Francis A. Hall   11/ 3/51-2
Mathews, R. Stockett, 9 Jan. 1855, Rachel H. Brooks, dau. of
    John   1/11/55-2
Mathews, Thomas, 9 Aug. 1853, Laura Ann Handy, dau. of
    Edward H.   8/12/53-2
Mathiot, Charles, 27 Dec. 1852, Margaret Mathiot, dau. of
    George   2/19/53-2
Mathiot, Octavian Laertes, 18 Oct. 1855, Annie Maria Nalls   10/19/55-2
Mathis, Daniel, 2 Dec. 1858, Catherine Smyth   12/ 4/58-2
Mathison, Alexander, 8 Mar. 1853, Mary Ann McGan   8/11/53-2
Matlock, Robt. F., Jr., 2 Sept. 1856, Mary Ann Egan   9/ 4/56-2
Matox, Robert, 25 May 1858, Harriet Bailey   5/27/58-2
Matson, Joseph, 23 Nov. 1853, Joanna Hemphill   11/29/53-2
Matthews, Alfred, 30 Nov. 1853, Julia Johnson   12/ 2/53-2
Matthews, Alonzo D., 20 May 1858, Sarah A. Campbell   5/22/58-2
Matthews, Aquila, 5 May 1859, Mary S. Denn   5/ 9/59-2
Matthews, Edward, 30 Dec. 1858, Charlotte Johnson   1/ 1/59-2
Matthews, Eli, 23 Oct. 1856, Clara W. Royston, dau. of
    Wesley   10/25/56-2
Matthews, Emerson L., 13 June 1854, Lottie E. Waters, dau. of
    R. C. J.   6/14/54-2
Matthews, James E., 20 July 1851, Amelia M. Wiegand   7/22/51-2
Matthews, Samuel H., 11 Sept. 1860, Ruth Hannah Branson, dau.
    of Joseph   9/13/60-2
Matthews, Thomas, 25 Feb. 1860, Ann Maria Sims   2/28/60-2
Matthews, William, 15 Sept. 1857, Elizabeth Ellen Leather-
    berry   10/17/57-2
Matthews, William, 19 Sept. 1858, Elizabeth A. Trezise   9/21/58-2
Matthews, Wm. B., 12 June 1856, Nannie Dorsett, dau. of
    (Col.) Wm. N.   6/14/56-2
Mattingly, John L., 17 July 1859, Mary C. Mules   8/ 3/59-2
Mattingly, Thomas H., 20 Dec. 1857, Sophia Welch   1/ 1/58-2
Maulsby, Phil. B., 27 Apr. 1858, Maria Kate O'Laughlin   4/29/58-2
Maupin, Logan W., 10 Sept. 1857, Amanda A. Skinner   9/12/57-2
Maury, John, 2 Oct. 1856, Fannie A. Sours, dau. of Thos. A.   10/ 3/56-2
Maxfield, Levi, 24 Jan. 1855, Elizabeth Downey, dau. of
    George   1/26/55-2
Maxville, John, 2 Jan. 1853, Margaret Nolan   1/ 5/53-2
Maxwell, David, 9 Jan. 1851, Mary Dunn   1/10/51-2
Maxwell, David, 13 Mar. 1856, Catharine M. Ford, dau. of
    (Rev.) William   3/20/56-2
Maxwell, Henry, 17 Mar. 1856, Mary A. Presbury   3/21/56-2
Maxwell, John, 17 Nov. 1853, (Mrs.) Eliza C. Widney   11/26/53-2
Maxwell, John S., 2 Nov. 1858, Sallie M. Magaw, dau. of
    Robert T.   11/ 9/58-2
Maxwell, William, 27 Dec. 1859, Kate A. Duff   1/31/60-2
Maxwell, William Henry, 19 Jan. 1851, Charlotte Rose   1/24/51-2
Maxwell, William John, 15 Nov. 1855, Ellen Kelly   11/17/55-2
Maxwell, Wm. D., 2 Oct. 1851, Lydia E. Millholland, dau. of
    Robert D.   10/ 4/51-2
Maxwell, Wm. G., 15 Sept. 1859, Amelia Walter   9/17/59-2
May, Dominick M. H., 11 Apr. 1855, Mary V. Lilly   4/13/55-2

May, George, 2 June 1859, Elizabeth Arabella Palmer, dau. of
   John J.   6/23/59-2
May, James, 16 Jan. 1855, Jane McDougall   1/17/55-2
Mayer, Beverly R., 27 Oct. 1853, Bettie Wright, dau. of
   Charles U.   10/29/53-2
Mayhew, William E., 3 Dec. 1856, Abby Elizabeth Poor   12/12/56-2
Maynadier, John H., 13 Dec. 1855, Laura Matilda Littig, dau.
   of (Dr.) Thos.   12/18/55-2
Maynidier, Joseph, 5 July 1855, Rose Gallego, dau. of (Capt.)
   Francis   7/13/55-2
Mayo, John C. (Dr.), 19 May 1851, Mary Lewis Stovin, dau. of
   Charles J.   5/22/57-2
Mays, Charles W., 27 Dec. 1859, Ann R. Carter   12/28/59-2
Mays, John P., 7 June 1860, Dorcas Hicks   6/ 9/60-2
McAdams, James, 15 Jan. 1856, Melvinia Toner   1/21/56-2
McAdams, Patrick, 29 Apr. 1855, Margaret Gallagher   5/ 1/55-2
McAdams, Peter, 23 Aug. 1860, Kate M. Morrison, dau. of
   Cornelius   11/10/60-2
McAfee, William, 9 Jan. 1855, Caroline Corbell   1/11/55-2
McAlister, James, 27 Oct. 1859, Kate Broughton, dau. of James   11/ 4/59-2
McAlister, Richard, 27 May 1858, Margaret A. O'Neill, dau. of
   Daniel   5/29/58-2
McAllister, H. Clay, 27 Oct. 1859, Sarah E. Reiley   10/31/59-2
McAllister, Jas., 25 Mar. 1857, Julia Hoofnagle   4/21/57-2
McAllister, Nathan, 1 Nov. 1853, Julia Ann Walker   11/ 3/53-2
M'Cauley, J. A. (Rev.), 8 July 1851, R. M. Lightner, dau. of
   John   7/14/51-2
McAuliffe, John, 4 Mar. 1851, Mary Ann Nunan   3/ 7/51-2
McAvoy, John F., 15 Jan. 1857, Elizabeth Berry   2/ 9/57-2
McAvoy, Joseph, 3 Sept. 1852, Margaret Kennedy   9/ 4/52-2
McBee, William, 2 June 1860, Sarah E. Barrett   6/ 5/60-2
McBride, John, 20 Dec. 1853, Mary Toner   12/23/53-2
McBride, Wm. Henry, 29 Sept. 1858, Maggie Wells   10/ 1/58-2
Mc C-(?)-odden, Edward, 9 Mar. 1852, Martha Anderson   3/11/52-2
McCabe, James, 29 May 1859, Marinda Wright; corrected copy   6/ 6/59-2
McCabe, Jefferson, 13 May 1852, Louisa R. Nichols   5/19/52-2
McCabe, John, 23 Nov. 1857, Mary Ann Kerns   11/28/57-2
McCaddin, J. Francis, 26 Dec. 1859, Isabella A. Leckey   12/31/59-2
McCaffery, John J., 18 Oct. 1855, Mary E. Daley; 10/26/55-2   10/27/55-3
McCaffrey, Frank J., 11 Nov. 1856, Magie A. Quigg, dau. of
   James   11/15/56-2
McCaffrey, J. Hughes, 5 Feb. 1852, Mary Jane Kennedy   2/16/52-2
McCaffrey, James, 19 Jan. 1850, Mary Jane Gunby   1/25/54-2
McCaffrey, Patrick, 12 Feb. 1854, Mary Fleming   3/ 1/54-2
McCahn, Daniel, Jr., 12 Apr. 1858, Mary McDermott, dau. of
   William   4/14/58-2
McCain, John W., 23 Feb. 1854, Mary E. Orem   2/25/54-2
McCall, Edward, 8 Aug. 1859, Bridget Riley   8/10/59-2
McCall, James A., 20 Oct. 1851, Emily J. T. Collins   10/23/51-2
McCall, James F., 3 Nov. 1859, Avarilla P. Whitaker   10/ 4/59-2
McCall, John, 12 July 1857, Eliza Reilly   7/14/57-2
McCall, John B., 2 June 1856, Alice A. Simpson   7/ 5/58-2
McCambridge, Dennis J., 29 Jan. 1860, Mary Jane Rooney   1/30/60-2
McCamman, John, 7 Aug. 1853, Mary Templeton   8/11/53-2
McCamman, Thomas S., 12 Sept. 1860, Jemima Paterson   9/17/60-2
McCann, John R., 7 Oct. 1851, Sarah E. Collins   10/ 9/51-2
McCann, Michael, 25 Nov. 1860, Mary Tally   11/29/60-2
McCart, John, 7 Apr. 1853, B. A. Riley   4/11/53-2
McCarter, William, 7 Nov. 1854, Elizabeth Jane McHale   11/16/54-2
McCarthy, Eugene, 23 Nov. 1851, Catherine Roche   11/25/51-2
McCarton, Peter, 19 Sept. 1852, Catharine Curlay   9/20/52-2
McCarty, Daniel, 24 Aug. 1856, Mary Elizabeth Rudolph, dau. of
   Martin   9/ 1/56-2
McCarty, John, 19 Feb. 1854, Bridget McMahon   2/23/54-2
McCauley, Charles A., 24 Jan. 1853, Margaret A. Gosnell   1/31/53-2

McCauley, John, 13 Apr. 1852, Mary Ann Martin   4/16/52-2
McCauley, Joseph, 26 June 1860, Deborah J. Preston   6/27/60-2
McCauley, Reuben A., 12 Jan. 1857, Mary E. Abbott   2/14/57-2
McCauley, Wm. F., 18 May 1858, Arabella Adams, dau. of (Capt.)
     John G.   5/21/58-2
McCaulley, Wm. E., 24 July 1855, Susan E. Hassell   7/26/55-2
McCaulley, Wm. E., 24 July 1855, Susan E. Lassell; corrected
     copy   7/27/55-2
McCausland, Thomas, 25 Mar. 1856, Jane Hannah   3/29/56-2
McCausland, Wm. J., 31 Dec. 1855, Annie Hunter   1/ 2/56-2
McCawley, Joseph, 23 June 1857, E. A. Vinson   6/30/57-2
McCay, Henry H., 3 Nov. 1853, Caroline Betteley   11/ 4/53-2
McCay, Joshua P., 1 Mar. 1853, Emma L. B. Gray   3/ 7/53-2
McCeney, Thomas, 24 Sept. 1854, Mary Owens   9/28/54-2
McCevey, John, 15 May 1854, Janette Looper   5/30/54-2
McClain, John E., 3 Apr. 1854, Sarah Ann Maskell   4/ 5/54-2
McClatchey, James, 22 Aug. 1855, Sarah A. Gray   4/ 7/56-2
McClatchy, John F., 13 Sept. 1852, Rachel Ann Sewell   9/15/52-2
McClavey, Arthur, 25 Dec. 1853, Mary Taylor   12/29/53-2
McClayton, J. R., 24 Dec. 1853, M. J. Williams   1/24/54-2
McClayton, James; no date given, Martha R. Davis   5/30/54-2
McClean, William, 11 June 1855, Fannie R. Riggin, dau. of
     Jacob   6/18/55-2
McClellan, James, 31 May 1853, Caroline F. Collins   6/ 3/53-2
McClelland, George, 5 July 1852, (Mrs.) Ann O. Wallace   7/ 8/52-2
McClelland, George W., 20 Oct. 1852, Mary E. Smith   10/23/52-2
McClenaghan, John, 2 Jan. 1859, Elizabeth Phillips   1/ 7/59-2
McClenahan, H. B., 2 Aug. 1853, L. McComas   8/11/53-2
McClenahan, H. B., 2 Aug. 1853, Maria L. McComas; corrected
     copy   8/13/53-2
McClenan, John, 1 June 1858, Priscilla J. Ayres   11/30/58-2
McClintock, John (Rev.), 9 Oct. 1851, Catharine W. Emory   10/13/51-2
McClintock, Samuel, 2 Nov. 1857, Laura Moore   11/ 4/57-2
McClure, Christopher C., 16 Apr. 1857, Mary D. Strow   5/ 5/57-2
McClure, George D., 16 May 1860, Emma H. Most   5/24/60-2
McClure, James A. L., 13 Dec. 1859, Sue Stansbury, dau. of
     John S.   12/20/59-2
McClymont, Alexander, 13 Oct. 1857, Susan E. Johnson   10/16/57-2
McColgan, James, 28 Aug. 1859, Maggie O'Connell   9/ 1/59-2
McCollam, John J., 7 Jan. 1851, Drucilla Balderston   1/14/51-2
McCollem, Hugh, 16 Oct. 1851, Sarah Campbell   10/22/51-2
McColm, Robt. B., 22 Feb. 1854, Elizabeth A. Griffith   5/ 5/54-2
McComas, Geo. A., 19 Oct. 1859, Nannie E. Blades   10/25/59-2
McComas, George C., 22 Dec. 1856, Sarah E. Griffin   12/27/56-2
McComas, George M., 28 Jan. 1852, Margaretta Witmer   2/ 4/52-2
McComas, Isaac T., 17 May 1859, Sallie Slicer   5/18/59-2
McComas, J. Lee (Dr.), 25 Nov. 1858, Ellen M. Wheeler, dau. of
     (Maj.) M.   11/30/58-2
McComas, James A., 8 June 1852, Annie E. Ellison   6/11/52-2
McComas, Thomas W., 11 May 1852, Mary E. McDowell, dau. of
     George H.   5/13/52-2
McComas, Wm. W., 3 Aug. 1852, Mary Ann Liddell   8/ 9/52-2
McConkey, S. D., 28 Feb. 1855, Louisa G. Whiteford   3/ 1/55-2
McConkey, William, 11 May 1853, Margaret A. Hunt, dau. of
     Jesse   5/12/53-2
McConnell, James, 31 May 1853, Ann Haney   6/ 2/53-2
McConnell, John F., 8 May 1860, Mary Jane Fisher   5/14/60-2
McCord, William D., 27 Nov. 1855, Charlotte L. Tarr, dau. of
     Edwin S.   11/28/55-2
McCormick, Charles (Dr.), 17 Apr. 1855, (Mrs.) Ann Wells, dau.
     of Richard Iglehart   4/18/55-2
McCormick, Francis, 13 Dec. 1851, Bridget Burke   12/17/51-2
McCormick, James, 22 June 1853, Mary Ann Rorke   6/26/53-2
McCormick, James H. C., 1 Feb. 1860, Mary E. Parsons   2/ 6/60-2
McCormick, John, 11 Apr. 1851, Margaret Hammond   4/14/51-2

```
McCormick, John, 24 Feb. 1858, Letitia Miller                    3/27/58-2
McCosker, Thomas, 20 Oct. 1859, Anne McSweeny                   10/24/59-2
McCourt, Michael, 17 Nov. 1853, Elizabeth Ann Mount            12/19/53-2
McCovens, Alfred, 1 Dec. 1853, Mary Bailey                     12/ 3/53-2
McCoy, Arch'd. S., 15 June 1853, Henrietta Colins               6/18/53-2
McCoy, Henry, 12 Jan. 1860, Leah A. Todd, dau. of (Capt.)
    Nathan                                                      3/21/60-2
McCoy, James, 6 Oct. 1852, Elizabeth Fefel                     10/14/52-2
McCoy, James, 13 Feb. 1857, Earean Askton                       2/16/57-2
McCoy, Joseph, 10 Feb. 1859, Elizabeth A. Medcalf               3/21/59-2
McCoy, Robert, 1 Feb. 1852, Zorah Brashears, dau. of J. Bradley 2/ 2/52-2
McCoy, Samuel, 14 May 1851, Josephine Louise Johnson            5/16/51-2
McCoy, Stephen Sheppard, 7 Dec. 1858, Susannah Armstrong       12/ 9/58-2
McCracken, James, Jr., 2-(?) Feb. 1852, Rachel E. J. Shoe-
    maker, dau. of (Capt.) Geo.                                 2/25/52-2
McCracken, Joseph, 5 Feb. 1856, Nicey J. Richardson             2/ 8/56-2
McCracken, William, 10 June 1860, (Mrs.) Lucie Crook            6/12/60-2
McCray, Joseph, 4 Sept. 1855, Emma Jane Bucher                  9/ 6/55-2
McCready, Edward, 5 June 1851, Catherine Shelton                6/10/51-2
McCready, J. Wesley, 3 May 1858, Elizabeth Martin               5/28/58-2
McCreery, James, 29 July 1851, Fanny M. Crawford, dau. of
    Millar                                                      8/15/51-2
McCristal, Johm, 13 Aug. 1857, Frances Byrnes                   9/ 1/57-3
McCubbin, William, 12 Oct. 1856, Elizabeth McAbee              10/20/56-2
McCubbin, William L., 12 July 1859, Amanda V. McComas           7/14/59-2
McCubbins, John D., 23 Mar. 1854, Anna M. Hall, dau. of
    John H.                                                     3/30/54-2
McCullough, Andrew J., 21 May 1854, Barbara Ann Minnick         5/27/54-2
McCullough, Archibald, 13 Feb. 1854, Martha Matilda Rhinehart   2/16/54-2
McCullough, John, 12 Feb. 1856, Isabella Thompson               2/14/56-2
McCullough, John G., 24 Feb. 1856, Ann E. Wood                  3/ 4/56-2
McCully, Clinton, 20 Jan. 1854, Elizabeth D. Danels, dau. of
    (Commodore) J. D.                                           1/23/54-2
McCurdy, James, 22 July 1855, Amanda Jane Sevier, dau. of
    James                                                       8/ 6/55-2
McCuskar, Philip, 8 June 1852, Alice Bradley                    6/12/52-2
McDaniel, James C., 29 May 1851, Alethea B. Jessop              5/30/51-2
McDaniel, James L., 25 Mar. 1857, Lizzie A. S. Watkins, dau. of
    Thos. C.                                                    3/27/57-2
McDaniel, Robert J., 6 Sept. 1857, Mary J. W. Baily            9/16/57-2
McDermot, Thomas, 3 Jan. 1860, Elizabeth Reynolds              2/14/60-2
McDermott, Chas. T., 10 Apr. 1851, Harriet Ann Mezick          4/15/51-2
McDermott, James, 29 Aug. 1854, (Mrs.) Mary De Young           9/ 2/54-2
McDermott, Roderick, 28 Dec. 1852, Jane McKinney               2/ 8/53-2
McDermott, William T., 6 Feb. 1851, Elizabeth M. H. Mackall,
    dau. of Benjamin and Sarah A.                              2/13/51-2
McDermott, Wm. J., 27 Apr. 1854, Francis Van Horn              5/ 1/54-2
McDonald, George, 15 Mar. 1857, Barbara F. Pilsch              4/ 1/57-2
McDonald, Jas., 19 July 1851, M. A. Celena Chambers            7/23/51-2
McDonald, Samuel, 25 Aug. 1852, Mary Lavenia Pickett           8/31/52-2
McDonald, Sween, 3 Feb. 1852, Isabel Johnson                   2/ 6/52-2
McDonald, Thomas, 22 Oct. 1856, Emma Dorman                   11/13/56-2
McDonald, Thomas J., 5 July 1855, Fanny John Chiveri           7/18/55-2
McDonel, John R., 16 Sept. 1852, Mary Krout, dau. of John     10/ 8/52-2
McDonnell, Geo., 8 Sept. 1851, Bridget Clarence                9/22/51-2
McDonnell, John T., 8 Oct. 1854, Emma D. Jones                10/12/54-2
McDonough, J. Edwin, 14 Aug. 1851, Sallie A. Bradford          8/28/51-2
McDowell, Edward G., 12 Dec. 1860, Beata Mayer, dau. of Brantz 12/14/60-2
McDowell, Elijah, 23 Nov. 1852, Anna M. Philbert              11/24/52-2
McDowell, James, 13 Sept. 1851, Martha Cooke                   9/27/51-2
McDowell, James, 22 Apr. 1852, Annie E. Smith, dau. of Leonard 4/24/52-2
McDowell, John, 29 Sept. 1852, Harriet J. Barton             10/11/52-2
McDowell, John, 14 Aug. 1859, Mary E. Heigle                   9/ 6/59-2
McDowell, William, 27 Sept. 1859, Joanna Peddicord            9/28/59-2
McElderry, John J., 9 Sept. 1852, Mary J. Nickols             9/16/52-2
```

McElfatrick, John B., 12 Jan. 1851, Susan C. Dill   1/17/51-2
McElfresh, Charles (Rev.), 17 Feb. 1853, Mary Louisa Turner   2/18/53-2
McElhaney, Alexander, 27 Apr. 1854, Catharine Bert   4/29/54-2
McElhenny, George Dennis, 23 Oct. 1855, Henrietta Green, dau. of
     Joseph and Mary E.   12/28/55-2
McElroy, Daniel, 6 Sept. 1860, Margaret Cain   9/11/60-2
McElroy, James, 12 Oct. 1851, Mary R. McWilliams   1/14/52-2
McElroy, James, 15 July 1859, Mary Elizabeth Ennis   7/20/59-2
McElroy, James, 3 Oct. 1860, Kate Bonn   10/ 8/60-2
McElroy, John M., 25 Dec. 1859, Dorothia E. Muckelroy, dau. of
     John   12/30/59-2
McElroy, Matthew, 28 Jan. 1859, Mary Hunter   1/31/59-2
McElroy, William D., 30 Mar. 1858, Margaret E. Maccubbin   4/15/58-2
McEnrowe, J., 1 May 1858, Catherine Reilly   5/ 4/58-2
McEboy, Michael, 12 June 1859, Anne Rooney   6/13/59-2
McFadden, John H., 15 Mar. 1860, Louisa McFadden   3/17/60-4
McFarland, James Henry, 26 July 1859, Charlotte Keifel   7/27/59-2
McFarland, James S.; no date given, Marion Carr   3/19/55-2
McFarland, John, 3 Aug. 1854, Ellen Ha-(?)-igan   8/ 7/54-2
McFarland, John M., 10 Nov. 1853, Louisa M. Stewart   11/11/53-2
McFarland, William H., 9 May 1858, Mary Julia May   5/14/58-2
McFarlane, John H. (Capt.), 15 Mar. 1857, Charlotte E. White,
     dau. of (Capt.) Richard   3/19/57-2
McFaul, Alexander, 18 Mar. 1856, Elizabeth Ann Martin   6/24/56-2
McFaul, Daniel, 20 Aug. 1857, Mary Lizzie Unkle, dau. of
     Frederick   8/22/57-2
McGaghy, Sam'l., 8 Jan. 1852, Agnes B. Ross   1/12/52-2
McGahan, William, 4 Apr. 1851, Mary Neeley   4/26/51-2
McGall, J. H., 23 Sept. 1858, Sarah Gamble   10/ 9/58-2
McGarigle, David, 12 Oct. 1856, Ann Gallagher   10/18/56-2
McGarity, Bernard Wm., 19 Feb. 1860, Mary Ann Corrighan   2/25/60-2
McGarity, James, 25 Nov. 1856, Ann Cassidy   11/27/56-2
McGaw, James E. T., 5 July 1857, Martha A. Brooks   8/ 4/57-2
McGee, James F.; no date given, Sarah Virginia King   2/10/51-2
McGee, Joseph H., 29 Mar. 1853, Ellen C. Ennis   3/30/53-2
McGee, Thos. C., 4 Nov. 1852, Mary E. Long, dau. of Reuben S.   11/ 6/52-2
McGill, Wm. A., 6 Aug. 1856, Hannah Jane Watson   11/ 4/56-2
McGilley, John C., 17 Sept. 1854, Jane E. Gallagher   9/25/54-2
McGinn, Robt. C., 22 Feb. 1859, Lizzie Wright, dau. of Robt.   2/25/59-2
McGinnis, J. R., 27 Mar. 1854, Margaret A. Thompson, dau. of
     John A.   3/29/54-2
McGinnis, John Gerard, 8 Nov. 1859, Mary J. Jones   11/15/59-2
McGinnis, Richard, 16 Sept. 1858, (Mrs.) Susan B. Richardson   1/28/59-2
McGinnis, Wm. Geo., 27 May 1851, Mary Ann Spies   5/29/51-2
McGivney, Jas., 31 Aug. 1851, Mary A. Stack   11/12/51-2
McGlone, Thomas, 16 Feb. 1858, Margaret Heahs   2/25/58-2
McGnieve, Thomas, 19 June 1853, Ann McNeal   6/24/53-2
McGonigle, Daniel, 6 Mar. 1859, Margaret Stark   3/12/59-2
McGowan, George, 20 Dec. 1852, Martha Connolley   1/17/53-2
McGowan, Henry, 4 Sept. 1851, Mary A. Bevan   12/23/51-2
McGowan, John, 7 Apr. 1859, Eliza Hartens   4/ 9/59-2
McGowen, Hugh, 7 Oct. 1852, Mary Emily Jameson, dau. of
     William   10/12/52-2
McGowin, William, 14 Dec. 1856, Bridget Perry   12/27/56-2
McGraft, James A., 30 Dec. 1852, Priscilla Taylor   12/31/52-2
McGrane, Patrick, 19 June 1851, Mary Dunn   6/23/51-2
McGrath, David, 18 Sept. 1855, Jane Phillips   10/18/55-2
McGraw, James, 27 Oct. 1852, Mary Louisa White, dau. of (Capt.)
     William   10/28/52-2
McGraw, Michael, 20 Apr. 1854, Sarah Teresa O'Ferrall   4/21/54-2
McGready, John, 3 Jan. 1857, Josephine M. Rowe   10/ 5/57-2
McGrevy, Solomon, 29 June 1858, Susan B. Salisbury   7/ 2/58-2
McGrew, William, 3 Feb. 1857, Jane F. McKee   2/ 6/57-2
McGuffin, James, 7 Sept. 1851, Mary Fisher   9/ 9/51-2
McGuigan, James, 30 May 1859, Mary McLaughlin   8/15/59-2

McGuire, Geo. W., 16 Nov. 1858, Amelia Smith	11/18/58-2
McHenry, J. Howard, 25 June 1855, Sally Nicholas Cary, dau. of Wilson M.	6/27/55-2
McHugh, William, 17 Apr. 1854, Mary Hoban	5/ 3/54-2
McIlwain, Wm. W. F., 10 Jan. 1860, Beulah Adams	1/11/60-2
McIntire, David, 26 Nov. 1857, Annie Maria Preston, dau. of John	12/ 3/57-2
McIntosh, John M., 9 Sept. 1852, Nora Ann Berry, dau. of Edmund	9/15/52-2
McIntyre, James, 1 May 1856, Mary Donaghue	5/ 3/56-2
McIntyre, Owen, 4 Sept. 1856, Catherine Kelley	9/ 9/56-2
McIntyre, Peter, 5 July 1854, Catherine Bannon	7/ 7/54-2
McKay, James, 21 Oct. 1852, Mary McDougal	10/22/52-2
McKay, John Thomas, 17 Nov. 1859, Mary S. Harde, dau. of Benjamin C.	11/19/59-2
McKay, Peter, 17 Oct. 1860, Christiana C. Muirhead	10/24/60-2
McKay, Wm. F., 4 Feb. 1852, Lydia Kroh	2/10/52-2
McKechnie, Nevail, 7 Sept. 1854, Mary Bruce	9/29/54-2
McKee, Charles A., 2 June 1853, (Mrs.) Eliza A. Preston	6/ 4/53-2
McKee, James, 20 June 1855, Isabella C. Osbourn, dau. of (Rev.) James	6/23/55-2
McKee, James A. (Rev.), 26 Oct. 1854, Margaret Ann Workman, dau. of John	10/31/54-2
McKee, M. F., 2 June 1858, Anna Leonora Wheeler, dau. of John D.	6/ 3/58-2
McKee, Wm. F., 20 Sept. 1860, Sophia Jenkins, dau. of Robt.	9/24/60-2
McKeever, Isaac, 24 July 1837, Sarah A. St. John	7/26/52-2
McKeever, John, 24 Dec. 1854, Julia Nugent	12/28/54-2
McKeldin, Robert Edward, 15 Jan. 1860, Mary Jane Baldner	3/23/60-2
McKelvey, Alfred *, 15 Nov. 1859, Cass Librand	11/21/59-2
McKenna, Robert, 22 July 1851, (Mrs.) Caroline S. Jenkins	7/24/51-2
McKenna, T. James, 24 Nov. 1859, Mary Ann Sulivan, dau. of Eugene	11/26/59-2
McKenna, William, 20 July 1853, Jane Donovan	10/13/53-2
McKenney, Edward, 7 Dec. 1851, Anna Osborn	12/11/51-2
McKenney, John D., 2 Nov. 1858, Anna Croggon, dau. of Wm. Newton	11/ 3/58-2
McKenney, Thos., 23 June 1852, Isabella Mooney	6/24/52-2
McKenny, Samuel W. (Capt.), 20 Dec. 1851, Agness B. McMahon	12/24/51-2
McKenzie, Evan, 5 July 1860, Naomi Gosnell	7/27/60-2
McKernan, Thomas, 17 Sept. 1854, Mary A. Quinn	9/26/54-2
McKew, Dennis, 26 Apr. 1853, Victorine S. Bonenger	4/28/53-2
McKew, Edward J., 8 May 1856, Mollie Carrigan	5/10/56-2
McKew, Edward J., 15 May 1856, Mary A. Kerrigan	5/17/56-2
McKew, Francis, 25 May 1852, Mary Ann Plowman	6/19/52-2
McKewen, James, 1 Oct. 1854, Susan Donnelly	10/ 4/54-2
McKewen, William F., 21 Dec. 1857, Elenora Gregory	1/ 6/58-2
McKibbin, Thomas A., 31 Oct. 1855, Julia A. Mopps	11/ 5/55-3
McKim, Hollins, 26 Apr. 1860, Eliza F. Voorhees, dau. of (Com.) P. F.	4/28/60-2
McKim, Isaac, 22 Feb. 1859, Louisa B. Church, dau. of B. T.	2/25/59-2
McKim, John F., 25 Sept. 1860, (Mrs.) Susan Ann Howard	9/27/60-2
McKim, Robert, 11 Dec. 1851, Ellen Moore	12/17/51-2
McKim, Robert V., 28 Dec. 1858, Mary S. Albert	12/31/58-2
McKimmie, George, 3 Apr. 1856, Abby Annie Merriam	4/ 4/56-2
McKinley, James, 10 Dec. 1857, Margaret Collins	12/15/57-2
McKinney, Saml. H., 27 June 1860, Mary Lizzie Averett, dau. of Wm. B.	6/29/60-2
McKinney, Valentine, 5 Oct. 1858, Margaret McAleney	10/ 9/58-2
McKiver, John, 16 Mar. 1859, Elizabeth Cunningham	4/ 1/59-2
McKnew, Jeremiah, 2 Nov. 1852, Rosalie B. Taylor	11/ 3/52-2
McKnight, James W., 3 July 1853, Ann Eliza McCauley	7/ 7/53-2
McKnight, Samuel J., 6 May 1852, Mary Carson, dau. of John	5/ 8/52-2
McLain, William, Jr., 16 Apr. 1857, Olevia Wolf	4/25/57-2
McLane, Allan; no date given, Ariadne Knight, dau. of E.	2/ 7/56-2

McLane, Chas., 15 Nov. 1860, Anna Thompson   11/21/60-2
McLane, Chas. E., 11 Jan. 1858, Bettie McGoodwin, dau. of
    James K.   1/21/58-2
McLane, John, 20 Apr. 1852, Cassandra Sinclair   4/29/52-2
McLaughlin, Andw., 21 June 1855, (Mrs.) Elizabeth Heaps, dau.
    of Fredk. Mitchell   6/23/55-2
McLaughlin, Charles, 14 Oct. 1853, Susannah Jane Haney   10/18/53-2
McLaughlin, Daniel, 17 July 1851, Regina Elder   7/25/51-2
McLaughlin, E. Kirby, 26 Dec. 1855, Mary Gale Highland, dau. of
    Dr. Henry   12/29/55-2
McLaughlin, Francis, 28 Sept. 1853, Mary Hart   10/ 1/53-2
McLaughlin, Irvin, Jr., 3 Oct. 1859, Charlotte P. Miller   10/15/59-2
McLaughlin, John, 30 Oct. 1851, Julia Virginia Fergusson   11/ 3/51-2
McLaughlin, John, 25 Apr. 1859, Harriet Heath   4/27/59-2
McLaughlin, John W., 19 Aug. 1856, Mary Jane Garner   8/28/56-2
McLaughlin, Philips, 20 Sept. 1855, Agnes C. Lipp   9/21/55-2
McLaughlin, W. J., 15 Apr. 1858, Charlotte M. Crosby   4/22/58-2
McLaughlin, Wm., 26 Apr. 1859, Mary Ann Stages   4/30/59-2
McLaughlin, Wm., 26 Apr. 1859, Mary Ann Sturges; corrected copy   5/ 2/59-2
McLaughlin, Wm. B., 20 Dec. 1853, Harriet Cornelia Linn, dau.
    of Wm. D. B.   12/28/53-2
McLean, Henry, 31 Mar. 1859, Sarah H. Smith   4/ 5/59-2
McLean, John, 8 June 1851, Mary Ann Grove, dau. of Jacob   6/14/51-2
McLean, John H., 7 July 1854, Margaret J. Phillips   7/ 8/54-2
McLean, Lewis A., 9 Sept. 1852, Matilda Crook   9/11/52-2
McLean, Robert, 16 June 1858, Amanda M. Rowley, dau. of R.   6/17/58-2
McLean, Samuel A., 24 Feb. 1852, Elizabeth E. Lambert   2/26/52-2
McLean, Wm., 1 Nov. 1858, Eliza J. Parks Lusk, dau. of John   11/ 3/58-2
McLeane, Samuel Ready, 22 May 1851, Harriet A. Slater, dau.
    of James   5/24/51-2
McLeary, Gideon B., 4 July 1855, Sallie J. Willis   7/18/55-2
McLevey, John, 15 May 1854, Janette Looker; corrected copy   5/31/54-2
McMachen, John H., 17 Nov. 1852, (Mrs.) C. C. Parsons   11/23/52-2
McMackin, John, 24 June 1856, Adeline E. Hedges   7/ 2/56-2
McMahon, John, 25 Dec. 1859, Kate Riley   1/ 6/60-2
McMahon, Peter, 12 Sept. 1859, Bridget Hanaway   5/ 1/60-2
McMahon, Robert T., 12 July 1855, Alphonsa Johnson   7/17/55-2
McManus, F. S. (Dr.), 2 Feb. 1857, (?) Sinclair   2/10/57-2
McManus, James, 4 May 1858, Catherine Hanly; corrected copy   5/ 7/58-2
McManus, James, 4 May 1858, Catherine Hauley   5/ 6/58-2
McManus, John, 2 Nov. 1855, Elizabeth Hutson   11/ 6/55-2
McManus, Robert, 13 Sept. 1857, Elizabeth Lyth   9/16/57-2
McManus, Wm., 16 Oct. 1856, Ellenorah Evatt, dau. of Edward   10/17/56-2
McMekin, Charles, 23 Mar. 1854, (Mrs.) Frances Bond   3/28/54-2
McMillan, J. A., 1 Nov. 1855, Mary L. Thomas   11/ 2/55-2
McMillan, John G., 5 Jan. 1852, Mary R. Derr   1/ 8/52-2
McMurbrie, Richard C., 29 Nov. 1853, Caroline Murray, dau. of
    Daniel   12/ 3/53-2
McMurrey, Lewis, 2 Jan. 1851, Jane Monaca McDermott   1/ 3/51-2
McMurtrie, Richard C., 29 Nov. 1853, Caroline Murray, dau. of
    Daniel; corrected copy   12/ 5/53-2
McNabb, Aaron H., 17 June 1856, Ann Rebecca Collins   6/21/56-2
McNally, John, 2 Jan. 1853, Mary Campbell   1/ 3/53-2
McNamar, Henry, 4 Oct. 1857, Jane B. Coyle   10/ 6/57-2
McNamara, James, 21 Feb. 1860, Margaret Donally   2/22/60-2
McNamara, William U., 3 Oct. 1859, Alexina Cullison   10/11/59-2
McNeal, Hugh, 14 July 1854, Mary Mahar   7/17/54-2
McNeal, Isaac Q., 21 Feb. 1853, Martha W. Larrimore   2/23/53-2
McNeir, Andrew S., 20 Nov. 1851, Mary Y. Hull   12/ 1/51-2
McNeir, George W., 13 Mar. 1856, Eliza A. Smick   3/15/56-2
McNelly, James A., 26 Oct. 1852, Susan Rebecca Standiford   10/28/52-2
McNew, Nathan, 2 Sept. 1855, Mary A. Riggs   9/11/55-2
McNinch, William, 1 Mar. 1857, Ann Jane Courtney   4/ 2/57-2
McPherson, David, 24 Feb. 1852, Margaret Horn, dau. of
    Asexander   2/26/52-2

```
McPherson, Duncan, 21 May 1854, Mary J. C. McDaughlia, dau.
     of James                                                    6/10/54-2
McPherson, John, 27 Mar. 1851, Sarah Jane Layons                 4/ 4/51-2
McPherson, John H. T., 31 Mar. 1853, Mary G. Henry               4/ 1/53-2
McPherson, Maynard, 8 Dec. 1857, Mary P. Fitzhugh, dau. of P.    12/16/57-2
McPherson, William, 15 July 1858, Hannah Beckley                 8/ 4/58-2
McPoland, Daniel, 11 Jan. 1851, Bridget Radden; corrected copy   1/24/51-2
McPoland, Daniel Geo., 11 Jan. 1851, Bridget Rodam               1/23/51-2
McQuaid, John, 20 Feb. 1860, Annie M. Fogarte                    2/25/60-2
McShaw, John, 17 Aug. 1852, Mary Elizabeth Vore                  8/21/52-2
McSherry, James, 22 Apr. 1852, Helen Mary Carbery, dau. of
     James                                                       4/23/52-2
McVey, Sam'l., 10 Feb. 1853, Helen Brown                         2/11/53-2
McVey, William T., 29 July 1859, Ida Virginia Litsinger, dau.
     of Richard                                                  3/27/60-2
McWilliams, Ezekiel, 29 July 1852, Mary E. Ruccale               7/31/52-2
McWilliams, James, 9 June 1858, Eliza Delany                     6/12/58-2
McWilliams, John J., 22 June 1859, Fannie Fitzpatrick            8/ 9/59-2
Mead, Benjamin F., 19 Aug. 1853, Sarah E. Wiezand                8/23/53-2
Mead, Samuel L., 7 Jan. 1851, Eliza Lawn                         1/14/51-2
Mead, Thomas Carrol, 7 Jan. 1851, Matilda Brown                  1/14/51-2
Mead, Wm. H., 14 Sept. 1858, Sarah E. Livingston                 9/17/58-2
Meads, Richard P., 1 Jan. 1855, Harriet A. Smith                 1/ 5/55-2
Meakim, Wm. T., 10 Feb. 1859, Charlotte F. Clark                 2/28/59-2
Mearis, Malcom W., 8 Mar. 1859, Ann B. Caughey                   4/21/59-2
Mearns, John, 5 Nov. 1851, Catharine Ann Ford                    11/ 8/51-2
Mears, Thomas H., 1 Mar. 1855, Martha Ann Robinson               3/ 3/55-2
Mecaslin, William T., 1 Dec. 1857, Alverta Chamberlin            12/ 3/57-2
Mechem, Thomas N., 2 Apr. 1854, Margaret Ann Larue               4/14/54-2
Medairy, John W., 20 Nov. 1855, Sue L. Stayman                   11/22/55-2
Medairy, Summerfield, 26 Oct. 1858, Debbie Owings Smith, dau.
     of Job                                                      10/30/58-2
Medcalfe, Charles, 16 Apr. 1851, Henrietta M. Barroll, dau. of
     James E.                                                    4/18/51-2
Medinger, Augustus C., 8 Sept. 1856, Hannah R. Pfaff             9/10/56-2
Medinger, Emanuel Jacob, 6 July 1857, Ann Catharine Delaney      7/13/57-2
Medinger, Henry G., 15 Dec. 1858, M. Sophronia Willis, dau. of
     Cornelius                                                   12/18/58-2
Medinger, John G., 29 Dec. 1856, Margaretta Schmenner, dau. of
     Daniel                                                      12/31/56-2
Mee, James *, 19 Feb. 1857, Catherine Dolan                      3/20/57-2
Meecelet, Francis, 28 Nov. 1854, Amelia Picquet, dau. of James   12/ 9/54-2
Meeds, James E., 10 Jan. 1859, Ariette Orndorff                  1/12/59-2
Meeke, Jno. B., 2 Nov. 1857, Sarah C. Cromwell                   11/ 7/57-2
Meekins, William K., 4 Jan. 1855, Elizabeth Pope                 1/ 9/55-2
Meeks, John W., 15 Oct. 1857, Catharine Egger                    10/23/57-2
Meeks, John W., 25 Sept. 1860, Lizzie Wolford                    9/27/60-2
Megary, Alex., 28 June 1859, Flavilla Shipley                    7/ 2/59-2
Megee, John C., 11 Sept. 1851, Isabella Heman                    9/15/51-2
Meginnis, C. G., 13 May 1857, S. E. U. Thompson                  5/14/57-2
Meguinney, Nicholas, 20 May 1858, Eliza Hood                     5/22/58-2
Mehegan, William A., 30 Jan. 1858, Ellen M. Nunan                2/ 2/58-2
Meigs, Gilbert O., 7 Dec. 1856, Mary A. Price                    12/ 9/56-2
Meiser, Conrad, 24 Jan. 1860, Cora E. Gravenstine, dau. of
     James H. and Emer Jane                                      1/27/60-2
Meixsel, Howard F., 14 Oct. 1856, Maria A. Peregoy, dau. of
     Caleb                                                       10/15/56-2
Melarky, John, 6 Aug. 1854, Maria Liddy                          8/ 9/54-2
Melchire, Edward, 7 June 1858, Mary C. Elliott                   6/29/58-2
Mellon, James, 28 Oct. 1860, Lucinda Elder                       10/30/60-2
Mellor, John K., 15 May 1851, Rachel A. Ensey                    5/16/51-2
Melvin, Geo. W., 30 Mar. 1851, Mary A. Porter                    4/ 1/51-2
Melvin, George F., 13 Jan. 1853, Georgeanna Fields               1/17/53-2
Menke, Meinard, 7 Oct. 1851, Elizabeth E. Eichhorn               10/15/51-2
```

Mensendieck, Frd., 13 Nov. 1855, Minna Grattendick   11/20/55-2
Mentzel, William, 13 May 1851, Lizzie A. Thomas   5/14/51-2
Mentzell, Edward, 7 Sept. 1858, Martha A. McDonald   9/ 9/58-2
Menzies, Francis B., 13 June 1860, (Mrs.) Christiana Jones 6/29/60-2
Menzies, James, 24 Nov. 1858, Mary Catherine Caples   11/30/58-2
Mercer, Geo. T., 21 Dec. 1859, Mary Lizzie Yost   12/22/59-2
Mercer, Henry R., 19 July 1855, Sarah Ann Sparks   10/11/55-2
Mercer, James, 20 Oct. 1860, Jane Keys   11/ 6/60-2
Mercer, James M., 26 Feb. 1860, Ella W. Hopkins   2/28/60-2
Mercer, Luther O., 1 Feb. 1854, Hester A. Burgess   2/ 3/55-2
Merceron, Victor J., 3 May 1853, Virginia C. Daix   5/ 5/53-2
Meredith, C. Personett, 7 Apr. 1857, C. Kuster   7/ 6/57-2
Meredith, R. B., 11 Feb. 1856, Mary A. Harris   3/ 5/56-2
Meredith, Richard L., 5 May 1851, Emily Thomas   5/ 7/51-2
Merrick, Charles F., 15 Apr. 1858, Susan F. Cloudsley   4/19/58-2
Merrick, James A., 11 Nov. 1851, Mary V. Claspy   11/12/51-2
Merriken, Francis M., 31 Jan. 1858, Eugenia Beastell   2/ 2/58-2
Merriken, John D., 13 Mar. 1857, (Mrs.) Sarah E. Coberth 4/ 1/57-2
Merriken, William, 23 Nov. 1852, Sarah Codling, dau. of James 4/27/53-2
Merrill, Henry M., 27 May 1852, Mary Gibson   6/ 1/52-2
Merritt, George W., 18 Nov. 1856, Mary A. Plummer   11/20/56-2
Merritt, Samuel, 19 Oct. 1854, Elizabeth Read   10/21/54-2
Merryman, George W., 4 Oct. 1859, Mary M. Grubb   10/ 6/59-2
Merryman, John, 18 Feb. 1858, Marian Wallace Haggerty, dau.
    of John R.   2/25/58-2
Merryman, John H., 16 Sept. 1852, Jemima McCauley   9/23/52-2
Merryman, Lewis, 25 Nov. 1852, Ellen W. Coal, dau. of
    Philemon   12/ 1/52-2
Merryman, Moses S. R., 17 May 1853, Sarah A. Heffner, dau. of
    (Rev.) Edward   5/20/53-2
Merryman, Samuel H. B., 25 Jan. 1859, Martha Adele Clunet 1/27/59-2
Merson, William G. W., 4 Dec. 1856, Louisa Dearing   12/ 6/56-2
Merssinger, William, 27 Sept. 1859, Mary Crawford   10/ 4/59-2
Messersmith, J. William, 2 Dec. 1851, Sarah F. Barron;
    corrected copy   12/ 6/51-2
Messersmith, William, 2 Dec. 1851, Sarah F. Barrow   12/ 4/51-2
Mesteyer, Charles, 4 Apr. 1853, Margaret Ann Patterson   4/23/53-2
Mettee, Albert R., 8 June 1858, Anna M. O'Brien, dau. of
    Chas. C. C.   6/10/58-2
Mettee, Charles Leonard, 20 Mar. 1851, Jane Rebecca Todd, dau.
    of (Dr.) Joseph   3/21/51-2
Mettee, John T., 13 Nov. 1853, Eliza Jane Summerson   11/17/53-2
Mettee, Lewis A., 15 Nov. 1853, Susan A. H. Dawson   11/17/53-2
Mettee, Milton D., 14 Nov. 1854, Caroline Dawson, dau. of
    Thomas R.   11/16/54-2
Metter, Job, 3 Dec. 1855, Alice Elliott, dau. of Robert and
    Edith   12/ 4/55-2
Metz, Henry, 23 Dec. 1852, Catharine Lindeman   12/24/52-2
Metz, Richard A. J., 6 Jan. 1853, Isabella J. Craig   1/ 8/53-2
Metzeratt, William G., 9 Nov. 1858, Henrietta C. Eisenbrant,
    dau. of C. H.   11/12/58-2
Meushaw, Charles H., 10 Mar. 1852, Hannah E. Merrill   3/12/52-2
Meushaw, John, 2 Sept. 1851, Mary Ann Griffin   9/16/51-2
Mewburn, James (Dr.), 11 Apr. 1854, Henrietta B. Pope   4/14/54-2
Meyer, Augt. G., 24 Nov. 1856, Cassie E. Riefle   11/27/56-2
Meyer, Frederick C., 30 May 1854, Julia A. Moor   2/28/55-2
Meyers, Augustus G., 6 Dec. 1853, Margaret A. McCaddin   12/17/53-2
Mezick, Thomas J., 9 June 1857, Annie B. Ridout, dau. of
    Horatio   6/15/57-2
Michael, Alexander D., 6 Mar. 1855, Ann E. Randall, dau. of
    D. A.   3/ 7/55-2
Michael, F. S., 7 Apr. 1856, Anna M. Wise   4/12/56-2
Michael, Geo. D., 8 Jan. 1860, Elizabeth Anderson   4/ 3/60-2
Michael, George W., 3 Sept. 1857, Mary S. Thompson   9/ 8/57-2
Michael, Henry C., 18 Jan. 1854, Cornelia F. Courtney   1/23/54-2

```
Michael, Henry J., 12 May 1857, Sarah J. Michael                5/14/57-2
Michael, John V., 8 Jan. 1856, Anna Maria Westrich              1/16/56-2
Michael, John W., 18 Mar. 1860, Celestia Flynn                  4/ 3/60-2
Michael, Wm. B., 20 May 1856, Helen E. Burnett                  5/21/56-2
Michael, Wm. H., 15 Oct. 1857, Sarah J. Mears                  10/16/57-2
Middlekauff, Morris E. (Dr.), 13 Apr. 1852, Maggie V. Kemp,
    dau. of Henry                                               4/14/52-2
Middleton, James H., 23 Aug. 1859, Virginia A. Webb            9/ 5/59-2
Middleton, John D., 25 Sept. 1860, Eliza Miles                 9/26/60-2
Middleton, Rob't. J., 9 Mar. 1852, Ann Demeila Griffin          3/11/52-2
Middleton, Thomas, 18 Dec. 1851, Mary E. Morton               12/20/51-2
Mignot, Louis R., 11 Jan. 1860, Zairah C. Harris, dau. of
    (Dr.) C. A.                                                 1/12/60-2
Milan, David L., 18 Sept. 1860, Emily Watts                    9/20/60-2
Milburn, John, 7 Sept. 1856, Mary J. Fairbanks                 9/17/56-2
Milburne, John S., 9 Mar. 1856, Tambazine Young, dau. of
    William H.                                                  3/11/56-2
Milde, George, 16 Mar. 1852, Elynna Revonott                   8/12/52-2
Miles, Ashton (Dr.), 30 May 1855, Mary Jane Stuart             6/ 4/55-2
Miles, Benjamin F., 21 Nov. 1859, Harriet E. Willis           12/ 5/59-2
Miles, Charles, 14 Dec. 1860, Mary E. Knight                  12/15/60-2
Miles, George H., 22 Feb. 1859, Adeline Tiers, dau. of E. W.   3/ 3/59-2
Miles, Joshua, 29 May 1855, M. Virginia Bosley, dau. of
    Benjamin                                                    5/29/55-2
Miles, R. H. (Col.), 16 July 1860, Mary Blades                 7/18/60-2
Miles, Thomas, 5 Jan. 1858, Margaret A. Johnson                1/ 9/58-2
Millar, Charles W., 11 Jan. 1854, Fanny C. Buchanan, dau. of
    James                                                       1/13/54-2
Millar, Frank H., 10 Apr. 1860, Eugenia L. Owings, dau. of
    (Dr.) O. H.                                                 4/12/60-2
Millar, John Marshall, 15 Nov. 1855, Eliza M. Miller, dau. of
    J. P.                                                      11/20/55-2
Millar, Walter M., 4 Nov. 1858, Susan B. Winn, dau. of Wm.    11/ 8/58-2
Miller, Alexander H., 3 Oct. 1858, Annie Augusta Naff, dau. of
    John H.                                                    10/28/58-2
Miller, Andrew J., 12 Jan. 1860, Julia A. Davis, dau. of Amos;
    corrected copy                                             1/16/60-2
Miller, Armstead (Rev.), 28 Apr. 1859, Eliza Ann Dickerson,
    dau. of R. James and Sophia                                4/30/59-2
Miller, Benjamin T., 24 Nov. 1853, Isabella N. Firth          11/28/53-2
Miller, Charles, 10 June 1856, Margaret Voltz                  8/27/56-2
Miller, Charles, Jr., 1 Dec. 1853, Elizabeth A. S. Marshall   12/ 9/53-2
Miller, Charles F., 15 Nov. 1860, Lizzie A. Miller, dau. of
    Tobias G.                                                  11/26/60-2
Miller, Chas., 29 July 1852, (Mrs.) Maria C. Hanes             7/31/52-2
Miller, David J., 11 Mar. 1851, Caroline Hinks                 3/15/51-2
Miller, Ed., 11 Nov. 1858, Mary M. Shipley, dau. of Sainl. L. 11/19/58-2
Miller, Edgar G., 16 Feb. 1853, Eliza T. Bevar, dau. of
    Samuel                                                      2/18/53-2
Miller, Edward D., 18 Oct. 1855, Mollie E. Boilman, dau. of
    Wendall                                                    10/20/55-2
Miller, Edward N., 25 Nov. 1858, Mary E. Green                12/ 4/58-2
Miller, Edward T., 30 Apr. 1851, Margaret Ann Devier           5/ 2/51-2
Miller, George C., 25 Jan. 1853, Mary J. Bishop                2/ 3/53-2
Miller, George H., 5 Aug. 1858, Carrie C. Kurtz                8/ 6/58-2
Miller, George W., 1 May 1851, Virginia A. Selby, dau. of
    Henry                                                       5/ 3/51-2
Miller, George W., 22 Jan. 1855, Charlotte H. Robinson         2/ 9/55-2
Miller, Henry, 13 Jan. 1853, Barbara Ellen Ward                1/19/53-2
Miller, Howard, 31 July 1851, Emfield Mason                    8/ 9/51-2
Miller, J. B., 10 June 1857, C. M. Bentz                       6/12/57-2
Miller, J. F., 7 Oct. 1851, Ann Rebecca Fickey, dau. of
    Frederick                                                  10/ 8/51-2
Miller, J. I., 2 Oct. 1860, Lida Hulls                        10/ 3/60-2
Miller, J. Oliver, 29 Sept. 1859, Martha F. Martin            10/20/59-2
```

```
Miller, Jacob, 11 Dec. 1856, Minerva V. Veeder            12/16/56-2
Miller, John, 12 June 1851, Mary Ann Bentley               6/13/51-2
Miller, John, 14 June 1855, Margaret A. Vickers, dau. of
    Joseph                                                 6/20/55-2
Miller, John, 7 Sept. 1856, Catherine Madden               9/10/56-2
Miller, John, 23 Sept. 1860, Emily Sharp                   9/29/60-2
Miller, John A., 15 Nov. 1860, Eliza Beardsley            11/19/60-2
Miller, John F., 28 Mar. 1860, Mary Couplan                4/ 3/60-2
Miller, John J., 20 July 1852, Margaret Elizabeth Wier, dau.
    of John R.                                             8/11/52-2
Miller, John J. H., 27 Oct. 1853, A. M. C. Buck           11/ 5/53-2
Miller, Joseph J. S.; no date given, Margaret A. Crandell  3/14/57-2
Miller, Lewis, 6 Apr. 1857, Mary Horst                     4/ 8/57-2
Miller, Perry G., 31 Oct. 1854, Sarah Rebecca Wilson      11/ 3/54-2
Miller, Rhinehart, 4 Oct. 1853, Elizabeth Heffner         10/ 7/53-2
Miller, Robert, 20 Apr. 1854, Margaret Guy                 4/26/54-2
Miller, Royal E., 6 Feb. 1851, Susan A. Perrie             2/ 7/51-2
Miller, Samuel, 20 Oct. 1853, Catherine S. Smith, dau. of
    John L.                                               10/25/53-2
Miller, Samuel, 30 May 1854, Mary C. Tydings               5/ 6/54-2
Miller, Samuel L., 14 Aug. 1859, Elizabeth Ann Belt        8/16/59-2
Miller, Sidney, 30 May 1854, Frances Moore                 6/ 1/54-2
Miller, Thomas J., 30 Oct. 1860, Alice H. Griffin, dau. of
    Levin                                                 11/ 8/60-2
Miller, William C., 26 Apr. 1855, Cordelia J. Price, dau.
    of Augustus M.                                         5/ 1/55-2
Miller, William H., 19 June 1851, Elizabeth Jane Sampson   6/20/51-2
Miller, William H., 19 Dec. 1852, Amelia J. Crishop        3/22/52-2
Miller, William H., 3 Jan. 1855, Agness Lamb               4/ 8/56-2
Miller, William H., 20 Feb. 1855, Mary C. Weyl, dau. of (Rev.)
    Chas.                                                  2/21/55-2
Miller, William H., 3 July 1855, Agness Lamb; corrected copy 4/10/56-2
Miller, William H., 1 July 1857, Lydia Coburn              7/ 7/57-2
Miller, William J., 10 Feb. 1859, Sarah McVay              3/ 4/59-2
Miller, Wm. B., 10 June 1855, Mary E. Gillispie            7/ 4/55-2
Miller, Wm. Henry, 3 Nov. 1854, Lizzie Tucker             12/13/54-2
Miller, Wm. P., 27 June 1860, Annie B. Carrick             7/ 7/60-2
Millholland, John G., 12 Aug. 1851, Ann J. Shaw            8/13/51-2
Millholland, Robt. D., 23 June 1853, Mary E. Knotts, dau. of
    (Rev.) George P.; 6/25/53-2                            6/28/53-2
Milligan, James, 22 Dec. 1853, Annie Hagan                12/24/53-2
Milliken, Wm. Henry, 13 Jan. 1857, Emily V. Richardson, dau.
    of Geo. W.                                             1/19/57-2
Milliman, George L., 26 Dec. 1854, Sarah A. Hoffman       12/27/54-2
Mills, Bernard (Dr.), 1 Dec. 1853, Mary C. Gore, dau. of
    Jabez                                                 12/ 5/53-2
Mills, Edward C., 13 Dec. 1860, Nellie M. Kent, dau. of
    Thomas R.                                             12/31/60-2
Mills, Franklin, 1 Nov. 1855, Margaret W. Coulter         11/ 3/55-3
Mills, George, 6 Dec. 1853, (Mrs.) Mary Ann Coburn        12/ 8/53-2
Mills, George A., 25 Oct. 1855, Sarah J. (?)-a-(?)-ds, dau.
    of Samuel                                             10/27/55-3
Mills, Henry, 30 Apr. 1853, Mary Ann Brown                 5/11/53-2
Mills, James I., 10 Aug. 1851, Eliza Jane Taylor           8/22/51-2
Mills, John J., 1 Jan. 1855, Mary C. Given                 1/ 5/55-2
Mills, Rufus, 10 Oct. 1859, Mary Jane Pratt               11/14/59-2
Mills, S. B. (Dr.), 14 Sept. 1854, Elizabeth Magruder, dau.
    of J. R.                                               9/15/54-2
Mills, Thomas A., 11 Nov. 1856, Eliza Collins             11/12/56-2
Mills, Thomas W., 11 July 1856, Rosabell Herkins           8/23/56-2
Mills, William E., 7 Aug. 1851, Eliza Ann Jacobs           8/ 8/51-2
Mills, York, 3 May 1855, Catharine Collins                5/ 5/55-2
Milnor, James P., 30 Mar. 1859, Virginia B. Stephens, dau. of
    Alexander                                              4/26/59-2
Milnor, Joseph K., 4 July 1851, Margaret A. Hoff           9/18/51-2
```

Milstead, Andrew J., 25 May 1856, Elizabeth A. Davis   6/19/56-2
Miner, Thomas F., 25 Jan. 1858, Mary E. Buxton   1/28/58-2
Mingo, James, 8 Aug. 1860, Maria Jackson   8/11/60-2
Minner, George P., 30 Dec. 1851, Sarah Jane Pennington   1/ 1/51-2
Minnick, Benjamin F., 1 Apr. 1856, Martha C. Ryder   4/ 3/56-2
Minnick, William F., 4 July 1852, Maria A. Brendel   7/15/52-2
Minnick, Wm., 17 Oct. 1852, Susan Ann Hipwell   10/18/52-2
Minnis, Timothy D., 8 Dec. 1857, Susannah A. Lineberger   12/19/57-2
Minon, Michael, 10 Sept. 1853, Catherine Welsh   9/13/53-2
Minton, Charles A., 2 June 1851, Emily G. Marriott, dau. of
    (Gen.) Wm. H.   6/ 5/51-2
Miser, John, 5 Oct. 1851, Elizabeth Gardner   10/11/51-2
Miskimon, Samuel, 1 Mar. 1859, Mary Ann O'Brine   3/30/59-2
Miskimon, Thomas J., 2 Feb. 1860, Matilda A. Walker, dau. of
    Samuel A.   2/ 4/60-2
Mister, Severn F., 19 June 1855, Mary E. Anderson   6/21/55-2
Mister, Stevern F., 27 May 1852, Sarah E. Wilson   5/28/52-2
Mitchel, George W., 20 Aug. 1854, Ann Eliza Lasgwell   8/24/54-2
Mitchell, David C., 28 July 1857, Emma F. Betton   8/ 1/57-2
Mitchell, Frederick J., 23 Nov. 1859, Catherine S. Gwynn   11/26/59-2
Mitchell, G. Afred (Dr.), 28 Nov. 1854, Sarah J. McMulin   12/ 1/54-2
Mitchell, George, 24 Feb. 1852, Mary Jane Johnston   2/28/52-2
Mitchell, George, 3 Feb. 1857, Catherine Connely   2/ 7/57-2
Mitchell, George A., 12 Aug. 1856, Elizabeth Ann Gibbons, dau.
    of Thomas   8/15/56-2
Mitchell, George W., 1 June 1860, Margaret Spear   6/ 4/60-2
Mitchell, Henry, 28 Oct. 1851, Susan Holly   10/25/51-2
Mitchell, J. G., 14 June 1853, Debbie O. Cockey   6/16/53-2
Mitchell, James, 30 Apr. 1860, Margaret A. Lee   5/ 3/60-2
Mitchell, James H., 12 May 1859, Maggie T. Moore   5/14/59-2
Mitchell, James R., 24 Dec. 1860, Jane Kelso, dau. of Wm.   12/28/60-2
Mitchell, Johm, 6 July 1851, (Mrs.) Ann Hook   7/10/51-2
Mitchell, John, 24 Feb. 1859, Ann Donnelly   6/30/59-2
Mitchell, John A., 5 Apr. 1853, M. Kate Gregory   4/ 7/53-2
Mitchell, John T., 22 Nov. 1853, Maria L. Newton   11/23/53-2
Mitchell, John W., 23 Apr. 1858, Elizabeth Flannigan   4/27/58-2
Mitchell, Joseph B., 31 Mar. 1851, Georgianna Gordon, dau. of
    (Capt.) Geo.   4/ 1/51-2
Mitchell, Joseph H., 25 Feb. 1858, Cassandra W. Daniels, dau.
    of Walter   3/11/58-2
Mitchell, Joshua, 12 July 1853, Ann Maria Haines   7/18/53-2
Mitchell, Levin H., 1 June 1854, Britt Ann Harris   6/ 3/54-2
Mitchell, Levin Henry, 21 Jan. 1851, Margaret Gambler   1/23/51-2
Mitchell, Lewis A., 17 Feb. 1857, Margaret A. Jones   2/20/57-2
Mitchell, Marcellus A., 7 Dec. 1858, Henrietta E. Smith   12/ 8/58-2
Mitchell, Richard H., 15 Oct. 1857, Elizabeth Farnandis, dau.
    of Walter; 10/17/57-2; 10/19/57-2   10/20/57-2
Mitchell, Robert, 4 Nov. 1851, Julia A. Deppich; corrected
    copy   11/17/51-2
Mitchell, Robert, 4 Nov. 1851, Julia A. Teppick   11/15/51-2
Mitchell, Robert, 20 Dec. 1851, Mary E. Williams   12/20/51-2
Mitchell, Robert, 11 Nov. 1856, Ann S. Wink   11/13/56-2
Mitchell, Robt. M., 15 Oct. 1856, Mary A. Foy, dau. of Jas. 10/22/56-2
Mitchell, Thomas A., 24 July 1851, Isabel C. Mayo   7/29/51-2
Mitchell, Thomas E., 19 Feb. 1856, Mary E. McGowan   2/22/56-2
Mitchell, W. H., 9 Aug. 1860, Mary C. Peiarcy   8/15/60-2
Mitchell, Walter A., 7 Oct. 1856, Susan Thomas   11/ 1/56-2
Mitchell, Wm., 28 Jan. 1851, Adar Collins   2/ 1/51-2
Mitchell, Wm. H., 23 Dec. 1856, Elizabeth A. Cole   12/30/56-2
Mitchell, Wm. J., 30 June 1858, Anna R. Riley   7/12/58-2
Mitchell, Zebd., 14 Jan. 1858, (Mrs.) Mary F. Ennis   1/29/58-2
Mitchell, Zechariah, 3 Feb. 1860, Mary H. Dennis   2/ 4/60-2
Moale, John T., 23 Oct. 1854, Caroline Reister   10/25/54-2
Moales, Frederick, 16 Aug. 1860, Mary Johnson   8/18/60-2
Mobbs, George, 22 Oct. 1854, Mary Ann Skipper   10/31/54-2

```
Mockbee, Richard, 7 Nov. 1855, Delia Amanda Whitney, dau.
     of Daniel                                                11/ 9/55-2
Moelling, Edward, 15 Oct. 1853, Virginia Leach               10/18/53-2
Moffitt, Robert; no date given, Margaret Ann Richards         4/ 3/60-2
Moffitt, Robert, 3 Apr. 1860, Ann Richards; corrected copy    4/ 9/60-2
Moffitt, Thomas, 20 May 1853, Fanny Little                    5/27/53-2
Mohler, James W., 22 Oct. 1856, Julia V. Larsh, dau. of (Dr.)
     Silas                                                   10/23/56-2
Mohun, Lanahan M. P., 31 Dec. 1850, Rosella A. Brawner        1/14/51-2
Mok, George W., 21 Apr. 1853, Hannah A. Kinsey, dau. of Stacy 4/23/53-2
Moleswirth, Asbury, 21 Jan. 1858, Elizabeth Diffey            1/25/58-2
Molligan, John, 21 Apr. 1851, (Mrs.) Elizabeth McShane        4/23/51-2
Molonee, Lawrence, 12 Apr. 1853, Sarah Whitworth              4/14/53-2
Molony, Edmund, 9 Jan. 1855, Josephine C. Cormick             1/16/55-2
Molony, Samuel, 7 Sept. 1854, Kathleen O. Moore, dau. of
     (Capt.) George                                          10/12/54-2
Monaghan, Patrick, 6 May 1860, Rose Hughes                    5/10/60-2
Mongar, Leon, 5 Feb. 1856, Anna E. Ball, dau. of W. D.        2/11/56-2
Mongolar, John, 7 Aug. 1854, Melvina Brown                    8/ 9/54-2
Monk, Solomon, 19 Sept. 1858, Cornelia Nichols               10/28/58-2
Monk, William H., 1 Mar. 1857, Marriam A. B. Plummer          3/ 6/57-2
Monks, John C., 5 Mar. 1857, Talitha E. Whitaker              3/ 7/57-2
Monroe, James, 5 Mar. 1854, Mary A. Dunn                      3/ 9/54-2
Monroe, Thomas Truman, 16 Dec. 1852, M. Eliz. Fowler         12/17/52-2
Monroe, W. R. (Rev. Dr.), 18 Sept. 1852, Fannie A. Tittle,
     dau. of Jeremiah                                         9/20/52-2
Monroe, Wm. W., 10 Nov. 1856, Susan A. Moore                 11/15/56-2
Montague, Peter, 1 Nov. 1858, Fanny Sykes                     1/ 3/59-2
Montague, Richard, 31 July 1853, Catharine Thomas             8/ 3/53-2
Montague, Wm. L., Jr., 25 Feb. 1858, Sallie Howard Love       2/26/58-2
Montell, Francis Montague, 12 Nov. 1857, Jane Norwood, dau.
     of John                                                  2/ 3/58-2
Montgarett, Jos., 2 Dec. 1852, Elizabeth Laurence, dau. of Wm. 12/ 6/52-2
Montgillian, Lewis, 14 Jan. 1851, Mary Ann Duvall             1/15/51-2
Montgomery, Asel, 23 July 1857, Harriet Ann Wells            10/ 7/57-2
Montgomery, D. E., 26 Apr. 1855, Ellen Smith, dau. of N. R.   4/28/55-2
Montgomery, David, 24 May 1860, Mary A. Vickers               6/ 8/60-2
Montgomery, Elias, 31 July 1851, Josephine Levay; corrected
     copy                                                     8/ 4/51-2
Montgomery, Elias, 31 July 1851, Josephine Savey              8/ 2/51-2
Montgomery, John B., 25 Oct. 1859, Mary E. Boarman, dau. of
     Ignatius and Sarah                                      11/22/59-2
Montgomery, Samuel, 17 Aug. 1851, Lorettia Keefer             8/20/51-2
Montgomery, Samuel, 5 May 1853, Ann Maria Potter              5/10/53-2
Montgomery, William T. (Dr.), 2 Oct. 1855, Mary H. Latimer,
     dau. of William G.                                      10/ 6/55-2
Moody, Horace, 28 Aug. 1860, Mary Josephine Madden            9/ 1/60-2
Moody, Wm., 27 Oct. 1857, Mary E. Faucett                     6/29/58-2
Moon, Edward H., 17 Feb. 1857, Ruth Virginia Eden             2/24/57-2
Mooney, Charles, 7 Oct. 1856, Susan White, dau. of (Capt.) David
     H.                                                      10/15/56-2
Mooney, John, 12 Apr. 1852, Mary Ann O'Hanlon                 4/17/52-2
Mooney, Thomas, 5 Oct. 1857, Catherine Elizabeth Mooney      10/28/57-2
Mooney, William, 1 June 1852, Mary J. Andrews                 6/ 2/52-2
Mooney, William, 11 June 1856, Elizabeth George              7/ 8/56-2
Moore, Charles, 11 Feb. 1857, Alverta P. Caughey              2/13/57-2
Moore, Charles S., 26 July 1860, Mary Ann Toppin, dau. of
     Andrew and Lucy                                          7/28/60-2
Moore, Edward, 29 Apr. 1858, Eliza J. Hall                    5/ 5/58-2
Moore, Geo. W., 16 May 1851, Margaret A. Chilcotte;
     5/19/51-2                                                5/20/51-2
Moore, George Washington, 6 Sept. 1860, S. Morow             9/11/60-2
Moore, Henry, 13 Jan. 1857, Virginia C. Houston, dau. of
     John F.                                                  1/16/57-2
Moore, Henry W., 28 Aug. 1860, Catharine Ritter              8/31/60-2
```

Moore, Isaac, 27 Mar. 1856, Rosetta Graves, dau. of David and Phebe	3/29/56-2
Moore, J. Faris, 7 Dec. 1853, Mary E. Rice	12/10/53-2
Moore, James A., 12 Sept. 1854, Rachael E. Deputy	9/13/54-2
Moore, James B., 15 Nov. 1855, Anna Mary Martin, dau. of Ephraim	11/17/55-2
Moore, James W., 1 Dec. 1859, Susan Moore	12/ 3/59-2
Moore, John, 11 Dec. 1853, Susanna Battee	12/13/53-2
Moore, John, 30 Jan. 1859, Mary Jane Barnes	2/ 1/59-2
Moore, John A., 17 Nov. 1859, Kate E. Bowen	11/21/59-2
Moore, John H., 5 Mar. 1851, Rebecca A. Cunningham	3/11/51-2
Moore, John Thomas, 7 Aug. 1855, Mary Elizabeth Stockett	8/13/55-2
Moore, L. B., 13 Sept. 1853, Letitia Lemon	9/21/53-2
Moore, Levi, 19 Apr. 1859, Terresey Allice	4/21/59-2
Moore, Matthew, 22 Apr. 1858, Emma Guie, dau. of Robt.	4/26/58-2
Moore, Nathaniel, 27 Jan. 1853, Ann Smith	2/ 1/53-2
Moore, Thomas H., 13 May 1852, Kate De'valin, dau. of Hugh	5/15/52-2
Moore, Thomas M., 6 May 1857, Lizzie S. Roberts	5/ 7/57-2
Moore, William, 1 Oct. 1853, Easter Cook	10/ 5/53-2
Moore, William, 16 Feb. 1856, Mary Stratton	10/ 2/56-2
Moore, William H., 3 Nov. 1857, Harriet V. Clary; corrected copy	11/12/57-2
Moore, William H., 3 Nov. 1857, Harriet V. Clay	11/11/57-2
Moore, William H., 6 Sept. 1860, Rachel Hart	9/10/60-2
Moore, William Henry; no date given, Susan E. Waldo	11/ 2/58-2
Moore, William Henry, 21 Oct. 1858, Susan E. Waldo; corrected copy	11/ 3/58-2
Moore, William T., 1 May 1851, Mary E. Gorman	5/ 6/51-2
Moore, Wm. H. H., 2 Mar. 1854, Amanda Pettit, dau. of James	3/ 6/54-2
Moorehead, W. H., 12 Dec. 1854, Lizzie A. Quincy, dau. of (Capt.) John D.	12/14/54-2
Mooringstar, Adam, 5 Nov. 1857, Sarah Ellen Cunningham	12/10/57-2
Mopps, Amos S., 12 Jan. 1859, Annie Bell	1/19/59-2
Mopps, James S., 12 Jan. 1859, Anna Bell; corrected copy	1/21/59-2
Moran, David, 22 June 1858, (Mrs.) Ann Curran	6/23/58-2
Moran, Josephine Augustine, 20 Aug. 1857, Margaret Ann Quinn	8/21/57-2
Moran, Thomas L., 22 Nov. 1855, Sarah C. Chase	11/29/55-2
Morawetz, Leopold F., 24 May 1855, Elise Meyer	5/25/55-2
Moray, A. H., 20 Jan. 1859, (Mrs.) P. S. Keavins	9/24/59-2
Moree, Abraham, 19 Feb. 1854, Amanda J. Capels	2/22/54-2
Morehiser, John S., 2 Apr. 1855, Sarah Ann Howard	4/ 4/55-2
Moreland, Wm. H., 14 July 1859, Emily L. Kinnamon	7/15/59-2
Moreton, William S., 16 May 1860, Sarah C. White	5/17/60-2
Morgan, Benjamin, 6 Jan. 1859, Dorothea Agnes Clayton, dau. of J.	1/10/59-2
Morgan, Charles Snowden, 17 July 1853, Hester Ann Tutte	8/ 3/53-2
Morgan, Daniel, 7 Aug. 1855, (Mrs.) Mary Jane Jackson	8/15/55-2
Morgan, Daniel T., 9 Sept. 1858, Mary C. Mattingly	9/15/58-2
Morgan, G. E. (Dr.), 28 Apr. 1852, Caroline Y. Peyton, dau. of (Rev.) Velverton	5/ 1/52-2
Morgan, George, 15 Nov. 1855, Frances Dudley	11/20/55-2
Morgan, George T., 16 Jan. 1859, Mary Cragg	2/ 1/59-2
Morgan, George W., 13 Feb. 1851, Ann Maria Fish	2/14/51-2
Morgan, Hugh, 23 Nov. 1856, Georgiana Bouram	12/ 9/56-2
Morgan, J. Asbury, 28 Dec. 1852, Catharine Emory	12/29/52-2
Morgan, J. Louis, 4 Feb. 1858, Margaret E. Hahn	2/ 9/58-2
Morgan, James, 4 Sept. 1855, Sarah A. Prettyman	9/13/55-2
Morgan, James S., 1 Dec. 1853, Henrietta S. Love	12/ 2/53-2
Morgan, Jeremiah, 20 Dec. 1852, Anna Redden	12/23/52-2
Morgan, Robert C., 9 Oct. 1856, Elizabeth M. Wood, dau. of (Dr.) Wm. Maxwell	10/21/56-2
Morgan, T. A. (Rev.), 9 Mar. 1854, Caroline F. Dallam, dau. of (Dr.) Wm. M.	3/11/54-2
Morgan, William R., 15 Jan. 1851, Sarah A. Fitzpatrick, dau. of Jno.	1/17/51-2

Morines, William John, 24 Oct. 1858, Susanna E. Tolson	11/ 3/58-2
Morley, J. C., 31 Oct. 1856, M. J. Adams	11/ 1/56-2
Morningstar, George W., 24 May 1860, Nancy Jane Bitzer	5/25/60-2
Morray, Patrick, 5 Jan. 1853, Catharine Smith	1/18/53-2
Morrill, Owen T., 5 Jan. 1860, Sarah J. Hicks	1/ 9/60-2
Morris, Edwin F., 8 Sept. 1852, Mary Ann Norris	9/10/52-2
Morris, G. W., 28 Apr. 1853, D. C. Eckardt	4/30/53-2
Morris, Harry, 7 Jan. 1858, Mary Ellen Logsdon, dau. of John	1/ 9/58-2
Morris, Jacob, 7 Mar. 1855, Annie E. Morris, dau. of Levin	3/13/55-2
Morris, John A., 15 July 1853, Sarah R. Allen	7/23/53-2
Morris, John S., 12 Feb. 1857, Matilda L. Williams	2/14/57-2
Morris, John T., 25 May 1852, Hannah Clementine Heagy, dau. of (Capt.) James	5/27/52-2
Morris, L. F., 25 Oct. 1859, Lizzie A. Wright	10/27/59-2
Morris, Stephen, 2 Feb. 1858, Bridget T. McCann	2/ 5/58-2
Morrison, Benjamin, 27 Feb. 1855, Sarah Mathews	3/ 1/55-2
Morrison, Henry Whitely, 21 Oct. 1856, Laura Jessop	10/22/56-2
Morrison, Hugh, 17 Nov. 1853, (Mrs.) Julia Feelemyer	12/ 1/53-2
Morrison, Hugh A., 27 Sept. 1859, Mary M. E. Spicer	9/29/59-2
Morrison, James, 15 Apr. 1851, Catharine Foring	4/17/52-2
Morrison, James S., 10 Sept. 1851, Susan Burnham; 9/12/51-2	9/13/51-2
Morrison, Jas. M. (Dr.), 12 June 1860, Laura M. Startzman	6/16/60-2
Morrison, Jefferson, 24 Oct. 1854, Elizabeth Planter	10/26/54-2
Morrison, John H., 16 Sept. 1855, Martha Warfield	9/19/55-2
Morrison, Louis, 26 Apr. 1859, Mary P. Cann	4/27/59-2
Morrison, Theodore, 24 Nov. 1853, Margaret Burge	11/26/53-2
Morrison, William, 1 Nov. 1855, Fannie W. Evans, dau. of Thomas W. Turner	12/11/55-2
Morrison, Wm. T., 4 Jan. 1859, Cassandra Petticord	1/11/59-2
Morriss, Wm. W., 28 July 1853, Lydia Shaver	8/ 1/53-2
Morrow, David, 17 May 1860, Caroline V. Miller	5/19/60-2
Morrow, George G., 22 Feb. 1858, Eliza J. Chamberlin	2/25/58-2
Morrow, John, 6 Sept. 1860, Ann J. Wood; 9/10/60-2	9/11/60-2
Morrow, William, Jr., 26 May 1853, Caroline Ritter, dau. of J. and Margaret	5/30/53-2
Morrow, Wm. T., 15 June 1856, Debora E. Brow	7/31/56-2
Morse, Charles, 28 Dec. 1857, Johanna H. L. Richers	12/30/57-2
Morse, Thos. W., 2 May 1855, Catharine S. Heddinger	5/ 4/55-2
Morsell, Quincy A., 4 May 1858, C. L. Gambler	5/ 8/58-2
Morsell, Richard T., 2 Dec. 1858, Mary A. Pratt, dau. of Henry R.	12/ 9/58-2
Mortimer, Edwin, 22 Nov. 1858, Ella E. Farley	11/27/58-2
Mortimer, John W., 8 Dec. 1857, Virginia A. Hall	12/12/57-2
Mortimer, William, 30 Nov. 1855, Margaret Wright	12/ 4/55-2
Morton, Francis C., 13 Oct. 1853, Fanny E. Edwards	10/22/53-2
Morton, George C., Jr., 16 Jan. 1858, Harriet Anna Light	1/18/58-2
Morton, Patrick, 31 Jan. 1858, Mary McCoy	2/ 2/58-2
Morton, Samuel P., 20 Aug. 1860, Maggie Wiegel	8/21/60-2
Morville, P. Wilson, 27 Oct. 1856, Susan E. Andrews, dau. of (Capt.) Elijah	10/30/56-2
Moss, James E., 2 June 1859, Adeline S. Melhorn	6/ 4/59-2
Moss, John D., 5 Jan. 1854, Hannah R. Howard	1/ 7/54-2
Most, John T., 31 July 1856, Eliza Jane Scott, dau. of James	8/ 4/56-2
Mottu, Theodore, 18 Mar. 1851, Mary Elizabeth Harvey, dau. of Thomas	3/20/51-2
Mount, Thomas L., 29 Nov. 1860, Sophia L. Keener, dau. of Christian	12/ 4/60-2
Mowbray, James H., 21 July 1856, Sarah B. Cole	7/23/56-2
Mowbray, Jas. H., 8 Nov. 1859, Agnes E. Russell, dau. of (Capt.) Geo. W.	11/11/59-2
Mowbry, Thomas, 10 Jan. 1854, Susan Y. Creighton	1/12/54-2
Moxley, Thomas, 12 Jan. 1854, Jane T. Payne	1/13/54-2
Moxley, Walter, Jr., 5 Oct. 1858, Frances E. Ellison	10/ 7/58-2
Moyer, William, 16 Oct. 1851, Ann Bosley	10/17/51-2
Muir, Alex. F., 7 Mar. 1855, Elizabeth Elliott	3/ 9/55-2

Muir, John A., 3 May 1853, Sarah Ann Zeigler   5/ 5/53-2
Muir, Robt. D., 19 Sept. 1859, Susan Stith Hepburn, dau. of
     Jno. M.   9/22/59-2
Muirhead, Samuel D., 1 Dec. 1859, Ruth R. Disney   12/ 3/59-2
Muirhead, Wm., 29 June 1857, Mary Ann Ward   7/ 2/57-2
Muldoon, James, 26 Feb. 1854, Sarah A. V. Hitzelburger   2/28/54-2
Mules, Daniel W., 10 Feb. 1857, Margaret J. Crockard, dau. of
     John   2/13/57-2
Mules, Nathaniel P., 8 Jan. 1856, Mary S. Purden   1/15/56-2
Mules, Thomas H., 17 Apr. 1851, Elizabeth M. Jenkins, dau. of
     Thomas   4/19/51-2
Mulholland, Francis, 2 Sept. 1858, Imogene Webb, dau. of John
     and Ann; corrected copy   9/21/58-2
Mulholland, Francis, 2 Sept. 1858, Josephine Webb   9/ 4/58-2
Mullan, James, Jr., 17 Feb. 1852, Mary Ann Gallaway   2/19/52-2
Mullan, John P., 1 Jan. 1855, Emily S. Small   1/ 3/55-2
Mullan, William H., 8 June 1858, Alice E. O'Donald   6/12/58-2
Mullen, John, 11 June 1857, Mary Ann Craig   6/16/57-2
Mullen, Mordecai, 3 Nov. 1857, (Mrs.) Ann Carmine   11/11/57-2
Muller, Henry A., 8 Sept. 1856, Sophia M. Harman   9/10/56-2
Muller, Jno. R. (Dr.), 16 Feb. 1860, Ellen R. Price   2/23/60-2
Mullikin, Jas. McE. (Dr.), 4 Dec. 1856, (Mrs.) Margaret D.
     Hammond   12/11/56-2
Millikin, Thomas McKildry, 12 June 1856, Lizzie Rind, dau. of
     Samuel   6/13/56-2
Millin, John, 29 Aug. 1858, Mary Lizzie McAlear   9/18/58-2
Mullin, Michael, 1 Aug. 1854, Adeline Yeager   8/ 4/54-2
Mullin, Michael, 6 Feb. 1859, Matilda Jane France   2/12/59-2
Mullinix, Joseph, 13 Oct. 1853, Levina Lawton   11/ 2/53-2
Mumma, David, 22 Sept. 1858, Mary Ann Hall   9/29/58-2
Mumma, Edward W. (Dr.), 15 Oct. 1852, Sarah T. Baker;
     12/ 4/52-2   12/ 6/52-2
Mumma, John T., son of John, 21 Oct. 1852, Sarah Catharine
     Lenndus, dau. of George   10/25/52-2
Munder, Charles F., Jr., 11 Nov. 1851, Priscilla R. Price,
     dau. of David   11/17/51-2
Munder, Theoph. F., 16 Nov. 1858, Emiline Inderrieden   12/ 3/58-2
Mundorff, Isaac, 22 Nov. 1859, Kate Triplett   12/ 3/59-2
Munn, George, 30 Mar. 1853, Mary C. Burns   4/ 2/53-2
Munroe, James, 25 May 1852, Matilda R. Walter, dau. of Geo.   6/ 3/52-2
Muray, Edward, 22 Sept. 1856, Laura V. Jones   9/24/56-2
Murdoch, Wm. T., 8 Feb. 1860, Louisa Tucker, dau. of John   2/15/60-2
Murdock, E. F., 11 July 1853, Catherine Plowman   7/13/53-2
Murfee, James T., 28 Dec. 1854, Martha Sarah Councill   1/ 1/55-2
Murphy, Daniel, 6 Mar. 1851, Ann Eliza Corletto, dau. of
     Francis   3/18/51-2
Murphy, Frances P., 31 Oct. 1859, Ellen Scanlon   11/ 2/59-2
Murphy, Geo. W., 14 Nov. 1852, Caroline M. Duffy   11/15/52-2
Murphy, Geo. W., 13 May 1856, Anna M. Kiethley, dau. of
     John and Rebecca J.   5/20/56-2
Murphy, George W., 30 Oct. 1855, Kate E. Will   11/ 1/55-2
Murphy, Henry, 9 July 1857, Mary Ann Duffy   7/11/57-2
Murphy, Henry, 30 Dec. 1858, Ann E. Conner   3/22/59-2
Murphy, Isaac S., 12 Jan. 1860, Margaret S. Dorman   1/14/60-2
Murphy, Jesse A., 5 Nov. 1854, Rachel C. Schaffer, dau. of
     Jacob   11/11/54-2
Murphy, John, 17 June 1852, Margaret E. O'Donnoghue, dau. of
     T.   6/24/52-2
Murphy, John, 30 July 1854, Jane McGugan   8/ 4/54-2
Murphy, John W., 14 Feb. 1856, Mary Virginia L'anson, dau. of
     Richard M.   3/ 1/56-2
Murphy, Patrick, 8 June 1860, Annie Shepperd   6/11/60-2
Murphy, Peter, 3 Oct. 1857, Catherine Carroll   10/ 6/58-2
Murphy, Robert, 10 Dec. 1856, Emma V. Merrick   12/19/56-2
Murphy, Thomas, 1 May 1853, Louisa Webster   5/10/53-2

Murphy, Thomas, 29 July 1853, Mary Hughes	8/ 5/53-2
Murphy, Thomas A., 16 Oct. 1855, Isabella Smith	10/22/55-2
Murr, Jacob, 25 Dec. 1859, Mary Celina Wigner	12/29/59-2
Murr, Wm., 10 Feb. 1856, Mary A. Harrison, dau. of Basil	2/13/56-2
Murray, Albert, 18 May 1858, Adelaide Merchant	5/20/58-2
Murray, Francis, 1 Apr. 1851, Margaret L. Wilson	4/ 6/52-2
Murray, Francis, 20 Apr. 1852, Susan Williams	4/29/52-2
Murray, Jesse H., 14 Apr. 1852, Amelia A. Tracey	4/16/52-2
Murray, John Hays, 8 Dec. 1859, Victoria Johnson	12/12/59-2
Murray, Richard C., 30 Apr. 1857, (Mrs.) Ellen Doyle	7/23/57-2
Murray, Robert C., 30 Apr. 1857, (Mrs.) Ellen Doyle	7/ 2/57-2
Murray, Samuel, 22 Nov. 1860, (Mrs.) Eliza Robinson	11/24/60-2
Murray, Thomas, 27 Oct. 1859, Louisa V. Herbert	10/29/59-2
Murray, Thomas, 11 Sept. 1860, Kate Tolan	9/19/60-2
Murray, Wm. J., 8 Feb. 1855, Mary J. Anderson, dau. of Wm.	2/13/55-2
Murrey, James, 14 Jan. 1858, Catherine Murphy	2/19/58-2
Murry, John R., 1 May 1856, Mary A. Griffin, dau. of John	5/ 5/56-2
Murry, William, 1 June 1857, Emily J. Williams, dau. of	
John and Sophia E.	6/ 3/57-2
Muskell, Joseph H., 13 July 1859, Margaret Ann Fisher	7/16/59-2
Mussee, William R., 27 Nov. 1856, Fannie J. Davis	12/ 1/56-2
Musselman, J., 23 Dec. 1852, Elizabeth Isaacs, dau. of John	12/25/52-2
Musselman, Wm. Henry, 31 Oct. 1854, Mary M. Huster	11/ 2/54-2
Musser, James G., 4 July 1852, Catharine Kelly	10/13/52-2
Muth, Francis, 25 Jan. 1855, Theresa A. Wittenauer	1/31/55-2
Muth, John P., 4 May 1858, Mary Berger	5/ 7/58-2
Muth, Sebastion A., 16 May 1859, Margaret Einhorn	5/17/59-2
Muthert, August, 9 Oct. 1856, Ann Eliza La Port, dau. of Henry	10/11/56-2
Myer, D. Webster, 3 Nov. 1859, Laura A. Huffington	11/ 4/59-2
Myer, Geo. W., 9 Oct. 1851, Mary Jane Myers	10/14/51-2
Myerly, John J., 10 Jan. 1856, Caroline D. L. Ridgely	2/ 5/56-2
Myers, A. A., 1 Mar. 1859, Kate Lowell	4/ 5/59-2
Myers, A. J., 26 Jan. 1854, Mary F. Griffith	1/28/54-2
Myers, Alexius Joseph, 23 Jan. 1855, Julia Ann Stansbury	1/25/55-2
Myers, Charles, 23 Oct. 1859, Barbara Ritter Price	10/25/59-2
Myers, Charles A., 27 Sept. 1860, Susan Sanders	10/ 2/60-2
Myers, Geo., 12 May 1857, Josephine L. Morris, dau. of James	5/16/57-2
Myers, George, 14 Oct. 1858, Catharine Slyder	10/18/58-2
Myers, Herman, 11 May 1856, Susanna Katz	5/13/56-2
Myers, Isaac, 25 Feb. 1858, Emma V. Morgan	3/26/58-2
Myers, J. Oliver, 3 Apr. 1860, Mary Reed Yarborough, dau. of	
(Col.) Edward	4/ 9/60-2
Myers, Jacob J., 12 Jan. 1860, Mary J. Boyd	1/13/60-2
Myers, James A.; no date given, Susanna T. Bowen	4/20/60-2
Myers, James A., 19 Apr. 1860, Susie J. Bowen; corrected copy	5/ 7/60-2
Myers, John, 18 Apr. 1852, Mary Haley	4/20/52-2
Myers, John, 22 Mar. 1858, Mary Jane Johnson	4/24/58-2
Myers, John H., 27 Mar. 1851, Mary E. McCullough	4/ 5/51-2
Myers, John H., 29 Apr. 1856, Elizabeth Frances Reed, dau. of	
John; 4/30/56-2; 5/ 1/56-2	5/ 2/56-2
Myers, John Henry, 4 June 1854, Julia Ann Miller	6/ 6/54-2
Myers, Leonard, 24 June 1856, Marion Smith	6/28/56-2
Myers, Oliver P., 29 May 1859, Eliza E. Armiger	5/31/59-2
Myers, Philip, 24 Feb. 1853, Adelaide Porter	2/25/53-2
Myers, William (Capt.), 27 Nov. 1856, (Mrs.) Rebecca J. Hanna	12/ 2/56-2
Myers, William H., 18 Feb. 1858, Mary J. Little	3/20/58-2
Nace, Geo. Washington, 21 June 1858, Mary Ann Hoffman	7/13/58-2
Nace, John M., 26 July 1859, Anna R. Wiker	8/ 1/59-2
Nachman, G., 29 Mar. 1857, Rebecca Demelman	4/ 1/57-2
Nagel, August Jacob, 28 June 1857, Eliza A. Williamson	8/ 7/57-2
Nagle, Charles W., 25 Oct. 1860, Annie Wilcox	10/30/60-2
Nash, John, 9 Oct. 1854, Anna Shields; 10/11/54-2	10/12/54-2
Nash, John W. (?) Sept. 1852, Nancy S. Humphreys	9/ 7/52-2
Nash, Robert H., Jr., 11 Oct. 1853, Josephine A. Smith	10/15/53-2
Nash, Thomas S., 24 Apr. 1860, Catharine J. Willayrd	4/28/60-2

Nason, James S., 8 June 1854, Annie S. Foster; corrected copy   6/14/54-2
Nason, James S., 9 June 1854, Annie S. Foster   6/13/54-2
Nason, William C., 3 June 1858, Louise Miller   6/ 5/58-2
Navy, George W., 1 Sept. 1859, Loretta Estelle Cobb   9/ 3/59-2
Naylor, Nelson W., 8 Feb. 1852, Elenora Langley   2/19/52-2
NcCabe, James, 29 May 1859, Marinda Wright   6/ 4/59-2
Ncolfenden, Thomas, 24 Nov. 1853, Jane Anna Marsden   11/26/53-2
Neal, B. F. (Hon.), 26 May 1857, Azubah Haines   5/27/57-2
Neal, George H. C., 20 Mar. 1855, Ann Amelia Tongue, dau. of
    J. Robt.   3/21/55-2
Nearman, Charles, 3 Sept. 1854, Hannah M. Haney   9/25/54-2
Neavitt, John A., 14 Aug. 1856, (Mrs.) Emala Harvey   8/18/56-2
Needham, George F., 27 June 1853, N. Maria Ross, dau. of
    Warren   7/12/53-2
Neely, Edward B., 5 May 1852, Charlotte Slagle, dau. of J.   5/12/52-2
Neely, John (Rev.), 7 Sept. 1852, Rebecca S. Dorsey, dau. of
    (Dr.) Wm. H.   9/ 8/52-2
Neely, Thomas, 1 Mar. 1860, Caroline H. Schiermer   3/ 3/60-2
Neff, John (Dr.), 20 Dec. 1860, Abby H. Brownson   12/27/60-2
Neidhamer, John George, 26 Sept. 1855, Mary Catharine Schuh   10/23/55-2
Neighoff, Joseph, 12 Sept. 1852, Josephine Winks   9/16/52-2
Neild, Hugh, 11 Dec. 1855, (Mrs.) Mary Ann Reay   12/12/55-2
Neilson, Andrew J., 12 Apr. 1853, Sarah R. Bewley   4/21/53-2
Neiman, Edward, 25 Nov. 1858, Josephine Bannenberg   11/27/58-2
Neimeyer, Friederich, 30 Mar. 1854, Elizabeth Frank   4/ 1/54-2
Nelson, James, 25 Nov. 1855, Sarah E. Ozmon   12/ 1/55-2
Nelson, Nicholas H., 4 Nov. 1858, Elizabeth B. Amos   11/ 5/58-2
Nelson, Peter, 14 Mar. 1852, Louisa Shaw   3/17/52-2
Nelson, R. W. (Dr.), 23 May 1854, Ellen Jones, dau. of Hiram   5/25/54-2
Nelson, William L., 12 Oct. 1852, Sarah R. Rose, dau. of
    Peyton R.   10/13/52-2
Nesmith, John F., 21 Aug. 1860, Mary C. Place   8/25/60-2
Ness, Alfred S., 27 Apr. 1852, Anna E. Larrabee   5/ 1/52-2
Ness, George W., 9 May 1854, Joanna R. Thomas, dau. of Jos. B.   5/11/54-2
Netre, Ferdinand, 17 May 1860, Sarah Curry   9/15/60-2
Neupot, Boston, 22 Feb. 1855, Rachel McCoy   2/24/55-2
Neuslein, Nickloss, 13 Jan. 1851, Northburga Grendelmeyer   1/15/51-2
Nevaker, Charles B., 21 Sept. 1853, Sarah J. F. Wooden   9/29/53-2
Neville, James H., 27 July 1857, Susan Robinson   7/29/57-2
Neville, John W., 30 Aug. 1853, Martha E. Ogle   10/24/53-2
Neville, Wm. J., 25 July 1854, Mary H. Nelson   8/ 2/54-2
Nevin, Enoch M., 13 Dec. 1854, Sarah A. Williams   12/20/54-2
Nevins, John, 11 Mar. 1852, Margaret Jane McDowell   3/15/52-2
Nevker, John W., 20 July 1851, Jane Catherine Fentress, dau.
    of Louis   7/25/51-2
Newborn, Jonathan, 27 July 1852, Mary Ann Grannruth   7/31/52-2
Newcombe, John Curtis, 10 Nov. 1859, Mary Reynolds Douglas, dau.
    of William   11/14/59-2
Newell, Samuel T., 24 Sept. 1851, Amanda A. Lloyd   10/ 4/51-2
Newgent, Michael, 11 Jan. 1852, Mary C. Standiford   1/15/52-2
Newgent, Samuel A., 4 July 1859, Frances A. Swan   8/ 8/59-2
Newgent, Sylvester T., 4 July 1855, Matilda A. McClenahan   8/17/55-2
Newhouse, John H., 8 Mar. 1858, Margaret Penn   3/10/58-2
Newkirk, Chas. H. V., 28 Apr. 1853, Mary R. Baker, dau. of
    Henry   5/ 2/53-2
Newkirk, Henry V., 10 Sept. 1854, Josephine Price   9/13/54-2
Newman, Jacob E., 15 July 1856, Anna E. Laws   7/17/56-2
Newman, John, 1 Jan. 1852, Elizabeth Askings, dau. of Basil and
    Hannah   1/ 3/52-2
Newman, Lawson J., 15 Jan. 1858, Lavilla M. McLanhan   2/16/58-2
Newman, William W., 6 Dec. 1855, Margaret Ann Merryman, dau.
    of Samuel   12/11/55-2
Newton, Alfred C., 4 Aug. 1853, Sophia Cook   8/ 6/53-2
Newton, Josiah V., 13 Oct. 1857, Elenora Bryan, dau. of C.   10/14/57-2

Newton, William M., 10 Oct. 1852, Lucy R. Leeland, dau. of
    Baldwin M.   10/13/52-2
Newton, William Thomas, 1 Feb. 1852, Mary Free   2/ 2/52-2
Ney, Joseph, 6 Oct. 1858, Rebecca Gager, dau. of Jacob   10/ 8/58-2
Nice, George A., 8 Oct. 1851, Alverda M. Hunt   10/13/51-2
Nicely, H. C., 31 July 1860, H. L. Shryock   8/18/60-2
Nicholas, Benjamin F., 17 July 1859, Mary Jane Duncan   7/19/59-2
Nicholas, Charles, 17 Apr. 1860, (Mrs.) Elizabeth Russell   4/19/60-2
Nicholls, James W., 2 July 1851, Mary Ann Pitts   7/ 4/51-2
Nicholls, Nelson, 3 Aug. 1855, Rahama L. Charton   8/ 6/55-2
Nicholls, Reuben H., 13 Oct. 1853, Catharine B. Rea   10/14/53-2
Nicholls, Wm. I., 14 Oct. 1851, Harriet E. Linthicum   10/16/51-2
Nichols, Charles W., 10 Oct. 1854, Mary E. Mannakee   10/13/54-2
Nichols, George M., 7 Feb. 1853, (Mrs.) Catharine Chizem   2/10/53-2
Nichols, Isaac, 23 Nov. 1854, Adeline Carr   11/28/54-2
Nichols, J. Stewart, 20 Mar. 1860, Maggie P. Naylor   4/ 6/60-2
Nichols, Joseph Benton, 28 Nov. 1857, Matilda Bailiss   11/30/57-2
Nichols, Levin, 11 Nov. 1858, Henrietta Gould   11/13/58-2
Nichols, Thomas, 23 Dec. 1856, Kezia Jane Wells   12/25/56-2
Nicholson, Abrm, 13 Dec. 1855, Lydia Ann Frazure   12/15/55-2
Nicholson, Arthur T., 31 Aug. 1856, Amanda E. Sprucebank   9/ 2/56-2
Nicholson, George, 19 Jan. 1854, Maria Finnell   1/25/54-2
Nicholson, Henry, 15 Mar. 1858, Kate E. Machen   3/17/58-2
Nicholson, Henry F., 7 Feb. 1854, Harriet A. Tucker   2/ 9/54-2
Nicholson, Henry Q., 11 June 1855, Emmie S. Feelemyer   6/14/55-2
Nicholson, Jacob C., 25 Oct. 1859, (Mrs.) Lucretia H. Shreck 10/29/59-2
Nicholson, Jacob K., 14 Feb. 1856, Matilda A. Mott   2/26/56-2
Nicholson, James A., 18 Dec. 1860, Laura V. Turner, dau. of
    Lewis   12/21/60-2
Nicholson, James S., 1 July 1851, Wilhamina Ann Armiger   7/ 2/51-2
Nicholson, Joseph J. (Rev.); no date given, Ellen Blaine Lyon 7/23/51-2
Nicholson, Michael, 24 Jan. 1856, Georgeanna Bettson   2/15/56-2
Nicholson, Samuel, 16 June 1858, Elizabeth Clark   9/ 9/58-2
Nicholson, T. A. (Dr.), 29 Nov. 1860, Catherine M. Wager   12/ 1/60-2
Nicholson, Washington, 28 Apr. 1859, Frances Cornelia Carter   5/ 2/59-2
Nicholson, Wm., 28 Feb. 1852, Margaret Sutton   3/ 5/52-2
Nicholson, Wm. H., 6 Feb. 1859, Margaret Kees   2/15/59-2
Nicholson, Wm. T., 8 Nov. 1860, Alverda Widerman, dau. of
    Saml. B.   11/10/60-2
Nickerson, Thos. S., 2 Dec. 1851, Mary Benson, dau. of
    Samuel Lucas   12/ 3/51-2
Nicklas, John, 17 Apr. 1855, Kate A. Justis   4/20/55-2
Nickles, Joseph, 9 Oct. 1860, (Mrs.) Abarilla Chandler   10/31/60-2
Nicolai, Chas. H., 22 Feb. 1855, Charlotte R. Turner, dau.
    of (Col.) J. Maybury   7/25/55-2
Nicoll, Benj. B., 15 Dec. 1850, Mary A. Taylor, dau. of Wm.   9/ 1/51-2
Nicols, Jas., 8 Dec. 1859, Olivia Richardson   12/10/59-2
Niehoff, Joseph A., 22 Dec. 1859, Susan V. Rogers   1/12/60-2
Nielsen, William, 12 Feb. 1854, Elizabeth Warner, dau. of
    Jacob   2/14/54-2
Niemyer, John, 14 July 1856, Elizabeth Ellen Granruth, dau. of
    Gustavus   8/ 5/56-2
Nilan, Thomas, 2 Aug. 1859, Catharine Madigan   8/ 3/59-2
Nimmo, James R., 28 Mar. 1853, Lizzie W. Jervis   4/ 1/53-2
Nimmo, Joseph C., 16 Apr. 1860, Sarah M. P. Cropper   4/20/60-2
Nippard, John R., 11 May 1857, Margaret S. Curtain   5/16/57-2
Niser, Samuel, 25 Mar. 1858, Georgianna Curley, dau. of Jas. W. 4/21/58-2
Nixon, William, 31 Mar. 1853, Elizabeth Miller   4/ 5/53-2
Noah, Jacob, 18 Jan. 1857, Bettie Katz   1/19/57-2
Noble, David S.; no date given, Milfred Tabb   1/ 4/55-2
Noble, Elisha, 4 June 1857, Elizabeth N. Bennett   6/ 6/57-2
Noble, Jas. R., 1 Aug. 1854, Mary E. Wickes   8/ 3/54-2
Noel, Samuel H., 10 Aug. 1854, Angeline White   8/25/54-2
Nohnes, James, 3 Dec. 1851, Emily Jane Miles   11/15/52-2
Nolan, James, 16 Nov. 1856, Bridget Cortney   11/26/56-2

```
Nolan, John, 26 Oct. 1851, Margaret A. Gilner                   10/29/51-2
Noland, William C., 2 Sept. 1851, Virginia Ensor                 9/ 5/51-2
Nolen, John C., 12 Apr. 1852, Mary Ellen Gosnell                 4/20/52-2
Nolen, T. Spencer, 4 Aug. 1859, Mary W. Readel, dau. of (Dr.)
    J. D.                                                        8/ 5/59-2
Noll, Adam, 13 Nov. 1859, Wilhelmina Dendy                      11/15/59-2
Nolting, Emil O., 1 Dec. 1858, Susan C. Horn, dau. of J. V.     12/ 2/58-2
Nonnes, Henry S., 15 Mar. 1857, Maria Bevans                     3/31/57-2
Noockogey, Geo., 25 Oct. 1855, Mary E. Jordan                   10/30/55-2
Norfolk, George R., 15 Oct. 1857, Joise A. Parrioth             10/19/57-2
Norfolk, Jas. R., 11 Feb. 1858, Susan C. Barkley                 2/16/58-2
Norfolk, John Wesley, 21 Sept. 1853, Almira Wooden               9/27/53-2
Norman, John, 19 June 1853, Margaret Byrne                       6/23/53-2
Norment, Richard B., 6 Oct. 1853, Margaret Anna Ward, dau. of
    (Rev.) Ulysses                                              10/ 7/53-2
Norris, Amos, 11 Mar. 1852, Jane Amelia Gwynn                    3/13/52-2
Norris, C. Sidney, 15 Sept. 1857, Elizabeth Cromwell, dau. of
    Richard, Jr.                                                 9/17/57-2
Norris, Charles Henry, 20 Feb. 1859, Mary Cassandra Atkinson     2/25/59-2
Norris, David Lee, 13 Oct. 1857, Laura A. Calwell               10/14/57-2
Norris, Edgar J., 4 Oct. 1859, Mary Jane Duford                 10/ 6/59-2
Norris, Edward, 24 Dec. 1854, Emaline Appleby                   12/27/54-2
Norris, George R., 23 Dec. 1855, Eliza Ann Aler                 12/25/55-2
Norris, H. L., 15 Mar. 1855, Annie M. Howard, dau. of
    Samuel                                                       3/19/55-2
Norris, Isaac H., 1 Jan. 1857, Mary Elizabeth D. Souder          1/ 3/57-2
Norris, J. Charles, 17 Sept. 1857, Mary Crawford                 9/22/57-2
Norris, J. Cloud, 1 Jan. 1852, Mary A. Schlosser, dau. of
    John W.                                                      1/16/52-2
Norris, Jacob, 11 Nov. 1858, Fannie A. Ensey, dau. of Lot       11/13/58-2
Norris, James T., 10 July 1858, Elizabeth C. Frederick           7/20/58-2
Norris, John B., 3 Mar. 1858, Martha E. Dixon                    3/ 5/58-2
Norris, John C., 27 Nov. 1860, Susan D. Rogers                  12/ 3/60-2
Norris, John W., 17 Jan. 1860, Susie Billingslea, dau. of Wm.    1/21/60-2
Norris, Saml. C., 2 May 1855, Julia F. Cox                       6/18/55-2
Norris, Thomas T., 30 Oct. 1856, Mary D. Ireland                11/ 1/56-2
Norris, William, 4 May 1852, Sarah R. Merriken                   5/ 6/52-2
Norris, William H., 15 July 1852, Mary Louisa Cooper             7/22/52-2
Norris, Wm. Henry, 20 Oct. 1853, Lizzie A. Bennett              10/22/53-2
North, Richard, 27 May 1858, Frances E. Parrott                  5/31/58-2
North, Robert, 7 May 1857, (Mrs.) Emily J. Price                 5/19/57-2
Norton, James M., 15 Dec. 1853, Mary Virginia Edwards           12/20/53-2
Norton, James W., 13 Feb. 1851, Lucretia Harper                  2/14/51-2
Norwood, Belt S., 16 May 1854, Isabel McElray                    5/19/54-2
Norwood, Benj. R., 30 Mar. 1852, Susan E. Thomas                 4/ 1/52-2
Norwood, Edward, 13 Apr. 1854, Juliet C. Hill, dau. of John E.   4/28/54-2
Norwood, James, 4 Oct. 1853, Margaret A. E. Dashields           10/ 6/53-2
Norwood, Jerome, 27 Mar. 1855, Sarah J. Coram                    3/29/55-2
Norwood, John E., 4 May 1853, Maria E. Burgess                   5/23/53-2
Norwood, Rufus, 27 Jan. 1858, Anne Hyatt                         1/29/58-2
Nowlen, Michael, 21 Sept. 1858, (Mrs.) Eliza Brophey             9/28/58-2
Nugent, James, 16 Apr. 1855, Mary Ann Drum                       4/20/55-2
Nugent, Jimmy *, 30 Nov. 1859, (Mrs.) Eveline Collins, widow
    of James                                                    12/ 7/59-2
Nugent, John, 5 Oct. 1852, Mary M'Mahon                         10/ 7/52-2
Nugent, Thomas A., 28 Odt. 1852, Catharine Vincent Murphy       11/ 1/52-2
Nulton, John B. C., 4 Feb. 1851, Louisa L. Metzgar, dau. of
    Daniel                                                       2/13/51-2
Numbers, Benjamin F., 2 June 1851, Catherine L. Holland          6/ 4/57-2
Numbers, William, 29 Sept. 1857, Sarah Numbers                  10/ 6/57-2
Numsen, N. G., 1 Nov. 1853, Matilda Cross, dau. of Samuel B.    11/ 2/53-2
Numsen, Peter, 3 May 1859, Cordella Brierly                      5/ 4/59-2
Numsen, Wm. N., 9 Oct. 1856, Mary C. Gerber                     10/15/56-2
Nuthall, Charles, 26 June 1857, Ann E. Sprague                  11/ 2/57-2
Nuthall, John L., 24 Feb. 1858, Sarah E. Hicks                   2/26/58-2
```

Nutter, Levin, 12 Aug. 1851, Sarah Wyatt   8/13/51-2
Nyce, Jacob Ridgway, 12 June 1860, Mary Elizabeth Gwaltney   6/14/60-2
Oakford, Charles A., 18 Oct. 1860, Emma A. Zollinger   10/27/60-2
Oarman, John, 16 Mar. 1856, Eliza Ogle   3/26/56-2
O'Bannon, L. W., 8 Apr. 1856, (Mrs.) Mary Chase, dau. of (Col.)
    D. S. Miles   5/ 7/56-2
Ober, Henry, 15 Jan. 1852, Caroline Burdine   1/17/52-2
O'Bold, Francis S., 10 Oct. 1855, Sarah J. Fleishell   10/18/55-2
O'Brien, Cornelius F., 2 Feb. 1858, Margaret F. Vernon   2/16/58-2
O'Brien, James, 18 July 1853, Eleanor M. O'Connor   7/23/53-2
O'Brien, John, 10 July 1854, Ann Louisa Steadey   7/13/54-2
O'Brine, William E., 25 Sept. 1855, Henrietta Wesly   10/ 2/55-2
O'Callaghan, Edward, 5 May 1853, Maria O'Neal   5/ 7/53-2
O'Callaghan, William, 1 Jan. 1855, Mary Shanahan   1/23/55-2
Oches, Chas. H., 1 July 1851, Isabella Young   7/ 3/51-2
O'Connell, Daniel, 15 July 1852, Eliza Jane Sullivan, dau. of
    Jeremiah   7/16/52-2
O'Connell, Patrick, 15 June 1856, Mary Ryan   6/19/56-2
O'Conner, Michael, 17 May 1851, Isabella Gardner   5/23/51-2
O'Conner, Michael, 28 Feb. 1854, Fanney Dailey   11/29/54-2
O'Conners, Michael, 28 Feb. 1854, Fanney Dailey; corrected
    copy; 11/30/54-2   12/ 1/54-2
O'Connor, Lawrence P., 9 Aug. 1853, Louisa Jones   8/11/53-2
O'Connor, William, 14 Sept. 1852, Henrietta Gain   9/15/52-2
O'Daly, Henry E., 3 Aug. 1851, Catherine C. Hartstonge   8/ 5/51-2
Odell, William C., 16 Oct. 1860, Elizabeth H. Choate, dau. of
    Herod   10/18/60-2
Odend'hal, John H., 26 Oct. 1859, Anne Rosalie Bobee   10/29/59-2
Odendhal, Sebastien, 24 Sept. 1857, Mary T. Devlin   10/13/57-2
Odle, Truman, 25 Apr. 1855, Mary A. Wilson   4/27/55-2
O'Donald, James F., 5 June 1856, Margaret E. Thompson   6/ 9/56-2
O'Donevan, John H., Jr., 29 May 1855, Maria Louisa Clagett, dau.
    of Eli   5/31/55-2
O'Donnell, Chas. Oliver, 1 Sept. 1852, Luzinha Jantha Pereira   9/13/52-2
O'Donnell, John, 30 Jan. 1851, Elizabeth Ann Medcalfe   2/ 6/51-2
O'Donnell, John Edward, 20 Nov. 1856, Elenora Adams   11/27/56-2
O'Donnoghue, Florence (Dr.), 16 June 1857, Nellie M.
    Stallings, dau. of (Lieut.) Joseph   6/17/57-2
O'Donohue, Daniel, 23 June 1859, Anne O'Conner   6/28/59-2
Oettinger, Moses, 16 May 1854, Louisa Rosenfeld, dau. of
    Simon   5/20/54-2
Ofaley, John R., 14 June 1857, Anne Cummins, dau. of John W.   6/16/57-2
Offner, John A., 17 Feb. 1852, Christiana C. Droste, dau. of
    John H.   2/20/52-2
Offut, John W. S., 26 Nov. 1856, Mary E. Beall, dau. of
    Horatio   11/28/56-2
Offutt, James W., 28 Dec. 1858, Agnes S. Hewitt, dau. of
    (Dr.) R. D.   1/ 6/59-2
Offutt, John F. C., 23 July 1857, Mary Elizabeth Cozine   7/25/57-2
Offutt, Thomas Z. (Dr.), 22 July 1856, E. A. Offutt, dau. of
    Samuel   7/24/56-2
Ogden, John W., 8 May 1855, Mary A. Watkins, dau. of Wm. W.   5/11/55-2
Ogell, George W., 6 Sept. 1854, Ann J. Adams   9/ 8/54-2
Ogier, John S., Jr., 2 Dec. 1852, Mary Elizabeth Burgeon   12/ 3/52-2
Ogle, Charles, 18 Dec. 1860, Emily J. Hoffman, dau. of Geo. W.   12/20/60-2
Ogle, Jeremiah, 25 June 1855, Elizabeth Rimby   7/10/55-2
Ogle, William F., 15 Sept. 1857, Caroline Peddicord   1/27/58-2
Ogle, Wm. Edward, 20 Dec. 1853, Hannah Fuller   12/29/53-2
O'Grady, Thos., 31 Jan. 1853, Mary Kenney   2/ 9/53-2
Ogsten, George W., 16 Nov. 1853, Harriet Wood Mills, dau. of
    Philo L.   11/18/53-2
Oherl, Thomas J., 15 Oct. 1857, Mary Elizabeth Stewart   10/21/57-2
Ohler, Elias, 20 May 1852, Josephine Louisa Laurence, dau.
    of Ham. D.   5/25/52-2
Ohler, Jacob H., 24 Mar. 1859, Martha A. J. Robinson   4/ 8/59-2

Old, Thos. (Dr.), 8 Mar. 1860, M. Jane Miller   3/10/60-2
Oldfield, Granville S., Jr., 15 Sept. 1852, Virginia Stevens   9/18/52-2
Oldfield, W. W., 23 Feb. 1857, Mary Ann Perry   3/12/57-2
Oler, John W., 10 June 1856, Sarah Balay   6/19/56-2
Oler, Richard, 20 Dec. 1860, Catherine S. Fowler, dau. of
      Philip W.   12/27/60-2
Oler, Wm. H., 16 Dec. 1858, (Mrs.) Helen McVey   12/20/58-2
Oleson, Alexander, 5 Mar. 1854, Elizabeth Patterson, dau. of
      John   3/ 8/54-2
Olhaber, Clement, 4 Sept. 1860, M. Olivia Thompson   9/10/60-2
Olive, Thomas, 4 Feb. 1855, Mary Ann Sprankling   2/ 7/55-2
Oliver, George, 23 Jan. 1851, Isabella McDowell   1/27/51-2
Oliver, John, 8 June 1852, Louisa W. Demortie   6/ 9/52-2
Oliver, John, 10 Jan. 1854, Margaret Watson   1/11/54-2
Oliver, John, 16 Jan. 1855, Susan Elsroad, dau. of Michael   1/18/55-2
Oliver, John, 5 Dec. 1859, Margaret G. Laughlin   12/16/59-2
Oliver, John, 5 Dec. 1859, Margaret J. Laughlin; corrected copy   12/17/59-2
Oliver, William, 22 Aug. 1854, Sarah McCoy   8/25/54-2
Olsan, L., 2-(?) Jan. 1854, Elizabeth Tamman   1/31/54-2
Ommenhausser, John J., 9 Nov. 1858, Victoria A. Beauchamp   11/11/58-2
O'Neal, Israel C., 18 Feb. 1860, (Mrs.) Annie E. Chandler   2/25/60-2
O'Neal, John L., 27 Mar. 1860, Dorcas M. Hammontree   3/28/60-2
O'Neill, Charles Z., 8 Mar. 1854, Deborah A. Burley, dau. of
      Isaac   3/30/54-2
O'Neil, Chas. C., 20 May 1851, Louisa A. Cornprobst, dau. of
      Ignatius   5/21/51-2
O'Neill, John, 3 Apr. 1851, Ruth Wilks, dau. of James, Jr.   4/ 5/51-2
O'Neill, Owen, 12 Feb. 1857, Elizabeth Burns, dau. of Phillip   2/14/57-2
Onion, James H. W., 29 Jan. 1860, Kate R. Murphy   2/13/60-2
Onion, John R., 2 Sept. 1858, Sarah A. Turner   9/ 4/58-2
Onion, W. F. H., 9 June 1853, Jane E. Griffith, dau. of
      (Dr.) Lewis   6/14/53-2
Oram, John H., 15 Jan. 1856, Margaret C. Valentine   1/17/56-2
O'Reilly, Bernard, 24 Dec. 1854, Margaret L. Kelly, dau. of
      James   12/28/54-2
Orem, J. Edward, 25 Feb. 1858, Biddy Jane Evans   2/27/58-2
Orem, Joshua, 29 Dec. 1852, Leonora M. Miller   12/31/52-2
Orem, Josiah, 31 July 1851, Caroline P. Skinner, dau. of
      William   8/ 2/51-2
Orem, Perry C., 13 June 1853, Catherine M. Sheeler, dau. of
      Anthony   6/22/53-2
O'Rourke, Luke, 8 July 1854, Mary R. Wright   9/15/54-2
Orrick, John C., 25 Feb. 1857, Anne Eliza Beckley   2/28/57-2
Orrick, John C., 13 May 1858, Elizabeth Dickson Smith, dau.
      of Jacob   5/14/58-2
Ortlip, Mahlon, 22 Feb. 1859, Mary Frances Dunoway   2/24/59-2
Osbeck, John F., 10 Nov. 1853, Anne E. Thompson   11/11/53-2
Osborn, Owen, 4 Dec. 1851, Sarah E. Taylor   12/ 6/51-2
Osborn, Wm. S., 18 Sept. 1860, Sannia M. Thompson   9/19/60-2
Osburn, Addison, 30 Nov. 1853, Massy G. Osburn   12/ 1/53-2
Osgodby, Thomas W., 2 Mar. 1853, Sarah L. Dubbs   3/23/53-2
Osterhus, J. A., 6 Oct. 1857, Elizabeth G. Pagels   10/12/57-2
Osterman, Jas. A., 29 June 1858, Margaret M. Linhard, dau. of
      (Capt.) Thos.   7/ 3/58-2
Otterback, Philip, 28 July 1848, Emma L. Miller; corrected
      copy   4/18/53-2
Otterback, Philip, Jr., 29 July 1848, Emma L. Miller   4/16/53-2
Otterson, James, 20 Feb. 1851, Jane S. Green   2/24/51-2
Ould, John, 18 June 1860, (?)   (?)   6/20/60-2
Ould, Marion H., 28 June 1855, Mary Susan Swift   6/30/55-2
Ourand, Joseph T. W., 11 Aug. 1857, Maggie Arthur, dau. of
      James, Sr.   8/14/57-2
Oursler, William W., 16 Jan. 1851, Ann Eliza Manly   1/20/51-2
Oursler, William W., 17 Nov. 1859, Melcena E. Talbot   11/19/59-2
Oursler, Charles H., 21 Oct. 1858, Mary E. Holbrook   10/22/58-2

Over, Anthony, 16 Sept. 1858, Margaret Shaney   9/21/58-2
Overton, James B., 21 Nov. 1854, Josephine Eaverson   11/25/54-2
Overton, James Blackburn, 21 Nov. 1854, Josephine Eaverson;
  corrected copy   12/ 9/54-2
Overton, John B., 23 Dec. 1852, Mary E. Pimm, dau. of John M. 1/ 7/53-2
Owens, B. Welch, 21 Apr. 1858, Maude A. Smith   4/24/58-2
Owens, Cornelius A., 27 Mar. 1856, Martha A. Tilghman   3/29/56-2
Owens, George W., 27 Mar. 1851, Ann W. Brownley   3/29/51-2
Owens, James, 15 Jan. 1853, Esther A. Hiss, dau. of Jesse L. 2/17/53-2
Owens, James E. (Dr.), 5 July 1853, Elizabeth R. Dorsey   7/ 7/53-2
Owens, John W. T., 31 Dec. 1854, Margaret Huggins   1/13/55-2
Owens, Richard, 24 Jan. 1856, Catharine Hazelup   1/26/56-2
Owens, Richard W., 19 Jan. 1860, Amelia Elizabeth Cook   1/27/60-2
Owens, Samuel, 26 Apr. 1857, Joanna Williams   4/28/57-2
Owens, Samuel W., 11 Oct. 1859, Sarah Winters   10/13/59-2
Owens, T. F., 24 Mar. 1852, Sarah A. Laws   3/25/52-2
Owens, Thomas (Dr.), 11 June 1860, K. Valeria Riley   6/30/60-2
Owens, Thomas, 6 Oct. 1860, Lizzie M. Dempsey, dau. of James
  and Elizabeth   10/10/60-2
Owens, Uriah F., 22 Dec. 1852, Dorothy Hopper   12/24/52-2
Owens, Wm.; no date given, Mary Ann O'Shea   5/19/59-2
Owings, B. Allen, 24 Feb. 1857, Mattie Massey, dau. of (Dr.)
  N. R.   2/25/57-2
Owings, Benjamin T., 18 Apr. 1852, Eliza Owings   5/11/52-2
Owings, G. Washington, 14 July 1859, Susannah Crooks   7/20/59-2
Owings, Henry, 2 May 1860, Amelia A. Owings   5/ 3/60-2
Owings, Israel E., 1 June 1851, Amelia Ann Dyer   6/ 4/51-2
Owings, J. Breneman, 24 Apr. 1855, Bithiah H. Spry   4/30/55-2
Owings, James W., 5 Sept. 1855, Mary Leeson   9/12/55-2
Owings, John B., 9 Nov. 1853, Henrietta V. Stork   11/11/53-2
Owings, Joshua, 26 June 1855, Serena J. Cadell   10/16/56-2
Owings, Levi T., 11 July 1855, Amelia V. Ditman   7/12/55-2
Owings, Thomas B., 18 May 1859, Virginia M. Aitken, dau. of
  (Dr.) James   5/19/59-2
Owings, Thomas D., 14 Apr. 1853, Laura J. Jenkins   4/19/53-2
Owner, James, 24 Feb. 1858, Mary E. Stuck   2/26/58-2
Oxworth, Daniel, 31 Jan. 1858, Laura V. Croggon   2/ 2/58-2
Ozmon, Greenbank, 25 Nov. 1858, Marion E. Hall, dau. of
  John H.   11/27/58-2
Ozmon, John W., 5 Jan. 1857, Margaret A. Arnold, dau. of
  Clemmend and Kezia   1/ 6/58-2
Padgett, John, 27 Nov. 1851, Anne Rollins   12/ 4/51-2
Padgett, Joseph H., 4 Oct. 1853, Mary Ann E. Smith   10/ 6/53-2
Padgett, Joseph M., 28 July 1853, Elizabeth B. Nally   7/30/53-2
Padgett, Reuben B., 29 Sept. 1853, Sophia Schminke, dau. of
  George   10/ 1/53-2
Padgett, Robert J., 27 July 1858, Ann J. Hamill   7/30/58-2
Page, Arthur, 12 Oct. 1852, Mary Jane Campbell   10/15/52-2
Page, Calvin, 11 May 1853, Lucretia Brewer   5/12/53-2
Page, Carter H, 24 Nov. 1857, Lelia Graham, dau. of Wm.   11/28/57-2
Page, Frank M., 26 Apr. 1854, Mary Victorine Vallette, dau. of
  Victor   4/29/54-2
Page, Lewis, 16 Aug. 1852, Harriet Lovecy   8/26/52-2
Page, R. Virgil, 8 Nov. 1860, Addie F. Townshend   11/13/60-2
Page, Thos., 27 Aug. 1853, Mary Magaline Pitt   8/31/53-2
Page, William, 10 Oct. 1852, Catherine E. Brian   5/ 3/53-2
Paine, Jas. R., 26 Oct. 1852, Sadonia Robertson   10/29/52-2
Paine, John A., 15 Nov. 1859, Mary A. Curtis   11/21/59-2
Painter, James E., 25 Dec. 1856, Sarah P. Bloomer   12/30/56-2
Palke, J. M., 19 July 1853, Lucinda S. Neel, dau. of (Col.)
  Thomas   7/30/53-2
Palmer, Andrew J., 1 Feb. 1859, Emily A. Davis   2/16/59-2
Palmer, Chas. H., 22 June 1852, Margaret Logan; 7/14/52-2   7/16/52-2
Palmer, Henry C., 1 July 1852, Arianna E. Mulliken, dau. of
  Thomas   8/ 3/52-2

156   MARRIAGES IN THE BALTIMORE SUN, 1851-1860

Palmer, Innis N. (Capt.), 17 May 1855, Kate Jones, dau. of
     (Capt.) Llewellyn   5/18/55-2
Palmer, John (Capt.), 22 Jan. 1857, Elizabeth Frances
     Creighton, dau. of (Capt.) Samuel   1/24/57-2
Palmer, John H., 10 Feb. 1857, R. Ella Thomas   3/ 4/57-2
Palmer, John M., 14 Oct. 1855, Ann E. Hixon   10/24/55-2
Palmer, John W., 2 June 1855, Henrietta Lee, dau. of Elisha   6/ 5/55-2
Palmer, Thomas (Capt.), 17 Nov. 1853, Emaline Wheatly   11/24/53-2
Palmer, Thomas, 7 Feb. 1854, M. Irene Hooper   2/ 8/54-2
Palmer, W. Henry, 15 Sept. 1857, Anna Maria Kieekhoefer, dau. of
     A. T.   9/24/57-2
Pamphilion, James T., 18 Feb. 1858, Ann Eliza M. Gehlor   2/20/58-2
Pancost, William P., 20 Nov. 1851, Rachel Ijams, dau. of
     Franklin F.   11/27/51-2
Paraway, John, 23 Dec. 1852, Celestia Ann Jones   12/25/52-2
Pardee, John A., 31 Oct. 1859, Hanna E. Button; corrected
     copy   11/ 8/59-2
Pardee, John H., 1 Oct. 1859, Hannah E. Button   11/ 7/59-2
Parish, D. Howard (Rev.), 1 Dec. 1859, Lizzie J. Brown, dau.
     of John S.   12/ 2/59-2
Parish, Richard, 11 May 1853, Sarah Sensney   5/13/53-2
Parke, Francis G., 7 June 1859, Mary E. Kerr, dau. of Andrew   6/14/59-2
Parke, Thos. H., 9 Jan. 1855, Annie Torbert, dau. of Saml.;
     corrected copy   1/17/55-2
Parker, Edwin L., Jr., 26 Feb. 1857, Jane Peters   2/28/57-2
Parker, Fred'k. L., 2 Aug. 1852, Elizabeth A. Knott, dau. of
     Jas. M.   8/ 5/52-2
Parker, Jacob, 17 Nov. 1859, Mary M. Free   12/12/59-2
Parker, Jacob, 17 Oct. 1859, Mary Margaret Free, dau. of
     Jefferson; corrected copy   12/12/59-2
Parker, Jacob, 17 Nov. 1859, Mary Margaret Free, dau. of
     Jefferson; corrected copy   12/13/59-2
Parker, James (Capt.), 23 Apr. 1851, Mary Jane Williams   4/25/51-2
Parker, John E., 9 Feb. 1859, Anne E. Dryden, dau. of
     Edwin S.   2/12/59-2
Parker, John W., 30 Sept. 1853, Sarah S. Clarke   10/ 1/53-2
Parker, Thomas H., 9 Jan. 1855, Annie Torbert, dau. of Saml.   1/16/55-2
Parker, William G. W., 12 Jan. 1860, Elizabeth Ann Thompson   1/13/60-2
Parkhill, John H. (Col.), 24 June 1856, Annie E. Sangston,
     dau. of George E.   6/27/56-2
Parkhill, William, 19 Feb. 1852, Annie M. Plungett   2/21/52-2
Parkinson, Joel B., 18 Sept. 1860, Mary Elizabeth Hynson,
     dau. of B. T.   9/20/60-2
Parks, Aquilla J., 5 Dec. 1852, Eliza Jane Lusk   12/ 6/52-2
Parks, Elijah, 18 Mar. 1858, Sarah C. Reed   3/20/58-2
Parks, George W., 3 Sept. 1858, Mary Ann Stevenson   10/ 5/58-2
Parks, James H., 1 June 1856, Sarah J. Rupp   6/ 2/56-2
Parks, John A., 10 Sept. 1854, Mary Catherine Bishop   9/13/54-2
Parks, Josiah, 14 Apr. 1852, Emeline Neal   4/16/52-2
Parks, Richard, 6 July 1854, Margaret Clarke   7/11/54-2
Parlett, Benjamin F., 29 Dec. 1859, Isabel C. Ashton, dau. of
     W. R.   12/31/59-2
Parlett, Hezekiah, 12 Nov. 1852, Sarah Ann Clark   12/ 7/52-2
Parlett, James B., 23 Feb. 1851, Elizabeth A. Parlett   3/10/51-2
Parlett, William D., 20 May 1852, Susan Scrivnor   5/21/52-2
Parott, W. J., 14 Mar. 1854, Margaret Guess   3/28/54-2
Parr, Augustus, 6 Feb. 1853, Rebecca A. Walker   2/ 8/53-2
Parr, Charles H., 21 Apr. 1853, Rebecca W. Day   4/27/53-2
Parr, Curles H., 21 Apr. 1853, Rebecca W. Day   4/22/53-2
Parr, John H., 31 Dec. 1850, Jane A. V. Edmonds   1/ 6/51-2
Parran, James R., 23 Nov. 1854, Alice Lockington, dau. of
     Joshua   11/28/54-2
Parran, Wm. J., 2 Dec. 1854, Sarah Rebecca Bourne, dau. of
     Jas. J.   12/ 4/54-2

Parrish, Charles J., 23 June 1852, Mary Jane Thompson, dau.
    of John T.   6/26/52-2
Parrish, Jacob, 9 Feb. 1853, Susan Barry   2/12/53-2
Parrish, James, 23 Nov. 1859, Sarah Young   11/26/59-2
Parrish, John Walker, 21 Nov. 1856, Sarah Ann Leatherberry   11/25/56-2
Parrish, Thos. A., 29 Nov. 1855, Eliza Holmes   12/ 3/55-2
Parsons, Eliphalet, 19 Nov. 1857, Susie A. Warner, dau. of
    Asa   11/25/57-2
Parsons, George F., 18 Oct. 1859, Mollie Sheets, dau. of
    Jacob   10/21/59-2
Parsons, James S., 4 May 1856, (Mrs.) Mary Dolbry   5/13/56-2
Parsons, Stephen P., 21 Dec. 1854, Ann E. Welch   12/23/54-2
Partridge, William A., 10 Apr. 1853, Marie A. Dove   4/19/53-2
Pascal, Marion A., 25 July 1852, Catherine Trammell   7/28/52-2
Pascault, Louis C., 7 Aug. 1856, (Mrs.) E. J. Bond   8/ 9/56-2
Paschall, Thomas, 5 Aug. 1852, Margaret L. Coombs   8/ 9/52-2
Pascoe, Charles; no date given, Annie E. Tomlinson, dau. of
    Henry   2/ 8/55-2
Pascoe, Isaiah, 21 Oct. 1852, Sarah Jane Turpin, dau. of
    Joshua   11/ 1/52-2
Passcay, James A., 18 Dec. 1855, Alvira Cullison   10/31/56-2
Pate, Charles L., 30 Sept. 1858, Margaret Underwood   10/ 2/58-2
Pate, Joseph H., 19 Mar. 1852, Catherine C. Collins   4/ 2/53-2
Pate, William, 14 Apr. 1855, Eliza A. Robbins   4/24/55-2
Paterson, James, 14 Jan. 1858, Mary Jefers   1/25/58-2
Paterson, Robert, 21 Jan. 1858, Margaret Christie   1/26/58-2
Patrick, Benjamin F., 8 Jan. 1856, Ione Palmer   1/ 9/56-2
Patrick, John H., 24 Feb. 1852, Charity G. De Valangin   2/26/52-2
Patten, Charles, 25 Nov. 1858, Ellenena Spencer   11/27/58-2
Patten, Geo.; no date given, Emma Patten, dau. of Richard   3/16/53-2
Patten, George, 26 Oct. 1854, Adelaide Lynch, dau. of Thomas   10/31/54-2
Patterson, David, 31 Jan. 1860, Mary McCann   3/ 7/60-2
Patterson, George A., 6 Mar. 1851, Martha C. Mann   3/10/51-2
Patterson, George W., 1 Aug. 1860, Mary E. Harrison   8/21/60-2
Patterson, Isaac, 9 Oct. 1853, Fanny Currey   10/10/53-2
Patterson, J. Orville, 26 Feb. 1852, Anna Jane B. De La Roche,
    dau. of Geo. F.   3/ 1/52-2
Patterson, James, 10 May 1853, Mary M. Maccan   7/27/53-2
Patterson, James, 15 Apr. 1855, (Mrs.) Catharine Kernan   6/10/56-2
Patterson, James, 9 July 1860, (Mrs.) Jennie Cochran   8/14/60-2
Patterson, Joseph, 7 May 1857, Susanna Gaines   5/ 8/57-2
Patterson, Joseph C., 24 July 1851, Frances Kelly   7/28/51-2
Patterson, Lloyd, 7 Mar. 1860, Eliza L. Horney   5/28/60-2
Patterson, Thomas N., 30 May 1855, Martha G. Keirle   5/31/55-2
Patterson, William, 8 Nov. 1855, Mary E. Lawder, dau. of
    Samuel M.   11/26/55-2
Pattison, John, 10 Apr. 1860, Emily Ann Mitchell   4/12/60-2
Pattison, Thos., 27 July 1852, Lizzie Morrison   7/29/52-2
Pattison, Wm. Winder, 30 Oct. 1851, (Mrs.) Mary Tubman   10/31/51-2
Paul, C. J. (Capt.), 16 May 1855, Louisa N. Mathews   5/17/55-2
Paul, Jennings, 9 May 1860, Agnes A. Thompson   5/19/60-2
Paul, Robert C., 12 Oct. 1852, Anne Eliza Miller   10/18/52-2
Pawley, Finley, 7 July 1859, Margaret Carnes   7/ 9/59-2
Pawley, John A. A., 19 Jan. 1860, Lizzie J. Barry   1/24/60-2
Paxson, Simmons, 31 May 1859, Hannah Jane Chapman   6/ 4/59-2
Paynter, Martin S. B., 19 Dec. 1850, Sarah Louisa Kobore   2/10/51-2
Peabody, J. D., 8 June 1852, Rosalba E. Beall, dau. of
    Richard B.   6/ 9/52-2
Peace, William E. (Dr.), 16 Nov. 1851, Sarah Alexander Magill,
    dau. of James   11/18/52-2
Peach, John, 15 Feb. 1855, Emma J. Carsner, dau. of Danl.   2/17/55-2
Peacock, Charles A., 23 Dec. 1855, Elenora C. Lafferty   1/ 9/56-2
Peacock, George W., 4 Nov. 1851, Ellen M. Seabright, dau.
    of Samuel   11/ 8/51-2
Peacock, John M., 1 June 1852, Rachel J. Wyant   6/ 3/52-2

Peacock, John R., 2 Jan. 1851, Permelia Jane Tolley   1/ 4/51-2
Peacock, Samuel, 17 Oct. 1853, (Mrs.) Mary Ann Kepler   10/27/53-2
Pearce, Davidson D., Sr., 7 Feb. 1854, (Mrs.) Eliza M.
     Hamilton   2/ 8/54-2
Pearce, James W.; no date given, M. Virginia Emery, dau. of
     J. B.   6/ 6/53-2
Pearce, John A. W., 7 Sept. 1854, Ruta Ann Mecasun, dau. of
     John   9/ 8/54-2
Pearce, John C., 1 Nov. 1855, Sarah A. Woods, dau. of
     Richard G.   11/ 5/55-3
Pearce, John G., 11 Mar. 1852, Jemima Elizabeth Brown, dau.
     of William   3/12/52-2
Pearce, John H., 30 June 1859, Sarah R. Demby   7/ 2/59-2
Pearce, N. B., 25 Jan. 1853, Nannie Kate Smith   3/21/55-2
Pearce, T. T. G. (Dr.), 29 Nov. 1855, Mary Eleanor Moores,
     dau. of (Dr.) Saml. Lee   12/ 1/55-2
Pearl, Samuel T., 12 July 1855, Mary Ellen Osbourn   7/24/55-2
Pearson, John, 6 Dec. 1853, Christina Bell   12/ 9/53-2
Pearson, John William, 7 Dec. 1856, Anna Eliza Osborn Mayhew   12/10/56-2
Peck, Nathaniel, Jr., 4 Nov. 1851, Caroline Maxfield   11/ 7/51-2
Peck, Thomas E., 28 Oct. 1852, Ellen C. Richardson   11/ 2/52-2
Peck, William H., 10 Nov. 1853, Elenore Gaines   11/12/53-2
Peddicord, George, 4 Dec. 1856, Sarah E. Steele   1/ 6/57-2
Peddicord, Henry A., 14 Nov. 1855, Mary E. Mercer   11/17/55-2
Peddicord, Theodore, 21 June 1860, Amelia Bowen   6/25/60-2
Peddicord, Wesley, 26 Feb. 1854, Sarah E. Lawrence   2/28/54-2
Pedro, Joseph, 26 Dec. 1859, Fanny Edkins, dau. of Joseph   12/28/59-2
Peed, James R., 2 May 1860, Maggie A. Young   5/ 9/60-2
Peed, James R., 2 May 1860, Margaret Ann Young, dau. of
     (Capt.) George; corrected copy   5/11/60-2
Peede, P. J., 24 Aug. 1858, Hetty M. Canzler   8/26/58-2
Peirce, Edward, 16 Oct. 1856, Sophia E. Kummer   10/20/56-2
Peirce, Elias H. (Dr.), 2 June 1857, Sallie C. Hardcastle   6/ 3/57-2
Peirce, G. H. (Dr.), 23 Sept. 1856, Jennie B. Hammond   9/26/56-2
Peirsol, Isaac D., 21 Jan. 1858, Maggie Thomas, dau. of George   2/ 2/58-2
Pikiffer, N. A., 9 Mar. 1854, Mary Metz   3/14/54-2
Pendergast, Charles H., 5 Nov. 1856, Louisa J. Lynch, dau. of
     James   11/ 6/56-2
Pendergast, James F., 23 Nov. 1852, Adelaide Lynch, dau. of
     James   11/25/52-2
Pendleton, Wm. M., 4 May 1858, Bettie Frisby, dau. of J.
     Edwards   5/22/58-2
Penington, Noble, 6 June 1857, H. Lousia Price   6/ 5/57-2
Penington, Stephen M., 13 June 1854, Matilda E. Herchfeldt;
     6/17/54-2   6/19/54-2
Penn, Jacob, 7 July 1853, Alice Jeffers; corrected copy   7/ 9/53-2
Penn, Samuel B., 22 Sept. 1859, Emily J. Croggan, dau. of
     Washington; corrected copy   9/26/59-2
Penn, Samuel B., 22 Sept. 1859, Emily J. Croggon   9/24/59-2
Penn, William Y., 30 Jan. 1859, Lizzie A. Warfield   2/14/59-2
Pennington, Charles J., 14 Apr. 1853, Elizabeth T. Winder, dau.
     of (Capt.) E. S.   4/20/53-2
Pennington, Charles P., 10 May 1855, Caroline A. Owens   5/12/55-2
Pennington, J., Jr., 6 May 1858, Elizabeth A. Stirling, dau. of
     Archibald   5/10/58-2
Pennington, John H., 15 Sept. 1853, Elizabeth Bostic   9/19/53-2
Pennington, Louis E., 4 Feb. 1851, Jane C. Janvier, dau. of
     W. B.   2/13/51-2
Pennington, William C., 21 Sept. 1858, Anna C. Fineberger   9/22/58-2
Pennock, Charles E., 5 Sept. 1855, Elizabeth Gibbens   9/ 7/55-2
Penny, Henry (Capt.), 31 Jan. 1854, Catharine A. Syme, dau.
     of James and Margaret   2/ 2/54-2
Pentz, Emory McK., 28 May 1860, Mary L. Whitaker; 5/30/60-2   5/31/60-2
Pentz, Jacob, 3 Apr. 1855, Mary W. Herster   4/ 9/55-2
Pentz, Joseph A. P., 13 May 1855, Isabella M. Humphreys   5/15/55-2

Pentz, William H., 12 July 1852, Virginia Wilson   7/26/52-2
Pentz, William S., 8 June 1854, Anna R. Sullivan   6/10/54-2
Peppler, Alexander, 28 Jan. 1851, Elizabeth Barnstricker   2/11/51-2
Perce, John, 28 Dec. 1852, Harriet A. Russell   1/15/53-2
Peregoy, C. E., 23 Sept. 1860, Mary A. Cochran   11/23/60-2
Peregoy, Jas., 4 Sept. 1856, Josephine C. Cocks   9/11/56-2
Peregoy, John H. W., 25 Dec. 1854, Margaret Rork   1/ 1/55-2
Peregoy, Joshua, 25 Oct. 1859, Julia A. Grim   11/23/59-2
Peregoy, William B., 3 Sept. 1851, Elizabeth C. McFarlane, dau.
     of John   9/ 9/51-2
Perine, Oliver, 26 Aug. 1852, Mary Catherine Hooker, dau. of
     Robert   9/ 2/52-2
Perine, Wesley S., 22 Jan. 1857, Rebecca J. Mays   1/26/57-2
Perkins, James, 27 Mar. 1853, Agnes T. Tomphson, dau. of
     William   4/ 1/53-2
Perkins, John, 16 Sept. 1856, G. V. Roberts, dau. of Wm.   9/19/56-2
Perkins, Otis B., 24 Dec. 1851, Frances Booth   12/30/51-2
Perkins, William, 8 Mar. 1855, Susan Machenheimer   3/10/55-2
Perkins, William J., 27 Apr. 1854, Elizabeth A. Spencer, dau.
     of Thomos   5/ 1/54-2
Perkins, Wm. H., 11 Jan. 1860, Laura Pochon   1/18/60-2
Perkins, Wm. H. H., 13 Sept. 1857, Amanda M. Ortlip   9/21/57-2
Perlasous, Alexander, 11 May 1858, Rebecca Lain   5/13/58-2
Perrie, J. B., 25 Feb. 1858, Mattie A. Conrad, dau. of Nelson   3/ 5/58-2
Perrie, Rinaldo W., 24 May 1859, Imogene Conrad, dau. of N.   5/30/59-2
Perrie, Thomas H., 19 Oct. 1860, Lottie C. C. Ames   10/23/60-2
Perrin, Wm. A., 3 June 1852, Margaret E. George, dau. of
     Joseph   6/12/52-2
Perry, A. Allen, 25 June 1856, Anna E. Stow, dau. of Thomas   7/ 2/56-2
Perry, Albert, 14 Oct. 1859, (Mrs.) Cornelia Bassett   10/17/59-2
Perry, Ancell Coats, 2 Aug. 1858, Susan Emeline Louisa Perry   8/ 3/58-2
Perry, Charles M., 25 Sept. 1856, Josephine A. Sharkey   9/29/56-2
Perry, Francis W., 19 Jan. 1860, Annie S. Robinson   6/21/60-2
Perry, Henry W., 11 Oct. 1854, Sarah Louisa Van Rostrum   10/19/54-2
Perry, James, 31 Dec. 1857, Emily Jane Coultrider   1/ 9/58-2
Perry, Michael C. H., 12 Nov. 1855, Mary E. Houck   11/15/55-2
Perry, Richard, 7 Apr. 1853, Sarah Hobbs   4/13/53-2
Perry, Thomas, 6 Mar. 1853, Nancy Martin   3/ 7/53-2
Personette, Thos. H., 30 Sept. 1855, Sarah E. Holmes, dau. of
     John E.   10/22/55-2
Pescud, Edward (Capt.), 12 Jan. 1854, Sarah R. Tucker, dau. of
     John H.; 1/14/54-2
                                                                    1/16/54-2
Peter, John T., 14 Oct. 1852, Caroline Seth   10/15/52-2
Peters, Henry, 21 Mar. 1853, (Mrs.) Jane Coleman   3/31/53-2
Peters, James, 6 Oct. 1859, Isabella N. Freeman, dau. of (Col.)
     Wm. H.   10/ 7/59-2
Peters, L. M., 4 Mar. 1850, Hannah George   8/23/59-2
Peters, Simon, 20 Sept. 1857, Letitia Ann Fisher   9/22/57-2
Peterson, Elias, 20 Jan. 1851, Margaret Ann Bradley   2/11/51-2
Peterson, John French, 10 Jan. 1856, Elizabeth Sarah Holmes,
     dau. of Samuel and Mary   2/18/56-2
Peterson, Lewis A., son of (Capt.) F., 21 July 1852, Isabel
     Witters, dau. of James   7/26/52-2
Pettibone, Philip (Dr.), 8 Jan. 1856, Willie Hans   1/10/56-2
Pettitt, Joseph D.; no date given, Ann Maria Talbott   12/10/52-2
Pettitt, Wm. F., 28 Apr. 1853, Elizabeth Spillmer   4/30/53-2
Peyton, Henry E., 12 May 1859, Mary Elizabeth Braden, dau. of
     Noble S.   5/14/59-2
Phalan, Nicholas; no date given, Martha Ann Clark   4/15/53-2
Phelps, Francis P. (Dr.), 12 May 1853, Mary R. Springer, dau.
     of (Col.) D. C.   5/13/53-2
Phelps, Geo. D., 19 Nov. 1856, Indiana R. Lindsay   11/22/56-2
Phelps, Nelson, 18 Jan. 1857, Elizabeth A. Shipley, dau. of
     Larkin   1/19/57-2

Phelps, R. Thompson, 29 Jan. 1856, Caroline F. Bond, dau. of
    Peter   2/ 2/56-2
Phelps, Richard J., 13 Feb. 1855, (Mrs.) Sarah A. Seveirs   2/17/55-2
Phelps, S. Ledyard, 3 Oct. 1853, Lizzie Maynadier, dau. of
    (Capt.) Wm.   10/ 4/53-2
Phelps, Silas, 7 Oct. 1852, Ellen Frances McLaughlin, dau. of
    Robert   10/ 8/52-2
Phelps, William, 17 Nov. 1859, Mary A. McRoberts   11/22/59-2
Phenix, Howard, 10 Feb. 1853, Elizabeth Blake, dau. of James
    Lugare   2/18/53-2
Phifer, John, 3 Oct. 1854, Christina Waltz   10/10/54-2
Philips, David, 6 July 1856, (Mrs.) Rebecca Guy   7/ 9/56-2
Philips, Henry, 7 Oct. 1858, Emma Seeger, dau. of Jacob   10/ 9/58-2
Philips, Hugh, 8 Feb. 1855, Mary Elizabeth Egan   2/12/55-2
Philips, J. Van Ness, 3 Aug. 1852, Laura Johnson, dau. of
    Clarence   8/ 6/52-2
Philips, Robert A. (?) Aug. 1860, Mary Virginia Sturgeon   11/19/60-2
Philips, Thos., 15 Aug. 1857, Rachel C. Watts, dau. of (Rev.)
    John   9/16/57-2
Phillips, Benjamin, 16 May 1852, Sarah J. Parrish   5/21/52-2
Phillips, Chas., 16 Dec. 1858, Margaret S. Cline, dau. of
    M. B.   12/24/58-2
Phillips, Edwin, 27 Dec. 1852, Margaretta Glenn, dau. of R. W. 5/10/54-2
Phillips, Geo. W., 3 Nov. 1852, Mary E. Alpha, dau. of (Capt.)
    Mitchel   11/ 6/52-2
Phillips, Harvey (Capt.), 2 Sept. 1852, Olevia H. Burnett, dau.
    of (Capt.) J. P.   9/ 4/52-2
Phillips, Isaac, 1 May 1851, Jemima Vickers   5/ 3/51-2
Phillips, James, 3 July 1860, (Mrs.) Martha A. Howarth   7/ 4/60-2
Phillips, James P., 16 Apr. 1860, (Mrs.) Mary G. Stansbury   4/20/60-2
Phillips, Jas. T., 1 Jan. 1851, Margaret Hudgin   1/ 4/51-2
Phillips, John, 30 Dec. 1852, Belinda Roberts   1/ 7/53-2
Phillips, John (Capt.), 5 July 1860, (Mrs.) Ann M. McGuyre   7/ 7/60-2
Phillips, John A., 25 Oct. 1860, Rebecca J. Lawton   11/ 6/60-2
Phillips, John B., 23 Nov. 1854, Annie M. Steuart, dau. of
    Edward   11/27/54-2
Phillips, Kep., 9 Feb. 1858, Louisa A. Best, dau. of (Rev.) H. 2/12/58-2
Phillips, Levin, 14 Jan. 1851, Elizabeth A. Tall   1/16/51-2
Phillips, Llewellyn, 17 May 1855, Emily D. Brunner, dau. of
    Daniel   5/19/55-2
Phillips, Peter F., 10 June 1857, Josephine Hughes   6/12/57-2
Phillips, R. R., 3 Nov. 1857, Maggie A. Thompson   11/ 5/57-2
Phillips, Richard S., 25 Sept. 1853, Nancy Marshall   12/24/53-2
Phillips, Robert (Capt.), 27 Mar. 1856, Henrietta Cook, dau. of
    Henry and Julia A.   4/ 9/56-2
Phillips, Robert H., 5 Mar. 1860, Ellen M. Berry   4/17/60-2
Phillips, Thomas, Jr., 23 Dec. 1855, Eliza Ramsey   12/24/55-2
Phillips, William (Capt.), 26 Oct. 1854, Annie Langford, dau.
    of Nathan G.   10/27/54-2
Phillips, William, 28 Apr. 1858, Isabella Clarke   4/30/58-2
Phillips, William B., 15 July 1851, Mary Ann Brett   7/17/51-2
Phillips, William G., 30 Mar. 1858, Mary Catharine Pumphrey, dau.
    of George S.   3/31/58-2
Phipps, Robert, 26 Dec. 1859, Mary J. Holland   12/28/59-2
Phoebus, John H., 4 June 1851, Elizabeth A. Boyd   6/ 7/51-2
Pic, John F., 1 Jan. 1854, Hannah McNamee   1/ 6/54-2
Picker, John C., 17 Jan. 1856, Kate Ortewine   1/19/56-2
Pickett, James H., 28 Oct. 1856, Catherine F. V. S. McAllister 11/ 3/56-2
Pickett, John T., 18 Oct. 1853, Kate Keyworth, dau. of Robert 10/22/53-2
Picking, C. S. (Dr.), 4 Oct. 1859, Margaret A. Taylor;
    10/ 6/59-2   10/ 7/59-2
Pierce, Andrew Jackson, 3 Sept. 1855, Mary C. Pentz   9/ 4/55-2
Pieroint, John; no date given, Naomi Widerman, dau. of S. B.   9/ 4/57-2
Pierpoint, Henry H., 15 Feb. 1860, Jane H. Wright   2/16/60-2
Pierpont, Charles H., 11 Dec. 1856, Eliza A. Sulliven   12/13/56-2

Piggott, Isabel M., 15 Dec. 1859, Samuel A. Appold   12/24/59-2
Pilcher, James V. B., 5 Sept. 1858, Margaret Jane Worford,
      dau. of Abraham and Elizabeth   9/ 7/58-2
Pilkinton, James E., 25 Oct. 1860, Annie D. Adams   10/29/60-2
Pillsberry, Richard H., 19 June 1860, Fannie Courtney, dau.
      of Jeremiah   8/10/60-2
Pilsch, Gotleib, 25 Jan. 1853, Jane Elizabeth Lovejoy   1/28/53-2
Pindell, Durham, 25 Nov. 1856, Emma Fowler   11/27/56-2
Pindell, Gassaway, 16 Jan. 1856, Sallie E. Kelley   1/19/56-2
Pindell, Lewis A., 21 Oct. 1858, Mary A. Langley   10/25/58-2
Pindell, Lewis H., Jr., 24 Oct. 1856, Margaret Ann Higgins   10/28/56-2
Pindell, Thomas George, son of (Col.) Thos., 11 Nov. 1852,
      Mary L. Brooks, dau. of Shadrack   11/13/52-2
Pindell, William T., 28 Nov. 1853, Mary L. Gray, dau. of
      Jonathan J.   12/ 7/53-2
Pinder, Robert, 7 July 1859, Mary A. Hueston   7/ 9/59-2
Pindle, William James, 22 Dec. 1859, Anna Maria Blake   12/24/59-2
Pinto, John V., 12 Mar. 1857, Deborah Woodcock   3/14/57-2
Piper, Frederick, 9 Nov. 1860, Mary E. Williams   11/20/60-2
Piper, Henry F., 5 Mar. 1857, Emma A. Hickman   3/ 7/57-2
Piper, J. H., 4 Oct. 1856, Margaret Beeler   10/ 6/56-2
Pitcher, Columbus O., 22 Sept. 1859, Charlotte A. Ledley   9/24/59-2
Pitcher, Thos. J., 23 Oct. 1851, Catherine Burns   10/25/51-2
Pitner, James, 22 May 1851, Mary F. Green   5/26/51-2
Pittmen, Edward G., 4 Dec. 1856, Alvira J. Barrett   12/ 9/56-2
Pitts, Thomas C., 3 Mar. 1853, Elizabeth Gunter   3/14/53-2
Plant, James T. K., 13 May 1852, Louisa M. Gorton, dau. of
      (Capt.) Wm. A.   5/17/52-2
Plant, John J., 4 July 1859, Harriet E. Bender   7/ 7/59-2
Plant, Joseph T. K., 13 May 1852, Louise M. Gorton, dau. of
      (Capt.) Wm. A.; corrected copy   5/19/52-2
Platt, Alexander, 14 July 1859, Delia Bussard   7/16/59-2
Platt, John F., 13 Feb. 1854, Elizabeth McPherson, dau. of
      Duncan   2/27/54-2
Pleasants, James Snowden, 25 Nov. 1858, Jane Plater Williams,
      dau. of (Col.) (?) Plater   12/ 2/58-2
Plett, George, 12 Apr. 1860, Mary Frances Sherer, dau. of
      Christopher   4/16/60-2
Plitt, Maxamilian, 1 Apr. 1858, Sophia Knipp   4/ 6/58-2
Ploughman, Daniel, 9 Jan. 1851, Mary Jane Vincent   1/11/51-2
Plowden, Edmund J., 16 Jan. 1855, Josephine V. Freeman, dau.
      of John D.   1/17/55-2
Plowman, Augustus, 1 June 1858, Ethelender Frances Mace, dau.
      of Stephen T.   7/ 3/58-2
Plowman, James T., 5 Oct. 1852, Sarah A. Hackney   10/ 8/52-2
Plowman, William Henry, 8 June 1854, Matilda M. James, dau.
      of John   6/12/54-2
Plum, Sol, 22 Aug. 1852, Sarah Hess   8/24/52-2
Plummer, Fayette, 17 Oct. 1854, Kate A. Gould   10/25/54-2
Plummer, James H., 23 Mar. 1855, Sarah Ann Davis   3/27/55-2
Plummer, Jarrett, 13 Oct. 1853, Sarah Heath   10/31/53-2
Plummer, Richard, 11 Nov. 1852, Elizabeth T. Hicks, dau. of
      Edward   11/17/52-2
Plummer, Thomas, 16 May 1853, Ellennora Dennison   5/21/53-2
Plummer, William E., 2 Oct. 1860, Johana Kelly   10/ 4/60-2
Plummer, William H., 11 July 1853, Mary E. Southcomb   7/19/53-2
Plummer, Wm. James, 1 Dec. 1859, Elizabeth Foy, dau. of Jas.;
      12/ 3/59-2   12/ 5/59-2
Plunkett, Jas., 31 Aug. 1851, Anna Higgins   9/16/51-2
Plyman, John, 8 Oct. 1851, Mary Ann Watkins   10/11/51-2
Poat, John, 6 Dec. 1860, Teresa McConnell, dau. of Hugh   12/ 8/60-2
Pochon, Jules L., 21 Aug. 1856, Sophia Dunnock   8/22/56-2
Pocock, Jesse, 27 Jan. 1853, Ellen Baty   2/ 1/53-2
Poe, Elliott O'Donnell, 18 Dec. 1851, Mary A. Steuart, dau. of
      H. H. and Ann   12/20/51-2

```
Pohlen, Henry, 6 July 1859, Mary E. Kinnear                    9/27/59-2
Poisal, T. Bond, 1 June 1858, Eliza G. Foster, dau. of B. W.   6/ 2/58-2
Poist, George W., 26 Oct. 1854, Elizabeth A. White           10/27/54-2
Poist, Jerome, 26 Nov. 1851, Ann Elizabeth Coyle, dau. of B.  11/29/51-2
Poist, Joseph S., 19 Sept. 1860, Rebecca Taylor               9/21/60-2
Pole, John Henry, 14 Dec. 1857, Margaret Ann Washington       1/16/58-2
Pole, William, 6 Nov. 1856, Sarah D. B. Steir                11/ 7/56-2
Polf, E. Hermann, 13 July 1856, Mary E. Phillips, dau. of Thos. 7/14/56-2
Polin, Thomas M., 25 Aug. 1851, Mary E. Williams              9/22/51-2
Pollard, Peter B., 2 Nov. 1852, Mary Ann Battee, dau. of Samuel 11/ 9/52-2
Polk, Robert M., 10 May 1853, (Mrs.) Mary Righter             5/18/53-2
Poller, Henry N., 9 Apr. 1854, Adelaide R. Rheim              4/12/54-2
Polley, Charles G., 25 Nov. 1858, Mary E. Doyle, dau. of Peter 12/ 2/58-2
Pollitt, Francis, 4 May 1858, Ann Matilda Rollins             5/ 5/58-2
Pomery, Wm. H., 6 Aug. 1857, Alice F. Crawford                8/ 7/57-2
Pomp, John, 22 Mar. 1855, Mary A. Watlington, dau. of (Capt.)
  Wm.                                                          3/24/54-2
Pond, R. S., 9 Mar. 1854, Anna R. Olwine; corrected copy       3/13/54-2
Pontier, John S., 25 Oct. 1858, Josephine M. Masters         10/29/58-2
Pool, Joseph, 21 June 1860, Susan J. Kelly                     6/23/60-2
Poole, Edwin R., 28 Oct. 1852, Susan J. Ager                 11/ 1/52-2
Poole, Fademon, 25 Feb. 1851, Ann Eliza Webb                   2/26/51-2
Poole, Perry, 16 Nov. 1853, Mary J. Read                     12/14/53-2
Pope, Charles, 17 Nov. 1857, Frances Martin, dau. of William 11/19/57-2
Pope, Daniel F., 23 Apr. 1857, Hannah M. Scharil, dau. of
  Isaac T.                                                     4/27/57-2
Pope, G. W., Jr., 1 Mar. 1856, Clara Virginia Wheeler, dau.
  of Asher S. and Elizabeth C. Kellogg                         3/ 4/56-2
Pope, George A., 11 June 1857, Hannah L. Betts, dau. of
  Richard K.                                                   6/13/57-2
Pope, John H., 24 Aug. 1851, Virginia Johnston                 8/28/51-2
Pope, William H., 13 Nov. 1860, Elizabeth S. Pugh            11/16/60-2
Pope, William H., 15 Nov. 1860, Elizabeth S. Pugh; corrected
  copy                                                        11/17/60-2
Poppham, William, 30 Dec. 1852, Margaret Berry                 1/ 1/53-2
Poppen, John F., 4 Sept. 1859, Priscilla Westerman            9/16/59-2
Porter, Andrew Jackson, 3 Jan. 1859, Rachel Ann Marrott        1/26/59-2
Porter, Charles Lawton, 2 Dec. 1851, Mary B. Loane           12/22/51-2
Porter, James, 14 July 1859, Eliza McKee                       7/16/59-2
Porter, James E., 5 Apr. 1855, Sarah J. Chisholm, dau. of
  James F.; corrected copy                                     4/18/55-2
Porter, James E., 5 Apr. 1855, Sarah J. Chisholmz              4/ 9/55-2
Porter, James P., 19 Apr. 1857, Mary Elizabeth Patterson, dau.
  of Joseph                                                    3/20/58-2
Porter, John, 29 May 1856, (Mrs.) Ellen Welch                  6/18/56-2
Porter, Nathan, Jr., 4 Oct. 1858, Ann Maria Spucebank        10/ 8/58-2
Porter, Robert M., 12 May 1853, Caroline Lavenia Loar, dau.
  of G.                                                        5/21/53-2
Porter, Samuel, 15 June 1858, Linda Jane Deiter                6/17/58-2
Porter, William E., 8 Apr. 1852, Sarah Paxton                  4/ 9/52-2
Porter, William T., 7 July 1859, Margaret J. Tomblinson        7/ 9/59-2
Ports, William F., 28 July 1860, Emma C. Hubard              11/ 1/60-2
Posey, Alfred, 27 Nov. 1853, Sarah Werrey                     11/28/53-2
Posey, John V., 20 Nov. 1855, Columbia Hammett               11/21/55-2
Posey, Midleton, 8 May 1851, Rebecca Trupulet                  5/10/51-2
Posliff, Wm., 8 Jan. 1854, Beatty Booth                        1/10/54-2
Potterfield, A. J., 18 Sept. 1854, Maria Weygandt             9/19/54-2
Potts, John, 1 June 1852, Margaret St. John                    6/ 3/52-2
Poultney, Thomas, Jr., 18 May 1859, Georgia McClelland, dau. of
  (Col.) John                                                  5/27/59-2
Powell, Charles Edward, 30 Apr. 1854, Julia Ann Barth          5/ 1/54-2
Powell, Elias, 31 Oct. 1854, Eliza Spilman Harris, dau. of
  Daniel R., Sr.                                              11/ 3/54-2
Powell, G. Washington, 28 June 1855, Caroline Amanda Morton,
  dau. of Dixon                                                6/29/55-2
```

Powell, Jesse, 28 Jan. 1856, (Mrs.) Sarah H. Morhiser   2/13/56-2
Powell, John, 14 June 1854, Mary Kernan, dau. of Jas.   6/17/54-2
Powell, John, 5 Sept. 1857, Johanna Kelly   9/10/57-2
Powell, John F., 29 Sept. 1853, Alice A. Tilvard, dau. of
    H. W.   10/ 3/53-2
Powell, Robert, 24 May 1858, Mary Jane Brackin   5/28/58-2
Powell, Samuel, 10 Dec. 1858, Emma Snead   12/14/58-2
Powell, Thomas Henry, 12 Sept. 1858, Eliza Jane   9/14/58-2
Powell, W. Angelo, 14 Apr. 1857, Regina Angela Gillmeyer   4/16/57-2
Powell, Washington, 20 Nov. 1853, Lydia Lynch   11/23/53-2
Powell, William W., 13 Oct. 1859, Josephine Turner   10/17/59-2
Powell, Wineburg Thomas, 16 Sept. 1855, Mary Ann McMacken   9/18/55-2
Powell, Wm. G., 26 June 1854, Elizabeth J. Cummings   8/ 3/54-2
Power, John, 12 Nov. 1855, Susie Bayzand, dau. of Wm. H.   11/13/55-2
Powers, John J., 15 May 1853, Margaret E. Mathews   5/27/53-2
Powley, Edwin, 27 May 1851, Elenora Knight   5/29/51-2
Prather, Josiah T., 6 Feb. 1851, Mary B. Dimond, dau. of (Capt.)
    William   2/15/51-2
Pratt, Charles, 27 Feb. 1860, Mary E. Graham   3/12/60-2
Pratt, John W., 3 Aug. 1852, Marriget A. R. Pratt   8/ 5/52-2
Pratt, Stephen H. (Dr.), 1 Dec. 1853, Priscilla Sophronia
    Johnson   12/12/53-2
Prattes, Tilghman, 25 Mar. 1851, (Mrs.) Lucy A. Henson   4/ 5/51-2
Prentice, Sumner, 11 May 1858, Elizabeth R. Woods   5/14/58-2
Prentiss, John, 6 July 1858, Sarah Watson   7/13/58-2
Prentiss, T. Melville, 7 Oct. 1858, Lizzie V. Taylor, dau. of
    William   10/11/58-2
Presan, Henry, 20 Nov. 1860, Sophia Lehmann   11/26/60-2
Presbury, Wm. W., 26 June 1854, (Mrs.) Anetta E. Smith, sister
    of (Mrs.) J. W. Winter   7/ 3/54-2
Prescott, Charles H., 1 Mar. 1852, Sarah A. Metezs, dau. of
    John A. and Sarah   3/10/52-2
Presstman, Benj'n. C., 16 July 1857, Frances Anita Renshaw   7/18/57-2
Presstman, S. Wilson, 6 Nov. 1856, Frances Lewis Fowle, dau. of
    William   11/ 8/56-2
Presstman, Thomas R., 30 May 1855, Louisa M. Mowell, dau. of
    Peter   6/ 2/55-2
Preston, J. Alexander, 25 Oct. 1860, Achsah Ridgely Carroll,
    dau. of James, Jr.   10/27/60-2
Preston, J. B., 6 Feb. 1855, Melissa V. Trump, dau. of
    Robert V. and Marianne   2/10/55-2
Preston, James B., 29 Apr. 1858, Mary A. Wilks   5/ 6/58-2
Preston, James Henry, 21 Apr. 1856, Eliza Jane Cullam   4/22/56-2
Preston, John D., 19 Feb. 1854, Mary Harvey   2/22/54-2
Preston, William, 2 July 1857, Mary Murray   7/ 7/57-2
Prettyman, E. Barrett, 6 June 1855, Lydia F. Johnston, dau.
    of (Capt.) Z. F.   6/15/55-2
Prevost, Alistides, 17 Aug. 1854, Constance P. Le Brun   8/26/54-2
Prevost, Euriale, 3 Nov. 1853, Valerie Bizouard   11/ 5/53-2
Price, Alfred C., 11 May 1852, Frances C. Evans   5/12/52-2
Price, Benjamin F. (Dr.), 5 Mar. 1857, Mary A. Harshberger   4/11/57-2
Price, Charles, 30 May 1858, Harriet Lewis   6/15/58-2
Price, Charles H., 14 Oct. 1855, Josephine Pierce   11/21/55-2
Price, David F., 4 Nov. 1852, Mary E. Pierce   11/ 6/52-2
Price, David J., 11 July 1855, Elizabeth P. Hudson   7/13/55-2
Price, Edgar S., 18 July 1859, Marian V. Bankhead   7/25/59-2
Price, Edward H., 11 Aug. 1853, Elizabeth C. Benson, adopted
    dau. of Elijah and Elizabeth C. Potter   8/13/53-2
Price, Edwin, 23 Aug. 1853, Mary Elizabeth Horney   8/24/53-2
Price, Eugene F., 27 July 1851, Mary Adams   7/29/51-2
Price, George R., 1 Mar. 1859, Mary E. Kremer, dau. of James F. 3/12/59-2
Price, George T., 25 Nov. 1860, Emma Jene Crop; corrected copy 12/31/60-2
Price, George T., 25 Nov. 1860, Emma Jene Cross   12/29/60-2
Price, George W. (Capt.), 15 Sept. 1853, Eliza A. Carter   9/21/53-2
Price, J. Ryland, 14 Mar. 1854, Kate Langdon   3/15/54-2

Price, Jacob, 10 Apr. 1860, Catharine Smith   4/11/60-2
Price, James, 24 Jan. 1853, Mary M. Marshall   1/31/53-2
Price, James B., 29 Sept. 1854, Sarah E. Croe   10/ 7/54-2
Price, John, 19 May 1853, Margaret Williams   5/23/53-2
Price, John A., 14 Sept. 1858, Martha Ellen Bull   9/15/58-2
Price, John F., 10 May 1860, Sarah A. Uppercue   5/23/60-2
Price, John H., 7 Mar. 1854, Matilda V. Evans, dau. of Daniel   3/10/54-2
Price, John T., 4 Nov. 1858, Matilda E. Hagerty   11/ 6/58-2
Price, Richard H., 30 Nov. 1853, Editith A. Moore   12/ 2/53-2
Price, S. C. (Dr.), 2 June 1858, E. M. Dyson   6/ 4/58-2
Price, Samuel S., 5 Jan. 1855, Margaret Shum   1/ 6/55-2
Price, Skelton, 14 Apr. 1853, Elizabeth Burnham   4/15/53-2
Price, Thomas, 22 Nov. 1860, Ellennor P. Phillips   11/26/60-2
Price, Thos. C., 27 Mar. 1851, Mary E. Scott, dau. of Samuel   4/15/51-2
Price, Thos. S., 22 Sept. 1851, Kate Malory   9/23/51-2
Price, Thos. T., 20 Jan. 1851, Mary A. Corbaley   1/22/51-2
Price, William, 26 May 1859, Josephine Brown   5/28/59-2
Price, William K., 31 Dec. 1850, Ann Eliza Cragg   1/ 3/51-2
Price, Wm. T., 9 Mar. 1854, Josephine A. Marshall, dau. of
   Philip   3/13/54-2
Prichard, George M., 25 Mar. 1856, E. J. Duyer   4/ 2/56-2
Prichard, Samuel H., 28 Feb. 1856, Harriet L. Kirby   3/ 1/56-2
Pridgeon, JOhn, 22 Dec. 1860, Ann Davis   12/27/60-2
Pridgeon, William R., 10 Feb. 1857, Georgiana A. Taylor   2/19/57-2
Pridham, Wm. F., 10 Feb. 1858, Ann W. Harrison Davidson   2/16/58-2
Prime, Wm. T., 14 July 1853, Harriet E. Brown, dau. of Adam C.   7/18/53-2
Primrose, William G., 2 May 1854, Margaret E. Daniker   5/ 4/54-2
Prince, Alexander H., 15 Oct. 1857, Anna A. Smith   11/19/57-2
Prince, Isaac, Jr., 15 Dec. 1852, Ann E. Grammer   12/16/52-2
Prince, John, 19 Oct. 1859, Johanna M. Evans   10/20/59-2
Prince, Thomas D., 14 Nov. 1852, Roberta S. Hawkins   11/20/52-2
Prince, Wm., 10 Nov. 1855, Mary Ellen Tally   11/13/55-2
Prince, Wm. H., 9 Mar. 1857, Sidney Ann McComas   3/19/57-2
Prinz, Hartman J., 12 June 1855, Maria Knote   6/14/55-2
Prior, Francis A., 21 Aug. 1853, Ann Jane King   8/30/53-2
Pritchard, Jas. T., 26 May 1854, Ruth S. Forsyth   5/27/54-2
Pritchard, Levin, 7 July 1859, Margaret Grant   7/16/59-2
Pritchard, William, 25 Dec. 1853, Louiza Ogden   12/30/53-2
Pritchett, George W., 7 June 1857, Mary F. Seward, dau. of
   James   6/30/57-2
Pritchett, Wm. L., 4 Nov. 1855, Mary E. Satterfield;
   11/ 8/55-2   11/ 9/55-2
Pritchett, Wm. T., 20 May 1858, M. J. White   5/24/58-2
Proctor, Chas., 13 Jan. 1853, Martha Kellis   1/15/53-2
Proctor, James, 13 Dec. 1860, Ann Lee   12/15/60-2
Proctor, Joseph A., 14 June 1859, Elizabeth E. Price   6/21/59-2
Proctor, Robert H., 25 Jan. 1859, Martha S. Athison   2/ 4/59-2
Proctor, Samuel T., 8 Nov. 1855, Ellen H. Cowman   11/12/55-2
Proud, George, 13 Oct. 1854, (Mrs.) Catherine Graydon   10/17/54-2
Prouty, Everitt, 12 Aug. 1858, Mary F. Chisholm   8/21/58-2
Prunty, John E., 27 Dec. 1859, Mary E. Wilber   8/ 8/60-2
Pryor, George E., 31 May 1860, Emma C. Staylor   6/ 7/60-2
Pryor, Richard, 23 Feb. 1851, Sarah Magness   2/28/51-2
Pryor, Stephen, 22 July 1859, Mary Anthony   7/27/59-2
Pugh, John E. (Dr.), 4 June 1856, Sallie E. Cocke   6/16/56-2
Pugh, William G., 8 Sept. 1858, Julia E. Morrow   9/11/58-2
Puhl, John Henry, 4 Sept. 1859, Ann Tenweeges   9/ 6/59-2
Pullen, Eugene H., 19 Apr. 1860, Mary H. Poole   4/24/60-2
Pumphrey, Chas., 21 Oct. 1852, Ann Eliza Cromwell   10/23/52-2
Pumphrey, Jas. B., 9 Mar. 1856, Agnes J. Cline, dau. of
   Henry and Maria   3/14/56-2
Pumphrey, Levi, 22 Jan. 1854, (Mrs.) Ellen Sweeting   1/26/54-2
Pumphrey, Lloyd P., 22 Aug. 1852, Rebecca Grimes   8/27/52-2
Pumphrey, Osbourn S., 1 Dec. 1857, Leonora S. Robinson, dau.
   of Benjamin   12/ 8/57-2

Pumphrey, Wm., 28 Oct. 1852, Georgeanna Cromwell   10/29/52-2
Purdy, William H., 9 Jan. 1856, M. Amanda Jones   1/12/56-2
Purenet, L. A., 4 Apr. 1860, Emily Cassin Baker, dau. of
    (Dr.) Wm.   4/12/60-2
Purnele, Thomas, 1 Apr. 1857, Mary Malinda Sutton   4/ 3/57-2
Purnell, Thomas, 1 Apr. 1857, Mary Malinda Sutton; corrected
    copy   4/ 4/57-2
Purvis, J. Armfield, 25 Nov. 1857, Annie R. Coale, dau. of
    Philemon   12/ 2/57-2
Purvis, Jas. F., Jr., 21 May 1857, Annie M. Roberts   5/26/57-2
Pusey, Littleton T., 9 May 1860, (Mrs.) Mary E. Bunting   5/11/60-2
Putman, Geo. W., 7 June 1856, Mary Ann Parker   6/ 9/56-2
Pyfer, P. M., 11 Sept. 1860, M. E. Gilliss, dau. of George   9/15/60-2
Quail, Robert R., 18 Oct. 1855, Elizabeth C. Haslup   10/23/55-2
Quailes, Edward, 24 Feb. 1853, Virginia P. Davis, dau. of
    (Rev.) John   3/ 1/53-2
Quanz, Antonie, 18 Feb. 1851, Mary Ann Shafer   2/19/51-2
Quay, Andrew E., 20 Dec. 1860, Virginia E. McKeldoe   12/22/60-2
Quay, John W., 6 Jan. 1859, Sarah A. Rowes   1/11/59-2
Quay, Wm. L., 6 Mar. 1851, (Mrs.) Mary E. Patterson   3/10/51-2
Quickly, Caesar, 26 Feb. 1852, Sarah Ann Sterrett, dau. of
    Jesse   2/27/52-2
Quickly, Elisha, 14 June 1857, Fanny Hatten   6/15/57-2
Quigley, William S., 29 Apr. 1852, Martha W. Reisinger   5/ 3/52-2
Quinan, Pascal A. (Dr.), 27 Dec. 1856, Sophie Adelaide
    Jackson, dau. of John G.   1/ 7/57-2
Quincy, Walter C., 4 Oct. 1853, Martha R. Smith   10/11/53-2
Quincy, William Henry, 1 Oct. 1851, Elizabeth J. Sisson   10/ 3/51-2
Quinlan, Joseph E., 8 July 1858, Margaret A. Bullen   7/10/58-2
Quinlan, Louis A., 23 Jan. 1851, Almira V. Williams   1/25/51-2
Quinn, Francis A., 30 Sept. 1855, Ellen Gordan   10/16/55-2
Quinn, Francis J., 26 Jan. 1855, Isabella McConvey   1/30/55-2
Quinn, James, 3 Aug. 1853, Ann Smith   8/30/53-2
Quinn, John, 19 Sept. 1858, Mary Barnes   10/23/58-2
Quinn, Thomas, 26 Sept. 1854, Eliza Young   9/28/54-2
Raborg, C. Henry, 30 Apr. 1855, Virginia C. Turner, dau. of
    T. W.   5/ 1/55-2
Raborg, Geo. G., 5 May 1853, Carrie M. Ross, dau. of Wm. B.   5/10/53-2
Radder, Henry R., 17 Apr. 1855, Mary L. Turner   4/18/55-2
Radecke, John, 15 Nov. 1859, Augusta Kabernagel   11/19/59-2
Rafley, William, 18 May 1853, Charity S. Harryman   7/13/53-2
Ragan, Martin, 24 Sept. 1851, Mary Ragan   9/26/51-2
Raiff, William H., 9 June 1859, Caroline Handy   6/16/59-2
Rainbow, Chas., 28 Aug. 1851, Sophia Mitchell   8/29/51-2
Rainey, Robert, 27 June 1858, Margaret Green   6/29/58-2
Rains, Charles A., 5 Sept. 1855, D. E. Parish   9/ 9/55-2
Rairdan, John, 30 July 1853, Margaret Cunningham   8/ 2/53-2
Raitt, H. Clay, 12 June 1860, Eliza P. Kennard, dau. of Geo. I.   6/13/60-2
Ralston, Robert, 30 Dec. 1858, Margaret Hunter   1/ 3/59-2
Ramborger, H. G. O.; no date given, Hannah Whipple   6/ 3/51-2
Ramborger, Horace Go., 14 Apr. 1858, Rosalba J. League, dau.
    of Geo. B.   4/16/58-2
Ramborger, Ozeas Heartle, 17 May 1853, Eller Arentrice   5/20/53-2
Ramsay, J. Glendy, 13 Jan. 1853, Hannah A. L. Shaffer, dau.
    of F. Littig   1/17/53-2
Ramsay, J. W. (Dr.), 18 May 1858, Jennie L. Hoffman, dau. of
    John H. and Louisa   5/28/58-2
Ramsay, John, 31 July 1856, Amanda M. F. Rowles   8/ 8/56-2
Ramsay, Robert B. (Capt.), 2 Aug. 1853, Emily Kelly, dau. of
    (Capt.) Matthew   8/ 6/53-2
Ramsey, Charles Z. R., 18 Nov. 1851, Anne E. Smith   11/20/51-2
Ramsey, Robert Jamieson, 7 Jan. 1851, Caroline C. Hamelin   1/ 9/52-2
Randall, John, 26 May 1853, Sarah Irvin   5/30/53-2
Randall, Samuel O., 19 Oct. 1854, Mary A. Ferry   10/21/54-2
Randel, Wm. T., 26 Aug. 1851, Mary Ann Williams   8/29/51-2

```
Randell, Robert, 2 Aug. 1860, Joanna Cleary                    8/21/60-2
Randle, Edward, 2 June 1851, Lear E. Jones                     6/ 4/51-2
Randle, Richard, 1 Jan. 1860, Mary E. Jones                    1/ 4/60-2
Randle, Wm. H., 29 Sept. 1851, Lydia Rimby                     9/30/51-2
Randolph, James T., 2 Sept. 1856, Mary Corrigan, dau. of B.    9/ 4/56-2
Rankin, R. G. (Dr.), 30 Sept. 1851, Margaret R. Green          10/11/51-2
Ransom, J. C., 27 Sept. 1855, Theresa Conner                   10/ 5/55-2
Rapin, Gerhard, 21 Feb. 1860, Angelica Mueller                 3/ 3/60-2
Rappold, John M., 8 Feb. 1852, Elizabeth Schufelerber          2/11/52-2
Rarick, John H., 10 Sept. 1854, Elizabeth A. Harvey            9/13/54-2
Rash, Christian, 11 Sept. 1851, (Mrs.) Mary Robinson           9/13/51-2
Rashbone, George C., 29 May 1854, Elizabeth Hoffman            5/30/54-2
Rasin, R. W. I., 19 June 1860, Margaret A. Johnson             6/21/60-2
Ratcliffe, L. E., 17 Aug. 1854, Mary C. Stuart                 8/21/54-2
Rathell, Henry H. A., 13 Feb. 1851, Sarah Rebecca Lee          2/21/51-2
Rathell, Samuel, 8 Feb. 1859, Mary E. Hickman                  2/10/59-2
Raub, Michael E., 2 Sept. 1856, Mary C. Winter                 9/ 5/56-2
Ravers, Dennard H. (Capt.), 3 Jan. 1855, Laura Zipporah Harring-
    ton                                                        1/ 5/55-2
Rawlings, Benjamin, 1 Nov. 1855, Josephine Victoria Patrick,
    dau. of L. D.                                              11/ 6/55-2
Rawlings, Charles H., 23 June 1853, Sarah J. S. Wilkinson,
    dau. of James T.                                           6/28/53-2
Rawlings, Chas. H., 14 Apr. 1859, Cecilia Reardon              4/16/59-2
Ray, Alfred, 29 Oct. 1856, Annie E. Gayle, dau. of (Capt.)
    Joseph R.                                                  11/ 7/56-2
Ray, Alfred, 2 Aug. 1859, Ella M. Gatch, dau. of (Capt.)
    Nicholas                                                   8/ 3/59-2
Ray, B. F., 30 June 1853, Ellen Clements                       7/14/53-2
Ray, Henry, 11 Sept. 1856, Martha Hoxen, dau. of Richard       9/18/56-2
Ray, Oliver, 2 Oct. 1856, Fannie E. Wysham, dau. of John       10/ 4/56-2
Ray, Thomas, 26 Apr. 1855, Mary McFadden                       5/ 5/55-2
Raybold, Thomas J., 3 June 1852, Clara A. Underwood, dau. of
    Jacob                                                      6/ 5/52-2
Raymo, Francis, 10 June 1856, (Mrs.) Mary E. Bush              6/12/56-2
Raymond, James H., 17 Nov. 1853, Robertine R. L. Allen, dau. of
    Robt. T.                                                   11/18/53-2
Raymond, Shepperd K., 10 June 1856, Lucy H. Balderston         6/13/56-2
Raysinger, Martin, 4 July 1852, Mary Catharine Merson          7/ 7/52-2
Rea, Charles H., 15 Dec. 1853, Julia H. Angel                  12/23/53-2
Read, Calvin, 29 Dec. 1858, Susan E. Rogers                    1/ 1/59-2
Read, Edwd. R., 8 May 1860, Carrie E. Larrabee                 5/10/60-2
Read, George T., 20 Feb. 1856, Caroline A. G. Summers          9/16/56-2
Read, John W., 22 June 1853, Lizzie Lowjenslager, dau. of
    (Capt.) Jacob                                              6/26/53-2
Read, Joseph E., 16 July 1854, Isabella Jane Murray            7/29/54-2
Read, Nelson S., 19 Jan. 1860, E. Virginia Richardson, dau. of
    John W.                                                    1/24/60-2
Read, Oliver, 1 Nov. 1860, Fannie V. Burchinal                11/14/60-2
Read, William George, 21 Feb. 1860, (Mrs.) Elizabeth A.
    Howard                                                     2/24/60-2
Read, William H., 12 Apr. 1854, A. Charlesina Rowins           4/17/54-2
Read, William H., 11 Oct. 1855, Julia A. Mason                10/25/55-2
Realey, Michael L., 15 Nov. 1855, Catharine J. Lum            11/17/55-2
Reaner, Wm. H., 25 June 1853, Bridget O'Brien                  6/28/53-2
Reaney, James, 18 Apr. 1854, Isabella McWhorter                4/19/54-2
Reaney, James, 10 May 1860, Rachel J. Warford                  5/11/60-2
Reay, Alfred W., 19 Mar. 1854, Marian A. Turner, dau. of (Col.)
    J. M.                                                      3/22/54-2
Reay, David, 31 Dec. 1851, Georgeanna Gardner                  1/ 6/52-2
Reay, George W., 22 Aug. 1858, Josephine Deady                 8/25/58-2
Reckert, George M., 1 June 1854, Mary E. Huster                6/19/54-2
Reckitt, Charles, Jr., 4 July 1860, Henrietta Jones            7/30/60-2
Reddish, Robert H., 14 Aug. 1856, Sarah A. Uhler               8/16/56-2
```

Redebaugh, William, 17 Jan. 1856, E. Z. K. Walker, dau. of
  Geo. W.   4/10/56-2
Redgrave, Samuel T., 9 Sept. 1856, Agnes Nolen   9/11/56-2
Redgrave, William S., 14 Apr. 1857, Kate L. Park, dau. of
  Robert J.   4/20/57-2
Redgrave, Wm. B., 26 July 1855, Annie R. Raborg, dau. of
  Goddard   7/30/55-2
Reece, Joshua, Jr., 22 Dec. 1858, Estelle Benson, dau. of
  (Capt.) Wm. R.   12/25/58-2
Reed, Alexander S., 2 Apr. 1851, Emma Mowbray   4/ 3/51-2
Reed, Amos W., 12 Mar. 1857, Frances C. Grimes, dau. of Jahiel   3/17/57-2
Reed, Charles H., 29 May 1853, Mary W. Parks   6/ 1/53-2
Reed, Henry C., 11 Oct. 1853, Kate King, dau. of Geo.   10/12/53-2
Reed, James A. (Dr.), 16 Dec. 1857, Emily E. Hutchings, dau.
  of (Col.) Wm.   12/30/57-2
Reed, James C., 18 Mar. 1851, Elizabeth B. Circle   3/20/51-2
Reed, James N., 5 Dec. 1854, Martha Wilson   12/18/54-2
Reed, John, 18 Dec. 1855, Kitty Ann Ebaugh   1/ 3/56-2
Reed, John H., 18 Mar. 1851, Frances Gerber   3/26/51-2
Reed, Joseph E. (Dr.), 16 May 1854, Margaret V. Mundorff   5/18/54-2
Reed, Joseph H., 21 Dec. 1854, Margaret A. Blackburn, dau. of
  John   12/22/54-2
Reed, Joseph H., 9 Nov. 1858, Rachel Ann Lee   12/ 7/58-2
Reed, Samuel J., 4 Apr. 1854, Mary Ann Parsons   4/ 6/54-2
Reed, William, 30 Mar. 1857, Rebecca Anderson   4/ 3/57-2
Reed, William E., 10 Dec. 1853, Sarah R. Reed; 12/15/53-2   12/16/53-2
Reed, William L., 24 Dec. 1851, Amanda Kate Forney, dau. of
  Isaac C.   12/30/51-2
Reed, Wm. H., 11 Sept. 1851, Eliza Gable   9/17/51-2
Reed, Wm. H., 25 Feb. 1858, Josephine P. Upton   7/10/58-2
Reeder, Charles H., 27 Aug. 1856, Josephine E. Long   9/ 5/56-2
Reeder, John H. (Dr.), 24 July 1856, Kate C. Harris   7/25/56-2
Reedy, Michael, 8 Nov. 1852, Margaret Ryan   11/13/52-2
Rees, John, 17 July 1856, Jane Seymour   7/20/58-2
Reese, Andrew, 25 Oct. 1855, Eleanora Young   10/29/55-2
Reese, Andrew, 17 Nov. 1858, Laura C. Horn   11/18/58-2
Reese, David, 11 Dec. 1851, Louisa Gabler, dau. of F. A.   12/13/51-2
Reese, Edward, 9 May 1854, Mary A. Gilpin, dau. of Saml.   5/10/54-2
Reese, Edwin F., 3 Dec. 1857, Kate W. Berryhill   12/ 5/57-2
Reese, Jacob, 24 Feb. 1859, Alvirda Maloney   2/26/59-2
Reese, John; no date given, Virginia Bowen   9/13/54-2
Reese, John E., Jr., 23 Nov. 1858, Alice Virginia Gibbs, dau.
  of H. M.   11/25/58-2
Reese, John L., son of (Rev.) A. A., 23 Oct. 1860, Nellie
  Blocher, dau. of Dan'l.   10/24/60-2
Reese, John S., Jr., 9 Nov. 1852, Arnoddena O. Focke, dau. of
  Fred'k.   11/11/52-2
Reese, Robert P., 31 Dec. 1850, Kezia R. Macartney   1/ 2/51-2
Reese, Stephen W., 18 Aug. 1859, Sarah J. Kugler   8/23/59-2
Reese, William J. D., 27 Mar. 1860, Elizabeth Barth   4/ 3/60-2
Reess, Samuel, 27 Oct. 1856, Mary Ann Smith   12/ 2/56-2
Reich, Wm., 20 Apr. 1853, Lucie J. Brown   4/21/53-2
Reichenbach, Frederick C., 15 Sept. 1853, Catharine Koyatsch   9/23/53-2
Reid, Aloysius, 18 Feb. 1851, Sarah Ann J. Feaster   3/ 5/51-2
Reid, J. D., 3 Jan. 1855, Henrietta O'Connor, dau. of Eugene   1/13/55-2
Reid, John A., 11 Oct. 1860, Margaret E. Personette   10/29/60-2
Reid, Williams Evans, 9 June 1859, Sarah Jane McDonald   8/ 1/59-2
Reid, Wm. H., 11 Aug. 1853, Malvina A. Blades   8/24/53-2
Reign, David M., 26 May 1853, Eleanor Ann Crooks   5/30/53-2
Reiley, J. McKendree, 1 Apr. 1856, M. Alcesta Stevenson, dau.
  of (Rev.) Wesley   4/ 3/56-2
Reilly, Denis, 1 Nov. 1860, Mary Connolly   11/ 3/60-2
Reilly, Jeremiah, 8 Nov. 1860, Mary Johnson   11/10/60-2
Reilly, John F., 9 June 1852, Kate Mullynix   6/15/52-2
Reilly, John J., 22 Aug. 1852, Harriet Ann Leishear   8/26/52-2

Reilly, P. D., 30 Aug. 1860, Maggie Bradley	9/ 6/60-2
Reilly, Philip, 16 May 1852, Alice Clark	5/18/52-2
Reilly, Robert, 22 July 1860, Virginia Meyers	7/31/60-2
Reilly, Thomas, 18 Dec. 1859, Margaret McCormac	12/24/59-2
Reily, Michael J., 9 Feb. 1859, Kate T. Gibson	2/15/59-2
Reindollar, J. T., 22 Dec. 1853, Josephine B. Vernay	12/23/53-2
Reineker, Charles H. C., 5 Apr. 1855, Emeline F. Watts	5/25/55-2
Reinhart, A. H., 2 Sept. 1852, Maria Plain	9/ 4/52-2
Reinhart, George, 22 June 1851, Alverda Morgan	8/ 8/51-2
Reinicker, J. Frederick, 25 May 1854, Laura A. Graves	5/27/54-2
Reister, Mathias, 21 Apr. 1857, Josephine McIntire	4/29/57-2
Reiter, Abraham, 8 July 1855, Mary Jane Willson	7/10/55-2
Reiter, Joseph F., 27 Nov. 1851, Mary Ann E. Mooney	11/29/51-2
Reiter, Philip B., 13 Sept. 1853, Lucretia Letournau	9/15/53-2
Remly, Geo. W., 13 Sept. 1855, Amelia Rogge	9/17/55-2
Remmey, Theodore R., 26 Sept. 1860, Margaret A. Euel	9/28/60-2
Ren-(?)-knapp, A., 21 Aug. 1854, Mary E. Norflet	8/29/54-2
Rendall, George, 4 Dec. 1857, Mary E. Dinsmore	12/ 5/57-2
Renehan, William, 20 Nov. 1860, Augusta Benzinger, dau. of (Col.) M.	11/21/60-2
Renner, Thomas, 10 Jan. 1859, Sarah Ann Adams, dau. of James	1/11/59-2
Renous, Edw'd. G., 14 Oct. 1852, Ethalinda C. Harrison	10/16/52-2
Renshaw, Lemuel, 2 Jan. 1851, Sarah A. J. Clark	1/ 6/51-2
Renshaw, Robert H., 26 Apr. 1859, Lucy Carter	4/28/59-2
Repplier, John G., 21 Jan. 1851, Agnes Mathias, dau. of Jacob	1/23/51-2
Repstock, Franklin, 16 May 1853, Sarah Ann Welts	5/18/53-2
Resch, George Philip, 22 Jan. 1854, Catherine Smith	1/24/54-2
Retter, John, 6 May 1852, Elizabeth G. Ford	5/ 8/52-2
Reuter, Charles, 18 Dec. 1860, Ellen Frantz	12/20/60-2
Revell, James, 19 July 1860, E. Janie Cowan	7/20/60-2
Revell, Thomas Daniel, 1 May 1857, Mary Ann Dove	5/ 5/57-2
Rever, Ferdinand N., 29 Dec. 1850, Wilhelmine Catherine Hunichenn	1/ 2/51-2
Rey, Jesse K., 14 Oct. 1852, Adelaid Dippell	10/15/52-2
Reyburn, John S., 2 Sept. 1851, Rebecca Small	9/ 8/51-2
Reynolds, Bernard J., 15 Apr. 1858, Bridget Dunican	5/27/58-2
Reynolds, C. A. (Lieut.), 13 Nov. 1856, Annastatia Butler, dau. of John	11/15/56-2
Reynolds, Columbus, 2 May 1858, Caroline Johnson	5/20/58-2
Reynolds, Edward H., 9 Apr. 1854, Bridget Smith	4/18/54-2
Reynolds, Henry R., 15 Feb. 1855, (Mrs.) Mary E. Brooking	2/17/55-2
Reynolds, James, 27 Jan. 1859, Jane V. Calloway	1/29/59-2
Reynolds, Joel, 28 Aug. 1851, Eliza Taylor	8/30/51-2
Reynolds, John N., 25 Sept. 1856, Margaret Jane Hamilton, dau. of James	9/30/56-2
Reynolds, Joseph, 19 Dec. 1852, (Mrs.) Elizabeth Ann Roberson	1/ 3/53-2
Reynolds, Joseph W., 27 Dec. 1860, Maggie A. Tucker	12/28/60-2
Reynolds, Samuel, 28 July 1859, Annie Walmsley	8/29/59-2
Reynolds, Samuel H., 28 Mar. 1854, Rebecca A. Forde	3/30/54-2
Reynolds, Wesley W., 8 Oct. 1857, Kate App, dau. of John	10/21/57-2
Reynolds, William G., 25 Sept. 1860, Dorcas Rebecca Brome, dau. of William H.	9/27/60-2
Reynolds, Wm. J., 8 June 1853, Jane Ann Somervile, dau. of Wm.	6/14/53-2
Reynolds, Wm. J., 30 Aug. 1857, Catharine Lyons	8/31/57-2
Rhea, Robert W., 17 Aug. 1858, Columbis Wroten	8/18/58-2
Rhine, Luther P., 25 Dec. 1856, Caroline Madison	12/27/56-2
Rhine, S. G., 11 Aug. 1858, E. Herrman, dau. of A.	8/12/58-2
Rhoades, James H., 6 Mar. 1851, Ellen Earp	3/11/51-2
Rhoads, John R., 31 July 1851, Caroline C. Morgan	8/ 1/51-2
Rhoads, Willard, 16 May 1853, Eliza A. Merritt	5/20/53-2
Rhoddes, James, 27 Oct. 1853, Eliza J. Dalton	11/ 2/53-2
Rhodes, A. C., 17 Nov. 1852, Virgie C. Hewitt, dau. of Peter	11/22/52-2

Rhodes, Edgar Eugene, 10 Nov. 1852, Eliza T. Norris, dau. of
    Joseph, grandau. of Daniel Hoffman   11/11/52-2
Rhodes, J. Peter, 4 May 1854, Mary A. Cullum, dau. of J.
    and N.   5/ 9/54-2
Rhodes, John F., 14 Aug. 1858, Margaret Jory   9/21/58-2
Rhodes, Samuel P., 26 Oct. 1857, Margaret J. Curry   10/28/57-2
Rhuark, Thomas (Capt.), 4 Jan. 1857, Rebecca Y. O. Hollings-
    head   1/ 6/57-2
Rial, Michael K., 6 Sept. 1857, Jane McManes   9/21/57-2
Rial, William, 29 Nov. 1853, Esther A. Adams   12/ 2/53-2
Ricards, John R., 13 Oct. 1853, F. V. Ricards   3/ 1/54-2
Rice, Chas., 23 Sept. 1852, (Mrs.) Ann E. Dimmett   9/30/52-2
Rice, Chas., 8 Mar. 1853, Almira Brown   3/21/53-2
Rice, F. (Maj.), 25 Apr. 1855, Kate L. Kraft, dau. of Jacob   4/30/55-2
Rice, Isaac A., 3 Sept. 1854, Amelia Rosenhaupt   9/ 5/54-2
Rice, Jacob, 8 Mar. 1854, Fanny Hable, dau. of Lewis   3/10/54-2
Rice, John H., 28 Apr. 1859, Sophie Mantz, dau. of Henry;
    4/30/59-2   5/ 2/59-2
Rice, Lewis, 17 Nov. 1858, Mary Kraft   11/27/58-2
Rich, Thomas R., 20 Nov. 1856, Lizzie Wilson, dau. of William   11/22/56-2
Richards, Edward C., 4 Dec. 1856, Ellen M. Tewksbury, dau. of
    G. D.   12/ 5/56-2
Richards, George W., 30 Aug. 1859, Mary F. Reed, dau. of
    Jacob   3/19/60-2
Richards, John H., 28 Oct. 1852, Jane Isabella McGovern   11/ 2/52-2
Richards, Joseph, 3 May 1855, Margaret Hunter   5/ 4/55-2
Richards, T. H. Bushey, 12 Jan. 1859, Kate Kelley, dau. of
    Thomas   1/19/59-2
Richards, Thomas, 1 May 1851, Charity Sanders   5/ 2/51-2
Richards, William H., 12 Nov. 1851, Sarah A. Reese   11/14/51-2
Richardson, Caleb, 26 Feb. 1856, Mary A. C. Hawkins   2/28/56-2
Richardson, Charles, 18 Nov. 1858, Sarah M. Greenfield   11/23/58-2
Richardson, Charles C. (Dr.), Harriet A. Counselman, dau. of
    Charles   10/ 2/56-2
Richardson, Geo. W., 26 Jan. 1851, Julia Birmingham   1/28/51-2
Richardson, J. Summerfield, 3 Sept. 1860, Sallie A. Montgomery,
    dau. of (Dr.) James   9/ 4/60-2
Richardson, James A., 31 May 1858, Nora A. Manny   6/ 4/58-2
Richardson, James M., 13 June 1854, Mary A. Gettier, dau. of
    George   6/16/54-2
Richardson, Jas. A., 28 May 1857, Sallie R. Merryman   5/29/57-2
Richardson, John, 20 Sept. 1854, Susan Hurst   9/26/54-2
Richardson, John F., 14 Sept. 1854, Rachel J. High   9/15/54-2
Richardson, John Henry, 6 Oct. 1859, Martha Ann White   10/12/59-2
Richardson, John R., 25 July 1855, Ann J. Godwin, dau. of
    Littleton S.   7/28/55-2
Richardson, Maurice, 2 Sept. 1856, Emma Jane H-(?)-dy, dau. of
    Edward   2/20/57-2
Richardson, Robert S., 10 Mar. 1853, Margaret S. Ennis   3/11/53-2
Richardson, Samuel M., 30 June 1853, Marilla A. Miller, dau. of
    Francis A.   7/ 1/53-2
Richardson, Samuel McD., 16 Jan. 1855, Hannah T. Robinson, dau.
    of (Capt.) Edwin   1/18/55-2
Richardson, Samuel S. (Dr.), 30 Apr. 1856, Ann M. Gambrill, dau.
    of Charles A.   5/ 2/56-2
Richardson, Wm. H., 1 Nov. 1860, Kate R. Hanson, step-dau. of
    Wm. H. McLean   11/ 8/60-2
Richardson, Wm. Henry, 2 June 1859, Harriet Ann Taylor   6/10/59-2
Richbutton, William, 22 Aug. 1855, Mary Augusta Clopper, dau.
    of F. C.   8/24/55-2
Richcreek, Israel, 11 May 1856, Mary Benson   5/12/56-2
Richey, Henry A., 7 Aug. 1860, Rachel F. McGeehan, dau. of
    Miles and Rachel   8/15/60-2
Richmond, Henry, 12 Jan. 1857, Laviniah H. Harris   5/ 8/57-2
Richmond, John W., 5 Aug. 1858, (Mrs.) Margaret Ann Boswell   9/22/58-2

Richstein, John, 16 Nov. 1852, Elizabeth Wherritt	11/18/52-2
Richstein, William, 7 Jan. 1857, Elenora Kerner, dau. of	
William, grandau. of George Kaylor	1/ 9/57-2
Richter, William, 8 June 1851, Mary Catherine Houck	6/10/51-2
Richter, William, 25 Oct. 1857, Ann Maria Bratt	10/28/57-2
Rickerby, Alfred, 11 Nov. 1851, Jane Teresa Rogers	11/17/51-2
Ricketts, George, 14 Dec. 1852, Louisa Walmsley	12/23/52-2
Ricketts, Granville C., 17 Oct. 1857, Florida B. Baltzer	10/26/57-2
Ricketts, Granville C., 2 July 1860, Mollie Braley	7/ 3/60-2
Ricketts, Samuel J., 28 Feb. 1858, Balinda Bowen	3/ 4/58-2
Ricktor, Elias, 6 Dec. 1857, Lisette Burger	12/11/57-2
Riddell, H. G., 16 Nov. 1856, Emma C. Crosby	4/27/57-2
Riddle, Beal D., 30 Nov. 1859, Belle Hume	12/ 6/59-2
Riddle, Chas. J., 24 June 1852, Louisa Day	6/26/52-2
Riddlemoser, G. W., 10 Nov. 1857, M. V. Barnaclo	11/12/57-2
Riddlemoser, Joseph, 2 Oct. 1860, Carrie Snyder, dau. of	
William	10/10/60-2
Rider, Edward, Jr., 14 Mar. 1855, Rebecca A. McCoakey, dau. of	
George W.	3/17/55-2
Rider, George, 30 Oct. 1856, Sarah Jane Smith, dau. of Cephas	11/ 1/56-2
Rider, Noah S. (Dr.), 18 Apr. 1853, A. Amanda Taylor, dau. of	
(Rev.) John S.	4/19/53-2
Ridge, William T., 16 Aug. 1859, Frances L. Robinson	8/24/59-2
Ridgeley, J. Selman, 19 Sept. 1851, Mary Smith	10/11/51-2
Ridgely, Benjamin Rush, 20 Sept. 1855, Mary Catharine Todd	9/22/55-2
Ridgely, Charles (Dr.), 20 Jan. 1857, Margaret Feinour	1/23/57-2
Ridgely, Charles L., son of (Capt.) Thos. P., 6 Apr. 1851,	
Mary Prudence Harris, dau. of Samuel	4/ 8/51-2
Ridgely, Chas., 27 Feb. 1858, M. S. Howard, dau. of James	3/ 8/51-2
Ridgely, George C., 13 Oct. 1853, Henrietta Ricketts, dau. of	
Thomas C.	10/19/53-2
Ridgely, J. S., 4 July 1851, Mary Smith; corrected copy	10/14/51-2
Ridgely, James L., Jr., 9 Oct. 1856, Annie M. O'Dell, dau. of	
Geo. E.; corrected copy	10/11/56-2
Ridgely, James L., Jr., 9 Oct. 1856, Annie M. O'Dree, dau. of	
Geo. E.	10/10/56-2
Ridgely, L. W., 21 Oct. 1856, Georgie Anna Rust, dau. of P. N.	10/23/56-2
Ridgely, Oliver D., 5 Dec. 1855, Harriet T. Crawford	12/11/55-2
Ridgely, Samuel, 21 Mar. 1854, Ann Eliza Robb, dau. of John	3/23/54-2
Ridgely, T. Graham, 7 Oct. 1851, Debbie Ridgely, dau. of	
(Dr.) M. S. Baer	10/ 9/51-2
Ridgeway, Henry, 17 Apr. 1855, Hester Gilley	4/19/55-2
Ridgly, Samuel, 22 Nov. 1851, Mary Ann Swan	11/25/51-2
Ridley, Dennis, 30 Oct. 1851, Margaret M. Knott	11/ 1/51-2
Riely, James, 4 Apr. 1858, Margaret Wiggins	4/ 6/58-2
Rieman, R. C., 22 Mar. 1853, Emily Adams, dau. of Jas. C.	3/26/53-2
Rigby, James H., 2 Mar. 1851, Sarah E. Glass	10/ 4/51-2
Rigdon, Robert M., 6 Nov. 1851, Augusta A. Robertson, dau. of	
John T.	11/14/51-2
Riggins, Joseph, 27 Mar. 1851, Mary R. Easton	3/31/51-2
Riggs, Benjamin H., 22 June 1851, Susanna V. Yeagers	6/24/51-2
Riggs, Femus D., 30 Jan. 1854, Sarah Coware, dau. of (Capt.)	
Thomas	6/28/54-2
Riley, Benjamin C. H., 20 May 1852, Eliza Jane Hamilton	5/25/52-2
Riley, Daniel L., 30 Mar. 1852, Catharine P. Barnes, dau. of	
Richard Kennard	4/ 3/52-2
Riley, George, 19 Sept. 1855, Mary Jane Jones	9/25/55-2
Riley, George W., 23 Dec. 1855, Sarah Weston Rouse	12/24/55-2
Riley, James, 26 Sept. 1860, Elizabeth A. Turner	10/ 2/60-2
Riley, John, 21 Oct. 1858, Mary Newkup	10/23/58-2
Riley, John C., 17 Dec. 1854, Mary A. Bowers	12/19/54-2
Riley, John J. G., 18 Feb. 1860, Annie E. Moody	2/22/60-2
Riley, John T., 20 June 1860, Charlotte A. Barnheart	6/27/60-2
Riley, Wm. H.; no date given, Ann Jane Younger	10/29/51-2
Rimby, Jacob, 25 Feb. 1851, Anna E. Butler	2/27/51-2

Rimmore, Wm., 26 Jan. 1853, Mary Ann Hooper   2/15/53-2
Rineman, John, 30 Dec. 1853, Henrietta Jenkins   1/13/54-2
Ring, Austin, 29 July 1852, Virginia C. Gemeney, dau. of John   7/30/52-2
Ring, Peter Clement, 2 Oct. 1851, Mary Catherine Boland   10/ 4/51-2
Ringgold, Fayette M., 20 Nov. 1854, Marcedes Lanas, dau. of
    Jose   2/ 2/55-2
Ringgold, George W., 26 Oct. 1856, Mary A. Engles   10/28/56-2
Ringgold, J. E., 26 Feb. 1852, Jane Frances Smith, dau. of
    Griffin   2/27/52-2
Ringgold, James P., 22 Sept. 1856, (Mrs.) Caroline Cisselberger 9/24/56-2
Ringgold, John P., 14 July 1853, Louisa A. Wickes, dau. of
    John   7/18/53-2
Ringgold, William J., 27 June 1852, Elizabeth Ann Sundereand   6/28/52-2
Ringold, Moses, 3 Nov. 1859, Martha Wilson   11/ 5/59-2
Ringold, Orlando, 11 Mar. 1855, Mary E. Bond   3/13/55-2
Ringrose, C. J., 17 Feb. 1852, Sarah Jane Patterson   2/19/52-2
Ringrose, John W. (Col.), 26 July 1859, (Mrs.) Sarah M.
    Marsolette   7/28/59-2
Ringrose, Walter, 20 Mar. 1851, Rachel M. Young   3/22/51-2
Rinn, John S., 5 Dec. 1852, Sarah Burns   12/ 6/52-2
Rippey, J. Duncan, 30 Oct. 1855, Lizzie G. Watts, dau. of
    John W.   10/31/55-2
Risley, Joseph H., 12 Dec. 1860, Mary E. Bishop, dau. of
    (Col.) E. B.   12/20/60-2
Ritchie, Jno., 5 May 1858, Bettie H. Manisbury, dau. of Wm. P. 5/ 6/58-2
Ritchie, Robert, 25 June 1857, Mary Ann Nicholson   6/27/57-2
Ritchie, Wm. H., 13 Oct. 1859, Elizabeth A. Ray   10/25/59-2
Ritter, Alfred, 19 Sept. 1858, Amanda Young   10/ 4/58-2
Ritter, David, 8 Oct. 1851, Elizabeth Arnold   10/ 9/51-2
Ritter, Eli, 7 May 1857, Louisa M. Lemlie   5/ 9/57-2
Ritter, John B., 7 Feb. 1858, Catherine Dorm   2/ 9/58-2
Ritter, Wm. H., 11 July 1859, Maria C. Dippell   7/16/59-2
Rittue, William, 11 May 1853, Elizabeth Turner   5/13/53-2
Rivell, John, 28 Sept. 1854, Mary Pollock   9/30/54-2
Rivers, John C. J., 5 Aug. 1858, Julia C. Plyman, dau. of John 8/10/58-2
Rixter, John, 9 Aug. 1860, Frances Duncan   8/25/60-2
Roach, Benjamin F., 11 Apr. 1854, Margaret P. Dennis   4/13/54-2
Roach, James M., 21 May 1851, (Mrs.) Mary C. Mathany   5/23/51-2
Roach, John A., 31 May 1853, Eugenia E. Clark, dau. of J. H.   6/ 3/53-2
Roach, Michael, 5 Feb. 1856, Emily Irwin   2/ 7/56-2
Roach, P., 6 Mar. 1859, Wineford Costelow   3/ 9/59-2
Roach, Stephen, 19 Aug. 1854, Isabella O'Neill   9/ 2/54-2
Roads, John L., 23 Oct. 1851, Margaret A. Clazy   10/24/51-2
Roads, Joseph W., 3 July 1853, Cordelia Green, dau. of George   7/ 8/53-2
Robb, Eliakin T., 30 July 1853, Viletta F.• Bishop, dau. of
    Richard R.   8/ 1/53-2
Robb, John A., Jr., 20 Nov. 1851, Mary C. Bell   11/21/51-2
Robb, Joseph, 31 Jan. 1860, Susie C. Jones, dau. of Israel   2/ 2/60-2
Robb, William H., 30 July 1857, Margaret A. Files   8/ 1/57-2
Roberson, James T., 29 Nov. 1860, Ellen Lee   12/ 1/60-2
Roberson, John, 5 Mar. 1857, Sarah Frances Moore   4/ 8/57-2
Roberts, Alexander B., 6 May 1860, Hester A. Langrill   5/18/60-2
Roberts, Alfred, 15 Oct. 1853, Mary E. D. Bowdle   11/16/53-2
Roberts, Augustus, 6 Aug. 1857, Elizabeth Brooks   8/12/57-2
Roberts, Charles C., 23 Mar. 1855, Sarah C. Biddle   4/ 5/55-2
Roberts, Charles H., 29 Mar. 1853, Sarah A. Jones, dau. of
    William   4/ 1/53-2
Roberts, Hugh, Jr., 22 Nov. 1859, Emma C. Mathaney   12/26/59-2
Roberts, J. McClain, 15 Oct. 1857, Eliza G. Albrater   10/17/57-2
Roberts, J. McClain, 15 Oct. 1857, Eliza G. Altvater; corrected
    copy   10/19/57-2
Roberts, John, 1 Sept. 1853, Sarah Ann James   9/ 7/53-2
Roberts, John, 1 Jan. 1857, Lizzie J. Sadler, dau. of (Capt.)
    Thomas   1/ 3/57-2
Roberts, John W., 14 July 1853, Ann T. Barcher   7/19/53-2

```
Roberts, Joshua, 2 Apr. 1860, Mary Barnett                          4/ 3/60-2
Roberts, Noah, 27 Aug. 1858, Louisa Lomax                           8/31/58-2
Roberts, Owen B., 22 Dec. 1853, Hester Ann Thomas                  12/24/53-2
Roberts, W. H., 26 Oct. 1852, Elizabeth D. Dobler                  10/28/52-2
Roberts, Wm. C., 1 Nov. 1860, Elizabeth Foot                       11/ 3/60-2
Roberts, Wm. Roy, 17 Sept. 1856, Jane C. Ney                        9/18/56-2
Robertson, G. M., 27 Mar. 1851, E. A. W. Tarr                       3/28/51-2
Robertson, Geo. M., 27 Mar. 1851, Emily Augusta W. Tarr, dau.
     of Edwin S.; corrected copy                                    3/29/51-2
Robertson, H. R., 8 May 1856, Mary A. Montague, dau. of Henry B. 5/14/56-2
Robertson, James W., 24 May 1853, Rebecca R. Hooker                 5/28/53-2
Robertson, Nathaniel C., 11 June 1857, Henrietta Esender            6/12/57-2
Robertson, Powhatan, 22 Dec. 1853, Lelia Bolling Bernard,
     dau. of John H.                                               12/31/53-2
Robertson, William, 21 Apr. 1853, Louisa Cole                       4/23/53-2
Robeson, Samuel, 14 Dec. 1851, Ruth Daughton                       12/20/51-2
Robey, J. Edward, 13 Apr. 1857, Melvina Oliver                      4/25/57-2
Robey, James T., 22 Jan. 1857, Sarah V. Howard                      1/28/57-2
Robier, Benjamin F., 25 July 1852, Catharine Ceila McDough          7/27/52-2
Robieson, Richard, 1 May 1851, Mary A. Horan                        5/ 3/51-2
Robins, Albert K., 15 Mar. 1860, Mary E. Bowen                      3/20/60-2
Robins, James B., 23 Nov. 1858, Mary C. Osterman, dau. of
     Augustus                                                      11/27/58-2
Robins, Wm. E., 12 June 1851, Margaret Stewart                      6/14/51-2
Robinson, A. C. (Dr.), 20 Jan. 1857, M. Louisa Hall, dau. of
     B. W.                                                          1/26/57-2
Robinson, C. B. (Dr.), 27 June 1859, P. Olevia Haslup               2/ 1/60-2
Robinson, Charles, 13 Apr. 1858, Elizabeth Olinton                  5/12/58-2
Robinson, D. Otley, 4 Sept. 1860, Theodora Chase, dau. of
     (Capt.) Stephen                                                9/ 7/60-2
Robinson, Davenport T., 20 May 1851, Ellenora Burneston, dau.
     of Issac                                                       5/22/51-2
Robinson, Edwin D., 11 June 1857, Maria L. Saylor                   6/16/57-2
Robinson, George, 9 June 1859, Ann Eliza Cook                       6/11/59-2
Robinson, Henry F., 2 Jan. 1851, Sarah A. H. Jenkins, dau. of
     Uriah                                                          1/24/51-2
Robinson, James, 12 Nov. 1854, Mary Ann Lewin                      12/29/54-2
Robinson, James, 11 Aug. 1857, Frances A. Fontz                     8/18/57-2
Robinson, James B., 3 Jan. 1856, Ellen E. Bond                      1/21/56-2
Robinson, James D., 21 Jan. 1856, R. Virginia Moody, dau. of
     John H.                                                        1/22/56-2
Robinson, James R., 1 Sept. 1857, Mary Elizabeth Butler            10/ 3/57-2
Robinson, James R., 1 Sept. 1857, Josephine M. Langley             10/ 3/57-2
Robinson, James S., 16 Nov. 1852, Mary Henshaw                     11/24/52-2
Robinson, James S., 25 Nov. 1857, Aramanella M. Shipley, dau.
     of Wm.                                                        12/ 8/57-2
Robinson, John, 28 Oct. 1854, Mary Ellen Mackey; corrected
     copy                                                          11/13/54-2
Robinson, John, 28 Oct. 1854, Mary Ellen McRey                     11/ 6/54-2
Robinson, John E., 10 June 1856, (Mrs.) Ellen Freeman
     Creamer, dau. of Henry Mourer                                  7/ 7/56-2
Robinson, John T., 22 Apr. 1855, Margaret J. Rutter                4/27/55-2
Robinson, John W., 10 Dec. 1860, Mary E. Riley                     12/29/60-2
Robinson, Joshua, 28 Sept. 1851, Mary Elizabeth Grove, dau.
     of John                                                       10/ 8/51-2
Robinson, Josiah F., 19 Dec. 1859, Anne Eliza Marshall            12/20/59-2
Robinson, Lewis H., 12 June 1859, Rebecca Cornelia Burnham,
     dau. of Samuel                                                 7/18/59-2
Robinson, Richard, 3 Aug. 1860, Emma J. Harford                     9/12/60-2
Robinson, Richard H., 21 Aug. 1852, Margaret Jane Gray;
     9/ 2/52-2                                                      9/ 4/52-2
Robinson, Thomas S., 6 Nov. 1856, Elizabeth Street                11/ 8/56-2
Robinson, William D., 11 June 1859, Emma M. Benson                  1/19/60-2
Robinson, Wm., 25 Oct. 1851, Sarah J. Nichol                      10/28/51-2
Robinson, Wm., 8 May 1854, Mary A. Beacham                          5/26/54-2
```

```
Robinson, Wm. C., 18 Nov. 1858, Isabella Rowland, dau. of
   Joseph                                                    12/18/58-2
Robinson, Wm. H., 19 Oct. 1852, Sarah E. Dehaven            10/21/52-2
Robinson, Wm. M., 24 Nov. 1857, Lizzie H. Waters            11/26/57-2
Robinson, Wm. T., 19 Aug. 1851, Ann Elizabeth Wooden         8/22/51-2
Robinson, Wm. T., 22 Dec. 1858, M. A. Reed                  12/25/58-2
Robison, Edward R., 25 Oct. 1858, Sarah C. Brady            10/27/58-2
Robson, John Q. A., 14 Dec. 1854, Ann E. Clark              12/16/54-2
Roche, Charles M., 28 Apr. 1859, Madora L. Lentz, dau. of
   Chas. W.                                                  5/ 9/59-2
Roche, George J., Jr., 4 May 1854, Anna Jane Jones           5/ 8/54-2
Rochester, Matthew N., 3 Apr. 1860, Anna McQuaid             4/ 5/60-2
Rochester, William, Jr., 22 Dec. 1857, Julia Ann Jones, dau.
   of William                                                1/ 7/58-2
Rock, Albert, 25 July 1852, Anna Seitz                       7/29/52-2
Rock, Henry, 25 June 1857, Mary J. Jarboe                    6/27/57-2
Rock, Thos., 18 Jan. 1852, Elizabeth Day                     1/20/52-2
Rode, William, 3 Aug. 1851, Emeline E. Reily                 8/ 8/51-2
Roden, William Henry, 19 Aug. 1858, Harriet Ann Davis        8/21/58-2
Rodenmayer, Francis T., 20 Apr. 1854, Elizabeth Howard, dau.
   of John P.                                                4/21/54-2
Rodewald, Henry, 3 Oct. 1855, Eliza Rodewald, dau. of Henry 10/ 4/55-2
Rodgers, Alfred C., 19 Apr. 1859, Agnes Lowering, dau. of Wm. 4/21/59-2
Rodgers, Alfred C., 19 Apr. 1859, Agnes Lowery, dau. of Wm.;
   corrected copy                                            4/22/59-2
Rodgers, George H., 14 Jan. 1851, Mary S. Evans, dau. of
   Isaac, Sr.                                                1/15/51-2
Rodgers, Hiram P., 9 Feb. 1854, Ann R. Williams              2/13/54-2
Rodgers, Jno. J. (Capt.), 6 Jan. 1851, Kate J. Saunders      1/ 8/51-2
Rodgers, John B., 18 Dec. 1859, Jane E. Rielley              2/22/60-2
Rodgers, John C., 23 Nov. 1857, Elizabeth J. Fisher, dau. of
   William                                                  12/10/57-2
Rodgers, Samuel (Rev.), 23 Feb. 1852, Angeline Nicholson     2/24/52-2
Rodriguez, Philip, 20 Nov. 1852, Margaret A. Roane, dau. of
   (Mrs.) Margaret Brennan                                  11/29/52-2
Roe, Robert, 17 July 1851, Harriet Duberry                   7/19/51-2
Roe, Samuel H., 28 Nov. 1853, Sarah J. Botterell            12/ 2/53-2
Roe, William (Capt.), 21 June 1857, Adelaide T. Reamy        7/ 7/57-2
Roessler, Gotthelf Ferdinand Robert, 24 Nov. 1852, (Mrs.) Mary
   Ann Koethen                                              11/27/52-2
Roger, Narcisse, 7 June 1855, Catharine Peters               6/12/55-2
Rogers, Arthur Lee, 23 Nov. 1858, Charlotte Rust, dau. of
   (Gen.) George                                            11/24/58-2
Rogers, C. Howard, 17 May 1860, Lizzie Tyler Belt, dau. of
   Truman                                                    5/22/60-2
Rogers, Charles W., 25 Nov. 1858, Catherine A. H. Giles, dau.
   of Walter                                                11/27/58-2
Rogers, Chas. Lyon, 18 May 1858, A. Rebecca Grogan           5/22/58-2
Rogers, Chas. R., 15 May 1856, Harriet B. Forman             5/17/56-2
Rogers, E. Stanley, 29 Nov. 1860, Mary Ege, dau. of E. G.   12/ 1/60-2
Rogers, Evans, 19 May 1853, Gertrude Ambler Scribner, dau. of
   Samuel                                                    5/20/53-2
Rogers, George W., 21 Oct. 1852, Caroline Metzgar           10/28/52-2
Rogers, J. L., 16 Sept. 1852, Virginia R. Babcock            2/17/53-2
Rogers, James S., 18 Oct. 1854, M. Virginia Leef, dau. of
   Henry                                                    10/21/54-2
Rogers, John A., 12 Jan. 1858, Louisa Mantz                  1/13/58-2
Rogers, P. J., 14 June 1859, Margaret Onthank                7/18/59-2
Rogers, Randolph; no date given, Rosa Ignatia Gibson, dau. of
   Henry                                                     9/ 5/52-2
Rogers, W., 18 May 1857, Mary Jones                          7/11/57-2
Rogers, William, 22 Sept. 1851, Mary Adelaide Booth, dau. of
   Jos.                                                     10/11/51-2
Rogers, William, 16 June 1853, Hannah Elizabeth Shepherd     6/17/53-2
Rohde, Martin, 17 June 1860, Margaret Schuster               6/21/60-2
```

```
Rohler, Wm., 2 Dec. 1856, Mary A. Gyke                        12/ 4/56-2
Rokess, John Washington, 16 Feb. 1855, Ann Maria Hooper        2/23/55-2
Roland, Emich, 5 Dec. 1854, Mary A. Rutter                    12/ 9/54-2
Rolle, Justin Albert; no date given, Helen M. Lueber, dau. of
    Francis                                                    1/ 8/58-2
Rollins, Edward, 31 Dec. 1851, Mary Jane Field, dau. of (Capt.)
    Lorenzo D.                                                 1/ 2/52-2
Rollins, Isaac H., 5 Feb. 1857, Sarah A. E. League             2/ 7/57-2
Rollinson, Edward, 9 Apr. 1858, Isabella Simpson               4/12/58-2
Rondo, B., 5 Aug. 1858, Laura Taylor Shaw, dau. of Richard;
    corrected copy                                             8/10/58-2
Roney, Thomas, 9 Oct. 1856, Fannie Robertson                  10/15/56-2
Rooke, Camillus (Capt.), 25 Oct. 1858, Teresa R. Wheeler, dau.
    of John D.                                                10/26/58-2
Rooker, J. Q., 11 Dec. 1853, M. F. Mullay, dau. of J. M.      12/15/53-2
Rooney, James, 3 Aug. 1858, (Mrs.) Ann McDonald                8/ 5/58-2
Rooney, Michael D., 3 Jan. 1858, Kate Flynn                    1/ 6/58-2
Rooney, Nicholas, 15 Mar. 1853, Mary Right                     3/26/53-2
Rooney, P. H., 24 Dec. 1850, Isabella E. Painter               1/ 2/51-2
Roose, William S., 20 May 1858, Jane Stephenson, dau. of John  5/21/58-2
Root, Henry R., 10 May 1859, Elizabeth V. Slater, dau. of
    George                                                     5/12/59-2
Root, Richard, 22 Dec. 1853, Ann P. Brockman, dau. of Calvin  12/29/53-2
Ropes, Archer, 13 Jan. 1852, Emilie W. Tucker                  1/16/52-2
Rose, J. Benjamin, 27 May 1856, Laura Virginia Purnell, dau.
    of Chas. B.                                                5/28/56-2
Rose, Jacob J., 5 Aug. 1852, Alice A. Cunningham              10/ 5/52-2
Rose, John, 3 June 1852, Mary E. Hall, dau. of C. A.           6/ 4/52-2
Rose, John, 10 Nov. 1853, Minerva A. Selby                    11/16/53-2
Rose, John, 22 Oct. 1857, Mary Elizabeth Meyer               10/26/57-2
Rose, John T., 12 Feb. 1854, Sarah A. Dagnar                   2/14/54-2
Rose, Peter, 2 Apr. 1851, Mary S. Mitchell, dau. of James
    and Huldah                                                 4/ 8/51-2
Rosenberg, Peter, 10 Jan. 1854, Sarah Louisa Adams             1/16/54-2
Rosenberger, James A., 11 Sept. 1855, Jennie M. Thomas         9/14/55-2
Rosenberger, Philip, 21 Aug. 1860, Maria F. Simpson            8/29/60-2
Rosensteel, Joseph L., 2 Oct. 1856, Fannie Gold, adopted dau.
    of Peter F.                                               10/ 6/56-2
Rosenstock, Samuel, 1 Nov. 1853, Amelia Herzberg, dau. of
    Meyer                                                     11/ 2/53-2
Rosewag, Chas. F., 9 Mar. 1852, Lucy Lill Billups, dau. of
    (Capt.) Richard, grandau. of George Gayle; corrected
    copy                                                       3/12/52-2
Ross, Aaron, 2 Dec. 1851, Catharine Linzey, dau. of Wm.       12/ 4/51-2
Ross, Abner C., Jr., 22 Dec. 1857, Laura Virginia Burdick     12/28/57-2
Ross, David J., 26 Oct. 1858, Julia M. Weaver                10/29/58-2
Ross, Henry W., 12 June 1860, Catharine A. Peregoy, dau. of
    James C.                                                   6/14/60-2
Ross, James (Rev.), 31 Oct. 1854, Susannah Barnes, dau. of
    David                                                     11/ 2/54-2
Ross, Jas. F., 14 Sept. 1851, Henrietta Fredericka Prince, dau.
    of Wm.                                                     9/15/51-2
Ross, Napoleon, 2 Mar. 1853, Henrietta Busey                   3/ 5/53-2
Ross, Robert, 12 July 1858, Mary E. Tubman                     7/14/58-2
Ross, Thomas; no date given, Jane Monney                       4/14/52-2
Ross, William T. H. (Dr.), 19 Nov. 1857, Jane C. Clendinen    11/23/57-2
Rossie, James B., 6 Jan. 1859, Josephine E. Stephens           1/10/59-2
Rossiter, John F., 20 Mar. 1856, Mary A. Smith, dau. of
    Samuel C.                                                  3/24/56-2
Roszwag, Charles F., 9 Mar. 1852, Lucy L. Billups              3/11/52-2
Roten, James Thomas, 12 Feb. 1856, Mary Jane Bramble           2/14/56-2
Roten, Perry J., 18 Mar. 1856, Dorathy A. Tuxford             3/24/56-2
Roten, Samuel, 31 Oct. 1855, Julia Ann Peek                   11/ 2/55-2
Rothel, Thomas, 25 Dec. 1855, Elizabeth Ellen Sears          12/31/55-2
```

Rothschild, L., 3 Apr. 1853, Sarah Hartz, dau. of Tobias   4/13/53-2
Rott, Richard, 25 Mar. 1851, Margaret A. Catlin   4/16/51-2
Rouch, John H., 14 Oct. 1852, Sarah Jane Bowen, dau. of
    Benjamin   10/28/52-2
Rouchester, George, 22 Nov. 1852, Amanda Boone, dau. of
    Henry D.   12/14/52-2
Rouck, Jesse, 22 Nov. 1860, Mary E. Akehart   11/24/60-2
Rounds, William, 16 Sept. 1860, Eliza Duffey   9/22/60-2
Rountree, Jno., 8 Apr. 1860, Mary E. Stoutsberger   6/15/60-2
Rourk, John A., 23 Jan. 1859, Elizabeth Hindes   1/25/59-2
Rourk, Michael A., 19 Apr. 1853, Martha A. Crop   5/ 2/53-2
Rourke, Michael J., 18 Oct. 1857, Kate Rousselet   10/30/57-2
Rous, James W., 17 Sept. 1851, R. G. Lindsey; 9/29/51-2   9/30/51-2
Rouse, Thomas J., 11 Apr. 1853, Rebecca Inloes   4/13/53-2
Rousse, J. F., 9 Oct. 1856, Martha Coss, dau. of Geo.   10/13/56-2
Roussel, Ameidei, 27 Feb. 1857, Emma Mallet   3/ 2/57-2
Rousselat, Charles A., 24 Apr. 1855, (Mrs.) Bridget Laughran   4/25/55-2
Roussell, Anton Ferdinand, 1 May 1859, Augusta Bruns   5/10/59-2
Roux, George S., 2 Aug. 1860, M. Lizzie Mitchell, dau. of
    Judson   8/16/60-2
Rowe, John L., 29 July 1851, Margaret A. Bronson   7/31/51-2
Rowe, R. Temple, 6 Dec. 1853, Lavininia Greenwood, dau. of
    Wm. S.   12/ 8/53-2
Rowe, William B., 28 Sept. 1854, Eliza J. Bates   9/30/54-2
Rowles, John, 1 June 1859, Rachel Galloway   6/ 2/59-2
Rowles, William D., 28 Aug. 1851, Mary Jane Crowther   8/30/51-2
Rowlett, Richard, 9 Nov. 1853, Jane Deady, dau. of John   11/11/53-2
Rowley, Edward L., 17 Nov. 1859, Amelia Jane Hilditch   11/21/59-2
Royston, Bosley, 2 Mar. 1853, Mary Ann Shelly   3/ 3/53-2
Royston, N. Bowen, 15 July 1851, Harriet Elizabeth Lambdin   7/17/51-2
Ruark, Thomas L., 29 Nov. 1860, Serah E. Maddux   12/ 1/60-2
Rubins, James B., 23 Nov. 1858, Mary C. Osterman, dau. of
    Augustus   11/25/58-2
Ruckle, William S., 8 Apr. 1852, Sarah B. Northam   4/12/52-2
Ruddach, Joseph H., 22 Nov. 1856, Sarah Griffith   11/25/56-2
Rudiger, Adolph, 11 July 1858, Augusta Roske   7/12/58-2
Rudisell, Thomas, 9 Feb. 1860, (Mrs.) Charlotte Heiner   2/10/60-2
Rudolph, Columbus, 21 Sept. 1857, Emeline Henderson   9/24/57-2
Rudolph, Martin B., 9 Oct. 1859, Elizabeth Wood   10/13/59-2
Ruff, G. F., 26 May 1853, Isabel Sheeler, dau. of Anthony;
    corrected copy   5/31/53-2
Ruff, G. Frederick, 26 May 1853, Isabel Sheeler, dau. of
    Anthony   5/28/53-2
Ruff, Henry, 18 June 1857, S. Althea Street   6/19/57-2
Ruff, Jacob, 26 Jan. 1858, Rosa C. M. Waldner, dau. of Jacob P.   1/28/58-2
Ruff, John Wesley, 17 June 1858, Georgianna Morsell   6/19/58-2
Ruger, Oliver J., 3 May 1859, Fannie C. Mortimer, dau. of
    (Col.) C.   5/ 6/59-2
Ruhol, John, 30 Jan. 1856, Louisa Kerby   2/ 1/56-2
Ruhrah, D. C., 1 June 1859, Mollie A. Pincknaur   6/ 3/59-2
Ruley, John M., 13 Dec. 1859, Alexina Marshall   12/24/59-2
Ruley, P. W., 8 Oct. 1854, Annora Birmingham   10/19/54-2
Rundle, William, 12 Apr. 1856, Amanda M. Waters   11/10/56-2
Runelle, Samuel S., 29 July 1860, Mary Ann Wilt   11/ 6/60-2
Rupley, Admiral, 19 Mar. 1855, Sarah D. Ensor   4/19/55-2
Rupp, Edward S., 23 Feb. 1854, Frances A. Smith, dau. of
    Nicholas   3/ 6/54-2
Rupp, Jacob, 19 June 1851, Sarah Ann Kelley   7/ 3/51-2
Rupp, Reuben F., 9 Jan. 1855, Jane H. Allen   1/11/55-2
Rupp, Wm., 26 July 1852, Rebbecca C. Thomas   8/17/52-2
Rush, Anthony, 19 Dec. 1858, Martha Swann   12/20/58-2
Rusk, Edwin W.; no date given, Margaret Campbell   7/ 2/58-2
Rusk, Thomas J., 16 May 1855, Eliza E. Murphy, dau. of J. D.   5/19/55-2
Ruskell, George, 10 Apr. 1856, M. Lizzie Carter, dau. of David   4/16/56-2
Russell, Aaron, 22 Nov. 1860, Catherine Jacobs   11/24/60-2

Russell, Andrew, 11 Mar. 1852, Eleanor Bowen   3/16/52-2
Russell, E. Walton, 24 Sept. 1860, M. Elizzie Goldsmith, dau.
    of John   9/25/60-2
Russell, Elijah J., 4 Aug. 1858, Caroline Brown, dau. of John 8/14/58-2
Russell, Frederick, 10 Apr. 1856, Mary Reid   4/16/56-2
Russell, John, 22 Aug. 1856, Rebecca Brambill   8/30/56-2
Russell, John A., 19 July 1855, Emily H. Webb, dau. of Henry   7/24/55-2
Russell, Michael, 14 Mar. 1855, Mary A. Morrow   4/ 5/55-2
Russell, Michael D., 27 Feb. 1859, Mary C. O'Brien   3/17/59-2
Russell, Patrick, 31 July 1853, Matilda Gelaspy   8/ 2/53-2
Russell, Thomas P., 7 June 1852, Elizabeth A. Mules   6/ 9/52-2
Russell, William, 10 May 1853, Mary Grace Mayer, dau. of
    George Lewis   5/14/53-2
Russell, William, 22 Dec. 1857, Susanna S. Wood, dau. of
    Thomas   12/25/57-2
Russell, William, 6 Sept. 1860, Annie Streetts, dau. of
    Mansfield   9/11/60-2
Russell, William H., 20 Oct. 1857, Mary V. Short   10/26/57-2
Russell, William T., 24 July 1851, Rosanna Patterson   7/28/51-2
Rust, George T., 6 Oct. 1859, Rebecca C. Yellott, dau. of
    John   10/ 7/59-2
Rust, John, 15 Apr. 1852, Elizabeth A. Taylor   4/17/52-2
Rust, Paul, 21 Mar. 1853, Catharine Lineberger   3/24/53-2
Rutherdale, Joseph, 7 Nov. 1854, Margaret Evitt   11/10/54-2
Rutherdale, Robert, 1 June 1853, Martha Mason   6/ 2/53-2
Rutherford, Alexander, 28 Mar. 1853, Ellen Keats   4/ 6/53-2
Rutledge, A., 8 Jan. 1857, Ariel Amos   1/10/57-2
Rutter, Edward J., 22 May 1851, Annie Eliza Littig   5/24/51-2
Rutter, John, 18 Oct. 1860, Julia A. C. Nagle   10/23/60-2
Rutter, John A. J., Jr., 23 Jan. 1851, Margaret E. Walker   1/24/51-2
Rutter, Philip, 13 Jan. 1853, Aurora C. Johnson, dau. of Wm. H. 1/19/53-2
Rutter, Thomas C., 4 Jan. 1855, Laura Bombarger   4/ 5/55-2
Ryan, E. J., 25 Aug. 1856, Sarah Y. Brannan   10/ 9/56-2
Ryan, Edward, 5 July 1858, Ellen Burnell   7/13/58-2
Ryan, James, 23 Nov. 1858, Ellen Broderick   11/25/58-2
Ryan, John, 23 Dec. 1852, Charlotte Eliza Lee   12/29/52-2
Ryan, John, 16 Aug. 1853, Kate Buckley   8/24/53-2
Ryan, John, 14 Dec. 1854, Susan J. Keener   12/16/54-2
Ryan, John, 6 Oct. 1859, Priscilla Ford   10/15/59-2
Ryan, John F., 10 May 1859, Margaret E. Meagher   6/ 1/59-2
Ryan, Michael, 13 Oct. 1857, Jane N. Bagwell   10/14/57-2
Ryan, Thomas, 1 Aug. 1858, Mary Elizabeth Gould   9/ 3/58-2
Ryan, Timothy, 14 Jan. 1855, Mary W. Shortall   1/17/55-2
Ryen, Wm. H., 6 Feb. 1851, Rebecca A. Walker, dau. of (Col.)
    S. D.   2/ 7/51-2
Ryer, Randolph, 14 June 1852, Lauretta Ross, dau. of Andrew
    Hazlehurst   6/17/52-2
Ryther, E. A., 25 Nov. 1856, Margaret Spicer   11/27/56-2
S-(?), M. H., 20 Apr. 1852, Catharine Rigney, dau. of Thos.
    Cusack   4/22/52-2
S-(?)-haum, Lewis, 22 May 1856, Mary E. Sexton   7/ 1/56-2
Sadler, Jos. W., 26 Sept. 1858, Susannah Ayers   9/28/58-2
Sadler, Solomon H., 7 Oct. 1856, Caroline A. Willson   10/ 8/56-2
Sadler, William, 4 Oct. 1854, Martha Welch   10/12/54-2
Sadtler, Andrew, 5 Jan. 1851, Barbara Rice   1/16/51-2
Saffell, James, 10 Nov. 1857, Annie E. Webb   11/12/57-2
Saffell, Richard H., 23 Dec. 1852, Christianna Clough   1/ 6/53-2
Safford, N. P., 17 Mar. 1859, Susannah V. Perkins   3/19/59-2
Sage, Henry B.; no date given, Caroline L. Goldsmith   1/ 9/57-2
Sagle, Joseph R., 6 May 1856, Ellen R. Lane   5/ 8/56-2
Sahm, Jacob, 29 Aug. 1855, Mary A. H. Amey, dau. of Henry   9/12/55-2
St. John, James, 9 Nov. 1854, Catharine Thompson   11/14/54-2
Sales, Philip, 26 Feb. 1857, Sarah E. Moxley, dau. of Walter   2/28/57-2
Sales, Wm. H., 9 Nov. 1852, Barbara Bowzer, dau. of (Mrs.)
    Lydia   11/10/52-2

```
Salinas, Charles H., 14 Mar. 1860, Annie Elfing Swiggett, dau.
    of William H.                                               3/22/60-2
Salmon, P. Adolphus, 27 Dec. 1859, Kate A. Neilson             1/ 2/60-2
Salp, Henry, 9 June 1851, Ann E. Fisher                        6/12/51-2
Sampson, James, 1 Apr. 1851, Mary Ward                         4/ 3/51-2
Sampson, Rezin B., Jr., 5 July 1855, Elizabeth Mask            7/10/55-2
Sanburn, Thomas S., 13 Mar. 1851, Charlotte Marew              3/15/51-2
Sanders, Barney, 24 June 1855, Rachel A. Foreman               6/28/55-2
Sanders, Geo. B., 1 Jan. 1854, Susanna H. Daneker              1/ 3/54-2
Sanders, Geo. W., 12 July 1853, Susan B. Thompson              7/13/53-2
Sanders, J. Mason, 10 Apr. 1860, Ann Ophelia Shryock           4/14/60-2
Sanders, John F., 12 Dec. 1853, Elizabeth A. Hubbard          12/15/53-2
Sanders, John H., 5 Apr. 1855, Susan E. G. Kirkwood, dau. of
    John and Ann                                               4/10/55-2
Sanders, William, 19 June 1853, (Mrs.) Martha Pearce           6/21/53-2
Sanderson, John, 25 Sept. 1851, Ann Norwood                    9/26/51-2
Sanderson, John, Jr., 10 Nov. 1856, M. A. Bond                11/12/56-2
Sands, Edwin, 12 Jan. 1854, Elizabeth Sewall                   1/19/54-2
Sands, Henry R., 5 Nov. 1860, Sarah C. Walters                11/12/60-2
Sands, James, 20 Sept. 1860, Lottie Virginia Kilgrove          9/28/60-2
Sands, Samuel, 9 Dec. 1852, (Mrs.) Anna J. Buck               12/13/52-2
Sanford, Daniel A., 9 June 1859, Sophia Robinson               6/14/59-2
Sangston, G. E., Jr., 3 May 1860, A. Rebecca Cecil, dau. of
    Owen                                                       5/ 7/60-2
Sangston, James A., 6 June 1854, Laura F. Sangston             6/ 7/54-2
Sank, Joseph H., 27 Jan. 1859, (Mrs.) Jane L. Martin           1/29/59-2
Sanks, Corbin, 25 Mar. 1855, Elizabeth Hirsh                   3/28/55-2
Sanks, Jas. Reily, 21 June 1860, Susana Dutton                 6/23/60-2
Sanner, Isaac S., 14 July 1860, Eleanora Fry                   7/20/60-2
Sanner, James B., 24 Dec. 1854, Ann Maria Beetley, dau. of
    (Capt.) John                                              12/30/54-2
Sanner, John A., 26 May 1852, Ann Maria Watkins                5/28/52-2
Sansbury, John W., 1 Feb. 1855, Susanna Anderson               2/ 3/55-2
Sansbury, R. T., 7 Mar. 1855, Sarah A. Reynolds                3/15/55-2
Sansbury, Richard T., 8 Mar. 1855, Sarah A. Reynolds           3/20/55-2
Santmyer, John H., 3 Oct. 1855, Emma J. Terry                 10/ 8/55-2
Sapp, Andrew J., 26 Oct. 1856, Sarah Jane Wright              10/29/56-2
Sapp, Benjamin Franklin, 17 Nov. 1857, Mary Ann Litsinger     1/ 5/58-2
Sapp, Charles, 27 Oct. 1859, Alice C. Parsons                10/28/59-2
Sapp, Daniel, 24 Oct. 1855, Mary Jane Pennington             10/25/55-2
Sapp, David S., 3 July 1853, Sophia C. Pindell, dau. of Louis  7/ 6/53-2
Sapp, J. O., 27 Mar. 1851, Mary Ann Harford                    3/31/51-2
Sapp, John F., 16 Oct. 1859, Mary F. Stanford                 10/19/59-2
Sapp, Wm. J., 10 Nov. 1852, Jemima Jane Bryant                11/12/52-2
Sappington, Otis B., 23 Apr. 1856, Sallie M. Crane             4/26/56-2
Sappington, Rich'd. (Dr.), 18 Oct. 1854, Aralanta R. Smith    10/21/54-2
Sarlouis, B., 31 Aug. 1856, Amalie Marcusi                     9/ 3/56-2
Sattler, Wm., 1 Mar. 1853, Kate Sadtler, dau. of Philip B.     3/ 4/53-2
Sauerwein, Francis D., 15 Dec. 1859, Mary V. McCabe            2/ 7/60-2
Sauffer, Samuel B., 11 Mar. 1851, Eliza E. Buchanan, dau. of
    J. M.                                                      3/15/51-2
Saulsbury, Andrew C., 25 July 1854, Kate L. Ross               7/27/54-2
Saulsbury, Andrew J., 6 Mar. 1853, Julia A. Davids             3/ 7/53-2
Saulsbury, James, 3 Oct. 1858, Margaret A. Goodwin            10/ 8/58-2
Saumenig, Henry W., 26 Feb. 1857, Sarah C. Saumenig            2/28/57-2
Saunders, B. J., 2 May 1854, Mary Ann Lloyd                    5/ 6/54-2
Saunders, Carter A., 28 June 1859, Lute R. Hill, dau. of Thomas 7/ 1/59-2
Saunders, George C., 13 Sept. 1858, Rebecca J. Alexander      11/22/58-2
Saunders, George E., 26 Jan. 1857, Maria C. Tall               1/27/57-2
Saunders, Henry, 18 Nov. 1858, Ann Eliza Mahoney              12/ 2/58-2
Saunders, Jas. S., 13 Nov. 1851, Mary Ann Macklin             11/15/51-2
Saunders, John, 25 Sept. 1851, Rachel A. Brown                 9/27/51-2
Saunders, John S., 14 Apr. 1857, Virginia Johnson              4/18/57-2
Saunders, Prince H. B., 7 Apr. 1857, Lucinda W. Mitchell       4/29/57-2
Saunders, William H., 30 Jan. 1855, Sarah S. Smith             2/ 1/55-2
```

Saune, Christian, 20 Oct. 1856, Louisa Clauttice   10/31/56-2
Sauner, George W., 14 Nov. 1855, Eliza A. Hayd   11/22/55-2
Sauner, John H., 6 May 1851, Elizabeth Ann Seltigh, dau. of
     John G.   5/ 8/51-2
Sauter, Chris N., 9 Dec. 1858, Mary Frances Brosenne   12/14/58-2
Savage, Charles E., 29 Jan. 1856, Carrie H. Williams   7/31/56-2
Savage, Lycurgusie E., 16 Nov. 1852, Amelia J. C. Yager, dau. of
     Joseph   11/18/52-2
Savagh, Joseph L., 27 Nov. 1856, Julia Gold Wonn   12/ 2/56-2
Savill, Francis, 20 Jan. 1851, Margaret Williamson   2/ 6/51-2
Savin, Marcus D., 26 June 1860, Annie E. Williams   6/28/60-2
Savoy, Ransom, 16 Jun. 1859, Maria Green   6/20/59-2
Sawkins, Alfred H., 17 Apr. 1856, Mary A. Buckley   6/ 2/56-2
Sawkins, F. A., 20 Feb. 1855, G. Whitley   8/29/55-2
Sawkins, J. G., 27 Mar. 1855, Mary H. Brodie   4/ 5/55-2
Sawyer, Walter, 6 July 1852, Maria Kain   7/ 7/52-2
Saxten, Wm. A., 18 Apr. 1859, Sallie S. Abercrombie, dau. of
     James   4/30/59-2
Sbisa, Joseph (Capt.), 10 June 1852, Sarah Virginia Follin   6/14/52-2
Scaggs, James S., 6 Dec. 1853, Martha C. Boteler   12/ 7/53-2
Scaggs, Lemuel, 23 Oct. 1854, (Mrs.) Margaret A. Rasin   10/30/54-2
Scarborough, Amos W., 15 Jan. 1852, Sarah Chaney   5/20/52-2
Scarborough, Jno. T., 8 Mar. 1855, Pauline M. Durkee   4/ 2/55-2
Scarburgh, Mitchell T., 6 Aug. 1858, Mary H. Young   8/10/58-2
Scarf, J. L., 17 May 1859, Emeline Smithson   5/18/59-2
Scarff, Thomas T., 27 Mar. 1853, Angelina Margerum   4/ 7/53-2
Scarff, Wm. T. (Dr.), 25 Nov. 1858, Sarah Margaret Lauder,
     dau. of Charles   11/27/58-2
Scarlett, William G., 18 Dec. 1860, Corrilla C. Armstrong   12/20/60-2
Scaum, Charles, 19 July 1853, Mary Elizabeth Collins   7/23/53-2
Schaefer, Adam, 3 Aug. 1857, Catherine Munduff   8/ 8/57-2
Schaeffer, Edward K., 3 June 1852, Elizabeth Morton, dau. of
     John A., Jr.   6/ 5/52-2
Schaer, John F., 20 Sept. 1859, Emma E. Schulz   9/21/59-2
Schaeffer, Martin, 26 May 1851, Mary Ann Kemp   5/28/51-2
Schaeffer, William G., 10 June 1858, Ada Milley, dau. of John 6/11/58-2
Schafer, George F., 3 May 1851, (Mrs.) Minna Strohmeyer   5/ 6/51-2
Schaffer, Fred. Littig, Jr., 10 Nov. 1859, Georgia Lauderman,
     dau. of Henry R.   11/12/59-2
Scharf, William J., 6 Apr. 1858, Sarah V. Knight   4/ 8/58-2
Scharff, John H., 14 July 1859, Margaret E. Walker   7/30/59-2
Schaum, F., Sr., 11 Mar. 1854, (Mrs.) C. Buckleman   3/13/54-2
Schaum, Lewis, 28 Feb. 1860, Mary C. Beather   3/ 3/60-2
Schaum, Lewis, 28 Feb. 1860, Mary C. Reather; corrected copy   3/ 5/60-2
Schaum, William L., 16 Feb. 1858, Martha A. Cunkle   2/19/58-2
Scheer, Valentine, 11 Aug. 1859, Mary A. Sener   8/12/59-2
Scheerer, Geo. Wm., 17 Sept. 1854, Margaret E. Voglesong   9/19/54-2
Scheib, J., 23 Nov. 1851, Margaret A. Wittig   11/29/51-2
Scheker, Samuel, 21 Sept. 1853, Sarah F. Major   9/23/53-2
Scheldt, Henry J., 11 Feb. 1856, (Mrs.) Sarah Jackson   3/13/56-2
Schenckel, Conrad, 26 Jan. 1851, Elizabeth Snyder   1/28/51-2
Scheurer, John G., 16 Nov. 1858, Jane S. Hickman; corrected
     copy   12/ 1/59-2
Scheurer, John O., 18 Nov. 1859, Jane S. Hickman   11/30/59-2
Schiebler, Henry K., 6 Oct. 1857, Sarah J. Marten   10/17/57-2
Schlighting, L., 27 Dec. 1852, Mary Egan   1/ 8/53-2
Schmidt, John Jacob, 10 Aug. 1857, Susan Agnes Richardson,
     dau. of George   8/21/57-2
Schmidt, P. D., 17 Aug. 1852, E. H. Muhlofer   8/19/52-2
Schmidt, Simeon, 24 Nov. 1859, Anna Maria Berenstecher   11/24/59-2
Schmidt, William, 25 Apr. 1860, Charlotte Hax   5/ 1/60-2
Schmidt, Wm. J., 2 Apr. 1857, Mary Virginia Scott   4/ 3/57-2
Schmitt, Joseph, 3 June 1859, Mary Emma Hanson   7/ 6/59-2
Schmuk, Lewis, 6 Feb. 1851, Maria Christ   2/ 8/51-2
Schoe, Lewis, 20 July 1851, Sarah J. Batteaus   7/22/51-2

Schofield, Arsemus, 19 Sept. 1854, Mary Jane Hennace	9/22/54-2
Schofield, Henry, 14 Sept. 1859, Barbara L. Dames, dau. of William and Alesea	9/17/59-2
Schomann, John, 1 Sept. 1858, Kate Fisher	9/ 3/58-2
Schone, H. H., 9 Nov. 1857, (Mrs.) D. Ellman	11/11/57-2
Schoolcraft, James, 10 Apr. 1856, Jane Pierce	9/19/57-2
Schooley, Presley M., 27 Feb. 1851, Mary Jane Adams	3/ 3/51-2
Schoolherb, Samuel, 27 Aug. 1854, Bertha Rosenthal	8/29/54-2
Schoolherr, Louis, 10 July 1859, Sarah Strauss	7/12/59-2
Schott, John, 18 Nov. 1858, Louisa M. Brandau, dau. of (Rev.) G. H.	11/23/58-2
Schott, John, 30 Dec. 1858, Mary R. Schroeder	1/ 8/59-2
Schreiner, Charles, 18 Nov. 1860, Lottie A. Baltzell	11/20/60-2
Schriver, Alfred, 22 Mar. 1860, (Mrs.) Hannah A. Woods	3/24/60-2
Schroder, Henry C., 18 Feb. 1855, Anne E. McWilliams	2/20/55-2
Schroder, Jacob W., 22 Apr. 1855, Matilda Cooper	10/ 2/55-2
Schroder, Richard T., 28 Feb. 1858, Elizabeth F. Woods	3/ 3/58-2
Schroder, Seigesmund C., 17 Apr. 1853, Caroline A. Free	4/20/53-2
Schroeder, Charles H., 26 Apr. 1854, Fanny Adelaide Sayre, dau. of Wm.	5/ 3/54-2
Schroeder, George L., 22 Mar. 1859, Catharine Young	3/24/59-2
Schugard, John C., 22 June 1858, Mary G. Dolfield	6/23/58-2
Schultz, Alexander, 29 May 1856, Lizzie Myer, dau. of John J.	5/30/56-2
Schultz, Augustus, 8 Sept. 1852, Biddy Magan	9/13/52-2
Schultz, Edw'd. T., 18 Nov. 1852, Susan R. Martin, dau. of David	11/22/52-2
Schultz, Louis H., 7 Mar. 1859, Nettie Thater	3/ 9/59-2
Schultze, John H., 5 Dec. 1852, Mary Ann Davis	12/ 7/52-2
Schulz, Charles Louis, 30 Nov. 1859, Sophia Henrietta Schaer	12/ 2/59-2
Schumaker, Carston H.; no date given, Mary M. Scheir, dau. of Chas. and Margaret	11/ 7/56-2
Schwab, Israel, 8 June 1856, Rose Reichenberger	6/10/56-2
Schwab, Solomon, 12 Nov. 1854, Helen Bauer, dau. of H.	11/14/54-2
Schwartze, John, 16 Mar. 1854, Arietta W. Willis	3/17/54-2
Schwarz, Gustav, 21 Dec. 1858, Josephine M. Grant, dau. of Jos. P.	12/25/58-2
Schwatzhaupt, Charles, 10 Oct. 1859, Margaretta Meyers	10/13/59-2
Schwearer, John A., 10 July 1859, Christina W. Buchta	8/ 8/59-2
Schweizer, Chas. M., 26 May 1856, Agnes F. Simpson	6/ 2/56-2
Schwrar, Philip G., 11 Mar. 1852, H. Kent Hall, dau. of (Col.) Wm.	3/16/52-2
Scoggins, Samuel R., 12 Jan. 1858, Mary J. Askey	1/14/58-2
Scott, A. O., 2 Apr. 1853, Jane B. Wilson	4/ 4/53-2
Scott, A. P., 20 July 1852, Ella T. Coyle, dau. of Charles	7/21/52-2
Scott, Abel F. (Capt.), 3 Mar. 1851, Eliza Jane Little, dau. of (Capt.) George	3/10/51-2
Scott, Albert G., 6 June 1860, (Mrs.) Eunice C. Watrous	6/ 9/60-2
Scott, Charles A., 27 Dec. 1859, Mary E. Parker	12/29/59-2
Scott, Charles J., 7 Apr. 1853, Margaret R. Shipley	4/11/53-2
Scott, Edwd. R., 30 Aug. 1855, Elizabeth A. Tingle, dau. of John	9/ 4/55-2
Scott, Edwd. R., 30 Aug. 1855, Elizabeth H. Tingle, dau. of John; corrected copy	9/ 5/55-2
Scott, Eli, 24 Jan. 1854, (Mrs.) Alvesta Clifford, dau. of Geo. Richstein	1/26/54-2
Scott, Ephraim, 23 Jan. 1859, Ellenora Davis	1/25/59-2
Scott, Francis H., 26 June 1854, A. Cordelia Lansdale	6/27/54-2
Scott, Francis P., 25 Aug. 1851, Mary Elizabeth Grice	8/26/51-2
Scott, George, 17 May 1858, Ann Maria Price	5/19/58-2
Scott, George Littig, 6 Dec. 1859, Mary Hopkins, dau. of (Dr.) Wakeman H.	12/ 9/59-2
Scott, Greenberry, 22 July 1858, Margaret Finly	7/24/58-2
Scott, Henry B. (Dr.), 17 Oct. 1854, Rebecca C. Travers, dau. of D. B.	10/21/54-2
Scott, Henry E., 28 Jan. 1858, Jane M. Patterson	6/ 4/58-2

```
Scott, Isaac, 13 Feb. 1851, Josephine Lava                    2/15/51-2
Scott, James, 10 Sept. 1857, Annie E. Atwell, dau. of Joseph  9/15/57-2
Scott, James, 27 Jan. 1859, Eliza Ann Kirk                    1/28/59-2
Scott, Jesse, 25 May 1851, (Mrs.) Elizabeth Ex                5/27/51-2
Scott, Job, 5 Oct. 1854, M. Fannie Kirby, dau. of Thos. R.   10/10/54-2
Scott, John, 10 Jan. 1851, Mary Jane Deaver, dau. of Amos and
  Eliza                                                       2/11/51-2
Scott, John C., 24 July 1856, Alcinda E. Ricter             10/25/56-2
Scott, John H., 23 May 1852, Araminta Beck                    5/31/52-2
Scott, John H., 26 June 1856, Sarah Ann Marine                6/28/56-2
Scott, John R., 27 Aug. 1860, C. Ann Emily Denny, dau. of
  Benj., Jr.                                                  8/29/60-2
Scott, Joseph, 22 Nov. 1860, Sevilla Sefton                  11/24/60-2
Scott, Martin P. (Dr.), 24 Oct. 1854, Pocahontas C. Bernard,
  dau. of John H.                                            11/17/54-2
Scott, R. S., 17 Apr. 1856, Ellen E. Godwin, dau. of Wm. M.   4/22/56-2
Scott, Robert, 16 Oct. 1851, Susan Morrison                  10/20/51-2
Scott, Samuel, 19 June 1855, Ann Colwell                      6/21/55-2
Scott, Sewell B., 10 Feb. 1859, Achsah G. Davis, dau. of (Dr.)
  C. S.                                                       2/12/59-2
Scott, Stephen, 10 Apr. 1856, Ellen Jackson                   4/11/56-2
Scott, Upton, 26 Jan. 1854, Rebecca P. Aiken, dau. of George  2/14/54-2
Scott, William, 20 Mar. 1851, Mary Ann McCormick              3/22/51-2
Scott, William, 24 July 1851, Mary Ellen Jackson              7/25/51-2
Scott, William, 2 Mar. 1852, Ann R. Stiver                    3/ 4/52-2
Scott, Wm. Graham, 17 Dec. 1854, Annie Virginia Devlin, dau. of
  John S.                                                    12/25/54-2
Scotti, Henry E., 28 Jan. 1858, Jane M. Patterson            6/ 7/58-2
Scrivener, James E., 16 June 1859, Kate Garner                6/18/59-2
Scrivener, Lewis, 11 Nov. 1857, Elizabeth A. Schillenberger  11/19/57-2
Scrivener, Thomas S., 11 Dec. 1855, Catherine French, dau. of
  E.                                                         12/12/55-2
Scrivner, John W., 29 May 1860, Margaret Lydia Biddinger;
  5/30/60-2                                                   5/31/60-2
Scrocgons, George, 6 Sept. 1853, (Mrs.) Mary Jane Dockins    9/ 9/53-2
Scroggins, William H., 25 Dec. 1858, Rebecca Jones          12/27/58-2
Scully, Danl., 18 Feb. 1855, Frances Byans                   3/ 2/53-2
Scully, James, 17 July 1860, Ellen Noughton                  7/28/60-2
Scwatka, Francis A., 31 Mar. 1859, Elizabeth Joyce           4/ 4/59-2
Seaman, William A., 5 Feb. 1857, Barbara E. Drost, dau. of
  John H.                                                    2/ 9/57-2
Sears, H. H., 20 June 1860, Winnie T. Wheelwright            6/30/60-2
Sears, S. W. (Rev.), 22 Feb. 1859, Elizabeth R. McCahan      2/28/59-2
Sears, W. H., 14 Mar. 1854, Margaret E. Morgan               3/17/54-2
Sears, William, 29 June 1852, (Mrs.) Emma Cecilia Lassar     7/ 3/52-2
Seatle, Henry A., 17 May 1856, Matilda A. Venabels           7/31/56-2
Seawell, John Tyler, 26 Oct. 1852, Fanny E. Jackson, dau. of
  (Maj.) Wm.                                                10/28/52-2
Sebourn, Joseph B., 14 Nov. 1854, Sarah Baker               11/15/54-2
Sebree, John J., 10 Nov. 1859, Anna M. Davis                11/19/59-2
Seccombs, Joseph, 15 May 1851, Catherine A. Bowen            5/17/51-2
Secrist, Jacob, 10 July 1856, Elizabeth Kivler               7/12/56-2
Sedecum, Benjamin, 27 May 1855, Ann Rebecca Wade            10/29/55-2
Sedecum, John, 18 July 1858, M. A. Wade                      9/29/58-2
Sedgwick, John T., 29 Mar. 1860, Elizabeth Boardley          3/31/60-2
Seebode, Charles F., 14 Jan. 1855, Martha Davis              1/16/55-2
Seebode, Chas. F., 2 July 1856, Anna J. French               7/ 4/56-2
Seemuller, John R., 1 Jan. 1856, Mary E. Trimble             1/ 3/56-2
Segerman, John J., 27 Jan. 1856, Jane A. Yates               2/ 1/56-2
Seidenstricker, A. H., 14 Dec. 1854, Harriet B. Davis, dau. of
  Geo. W.                                                   12/16/54-2
Seidenstricker, John B., 11 Nov. 1851, Mary H. Cragg        11/14/51-2
Seidenstricker, John W., 21 Nov. 1854, Belinda C. Boozer    12/ 6/54-2
Seipp, William, 2 Sept. 1854, Mary E. Zapp                   9/ 6/54-2
Seitsig, Philip, 5 Nov. 1856, Margaret McClain              11/ 7/56-2
```

Seitz, Conrad G., 27 Sept. 1855, Catharine Trogler   9/29/55-2
Selby, John S., 21 June 1860, Margaret R. Conradt, dau. of
    G. M.   6/22/60-2
Selby, Mordecai, 11 Mar. 1851, Martha E. Scrivner   3/14/51-2
Selby, N. Richard, 6 Oct. 1859, Mary Ellen Goldsborough, dau. of
    Wm. J.   10/12/59-2
Seligman, Sigmund J., 12 Mar. 1854, Hannah Getz, dau. of Louis   3/14/54-2
Sellar, Alexander, 14 Apr. 1858, Mary L. Chase, dau. of J. H.   4/15/58-2
Sellers, Amanuel, 16 June 1857, Margaret E. Hopwood   6/22/57-2
Sellers, J. Henry, 18 May 1859, Ella C. Curtis, dau. of John D.   5/26/59-2
Sellman, Alexander, 8 Apr. 1852, Hester A. Lowyada   4/ 9/52-2
Seltzer, Wm. H. D., 30 Dec. 1856, Lizzie M. Lindsey   1/ 3/57-2
Selvage, William, 12 Aug. 1858, Ellen Bowers   8/14/58-2
Selway, Frederick, 4 July 1852, Ann Hubbard   7/ 7/52-2
Selway, William, 18 May 1857, Mary V. Pridgeon   5/21/57-2
Senseney, George F., 4 Nov. 1851, Mary Helen Gallaher, dau. of
    John S.   11/11/51-2
Serman, John, 12 Jan. 1858, Theodocia E. Leonard   1/14/58-2
Serrin, Dan'l. C., 14 Jan. 1851, Catherine Miller   1/17/51-2
Serrin, William D., 6 Nov. 1851, Sarah A. Camberland   11/10/51-2
Sessford, George A., 12 Sept. 1852, Mary Ann Isaac   9/14/52-2
Severe, William, 31 Jan. 1857, Mary A. Williamson   2/ 7/57-2
Severe, Wm. Thomas, 14 July 1859, Henrietta Jane Harris   7/18/59-2
Sevier, Wm. H., 16 Aug. 1852, Susannah Cowman, dau. of Richard
    and Mary Ann   9/16/52-2
Seving, John R., 17 Apr. 1851, Sarah A. Zimmerman   4/19/51-2
Seward, Edward S., 29 May 1851, Drucilla C. Ward   6/ 4/51-2
Seward, Levin J., 11 June 1854, Sarah C. James   6/13/54-2
Seward, William E., 1 Jan. 1851, Anner Louisa Oldner   1/ 3/51-2
Seward, William H. (Capt.), 31 May 1853, Elizabeth M. Aikman   6/ 3/53-2
Sewell, John T., 7 Feb. 1856, Amelia A. Layfield; 2/16/56-2   2/18/56-2
Sewell, Perry V., 1 May 1851, Hester Ann Tarter, dau. of Henry   5/ 3/51-2
Seymore, David F., 30 Dec. 1852, Ann L. Hann   1/ 4/53-2
Seymour, Samuel, 28 Oct. 1855, Sarah A. Skipper   10/30/55-2
Seymour, William C. S., 6 Oct. 1859, Mary E. Goodman   10/11/59-2
Seymour, Z. A., 7 May 1854, Margaret Dixon   5/ 9/54-2
Seys, Henry H. (Dr.), 17 Nov. 1853, Hattie H. Foote, dau. of
    (Hon.) A.   11/22/53-2
Sh-(?)-gars, James, 11 Aug. 1853, Margaret A. Four-(?)-man   8/19/53-2
Shade, David, 28 May 1857, Sarah Urilla Amey, dau. of John R.   6/ 9/57-2
Shaeffer, William H., 20 Nov. 1860, Sarah E. Ousler   11/21/60-2
Shaffer, Chas., 14 Sept. 1851, Ellenor Elizabeth Kurtz   9/23/51-2
Shaffer, Chas. H., 27 May 1856, Catharine J. Christopher, dau.
    of Michael and Mary Ann   6/ 4/56-2
Shaffer, Daniel, 4 Sept. 1859, Elizabeth E. Wood   9/12/59-2
Shaffer, Fred. Littig, Jr., 10 Nov. 1859, Georgia Louderman,
    dau. of Henry R.; corrected copy   11/15/59-2
Shaffer, George T., 25 Mar. 1860, Mary E. Santflaben   5/18/60-2
Shaffer, John W., Jr., 3 Oct. 1859, Caroline H. Smith   10/ 5/59-2
Shaffer, Thomas H., 27 Apr. 1854, Rose Ann Meekum   4/29/54-2
Shaffner, Peter R., 21 Dec. 1851, Ann C. Solomon   12/27/51-2
Shakespear, Nathan, 15 Nov. 1855, Matilda A. Crouch   11/17/55-2
Shakespeare, Jonathan, 15 Nov. 1855, Amanda A. Crouch;
    corrected copy   11/19/55-2
Shakspear, Oliver P., 29 Apr. 1857, Eliza Jane Freeburger   5/30/57-2
Shallus, Frank H., 11 May 1858, Isabel Cursey   5/13/58-2
Shan, Bernard, 27 May 1857, Mary Simpson   6/ 5/57-2
Shanahan, Patrick, 30 Mar. 1856, (Mrs.) (?) Freeley   4/ 1/56-2
Shane, Edward M., 22 Jan. 1857, Henrietta Gray   2/ 6/57-2
Shane, George R., 10 Dec. 1851, Margaret Merson   12/13/51-2
Shane, Irvin A., 24 Oct. 1860, Mary E. Stuart   10/25/60-2
Shane, Joseph W., 1 June 1854, Amand C. Geleach   6/ 6/54-2
Shaney, John A., 1 Jan. 1852, Mary Jane Rodgers   1/ 6/52-2
Shank, George W., 10 Nov. 1857, (Mrs.) Barbary Panks   11/13/57-2
Shanks, Thomas, 7 July 1852, Priscilla D. Lester   7/12/52-2

Shannon, Geo. B., 31 Aug. 1858, Victoria Corry, dau. of
    William   9/ 8/58-2
Shannon, James, 13 Jan. 1859, Julia Ann Hakesley   1/15/59-2
Shannon, Wm. A., 22 Feb. 1859, Rhoda East   2/23/59-2
Sharer, Wm. G., 23 Dec. 1853, Rachel P. Perne, dau. of
    Maulden   12/24/53-2
Sharnitsky, John, 8 Apr. 1860, Adelaide Rudigier   4/10/60-2
Sharp, A. P., 16 Jan. 1851, Anna H. Matthews, dau. of Joshua 1/20/51-2
Sharp, Charles, 26 June 1856, Esther E. Leatherburry   7/ 2/56-2
Sharp, Henry, 24 June 1858, (Mrs.) Laura Miller   6/26/58-2
Sharp, Isaac Byron, 12 June 1860, Nettie Bennett, dau. of (Col.)
    A. B.   6/28/60-2
Sharp, William H. H., 17 Sept. 1859, Fannie Rayhice   9/20/59-2
Sharply, Samuel D., 23 June 1859, Mary E. Taylor   7/ 7/59-2
Shauck, Jarerett M., 20 May 1852, Emily C. Berry   5/21/52-2
Shaul, Benjamin L., 27 Dec. 1859, Esther A. Culver   12/28/59-2
Shaul, Joseph W.; no date given, Amanda Gelbach, dau. of
    Nathan and Mary Ci-(?)-bin, adopted dau. of George and
    Ana   6/16/54-2
Shaw, Arthur, 20 Aug. 1854, (Mrs.) Eliza McFadden   8/29/54-2
Shaw, Bernard, 13 Mar. 1853, Susan C. Cook   3/15/53-2
Shaw, Bernard, 27 May 1857, Mary Simpson   6/ 4/57-2
Shaw, Christopher, 4 Feb. 1857, Julia A. Langdon, dau. of
    Giles S.   2/ 5/57-2
Shaw, Daniel J., 10 Mar. 1853, Susan R. Vore   3/12/53-2
Shaw, Emanuel, 6 Oct. 1859, Sarah Jane Fort   10/14/59-2
Shaw, George S., 29 Apr. 1858, Amelia R. Waidner, dau. of
    Louis A.   5/ 1/58-2
Shaw, Greenbury W., 10 Feb. 1859, Ann Eliza Travers   2/11/59-2
Shaw, John Eyres, 13 Apr. 1858, Ann Rebecca Watkins   4/19/58-2
Shaw, Richard J. E., 17 Dec. 1855, Henrietta Jeffers   12/20/55-2
Shaw, Thomas J., 24 May 1853, Mary Ann Fonce   5/26/53-2
Shaw, William H., 21 Apr. 1853, Annie E. Kelley, dau. of Wm. P. 4/23/53-2
Shawn, Samuel Charles, 5 July 1855, Mary Jane Nally, dau. of
    Richard and Mary   7/ 7/55-2
Shay, W. C. (Col.), 15 Apr. 1858, Annie Upp, dau. of Henry 4/22/58-2
Shea, William, 24 Aug. 1851, (Mrs.) Sarah Hacket   9/ 4/51-2
Sheafer, C. F. (Dr.), 2 June 1859, J. Ellie Caufman, dau. of
    H. W.   6/ 6/59-2
Shearer, William, 16 Sept. 1858, Agnes Carr   9/18/58-2
Shearwood, Charles W., 1 Dec. 1859, Catherine J. Hart   12/ 6/59-2
Sheehan, James A., 10 July 1855, Ellen A. McElroy, dau. of
    John   7/14/55-2
Sheehan, Maurice, 11 Feb. 1855, Mary R. Kelly   2/15/55-2
Sheehan, Thomas, 28 Oct. 1860, Catherine Casidy   10/30/60-2
Sheets, James M., 9 Sept. 1852, Caroline L. Miller   9/13/52-2
Sheets, Wm. H., 16 Feb. 1858, Mary A. Peercell   2/19/58-2
Sheetz, Geo. T., 30 Dec. 1852, Rebecca Jane Jackson, dau. of
    (Capt.) A. I. W.   1/ 4/53-2
Sheetz, Henry C., 25 Apr. 1852, Maria Fitzpatrick   4/26/52-2
Sheffield, George W., 29 Jan. 1857, Anna M. Fell, dau. of
    Phillip S.   1/31/57-2
Sheffield, James, 27 Dec. 1858, (Mrs.) Rosabella Drake, dau. of
    Andrew Armstrong   1/26/59-2
Sheffield, John P., 6 Nov. 1852, Mary A. Evans   11/16/52-2
Shehan, Daniel, 27 Feb. 1857, Mary Kelly   3/ 3/57-2
Shehan, Edward, 17 Aug. 1858, Catherine O'Neill   10/ 4/58-2
Shehan, George A., 29 July 1858, Catherine Louisa Davis   1/22/59-2
Shekell, C. F., 19 Sept. 1853, Mary Eliza Leavitt, dau. of
    John   10/ 1/53-2
Shekell, Richard A., 15 Nov. 1853, Lottie A. Edmonston, dau. of
    J. A.   11/22/53-2
Sheldon, James, 23 Dec. 1852, Rachel Mason   12/28/52-2
Sheldon, Robert, 26 Sept. 1859, George Ellen Russell, dau. of
    James and Martha   1/11/60-2

Shenkel, Philip C., 18 Feb. 1858, Caroline Dickel   3/12/58-2
Shennick, John H., 1 June 1858, Frances E. Willis   6/ 7/58-2
Sheperd, John, 11 Oct. 1853, Jane Hopkins   10/19/53-2
Shepherd, George T., 10 July 1851, Susanna R. A. Spicer   7/14/51-2
Shepherd, William H., 7 Jan. 1851, Augusta S. Moffitt, dau. of
    William   1/ 9/51-2
Shepherd, Wm. Hy., 10 Dec. 1856, M. Pattison Keene, dau. of
    Richard C.   12/11/56-2
Sheppard, John, 26 Jan. 1853, Harriet Edel, dau. of Josiah   2/ 3/53-2
Sheppard, John T., 12 Apr. 1851, Isabella G. Barrett   9/ 2/51-2
Shepperd, James Henry, 2 Feb. 1851, Hetty Maria Markes   2/ 8/51-2
Shepperd, N. C. (Dr.), 18 Oct. 1859, E. Laura Meeds, dau. of E. 10/28/59-2
Sheppherd, Edwin T., 13 Dec. 1859, Marguirite A. Stephenson,
    dau. of John   12/15/59-2
Sheradine, Luther, 1 Jan. 1852, Mary Jane Baker   1/ 5/52-2
Sherar, Albert, 23 Aug. 1856, Maggie McConner, dau. of M.   12/25/56-2
Sherar, Albert, 28 Aug. 1856, Maggie O'Conner, dau. of M.;
    corrected copy   12/27/56-2
Sheridan, Wm. H. (Dr.), 31 Oct. 1854, Ellenora Cook, dau. of
    Wm.; corrected copy   11/ 3/54-2
Sheridan, Wm. R. (Dr.), 31 Oct. 1854, Hanora Cook, dau. of Wm.   11/ 2/54-2
Sherlock, William, 17 Dec. 1860, Caroline Glenn   12/21/60-2
Sherman, Wm. R.; no date given, Mary D. Colscott   12/22/58-2
Sherrer, John, 7 Sept. 1856, Jane M. Moffitt   9/10/56-2
Sherwood, George W., 28 Nov. 1854, Mary A. Hardesty, dau. of
    R. C.   11/29/54-2
Sherwood, Wm. Jesse, 2 Sept. 1858, Mary Ellen McKewin   9/ 7/58-2
Shewbrooks, Thomas F., 27 Mar. 1856, Laura E. K. Day   3/29/56-2
Shields, John, 14 Nov. 1851, (Mrs.) Agnes Fulton   11/24/51-2
Shields, Geo. W., 22 May 1860, Matilda Chapman   5/24/60-2
Shields, John A., 29 Jan. 1852, Mary Jane Dilworth   2/ 2/52-2
Shillington, Joseph (Col.), 5 May 1856, Lizzie Cummings   6/ 6/56-2
Shillington, Joseph (Col.), 5 June 1856, Lizzie Cummings;
    corrected copy   6/ 7/56-2
Shipley, Andrew W., 12 Apr. 1855, Fanny C. Lane   4/17/55-2
Shipley, Brice G., 27 Jan. 1859, Mary A. Bleakley, dau. of
    Saml. H.   1/31/59-2
Shipley, Columbus G., 9 Sept. 1852, Sarah V. Stiver   9/13/52-2
Shipley, Francis M., 2 Aug. 1855, Emily V. Hooper   8/ 7/55-2
Shipley, George E., 23 Feb. 1858, Mary Jane Harman, dau. of
    Andrew, Jr.   2/25/58-2
Shipley, George W., 18 Dec. 1853, Mary M. Skipper   12/29/53-2
Shipley, Henry B., 26 Oct. 1859, Susan Bidinger   12/19/59-2
Shipley, John T., 1 May 1859, Virginia E. Walters   5/11/59-2
Shipley, John W., 3 Mar. 1859, Mary E. Kircher   3/ 5/59-2
Shipley, Johnzee L., 10 Dec. 1856, Louisa A. Gawthrop   12/17/56-2
Shipley, Lovelace, 27 June 1853, Harriet R. Gosnell, dau. of
    William   6/29/53-2
Shipley, Plummer, 9 June 1857, Rebecca Duwees   6/10/57-2
Shipley, Richard, 2 Dec. 1852, Agnes C. Quail, dau. of James R. 12/ 4/52-2
Shipley, Samuel T., 7 Dec. 1852, Mary E. Worthington, dau. of
    Rezin H.   12/14/52-2
Shipley, Talbott G., 7 Dec. 1854, Elizabeth W. Dorsey;
    12/12/54-2   12/13/54-2
Shipley, Theodore H., 20 Nov. 1851, Susanna C. Rowles   11/24/51-2
Shipley, Thomas H., 14 July 1859, Ann Maria Sindall   7/27/59-2
Shipley, Thos., 28 Oct. 1852, Mary Burke   11/ 1/52-2
Shipley, Wm. B., 29 Nov. 1860, Eliza Jane Coursey   12/ 1/60-2
Shirey, John, 25 Jan. 1860, Sarah E. A. Mercer   1/30/60-2
Shirk, Isaac, 2 Dec. 1852, Catharine S. Orrick, dau. of Wm. K.   12/ 3/52-2
Shirley, Walter, 6 Apr. 1854, E. Sophia Bosley, dau. of Amon   4/12/54-2
Shivers, John, 7 June 1857, Sarah E. Sullivan   6/ 9/57-2
Shivers, Nicholas, 24 Feb. 1853, Eveline Melvina Gorthrop   2/28/53-2
Shock, F. A., 14 Jan. 1857, Virginia Scott, dau. of Andrew   1/17/57-2
Shockley, Lizzie, 21 Nov. 1859, G. P. H. Sinsz   11/22/59-2

Shoemaker, George W., 16 Apr. 1855, Mary Virginia Bradley   4/19/55-2
Shoemaker, Lewis W., 13 Jan. 1853, Mary R. Parks   1/15/53-2
Shoemaker, Samuel M., 28 Dec. 1853, Augusta C. Eccleston, dau.
     of (Hon.) John B.   1/ 2/54-2
Shoemaker, Thomas E.; no date given, Sarah Jane Hubbard   8/ 8/57-2
Shoeman, Frederick, 6 May 1858, Sophia L. Kraus   5/11/58-2
Shook, Jacob, 18 Jan. 1858, Laura Jane Mitchell   1/22/58-2
Short, Benj. F., 24 July 1856, Elizabeth Guyton   8/ 1/56-2
Short, John H., 2 Dec. 1852, Elizabeth A. Parker   12/ 4/52-2
Shorter, William T., 6 Oct. 1853, Laura A. R. Sanner   10/10/53-2
Shott, Joseph A., 11 Dec. 1853, Sarah Elizabeth Evans, dau.
     of William   12/14/53-2
Shott, Joseph A., 1 June 1859, Molley A. Keenright, dau. of
     Nicholas   6/ 9/59-2
Showacre, George W., 11 Mar. 1851, Mary Ann Bertline Thomas   3/13/51-2
Showacre, Josiah S., 10 July 1860, Sophia E. Barnes   8/30/60-2
Showalter, Henry, 24 Aug. 1852, Elizabeth Cecilia Robinson;
     corrected copy   8/31/52-2
Showalter, Wm. Henry, 24 Aug. 1852, Eliza Cecilia Robinson   8/25/52-2
Shreck, J. W. F., 31 Mar. 1853, Margaret A. Jeffers, dau. of
     Benjamin   4/ 2/53-2
Shreck, William C. W., 31 Mar. 1853, Eliza G. Gaw, dau. of
     William   4/ 5/53-2
Shreeve, Jesse (Rev.), 16 Oct. 1856, Margaret A. Huppman   10/17/56-2
Shreiner, George Washington, 9 May 1858, Mary B. Sprucebank   5/12/58-2
Shreve, James H., Jr., 8 Dec. 1857, Carrie E. Ray   12/14/57-2
Shriner, Peter, 17 June 1857, Kate Louisa Ness   6/20/57-2
Shriver, A. J., 31 Mar. 1858, Jenny Brown   4/ 1/58-2
Shriver, D. C., 14 Oct. 1856, Louisa Farnham   10/15/56-2
Shriver, Henry C., 10 May 1855, Hannah S. Bennett, dau. of
     John   5/12/55-2
Shriver, Thomas W., 14 Aug. 1851, Anna Sturdy   8/16/51-2
Shriver, William, Jr., 15 May 1860, C. Roberta Lyon   5/28/60-2
Shroder, Joseph, 27 Jan. 1859, Christina Pffifer   3/10/59-2
Shrotte, William T., 28 Mar. 1853, Maria L. Jones   4/12/53-2
Shryer, George F., 28 Apr. 1853, Mary Evans, dau. of
     Washington   5/ 2/53-2
Shryock, Wm. Henry, 7 Apr. 1857, Eliza J. Foxcroft, adopted
     dau. of Wm. H. Blass   4/ 8/57-2
Shubrook, William H., 3 Nov. 1853, Kezia Love   11/15/53-2
Shuck, Jacob, 10 Jan. 1854, Anna McCuen   1/16/54-2
Shuck, Jacob, 18 Jan. 1857, Laura Jane Mitchell, dau. of
     Washington   2/ 5/58-2
Shue, William Henry, 28 Sept. 1852, Christiana Lee   10/ 5/52-2
Shultz, Alfred, 29 June 1860, Cornelia Smith   11/14/60-2
Shultze, Augustus D., 28 Sept. 1858, Indiana A. Fuller   10/ 1/58-2
Shuman, S. T., 12 Oct. 1859, Florence W. Norris   10/15/59-2
Shunk, James F., son of (Gov.) Francis R., 10 Mar. 1858,
     Rebecca Black, dau. of (Hon.) Jeremiah S.   3/17/58-2
Shyne, Michael R., 3 Mar. 1851, Catharine O'Bryan   3/ 4/51-2
Siberry, Edw'd., 26 Aug. 1852, Elily Grimes   9/ 7/52-2
Sibrett, William H., 1 Jan. 1855, Mary J. McKee   2/19/55-2
Sickel, John L., 11 Jan. 1859, Emily J. Brooks, dau. of Wm.   1/13/59-2
Siddons, William, 14 Oct. 1857, Mary Frances Cunningham, dau. of
     John T.   10/17/57-2
Siebert, John, 2 Nov. 1856, Margaret Herz   11/ 4/56-2
Silence, Charles Andrew, 1 Sept. 1857, Anna Catherine Collins   9/ 2/57-2
Silver, Amos, 15 Nov. 1852, Sarah Ann Evans   11/19/52-2
Sim, Robert, 28 Apr. 1853, Martha Thompson   4/30/53-2
Simmons, Francis, 14 Oct. 1853, Anna Elizabeth McWilliams   10/12/53-2
Simmons, Isaac S., 18 Nov. 1851, Mary Ann G. Shipley   11/27/51-2
Simms, Albert C., 12 June 1860, Clara L. Mitchell   6/22/60-2
Simms, James, 6 Jan. 1853, Priscilla Painter   1/ 8/53-2
Simms, Richard E., 1 Feb. 1853, Fanny L. G. Stearns, niece of
     Alphifus Hyatt   2/ 2/53-2

Simms, William Henry, 19 June 1858, Josephine Keys	6/21/58-2
Simon, Wm., 11 Jan. 1854, Hannah Weglein, dau. of A.	1/13/54-2
Simond, Jos. Easton, 9 Jan. 1853, Sarah D. Cord	1/12/53-2
Simonson, John W., 13 Sept. 1860, Rosa B. Bunting	9/29/60-2
Simpers, Amos E., 24 Sept. 1855, Eliza J. Akers	9/25/55-2
Simpson, Alexander, 9 Feb. 1860, Agnes Greer	2/11/60-2
Simpson, E. Ford, 13 Jan. 1853, Ada Shipley, dau. of Benj.	1/14/53-2
Simpson, Falk, 5 Mar. 1854, Mina Kraut	3/ 8/54-2
Simpson, George, 8 Nov. 1853, Rachel Booth	11/11/53-2
Simpson, George B., 3 Oct. 1855, Isabel Perry, dau. of Jeremiah	10/ 5/55-2
Simpson, George B., 17 Feb. 1857, Louisa Jane Preuss	2/23/57-2
Simpson, George L., 1 Sept. 1860, Maggie J. L. Newman	9/ 5/60-2
Simpson, George W., 5 July 1860, Mary Cookes	7/ 9/60-2
Simpson, Henry C., 7 Mar. 1858, Mary Rebecca Harryman	3/ 9/58-2
Simpson, James, 31 July 1853, Eliza J. McEllwain	8/ 8/53-2
Simpson, John Alpha, 18 Oct. 1859, Emily Virginia Phillips	10/22/59-2
Simpson, John T., 16 May 1855, Elizabeth Jane Busick	5/17/55-2
Simpson, John T., 15 Nov. 1860, Sarah A. Vanhorn	11/20/60-2
Simpson, Luther R., 21 Aug. 1851, Frances A. Boyle	8/26/51-2
Simpson, Thomas B., 28 Mar. 1854, Eliza Ann Starr, dau. of G. W.	3/30/54-2
Simpson, Thomas V., 4 Apr. 1858, Hester A. Armstrong	5/ 7/58-2
Simpson, Wm. B., 11 Feb. 1855, Catharine Armstrong	2/12/55-2
Simpson, Wm. R., 22 Jan. 1857, Anna M. Smick	1/27/57-2
Sims, John, 19 Sept. 1858, Martha Ann Willis	9/21/58-2
Sindall, John T., 14 June 1860, Ann E. Markley	7/ 4/60-2
Singleton, Thomas H., 26 Dec. 1860, Susan Jane Brooks	12/28/60-2
Sisco, James, 11 Mar. 1860, Elizabeth Chew	3/13/60-2
Sisselberger, Andrew, 31 Mar. 1859, Mary Hunter	11/30/59-2
Sitler, Alexander J., 6 June 1858, Martha A. R. Tolson	6/10/58-2
Sims, Thomas, 18 June 1857, Mary A. Champhee	8/14/57-2
Simson, Robert, 21 May 1854, Mary Ann Shipley	11/14/54-2
Simson, Walter, 3 Sept. 1853, (Mrs.) Elizabeth Smith	9/ 9/53-2
Simund, James Easton, 9 Jan. 1853, Sarah D. Cord; corrected copy	1/13/53-2
Sinclair, Charles W., 30 May 1854, Victorine W. Niles	6/ 1/54-2
Sinclair, George W., 25 Mar. 1856, Ellen Wald	3/31/56-2
Sinclair, William M., 3 Dec. 1854, Madaline Colbert	12/ 5/54-2
Sindall, S. L., 18 June 1857, Maggie E. Isaacs, dau. of Jonathan	6/24/57-2
Singafoos, John F., 3 July 1853, Ann Eliza Shaffer	7/19/53-2
Single, Daniel, 24 Sept. 1854, Ann Eaton	9/30/54-2
Singleton, John N., 16 Aug. 1854, Sallie Smith, dau. of James Baxter	8/17/54-2
Sinn, Wm. E., 30 May 1852, Anna Eliza Bonn	6/ 7/52-2
Sinskey, John William, 24 June 1856, Sarah J. Granrath	7/ 1/56-2
Sisson, Martin A., 7 Feb. 1856, Kate N. Stewart, dau. of John	2/ 8/56-2
Skaggs, Henry S., 17 Mar. 1858, Lydia R. Ford, dau. of Wm.	4/ 9/58-2
Skillman, George R., 22 Apr. 1858, Mary E. Pierce	4/24/58-2
Skinner, James H., 21 May 1856, Joshuanna German, dau. of Joshua	5/28/56-2
Skinner, James W., 2 Nov. 1851, Ellen Phelps	11/ 4/51-2
Skinner, John J., 9 Oct. 1856, Margaretta M. Teal	10/10/56-2
Skinner, Joseph H., 25 June 1857, Sarah Amanda Hall	7/ 3/57-2
Skinner, O. C., 1 Sept. 1853, Sarah J. Witon, dau. of Henry	9/ 2/53-2
Skinner, Robert C. (Capt.), 31 Jan. 1853, Martha A. Blunt	2/ 1/53-2
Skinner, Samuel T., 10 Feb. 1853, Rachael A. Willis	3/18/53-2
Skinner, Thos. E., 8 Mar. 1853, Martha H. Meginniss	3/10/53-2
Skinner, Thomas B. (Capt.), 16 Oct. 1851, Sarah R. German	10/18/51-2
Skinner, Thos. R. (Capt.), 11 June 1853, Priscilla Bucey	6/15/53-2
Skinner, William H., 26 Apr. 1854, Martha Ann Wilson	4/27/54-2
Skinner, Wm. T., 24 May 1857, Laura V. Steadman	6/ 3/57-2
Skipper, John W., 28 Dec. 1859, Mary C. Dorman	1/10/60-2
Skipper, Joseph, 27 Nov. 1859, E. Ann Arnold	11/29/59-2

```
Skivington, David, 20 June 1855, Catharine McDermott          6/21/55-2
Skyler, John, 1 Sept. 1859, Caroline Deater                   9/ 3/59-2
Slack, Amos W., 9 Aug. 1857, Eliza J. Ward                    8/17/57-2
Slack, John, 15 Feb. 1853, (Mrs.) Jane Sutton                 2/26/53-2
Slack, John W., 14 Oct. 1851, Martha R. Broome               10/16/51-2
Slacum, James L., 1 May 1856, Mary C. Winchester              5/ 5/56-2
Slade, J. Albert, 7 Sept. 1855, Hettie A. Barr                9/12/55-2
Slagle, Charles W., 8 Nov. 1860, Rachel A. Matthews          11/10/60-2
Slagle, Henry C., 29 Dec. 1858, Jane Faukland                12/31/58-2
Slane, John W., 11 May 1857, Bridget Droney                   5/12/57-2
Slasman, Alexander, 20 July 1857, Sarah Rebecca West          7/22/57-2
Slater, George Washington, 13 Aug. 1855, Ann Glenn           9/14/55-2
Slater, Henry, 3 May 1853, Susan Porter                      5/16/53-2
Slater, John H. C., 30 May 1854, Harriet P. Reay             6/ 1/54-2
Slater, John L., 21 Sept. 1859, Olive Shorey                 9/27/59-2
Slater, Robert J., 31 July 1856, Lydia F. Glass, dau. of Isaac  10/ 9/56-2
Slater, Samuel J., 9 June 1859, Kate Robb                    6/13/59-2
Slater, William, 8 June 1858, Mary E. McAllister             6/11/58-2
Slaughter, Daniel, 10 Nov. 1859, Margaret Dorsey            11/12/59-2
Slauter, Adolph F., 2 Oct. 1859, Georgeann Heslin           10/13/59-2
Sleade, Lewis, 21 May 1855, (Mrs.) Mary Bealey               5/23/55-2
Sleeper, John C., 28 Apr. 1859, Asia Booth, dau. of Junius B.  4/30/59-2
Slepper, G. A., 30 Oct. 1856, (Mrs.) Cecelia Chenoweth      12/30/56-2
Slevin, Michael, 2 Aug. 1857, Margaret McDermott             8/13/57-2
Slicer, Henry W., 15 Dec. 1856, Rosabella Cooper            12/17/56-2
Slincer, James B., 16 Dec. 1858, Mary M. C. Thomas          12/18/58-2
Slingluff, Upton, 15 Aug. 1855, Mary F. Cookey, dau. of (Maj.)
     Jos.                                                    8/16/55-2
Sloan, Hugh, 7 July 1854, Mary Collins                       7/27/54-2
Sloan, James, Jr., 26 Apr. 1860, Abbie L. Huppman            5/ 2/60-2
Sloan, John Q., 9 Oct. 1851, Lizzie C. Richstein            10/11/51-2
Sloan, Samuel A., 2 Feb. 1854, Mary C. Allderdice, dau. of
     Abraham                                                 2/ 4/54-2
Sloane, Francis J., 11 Feb. 1858, Ella Young, dau. of James  2/13/58-2
Sloann, Hugh, 7 July 1854, Mary Cullen                       7/26/54-2
Slocum, Stephen T., 17 May 1853, Mary Jane Lamy, dau. of John B.  5/31/53-2
Slodfeld, Frederick L. D., 2 Jan. 1851, Henrietta Melchoir   1/ 4/51-2
Slothower, Geo. E., 4 Sept. 1855, Maria R. Randall           9/14/55-2
Slye, A. B., 29 Dec. 1857, Susan R. Sothoron                12/31/57-2
Small, Bruce, 30 Sept. 1858, Fannie J. Fowler               10/11/58-2
Small, George, 13 Jan. 1852, Mary Grant Jackson, dau. of
     (Capt.) Wm. A.                                          1/15/52-2
Small, Jacob, 9 Oct. 1860, Rebecca Hopkins, dau. of James   10/11/60-2
Small, Latimer, 19 June 1860, Mary S. Wilson, dau. of Wilson  6/20/60-2
Small, Leon, 10 Feb. 1859, Caroline Rebecca Cook             2/12/59-2
Small, William, 20 May 1852, Emily Adam, dau. of John        5/25/52-2
Smardon, John G., 2 Mar. 1851, Ann R. Butler, dau. of Larkin  3/ 5/51-2
Smedley, Jonathan H., 13 Nov. 1856, Christiana R. Golds-
     borough                                                11/17/56-2
Smelcer, Chas. A., 4 May 1852, Caroline C. Stewart           5/ 8/52-2
Smick, Peter W., 23 July 1857, Marianne Knox; corrected copy  8/ 5/57-2
Smick, Peter W., 30 July 1857, Marianne Knox                 8/ 3/57-2
Smiley, James, 22 Nov. 1855, Isabella Greenwood             11/26/55-2
Smiley, Wm., 27 Jan. 1853, Anna Phillips                     2/ 1/53-2
Smith, Alexander, 29 Sept. 1860, Elizabeth Hawkins          10/ 1/60-2
Smith, Alison, 3 Dec. 1857, Sarah A. Wright                 12/ 4/57-2
Smith, Andrew, 11 Aug. 1851, Margaret Horner                 8/16/51-2
Smith, Asa H., 12 Apr. 1855, Emily S. Marriott               5/10/55-2
Smith, Augustine J., Jr., 6 Mar. 1855, Sarah Chew O'Donnell,
     dau. of John                                            3/ 7/55-2
Smith, B. B., 1 Aug. 1859, Eveline V. LeGrand                8/ 2/59-2
Smith, Berwick B. (Dr.), 20 Apr. 1854, Nannie W. Moale, dau.
     of (Col.) Saml.                                         4/25/54-2
Smith, C. DeWitt, 18 Oct. 1859, Elizabeth Howard Meredith, dau.
     of James                                               10/25/59-2
```

Smith, C. Roberts, 1 Dec. 1857, Carrie P. Fowble, dau. of	
W. H.	12/ 3/57-2
Smith, Charles, 11 May 1854, Mary Ellen Jackson	5/13/54-2
Smith, Charles, 2 Dec. 1858, Moseline Frncis	12/ 4/58-2
Smith, Charles Henry, 10 Aug. 1853, Ann Maria Bathell	8/13/53-2
Smith, Charles W., 13 Sept. 1857, Mary Ann Madden	9/26/57-2
Smith, Charles Winston, 10 Jan. 1859, Rebecca Hart	1/11/59-2
Smith, Chas., 10 May 1858, Rachel Ann Sanders	5/12/58-2
Smith, Chas. C., 28 May 1856, Lydia R. Griffith	6/13/56-2
Smith, Chas. F., 2 Sept. 1852, Matilda Bowen	9/14/52-2
Smith, Cornelius, 4 Oct. 1860, Hannah Lemmon	10/ 6/60-2
Smith, Cyrus E., 17 May 1853, Harriet Haney	5/21/53-2
Smith, D. C., 19 Nov. 1860, Lucretia H. Duvall, dau. of Allen	11/26/60-2
Smith, Ebenezer, 22 June 1853, Jane Scott	6/28/53-2
Smith, Edwin, 20 Dec. 1855, Susannah Peters, dau. of William	12/22/55-2
Smith, Edwin H., 6 Feb. 1855, Virginia C. Lownds	2/ 7/55-2
Smith, Elijah, 30 Oct. 1853, Eliza Thompson	11/ 1/53-2
Smith, F. G., 3 July 1854, Rachel Pearson	7/ 6/54-2
Smith, Francis, 2 Mar. 1852, Harriet L. Parmelee	3/ 3/52-2
Smith, Frank C., 15 Jan. 1856, Alice Bussey	1/19/56-2
Smith, Frederick, 8 Sept. 1857, Amelia Wise	9/10/57-2
Smith, Fred'k., 28 Oct. 1852, (Mrs.) Maria F. Baurgelt;	
11/ 1/52-2; 11/ 2/52-2	11/ 3/52-2
Smith, G. W. P., 15 Jan. 1856, Elmira C. Purnell, dau. of	
John F.	2/ 7/56-2
Smith, Geo. T., 11 July 1853, Margaret A. Green	7/26/53-2
Smith, Geo. W., 23 Nov. 1852, Isabella E. Dix	12/ 6/52-2
Smith, Geo. W., 27 June 1858, Henrietta Northern	6/29/58-2
Smith, George, 18 Dec. 1851, Sophia Sampson	12/20/51-2
Smith, George A., 12 July 1860, Catherine Moylan	7/17/60-2
Smith, George C., 21 Dec. 1851, Sarah E. Slaughter, dau. of	
John T.	12/23/51-2
Smith, George W., 16 Nov. 1859, Mary A. Degaw	11/21/59-2
Smith, Henry, 30 Jan. 1851, Olivia Harvey	2/ 1/51-2
Smith, Henry, 14 Sept. 1851, Mary Ann Gordon	9/18/51-2
Smith, Henry, 7 Feb. 1854, Ann M. Britt	2/18/54-2
Smith, Henry, 21 Dec. 1854, Josephine V. Tilyard	12/25/54-2
Smith, Henry, 2 Oct. 1859, Sarah Jane Howard	10/ 4/59-2
Smith, Henry C., 15 Sept. 1853, Eliza Tash	9/24/53-2
Smith, Henry C., 21 June 1859, Pattie Harbert, dau. of	
Charles	6/27/59-2
Smith, Henry Jacob, 7 Jan. 1858, Ann Eliza Merson	1/12/58-2
Smith, Herman W., 8 Feb. 1851, Martha Backman	2/12/51-2
Smith, Isaac, 7 Oct. 1860, Sarah Thomas	10/ 9/60-2
Smith, Isaac M., 26 Sept. 1853, Virginia Delany	9/27/53-2
Smith, Isaac N., 17 July 1855, (Mrs.) Sarah L. Hall	7/19/55-2
Smith, J. Edward, 17 Aug. 1852, Mary E. Segerman	8/19/52-2
Smith, J. H., 10 May 1860, Mattie Tyler, dau. of Wm., niece	
of (Pres.) Jno.	5/15/60-2
Smith, J. Jacob, 6 Jan. 1855, Joseba E. Gardner, dau. of Wm.	1/16/55-2
Smith, J. W., 16 Apr. 1857, Rosa A. Martin	4/25/57-2
Smith, J. Wilson, 23 Feb. 1853, Amelia Shipley, dau. of Henry	2/25/53-2
Smith, James, 1 Nov. 1853, Elizabeth A. Gessforo	11/10/53-2
Smith, James, 14 Sept. 1857, Fanny Coupland, dau. of Richard	9/16/57-2
Smith, James, 29 July 1860, Christianna Magaw	9/13/60-2
Smith, James, 20 Dec. 1860, Alice Vernay	12/21/60-2
Smith, James F., 12 Mar. 1857, Elizabeth A. Adams	3/24/57-2
Smith, James H., 8 Jan. 1852, Anna E. Brown	1/10/52-2
Smith, James H. (Capt.), 19 May 1853, Sarah E. Morris	5/21/53-2
Smith, James J., 1 Jan. 1854, Mary Spear	1/ 6/54-2
Smith, James L., 29 Mrs.) Lucinda L. Hough	3/31/54-2
Smith, James L., 6 Nov. 1855, (Mrs.) Mary F. Daly	11/ 7/55-3
Smith, James M., 29 Nov. 1859, Elizabeth Jones	12/ 8/59-2
Smith, James P., 22 Apr. 1856, Margaret M. Darnall	4/25/56-2
Smith, James R., 25 May 1857, Mary M. Steel	6/ 2/57-2

```
Smith, James Rogers, 8 Apr. 1853, Mary A. E. Cononlly        5/21/53-2
Smith, James T., 24 May 1860, Emma E. Peck                   5/26/60-2
Smith, Jas. T., 2 Apr. 1955, Mary F. Starr                   4/ 6/55-2
Smith, John, 3 Mar. 1851, Kate High, dau. of William         3/ 8/51-2
Smith, John, 4 Oct. 1855, Hannah Pervines                   10/ 5/55-2
Smith, John, 14 Apr. 1857, Mary Monahan                      4/20/57-2
Smith, John, 22 Nov. 1859, Mary Beziat                      12/ 8/59-2
Smith, John Alexander, 4 Nov. 1852, Susannah McKendree, dau.
  of Joshua Holland                                         11/10/52-2
Smith, John D., 29 Mar. 1859, Mattie Blass                   4/ 1/59-2
Smith, John E. (Capt.), 6 Sept. 1859, Amanda M. Rollins      9/ 7/59-2
Smith, John F., 25 May 1858, Ann Rebecca Tarter              6/ 1/58-2
Smith, John H., 30 May 1853, Ada Haywood                     6/ 2/53-2
Smith, John H., 4 June 1855, Rose Braceland                  6/ 6/55-2
Smith, John H., 23 Dec. 1859, Mary Jane Hill                 1/12/59-2
Smith, John L., 11 June 1857, Virginia C. Smith, dau. of
  James Lownds                                               6/12/57-2
Smith, John M., 14 Apr. 1853, Margaret A. Patterson          4/18/53-2
Smith, John W., 1 June 1857, Mary L. Blacklar                6/ 4/57-2
Smith, Joseph, 10 Apr. 1851, Martha A. Bond, dau. of L. W.   4/16/51-2
Smith, Joseph, 11 Aug. 1853, Ann E. Clarkekey, dau. of Abner 8/16/53-2
Smith, Joseph E., 30 Jan. 1851, Mary Jane Wilsa              2/ 3/51-2
Smith, Josiah, 28 Jan. 1851, Elizabeth Jane Clash            1/29/51-2
Smith, Levin A., 22 Dec. 1853, Annie M. Ballard, dau. of A. H. 12/28/53-2
Smith, Martin, 28 Oct. 1857, Margaret Jane Barclay          10/29/57-2
Smith, Martin L., 20 May 1858, Mollie P. Brown               5/26/58-2
Smith, Michael, 3 July 1851, Eliza Ann Richardson            7/ 9/51-2
Smith, Michael, 1 Mar. 1859, Rosanna Mulligan                6/ 7/59-2
Smith, O. J., 16 Dec. 1859, Annie McWilliams                 7/ 4/60-2
Smith, Peter, 3 Apr. 1855, Mary R. Magruder                  4/ 4/55-2
Smith, Peter, 15 Jan. 1860, Sarah Mars                       2/ 9/60-2
Smith, Prince Albert, 16 Aug. 1860, Catharine Maxfield       8/17/60-2
Smith, R. A., 16 July 1860, Delia Shaw                       7/23/60-2
Smith, R. P., 7 Jan. 1858, Cassie Howlett, dau. of John Q.   1/12/58-2
Smith, Reuben R., 20 Oct. 1856, Jane E. Patmor              12/ 5/56-2
Smith, Richard A., 5 Aug. 1852, Lizzie A. Hergesheimer, dau.
  of Chas.                                                   8/10/52-2
Smith, Robert, 30 Mar. 1852, Sarah Neely                     4/ 1/52-2
Smith, Robert H., 26 Dec. 1856, Sallie E. Jefferson, dau. of
  James                                                      1/ 7/57-2
Smith, Robert H., 28 Dec. 1857, Amanda E. Wilson             1/ 9/57-2
Smith, Robert Z., 23 May 1859, Lilly Murphy                  5/25/59-2
Smith, Rob't. W., 21 Oct. 1852, Amelia Frances Brown, dau. of
  Samuel                                                    11/ 6/52-2
Smith, Sam'l., 11 Mar. 1852, (Mrs.) Margaret Macallister     4/ 2/52-2
Smith, Sam'l. A., 2 Sept. 1852, Harriet Hanson               9/14/52-2
Smith, Sam'l. H. C., 29 Dec. 1851, Mary E. Wise             12/30/51-2
Smith, Sam'l. N., 26 Oct. 1851, Susan L. Townsend           11/ 1/51-2
Smith, Samuel, 12 Dec. 1853, Lucinda Hawkins, dau. of Charles 12/16/53-2
Smith, Samuel, 7 June 1855, Sarah J. H. Day                  6/ 8/55-2
Smith, Samuel, 11 June 1856, Emily Brown                     6/14/56-2
Smith, Samuel A., 23 June 1856, Catharine Dolbow             6/25/56-2
Smith, Thomas, 22 Oct. 1857, Harriet Ann Dickerson          10/24/57-2
Smith, Thomas B., 23 May 1858, E. A. Kirk, dau. of Samuel    5/25/58-2
Smith, Thomas R., 5 Mar. 1854, Sarah J. Spicer               3/ 9/54-2
Smith, Thos. H., 3 Dec. 1851, Mary Jane Collins             12/ 5/51-2
Smith, W. T., 20 Aug. 1855, J. A. Bayley                     9/ 3/55-2
Smith, Walter C., 22 Dec. 1856, Eliza Sidney Buchanan, dau. of
  Robt. S.                                                  12/30/56-2
Smith, William, 5 Dec. 1854, Susan Stapleford               12/ 7/54-2
Smith, William, 4 Jan. 1859, Anna McPherson                  1/ 6/59-2
Smith, William, 20 June 1859, Adeline E. Holtz               7/11/59-2
Smith, William B., 4 Sept. 1856, Elizabeth A. Hush           9/ 9/56-2
Smith, William B., 11 Nov. 1856, Martha E. Mays             11/13/56-2
```

Smith, William H., 29 Sept. 1859, Sophia Sargent Tucker, dau.
   of Enoch; 10/ 1/59-2   10/ 3/59-2
Smith, William H., 25 June 1860, Frances Elizabeth Hart   2/26/60-2
Smith, William Hamilton, 26 Aug. 1858, Thomasina H. Thrall   8/30/58-2
Smith, William J., 12 Sept. 1852, Sarah Ann Kimmell   9/16/52-2
Smith, William J., 5 Jan. 1858, Laura A. Llewellin   1/14/58-2
Smith, William P., 27 Feb. 1851, (Mrs.) Sarah E. Bishop, dau. of
   Joseph K. Holdon   2/28/51-2
Smith, William T., 11 Jan. 1859, Ann Rebecca Wilkinson   1/14/59-2
Smith, William Z., 7 Jan. 1851, Martha Jane Baxter   1/10/51-2
Smith, Witington, 8 Dec. 1859, (Mrs.) Anna E. Harisson   12/10/59-2
Smith, Wm., 23 July 1857, Rachel Lucas   7/27/57-2
Smith, Wm., 23 July 1857, Rachel Ann Lucas; corrected copy   7/27/57-2
Smith, Wm. B. (Capt.), 6 Aug. 1856, Lucy A. Brown   8/16/56-2
Smith, Wm. C., 7 Nov. 1860, Kate C. Venable, dau. of Geo. W. 11/ 8/60-2
Smith, Wm. F., 11 Oct. 1860, L. S. Nicholson   10/18/60-2
Smith, Wm. H., 5 Apr. 1855, Emily J. Dickson   4/ 7/55-2
Smith, Wm. H., 10 May 1860, Mary E. Cornish   5/12/60-2
Smith, Wm. O., 8 May 1851, Fanny Elizabeth Wolf   5/15/51-2
Smith, Wm. R., 11 Oct. 1860, L. S. Nicholson   10/13/60-2
Smithson, John F., 8 May 1851, Emily Tipton   5/10/51-2
Smoot, Alleghany, 1 June 1856, Susan L. Miller, dau. of J. P. 6/ 3/58-2
Smoot, C. C., Jr., 2 Nov. 1854, Susan A. Smoot, dau. of H. B. 11/13/54-2
Smoot, J. W., 18 Nov. 1856, Mary McKenna, dau. of Patrick   11/22/56-2
Smoot, John H., 30 Jan. 1851, Julia Duvall, dau. of (Col.)
   Daniel   2/ 3/51-2
Smouse, Thomas, 10 Apr. 1860, E. Josephine Gallaway, dau. of
   Thomas A.   4/19/60-2
Smyrk, Alfred E., 5 Jan. 1854, Ann Eliza Gray   1/ 9/54-2
Smyser, Adam, Jr., 22 June 1855, Kate Botterill   8/15/55-2
Smyser, Zachariah L., 8 Sept. 1857, Annie M. Sanders; corrected
   copy   9/14/57-2
Smyser, Zeohariah L., 8 Sept. 1857, Annie M. Sanders   9/12/57-2
Smyth, Geo., 12 Oct. 1854, Providence Disney   10/20/54-2
Snavely, Joseph F., 3 Mar. 1857, Elizabeth Ann Bush   3/ 5/57-2
Snider, J. Adrian, 1 Aug. 1855, Cordelia Lake   8/ 2/55-2
Snow, Charles H., 15 June 1852, Ellen Inloes, dau. of William 6/21/52-2
Snow, Edward J., 26 Feb. 1851, Mary E. Inloes, dau. of Wm.   3/ 5/51-2
Snowden, John, 16 June 1857, Sarah E. Hopkins, dau. of Basil B. 6/18/57-2
Snowden, Robert, 7 Mar. 1860, Mary A. Sters   3/10/60-2
Snowden, William, 29 Apr. 1857, Adelaide Warheat, dau. of
   (Dr.) Gustavus   5/ 7/57-2
Snyder, Daniel W., 8 May 1855, Blendia A. Constable; corrected
   copy   5/12/55-2
Snyder, Daniel Webster, 8 May 1855, Belinda Ann Constable   5/10/55-2
Snyder, George, 21 Oct. 1852, Ann Maria Em-(?), dau. of
   John V.   10/22/52-2
Snyder, Henry, 5 June 1854, Maria M. Swain   6/ 7/54-2
Snyder, Henry R., 12 Sept. 1851, Mary Rosanna Rogers Slathour,
   dau. of Catharine Rogers and John   10/11/51-2
Snyder, J. Henry, 30 Dec. 1852, Eliza Jane Brawner, dau. of
   Andrew   1/ 1/53-2
Snyder, Jacob C., 8 Feb. 1854, Eliza Ann Hamilton, dau. of
   John; corrected copy   2/11/54-2
Snyder, Jacob G., 8 Feb. 1854, Clara Ann Hamilton, dau. of John 2/10/54-2
Snyder, John H., 20 Jan. 1852, Martha Ann Baurgelt   1/22/52-2
Snyder, John H., 5 Jan. 1854, Josephine Mask   1/ 6/54-2
Snyder, Joseph T., 14 May 1856, Sarah Louisa Cunningham   5/21/56-2
Snyder, Walter, 25 Sept. 1860, Mary R. Clagett   9/26/60-2
Snyder, William, 23 Dec. 1857, Ann Rebecca Sylvester   12/25/57-2
Sollers, Geo. L., 16 Aug. 1860, Martha A. Johnston   8/17/60-2
Sollers, Jas. H., 1 Jan. 1858, Linda J. Whorton   1/ 4/58-2
Sollers, John J., 21 Nov. 1860, Kate L. Unlack   11/24/60-2
Solomon, Rob't., 23 Sept. 1851, Matilda Allen   9/27/51-2
Solomon, Samuel L., 22 Nov. 1855, Olevia League   11/26/55-2

Somervell, Charles Sewell, 1 Dec. 1853, Margaret Elizabeth
    Weems, dau. of (Dr.) L. L.   12/ 9/53-2
Sommer, John P., 12 Nov. 1857, Mary B. Wirth   11/13/57-2
Sommerlock, John F., 5 Sept. 1855, Anna Wilkins   9/ 7/55-2
Sommers, H., 5 Sept. 1855, Lena Oppenheimer, dau. of D.   9/11/55-2
Sommerville, James P., 16 Feb. 1851, Emily A. Pryor, dau. of
    Edward   2/25/51-2
Sonnehill, Lewis, 17 Oct. 1852, Barbara Prag, dau. of A.   10/18/52-2
Soper, Edward H., 13 Nov. 1859, Melissa Jones   11/15/59-2
Soper, Geo. F. D., 22 Feb. 1853, Jane Carrol   2/23/53-2
Soper, John H., son of Henry G., 14 Feb. 1854, Annie Pierce,
    dau. of Peter P.   2/16/54-2
Sorrel, William S., 2 Sept. 1858, Mary Ellen Snoden   9/ 4/58-2
Souder, David W. F., 23 June 1859, Mary A. Stewart   7/23/59-2
Southard, James, 22 Mar. 1858, Mary Elizabeth Suter   6/15/58-2
Southcomb, A. S., 22 Jan. 1855, Maria Henderson   1/25/55-2
Southey, James L., 24 July 1853, Adeline Cole   7/28/53-2
Spaight, Jeremiah, 9 Feb. 1860, (Mrs.) Allethea A. Whitlock   2/14/60-2
Spalding, B. D., 6 Jan. 1853, Priscilla Moore, dau. of H. A.   1/10/53-2
Spalding, J. Willett, 1 Mar. 1859, Frances Clara Fatterman,
    dau. of W. W.   3/10/59-2
Spamer, Charles C., 18 Mar. 1860, Margaret Spangler   3/20/60-2
Spamer, Henry, 8 Sept. 1860, Elizabeth Hiney Erling   9/11/60-2
Spangler, James A., 20 Nov. 1856, Julia Keilholtz   11/22/56-2
Spangler, John F., 28 Jan. 1858, Mary M. Coulter, dau. of
    (Dr.) Mifflin   1/29/58-2
Spargo, Jonathan, 16 Dec. 1859, Susan Calloway   12/19/59-2
Spargo, William, 2 Feb. 1858, Eliza Harry   2/ 4/58-2
Sparklin, Edward M., 15 Feb. 1857, Ann Daly   2/21/57-2
Sparklin, William B. F., son of (Rev.) Samuel, 26 Nov. 1857,
    Hester A. Booth   12/ 1/57-2
Sparks, Edward R., 5 June 1851, Rachel Miles   6/13/51-2
Sparks, Levi, 8 July 1852, (Mrs.) Elizabeth McCurley   7/12/52-2
Sparks, Richard P., 28 Nov. 1859, Emily Frances Jones, dau. of
    (Capt.) Lemuel   12/ 1/59-2
Sparks, Robert, 17 Dec. 1857, Catherine Hammond, dau. of
    Walter C.   12/19/57-2
Sparks, S. Edward, 29 Nov. 1855, Mary Ann Amey   12/ 3/55-2
Sparrow, Daniel, 2 Nov. 1857, Eliza Bryan   11/ 5/57-2
Sparrow, Josephus, 3 Nov. 1856, Sarah Jane Campbell   11/ 8/56-2
Spaulding, Basil D., 6 Jan. 1853, Sarah Ann Priscilla Moore   1/ 8/53-2
Speake, R. H. (M.D.), 1 Oct. 1851, Georgina F. Weaver, dau. of
    (Capt.) William A.   10/ 4/51-2
Speake, Wm. F. (Rev.), 30 Oct. 1855, Mary Radcliff   11/ 1/55-2
Speaks, John W., 21 Dec. 1851, Sarah C. Willson   12/24/51-2
Spear, John W., 13 Oct. 1853, Amanda J. Lucas, dau. of (Capt.)
    Thomas   10/15/53-2
Spears, Robert J., 28 Apr. 1857, Elizabeth C. Graham   4/29/57-2
Speck, Wm., 28 May 1852, Mary Baker   5/31/52-2
Spedden, Edward, 7 June 1853, Emily C. Bender   6/ 8/53-2
Spedden, Edward, 29 Mar. 1855, Martha M. Barron   3/31/55-2
Spedden, John; no date given, Elizabeth Abey   11/21/57-2
Spedden, John M., 24 July 1851, Margaret C. Lee, dau. of
    James H.   7/29/51-2
Spedden, Wm. H., 22 Nov. 1859, Margaret J. G. Armstrong   11/26/59-2
Spedden, Wm. L., 21 Apr. 1852, Hellen Francis Kearney   6/12/52-2
Speddin, George A., 16 Jan. 1851, Mary Jane Sewell, dau. of
    Thos. H.   1/21/51-2
Speelman, Frederick, 20 May 1852, Mary C. Hand   6/ 8/52-2
Spelman, John H., 5 Nov. 1854, Mary Gandenbein   11/ 7/54-2
Spence, George W., 19 July 1852, Mary Ann Kelley   8/14/52-2
Spence, James C., 23 Nov. 1858, Harriet C. Reid, dau. of
    Charles   11/29/58-2
Spence, John H., 25 May 1854, Sarah Jane Stone   5/29/54-2
Spencer, Daniel M., 30 Oct. 1860, Anne E. Lecompte   11/12/60-2

Spencer, David, 25 Dec. 1860, Catharine A. Stone	12/27/60-2
Spencer, John M., 3 Feb. 1859, Sarah Elizabeth Jenkins, dau.	
of Wm. M.	2/ 4/59-2
Spencer, Joseph H., 18 Jan. 1854, Lavinia Cope, dau. of J. J.	1/24/54-2
Spencer, Oliver J., 17 Apr. 1857, Rachel Green	5/20/57-2
Spencer, Philip, 18 Oct. 1858, Elizabeth Camell	10/21/58-2
Spencer, T. H., 31 Jan. 1856, Ann A. Atwell	3/ 3/56-2
Spencer, Thomas J., 1 Feb. 1854, Mary A. E. Long	2/ 3/54-2
Sperlein, George, 12 Aug. 1855, (Mrs.) (?) Lohmais	8/17/55-2
Sperry, Benj. W., 2 Sept. 1851, Amelia C. Herner	9/ 8/51-2
Sperry, Benj. W., 2 Sept. 1851, Amelia C. Kerner; corrected	
copy	9/10/51-2
Spicer, Clarke, 18 Nov. 1860, Susanna Flemming	11/27/60-2
Spicer, Frank M., 21 Dec. 1858, Maria E. Colley, dau. of	
John W.	12/28/58-2
Spicer, George W., 9 Sept. 1856, Elizabeth Kindig	9/15/56-2
Spicer, J. Augustus, 6 Dec. 1855, Lizzie S. Lee	12/14/55-2
Spicer, Jas., 16 May 1860, Sarah Ann Burnham	5/19/60-2
Spicer, Philip M., 16 July 1857, M. L. Reigle	7/21/57-2
Spicknall, Wm. H., 29 Feb. 1860, Mollie M. Plummer	3/ 2/60-2
Spies, Jacob, 19 Nov. 1857, Caroline Smith, dau. of Christian	11/20/57-2
Spilcker, G. H., 19 Nov. 1857, Emma Sadtler, dau. of	
Philip B.	11/24/57-2
Spiller, Robert M., 18 Nov. 1857, Augusta Maltby, dau. of	
Elbridge	11/25/57-2
Spillman, Thomas A., 26 Apr. 1852, Henrietta Barou, dau. of	
John E.	5/17/52-2
Spilman, A. H., 6 July 1854, Sophia C. Smith, dau. of Saml.	7/10/54-2
Spilman, James D., 31 Oct. 1860, E. J. Cator	11/ 1/60-2
Spilman, James H., 31 May 1859, Elizabeth A. Rice	6/ 3/59-2
Spilman, Robert L., 27 Dec. 1859, Annie H. Pattison	12/29/59-2
Spindler, Peter A., 15 May 1860, Mary M. McGlane	7/11/60-2
Spindler, Peter A., 15 May 1860, Mary M. McGlone; corrected copy	7/12/60-2
Spinger, Geo. A., 5 June 1853, Cornelia R. Beltz, dau. of	
(Dr.) Henry; corrected copy	6/11/53-2
Spinger, George A., 5 June 1853, Cornelia R. Beltzs	6/ 7/53-2
Sponsler, John, 23 Feb. 1853, Mary Ann Gaubert	2/25/53-2
Sprankling, Edward M., 15 Feb. 1857, Anna Daly	2/23/57-2
Sprankling, John, 16 May 1859, Caroline Kuszmaul	5/20/59-2
Sprigg, Wm., 27 May 1858, Harriet Green	5/29/58-2
Spring, Robert, 4 June 1851, Mary Catharine McKinley	6/ 5/51-2
Springer, J. Henderson, 3 June 1858, Eliza S. H. Carter, dau.	
of Durden B.	6/ 7/58-2
Sprouse, Anthony, 26 Aug. 1852, Elizabeth Smith	8/30/52-2
Sprowl, James, 23 Jan. 1854, Margaret Taylor	1/25/54-2
Sprucebank, Abram, 19 Aug. 1851, Elizabeth Jane Mudd	8/21/51-2
Sprusebanks, James, 10 Oct. 1856, Cecele Ann Miles	11/17/56-2
Spurrier, Grafton D., 21 Nov. 1860, Elizabeth K. Fibby	
Gouverneur, dau. of Saml. L., grandau. of (Pres.) James	
Monroe	11/27/60-2
Spurrier, William, 16 May 1858, Mary C. Frizzell	5/20/58-2
Squires, John O., 27 Mar. 1860, Mary O'Brien	4/ 6/60-2
Staats, Elijah, 29 July 1856, Elizabeth A. Payne	7/30/56-2
Stabler, Edward H., 15 June 1859, Louisa M. Field	7/ 1/59-2
Stabler, William, 19 Aug. 1858, Elizabeth Gallagher	8/20/58-2
Stabline, Theodore, 11 Jan. 1857, Mary Ellen Agnes Leadbeater	1/19/57-2
Stack, Garrett, 23 Sept. 1855, Elizabeth Kelly	11/26/55-2
Stafford, Lawrence, 4 Oct. 1860, Mary McPherson, dau. of	
Duncan	10/ 6/60-2
Stafford, William J. (Capt.), 6 Mar. 1855, Caroline E.	
Gardner, dau. of Wm.	3/ 8/55-2
Stagle, Charles, 8 Nov. 1854, Elizabeth Lee	11/15/54-2
Stahl, Edward L., 1 Apr. 1852, Laura A. Kurtz, dau. of Jacob	4/ 3/52-2
Stahl, John, 12 Apr. 1857, Emma Mallory	4/17/57-2
Stahl, Walter, 26 July 1857, Jane Bradley	7/30/57-2

```
Stalfort, John H., 18 Oct. 1860, Medora J. Schwartz, dau.
    of Juline and Catharine                                   10/19/60-2
Stall, Andrew J., 3 Aug. 1856, Harriet Ann Rotin             8/ 5/56-2
Stall, William, 18 Nov. 1860, (Mrs.) Amanda J. Brown, dau. of
    John Fowler                                              11/20/60-2
Stallings, John W., 18 July 1853, Fanny Bussey                7/28/53-2
Stallings, William C., 16 Nov. 1855, Ann C. Chandler         11/17/55-2
Stammen, Charles G., 27 Sept. 1855, Lydia Ann Mettee          9/29/55-2
Stamp, Mordecai R., 13 Feb. 1855, Mary Ann McKee, dau. of
    Alexander                                                 2/23/55-2
Standiford, Edward P., 17 Dec. 1851, Amelia E. Henning, dau. of
    David                                                    12/18/51-2
Standiford, J. B., 25 Nov. 1856, Hester A. Smith             11/28/56-2
Standiford, John, 29 Sept. 1852, Mary Louisa House           10/ 8/52-2
Standiford, Nicholas J., 10 Feb. 1853, Mary Ann Galoway       2/12/53-2
Stanforth, Richard (Dr.), 4 May 1858, Martha W. Robertson, dau.
    of Thomas E.                                              5/ 5/58-2
Stanley, James, 29 Nov. 1860, Milley Matilda Thompson        12/ 1/60-2
Stanley, John, 1 Feb. 1854, Catharine A. Grammer              2/ 3/55-2
Stanley, Oliver, 24 Dec. 1855, Elizabeth Ann White           12/27/55-2
Stansberry, John, 2 Feb. 1860, Virginia Pole                  2/10/60-2
Stansbury, George H., 19 Feb. 1860, Emma Chase                3/ 8/60-2
Stansbury, John S., 17 June 1858, Elizabeth A. Tauney         6/19/58-2
Stansbury, John S., 2 Feb. 1860, Annie V. Pole                2/21/60-2
Stansbury, Albert, 20 June 1852, Fanny A. Jones, dau. of (Capt.)
    James                                                     6/23/52-2
Stansbury, Augusta M., 28 July 1856, Jane Callender Patterson 8/ 4/56-2
Stansbury, Chas. T., 3 Aug. 1854, Mary V. King                8/ 5/54-2
Stansbury, Darius, 18 Jan. 1853, Virginia Denmead             1/22/53-2
Stansbury, Elijah M., 31 May 1855, Elizabeth S. Miles         6/23/55-2
Stansbury, George R., 10 Oct. 1854, Elizabeth McDowell        1/16/55-2
Stansbury, Henry O., 9 Nov. 1854, Jane W. Keyworth           11/13/54-2
Stansbury, Jas., 10 June 1857, Eliza Hamilton                 8/21/57-2
Stansbury, Jas. E., 16 Sept. 1851, Atway Sword, dau. of
    John W.                                                   9/17/51-2
Stansbury, Jesse J., 6 May 1852, Margaret Ann Crowther        5/ 8/52-2
Stansbury, John L., 10 June 1851, Mary O. Smith               6/12/51-2
Stansbury, Jos. S., 1 May 1851, Georgeanna Norris             5/ 3/51-2
Stansbury, Nathaniel, 2 Oct. 1851, Hannah A. Baker           10/ 8/51-2
Stansbury, Rich'd. C., 24 Feb. 1852, Mary Elizabeth Bond      2/25/52-2
Stansbury, Smith, 29 May 1855, Annie Maria Stansbury          6/ 4/55-2
Stansbury, William G., 8 June 1853, Mary E. Hahns             6/10/53-2
Stanton, John, 15 Feb. 1856, Sally Kelly                      2/18/56-2
Stanton, Thomas, 22 July 1851, Elizabeth Willet               7/25/51-2
Stanton, Wm., 20 May 1851, Catherine Owings                   5/22/51-2
Stapleford, Alfred F., 7 Sept. 1857, Rebecca E. Foreman       9/17/57-2
Staples, Eben, 12 May 1857, Julia S. Dashiells                5/14/57-2
Stapleton, Laertus C., 18 Feb. 1851, Christiannie Baldwinn,
    dau. of Robert                                            4/11/51-2
Starkey, John G., 24 June 1858, Mary C. Cunningham            6/26/58-2
Starr, J. Taylor, 5 June 1856, Jane Roberts                   6/ 9/56-2
Starr, James H., 9 Apr. 1854, Sarah Jane Howard               4/12/54-2
Starr, John, 18 Apr. 1854, Martha Kendell, dau. of William J.;
    corrected copy                                            4/27/54-2
Starr, John, 18 Apr. 1854, Martha Kerdell                     4/26/54-2
Starr, Robert, 2 Oct. 1855, Maria Frances Johnston           10/ 4/55-2
Start, Wm. A. (Capt.), 9 July 1860, Sarah Elizabeth Plummer   7/11/60-2
Starr, Wm. T., 24 June 1858, Elizabeth D. Smith               2/28/58-2
Startzman, David, 16 Sept. 1855, Sarah Ann Miller             9/19/55-2
Startzman, John, 13 Mar. 1860, Mollie A. Jackson              3/17/60-4
Staubus, Solomon, 26 Dec. 1854, Catharine Rusmisel           12/27/54-2
Stauff, Henry, 27 May 1858, Caroline Fischer                  6/ 1/58-2
Stauffer, Henry, 30 Sept. 1858, Sarah S. Cairnes            10/ 2/58-2
Stauten, John, 28 Aug. 1855, (Mrs.) Susannah McFaddon         9/27/55-2
```

```
Stauter, John, 28 Aug. 1855, (Mrs.) Susannah McFadlon;
    corrected copy                                        9/28/55-2
Staylor, Andrew J., 4 June 1852, Mary Jane Groscup        6/26/52-2
Staylor, George W., 30 May 1852, Mary Washington, dau. of Henry  6/ 1/52-2
Staylor, John, Jr., 21 Sept. 1854, K. Lutts, dau. of John F.
    and Mary                                              9/27/54-2
Staylor, John J., 25 Jan. 1853, Ann Andrews               1/27/53-2
Staylor, Philip A., 8 Oct. 1855, Harriet Riggle           10/17/55-2
Staylor, Philip J., 31 Oct. 1859, Laura Virginia Valentine  11/21/59-2
Staylor, Philip J., 13 Nov. 1859, Virginia Valentine;
    corrected copy                                        11/26/59-2
Staymer, William H., 11 Sept. 1853, Sarah E. McGrath       9/13/53-2
Stead, E. Briggs, 10 Apr. 1855, Matilda Lavinia Hagthorp,
    dau. of Edward                                        4/11/55-2
Steble, Jos. W. (Dr.); no date given, Elenora Curtis, dau. of
    (Dr.) J. L.                                           7/27/54-2
Steed, Richard H. (Capt.), 26 Dec. 1856, Maria Elmira Myers  1/12/57-2
Steed, Richard H. (Capt.), 26 Dec. 1856, Maria Elmira Myles;
    corrected copy                                        1/13/57-2
Steele, J. Wesley (Dr.); no date given, Maggie J. Smith   3/10/60-2
Steele, James H., 21 Apr. 1857, Margaret E. Watkins, dau. of
    (Col.) John W.                                        4/23/57-2
Steele, John, 15 Apr. 1851, (Mrs.) Elizabeth Linville     4/17/51-2
Steever, Alexander, 28 Dec. 1856, Elizabeth A. Sauerhoff, dau.
    of John F.                                            1/21/57-2
Steever, Lafayette, 15 Jan. 1856, Catharine E. Sapp       1/17/56-2
Steffe, Lewis, 18 Jan. 1852, Catharine Thompson           1/24/52-2
Steffee, George, 31 July 1853, Anna Massey                8/ 8/53-2
Steiff, John L., 3 May 1855, Hannah A. Clifford, dau. of John  5/ 4/55-2
Steigelman, Columbus, 20 Aug. 1857, Catherine T. Norman   8/22/57-2
Stein, Myer, 12 Nov. 1851, Rose Rosenstock, dau. of Gershon  11/13/51-2
Stein, William, 11 June 1860, Mary G. Sorgler             6/12/60-2
Steinacker, Geo. T., 18 Feb. 1855, Agnes Clarkson Toamey  2/27/55-2
Steinbach, George P., 21 June 1859, Caroline E. Bruehl, dau. of
    Justus                                                6/25/59-2
Steiner, William, 11 June 1860, Mary E. Sorgler           6/19/60-2
Steinman, Charles L., 5 Apr. 1853, Mary C. Creighton      4/ 6/53-2
Steiver, Ferdinand, 16 Mar. 1858, Mary E. Dalrymple       1/ 8/59-2
Stembler, John A., 7 Dec. 1858, Margaret H. Cassady       12/15/58-2
Stenger, August, 28 Apr. 1853, Mary A. Snow, dau. of (Capt.)
    John                                                  5/ 2/53-2
Stephens, Alexander W., 8 June 1853, Josephine Boyd       6/10/53-2
Stephens, James H., Jr., 16 July 1857, Sarah Jane Hobbs   7/23/57-2
Stephens, James M., 27 Feb. 1851, Camilla E. Norwood, dau. of
    Thos. D.                                              3/ 5/51-2
Stephens, L. G., 24 Jan. 1857, Caroline M. Wall, dau. of
    Daniel                                                1/28/57-2
Stephens, P. (Col.), 30 Mar. 1852, Maria E. Goodloe       4/ 8/52-2
Stephens, Thomas A., 6 Mar. 1856, Mary L. Soran, dau. of
    Charles                                               3/ 7/56-2
Stephenson, Thomas John, 13 Nov. 1856, Sophia Hill, dau. of
    Alexander                                             11/15/56-2
Sterling, John H., 24 Aug. 1859, Susan B. Slade           8/25/59-2
Sterling, William H., 22 Apr. 1856, Mary A. Clarke, dau. of
    (Capt.) William                                       4/23/56-2
Stern, Henry, 9 May 1853, Caroline Hamburger              5/10/53-2
Stern, John, 7 Feb. 1856, Elizabeth St. Clair             2/12/56-2
Stertz, John Henry, 10 Aug. 1851, Ellenora Shoenberger    8/12/51-2
Steuart, Charles B., 2 Jan. 1851, Ellen F. Clark          1/ 4/51-2
Steuart, Chas. T., 27 Jan. 1853, Isa C. Marmelstein       1/29/53-2
Steuart, George H. (Capt.), 14 Jan. 1858, Maria H. Kinzie,
    adopted dau. of (Maj.) D. Hunter                      1/29/58-2
Steuart, Jas. A. (Dr.), 25 Feb. 1851, Sally Baxter        2/27/51-2
Steuart, Richard S., 27 May 1856, Georgia R. Gist, dau. of Wm.  5/28/56-2
Stevens, A. R., 1 Nov. 1853, Maria H. Stone               11/ 3/53-2
```

Stevens, Edward T. (Dr.), 28 Apr. 1853, Mary Catharine Holbrook,
   dau. of P. M.   4/29/53-2
Stevens, Francis G., 11 Sept. 1855, Julia E. Salgues   9/13/55-2
Stevens, George G., 10 May 1855, Margery J. McGuire   5/12/55-2
Stevens, James J., 28 June 1851, Ellen D. B. Harris   7/ 1/51-2
Stevens, James S., 5 Nov. 1855, Cornelia T. Gifford   11/ 9/55-2
Stevens, Jno. M., 26 Aug. 1856, Henrietta Gartaide, dau. of
   Jno.   8/28/58-2
Stevens, John G., 14 May 1855, Kate L. Marsters, dau. of
   Richard   5/21/55-2
Stevens, Joseph, 9 Sept. 1851, Barbara Wisebaugh   9/16/51-2
Stevens, Joseph, 5 Nov. 1857, Sarah A. Thompson   11/10/57-2
Stevens, Josiah C., 21 Jan. 1858, Sarah M. Mullikin   1/23/58-2
Stevens, Pratby J., 27 Nov. 1856, Adelaide M. Lutz   12/16/56-2
Stevens, Robert, 6 Nov. 1853, Ellen Harvey   11/ 8/53-2
Stevens, Richard M., 3 May 1860, Mary A. Stedding   5/28/60-2
Stevens, Samuel A., 15 June 1857, Frances L. Ames   6/23/57-2
Stevens, Sylvester, 1 Aug. 1855, Harriet O. Leach   8/17/55-2
Stevens, William E., 14 Dec. 1854, Crissy Relkey   12/18/54-2
Stevenson, Benjamin, 14 Sept. 1854, Sarah Brown   9/16/54-2
Stevenson, Charles C., 10 Apr. 1855, Ruth A. Griffith, dau. of
   Howard   4/12/55-2
Stevenson, Charles P. (Dr.), 13 May 1858, Martha Metzger, dau. of
   Daniel   5/14/58-2
Stevenson, George W., 2 Jan. 1854, Susan Chamberlain   1/ 4/54-2
Stevenson, J. M., 9 May 1854, Margaretta E. Paxton, dau. of
   (Col.) J. D.   5/15/54-2
Stevenson, John, 29 Sept. 1859, Mary Guy   9/30/59-2
Stevenson, Joshua S., 8 July 1856, Emily J. Haase   7/ 9/56-2
Stevenson, Wm. D., 25 Mar. 1856, Annie T. Russell, dau. of
   Thomas   4/ 1/56-2
Steward, Henry, 28 Apr. 1853, Emily Johnson   4/29/53-2
Steward, John, 12 June 1856, Priscilla Campher   6/14/56-2
Stewart, Alexander, 31 July 1851, Caroline F. Garrett   8/ 2/51-2
Stewart, Alexander, 26 Dec. 1852, Matilda A. Cruit   12/27/52-2
Stewart, Andrew J., 19 Dec. 1860, Margaret A. Elingsworth, dau.
   of Wm.   12/20/60-2
Stewart, Arthur, 5 Feb. 1857, Ann King   2/ 6/57-2
Stewart, Charles R., 18 July 1854, Virginia Jamisen, dau. of
   C. C.   7/20/54-2
Stewart, Chas. H., 14 Nov. 1855, Laura J. Chester, dau. of
   William   11/15/55-2
Stewart, Daniel, 3 Aug. 1853, Margaret Marshall   8/ 8/53-2
Stewart, Daniel, 12 June 1859, Ann L. Duncan   6/16/59-2
Stewart, Edw'd. F., 14 Jan. 1851, Sarah Stewart   1/22/51-2
Stewart, Edwin R., 18 July 1854, Marietta McNew   8/19/54-2
Stewart, George, 2 June 1859, Mary Riley   6/14/59-2
Stewart, George H., 13 Mar. 1859, Laura E. Sayre, dau. of
   James T.   3/16/59-2
Stewart, J. J., Jr., 1 May 1854, Mary Baynes, dau. of Jas. 5/ 8/54-2
Stewart, James, 25 Sept. 1854, Jane Drummond   9/27/54-2
Stewart, James M., 13 Dec. 1859, Sarah D. Harris   1/ 6/59-2
Stewart, Jas. S., 31 Dec. 1858, Annie E. Keirle, dau. of
   Washington T.   1/ 4/58-2
Stewart, John, 12 July 1853, Mary Jane Patterson   7/14/53-2
Stewart, John, 20 Oct. 1853, L. Josephine Moulton, dau. of
   Joseph W.   10/26/53-2
Stewart, John, 10 Sept. 1854, Harriet Jane McFarland   9/11/54-2
Stewart, John, 19 July 1859, Sarah Ann Kelly   7/22/59-2
Stewart, John F., 9 Nov. 1856, Catharine A. Stieber   11/11/56-2
Stewart, John F., 9 Nov. 1856, Catharine A. Stitcher; corrected
   copy   11/12/56-2
Stewart, John H., 1 Jan. 1853, Rebecca McMaster   1/ 3/53-2
Stewart, John M., 11 Aug. 1859, Anne E. Morrow   8/15/59-2

```
Stewart, John T., 4 Nov. 1851, Sarah E. Kennedy, dau. of
     Thos. A.                                                   11/27/51-2
Stewart, Joseph, 30 Sept. 1852, Rachel Sparks, dau. of Laban    10/ 2/52-2
Stewart, Joseph, 24 Jan. 1854, Eliza Fultz; 1/27/54-2            1/28/54-2
Stewart, Joseph, 12 June 1860, Rebecca Stewart                   6/14/60-2
Stewart, Joseph S., 1 Feb. 1855, Margaret M. Stewart             2/ 5/55-2
Stewart, S. M., 8 Apr. 1855, Elizabeth A. Sommer                4/10/55-2
Stewart, Thomas, 27 May 1858, Matilda Long                      6/12/58-2
Stewart, Walter, 3 Nov. 1858, Margaret Stewart                  11/ 5/58-2
Stewart, William, 18 Jan. 1855, Charity Bell                    1/20/55-2
Stewart, William H., 25 Apr. 1852, Catharine Donahoe            5/ 4/52-2
Stewart, Wm. S., 19 Jan. 1851, Clara Schae-(?)-ler              1/30/51-2
Stickel, Joseph, 31 May 1853, Mary A. Cooley                    6/ 2/53-2
Stiefel, Edward W., 1 Dec. 1858, Jane W. Holtzman, dau. of
     Wilhelm                                                    12/ 2/58-2
Stiefel, Julius, 15 June 1856, Emma Levin                       6/18/56-2
Stier, Upton, 10 Dec. 1857, Virginia C. Chaston, dau. of
     Stanislaus                                                 12/19/57-2
Stile, Upton, 10 Dec. 1857, Virginia C. Chilon                  12/18/57-2
Stiles, William (Dr.), 19 June 1856, Margaret Lyford;
     6/20/56-2                                                  6/21/56-2
Stinchcomb, James H., 2 Mar. 1854, Ary E. Frizzell, dau. of
     Beal                                                       3/22/54-2
Stinchcomb, John A., 22 Sept. 1856, Sophia Dawson, dau. of
     (Capt.) Wm. H.                                             9/24/56-2
Stinchcomb, Noah S., 26 May 1857, Mary E. Younger               5/28/57-2
Stinchcomb, Samuel S., 9 Oct. 1856, Elizabeth J. Cole, dau. of
     William; corrected copy                                    10/11/56-2
Stinchcomb, Samuel T., 9 Oct. 1856, Elizabeth Cole              10/10/56-2
Stinchcomb, Thomas W., 18 Dec. 1853, Ann Rebecca Chard          12/21/53-2
Stinchecomb, Chas., 2 Jan. 1851, Ann Disney                     1/10/51-2
Stine, N. H., 6 Dec. 1857, Amelia Rider, dau. of Moses          12/ 7/57-2
Stinson, Richard, 27 Jan. 1856, Margaret Sisco                  1/28/56-2
Stinson, Wm. H., 25 Nov. 1858, Eugenia G. Warfield, dau. of
     (Dr.) Gustavus                                             11/29/58-2
Stirling, Archibald, Jr., 13 June 1855, Nannie Steele Lloyd,
     dau. of Daniel                                             6/15/55-2
Stirling, Douglass, 12 Apr. 1859, Cornelia H. Elder, dau. of
     George H.                                                  4/14/59-2
Stirling, Wm. H., 10 July 1856, Sallie H. Miller                7/12/56-2
Stirn, D., 16 Aug. 1860, Maggie A. Posey                        9/ 1/60-2
Stivers, Thomas, 15 July 1858, Mary Covall                      7/17/58-2
Stockbridge, Clarence M., 25 Apr. 1858, Ida L. Monnier, dau. of
     (Dr.) J. V. T.                                             6/15/58-2
Stockett, Charles H., 10 Sept. 1854, Anna M. Chaney             9/25/54-2
Stockett, James B., 13 July 1853, Martha Ann Smith              7/16/53-2
Stockett, James P., 25 Oct. 1859, Ellen McCurdy                 10/28/59-2
Stocksdale, Jas. F., 3 June 1858, Jennie Owens                  6/ 5/58-2
Stocksdale, Sleas L., 2 Dec. 1852, Sarah J. Hiser, dau. of
     Wm. R.                                                     12/10/52-2
Stocksteale, Noah, 24 Mar. 1857, Ellen Gettier                  3/26/57-2
Stoddard, George W., 27 May 1858, Jennie Barker                 5/29/58-2
Stoddard, James W., 4 May 1851, Kitty P. Bool, dau. of John     5/ 6/51-2
Stoddard, John, 24 Feb. 1852, Ann Donaldson                     3/ 2/52-2
Stoddard, Marshall W., 2 Apr. 1859, Kate B. Snyder, dau. of
     Samuel; 4/25/59-2                                          4/26/59-2
Stoddart, Albert M., 10 Oct. 1853, Kate J. Menzies, dau. of
     Jas.                                                       10/12/53-2
Stoddart, William F., 4 Nov. 1852, Johanna Keiley               11/13/52-2
Stoltz, Gustavus, 20 Sept. 1854, Mary Cramar                    9/21/54-2
Stone, A. Augustus, 29 Apr. 1857, Mary H. Parsons               4/30/57-2
Stone, Benjamin F., 27 Oct. 1853, Helen A. Stone                10/31/53-2
Stone, Howard, 15 May 1856, Mary A. Teson                       6/17/56-2
Stone, J. H. *, 20 June 1852, Catherine Stevens                 6/23/52-2
Stone, James H., 15 Nov. 1860, Sallie S. Greer                  11/28/60-2
```

```
Stone, John T., 2 Feb. 1858, Emeline McNew                        5/ 4/58-2
Stone, Richard O., 19 Mar. 1860, Elizabeth Paddington             3/28/60-2
Stonesifer, Amos, 4 Mar. 1858, Fannie Garaghty, dau. of James     3/ 6/58-2
Stoops, James, 24 Oct. 1856, M. Caroline Browne, dau. of
    Benj. O.                                                     10/27/56-2
Storey, John W., 19 July 1860, Sallie M. Stover                   7/21/60-2
Storm, Edwin L., 2 Dec. 1858, Sallie A. Keagey                   12/ 7/58-2
Storm, Jeremiah, 11 May 1858, Lisette Garrald                     5/12/58-2
Story, John T., 31 Aug. 1858, Emily Burke                         9/ 4/58-2
Stott, Isaiah, 8 May 1853, Margaret Griffith                      6/ 8/53-2
Stouffer, D. P., 28 July 1858, Sarah J. Nicholson                 9/29/58-2
Stout, Henry L., 13 Mar. 1853, Harriet A. Bishop                  3/17/53-2
Stoutsenberg, Geo., 23 Jan. 1853, Amanda Barr-(?), dau. of
    John                                                          1/26/53-2
Stracke, Jacob, 22 Jan. 1855, Mary Ann Dunny                      2/ 6/55-2
Strains, Caleb, 9 Sept. 1855, Rachel E. L. Green                  9/11/55-2
Strandberg, Daniel, 19 May 1851, Eliza J. Shepherd                5/21/51-2
Strandberg, H. J. (Capt.); no date given, (Mrs.) Carrie A.
    Seegan                                                       10/ 3/60-2
Strane, George, 22 Jan. 1855, Margaret Sullivan                   1/23/55-2
Straughn, Levin E., 25 May 1859, Annie E. Barnett                 6/ 3/59-2
Straughn, William J., 9 Aug. 1859, Roselia C. Kerr                8/16/59-2
Strausbaugh, Aloysius, 4 June 1857, Ann Estelle Kerkham           6/17/57-2
Strausbaugh, Jacob W., 10 Feb. 1852, Sarah A. McSherry            2/14/52-2
Streeper, Charles, 20 Mar. 1851, Amanda L. Lyon, dau. of John B.  5/ 3/51-2
Street, David, 25 Sept. 1854, Mary S. Hamelin                     9/26/54-2
Street, J. Thomas, 16 Dec. 1856, Demelia Virginia Gallaway, dau.
    of (Capt.) Wm.                                               12/18/56-2
Street, John T., 16 Dec. 1856, Virginia D. Galloway              12/17/56-2
Streets, Thomas, 1 Jan. 1852, Julietta C. Hagthrop                1/ 2/52-2
Strible, John, 27 May 1858, Adeline O. Durkee                     5/29/58-2
Stribling, C., 7 Dec. 1852, Emma J. Nourse, dau. of
    Benjamin F.                                                  12/10/52-2
Striewig, Samuel, 30 June 1853, Savilla Marks                     7/ 9/53-2
Strohler, John W., 3 Dec. 1854, Catherine Houtsings              12/ 5/57-2
Strohm, Frederick, 29 Dec. 1853, Mary S. Wailes                  12/31/53-2
Stromberger, Frederick, 23 Dec. 1851, Mary E. Murray             12/27/51-2
Strong, Ed-(?)-y N. M., 21 Dec. 1851, Martha Ann Christopher,
    dau. of Michael and Mary                                     12/23/51-2
Strong, Thomas A., 10 Dec. 1857, Rebecca Audoun Chamberlain      12/11/57-2
Strother, Henry St. G., 18 Apr. 1854, Mary E. White              4/19/54-2
Struck, John B., 26 Nov. 1857, Catherine Wagner                  12/ 1/57-2
Stuart, Dilman S., 23 Dec. 1851, Mary M. Bell                    12/23/51-2
Stuart, Henry L., 13 Mar. 1853, Harriet A. Bishop                 3/16/53-2
Stuart, Henry W., 22 Nov. 1856, Margaret Johnson                 11/27/56-2
Stuart, Samuel, 3 Nov. 1853, Elizabeth Clotworthy                11/ 5/53-2
Stuart, Wm. Bruce, 13 July 1857, (Mrs.) Hannah Carter             7/29/57-2
Stubbins, B. A. (Dr.), 2 Mar. 1857, V. J. Roberts                 3/ 4/57-2
Stubbins, Joseph T., 8 Nov. 1860, Keziah Ambrose                 12/15/60-2
Stubbs, Wm. O., 13 Jan. 1853, Mary E. Vinzant                     1/17/53-2
Stuck, Charles, 17 Jan. 1854, Margaret Ann Mitchell               2/ 1/54-2
Stump, James, 14 Apr. 1852, Emeline Airey                         4/16/52-2
Stump, John W., Jr., 23 Aug. 1854, Mary M. Birdsall              10/ 4/54-2
Sturdy, Edward, 9 June 1857, Mary Ann Wisnom                      6/12/57-2
Sturgeon, Freedes, 26 Sept. 1853, Mary E. Hatch                   9/28/53-2
Sturgeon, Henry D., 20 Dec. 1853, Elizabeth Hammell              12/24/53-2
Sturgeon, John D., 20 Dec. 1853, Elizabeth Hammill               12/23/53-2
Sturts, Jacob, 12 Apr. 1853, Caroline Roch                        4/15/53-2
Sudman, Henry, 16 Aug. 1857, Annie Flynn                          9/22/57-2
Suell, Richard, 30 Sept. 1854, Elizabeth Allen                    4/23/55-2
Suit, S. Taylor, 13 Dec. 1859, A. B. Willmarth, dau. of A. F.    12/16/59-2
Sulfner, Adolphus, 27 Mar. 1853, Minerva Curtis                   3/29/53-2
Sullins, David H., 27 Mar. 1859, Mary J. Reese                    3/29/59-2
Sullivan, James, 1 Apr. 1852, Josephine E. Wilson                 4/15/52-2
Sullivan, John F., 12 July 1858, Emma Larsh                       7/14/58-2
```

```
Sullivan, Richard William, 17 June 1851, Mary Ann Aloysius,
    dau. of (Mrs.) Catharine DeWitt                              6/21/51-2
Sullivan, Samuel, 16 Jan. 1851, Mary Renn                        3/10/51-2
Sullivan, William H., 11 Dec. 1859, Mary Jane Miller            12/21/59-2
Sullivan, William S., 29 Oct. 1857, Hannah E. Wilcox            10/31/57-2
Sullivan, William Wesley, 12 Aug. 1860, Sarah A. Riggs           9/ 1/60-2
Sullivan, Wm. S., 17 May 1854, Rebecca Ann Senderling            5/20/54-2
Sumalt, Henry M., 9 Nov. 1859, Martha J. Mules                  11/14/59-2
Summers, George D.; no date given, Rosena Catherine Schaffer,
    dau. of Jacob                                               11/23/59-2
Summers, Samuel, Jr., 24 Dec. 1854, Jane Jackson Wilson         12/30/54-2
Summers, Thos. B., 6 Jan. 1852, Caroline Kone                    1/ 8/52-2
Summerville, Charles Henry, 14 Aug. 1860, Hannah Ann Watkins     8/16/60-2
Summerville, Peter, 23 June 1859, Margaret Ann Grason            6/25/59-2
Sumwalt, Albert W., 20 Oct. 1857, Mary J. Haugh                 10/22/57-2
Sumwalt, James H., 10 Dec. 1857, Mary A. Lee                    12/16/57-2
Sumwalt, John E., 23 Jan. 1853, Mary Elizabeth Walton            1/25/53-2
Sumwalt, Wm. L., 1 Mar. 1855, Martha B. Hammons                  3/ 3/55-2
Sunderland, Beverly W., 8 June 1851, Mary Coleman                6/10/51-2
Sunderland, John W., 18 Apr. 1854, Mary E. Morine                4/22/54-2
Super, Daniel, 14 Sept. 1852, Henerietta Alexina Moore, dau.
    of John                                                      9/18/52-2
Super, Wm. H., 19 Oct. 1859, Marcella V. Atkinson, dau. of
    George                                                      10/25/59-2
Suter, J. H., 17 May 1855, Mary Jane Kidd, dau. of Churchill;
    corrected copy                                               6/ 7/55-2
Suter, J. H., 17 May 1855, Sarah Jane Kidd, dau. of Churchill    6/ 6/55-2
Suter, James W., 16 Oct. 1856, Sallie L. West, dau. of Benj.    10/18/56-2
Suter, Jas. W., 19 May 1859, Bella G. Leel, dau. of Henry        5/21/59-2
Suter, John T., 22 Sept. 1853, Louisa Weybourn                   9/24/53-2
Suton, John W., 26 Mar. 1858, Mar R. Ross                        3/31/58-2
Suton, Joseph L., 18 Aug. 1853, Martha W. Ballard                9/ 6/53-2
Sutton, Andrew J., 23 Nov. 1851, Mary A. Crane, dau. of (Col.)
    George                                                      12/ 2/51-2
Sutton, Benj. F., 1 Dec. 1853, Mary Jane Haines                 12/ 3/53-2
Sutton, Edward, 2 June 1856, Frances E. Callender                6/ 3/56-2
Sutton, George H., 4 May 1852, Jane Parkhill                     5/ 6/52-2
Sutton, Jas., 28 Oct. 1852, Catherine Isabella Locke            10/30/52-2
Sutton, Jonathan, 12 Apr. 1855, Ruth Ann Sanks                   4/18/55-2
Sutton, Robt. B., 7 Dec. 1853, Julia Biscoe, dau. of Langley    12/ 9/53-2
Sutton, Wm., 30 Sept. 1852, Elizabeth Chanceaulme               10/ 1/52-2
Swagley, Chas. H., 19 Aug. 1851, (Mrs.) L. V. Gardnar            9/ 2/51-2
Swail, Daniel Henry, 7 July 1859, Margaret Ann Hesson            7/11/59-2
Swain, G. Edwin, 3 July 1859, Lucy A. Clarke                     7/ 4/59-2
Swain, Robt. C. E., 14 July 1853, Kate Amoss, dau. of James      7/16/53-2
Swancoat, R. J., 14 Nov. 1855, Emma R. Day                      11/15/55-2
Swann, Jno. W., 2 Jan. 1859, Anna E. Jennings                    1/ 4/59-2
Swann, Thos. Mercer, 24 Feb. 1857, Sallie M. McDonald            3/ 4/57-2
Swearingen, James, 21 Dec. 1858, Martha D. Joslen                1/ 5/59-2
Sweeney, David, 5 Jan. 1858, Ellen Ward                          1/11/58-2
Sweeney, M. B. (Rev.), 16 May 1853, Margaret M. Lyford, dau. of
    William G.                                                   5/17/53-2
Sweeney, Peter, 14 May 1854, Margaret E. Hart; 5/19/54-2         5/20/54-2
Sweeney, T. Campbell, 8 Jan. 1857, Sue H. Hutchinson             1/13/57-2
Sweeney, W. H., 27 Feb. 1857, Elizabeth Ann Phillips             3/11/57-2
Sweeny, Alfred, 11 Mar. 1852, Sarah E. Lee                       3/16/52-2
Sweeny, Louis D., 4 Oct. 1855, Eliza G. Miller                  10/ 5/55-2
Sweeny, Pat'k., 17 Feb. 1852, Ellen Holten                       2/19/52-2
Sweet, Charles, 3 Feb. 1858, Alice B. Barton                     4/ 7/58-2
Sweet, Wm. H., 29 Jan. 1852, Frances C. Markland                 2/ 9/52-2
Sweeting, Benjamin F.; no date given, Jane Ball                  7/22/52-2
Swift, George W., 28 Mar. 1854, Elizabeth Ward                   4/ 6/54-2
Swift, Myron C., 16 Nov. 1852, Virginia Helen League, dau. of
    Geo. Brown                                                  11/18/52-2
Swift, Wm. Henry, 31 Jan. 1855, Elizabeth A. Slade               2/ 3/55-2
```

Swindell, Chas. E., 4 Nov. 1858, Mary E. Bierbower, dau. of L.   11/ 8/58-2
Swindell, James E., 24 Aug. 1852, Elizabeth Lawson, dau. of
    David   8/31/52-2
Switzer, Francis A., 19 Feb. 1856, Ann J. G. Bussard   2/23/56-2
Switzer, George Frederick, 17 Nov. 1858, Mary B. Hamilton,
    adopted dau. of John and Mary Ann   11/22/58-2
Switzer, John W., 19 May 1859, Martha A. Wright   5/25/59-2
Switzer, William F., 28 Aug. 1851, Elizabeth E. Pearce   9/ 4/51-2
Sykes, David, 1 May 1856, Mary J. Frederick   5/ 8/56-2
Sylvester, Edward C., 20 Dec. 1860, Ellen F. Wright   12/22/60-2
Sylvester, Thomas H., 8 Feb. 1855, Susan Hanson   2/ 9/55-2
Szezuthowski, Mickal, 11 Jan. 1857, Josephine C. B. Youse   1/16/57-2
Szmelenyi, Erneste, 29 July 1851, Mary M. Bayley   7/30/51-2
Tabele, Joseph H., 10 Nov. 1857, Mary E. Fitzpatrick, dau. of
    John M.   11/19/57-2
Tacker, Isaac, 21 May 1857, (Mrs.) Sarah C. McDonnall   5/26/57-2
Taggart, John F., 16 Sept. 1851, Martha Newell; corrected copy   9/19/51-2
Taggart, John H., 16 Sept. 1851, Martha Newell   9/18/51-2
Talbot, Edward K., 8 July 1851, Martean Pennington   8/25/51-2
Talbott, Adam D., 1 Oct. 1857, Mary Ann Cockey, dau. of
    Joshua F.   10/ 7/57-2
Talbott, Benjamin, 16 Dec. 1856, Sarah Virginia Martin   12/18/56-2
Talbott, Chas. M., 5 Jan. 1860, Eugenia D. Hooper, dau. of
    Wm.   1/12/60-2
Talbott, Geo. W., 27 Aug. 1851, Rachel Amanda Vermillion   11/ 5/51-2
Talbott, Henry F., 19 Mar. 1857, Eliza A. Crosby   3/20/57-2
Talbott, Sam'l. C., 31 Mar. 1852, Ann Maria Rickter   4/ 5/52-2
Talbott, Walter M., 11 Nov. 1857, Harriet M. Muncaster, dau. of
    E. M.   11/14/57-2
Talbott, William, 16 June 1851, Mary Jane Vandegrift   6/17/51-2
Talbott, Wm., 2 May 1853, Margaret Stewart   5/ 6/53-2
Tall, George W., 17 Aug. 1858, Amanda B. Jones   8/25/58-2
Tall, James, 5 Mar. 1857, Mary Humphreys, dau. of Henry   3/11/57-2
Tall, Thomas A., 26 June 1856, Mary C. Poor   6/28/56-2
Tall, Washington, 12 Jan. 1854, Sarah Elizabeth Humphreys, dau.
    of Henry   1/16/54-2
Tall, Young, 30 Jan. 1856, Elizabeth Street   2/ 6/56-2
Tallent, William, 31 Oct. 1853, (Mrs.) Sarah Sauscer   11/ 4/53-2
Tammen, John Frederick, 4 Sept. 1856, Anna E. Clautice, dau. of
    Wm.; corrected copy   9/ 9/56-2
Taney, Joseph A., 28 June 1855, Ann Louisa White, dau. of
    Ambrose A.   7/ 2/55-2
Taneyhill, Ericcson H., 28 May 1851, Mary E. D. Taneyhill   5/29/51-2
Tanner, George, 6 May 1853, Mary Green   5/14/53-2
Tannuere, John Frederick, 4 Sept. 1856, Anna C. Clautice, dau.
    of Wm.   9/ 6/56-2
Tapscoll, Wm. C., 11 June 1857, Martha V. Norwood, dau. of John 6/13/57-2
Tarby, Chas. H., 7 Oct. 1852, Laura M. Bancroft   10/27/52-2
Tarlton, J. H. T., 21 May 1853, Jane P. Baldwin   6/ 2/53-2
Tarman, Z., 19 Oct. 1852, Laura F. Horton   10/23/52-2
Tarman, Z., 29 Nov. 1855, Virginia Reside, dau. of Wm.   12/ 6/55-2
Tartar, Henry B., 4 Dec. 1855, Lucinda Bradix   12/ 6/55-2
Tarter, Lewis H., 16 Mar. 1856, Emily A. Braddox   3/18/56-2
Tate, Andrew, 11 Oct. 1852, Hannah Chalfant   10/12/52-2
Tate, Charles M., 12 Apr. 1859, Mary Louisa Dell, dau. of
    George B.   6/13/59-2
Tate, John J., 22 Feb. 1855, Mary E. Gilley   2/26/55-2
Tate, Perry J., 3 June 1856, Sarah E. Hughes   6/ 7/56-2
Tate, Tom T., 11 Dec. 1856, Louisa M. Crouch   12/16/56-2
Tate, William, 25 June 1860, Margaret Elizabeth Schley   2/26/60-2
Tatspaugh, William H., 2 Jan. 1851, Laura V. Hatton   1/ 4/51-2
Tatum, Joseph J., 2 Nov. 1857, Eliza Nichols   11/ 6/57-2
Taylor, Abednego, 31 Dec. 1850, Sarah S. Matthews   1/ 4/51-2
Taylor, Abednego, 30 Aug. 1858, Drucilla F. Byrd   9/ 1/58-2
Taylor, C. T., 30 July 1857, Mary F. Miller   8/ 4/57-2

```
Taylor, E. G., 16 May 1859, Caroline King                        5/28/59-2
Taylor, E. H., 16 June 1858, J. Trail                            6/18/58-2
Taylor, Edward J., 13 Apr. 1852, Ann Eliza Aitcheson             4/24/52-2
Taylor, Elias, 18 Nov. 1858, Martha L. Davis; 11/23/58-2        12/20/58-2
Taylor, Ezekiel, 8 Dec. 1856, Nancy E. Callahan                 12/12/56-2
Taylor, Geo. E., 28 Dec. 1852, Mary Larkins                      1/ 5/53-2
Taylor, George, 2 June 1859, Harriet Walker                      6/10/59-2
Taylor, Hezekiah B., 28 Sept. 1859, Elizabeth A. Horn            9/30/59-2
Taylor, Horace W., 17 Apr. 1854, Ama A. Robinson                 4/24/54-2
Taylor, Isaac J., 17 Jan. 1860, Ella Nizer, dau. of (Rev.)
     Thomas A.; corrected copy                                   1/21/60-2
Taylor, Isaac J., 17 Jan. 1860, Ella Wizer, dau. of (Rev.)
     Thomas A.                                                   1/20/60-2
Taylor, J. Holmes, 15 Feb. 1855, Emily D. Freeman, dau. of
     (Hon.) John                                                 2/22/55-2
Taylor, James, 27 Oct. 1853, Esther Jane Robinson              10/29/53-2
Taylor, James, Jr., 24 Feb. 1857, Annie H. Gault, dau. of
     (Capt.) C. L.                                               4/ 7/57-2
Taylor, James Lewis, 9 Nov. 1858, Hannah F. Jones, dau. of
     (Col.) Wilson                                              11/11/58-2
Taylor, John, 20 Jan. 1853, Mary Jane Haliday                    1/22/53-2
Taylor, John D., 12 Mar. 1860, Sarah J. Forney, dau. of Isaac    9/26/60-2
Taylor, John G., 4 Mar. 1852, Mary Lucretia Hoyet Willcox        3/17/52-2
Taylor, John H., 18 Feb. 1858, Sarah E. Green                    2/20/58-2
Taylor, John W., 9 Jan. 1855, Margaret C. McClure                1/16/55-2
Taylor, John W., 17 Nov. 1859, Margaret Rebecca Cecill           3/28/60-2
Taylor, Joseph, 19 Mar. 1858, Alice Ann Owings                  11/ 8/59-2
Taylor, Joseph S., 28 Feb. 1860, Annie B. Constable              3/ 2/60-2
Taylor, Marion M., 2 May 1853, Sarah V. Scott                    5/28/53-2
Taylor, Moses R., 16 Feb. 1858, Hannah Ann Garrett               2/18/58-2
Taylor, Samuel, 27 July 1854, Frances J. Brown                  10/27/54-2
Taylor, Samuel, 2 Sept. 1856, Martha Stocket                     9/ 4/56-2
Taylor, Samuel T., 1 July 1851, Cassandra J. Reed                7/ 4/51-2
Taylor, Thadius, 26 Apr. 1854, Julia Braughton                   4/27/54-2
Taylor, Thomas, 30 Aug. 1853, Agness R. Boring                   9/ 2/53-2
Taylor, Thomas, 9 Mar. 1854, Julia Ann Mullen                    3/23/54-2
Taylor, Thomas, 6 May 1860, Mary C. Taylor                       5/16/60-2
Taylor, Thomas L., 12 Mar. 1857, Harvey A. Mittan, dau. of
     Wm. H.                                                      3/16/57-2
Taylor, Thos. R., 1 Oct. 1856, Lucie A. Sturtevant             10/10/56-2
Taylor, W. W., 16 Apr. 1856, Ellen B. Hayes, dau. of Henry       4/18/56-2
Taylor, William; no date given, Mary Y. Butler                   5/15/51-2
Taylor, William, 28 Mar. 1854, Martha J. Shoemaker               4/ 5/54-2
Taylor, William, 28 Sept. 1854, Rachel Ann Grinage               9/30/54-2
Taylor, William, 4 Oct. 1855, Mary Ann Watson                   10/ 5/55-2
Taylor, William A., 27 Oct. 1857, Sophia M. Searly             10/29/57-2
Taylor, William C., 10 Aug. 1858, Mahala A. Sudery               8/12/58-2
Taylor, William H., 28 Aug. 1855, Ann E. Crooks                  9/ 1/55-2
Taylor, William H., 31 Oct. 1856, Martha F. Curley              11/ 3/56-2
Taylor, William S., 30 Sept. 1852, Margaret E. Anderson         10/ 2/52-2
Taylor, Wm. H., 17 Aug. 1853, Josephine K. Norris, dau. of
     Benjamin B.                                                 8/18/53-2
Taylor, Wm. T., 15 Feb. 1852, Amanda Wright                      5/ 3/52-2
Taylor, Wm. T., 17 Oct. 1853, Mary E. Muir                      11/ 5/53-2
Tayman, William, 12 Oct. 1857, (Mrs.) Margaret A. Hunt;
     10/17/57-2                                                 10/19/57-2
Teackle, John H. (Dr.), 22 Feb. 1859, Mary E. Parker             2/24/59-2
Teal, George McK., 11 Nov. 1851, Mary A. Clark; corrected
     copy                                                        4/13/52-2
Teal, James R., 5 Nov. 1856, Susan Brashears, dau. of J. B.     11/ 7/56-2
Teal, Samuel W., 24 Feb. 1857, Susanna Teal                      3/ 5/57-2
Tebbz, D. H., 28 Nov. 1855, Martha E. Stewart                   11/29/55-2
Teemey, Henry, 16 Feb. 1860, Lizzie Meyer                        2/23/60-2
Teenan, Patrick, 18 Sept. 1860, Minta McLaughlin                 9/19/60-2
Tegeler, George, 31 May 1852, Elenora Schaeffer                  6/ 3/52-2
```

```
Tegmeyer, John H., 21 June 1853, Laura M. Staub              6/24/53-2
Temperley, John, 1 July 1851, Mary E. Richardson             7/ 4/51-2
Temple, Thomas, 10 July 1851, (Mrs.) Ann Buly                7/14/51-2
Temple, William C., 29 May 1860, Amanda C. Jackson           6/ 1/60-2
Temps, William Henry, 8 Nov. 1851, Virginia Elizabeth Carroll 11/12/51-2
Tenain, John J., 20 Dec. 1853, Sarah J. Legrand             12/23/53-2
Tenley, Rob't. Theodore, 13 Sept. 1852, Mary Elizabeth Tennant 1/24/53-2
Tennant, William, 10 Apr. 1853, (Mrs.) Susan White           4/30/53-2
Tennent, John C., 11 June 1858, Sallie T. Potter, dau. of
    John R.                                                  6/15/58-2
Tennent, Robert, 3 Dec. 1857, Mary C. Koburn                12/ 4/57-2
Tennison, A. C., 24 Dec. 1853, J. S. L.                     12/26/53-2
Tennison, Oliver, 23 July 1857, (Mrs.) Margaret Ann Buck     7/24/57-2
Tennison, W. H., 31 July 1853, (Mrs.) M. A. Hoshal           8/ 5/53-2
Tensfield, Arnold, 14 May 1851, Mary Jane Pearce, dau. of Obed 5/17/51-2
Tensfield, Charles M., 6 Aug. 1855, Gertrude MacBeth         8/ 8/55-2
Terral, Nicholas, 16 Jan. 1851, Juletty Smith               1/21/51-2
Teurtley, Thomas, 13 Feb. 1854, Anne Anderson               2/15/54-2
Thalheimer, Joseph, 27 Dec. 1855, Margaret Dill             1/ 1/56-2
Thatcher, Jesse R., 11 Oct. 1853, Matilda A. Daniels        10/15/53-2
Thawley, Thomas W., 4 Apr. 1854, Louisa Kriel               6/ 5/54-2
Theasher, Isaac, 28 Nov. 1854, Mary J. Bartholow            11/29/54-2
Thirlkel, Thomas H., 7 Nov. 1858, Mary J. Haynes            11/13/58-2
Thirlkeld, James B., 19 Sept. 1853, Elizabeth Weaver, dau. of
    Wm.                                                      9/24/53-2
Thistle, David, 5 June 1853, Hannah R. Shanklin, dau. of
    Robert                                                   6/ 6/53-2
Thom, J. P. (Dr.), 6 Oct. 1857, Ella L. Wright, dau. of
    W. H. D'c.                                              10/ 8/57-2
Thomas, (?); no date given, Mary C. Davidson                5/25/54-2
Thomas, A. Wayne, 27 June 1860, Mary Becktel                6/28/60-2
Thomas, Allen, 8 Jan. 1857, Octavie Bringier, dau. of M. D.  2/12/57-2
Thomas, Andrew, 18 Jan. 1854, Arietta Jane Burgess          1/20/54-2
Thomas, B. M., 2 Nov. 1854, Lenora A. Silence              11/ 4/54-2
Thomas, Charles A., 9 Nov. 1854, Mary M. Gettear           11/11/54-2
Thomas, Charles L., 24 June 1857, Anna Hine                11/23/57-2
Thomas, Cornelius; no date given, Mary Clare Boarman       10/ 9/56-2
Thomas, Cornelius, 7 Oct. 1856, Mary Clare Boarman; corrected
    copy                                                   10/10/56-2
Thomas D. W. (Dr.), 6 Sept. 1854, Maria Meredith Piet       9/ 8/54-2
Thomas, David H., 15 May 1856, Eliza Baker                  5/17/56-2
Thomas, Delamere, 29 Nov. 1853, Sarah A. England           11/30/53-2
Thomas, Edward C., Jr., 18 Dec. 1856, Mary J. Gere         12/20/56-2
Thomas, Elias, 9 Dec. 1852, Louisa McKnew                  12/14/52-2
Thomas, Francis J., 1 Mar. 1857, Susanna R. Rooker          7/ 2/57-2
Thomas, Franklin, 2 May 1853, Mary Elizabeth Turner         5/ 5/53-2
Thomas, George P., 28 Nov. 1854, Maria L. Kemp             11/29/54-2
Thomas, George W., 25 Mar. 1854, Catherine J. Bailey        3/27/54-2
Thomas, Henry G., 6 Feb. 1856, Virginia Adelaide Batton, dau.
    of T. F.                                                2/18/56-2
Thomas, Henry H., 4 May 1852, Eleanor Linthicum, dau. of Wm. 5/ 6/52-2
Thomas, Henry T., 26 July 1853, (Mrs.) Maria Young          8/ 2/53-2
Thomas, J. (Capt.), 7 Dec. 1852, (Mrs.) Kiturh Benderson   12/ 9/52-2
Thomas, J. D. (Rev.), 13 Oct. 1859, M. E. Buckey          10/14/59-2
Thomas, Jacob B., 27 Jan. 1852, Lizzie A. Norwood           1/30/52-2
Thomas, James Carey (Dr.), 12 Oct. 1855, Mary Whitall, dau. of
    John M.                                                11/ 2/55-2
Thomas, Jas. Gale, 14 Feb. 1856, Harriet Ann Tucker         3/ 5/56-2
Thomas, John, 14 Sept. 1851, Margaret Ann Wallace           9/16/61-2
Thomas, John, 19 Nov. 1851, Isabella McClausland           12/13/51-2
Thomas, John, 19 Oct. 1854, Elizabethton A. Tustin         10/21/54-2
Thomas, John, 7 oct. 1855, Drady Mathis                    10/ 9/55-2
Thomas, John H., 8 Apr. 1852, Emily Gordon                  5/ 1/52-2
Thomas, Johnson P., 24 June 1851, Emma A. McDonald          6/26/51-2
Thomas, Joseph, 5 May 1858, Jane James                      5/ 7/58-2
```

Thomas, Joseph, 24 Apr. 1859, Sophia Paroway   4/26/59-2
Thomas, Joseph A., 4 Oct. 1852, Martha M. Redgrave   11/ 5/52-2
Thomas, Joshua, 13 July 1857, Maria E. Rennell   7/16/57-2
Thomas, Lewis, 3 May 1860, Emis Louisa Ford   5/ 4/60-2
Thomas, Matthew, 1 Mar. 1860, Hannah Waters   3/ 3/60-2
Thomas, Piere, 29 Jan. 1852, (Mrs.) Almira Malvina Rouse   2/11/52-2
Thomas, Richard, 18 Feb. 1851, Elizabeth Butler   3/ 7/51-2
Thomas, Richard, 1 Mar. 1853, Elizabeth Hitch   3/16/53-2
Thomas, Richard H. (Dr.), 9 Feb. 1859, Deborah C. Hinsdale,
     dau. of Henry   2/18/59-2
Thomas, Saml. L., 15 Dec. 1853, Caroline M. Simpson   12/20/53-2
Thomas, Saml. W., 22 Sept. 1858, Ellen A. Moon, dau. of
     Edward   9/30/58-2
Thomas, Samuel K. J., 6 May 1856, Rebecca J. Cadell   5/ 9/56-2
Thomas, Shadrach, 15 Mar. 1857, Sophia Makes   3/17/57-2
Thomas, Sterling, 25 July 1855, (Mrs.) Mary Ann Johnson   7/30/55-2
Thomas, William, 4 Nov. 1852, Amelia Davis   11/ 8/52-2
Thomas, William H., 22 Mar. 1859, Lavinia Fowler   3/29/59-2
Thomas, William H., 2 Nov. 1859, Suesie Hanna   11/ 8/59-2
Thomas, William Henry, 16 Jan. 1859, Rachel Ann Harryman   1/18/59-2
Thomas, William J., 28 Nov. 1853, Mary E. Smith, dau. of
     Joseph   12/19/53-2
Thomas, William O., 11 Apr. 1855, Emily Durham   4/12/55-2
Thomas, Wm., 19 Apr. 1860, Ann L. A. Davis, grandau. of Jacob
     Dunham   5/ 7/60-2
Thomas, Wm. W., 11 Sept. 1854, Margaret A. Baker   9/18/54-2
Thompson, Andrew J., 14 Dec. 1853, Sarah Amelia Coumbes   12/19/53-2
Thompson, Benjamin F., 18 Aug. 1859, Emily Jane Wilson   8/30/59-2
Thompson, Charles H., 16 Apr. 1857, Matilda J. Whitaker   4/18/57-2
Thompson, Charles L., 21 Oct. 1857, Mary A. Rainier   12/12/57-2
Thompson, Charles P., 8 Mar. 1860, Fannie D. Bowen   3/17/60-4
Thompson, Daniel, 13 Dec. 1853, (Mrs.) Sarah Jane Gwyn   12/17/53-2
Thompson, Dennis C., 29 Aug. 1854, Sallie E. Tuck   9/ 1/54-2
Thompson, Geo. H., 30 Mar. 1851, Lavinia Betts   4/15/51-2
Thompson, Geo. W., 16 Mar. 1852, Sarah Jane Witherstine   3/31/52-2
Thompson, George A., 1 Jan. 1857, Mary J. Carback   1/ 3/57-2
Thompson, George H., 22 Feb. 1855, Ann C. Smith   3/ 5/55-2
Thompson, George M., 26 May 1853, Ann E. Tipton   6/18/53-2
Thompson, George R., 14 June 1853, Sarah V. Graves   6/17/53-2
Thompson, George W., 9 Sept. 1856, Sarah E. Merson   9/15/56-2
Thompson, Goldsmith, 10 Jan. 1860, Anna Elizabeth Wilson   1/13/60-2
Thompson, Henry E., 3 Dec. 1857, Harriet A. Trusty   12/ 5/57-2
Thompson, Henry Wm., 4 July 1854, Martha Powell   7/ 7/54-2
Thompson, Jason, 16 Mar. 1852, Delilah Jessup   3/23/52-2
Thompson, John A., Jr., 15 July 1856, Mary Francis Scharf, dau.
     of Wm. J.   7/19/56-2
Thompson, John C. (Dr.), 24 Feb. 1858, Bettie C. Prine, dau. of
     David   2/25/58-2
Thompson, John D., 29 June 1854, Louisa A. Robinson, dau. of
     Thomas   6/30/54-2
Thompson, John S., 15 June 1854, Eliza Jane Paul   6/27/54-2
Thompson, John T., 7 June 1852, Julia Coulter   6/17/52-2
Thompson, John W., 15 May 1855, Martha A. Gould   5/19/55-2
Thompson, Joseph B., 26 Dec. 1860, Augusta A. Rigdon   12/28/60-2
Thompson, Joseph R., 26 Feb. 1851, Rebecca D. Cooper   2/27/51-2
Thompson, Levis B., 20 May 1855, Ann Elizabeth Barton, dau. of
     Samuel S.   6/12/55-2
Thompson, Mahlon, 16 Dec. 1851, Angeline Whitaker   2/ 4/52-2
Thompson, Nicholas Otis, 27 July 1854, Mary C. Wilson, dau.
     of Jacob   7/29/54-2
Thompson, Oliver, 2 Nov. 1858, Ann Montell   11/10/58-2
Thompson, Owen, 23 Dec. 1852, Olevia E. Ketler   12/29/52-2
Thompson, R. W. (Dr.), 3 July 1851, Janey E. Graves, dau. of
     Rob't.   7/ 8/51-2
Thompson, Richard, Jr., 14 Nov. 1860, Susan M. Hill   11/16/60-2

Thompson, Robert, 5 Nov. 1857, Ellen Clary   12/18/57-2
Thompson, Robert B., 13 Apr. 1852, Catharine Hedrick   4/14/52-2
Thompson, Robt. A., 21 Nov. 1854, Maria A. Mettee, dau. of
    (Mrs.) Catharine Frisbee   12/ 5/54-2
Thompson, Saml., 7 Mar. 1859, Lottie Price   3/16/59-2
Thompson, William, 29 June 1852, Sarah E. Judd   7/ 1/52-2
Thompson, William, 6 July 1854, Georgeanna Sipple; corrected
    copy   7/15/54-2
Thompson, William, 7 July 1854, Georgeanna Sipple   7/14/54-2
Thompson, William, 12 Oct. 1856, Matilda Caroline Files   10/15/56-2
Thompson, William Bryce, 10 Aug. 1858, Ellen P. Chapman, dau.
    of Wm.   8/12/58-2
Thompson, William C., 15 Oct. 1851, (Mrs.) Maria Warring   1/ 5/52-2
Thompson, William D., Jr., 3 July 1860, Josephine L. Brien   7/ 4/60-2
Thompson, William E., 2 Feb. 1859, Elizabeth Smith   9/ 5/59-2
Thompson, William S., 4 May 1852, Margaret Southgate   5/ 5/52-2
Thompson, Wm. A., 25 May 1852, Mary Lancaster   5/29/52-2
Thompson, Wm. H., 6 May 1856, M. E. Thomas   5/ 8/56-2
Thomson, James S., 4 Feb. 1851, Maria C. Working   2/ 6/51-2
Thomson, John D., 19 Apr. 1853, Eliza B. Thompson   4/20/53-2
Thomson, William H., 9 Feb. 1851, Martha E. Merson   2/11/51-2
Thorington, Francis A., 27 Sept. 1857, Rebecca A. Rote   9/29/57-2
Thorn, Owen; no date given, Margaret E. Piggott   10/21/57-2
Thornley, John (Dr.), 2 Apr. 1856, Mary D. Pearce, dau. of
    Nathaniel   4/ 3/56-2
Thornton, James (Capt.), 30 Mar. 1860, Louisa Jones, dau. of
    (Capt.) Jacob   3/31/60-2
Thornton, John, 20 Dec. 1855, Mary Cecelia Fisher, dau. of Wm.   12/22/55-2
Thornton, Oscar A., 15 June 1856, Carrie E. Billings   7/ 2/56-2
Thornton, Samuel, 6 Oct. 1859, Eliza Stockett, dau. of
    Amanuel and Elenora; corrected copy   11/18/59-2
Thornton, Thomas, 16 Nov. 1856, Mary E. Taylor   11/22/56-2
Thornton, Benjamin F., 5 July 1859, Margaret B. Creighton, dau.
    of (Capt.) J. R.   7/11/59-2
Thournton, Thomas H., 11 Nov. 1855, Sarah J. Lockwood   12/24/55-2
Thrall, George E., 5 June 1855, Thomasina H. Gist, dau. of
    (Col.) Thomas Hammond   6/13/55-2
Thrasher, J. E.; no date given, Mollie E. Bowles   5/ 7/59-2
Thruston, Charles B., 10 Dec. 1857, Rosalie Gantt   12/11/57-2
Thurnauer, Charles, 15 June 1859, Adeline Weglein, dau. of A.   6/16/59-2
Thursby, Robert, 8 Nov. 1853, Louisa C. Remmey, dau. of Edward   12/ 1/53-2
Thursby, Robert A., 8 Nov. 1853, Louisa C. Remmey, dau. of
    Edward   11/26/53-2
Thursby, Wm. E., 30 Sept. 1858, Mary A. Hobbs   10/ 2/58-2
Thurse, David U., 28 Dec. 1854, Henrietta O. Kennard, dau. of
    Richard   1/ 1/55-2
Thurston, Isaac, 4 May 1851, Rebecca Fowler   5/ 9/51-2
Thurston, Samuel, 6 Oct. 1850, Eliza Stockett, dau. of Andrew
    and Elenora   11/17/59-2
Thurston, Samuel T., 14 Sept. 1859, Hester Ann Thurston   9/19/59-2
Tice, Bartholomew, 5 Dec. 1852, Caroline Roof   12/ 8/52-2
Tietjen, John, 20 Apr. 1852, Cecelia O'Donald   4/23/52-2
Tiffany, Francis, 14 Oct. 1852, Esther Allison Brown, dau. of
    George J.   10/16/52-2
Tilden, Thomas W., 12 Nov. 1859, Helen Dawson   11/14/59-2
Tilghman, Charles W., 26 Oct. 1852, Eliza Ann Hackett, dau. of
    George A.   10/28/52-2
Tilghman, James (Capt.), 6 Feb. 1851, (Mrs.) Sarah Augusta
    Steele   2/ 7/51-2
Tilghman, John O., 12 Feb. 1852, Margarett Waters   2/14/52-2
Tilghman, John O., 12 Feb. 1852, Margaret Weaver; corrected
    copy   2/16/52-2
Tilghman, Wm. J., 2 May 1857, Sallie H. Williams   6/ 4/57-2
Tillion, Frederick, 4 July 1858, Ellen Mulligan   11/ 6/58-2
Tillman, William, 10 Apr. 1851, Susannah Greenwood   4/11/51-2

```
Tillman, William H., 26 Feb. 1857, Araminta Clark              2/28/57-2
Tilyard, Alfred H., 7 Oct. 1852, Mary A. Brown                 10/11/52-2
Timanus, John T., 11 Dec. 1856, Fannie A. Carrol, dau. of
     David                                                     12/15/56-2
Timbs, John K., 4 Sept. 1856, Carrie Meeds, dau. of William     9/11/56-2
Timmons, J. Edwin, 24 Nov. 1859, Sallie E. Wilson              12/ 3/59-2
Timpson, Thos., 4 Jan. 1854, Sarah J. Moulton                   1/ 5/54-2
Tindell, Peter, 8 Apr. 1852, Mariam Elvina Thompson             4/13/52-2
Tindle, Robt. W., Jr., 17 Feb. 1859, S. Lizzie Wagart           2/19/59-2
Tindle, William H., 24 May 1853, Anna J. Lowry                  5/31/53-2
Tinker, George W., 10 May 1855, Mary E. Ford Walston, dau. of
     Leanurn                                                    5/21/55-2
Tinker, George W., 10 May 1855, Mary E. Ford Walston, dau. of
     Lemira; corrected copy                                     6/26/55-2
Tipton, Shadrach W., 6 Nov. 1856, Sarah A. Leaf                11/14/56-2
Tipton, Thomas, 10 May 1853, Dianah Albaugh, dau. of Wm.        8/19/53-2
Tipton, William Henry, 10 July 1851, Mary Elizabeth Selby       7/15/51-2
Tiskner, Wm., 19 Oct. 1854, Maria Harven                       11/ 1/54-2
Todd, Charles, 8 Jan. 1856, (Mrs.) Jane Hamsey                  1/16/56-2
Todd, George (Capt.), 20 Nov. 1853, Maria Cook                11/21/53-2
Todd, John H., 31 May 1857, Mary Ann Stinson                    6/15/57-2
Todd, Martin (Capt.), 1 Nov. 1855, Ann Emily Cooper, dau. of
     Robert and Ruth                                           11/ 7/55-3
Todd, Thomas B., 18 Nov. 1857, Mary E. Rockwell                11/21/57-2
Todd, Wm. W., 30 Aug. 1851, Honora Gregg                        9/ 2/51-2
Todhunter, Isaac F., 22 Sept. 1852, Emma Keyworth, dau. of
     (Maj.) Robert                                              9/23/52-2
Toel, Gustav, 20 Sept. 1854, Eline Von Santen                   9/22/54-2
Toffling, John H., 14 Apr. 1852, Elmira Matthews                4/16/52-2
Tole, Thomas, 3 Jan. 1853, Mary Kay Anag-(?)                    1/12/53-2
Tolley, John A., 8 July 1851, Mary A. Gurney                    7/10/51-2
Tolson, Daniel, 24 May 1859, Mary M. Scott                      5/27/59-2
Tolson, John A. R., 4 Mar. 1851, Anna E. G. Cline, dau. of
     Henry                                                      3/14/51-2
Tomes, William, 20 Nov. 1851, Mary Ann Cook                    11/22/51-2
Tolson, William E., 18 Oct. 1860, Susanna S. Henson            10/23/60-2
Tomlinson, David B., 22 Dec. 1853, Elizabeth Wilson             1/11/54-2
Tomlinson, William, 1 Sept. 1857, Sarah Clemson                 2/ 5/58-2
Toner, John, 12 Apr. 1856, Rosanna McMahon                      5/ 3/56-2
Toner, Joshua, 21 Jan. 1858, Maria Munahan                      1/23/58-2
Toner, Thomas E., 23 Nov. 1854, Hester E. Thomas               11/25/54-2
Tonge, Samuel D., 15 Dec. 1859, Belle H. Grafton, dau. of Mark 12/19/59-2
Toogood, Edw'd., 3 Apr. 1851, Ellenora Keys; corrected copy     4/ 7/51-2
Toogood, Edw'd., 3 Apr. 1851, Ellenora Kings                    4/ 5/51-2
Toole, John A., 17 Apr. 1852, Bridget Montecue                  5/ 3/52-2
Toomey, Joseph H., 8 Oct. 1856, Christina Ourspung             10/11/56-2
Toor, Oliver, 20 Oct. 1858, Mary Elizabeth Bookhultz           12/15/58-2
Tormey, Leonard J., 21 Nov. 1860, Ellen M. Jenkins, dau. of
     Alfred                                                    11/23/60-2
Torrington, James, 3 Dec. 1860, Mary Ann Coggins               12/11/60-2
Touson, John P., 5 Oct. 1857, Mary E. Parsons                  10/21/57-2
Towles, James, 10 Feb. 1859, Josephine Isabel Whittington       2/11/59-2
Towner, John Lester, 26 Feb. 1851, Eliza Stewart                2/27/51-2
Towns, Robert, 15 Mar. 1860, Frances A. Kirby                   3/21/60-2
Towns, Robert (Capt.), 15 Mar. 1860, Frances A. Kirby, dau. of
     (Capt.) Edward; corrected copy                             3/24/60-2
Townsend, Francis H., 2 June 1860, Eliza A. Clendinen           6/ 9/60-2
Townsend, James A., 3 Nov. 1853, Adeline Duncan                11/ 7/53-2
Townsend, John, 22 Oct. 1857, Matilda Gough                    10/26/57-2
Townsend, John C., 25 Nov. 1852, Mary M. Hebb, dau. of John    11/30/52-2
Townsend, Lemuel P., 17 Feb. 1859, Sallie E. Orndorff, dau. of
     Wm.                                                        2/19/59-2
Townsend, Robert S., 30 May 1854, (Mrs.) Mary J. Scholar        6/ 7/54-2
Townsend, Wilson, 16 Oct. 1856, Mary L. W. Robey, dau. of
     W. W.                                                     11/13/56-2
```

Towson, Charles, 14 Feb. 1860, Mary A. Wonderly	2/16/60-2
Towson, Jehu J., 18 Sept. 1851, Mary E. Walker	9/22/51-2
Towson, Wm. H., 28 Apr. 1856, Martha Jane Green	5/ 6/56-2
Tr-(?)-tt, Samuel E., 14 Nov. 1853, Laura J. Soran	11/15/53-2
Tracey, Edward M., 18 Dec. 1854, Mary E. Eccleston	12/19/54-2
Tracey, James S., 2 July 1857, Mary Ambrosia Conelly	7/ 8/57-2
Tracy, Frank W., 23 Oct. 1855, Sarah E. Jones	11/ 8/55-2
Tracy, Joseph, 30 May 1853, Joanna Keppler Sweeny, dau. of Thomas	7/ 8/53-2
Trail, R. H., 14 Mar. 1854, Maria L. Hanna	5/16/57-2
Trainer, James R., 1 Nov. 1855, Mary Elizabeth McDaniel	11/ 6/55-2
Trainer, John R., 20 June 1852, Eliza Jane Brown, dau. of Jacob S.	6/21/52-2
Trainor, George B., 11 Aug. 1853, Sarah Greenwood	8/13/53-2
Trammell, George W., 12 Aug. 1858, Kate Virginia Beacham	8/14/58-2
Travers, C. W., 12 Feb. 1857, Mary J. Pritchett	2/17/57-2
Travers, John H., 21 Feb. 1857, M. C. Navy	2/27/57-2
Travers, Philip L., 16 Oct. 1859, Barbara M. Dettentahler	10/26/59-2
Travers, Thomas H., 23 Nov. 1854, Eliza Jane Navy, dau. of Moses	11/25/54-2
Travers, William W., 15 June 1857, Alexina S. Wells	6/17/57-2
Treacy, John H., 9 Oct. 1854, Emily J. Miller	10/13/54-2
Treakle, H. Clay, 23 Dec. 1852, Mary J. Starr	12/27/52-2
Tredwell, Joseph B., 17 Feb. 1857, Annie Lochar	2/21/57-2
Treffenberg, Wm. A., 30 June 1857, Emily C. Sewell	7/ 2/57-2
Trego, John Thos., 18 Oct. 1853, Nellie J. Norris, dau. of Basil	10/20/53-2
Trego, Wm. H., 12 Feb. 1857, Ann Isabel Lovejoy	2/14/57-2
Treiber, M., 8 Feb. 1855, Bell E. Collins, dau. of (Rev.) J.	2/ 9/55-2
Treich, John B., 31 Mar. 1858, (Mrs.) Mary P. Bloxom	4/13/58-2
Tress, Edward Owen, 19 Aug. 1856, Mary Elizabeth Hanson, dau. of Geo. H.	10/13/56-2
Trexler, John L., 12 May 1857, Julia A. H. Jones, dau. of G.	5/16/57-2
Trimble, Henry C., 5 May 1853, Phebe D. Carr	5/ 7/53-2
Trimble, L. B., 13 Apr. 1858, Anne Calhoun Presstman	4/16/58-2
Trine, Henry, 17 July 1853, Louisa M. Giberson	7/19/53-2
Trippe, William J., 23 Mar. 1852, Elizabeth P. Trippe	3/26/52-2
Trohwitter, Charles, 4 Dec. 1856, Mary Elizabeth Meyer	12/ 6/56-2
Trost, John, 4 Jan. 1859, Henrietta Hesse	1/ 6/59-2
Trot, Robert, 27 Nov. 1860, Anna Joice	11/29/60-2
Trott, Jonathan, 16 Sept. 1852, Virginia R. Tatham; corrected copy	9/18/52-2
Trotten, Benjamin, 12 Feb. 1855, Ellen E. Merrick	2/14/55-2
Trought, Robert P., 15 June 1858, Rachel G. Henry	6/18/58-2
Troutman, John, 22 May 1858, Tamezene Hudgins	6/ 7/58-2
Trow, Orin C., 8 June 1858, Nina R. Petri	6/10/58-2
Trower, Jesse E., 24 June 1858, Sarah Fifell	6/28/58-2
True, Bartus, 10 Feb. 1857, Sarah Catherine Hamilton	2/18/57-2
Truefont, G. C., 3 Jan. 1853, M. A. Gibson, dau. of Henry Freyer	1/ 4/53-2
Truett, John, 7 June 1860, Rosetta Sheith	6/ 9/60-2
Truitt, David J. O. (Dr.), 17 Mar. 1858, Martha E. Bevans	4/ 7/58-2
Trumbo, John R., 26 Dec. 1859, Catharine E. Segafoose	12/31/59-2
Trumbo, William, 4 Sept. 1854, Elizabeth Arnold	9/13/54-2
Tschudy, C. Howard, 29 Sept. 1853, Eliza M. Keirle	10/ 3/53-2
Tschudy, John Coleman, 20 Mar. 1855, Sarah Jane Freeland, dau. of Egbert	3/22/55-2
Tschudy, William M., 22 Apr. 1852, Mary Elizabeth Gameny, dau. of John	4/27/52-2
Tshundy, James H., 15 Apr. 1852, Martha A. Walker	4/27/52-2
Tubman, B. Gaither, 23 Oct. 1855, Maggie J. Thomson	10/31/55-2
Tubman, Samuel M., 2 Mar. 1858, Agnes P. Rees, dau. of James	3/ 4/58-2
Tucker, Benjamin E., 14 Nov. 1860, Mary A. Furgison	11/16/60-2
Tucker, Charles C., 21 Apr. 1853, Mary Virginia Cross	4/23/53-2
Tucker, Charlie E., 17 July 1856, Emeline Glover	7/19/56-2

Tucker, Enoch G., 5 Dec. 1855, Mary Cecilla Henderson, dau.
   of John and Caturia   12/11/55-2
Tucker, H., 13 Feb. 1853, Elizabeth Ann White, dau. of
   Jacob and Eliza   2/17/53-2
Tucker, James H., 6 Oct. 1857, Lydia A. Tartar   10/ 8/57-2
Tucker, John H., 27 July 1852, Jane D. Hill, dau. of Thomas G. 7/28/52-2
Tucker, Samuel E., 11 Nov. 1856, Rebecca H. Murdoch, dau. of
   William   11/13/56-2
Tucker, Samuel P., 6 Oct. 1858, Catharine Ellen Mask, dau. of
   Isaac G.   10/12/58-2
Tucker, Wm. B., 9 Dec. 1852, Ann Maria Lusby   12/14/52-2
Tucker, Wolcott C., 22 Nov. 1855, Eliza Jane McConkey, dau.
   of Geo. W.   11/26/55-2
Tuckerman, William, 23 Apr. 1860, Harriet J. Story   4/25/60-2
Tuckey, Joseph M., 4 Mar. 1858, Margaret P. Wallace   3/ 6/58-2
Tudor, George R., 28 Aug. 1855, Laura Virginia Welsh   8/30/55-2
Tudor, J. Frank, 12 July 1859, Bettie J. Muligan   7/22/59-2
Tudor, Lewis, 8 Jan. 1857, Sarah W. Russell   1/15/57-2
Tudor, Robert G., 29 June 1857, Sarah S. Marshall   9/ 8/57-2
Tufts, Leonard D., 14 Apr. 1856, Margaret Hughes   4/18/56-2
Tulley, Alexander J., 15 May 1855, Sarah A. Denson   7/18/55-2
Tulley, Alfred H., 13 July 1856, Martha J. Batchelor   7/30/56-2
Tumey, Daniel, 6 Nov. 1859, Rachel Yeager   11/19/59-2
Tune, E. J., 1 Dec. 1858, Ginnie Courtney, dau. of J.   12/11/58-2
Tupe, Henry G., 8 Dec. 1859, Louisa S. Lemcke, dau. of
   Henhy H.   12/16/59-2
Turnbough, Conrad, 12 Aug. 1858, Isabella B. McClelland 8/19/58-2
Turnbull, Adam, 22 Jan. 1852, Lydia Shock   1/24/52-2
Turnbull, Albert, 6 Mar. 1857, Margaret Noos   3/ 7/57-2
Turner, A. H., 27 Sept. 1859, Mary Byrne   9/30/59-2
Turner, Charles, 5 June 1858, (Mrs.) L. Webster   6/14/58-2
Turner, Charles C., 25 Mar. 1851, Margarett Patterson, dau. of
   Edward   3/27/51-2
Turner, Charles E., 1 May 1856, Eliza Ellen Padgitt   5/ 6/56-2
Turner, Charles T., 30 July 1856, Margaret A. Crough   8/ 9/56-2
Turner, Eli, 21 Sept. 1854, Mary E. Ensor   9/23/54-2
Turner, Frederick S., 19 Mar. 1851, Margaret Jane Cook, dau. of
   Jacob   3/26/51-2
Turner, Geo. W. A., 18 Nov. 1852, Margaret Ann Ledley   11/24/52-2
Turner, George W., 21 Mar. 1854, Sarah E. Dorman, dau. of
   William   3/29/54-2
Turner, George W., 1 May 1856, Elizabeth Turner   7/ 3/56-2
Turner, J. H., 27 Sept. 1859, Mary Byrne; corrected copy 10/ 1/59-2
Turner, James W., 1 July 1860, Mary C. Lineberger   7/ 3/60-2
Turner, Jesse, 11 Mar. 1858, Eliza Blunt   3/18/58-2
Turner, John, 19 Sept. 1854, Cornelia A. Anderson   9/21/59-2
Turner, John, 28 Dec. 1854, (Mrs.) Catharine Stewart   1/ 2/55-2
Turner, John Wesley, 7 Aug. 1851, Mary Frances Sipler   8/14/51-2
Turner, Joseph, 8 July 1852, Mary J. Jewett   7/16/52-2
Turner, N. G. C., 8 May 1856, Mary E. Robinson   5/10/56-2
Turner, Thomas V., 10 Nov. 1852, Sarah Amelia Stevenson, dau. of
   Alexander   1/ 3/53-2
Turner, William, 28 Aug. 1851, Susannah Batchelor   9/ 2/51-2
Turner, William, 28 Aug. 1854, Elizabeth Frisdy   11/ 1/54-2
Turner, William, 22 Dec. 1858, Mary E. Clark   12/28/58-2
Turner, William A., 19 May 1857, Sidney Patterson, dau. of
   Edward   5/21/57-2
Turner, William H. F., 8 Nov. 1853, Sarah E. Scott   11/ 9/53-2
Turner, Zacharias, 28 Oct. 1851, (Mrs.) Louisiana J. Turner 10/26/52-2
Tuttle, Henry C., 24 Aug. 1857, Sabina Carroll   8/26/57-2
Tweedy, Samuel Augustus, 28 Feb. 1856, Celina F. Essex 3/ 3/56-2
Twilley, William Jesse, 24 May 1860, Mary C. Reese   5/26/60-2
Tyler, Charles H., 16 Dec. 1856, Lizzie Wright, dau. of (Dr.)
   J. J. B.   12/24/56-2
Tyler, Danl., 15 July 1855, Margaret A. Pearis   8/17/55-2

Tyler, Geo. H. (Capt.), 4 Dec. 1851, Henrietta Ross   12/ 6/51-2
Tyler, John Wesley, 2 Dec. 1860, Mary Ann Jones   12/ 4/60-2
Tysinger, Lewis, 28 Oct. 1851, Margaret Elizabeth Ager, dau.
    of Alex'r.   10/30/51-2
Tyson, James W., 1 Jan. 1851, Elizabeth W. Dawson, dau. of
    Mordecai   1/ 3/51-2
Tyson, Marshall, 14 July 1857, Catharine Ellen Smith, dau. of
    Matthew   7/15/57-2
Tyson, Richard W., 28 June 1853, Julia M. Howard, dau. of
    (Hon.) B. C.   6/30/53-2
Tyson, William, 16 Aug. 1855, Sarah Ann Brown   9/15/55-2
Uhl, John Howard, 20 Dec. 1854, Caroline Dana Jarvis, dau. of
    Russell, grandau. of (Hon.) Joshua Dana   1/13/55-2
Uhrbrock, Christian, 26 Aug. 1860, Susanna Swanwick   8/27/60-2
Uhrlaub, Edward, 17 Sept. 1851, Helena A. Deville   9/19/51-2
Ulman, Albert, 5 June 1859, Clementine Harriss   6/ 7/59-2
Ulman, Benjamin F., 23 Nov. 1856, Henrietta B. Benjamin, dau.
    of Levi   11/26/56-2
Umbaugh, M. H., 3 Aug. 1854, E. Ellen Scott   8/ 4/54-2
Underwood, Alfred J., 13 Nov. 1855, Susan C. Perkins   11/15/55-2
Underwood, James, 26 July 1858, Elizabeth Austin   8/ 5/58-2
Underwood, John, 5 Jan. 1851, Sarah J. Barton   1/ 9/51-2
Underwood, Joseph, 14 Nov. 1855, Mary E. Mullen   11/17/55-2
Underwood, Joseph A., 24 Apr. 1851, Virginia Kirby   4/26/51-2
Underwood, Jos. A., 24 Apr. 1851, Virginia Kirby, dau. of
    Samuel; corrected copy   4/28/51-2
Underwood, William B., 4 Mar. 1856, Mary E. Kerr   7/ 4/56-2
Underwood, William, Jr., 11 Apr. 1851, Martha A. Bollisae   5/ 2/51-2
Unger, Jacob H., 6 May 1856, Clara E. Wick   5/ 8/56-2
Unger, P. (Dr.), 22 May 1854, Hannah Evatt   5/23/54-2
Updegraff, Wm., 18 Jan. 1855, Laura A. Mobley   1/20/55-2
Uperman, Joseph, 28 Mar. 1854, Mary M. Metzger   4/ 3/54-2
Uppercue, Lewis F., 2 June 1856, Sarah A. Clifford; corrected
    copy   7/10/56-2
Uppercue, Lewis F., 2 July 1856, Sarah A. Clifford   7/ 3/56-2
Upperman, George, 19 June 1860, Elizabeth T. J. Highfield   6/21/60-2
Upshur, John B., 8 July 1858, Annie M. Andrews   8/23/58-2
Upshur, William Brown, 6 Nov. 1851, Catharine Teackle Neale   11/17/51-2
Upton, John W., 17 Feb. 1853, Mary E. Etzlen   2/18/53-2
Ureg, Philip, 30 Apr. 1854, Sebilla Bowers   5/13/54-2
Uthman, John T., 16 Nov. 1854, Martha G. Osborne   11/17/54-2
Utterback, A. W., 11 Oct. 1859, Virginia Tongue, dau. of J. R.   10/14/59-2
Vagt, Toelke, 31 Jan. 1858, Teresa Trautman, dau. of J. C.   2/ 3/58-2
Vail, George (Hon.), 30 Apr. 1856, Mary Lewis Lightfoot   5/ 2/56-2
Vain, Jas. J., 1 Dec. 1856, Mary Ellen Smith   12/ 2/56-2
Vale, Isaac G., 10 June 1852, Corilla Parsons   6/16/52-2
Valiant, Nicholas, 21 Apr. 1859, Eliza Botterill   4/23/59-2
Valiant, Samuel, 23 Dec. 1856, Sarah Brooks   1/ 1/57-2
Valiant, Samuel M., 11 Sept. 1860, Mary Ann Richardson   9/18/60-2
Vallee, Francis, 8 Oct. 1859, Elizabeth A. Galloway   5/21/60-2
Vance, James H., 23 May 1852, Mary F. Watts   5/26/52-2
Vancourt, J. B., 17 Jan. 1853, Amelia Mittnachtt, dau. of
    George H.   1/27/53-2
VanDaneker, John, 16 Dec. 1860, Annie Reynolds   12/22/60-2
VanDaniker, John, 9 Jan. 1853, Ann Maria Steward   1/11/53-2
Vandersloot, F. W. (Dr.), 16 Dec. 1856, Sarah G. G. Fife   12/19/56-2
VanDusen, Joseph B., 13 May 1856, Eleanora C. Richstein, dau.
    of George   5/15/56-2
Vanhollen, Geo., 12 Nov. 1857, Alice A. Hanney   11/16/58-2
Vanhorn, Edw. A. C., 5 July 1860, Mary Downs   7/ 9/60-2
Vanhorn, John, 8 Apr. 1854, Parnelia A. Wilson   4/11/54-2
Vanmeter, Jacob, Jr., 19 Nov. 1857, Annie McNeill Harness   11/21/57-2
Vanpelt, Benjamin F., 31 Aug. 1859, Ladora Gosnell   9/ 3/59-2
Vanphelt, Abraham, 14 Feb. 1856, (Mrs.) Mary J. Shaw   2/16/56-2
Vansant, George W., 8 Apr. 1860, Maggie A. Shuley   4/16/60-2

```
Vansant, John R., 10 Oct. 1858, Joanna M. Maher              10/19/58-2
Vansant, Joseph, 16 Oct. 1855, E. White                      10/18/55-2
Vansant, Joseph, 16 Oct. 1855, Ellen White; corrected copy   10/19/55-2
Vansant, Joshua A., 2 Mar. 1856, Mary Younger                 3/ 7/56-2
Vansant, Richard, 29 July 1853, Rebecca Webb, dau. of
     Richard; 9/ 8/53-2                                       9/ 9/53-2
Vansant, Thomas H., 17 June 1855, Catharine Houser            6/19/55-2
Vansant, William H., 8 Feb. 1859, Frances L. Leinert          2/14/59-2
VanWyck, John C. (Dr.), 7 Apr. 1858, Rosalie Taylor Berry,
     dau. of Henry R.                                         4/23/58-2
VanZee, Govert, 17 May 1852, D. H. Hollander                  5/19/52-2
Varley, Thomas P., 13 Oct. 1853, Caroline Rutt               10/18/53-2
Vaughan, James H., 11 Oct. 1858, Maria C. Dorsey             10/19/58-2
Veara, Francis, 24 Nov. 1853, Catharine S. High             11/26/53-2
Veith, John, 30 July 1856, Kate McAvoy                        8/ 1/56-2
Venable, Joseph G., 31 Dec. 1851, Caroline C. Hutchinson      1/10/52-2
Veogler, Henry, 29 May 1856, Amanda Rachel Seebold            6/ 2/56-2
Vernay, James L., 27 Jan. 1859, Lizzie Gosnell               1/29/59-2
Vernon, John, 14 Feb. 1853, Sarah E. Lookingland, dau. of
     Andrew                                                   2/28/53-2
Vernum, John A., 16 Feb. 1858, Ellen E. Newell, adopted dau.
     of Geo. W. Crouch                                        2/19/58-2
Vesey, John, 22 Jan. 1852, Ann E. Cusac                       2/ 2/52-2
Vick, B. W., 14 Sept. 1854, Eudora Higgins                    9/18/54-2
Vickers, Clement, 22 Sept. 1859, Jenny L. Moore               9/24/59-2
Vickers, George W., 2 June 1857, Elizabeth Saulisbury         6/20/57-2
Vickers, Jesse, Jr., 7 June 1855, Amanda E. Hughes            6/ 8/55-2
Vickers, Theodore, 16 June 1856, Mary Agnes Hall              6/25/56-2
Vickery, Wm. H., 28 Jan. 1854, Kate F. Wells, dau. of Peter   1/30/54-2
Victon, Henry, 15 Jan. 1854, Elizabeth Poblitte              1/21/54-2
Vinart, John, 15 Feb. 1855, Margaret Mayers                   2/19/55-2
Vincente, Edward P., 6 Sept. 1858, Louise Cook                9/ 8/58-2
Virtue, David B., 5 Apr. 1853, Rachel F. Cruett               4/ 8/53-2
Virture, William, 22 Mar. 1855, Eliza J. Lugan                3/27/55-2
Vocke, Fred. F., 25 Mar. 1858, Christine Hossback             3/30/58-2
Vogeler, Frederick, 16 Oct. 1860, Walesca Rasch              10/18/60-2
Vogelgesang, George L., 9 Sept. 1858, Wilhelmina D. Reichert  9/11/58-2
Vogelson, William H., 23 Jan. 1854, (Mrs.) Sarah V. Wheeler   1/25/54-2
Vogle, Lewis, 18 Mar. 1852, Catharine Yost                    3/20/52-2
Voglson, William H., 20 Sept. 1857, Annie Parsons             9/21/57-2
Vogt, L. Henry, 24 Nov. 1858, Mary E. Holmes                 12/ 1/58-2
Voice, George W., 17 Apr. 1856, Mary Emily Dill               4/25/56-2
Volandt, Wm. J., 11 Nov. 1857, (Mrs.) Elizabeth Z. Volandt   11/23/57-2
Volck, Adalbert J., 6 July 1852, Letitia R. Allen             7/ 7/52-2
Volk, John, 30 July 1854, Martha A. DeFord                    7/31/54-2
Volkmar, William, 6 Mar. 1854, Wilhelmina Dieffenbach         3/10/54-2
Vond, R. S., 9 Mar. 1854, Anna R. Olwine                      3/11/54-2
Vondersmith, Samuel, 11 Dec. 1860, Elizabeth Maloney         12/12/60-2
Von During, Frederick, 22 Dec. 1859, Elizabeth J. Letmate, dau.
     of Charles A.                                            1/14/60-2
Von Hoxar, Henry G., 1 May 1853, Lizzie C. Dinsmore, dau. of
     Thos.                                                   11/ 8/53-2
Von Witzleben, L. Arthur, 5 Jan. 1858, Isabel Cudlipp, dau.
     of F.                                                    1/25/58-2
Varden, Robert B., 2 Apr. 1857, Susan C. S. Corum             4/ 4/57-2
Von Hein, Otto, 1 Mar. 1856, Shady M. P. Donaldson            3/ 4/56-2
Vouse, William, 23 Dec. 1858, Fannie M. Stanton             12/28/58-2
W-(?)-arring, Geo., 15 Apr. 1852, Mary Jane Kaufman           4/22/52-2
Waddell, William A., 12 July 1853, Sarah E. Green, dau. of
     Robert                                                   7/15/53-2
Wade, Geo. W., 30 Dec. 1851, Maria Catherine Stewart, dau. of
     Jno.                                                     1/ 2/52-2
Wade, Henry, 1 June 1853, Ann Maria Davis                     6/ 7/53-2
Wade, John Jackson, 22 May 1855, Harriet Ann Morris           5/12/55-2
Waesche, Geo. W., 26 Feb. 1857, Belle W. Smith                3/ 3/57-2
```

```
Wagner, August, 20 Sept. 1853, Susan Gettler                    9/28/53-2
Wagner, Chas., 25 Nov. 1856, Kate Beck, dau. of Thomas         11/27/56-2
Wagner, George, 4 Apr. 1854, Caroline C. Doberer                4/ 7/54-2
Wagner, George L., 14 Nov. 1854, Eliza A. Chaney               11/27/54-2
Wagner, John Henry, 7 Jan. 1858, Louise Ewald                   1/ 8/58-2
Wagner, Levi Z., 29 Mar. 1860, Susie F. Goodhue, grandau. of
     Edward Norris                                              3/31/60-2
Wagner, Lewis, 4 Dec. 1856, Jane E. Armager                    12/ 9/56-2
Wagner, Philip, 8 May 1853, Margaret B. Lauderbach              7/12/53-2
Wagner, Wm. H., 13 Dec. 1855, Sarah F. Clark                   12/17/55-2
Wailes, Stephen C., 13 Oct. 1853, Leah A. Stanford, dau. of
     Thomas                                                    10/18/53-2
Waite, William A., 15 May 1859, Mary E. Fade                    5/17/59-2
Wake, John C., 18 June 1857, Mary Elizabeth Scarff              6/20/57-2
Wakeman, Lewis B., 28 Aug. 1855, Mary E. Layfield               8/30/55-2
Walden, John (Col.), 28 Feb. 1854, Virginia B. Fitzgerald       3/ 1/54-2
Waldman, W. C., 25 Oct. 1860, Julia A. Brohel                  10/31/60-2
Waldner, Francis, 9 Apr. 1855, Friederika Busman                4/11/55-2
Walker, Charles E., 7 Jan. 1857, Belle W. Hildt, dau. of (Rev.)
     George                                                     1/30/57-2
Walker, Charles Wesley, 1 July 1852, Jemima Ann Espy            7/ 5/52-2
Walker, Edwin, 4 Dec. 1860, Kate Keyser, dau. of James         12/ 6/60-2
Walker, George W., 4 Dec. 1860, Mary C. Hoffman                12/ 6/60-2
Walker, J. Edward, 20 Oct. 1857, Cornelia A. Sidwell, dau. of
     Hugh                                                      10/24/57-2
Walker, John, 4 May 1852, Helen Marr, dau. of John H. Kennedy   5/ 6/52-2
Walker, John, 1 Aug. 1854, Sarah Ann Hamilton, dau. of
     Samuel H.                                                  8/ 2/54-2
Walker, John W., 22 Apr. 1851, Susan Radcliffe                  4/25/51-2
Walker, Joseph, 28 Oct. 1856, Mary Ellen Peach, dau. of Saml.  11/ 8/56-2
Walker, Joshua, 28 Feb. 1855, Hattie C. Goodrich                4/11/55-2
Walker, Nathan W., 18 May 1854, Anna R. Scott                   5/20/54-2
Walker, Nathaniel C., 2 Apr. 1857, Mary Jane Corletto           4/ 3/57-2
Walker, Patrick Henry, 31 May 1860, Rosa B. Mittnacht           6/ 2/60-2
Walker, Samuel, 13 Jan. 1857, Elizabeth Whitaker                1/15/57-2
Walker, Samuel F., 26 May 1853, Georgianna M. Free              5/31/53-2
Walker, Thomas Douglass, 1 June 1854, Eleanor Virgnia Warwick   6/ 3/54-2
Walker, Washington L., 13 July 1859, Permelia C. Hall           7/14/59-2
Walker, William H., 20 Jan. 1859, Alvira Fallin, dau. of Daniel 1/24/59-2
Walker, William J., 1 Sept. 1860, J. M. Teresa Hobbs            9/ 4/60-2
Walker, Wm., 15 Apr. 1856, Susan G. Michael                     4/21/56-2
Wall, Charles A., 28 Apr. 1859, M. Louisa Gambrill, dau. of
     H. N.                                                      5/ 3/59-2
Wall, James E., 10 Jan. 1853, Jane Gray                         1/12/53-2
Wall, Jesse H. D., 12 June 1856, (Mrs.) Eliza Holt              6/14/56-2
Wall, Jos. W., 27 Jan. 1859, Mary S. McCollum                   2/ 2/59-2
Wallace, Francis Marion, 22 Mar. 1859, Wilhelmina Richardson,
     dau. of Thomas                                             3/23/59-2
Wallace, Geo. R.; no date given, Ella Jane Habliston            2/17/54-2
Wallace, Joseph H., 10 Nov. 1855, Martha A. Romine             11/14/55-2
Wallace, Richard D., 24 Aug. 1856, Magdalene Brown, dau. of
     Able and Magdalena                                         9/18/56-2
Wallace, Wm. H., 26 June 1856, (Mrs.) Sarah Jane Barton         6/28/56-2
Wallenberg, Herman, 14 July 1859, Elizabeth Gontrum             7/16/59-2
Waller, James W., 17 Feb. 1854, Emma A. C. Hunt                 2/20/54-2
Walling, George, 24 Sept. 1854, Lizzie Conly                   10/ 4/54-2
Wallingford, James, 11 Mar. 1852, Louisa Ingles                 3/13/52-2
Walmsley, Benjamin F., 22 Feb. 1852, Annie Atwood               2/25/52-2
Walmsley, Edwin, 29 Nov. 1860, Mary J. McGaw, dau. of James    12/25/60-2
Walmsley, Theodore, 15 Mar. 1858, Ella Tenly                    4/19/58-2
Walmsley, Wm. T., 31 Dec. 1851, Elizabeth A. Barnes; corrected
     copy                                                       1/ 7/52-2
Walmsley, Wm. T., 31 Dec. 1851, Elizabeth A. Burnes             1/ 6/52-2
Walpert, Frederick, 9 July 1856, Frederica Heurig               7/12/56-2
Walsh, James, 10 Nov. 1856, Bridget E. Molloy                  11/13/56-2
```

```
Walstrum, George W., 8 Oct. 1854, Sarah Winkelman              10/10/54-2
Waltemyer, F. G. F., 11 Feb. 1855, Ellen Wade                 2/13/55-2
Walter, Asbury H., 3 July 1855, Martha J. Newgent             8/15/55-2
Walter, Francis S., 14 Sept. 1854, Frederica L. Owens         9/15/54-2
Walter, Geo. K., 21 Sept. 1859, Susan Risteau                 9/26/59-2
Walter, Joseph E., 1 Sept. 1853, Sarah Tash                   9/16/53-2
Walters, Edwin, 4 Apr. 1860, Virginia C. Torian               5/31/60-2
Walters, Job, 8 May 1851, Ellen L. Slack                      5/ 9/51-2
Waltham, Charlton S., 29 July 1852, Maria M. Billingslea      8/ 5/52-2
Waltham, Thos. A., 26 Mar. 1851, Frances Pearson              3/29/51-2
Waltjen, Augustus F., 13 June 1853, Martha Lucinda Barton,
    dau. of Samuel S.                                         6/17/53-2
Waltjen, Henry, 1 Oct. 1857, Mary Horn                        10/ 3/57-2
Waltjen, John Jairot, 16 May 1853, Mary Elizabeth Bauer, dau.
    of Michael                                                5/24/53-2
Walton, Andrew J., 22 July 1851, Maria W. McCleary            7/26/51-2
Walton, Elisha, 28 July 1858, Sarah Jane Russell              7/29/58-2
Walton, John A. B., 10 July 1858, Bridget Croughen            8/13/58-2
Walton, John H., 8 Apr. 1858, Mary J. Nichols                 4/17/58-2
Walton, John H., 30 Sept. 1860, Eleanor Henry, dau. of
    Isaac and Mary                                            10/15/60-2
Waltz, John, 14 Aug. 1855, Mary Elizabeth Hobbs               8/24/55-2
Walworth, William Bailey, 3 Oct. 1854, Jeanie Gray, dau. of
    Henry W.                                                  10/ 6/54-2
Walzl, John H., 25 June 1857, Augusta A. Eisenbrandt          7/ 1/57-2
Walzl, Louis, 23 Sept. 1856, Elizabeth Catharine Weldon       9/25/56-2
Wampler, Lycurgus, 11 Mar. 1851, Elizabeth Zouck              3/12/51-2
Wampler, Wm. A., 16 June 1859, Mattie M. Pearre               6/20/59-2
Wancott, Daniel, 30 Oct. 1856, Anna Coltston                  11/ 4/56-2
Waner, J. W., 5 Jan. 1860, Virginia Orem                      1/13/60-2
Wannall, Chas. P., 17 June 1852, Mary A. Hollingshead         6/19/52-2
Waples, Wm. A., 25 May 1859, Eliza E. Ballard, dau. of
    Arnold W.                                                 5/26/59-2
Warburton, Samuel, 25 Dec. 1856, Emily V. Hilton              1/ 1/57-2
Ward, Alexander W., 12 July 1855, Sarah J. Hull               7/14/55-2
Ward, Franklin, 10 Dec. 1857, Ann M. Griffith                 12/12/57-2
Ward, George, 20 Mar. 1851, Susanna Richards                 3/21/51-2
Ward, George Walter, 13 Nov. 1855, Mary B. Stewart            11/27/55-2
Ward, J. Smith, 24 Aug. 1857, Octavia Ward                    8/25/57-2
Ward, John, 8 Sept. 1851, Mary Campbell                       9/22/51-2
Ward, John B., 1 May 1851, Louisa P. David, dau. of Edward W. 5/ 5/51-2
Ward, John W., 21 Feb. 1855, Milcha A. Sparrow                3/ 3/55-2
Ward, Joseph H., 26 Mar. 1857, Mary Jane Wells                3/31/57-2
Ward, Patrick, 12 Aug. 1855, Margaret McAtee                  8/15/55-2
Ward, Richard Henry, 19 Mar. 1857, Mary Elizabeth Trott       3/23/57-2
Ward, Robert H., 19 Jan. 1851, Emmeline Stoutsberger          3/11/51-2
Ward, Thomas H., 28 May 1855, Kate Fuhr                       5/20/56-2
Ward, Ulysses B., 1 Nov. 1855, Anne Waters                    11/ 2/55-2
Ward, William, 9 Nov. 1852, (Mrs.) Louise Startzman           11/11/52-2
Ward, William, 2 June 1856, Frances E. Bowen                  6/ 6/56-2
Ward, William, 3 Dec. 1857, Mary E. Moody, dau. of J. B.      12/ 4/57-2
Ward, William, 22 Dec. 1858, Ada T. Gambrill                  12/24/58-2
Ward, William, 3 Apr. 1860, Alenia Welsh                      4/ 4/60-2
Ward, Wm. J., 7 Oct. 1856, E. Josephine Dugan, dau. of
    Frederick J.                                              10/11/56-2
Ward, Yates, 23 Dec. 1851, Jeanette Virginia Jones, dau. of
    Thomas and Margaret                                       12/25/51-2
Warde, James, 7 Aug. 1853, Catharine V. Sullivan              8/10/53-2
Wardell, John R., 21 Dec. 1859, Mary A. Peters                1/ 7/59-2
Wardell, W. S., 20 June 1860, Annie V. Sims                   6/30/60-2
Warden, Hugh, 23 Sept. 1851, Alice M. Roney                   9/25/51-2
Warden, James, 23 May 1855, Sophia De Haven Herring, dau. of
    Henry                                                     5/26/55-2
Wards, Samuel E., 11 Oct. 1852, Louisa Donaldson              10/14/52-2
Ware, Aaron, 11 Oct. 1855, Hannah M. Harris                   10/17/55-2
```

```
Ware, Elias, Jr.; no date given, Anna M. Dimmitt, dau. of
    Charles R.                                                    6/ 4/53-2
Ware, George W., 8 Apr. 1860, Mary Ann Parrish                    4/11/60-2
Ware, James, 25 Aug. 1853, Elenora Lyon                           9/ 5/53-2
Ware, Joseph, 28 Sept. 1852, Susannah Carroll                    10/ 8/52-2
Ware, Thomas, 6 Oct. 1853, Louisa C. Rupley                      10/ 7/53-2
Wareham, John T., 6 July 1853, Susan E. Keen                      7/ 7/53-2
Warfield, August, 8 Dec. 1859, Kate A. Gaither, dau. of Perry    12/ 9/59-2
Warfield, Charles D., 17 May 1853, Isabella Warfield, dau. of
    (Dr.) Gustavus                                                5/20/53-2
Warfield, Enoch, 30 Sept. 1852, Flavilla Duvall                  10/ 1/52-2
Warfield, George, Jr., 25 Oct. 1860, Ellen Fryer, dau. of
    E. S.                                                        10/29/60-2
Warfield, John, 26 Jan. 1860, Mary C. Stewart                     2/ 1/60-2
Warfield, Joseph, 23 Feb. 1854, Rosannah Williams, dau. of
    Jephry and Sarah                                              2/25/54-2
Warfield, Joseph, 8 Dec. 1859, Margaret A. Garrett               12/17/59-2
Warfield, Lem. A., 21 Dec. 1852, Ada A. Miller, dau. of T. C.     1/ 4/53-2
Warfield, Magruder, 8 Nov. 1859, Mary E. Dorsey                  11/ 9/59-2
Warfield, Robert W., 23 Apr. 1855, Maranda J. Dunn                5/24/55-2
Warfield, Singleton, 28 Nov. 1859, Susan Ann Godwin              11/30/59-2
Warfield, Vachel B., 12 May 1853, Lavinia P. Shockley             5/14/53-2
Warfield, Wm. H., 4 Jan. 1859, Lottie Duvall, dau. of (Dr.)
    M. M.                                                         1/ 7/59-2
Warford, Thos. N., 23 Aug. 1860, Agnes C. Linthicum              8/28/60-2
Wargart, Bascom Henry, 11 June 1854, Susanna Richter             1/19/54-2
Warner, E. Russell, 28 Aug. 1850, Carrie M. Scheiff, dau. of
    John                                                         9/ 1/50-2
Warner, Franklin C., 18 Feb. 1858, Hannah H. Bruce, dau. of
    Bobert                                                        2/22/58-2
Warner, James, 15 Oct. 1855, Sarah Jane Hutchinson              10/23/55-2
Warner, Joseph F., 7 Oct. 1857, Laura V. Unfab, dau. of
    Charles                                                      10/14/57-2
Warner, Thomas, 25 Oct. 1855, Mary Frederica Cooper             10/27/55-2
Warner, William R., 18 Mar. 1857, Fannie A. Dewlin               3/21/57-2
Warren, John (Capt.), 8 Nov. 1855, Mary J. Bonneville           11/13/55-2
Warrick, George, 2 July 1853, Mary E. Thompson                   7/ 6/53-2
Warring, Erasmus G., 29 Aug. 1852, Julia L. Worthington          9/ 1/52-2
Warring, Thomas B., 1 Mar. 1855, Elizabeth A. Clark              3/14/55-2
Warrington, Wm. T. S., 11 Sept. 1853, Ann E. Taylor             9/13/53-2
Warthen, William R., 19 Dec. 1858, Margaret Ann Huges          12/23/58-2
Warthon, B. H., 24 June 1851, Henrietta Augusta Morrison        6/26/51-2
Wartman, A. C., 28 June 1855, Kate Boyd                          7/ 4/55-2
Washburton, Samuel, 25 Dec. 1856, Emily V. Hilton              12/31/56-2
Washer, Joseph, 1 Jan. 1860, Catharine Twaddle                   1/ 6/60-2
Wasmus, Frederick H., 1 June 1859, Sallie A. McDonough           6/28/59-2
Waterhouse, John, 16 Aug. 1854, Emeline S. Smith, dau. of
    James Baxter                                                 8/17/54-2
Waterman, James, 27 Feb. 1856, Sophia Patterson                  2/28/56-2
Waterman, Wm. J., 14 Jan. 1858, Mary S. Winder, dau. of Wm. S.   1/18/58-2
Waters, Andrew G., 2 July 1851, Antonia M. Womrath, dau. of
    Geo. F.                                                      7/ 3/51-2
Waters, Charles, 13 Feb. 1851, Ellen Magness                     2/17/51-2
Waters, Charles, 4 June 1860, (Mrs.) Elizabeth Blake             6/ 8/60-2
Waters, Charles E., 17 July 1860, Anne M. Easter, dau. of
    Hamilton                                                     7/20/60-2
Waters, Ed. G. (Dr.), 9 Mar. 1854, Augusta Hitch                3/11/54-2
Waters, H. Griffin, 24 Mar. 1853, Maria Louisa Denny, dau. of
    Benjamin                                                     3/28/53-2
Waters, Henry, 30 Sept. 1860, Margaret A. Anderson             10/13/60-2
Waters, James, 13 Dec. 1860, Caroline Robinson                 12/15/60-2
Waters, James B., 3 Feb. 1852, Ellen R. Young                    2/ 7/52-2
Waters, Jno. Summerfield, 30 Dec. 1850, Jeannie C. Darst         1/22/51-2
Waters, John, 8 Jan. 1853, Antoinette J. La Reintrie, dau. of
    J. L.                                                        1/10/53-2
```

Waters, Levin L., 6 Dec. 1859, Lucretia Jones, dau. of (Col.)
  Arnold E.   12/12/59-2
Waters, Richard, 8 Oct. 1857, Charlotte Blake   10/10/57-2
Waters, Somerset R., Jr., 14 Jan. 1851, Rachel Davis, dau. of
  Samuel and Hannah G.   1/16/51-2
Waters, Somerset R., 18 Dec. 1855, Rachel Ann Waters   12/20/55-2
Waters, Thomas, 25 Dec. 1860, Mary A. La Fevre   12/27/60-2
Waters, William, 10 May 1854, Mary E. Gibbs   5/13/54-2
Waters, Wm., 12 June 1851, (Mrs.) Emily Jane Spurrier   6/14/51-2
Waterworth, Robert O., 3 May 1858, Mary Jane Taylor   5/ 5/58-2
Watkins, Burlisson, 10 Dec. 1854, Elizabeth Augusta Burgess 12/15/54-2
Watkins, Geo. W., 26 Feb. 1852, Sarah Jane Maloney   2/27/52-2
Watkins, George, 7 Jan. 1858, Rachel Williams   1/12/58-2
Watkins, John H., 28 June 1853, Mary Ellen Davis   7/ 9/53-2
Watkins, John H., 23 Sept. 1856, Lizzie Rathell   10/ 1/56-2
Watkins, John Q. A., 24 Nov. 1852, Lizzie Ann Bryan, dau. of
  Christopher   11/30/52-2
Watkins, Mortimer S., 21 Apr. 1853, Maria Bowman   4/25/53-2
Watkins, Nicholas W., 10 July 1857, O. C. Benteen   7/13/57-2
Watkins, Richard G., 22 Apr. 1857, Lizzie Smith   4/27/57-2
Watkins, Rich'd. (Rev.), 5 Aug. 1852, (Mrs.) Ellen B. Kelly 8/ 7/52-2
Watkins, Rich'd. R. (Rev.), 5 Aug. 1852, (Mrs.) Ellen B.
  Ridout; corrected copy   8/ 9/52-2
Watkins, Thos. G., son of (Dr.) Wm. W., 3 Nov. 1860, Kate
  A. Welling, dau. of Henry   11/ 6/60-2
Watkins, Wm., Jr., 15 Jan. 1852, Susan M. Bowie   1/20/52-2
Watson, Henry R., 25 Nov. 1851, Frances Burris   11/27/51-2
Watson, James C., 10 Sept. 1851, Elizabeth Bell, dau. of
  Theodore   11/18/51-2
Watson, Robert, 21 Sept. 1852, Ann Oliver   9/30/52-2
Watson, William H., 19 July 1853, Amelia J. B. Randolph   7/20/53-2
Watson, William H., 28 June 1855, Kate Redding   7/ 2/55-2
Watson, William H., 21 Apr. 1858, Margaret Smith   4/22/58-2
Watt, Richard, 3 Jan. 1854, Juliet Almira Barow, dau. of
  John C.   1/ 5/54-2
Watt, William T., 5 Mar. 1860, Alexina Hubbard   3/ 8/60-2
Watters, Henry R., 9 Sept. 1853, Emily B. Forwood   9/21/53-2
Watts, Benjamin, 8 Sept. 1855, Mary A. H. Wise   11/17/55-2
Watts, Benjamin T., 23 Dec. 1857, Parmelia Carney   12/24/57-2
Watts, Gassaway, 3 July 1853, Ellen Carter   7/ 9/53-2
Watts, George W., 9 Sept. 1858, Emily V. Miles   9/23/58-2
Watts, J. Marion, 5 Apr. 1855, Harriet V. Perry   4/21/55-2
Watts, J. Thomas, 24 Oct. 1855, Nannie W. Prentice   10/27/55-3
Watts, James H., 20 Feb. 1859, Sarah E. Reed   2/23/59-2
Watts, John Andrew, 20 Sept. 1854, Louisa Anne Prichard   9/26/54-2
Watts, Rich'd. H., 20 July 1851, Barbary C. Brown   7/23/51-2
Watts, Sabreitt, 26 Oct. 1851, Lucinda Taylor   10/28/51-2
Watts, Thomas, 16 June 1859, Eliza Jane Baker   6/18/59-2
Watts, Thos. M., 16 Feb. 1854, Maria L. Nuthall, dau. of John W. 2/18/54-2
Watts, W. W., 24 May 1853, Susan Wiest   5/26/53-2
Watts, Wm. H., 3 Apr. 1851, Julia Ann Watts   4/ 7/51-2
Waugh, Beverly R., 25 Aug. 1853, Sarah S. Beatty, dau. of
  George   8/30/53-2
Waxter, William P., 29 Apr. 1860, Elizabeth Sprucebank   5/ 1/60-2
Way, A. J. H., 3 Nov. 1853, Kate Griffith   11/ 8/53-2
Way, David C., 26 Jan. 1860, Alice M. Maxwell   2/ 9/60-2
Way, George W., 14 Oct. 1852, Susanna Pope   10/18/52-2
Way, Henry, 12 Jan. 1854, Martha Richardson   1/13/54-2
Ways, Ignatius, 30 Apr. 1855, Jane E. Ridgely   5/12/55-2
Wayson, William H., 30 June 1857, Elizabeth Woodfield   7/ 2/57-2
Wealthy, John, 13 Dec. 1859, (Mrs.) Rosetta Jackes   1/ 5/60-2
Weatherby, Chas., 14 Dec. 1858, Maggie B. Harbert, dau. of
  Geo. W.   12/15/58-2
Weatherby, J. Emory, 21 July 1859, Millie De Bruder, dau. of
  Benjamin   7/23/59-2

Weatherstine, Chas. G., 18 Jan. 1852, Ann E. Purnell   1/31/52-2
Weatherston, John, 18 Mar. 1852, Mary E. Shipley   3/20/52-2
Weaver, Casper, 2 Dec. 1851, (Mrs.) Evline Tindle   12/ 4/51-2
Weaver, Casper, 10 Jan. 1854, L. Yingling   1/12/54-2
Weaver, Charles T., 29 June 1856, Laura J. Campbell   7/ 1/56-2
Weaver, Daniel L., 5 Sept. 1857, Arjyra S. M. L. Davis, dau.
     of Abel and Eliza Whitehurst   9/ 9/57-2
Weaver, Geo. R., 1 Dec. 1856, Fannie A. Baxley   12/ 6/56-2
Weaver, George W., 19 May 1853, Mary J. Flood   8/12/53-2
Weaver, Henry, 20 Apr. 1857, Catharine Houser   4/24/57-2
Weaver, Jacob Belville, 30 Oct. 1853, Elizabeth Ann Whorton,
     dau. of William   11/ 1/53-2
Weaver, James E., 8 Dec. 1856, Abigail A. Maoers   12/18/56-2
Weaver, James E., 26 July 1859, Eve M. Rogers, dau. of Elisha 7/28/59-2
Weaver, John Charles, 3 June 1858, Mary Jane Toomey, dau. of
     Josiah and Henrietta   6/ 5/58-2
Weaver, John J., 5 June 1854, Elizabeth A. Shipley, dau. of
     Hammond   6/16/54-2
Weaver, Lewis, 17 Jan. 1856, Margaret Poppe   1/19/56-2
Weaver, Thomas, 1 Sept. 1853, Susan Kelly   9/16/53-2
Weaver, Thomas, 21 Sept. 1857, Martha E. Turner, dau. of
     John   9/23/57-2
Weaver, Tobias E., 8 July 1856, S. E. Owens   7/24/56-2
Weaver, Wm. H., 30 Dec. 1851, Lizzie Jane Yeo, dau. of
     Alexander   1/ 2/52-2
Webb, C. Howard; no date given, Kate L. Mooney   9/15/57-2
Webb, C. Howard, 9 July 1857, Kate L. Mooney; corrected copy 9/17/57-2
Webb, Edward, 13 Oct. 1853, E. R. Burgee   10/15/53-2
Webb, Francis I. D., 16 Oct. 1860, Mary E. Postley; corrected
     copy   10/18/60-2
Webb, Francis J. D., 16 Oct. 1860, Mary E. Postley   10/17/60-2
Webb, Geo. D., 3 July 1859, Caroline Wheat   7/25/59-2
Webb, James, 9 Jan. 1853, Mary Brown   1/10/53-2
Webb, John, 21 Feb. 1860, Ann Maria Wells   4/ 2/60-2
Webb, John, Jr., 7 Feb. 1858, Margaret Coyne   5/ 6/58-2
Webb, John H., 8 Apr. 1856, Sarah Mayhew   4/12/56-2
Webb, John W., 24 Dec. 1856, Margaret A. Thompson   12/27/56-2
Webb, Robert, 2 July 1854, Mary Jane Cooper   7/13/54-2
Webb, Sam'l., 27 July 1851, Ann C. Phelan   7/30/51-2
Webb, Thos. H., 1 Mar. 1854, (Mrs.) Nancy Diggs   3/ 7/54-2
Webb, Vincent M., 8 Mar. 1859, Sarah A. Yeatman   3/10/59-2
Webb, William, 26 Oct. 1851, Mary Ellen Thompson   10/28/51-2
Webb, William George, 8 June 1851, Amanda C. Woods   6/11/51-2
Webbent, George, 28 Dec. 1856, Margaret A. Ennis, dau. of
     (Capt.) Joseph   1/ 7/57-2
Webber, Alexander G., 9 Nov. 1852, Estelle Maria Mannar, dau. of
     James B.   11/22/52-2
Weber, Henry, 24 Nov. 1853, Barbara Waldner   11/28/53-2
Weber, John, 19 Feb. 1854, Caroline Kan   3/ 3/54-2
Weber, John H., 10 Mar. 1857, Sophia Snyder   3/12/57-2
Weber, John Reisen, 1 Feb. 1857, Elizabeth Lechner   2/ 3/57-2
Weber, William F., 10 May 1859, Elizabeth C. Shaible; corrected
     copy   5/14/59-2
Weber, William F., 10 May 1859, Elizabeth C. Shauble   5/12/59-2
Webster, Edwin H., 6 June 1855, Caroline H. Earl   6/11/55-2
Webster, Geo. F., 8 Feb. 1854, Ellen Trail   2/ 9/54-2
Webster, H. W., Jr. (Dr.), 2 Apr. 1856, Kate E. Rizer   4/ 4/56-2
Webster, John M., 9 Sept. 1860, Eliza F. Cunningham   9/25/60-2
Webster, John T., 28 Aug. 1851, Mary Ann O'Donnell   8/30/51-2
Webster, Robert; no date given, Ellen Ann Dorsey, dau. of
     Gustavus   11/19/56-2
Webster, Stephen G., 10 June 1852, Jane Franklin   6/14/52-2
Webster, Thomas J., 20 Nov. 1856, Ann E. Gardner   11/25/56-2
Webster, Thomas W., 10 May 1853, Emma Mahaney, dau. of John 5/13/53-2
Wecker, Joseph, 7 Mar. 1859, Catharine Adelaide Kenney   3/ 8/59-2

Weckesser, Tobias W., 28 June 1859, (Mrs.) Mary Ann Ramsey   7/ 2/59-2
Wedge, W. S., 8 Apr. 1857, Margaret Higginbotham   4/14/57-2
Weedon, Alexander, 22 Nov. 1853, Elizabeth Cordelia Weedon;
  11/26/53-2   11/28/53-2
Weedon, James H., 8 Dec. 1857, Fannie E. Giddings, dau. of Jas. 12/12/57-2
Weedon, Tristram, 19 May 1852, Hannah M. Nickerson   5/21/52-2
Weeks, Benjamin, 1 Dec. 1853, Susan Wheeler   12/ 5/53-2
Weeks, Charles C., 2 Dec. 1857, Maggie S. Glassell, dau. of
  Wm. E.   12/ 7/57-2
Weeks, Edward C. N., 25 Dec. 1854, Kate Webb   12/27/54-2
Weeks, George H., 31 May 1859, Laura Babbitt, dau. of (Maj.)
  E. B.   6/ 4/59-2
Weeks, Gustavus, 18 Oct. 1860, Sarah Dorsey   10/27/60-2
Weeks, John H., 11 Dec. 1855, Mary E. Gray, dau. of Samuel   12/15/55-2
Weeks, Samuel F., 1 Nov. 1860, Lizzie Kate Dyott   11/15/60-2
Weeks, Wm. H., 8 Feb. 1855, Elizabeth Jane Underwood   2/10/55-2
Weems, Geo. W., 4 Oct. 1854, Rachel Anna D. Weems, dau. of
  (Dr.) David G.   10/ 5/54-2
Weems, Wm. M., 26 Apr. 1854, (Mrs.) Mary Manyhan Dempsey   4/26/54-2
Wehn, Phillip L., 25 Apr. 1859, Elizabeth Ann Erhart   4/28/59-2
Wehrheim, Philip, 11 Dec. 1859, Sibila Horbacher   12/16/59-2
Wehrly, George, 6 May 1857, Hattie B. Vinton, dau. of (Rev.)
  Spencer   5/ 8/57-2
Weiber, David, 30 Mar. 1858, Anna Niles Locke, dau. of Henry N. 3/31/58-2
Weiker, John, 11 Aug. 1853, Margaret Lightner   9/ 1/53-2
Weir, William J., 22 Dec. 1857, Margaret Campbell   2/23/58-2
Weirich, J. C., 16 Oct. 1851, Leah Jane Hedrick   11/ 1/51-2
Weise, William G., 11 June 1851, Margaret Gearhold   6/13/51-2
Weishampel, John F., Jr., 25 Oct. 1855, Mary Elizabeth Addeson,
  dau. of Samuel S.   10/27/55-3
Weitzel, Thomas, 25 Nov. 1854, Sarah Jane Loane, dau. of
  Joseph   1/ 3/55-2
Welby, Charles C., 4 Sept. 1860, Maggie E. Hartman, dau. of
  Isaac   9/ 8/60-2
Welch, Alexander G., 14 Nov. 1855, Bethea Muirhead   11/17/55-2
Welch, Charles, 21 May 1858, Judy Wislein   5/24/58-2
Welch, David, 26 Apr. 1855, Kate A. Boggs, dau. of John   5/ 5/55-2
Welch, James, 27 Apr. 1851, Julia Williams   5/26/51-2
Welch, Jno. L., 14 Oct. 1856, Louisa E. Robinson, dau. of E. W. 10/15/56-2
Welch, John, 15 July 1855, Frances Hobbs   7/17/55-2
Welch, Martin, 20 Dec. 1858, Kate Rositer   12/22/58-2
Welch, Samuel C., 21 Feb. 1858, Margaret A. Cushley   2/23/58-2
Welch, Warren (Dr.), 18 Sept. 1855, Mary A. Durst, dau. of
  John Felix   9/20/55-2
Wellener, John B., 12 May 1853, Susannah M. Alberger   5/16/53-2
Wellener, Thomas W., 12 Sept. 1859, Henrietta Coleman   9/14/59-2
Wellenner, Joseph W., 8 Nov. 1858, Margaret Rosalia Smith   11/13/58-2
Weller, George L., 13 Aug. 1860, Annie V. Johnson   8/14/60-2
Wells, Clinton G., 28 Oct. 1857, Esther A. League, dau. of
  Thomas M.   11/13/57-2
Wells, Jackson, 19 June 1857, (Mrs.) Caroline B. Manship   7/ 1/57-2
Wells, Joseph H., 9 Mar. 1854, Ellen G. Benson, dau. of
  (Capt.) Paul   3/ 9/54-2
Wells, Laban A., 23 Dec. 1851, Sarah G. Collins   1/ 5/52-2
Wells, Richard, 1 June 1858, Mary A. Daiger   6/ 4/58-2
Wells, Robert, 6 Sept. 1859, Alice J. Searley   9/ 9/59-2
Welsch, Joseph, 30 Sept. 1858, Ellen Kane   10/ 4/58-2
Welsh, Alonzo, 28 Feb. 1859, (Mrs.) Susan Morgan, dau. of
  Jacob Creamer   2/ 7/52-2
Welsh, Charles E., 18 Aug. 1858, Eliza C. Holden, dau. of
  Thomas L.   8/23/58-2
Welsh, Columbus, 30 Apr. 1857, Ellen Webb   5/ 1/57-2
Welsh, Henry H., 22 Aug. 1853, Susannah T. Oram, dau. of (Capt.)
  Joshua G.   8/29/53-2
Welsh, John W., 24 May 1851, Mary Voglesong   5/30/51-2

Welsh, Joseph M., 5 Mar. 1857, Lizzie Charles   3/ 7/57-2
Welsh, Peter, 11 Sept. 1853, Catherine Keefe   9/15/53-2
Welsh, Thomas; no date given, Maria S. Cherry, dau. of
     Talmadge   6/20/60-2
Welsh, William, 17 July 1856, Margaret A. French   7/25/56-2
Welsh, William C., 9 May 1859, Josephine Summers   5/24/59-2
Welsh, William H., 29 Nov. 1860, Sallie A. Wickes, dau. of
     (Col.) Joseph; 12/ 1/60-2; 12/ 4/60-2   12/ 6/60-2
Welsh, William O., 28 Apr. 1859, Eliza J. Woods   4/30/59-2
Welton, John W., 7 July 1852, Sarah Jane Howard   7/ 8/52-2
Wentworth, John W., 11 Oct. 1856, Sarah A. Burkins   10/20/56-2
Wenzell, Charles, 28 Oct. 1854, Georgeanna Ruth Foote, dau. of
     (Maj.) T.   11/18/54-2
Werdebaugh, John, Jr., 30 June 1851, Mary Jane Macelfresh   7/ 2/51-2
Werneburg, Frederick William, 26 Dec. 1858, Louisa Caroline
     Brack   1/ 1/59-2
Werner, Charles, 3 June 1860, Katharine Myers   6/ 5/60-2
Werner, Gustav, 30 Jan. 1852, Emilie Josephine Klunk   1/ 2/52-2
Werner, Louis, 25 July 1858, Frederica Grieberd   7/27/58-2
Wertz, John E., 7 Aug. 1856, Sarah A. McNelly   8/11/56-2
Werweck, John, 7 Feb. 1853, (Mrs.) Rebecca J. Patterson   2/ 9/53-2
Wesels, John, 14 Dec. 1854, (Mrs.) Margaret Cooper   12/19/54-2
West, Albert T., 27 May 1856, Frances Brooks   5/28/56-2
West, Henry W., 26 Apr. 1859, Roseanna McNally   4/29/59-2
West, James H., 11 Mar. 1856, Julia Eapesy   3/14/56-2
West, James H., 10 July 1856, Laura V. Elingsworth   7/12/56-2
West, James H., 3 Oct. 1859, Margaret A. Weaver   10/ 6/59-2
West, Robert, 23 Oct. 1859, Virginia Bangs   10/29/59-2
West, Thomas, 2 Nov. 1856, Emily Jane Fisher   11/ 4/56-2
West, William C., 2 June 1857, Mary Josephine Jameson, dau. of
     (Dr.) Charles   6/ 8/57-2
West, William H., 31 Oct. 1853, Mary E. Stanford, dau. of
     Thomas   11/ 3/53-2
West, William H., 1 Apr. 1857, Elizabeth A. Barrett   4/17/57-2
Westaway, William H., 4 Feb. 1858, Sophia Hudson   2/ 6/58-2
Westervelt, Richard L., 24 Sept. 1857, Mary A. Carson   9/28/57-2
Wetherald, Sam'l. B., 18 Sept. 1852, Anna Virginia Parker   9/21/52-2
Wetherly, James W., 17 Nov. 1853, Maria L. Ringgold, dau. of P. 11/21/53-2
Wetherstine, Thadeus, 4 May 1857, Emily E. Andrews   5/13/57-2
Wetmore, Theodore R., 22 Sept. 1859, Ellen D'Arcy, dau. of
     John N.   9/26/59-2
Wetmore, William, 5 Mar. 1856, Annie E. Dougherty, dau. of
     William C.; corrected copy   3/12/56-2
Wetnurl, William, 5 Mar. 1856, Annie E. Dougherty, dau. of
     William C.   3/11/56-2
Wetzel, Frederick, 8 Dec. 1859, Margaret Ann Shoemaker   12/12/59-2
Wever, Harman I., 24 July 1855, Elizabeth Henkel   7/28/55-2
Whalen, Oliver P., 9 Oct. 1860, Elizabeth Magness   10/11/60-2
Wharry, Robert N., 29 July 1860, Jennie Wilson   8/17/60-2
Wheary, Wm. H., 5 Jan. 1858, Eleanor M. Marston   1/13/58-2
Wheat, John A., 8 June 1854, Elizabeth D. Crawford, dau. of
     Robert K.   6/10/54-2
Wheatley, Benjamin, 6 July 1854, Mary E. Johnson   7/ 8/54-2
Wheatly, Edward J. (?) June 1856, Elizabeth Ann Cooper   6/ 9/56-2
Wheaton, David L., 15 Mar. 1857, (Mrs.) Susan R. Parker   3/16/57-2
Wheedon, Madison, 9 Oct. 1856, Sally A. Smith, dau. of James 10/18/56-2
Wheeler, Alfred, 13 July 1858, (Mrs.) Julia A. V. Sederberg   7/16/58-2
Wheeler, Bennet L., 25 Dec. 1855, Mary A. Ward   12/28/55-2
Wheeler, Charles A., 7 June 1855, Catherine Bokman   6/ 9/55-2
Wheeler, J. Columbus, 3 Sept. 1855, Sophia B. Medinger, dau.
     of C. A.   9/ 6/55-2
Wheeler, James, 16 May 1855, Sarah A. Woollen, dau. of James 5/17/55-2
Wheeler, James, 18 Nov. 1859, Susan Fisher   11/19/59-2
Wheeler, James H., 14 Jan. 1851, Susan Willamina Wamsley   1/18/51-2
Wheeler, John B., 2 Sept. 1856, Margaret L. Cook   9/10/56-2

Wheeler, John B., 2 Sept. 1856, Margaret L. Cook, dau. of
    Henry and Julia A.; corrected copy   9/20/56-2
Wheeler, Lewis H., 3 Oct. 1860, Mary H. Pomeroy   10/ 9/60-2
Wheeler, Madison, 9 Oct. 1856, Sally A. Smith, dau. of James   10/17/56-2
Wheeler, Tobias K., 1 June 1852, Elizabeth A. Dixon   6/ 3/52-2
Wheeler, William, 6 Oct. 1857, Eliza Stinchcomb   10/ 8/57-2
Wheeler, William A., 3 Apr. 1856, Letitta McLaughlin   5/13/56-2
Whelan, George W., 26 May 1853, Mary B. Haupt   6/ 4/53-2
Whelan, Louis N., 18 Nov. 1856, Rosa J. Foudriat, dau. of P. 11/20/56-2
Whelan, Michael, 21 Nov. 1852, Mary McAvoy   12/ 2/52-2
Whelan, Thomas, Jr., 27 Oct. 1853, H. Mary Gluck, dau. of
    John H. Duvall   10/28/53-2
Wheler, Thomas B., 9 June 1853, Mary M. Carns   6/11/53-2
Wheley, John, 27 Nov. 1856, Ann Carey   11/29/56-2
Wherrett, James M., 18 June 1851, Lucy Ann Elder   6/23/51-2
Wherritt, Geo. (Capt.), 4 May 1854, Mary B. Blackson   5/ 8/54-2
Wherritt, Thos. J., 15 Dec. 1859, Rebecca A. Lee   12/19/59-2
Whistler, George W., Jr., 1 June 1854, Julia Winas, dau. of
    Ross   6/ 2/54-2
Whitaker, Henry M., 10 Jan. 1854, Mary C. Miller   1/14/54-2
Whitaker, Joseph, 28 Sept. 1856, Adela Florence   9/29/56-2
Whitaker, Joshua, Jr., 18 Nov. 1856, Virginia H. Walker, dau. of
    Samuel   11/20/56-2
Whitcraft, Lewis, 21 Mar. 1859, Margaret Matthews   3/23/59-2
White, Alexander P., 1 Apr. 1858, Mary L. Realy   4/15/58-2
White, Alphonso (Dr.), 31 Jan. 1856, Verletta Disney   2/ 2/56-2
White, Asferry, 29 Nov. 1860, Caroline Fisher   12/ 1/60-2
White, Barney, 18 Mar. 1851, Rosanna Jane Anderson   3/22/51-2
White, Benjamin Nicholson, son of Thomas Spurrier, 10 Nov. 1859,
    Letitia Hannah Stratford, dau. of (Maj.) T.   12/ 6/59-2
White, Chas. A., 4 Mar. 1852, Elizabeth Spalding   3/ 5/52-2
White, Corneilius E., 27 Nov. 1856, Archie A. Gaines, dau. of
    Benj. P.   12/27/56-2
White, David, 23 Nov. 1859, Sarah E. Morgan, dau. of Edward 11/24/59-2
White, E. Hicks, 29 Jan. 1860, Sarah Kimmey   1/31/60-2
White, Frederick, 29 July 1856, Emma Turnbull   8/ 5/56-2
White, Geo. H. B., 15 May 1860, Fannie V. Withers, dau. of
    A. L.   5/17/60-2
White, Greensbury, 22 Apr. 1858, Sarah J. McVey   4/26/58-2
White, Harrison C., 22 Apr. 1858, Mary E. Harveycatter   5/15/58-2
White, Henry C., 6 Sept. 1859, Elizabeth Shaffer   9/23/59-2
White, Henry E., 31 Dec. 1858, Ada Forbes, dau. of John F. 1/ 5/58-2
White, Henry S., 19 Apr. 1859, Lucy E. Baker   4/22/59-2
White, James, 2 Apr. 1856, Mary A. Clark   4/ 5/56-2
White, James W., 25 Dec. 1860, Sarah Jane Eagleson   12/28/60-2
White, Jno. R., 19 Dec. 1860, Julia A. Degge, dau. of John L. 12/24/60-2
White, John, 28 June 1859, Eliza Jane White   10/28/59-2
White, John H., 26 Feb. 1852, Sarah A. Gayle, dau. of (Capt.)
    Jos. R.   2/28/52-2
White, Joseph L., 11 May 1852, Mary F. Saddler   5/12/52-2
White, Matthew, 27 May 1856, Sarah Jane Patterson   5/30/56-2
White, Michael, 29 Apr. 1854, Ann McEvoy   5/12/54-2
White, Orlando G., 3 May 1852, Sarah A. Folassen   5/ 4/52-2
White, Orlando G., 3 May 1852, Sarah A. Klassen, dau. of
    Chas.; corrected copy   5/ 5/52-2
White, Patrick, 7 July 1858, Elizabeth Shields   7/10/58-2
White, Peter, 3 July 1851, Margaret Ann Moore   7/ 4/51-2
White, Robert, 14 May 1851, Selina K. Mills   5/15/51-2
White, Samuel A., 15 Apr. 1855, Hannah J. Curran   4/24/55-2
White, Thaddeus W., 28 Dec. 1851, Maria Mitchell   1/ 5/52-2
White, Thomas, 13 Apr. 1858, Margaret J. Phillips   4/16/58-2
White, Welcome, 20 Oct. 1857, Marietta F. Read   10/23/57-2
White, Wesley F., 20 June 1854, Margaret Collins   6/22/54-2
White, William, 20 July 1857, Emily Ann Pow   8/10/57-2

White, William, 8 June 1858, Anna C. Stouffer, dau. of Jacob   6/10/58-2
White, William F., 13 Apr. 1859, Lavinia Lona   4/15/59-2
White, William, 18 Nov. 1859, Susannah Bellis, dau. of John   12/15/59-2
White, William F., 13 Apr. 1859, Lavinia Long; corrected copy   4/18/59-2
White, William P., 21 Oct. 1856, Julia A. Dorsey; corrected
     copy   10/29/56-2
White, William P., 21 Oct. 1856, Julia H. Dorsey   10/28/56-2
White, William T., 5 May 1853, Maria Lynch   5/10/53-2
White, Wm. J. H., 26 Apr. 1859, Emma E. Corms   4/29/59-2
Whitecar, James S., 11 Oct. 1854, Anna M. Murphy   10/13/54-2
Whiteford, Charles Henry H., 12 Sept. 1854, Eliza Jane
     Marshall   9/16/54-2
Whitehead, Wm. C., 4 Dec. 1856, Marion Bruce Crook, dau. of
     James   12/ 6/56-2
Whitehouse, George, 24 Dec. 1857, (Mrs.) Emma Welch   12/25/57-2
Whitehurst, Henry W., 11 Nov. 1858, Ella C. Mask, dau. of
     Charles W.   11/13/58-2
Whitelaw, John, 15 Jan. 1859, Emeline West   1/17/59-2
Whiteley, Calvin, 16 Mar. 1854, Harriet Westgardner, dau. of
     James Stone   3/18/54-2
Whiteley, John W., 2 June 1856, Mary Ann Pauner   6/ 4/56-2
Whiteley, Rob't. N., 15 Jan. 1853, S. C. Long; 1/17/53-2   1/18/53-2
Whitely, Wm. H., 4 Nov. 1852, Mary Tryan   12/29/52-2
Whitfield, Nathan B., 26 July 1857, Bettie Whitfield   7/28/57-2
Whiting, Edward, 30 Oct. 1856, Mary A. Wallace   11/19/56-2
Whiting, John H., 29 June 1857, Mary E. Tudor   9/19/57-2
Whitlock, John W., Jr., 24 July 1856, Almira Ann Frazier, dau.
     of James and Rachel   12/27/56-2
Whitlock, Robinson D., 2 May 1851, Frances E. McKinlay   5/ 5/51-2
Whitmarsh, George, 19 Nov. 1857, Elizabeth Ann Ijams, dau. of
     Franklin F.   11/21/57-2
Whitney, G. H., 15 Nov. 1860, Jane Harrison   11/17/60-2
Whitney, Geo. H., 24 July 1854, Ann Howell   8/ 7/54-2
Whitney, Geo. T., 6 Apr. 1852, Margaret E. Zeigler, dau. of
     Frederick   4/ 8/52-2
Whitney, Wm. N., 12 Jan. 1860, Harriet C. Kelly   1/23/60-2
Whitson, John, 12 June 1860, Almira Boone   6/20/60-2
Whittaker, Henry, 28 Nov. 1853, Martha E. Duncan, dau. of Wm.   12/ 7/53-2
Whittaker, Pallemon, 24 Dec. 1858, Eliza A. Groom   2/24/58-2
Whittaker, William J., 3 Jan. 1860, Margaret J. Laughlin   1/ 5/60-2
Whittemore, Edward, 1 Feb. 1859, Henrietta J. Cook   2/22/59-2
Whittemore, Lorman, 9 Aug. 1854, Anna M. Bell, dau. of John   8/12/54-2
Whittington, J., 10 May 1857, (?) Rielly   5/12/57-2
Whittington, John W., 27 Aug. 1857, Matilda R. Hammond   8/28/57-2
Whitworth, Charles W., 20 Jan. 1859, Kate Crooks   1/22/59-2
Whorton, John W., 14 May 1855, Mary Jane Craig, dau. of John   5/16/55-2
Whroten, James B. (Capt.), 16 Aug. 1853, Mary Slocum, dau. of
     George   8/17/53-2
Whyatt, William, 20 Oct. 1856, Rebecca Starr   12/30/56-2
Wibell, Geo. H., 25 Feb. 1857, Charlotte Squirs   2/27/57-2
Wible, David C., 24 Mar. 1853, Sarah Jane Joynes   3/26/53-2
Wick, Christopher, 20 Apr. 1854, Magdaline Fisher   4/21/54-2
Wickens, Edmund, 21 Dec. 1851, Plancina Scoefeild   1/ 8/52-2
Wicks, William, 1 Oct. 1857, Mary F. Gettier; corrected copy   10/ 9/57-2
Wicton, John, 9 June 1853, Henrietta Jones   6/15/53-2
Widderfield, Thomas E., 20 Nov. 1851, Ann Maria Almoney   11/24/51-2
Wiegan, W. Daniel, 23 July 1852, Louisa Hewett   7/27/52-2
Wiems, Charles Henry, 17 July 1856, Rebecca Oliver   7/19/56-2
Wien, Frederick A., 13 June 1853, Hester C. Wiegand   6/14/53-2
Wier, Thomas J., 27 Nov. 1860, Jane E. L. Bush   11/28/60-2
Wierman, N. M., 4 July 1853, Rosanna Martin   7/19/53-2
Wiest, Frederick A., 16 May 1854, Harriet S. Davis, dau. of
     William T.   5/20/54-2
Wigginton, William H., 9 Jan. 1859, Ellen J. V. Barnes   2/ 1/59-2
Wight, William, 1 Sept. 1852, Rachel Ann Norris   9/ 6/52-2

Wightman, Samuel M., 21 Oct. 1856, Emille M. Israel   10/24/56-2
Wightman, Wm. T., 7 Nov. 1854, Lou E. Jay, dau. of T. W.   11/ 9/54-2
Wilbourn, Lewis T., 10 Sept. 1855, Alice E. Wall, dau. of
    Daniel   9/11/55-2
Wilbur, Harrison, 28 Jan. 1851, Selina Ryland   1/31/51-2
Wilburn, William D., 12 Jan. 1860, Priscilla Cranford   1/20/60-2
Wilcox, Henry, 12 Sept. 1853, Emily Jane Strible   10/ 3/53-2
Wilcox, Henry Martin, 18 Oct. 1860, Emma V. Martin   10/20/60-2
Wilcox, J. Feniore, 6 Oct. 1853, Rebecca C. Wonn   10/22/53-2
Wilcox, John, 8 July 1857, Elizabeth Norwood   7/14/57-2
Wilcox, Mark, 15 June 1852, Ellen Lucas, dau. of Fielding, Jr.   6/18/52-2
Wilcoxen, Andrew J., 15 Apr. 1851, Anna M. Getzendanner, dau.
    of Daniel   4/17/51-2
Wilcoxson, Hanson T., 13 Feb. 1855, Mary K. Mason, dau. of
    Richard   2/19/55-2
Wildermuth, William, 11 Sept. 1856, Margaret Haas   9/13/56-2
Wiles, Aquila, 19 Mar. 1851, Priscilla P. Davis   3/21/51-2
Wiles, James, 2 Jan. 1851, Phebe Loflin   1/ 3/51-2
Wiley, Alexander, 10 Apr. 1860, Ann E. Walls   4/13/60-2
Wiley, Alexander, 10 Apr. 1860, Anne E. Wells; corrected copy   4/16/60-2
Wiley, Andrew J., 13 Feb. 1855, Margaret E. Aston   4/11/55-2
Wiley, Chas., 2 Mar. 1854, Elizabeth A. Downes   3/ 6/54-2
Wiley, James, 4 Sept. 1859, Lydia A. Ayres, dau. of Daniel H.   9/ 8/59-2
Wiley, John K., 13 Nov. 1853, Catharine Newton   11/19/53-2
Wiley, Joseph B., (?) Sept. 1858, Ellen A. Whipley   9/30/58-2
Wiley, Thomas, 16 Feb. 1854, Rebecca Ann Wiley, dau. of
    Matthew   2/18/54-2
Wiley, William, 19 Oct. 1854, (Mrs.) Julia A. Quirk   10/26/54-2
Wiley, William (Capt.), 28 Nov. 1854, Catharine Virginia
    Kellum, dau. of (Capt.) Lewis   11/29/54-2
Wilhelm, Chas. P., 21 Dec. 1854, Alcinda Frederick, dau. of
    Robert   12/28/54-2
Wilhelm, George, 23 Jan. 1860, Kunigunda Giete   1/25/60-2
Wilhelm, J. Milburn, 30 Dec. 1857, Hettie Clark   1/ 2/58-2
Wilhelm, John F., 24 Feb. 1856, Elizabeth Jane Wright   4/ 3/56-2
Wilhelm, Matthew H., 26 June 1856, Mary E. Foreman   6/28/56-2
Wilkerson, James, 16 Nov. 1854, Mary E. Galloway   11/22/54-2
Wilkins, Edward A., 22 Mar. 1855, Eugenia J. Botton, dau. of
    T. W.   4/19/55-2
Wilkins, George T., 6 Dec. 1855, Annie E. Manns, dau. of Wm. E.   12/ 8/55-2
Wilkins, Joseph (Dr.), 18 Jan. 1855, Anne Cleaves Pleasants,
    dau. of Wm. A.   1/22/55-2
Wilkinson, John Thomas, 6 Mar. 1856, Sarah Ellen Lambert   3/13/56-2
Wilkinson, John R., 10 Oct. 1854, Mary E. Holland, dau. of
    John G.   10/14/54-2
Wilkinson, Orlando A., 30 Nov. 1858, Mary A. Patton   12/20/58-2
Wilkinson, Thos. R., 15 Jan. 1857, Sarah Selvage, dau. of
    Thomas   1/19/57-2
Wilkinson, Thos. S., 26 May 1859, Fanny W. Hennett   5/27/59-2
Wilkinson, W. J., 23 Dec. 1856, Harriet Eugenia Blaney, dau. of
    James   12/31/56-2
Wilkinson, William, 24 June 1855, Narrissa Gregg, dau. of
    (Dr.) John   6/26/55-2
Wilkinson, William, 25 Apr. 1859, Sarah Haslam   5/ 2/59-2
Wilkinson, Wm. F., 6 Apr. 1852, Mary Ann Ross   5/ 4/52-2
Wilks, William, 1 Oct. 1857, Mary F. Gettier   10/ 8/57-2
Willard, Julius, 14 June 1859, Agnes A. Thompson   6/15/59-2
Willener, William F., 1 Dec. 1851, Margaret Ann H. Riley   12/ 8/51-2
Willet, Richard H., 16 Oct. 1860, Virginia T. Beall   10/19/60-2
Willett, Warren O., 10 Mar. 1857, Ellen F. Montgomery   3/12/57-2
Willey, Archibald, 16 Feb. 1851, Ann Maria Fowler, dau. of
    Jas. B.   2/20/51-2
Willey, Uriah, 24 June 1858, Margaret E. Dean   6/26/58-2
William, George A., 11 Jan. 1855, Edney R. Nash   1/15/55-2
Williams, Alexander, 25 Dec. 1853, Julia Wilson   12/28/53-2

Williams, Alexander, 29 May 1855, Lucinda Smith	5/31/55-2
Williams, Alexander, 20 Sept. 1860, Jemima Wise	9/22/60-2
Williams, Archibald D., 11 June 1855, Anna Robert	6/14/55-2
Williams, Carey W., 17 Jan. 1856, Elizabeth Smith	2/20/56-2
Williams, Charles, 4 Feb. 1851, Virginia E. Hussey, dau. of Copeland	2/ 8/51-2
Williams, Charles, 4 Jan. 1858, Jane Crocksell	1/ 5/58-2
Williams, Creamer, 14 Sept. 1860, Rachel A. Griffenberg	9/17/60-2
Williams, David, 20 Nov. 1851, Margaret Bordley	11/22/51-2
Williams, David M. C., 30 Oct. 1856, Elizabeth Fowler	11/ 1/56-2
Williams, Edward, 3 Sept. 1859, Millie V. Hoey, dau. of John	9/ 9/59-2
Williams, Emanuel, 11 Sept. 1853, Elizabeth Arnold	9/13/53-2
Williams, Geo. H., 17 Jan. 1854, Mary E. Williams	1/31/54-2
Williams, Geo. M., 13 Nov. 1860, Gertrude S. Long	11/16/60-2
Williams, George, 12 July 1860, Trecy Dorsy	7/14/60-2
Williams, George, 29 July 1860, Margaret G. Butler	8/25/60-2
Williams, H. J., 27 Feb. 1851, Olivia Hardesty, dau. of Charles R.	3/ 1/51-2
Williams, Henry, 16 Jan. 1851, Emily James	1/17/51-2
Williams, Henry, 25 Jan. 1855, Sophia Wyeth	1/27/55-2
Williams, Henry, 29 Sept. 1859, Ann Matilda Moore	10/ 1/59-2
Williams, Henry C., 10 Apr. 1856, Mary J. Butler	4/12/56-2
Williams, Henry H., 28 Feb. 1858, Isabella Whitaker	3/10/58-2
Williams, J. H., 24 June 1858, Anne Campbell	7/26/58-2
Williams, J. Overton, 21 Feb. 1860, Octavia Mannakee, dau. of John S.	3/ 3/60-2
Williams, James R.; no date given, Lizzie M. Lucas, dau. of Samuel	2/20/54-2
Williams, James R. (Dr.), 28 Oct. 1858, (Mrs.) Sarah H. Hughes	10/29/58-2
Williams, Jesse, 8 Nov. 1855, Matilda Rogers	11/10/55-2
Williams, John, 31 Dec. 1850, Sophia Johnson	1/ 3/51-2
Williams, John, 6 May 1860, (Mrs.) Julia Hutt	5/ 8/60-2
Williams, John, 7 Oct. 1860, Elizabeth Sullivan	10/ 9/60-2
Williams, John, Jr., 19 Apr. 1855, Cecelia A. Cunningham, dau. of George	4/21/55-2
Williams, John A., 6 Aug. 1860, Mary Adele Laroque, dau. of (Dr.) Edward	8/ 7/60-2
Williams, John E., 15 Jan. 1857, Ann Louisa Hahn	1/17/57-2
Williams, John H., 18 June 1857, Elizabeth Jane Eichelberger, dau. of J. H.	6/23/57-2
Williams, John M. (Dr.), 14 Sept. 1858, (Mrs.) Mary Ann Heckrote	10/ 4/58-2
Williams, John N., 10 May 1855, Susan Scott	5/14/55-2
Williams, John T., 1 May 1851, Rosetta Bateman	5/ 3/51-2
Williams, John T., 27 Oct. 1853, Rebecca Jane Hendry	11/ 1/53-2
Williams, John Waters, 6 Mar. 1860, Maggie E. Andrews	3/ 8/60-2
Williams, Joseph, 6 Apr. 1858, Susan Jane Mundarney	4/ 8/58-2
Williams, Michael, 25 Oct. 1860, Maria Janes	10/27/60-2
Williams, Nathan, 28 Sept. 1856, Mary A. Stinchcomb	1/ 6/57-2
Williams, Oscar, 19 Jan. 1858, Mary Lininger	1/23/58-2
Williams, Philip C., 12 Jan. 1858, Mary C. Whitridge, dau. of (Dr.) John	1/19/58-2
Williams, Pius W., 4 Nov. 1851, Henrietta Breast, dau. of Jas. A. and Eliza	11/11/51-2
Williams, Ramond W., 11 May 1854, Mary Watson	5/13/54-2
Williams, Thom G., 22 June 1854, Williamina W. Sangston	6/27/54-2
Williams, Thomas, 28 June 1854, Harriet A. Callume	7/ 3/54-2
Williams, Thomas C., 4 Jan. 1855, Mary Louisa Williamson	1/ 6/55-2
Williams, Thos. H., 29 Dec. 1859, Hester E. Watts	12/31/59-2
Williams, Thos. W., 28 Apr. 1853, Bessie K. Knease, dau. of Wm.	5/ 3/53-2
Williams, Wesley, 4 Jan. 1860, Henrietta Davis	1/13/60-2
Williams, William D., 13 Feb. 1851, Mary Ann Beers	2/15/51-2
Williams, William F., 13 Dec. 1853, Lydia Cadwalder	12/26/53-2
Williams, William H., 24 June 1852, Mary Winemiller	6/29/52-2

Williams, William H., 21 Mar. 1853, Barbara A. Hobbs	3/28/53-2
Williams, William K., 11 Apr. 1860, Sallie E. K. Sappington	4/19/60-2
Williams, Wm. P. (M. D.), 16 Sept. 1851, Annie Chapman	9/18/51-2
Williams, Wm. T., 26 June 1856, Actious P. Gill	6/30/56-2
Williams, Zadock, 16 Nov. 1854, Mary Morton	11/21/54-2
Williamson, Chas. A. J., 2 Mar. 1851, Ann Maria Cline	3/17/51-2
Williamson, Eiley S., 16 Mar. 1854, Lavina Pearce, dau. of Joseph	3/18/54-2
Williamson, James J., 20 June 1859, Cornelia A. Tarr	6/22/59-2
Williamson, John, 24 Apr. 1860, Evelyn Wysham	4/26/60-2
Willian, Miguel, 2 Aug. 1853, Amelia Memburg	8/ 4/53-2
Williar, Andrew J., 9 Aug. 1853, Betty A. Sparrow	8/11/53-2
Williar, Henry R., 9 Sept. 1852, Mary Elizabeth Heron, dau. of Alexander	9/13/52-2
Willig, George, 11 Oct. 1855, Susan A. Lafitte	10/13/55-2
Willinghan, James W., 2 June 1853, Sarah E. White	6/11/53-2
Willis, Henry, 6 Oct. 1852, (Mrs.) Ann Gould	10/ 9/52-2
Willis, John T., 16 Feb. 1858, Ann Elizabeth Pennington	2/23/58-2
Wills, Richard C., 28 Sept. 1856, Isabella V. Houston, dau. of James F.	10/ 2/56-2
Willis, Rich'd., 2 Oct. 1851, Emily A. O'Connor	10/ 7/51-2
Willis, Thos. R. P., 24 May 1851, Martha Welch	5/26/51-2
Willis, Wm. L. (Dr.), 5 May 1853, Frances A. Finley, dau. of Wm.	5/19/53-2
Willis, Wm. M., 28 June 1854, Mary A. Norwood	7/ 1/54-2
Willis, Wm. M., 27 Sept. 1858, Virginia Camp	9/29/58-2
Willmer, John S., 10 Aug. 1851, Arriminta Vanhorn	8/14/51-2
Willoughby, J. D. (Dr.), 8 July 1851, Martha E. Kernan, dau. of P.	7/11/51-2
Wills, Joseph F., 23 May 1855, Mary A. Calwell	8/ 9/55-2
Wills, Thomas K., 17 May 1855, Elizabeth Ayres	5/19/55-2
Wills, William G., 18 Mar. 1858, Emeline Osborn, dau. of Thomas	3/20/58-2
Willson, Isaac N., 13 Nov. 1856, Catherine Ann Isabella Campbell	11/17/56-2
Willson, Jacob H., 21 July 1859, Nancy Ann Limus	7/23/59-2
Willson, Jas. Henry, 4 June 1855, M. Clara MacCubbin	6/ 7/55-2
Willson, John W., 24 Mar. 1853, Rachel J. Matthews	3/26/53-2
Willson, Leonidas, 4 Apr. 1859, Maria E. Harris	4/ 7/59-2
Willson, Washington L., 24 Nov. 1853, Sallie L. Read, dau. of Wm.	11/28/53-2
Wilmer, Chas., 31 Oct. 1860, Harriet M. Rogers, dau. of Lloyd N.	11/ 1/60-2
Wilmer, W. J., 29 Nov. 1855, Sarah Jane Gaskins, dau. of Saml. S.	11/30/55-2
Wilson, A. C., 17 Nov. 1858, Emma J. Campton	11/24/58-2
Wilson, Alexander, 30 Dec. 1852, Sarah Jane Clendenen	1/ 5/53-2
Wilson, Archildbald, 11 Sept. 1856, Jane L. Ritchie	9/15/56-2
Wilson, Benjamin Edwards, 4 Dec. 1851, Ann Hynes	3/13/52-2
Wilson, C., 19 Apr. 1855, Ann Sprowl	4/21/55-2
Wilson, Charles, 18 Jan. 1854, Mary Ann Godfrey	1/24/54-2
Wilson, Charles A., 10 June 1858, Asenith E. Hall	6/14/58-2
Wilson, Christopher, Sr., 10 June 1852, (Mrs.) Mary Bageley	6/14/52-2
Wilson, Daniel, 22 Nov. 1860, Priscilla Harris	11/24/60-2
Wilson, David, 27 Dec. 1855, Jane Carr	1/ 1/56-2
Wilson, David, 20 Dec. 1860, Rachel Stephens	12/22/60-2
Wilson, Edward, 10 Mar. 1853, Sarah Ann Moore	3/12/53-2
Wilson, Edward, 19 Oct. 1854, Mary Ellen Diamond, dau. of William	10/27/54-2
Wilson, Ephraim K., 16 July 1856, Kate B. Steiger, dau. of Wm. T.	7/23/56-2
Wilson, Everett F., 23 Apr. 1857, Ann Jane Thompson	4/28/57-2
Wilson, Geo. W., 11 Aug. 1858, Sarah A. E. Lindsay	8/12/58-2
Wilson, George, 2 Feb. 1858, Alice Keelwright, dau. of Nicholas	2/ 6/58-2
Wilson, George, 7 Oct. 1858, (Mrs.) Lydia Demley	10/ 9/58-2

Wilson, Greenbury, 16 Apr. 1857, Alice McClanahan		4/18/57-2
Wilson, H. P. C. (Dr.), 16 June 1858, Alicia B. Griffith, dau. of (Capt.) David		6/17/58-2
Wilson, Henry K., 15 Dec. 1853, Mary Frances Strider		12/16/53-2
Wilson, Henry M. (Dr.), 7 Oct. 1851, Eliza Kelso Hollingsworth		10/ 9/51-2
Wilson, Henry P., 25 Oct. 1860, Georgia Hussey		10/26/60-2
Wilson, Isaac M., 28 Dec. 1854, Thomasina Balmer, niece of Thomas and Isabella Brown		1/ 2/55-2
Wilson, James, 16 Nov. 1852, Elizabeth Jones		11/18/52-2
Wilson, James A., 21 Oct. 1856, Henrietta Folks		10/24/56-2
Wilson, James M., 14 June 1859, Mary L. Latham, dau. of Arthur		6/29/59-2
Wilson, Jeremiah, 27 May 1858, Emeline Airs		6/ 1/58-2
Wilson, John, 12 July 1855, Mary A. Sponsler		7/19/55-2
Wilson, John, 17 Aug. 1856, Susan Sherwood		8/22/56-2
Wilson, John, 9 July 1857, (Mrs.) Eliza Thorne		7/10/57-2
Wilson, John A., 5 Nov. 1860, Mary G. Keenan, dau. of James		11/10/60-2
Wilson, John G., 1 Oct. 1855, (Mrs.) Elizabeth S. Bartholomew		10/11/55-2
Wilson, John Henry, 6 Jan. 1856, Louiza Moore		1/ 7/56-2
Wilson, John T., 14 Apr. 1857, Mary E. Farmer		4/17/57-2
Wilson, John T., 2 July 1857, Sarah C. Patterson		7/ 3/57-2
Wilson, John W., 9 Oct. 1860, Caroline L. Shirning		10/31/60-2
Wilson, Joseph, 5 May 1857, Usath McKinley		5/ 8/57-2
Wilson, Josiah, 14 Oct. 1858, Annie L. Watts, dau. of Richard		10/18/58-2
Wilson, Nathaniel J., 16 Nov. 1859, Ann Sophia Albaugh		11/29/59-2
Wilson, Robert, 30 Aug. 1852, Rebecca Ware		9/11/52-2
Wilson, Robert A., 26 Apr. 1859, Alice Anna Royston, dau. of Wesley		5/ 5/59-2
Wilson, Robert E., 21 Sept. 1854, Mary E. Luckett, dau. of Judson M.		9/22/54-2
Wilson, Robt. B., 17 June 1854, Mary Ann Ellis		7/ 6/54-2
Wilson, S. C. (Col.), 4 Dec. 1858, Carrie E. Walling		12/21/58-2
Wilson, Saml., 10 July 1856, Jane L. Burns		7/22/56-2
Wilson, Samuel, 26 Jan. 1854, Mary E. Tracey; corrected copy		3/ 8/54-2
Wilson, Samuel, 26 Jan. 1854, Mary E. Tracy		2/28/54-2
Wilson, Samuel, 27 Dec. 1854, Hannah E. Brundidge		1/ 3/55-2
Wilson, Samuel, 22 Mar. 1860, Sophia A. Stansbury, dau. of Hammond		3/27/60-2
Wilson, Samuel E., 2 Apr. 1857, Martha Wilson		4/ 4/57-2
Wilson, Thomas M., 1 May 1860, Jane Easton		5/ 4/60-2
Wilson, Thos. J., 3 Mar. 1852, Priscilla Brogden, dau. of David McC.		3/ 6/52-2
Wilson, V. Talbott, 10 Mar. 1859, Alverda Leffler, dau. of G. R. H.		3/18/59-2
Wilson, William, 1 Nov. 1853, Matilda Wilson		11/ 2/53-2
Wilson, William, 21 Apr. 1859, Sallie R. Beisel		4/27/59-2
Wilson, William, 8 Dec. 1859, Susan Myerly		12/ 9/59-2
Wilson, William A., 16 Feb. 1858, Ruth A. Street		3/ 3/58-2
Wilson, William B., 22 Mar. 1855, Ann M. Derry		4/ 4/55-2
Wilson, William H., 26 May 1853, Jane E. Davis		5/30/53-2
Wilson, William J., 21 Dec. 1856, Mary E. Raine		12/23/56-2
Wilson, William R., 1 Nov. 1860, Sarah E. Evans, dau. of H. P.		11/ 3/60-2
Wilson, William W., 30 Mar. 1856, (Mrs.) Ann Louisa Paca		3/30/57-2
Wilson, Wm., 16 Nov. 1852, (Mrs.) Maria Gaines		11/17/52-2
Wilson, Wm. H., 6 Jan. 1857, Malinda J. Colison		1/ 7/57-2
Wilson, Wm. H., 22 May 1859, Margaret A. Hartley		7/11/59-2
Wilson, Wm. W., 13 Jan. 1852, Mary E. Egerton, dau. of C. C., Sr.		1/14/52-2
Wilson, Wm. W., 10 May 1853, Anne E. Ferguson		5/12/53-2
Wilson, Young O., 22 Nov. 1853, Susan A. Reese, dau. of (Rev.) John L.		11/26/53-2
Wilton, R. P., 13 Dec. 1853, Fanny B. Bordley, dau. of J. B.		12/15/53-2
Wiman, Marcus, 29 Sept. 1852, Isabella McCleever		10/ 6/52-2
Winans, Ross, 9 Feb. 1854, Elizabeth K. West		2/11/54-2

Winans, Ross, Jr., 19 July 1855, Amelia M. Wentz, dau. of
    S. H. H.   8/17/55-2
Winchester, J. Marshall, 13 Nov. 1856, Anne Gordon Price, dau.
    of James E.   11/18/56-2
Winchester, Oliver A., 14 Sept. 1859, Carrie J. Brun   9/15/59-2
Winchester, S. G., 23 Nov. 1853, Micha A. Perine, dau. of
    Thos. J.   11/24/53-2
Winder, Charles S. (Capt.), 7 Aug. 1855, Alice Lloyd, dau. of
    (Col.) Edward   8/10/55-2
Winder, Henry, 8 Dec. 1853, (Mrs.) Mary Brown   12/10/53-2
Winer, Henry, 21 June 1859, Kate S. Sewel, dau. of Vachel   6/25/59-2
Wing, John H., 13 Apr. 1852, Helena Travers   4/15/52-2
Wing, Warren W., 1 Apr. 1851, Eliza Lugg, dau. of Benj.
    Franklin   4/ 5/51-2
Wingate, James B., 9 Feb. 1851, Lucy A. Oldham   2/11/51-2
Wingate, Samuel B., 6 Dec. 1855, Kate A. Ely   12/10/55-2
Wingfield, Henry, 26 Feb. 1860, Mary Alice Snow   2/27/60-2
Winingder, James, 9 Aug. 1859, Cordelia V. Cook   8/11/59-2
Winingder, Stephen, 9 Aug. 1855, Mary Jane Frazier   8/18/55-2
Winingder, Thomas, 6 Oct. 1857, Fannie Petherbridge   10/14/57-2
Winkleman, Frederick J., 14 Dec. 1852, Harriet Ann Lee   12/20/52-2
Winks, Samuel W., 14 Aug. 1856, Maria Cleary   10/16/56-2
Winneberger, George A., 29 May 1853, Aurelia Mason   5/31/53-2
Winsett, John R., 10 Nov. 1859, Sue B. Allen, dau. of Solomon   11/16/59-2
Winsey, Wm. H., 7 June 1860, Lydia Cobourn, dau. of Daniel
    and Ellen   6/ 8/60-2
Winter, John, 25 Jan. 1859, Annie Zentz   2/ 2/59-2
Winter, Philip, 21 Sept. 1852, Ellen R. Cropp   10/ 6/52-2
Winter, Wm. P., 23 Jan. 1856, Emma R. Newman, dau. of Henry   1/28/56-2
Winters, Francis, 2 Jan. 1855, (Mrs.) Elizabeth Brown   1/13/55-2
Winters, Rob't., 28 Feb. 1853, Mary Murphy   3/ 5/53-2
Winterson, Gassaway, 22 Dec. 1857, Jane E. Jones   12/25/57-2
Wirth, John A., 15 Sept. 1857, Clara M. Walter, dau. of
    William and Mary   9/17/57-2
Wirth, Joseph, 2 Aug. 1860, Rosina Catherine Traus   8/15/60-2
Wirth, Nicholas, 25 Sept. 1853, Frederica C. Stolpp, dau. of
    John Ludwig   9/28/53-2
Wise, A. B., 15 Sept. 1851, Margaret England   9/24/51-2
Wise, Jacob, 11 June 1856, Sally Gazan, dau. of Jacob   6/13/56-2
Wise, John W., 16 July 1857, Eleanora W. Fitzpatrick   7/23/57-2
Wise, Samuel, 5 June 1856, Elizabeth E. Ly-(?)-rand   6/11/56-2
Wise, William H., 3 Nov. 1859, Sarah V. Stanford, dau. of Henry   11/ 7/59-2
Wishart, Geo. G., 3 July 1851, Georeanna Turner   7/ 8/51-2
Wisher, Aaron, 5 Sept. 1854, Sedonia Chambers   9/ 8/54-2
Wisman, George, 5 Aug. 1860, Cassandre Shipley   8/ 9/60-2
Wisner, John B., 24 Nov. 1857, Amanda Lefferman, dau. of Wm.   11/26/57-2
Wisong, Jacob, 15 Jan. 1852, Mary Jane Duering, dau. of John S.   1/17/52-2
Wiswall, E. T., 4 Dec. 1856, Sophia M. Trowbridge, dau. of R.   12/ 5/56-2
Withers, John, 1 Aug. 1860, Jane Bowen   8/25/60-2
Witz, William, 2 June 1853, Elizabeth A. Irons, dau. of
    Emanuel   6/13/53-2
Wodetzsky, G. Emanuel, 12 Apr. 1855, Sarah C. Allen   4/14/55-2
Woehrlen, George, 19 May 1857, Julia Choupin   5/22/57-2
Wolf, Alonzo L., 31 Aug. 1856, Martha J. Boyd, dau. of Wm. A.   10/11/56-2
Wolf, Christian, 14 May 1854, Lorathea Stubenrauch   5/23/54-2
Wolf, E. A.; no date given, Elizabeth Taft   7/17/56-2
Wolf, E. A., 15 July 1856, Elizabeth Toft; corrected copy   7/19/56-2
Wolfe, Geo. H., 15 June 1858, Mollie A. Heagy, dau. of Jas.   6/16/58-2
Wolfe, William S., 22 July 1858, Kate A. Jones, dau. of
    Morris J.   7/23/58-2
Wolff, Alexander, 9 Sept. 1858, Harriet Evans   9/16/58-2
Woltjen, Charles, 10 May 1860, Lizzie Stalford, dau. of
    Frederick and Anna   5/11/60-2
Wonderly, George L., 5 Apr. 1859, Isabella Rogers   4/ 9/59-2
Wonn, Jas., 22 Dec. 1852, Sarah Yeark   12/30/52-2

Wonn, Joshua, 3 Nov. 1852, Ann E. Fry, dau. of Joseph   11/ 4/52-2
Wood, Chas. O'Neill, 29 Apr. 1852, Charlotta P. Coram   5/ 1/52-2
Wood, Elias, 24 May 1853, Amand M. Swomley   5/25/53-2
Wood, Henry C., 4 Apr. 1853, Sarah A. Smith, dau. of (Capt.)
     Geo. G.   4/ 7/53-2
Wood, J. R., 23 Dec. 1858, S. Musgrave   12/28/58-2
Wood, James H., 23 Aug. 1853, Mary A. Russell   8/25/53-2
Wood, John, 4 May 1851, Sarah Ann Parker   5/28/51-2
Wood, John D., 10 Aug. 1854, Mary Catharine Brushwell   8/14/54-2
Wood, Joseph W., 17 Dec. 1857, Ann E. Dowell   12/19/57-2
Wood, Joshua, 25 Sept. 1860, Julia Ann Orem; 10/ 1/60-2   10/ 2/60-2
Wood, Nicholas L., Jr., 2 Jan. 1856, Mary E. Welch   1/ 4/56-2
Wood, Orlando, 18 Jan. 1859, Virginia Guy   1/27/59-2
Wood, William, 15 Apr. 1851, Eliza Coward, dau. of (Capt.)
     Thomas   4/16/51-2
Wood, William, 11 Jan. 1859, Mary Louisa Dowell   1/22/59-2
Wood, William F., 21 Nov. 1859, Mary L. Brewer, dau. of James   11/23/59-2
Woodall, E. B. (Capt.), 16 Nov. 1853, Lizzie M. Malsberger   11/26/53-2
Woodall, Henry E., 3 Mar. 1859, Margaret A. Rictor   3/ 4/58-2
Woodall, James R., 28 June 1854, Priscilla E. Brown   7/10/54-2
Woodall, John T., 5 Aug. 1856, Permelia Bramble, dau. of (Capt.)
     T. and Sarah A.   8/ 7/56-2
Woodall, William E., 13 Nov. 1860, Mary E. Hooper, dau. of
     Benjamin A.   11/16/60-2
Woodburn, Charles H., 17 Aug. 1854, Ellen B. Cooney, dau. of
     Patrick   8/21/54-2
Woodcock, Charles P., 11 Dec. 1855, Sarah Ann Rictor   12/13/55-2
Woodcock, Theodore, 4 July 1853, Catharine J. Sho-(?)-k   8/ 6/53-2
Woode, Orlando, 14 Dec. 1850, Ashsha M. Hall, dau. of Joshua   2/18/51-2
Wooden, James M., 27 Sept. 1857, Susanna M. Colley, dau. of
     Richard   10/ 1/57-2
Wooden, John, 26 Oct. 1854, Mary Ann Horsford, dau. of (Capt.)
     James   10/30/54-2
Wooden, John W., 28 May 1853, Susanna C. Creagh   6/28/53-2
Wooders, David J., 7 Feb. 1853, Sarah J. Fields   2/10/53-2
Woodhouse, Wm. W., 2 June 1859, Annie M. Saunders, dau. of
     (Dr.) A. H.   6/11/59-2
Woodloe, Taverner W., 20 Nov. 1856, Mary Jane Mills   11/22/56-2
Woodroffe, William, 4 June 1855, Mary Eftufania Blacklar   6/12/55-2
Woodrow, Lewis H., 7 June 1860, Elizabeth Arthur   6/ 9/60-2
Woods, Henry B., 29 Sept. 1859, Susan Ringrose   10/ 6/59-2
Woods, Hiram, Jr., 29 June 1852, Helen A. Chase, dau. of Daniel   7/ 2/52-2
Woods, John, 2 Jan. 1854, C. Philomena Green, dau. of Terrence   1/ 7/54-2
Woods, Robert, 5 Oct. 1858, Elizabeth A. Holladay   10/ 9/58-2
Woods, Walter, 14 Jan. 1851, Mary M. Myers   1/15/51-2
Woodville, Edward, 8 Jan. 1855, Jane Hughes   1/10/55-2
Woodward, Charles A., 17 Dec. 1857, Margaret F. Askey   12/22/57-2
Woodward, David A., 30 Apr. 1851, Josephine Latty   5/ 3/51-2
Woodward, George F., 24 June 1857, Amelia E. Nigh   6/26/57-2
Woodward, John T., 22 Sept. 1853, Maria Rodgers   9/23/53-2
Woodward, Randolph, 6 Feb. 1852, Caroline Gardner   2/28/52-2
Woodward, Robert V., 14 Aug. 1851, Catherine Gulley, dau. of
     Philip   8/16/51-2
Woodward, William H., 27 Feb. 1851, Julia Richardson   3/ 1/51-2
Woodyard, Charles Edward, 8 Nov. 1860, Frances Ann Bias, dau. of
     Horace   11/13/60-2
Woolford, Stephen B., 26 July 1853, Eliza Grove Hamilton, dau.
     of George D.   7/27/53-2
Woolford, Thos. S., 22 Mar. 1859, Eliza A. Travers   3/24/59-2
Woollen, J. Rogers, 25 Nov. 1857, Virginia Clayton   12/ 3/57-2
Woollen, J. W., 19 June 1856, Ann M. Cain   6/23/56-2
Woolley, Charles C., 10 Nov. 1858, Elizabeth A. White   11/12/58-2
Woolside, Edward, 8 Jan. 1855, Jane Hughes   1/11/55-2
Wooters, William H., 11 Nov. 1856, Sarah A. Hughlett   11/13/56-2
Wooters, Wm. H., 20 Dec. 1853, Eliza Ann Granger   12/22/53-2

Wooton, John Walter, 9 Dec. 1858, S. Emelie Muir	12/11/58-2
Worcester, Samuel H. (Rev.), 11 Oct. 1855, Elizabeth A. Scott, dau. of Townsend	10/13/55-2
Worden, A. Graham, 12 June 1855, Jeannie Ogden Niles, dau. of (Col.) William	6/14/55-2
Worick, John, 14 Jan. 1851, Mary Todd	1/15/51-2
Workman, John, 4 Sept. 1851, Juliette De Lareintrie	9/ 9/51-2
Worley, A., 11 May 1858, Tamar E. Hopkins	5/13/58-2
Worly, Adam, 30 Apr. 1857, (Mrs.) Mary G. Heany	5/ 2/57-2
Worrell, Charles, 21 Oct. 1858, Mary C. Jones	10/27/58-2
Worrell, Wm. D., 3 Jan. 1855, (Mrs.) E. T. Ryan	1/ 8/55-2
Worsdell, Joseph, 2-(?) Dec. 1855, Mary Ann Dix	12/31/55-2
Worthen, William D., 29 Nov. 1860, Virginia F. Seuerhoff	12/11/60-2
Worthington, Amos D., 12 June 1851, Harriet D. Hall	6/17/51-2
Worthington, E. Price, 8 Nov. 1860, E. F. Reeder	11/12/60-2
Worthington, N., 9 May 1854, Nannie O'Rourke	5/11/54-2
Worthington, Thomas C., 8 May 1855, Charlotte E. Amos, dau. of John	5/21/55-2
Worthington, Thomas H., 23 Dec. 1851, Elizabeth M. Williams	12/25/51-2
Wright, A. W., 30 Apr. 1856, Lizzie E. Gardner	5/ 2/56-2
Wright, Alfred, 6 July 1858, Agnes Hunter; corrected copy	7/ 9/58-2
Wright, Charles Wesley, 10 May 1860, Amelia Amanda Offley	5/12/60-2
Wright, Chas. D., 24 May 1855, Ellen M. Byrne	7/10/55-2
Wright, Edward Curry, 1 July 1856, Elizabeth A. Foster	7/ 2/56-2
Wright, Edward M., 7 July 1851, (Mrs.) Ann Weller	7/ 9/51-2
Wright, Frank, 10 May 1859, Lizzie Perkins	5/21/59-2
Wright, George P., 3 May 1852, Ann Elizabeth Cooper	5/11/52-2
Wright, James, 13 Jan. 1851, Louisa Joiner	1/16/51-2
Wright, James, 16 Sept. 1852, Caroline H. Britt	9/18/52-2
Wright, James R., 6 July 1856, Elizabeth J. McCleary	7/18/56-2
Wright, John, 6 July 1858, Agness Hunter	7/ 8/58-2
Wright, John J., 21 Oct. 1856, Kate Dananger	10/24/56-2
Wright, John W., 23 Mar. 1852, Mary Jane Peters	3/25/52-2
Wright, John W., 3 July 1853, Amelia A. Wilson	8/ 2/53-2
Wright, John W., 5 June 1856, Abbie E. Cunningham	6/14/56-2
Wright, Joshua W., 27 May 1851, Margaret Anderson, dau. of (Major) A.	5/29/51-2
Wright, Luther, 5 Oct. 1853, Harriet Jane West	10/ 7/53-2
Wright, Mahlon, 10 May 1857, Caroline Jarrett	6/ 6/57-2
Wright, Robert, 3 June 1856, Sarah Ann Perkins	6/21/56-2
Wright, Robert, 17 June 1860, Charlotte Johnson	6/26/60-2
Wright, Robert H., 23 Mar. 1857, Cephonia J. Thomas	5/ 5/57-2
Wright, Robert H., 11 Oct. 1859, Rose McCurdy	10/29/59-2
Wright, Sylvester H., 6 Sept. 1859, (Mrs.) Margaret A. Cloude	9/ 8/59-2
Wright, William, 23 May 1854, Elizabeth Ayres	5/26/54-2
Wright, Wm. David, 29 Apr. 1852, Rebecca J. Ford	5/ 8/52-2
Wright, Wm. H., 8 Apr. 1851, Amelia G. Kerner	4/10/51-2
Wright, Wm. L., 25 July 1855, Martha A. Wright	8/ 9/55-2
Wright, Wm. R., 22 Feb. 1852, Elizabeth Wolford	2/24/52-2
Wrightson, Columbus K., 28 Dec. 1859, Elizabeth A. Ward	1/ 7/59-2
Wrightson, Thomas H., 1 Nov. 1855, Mary Ann Hopkins	11/ 3/55-3
Wrightson, Thomas S., 3 Oct. 1860, Mary J. Smith	10/17/60-2
Wrightson, William D., 14 Apr. 1857, Martha A. Thinsley, dau. of Wm. T.	4/18/57-2
Wroe, Everet, 27 Feb. 1851, Margaret E. Duvall, dau. of Marshum	3/ 7/51-2
Wroten, David J., 12 Sept. 1853, Mary A. Crockett	10/ 1/53-2
Wyant, Edw'd. J., 14 Feb. 1853, Maria Louisa Baitzel	6/16/53-2
Wyatt, Andrew J. (Capt.), 27 May 1857, Harriet D. Brown	6/ 5/57-2
Wyatt, Joshua G., 1 May 1855, Julia A. Pickett	5/ 3/55-2
Wyatt, Joshua G., 11 Jan. 1860, Kate D. Hurst, dau. of James G.	1/14/60-2
Wyett, John E. (Capt.), 17 June 1856, Georgeanna E. Shields	6/19/56-2
Wyett, John E. (Capt.), 17 June 1856, Georgianna E. Shields; corrected copy	6/20/56-2
Wyle, James H., 26 July 1857, Sarah Elizabeth Dennis	7/30/57-2

Wylie, W. J., son of J., 3 Sept. 1860, Mary Frances Stuart,
    dau. of George   9/ 4/60-2
Wyman, Albert, 1 June 1854, Martha J. Taylor   6/ 3/54-2
Wyman, John, 11 Mar. 1860, Josephine Harvey   3/31/60-2
Wynn, J. Robt., 26 Apr. 1855, Emma C. Gould   5/ 1/55-2
Wysham, Henry C., 15 July 1852, Anna Carrie McCeney   7/16/52-2
Wysham, Joseph, 16 June 1856, Josephine B. McCeney   6/18/56-2
Wysham, Louis N., 11 Nov. 1851, Virginia Carver, dau. of (Col.)
    Thomas H. Lee   11/13/51-2
Wyvel, William A., 25 Apr. 1858, Ruth Ann Jones   4/27/58-2
Wyvill, Samuel A., 7 June 1853, Margaret F. Fairchild   6/10/53-2
Yager, Andrew J., 13 Aug. 1851, Rebecca C. Isaacs, dau. of
    Wm. C.   8/16/51-2
Yater, John L., 2 Sept. 1856, Lucie A. Lilly   9/ 4/56-2
Yealdhall, Irvan, 12 Apr. 1860, Ellen E. Egleston   5/22/60-2
Yeatman, John R., 26 Dec. 1855, Laura A. King, dau. of
    George W.   12/27/55-2
Yelland, J. S., 3 Mar. 1859, Margaret A. M. Smardon   3/ 5/59-2
Yellott, Coleman, 2 Apr. 1851, Virginia Rust, dau. of (Gen'l.)
    Geo.   4/ 5/51-2
Yengling, Charles, 14 Nov. 1860, Catherine Rupport   11/17/60-2
Yeo, Thomas B., 2 Dec. 1852, Rachel Maynard Dull, dau. of James 12/ 6/52-2
Yerkel, Charles, 5 Dec. 1853, Mary E. Cunningham, dau. of W.   12/28/53-2
Yingling, David G., 20 Oct. 1853, Rachel H. Griffith   10/24/53-2
Yoe, Robt. W., 18 Apr. 1854, Ann M. Ireland   4/19/54-2
Young, Benjamin F., 13 Jan. 1857, Isabella E. Grooms
    Sherrinston, dau. of (Capt.) W.   1/15/57-2
Young, Charles H., 16 May 1853, Amand Baker   5/18/53-2
Young, David G., 20 Oct. 1853, Babara Ellen Bachaler   10/24/53-2
Young, Edwin R., 26 Dec. 1860, Sarah Hall, dau. of William P. 1/23/60-2
Young, Geo. W., 6 Apr. 1857, Lucretia Phillips Steward   4/ 8/57-2
Young, Harrison, 7 Sept. 1854, Elizabeth Jones   9/11/54-2
Young, Henry S., 15 May 1851, Lydia Lambourn   5/19/51-2
Young, Henry S., 6 May 1858, Anna M. Johnson   5/10/58-2
Young, James H., 8 Feb. 1854, Mary A. Bloomer   2/11/54-2
Young, James Z., 4 Jan. 1853, Julia A. Lowe   1/ 6/53-2
Young, Jas., 5 Jan. 1853, Elizabeth Stretch   1/ 7/53-2
Young, Jerry, 26 Nov. 1857, M. Virginia Ward, dau. of John 11/28/57-2
Young, Joseph H., 16 May 1857, Theresa E. Redden   10/ 2/57-2
Young, Joshua T., 1 Dec. 1856, Lizzie R. Scharff, dau. of
    Isaac T.   12/ 2/56-2
Young, Otis, 20 Sept. 1851, Mary Virginia Corbell   9/23/51-2
Young, Samuel C., 12 Feb. 1852, Eugenia Yerby   2/13/52-2
Young, Walter S., 29 Jan. 1852, Sarah Collins   2/ 3/52-2
Young, William, 28 May 1853, Catharine McConnel   5/30/53-2
Young, William, 14 May 1854, Caroline Strickland   5/16/54-2
Young, William, 8 May 1855, Lizzie Bowers   5/22/55-2
Young, William H., 23 Feb. 1860, Ada J. Thomas, dau. of
    David E.   2/27/60-2
Young, William J., 30 Oct. 1855, Mary E. Tyler   11/ 1/55-2
Young, William T., 15 Nov. 1853, Elizabeth Kummer Stitcher 11/17/53-2
Young, Wm., 31 Oct. 1859, Hannah C. Hooker   11/ 4/59-2
Young, Wm. T., 2 Dec. 1858, J. S. Backus   12/ 7/58-2
Younger, Jespher W., 26 Aug. 1851, Maria A. White   9/ 2/51-2
Zachary, Robert J., 18 July 1853, Emma T. Dolan   7/20/53-2
Zaell, Philip, 28 Mar. 1854, Sophia Green   4/ 3/54-2
Zapp, Jacob, 31 July 1859, Annie S. Seibert   8/ 2/59-2
Zedricks, Henry, 5 Dec. 1860, Rebecca Neil   12/ 8/60-2
Zell, Andrew, 17 Dec. 1857, Margaret Todd, dau. of William 1/ 2/58-2
Zell, Charles E., 15 May 1856, Maria McGinnis, dau. of
    Richard   5/17/56-2
Zell, Henry, 2 Nov. 1852, Margaret E. Greenfeld   11/10/52-2
Zell, Jacob, 26 Mar. 1856, Louisa Johnson   4/ 3/56-2
Zell, William, 6 June 1852, Rosanna C. Miller   6/10/52-2

Zerkel, Charles, 5 Dec. 1853, Mary E. Cunningham, dau.
    of W.   12/29/53-2
Zerweck, John, 7 Feb. 1853, (Mrs.) Rebecca J. Patterson;
    corrected copy   2/10/53-2
Zim, Anthony, 13 May 1856, Mary Elizabeth Myers   9/18/56-2
Zimmerman, Geo. A., 17 June 1852, Virginia C. Lafever   6/19/52-2
Zimmerman, John W., 1 May 1855, Eliza J. Taylor, dau. of John 5/ 2/55-2
Zimmerman, Karl, 27 Feb. 1853, Mary Elizabeth Heuring   3/ 1/53-2
Zimmerman, S. B., 9 Feb. 1859, Annie M. London, dau. of
    Henry A.   2/16/59-2
Zimmerman, William H., 26 June 1853, Harriet Becker   10/ 1/53-2
Zimmisch, Fred., 4 Mar. 1851, Louisa Green   3/ 6/51-2
Zini, Anthelmo, 13 May 1856, Mary Elizabeth Myer   9/19/56-2
Zoeller, Valentine, 12 Apr. 1857, Mary Streckfus   5/20/57-2
Zollickoffer, David K., 24 Oct. 1857, Ida Carter, dau. of
    (Col.) Geo. R.   10/29/57-2
Zollickoffer, David Keener, 9 Mar. 1859, Virginia Pierce 3/18/59-2
Zollinger, George N., 17 Nov. 1851, Frances A. Read, dau. of
    Robt.; corrected copy   12/15/51-2
Zollinger, George N., 11 Dec. 1851, Frances A. Read, dau. of
    Jno.   12/13/51-2
Zorbach, Charles P., 1 Mar. 1858, Mary Ruppert   3/ 2/58-2
Zurhorst, Frederick, 23 Mar. 1851, Lisette Kehrer   3/25/51-2
Zwissler, Theodore, 4 Jan. 1859, Eleanor Harburg   1/ 5/59-2
Zwissler, Theodore, 4 Jan. 1859, Eleanor Marburg; corrected
    copy   1/ 6/59-2

Additions

Jamart, Louis A., 19 Oct. 1852, Kate A. Seager, dau. of Thos. T.	10/21/52-2
James, William J., 29 Dec. 1853, Harriet W. Richardson	1/ 2/54-2
James, William Lewis, 5 June 1855, Susan Levian Mason	6/ 7/55-2
Scarff, Henry, 26 Apr. 1856, Jane L. Mordew	5/29/56-2
Williams, James, 30 Aug. 1860, Henrietta Williams	9/ 3/60-2

Corrections Appearing in Subsequent Issues of the Paper

Fraser, Frank S., 4 Dec. 1859, Mary M. Stigerwald; corrected copy

Green, Saml. F., 27 Dec. 1859, Lizzie R. Wright, dau. of John R.; corrected copy

Murray, Richard C., 30 Apr. 1857, (Mrs.) Ellen Doyle; corrected copy

Sansbury, Richard T., 8 Mar. 1855, Sarah A. Reynolds; corrected copy

Smith, Wm. F., 11 Oct. 1860, L. S. Nicholson; corrected copy

Stansbury, John S., 17 June 1858, Elizabeth A. Tauney; corrected copy

Steiner, William, 11 June 1860, Mary E. Sorgler; corrected copy

Street, J. Thomas, 16 Dec. 1856, Demelia Virginia Gallaway, dau. of (Capt.) Wm.; corrected copy

Sturgeon, Henry D., 20 Dec. 1853, Elizabeth Hammell; corrected copy

Thursby, Robert, 8 Nov. 1853, Louisa C. Remmey, dau. of Edward; corrected copy

Note:

Chenoweth, Mary A. should be filed under Hillyard, Charles

FAMILY INDEX

Bookhultz, Mary Elizabeth
  203
Bool, John 195
  Kitty P. 195
Boom, Elizabeth 129
Boon, Amanda 3
Boone, Almira 216
  Amanda 175
  Eliza 90
  Henry D. 175
  Martha E. 45
  Mary Sophia 100
  Rebecca 90
  Stephen 90
Booth, Asia 186
  Beatty 162
  Frances 157
  Hester A. 190
  Jos. 173
  Junius B. 186
  Mary Adelaide 173
  Mary E. J. 56
  Mary Jane 35
  Rachel 185
Booz, Ann Rebecca 117
  Benjamin 24
  Sarah E. 24
Booze, Anna E. 121
Boozer, Belinda C. 180
Bordley, Fanny B. 220
  J. B. 220
  Margaret 218
Borgelt, Emma 67
  George 67
Boring, Agness R. 199
Borroughs, Roselia 118
Bosee, Sallie T. 58, 59
Bosler, John 11
  Mary W. 11
Bosley, Amanda 85
  Amon 183
  Ann 147
  Ann Eliza 30
  Benjamin 142
  E. Sophia 183
  Elenora 51
  Elizabeth 51
  Ellen 30
  Fannie 48
  Gamaliel 30
  Jno. 48
  John A. 97
  Laura 97
  M. Virginia 142
  Priscilla S. 92
  Wm. 48, 51
Bostic, Elizabeth 158
Boston, Lavininia 34
  Mary 122
  Mary A. 4
Bostwick, Elizabeth A. 35
Boswell, Margaret Ann
  (Mrs.) 169
  Margera J. 75
  Rebecca 54
Bosworth, Martha Ann 116
Boteler, Ellen W. 99
  Joseph J. 99
  Marion Ellen 99
  Martha C. 178
Botter, Susanna W. 21
Botterill, Eliza 206
  Kate 189
  Mary A. 77
  Sarah J. 55, 173
Botton, Eugenia J. 217
  T. W. 217
Bottrell, Hannah M. 110

Boulden, Carrie C. 132
  Mary E. 102
Bouldin, Charles D. 98
  M. Amanda 98
Bouram, Georgiana 146
Bourke, Anne E. 113
  Mary 31
Bourne, Jas. J. 156
  Sarah Rebecca 156
Bowditch, Mary E. 60
Bowdle, Mary E. D. 171
Bowen, Agnes R. 9
  Amelia 158
  Balinda 170
  Benjamin 175
  Catherine A. 180
  Eleanor 176
  Elizabeth D. 123
  Elizabeth Marcella 17
  Emily 22
  Fannie D. 201
  Frances E. 209
  Jane 221
  Julia A. 102
  Kate E. 146
  Mary Ann (Mrs.) 24
  Mary E. 67, 172
  Matilda 187
  Sarah A. 92
  Sarah B. 102
  Sarah C. 64
  Sarah Jane 175
  Susie J. 149
  Virginia 167
  Wilkes 17
Bower, Ann Elizabeth 34
  Eliza J. 81
Bowers, Annie M. 101
  Ellen 181
  Lizzie 224
  Martin, Jr. 78
  Mary A. 170
  Nannie E. 127
  Sebilla 206
  Sophia F. 78
Bowie, Susan M. 211
  Virginia Anne 51
Bowles, Emma Morton 11
  Mollie E. 202
Bowley, Hester Ann E. 7
Bowlin, Mary Jane 7
Bowling, Mary V. 9
  Thomas 9
Bowman, Maria 211
Bowyer, Kate 29
  Theodore 29
Bowzer, Barbara 176
  Lydia (Mrs.) 176
Boyd, Dollie 83
  Elizabeth A. 160
  H. S. 28, 67
  James 126
  Jeanette 9
  John 9
  Josephine 193
  Kate 210
  Maggie 126
  Margaret 14
  Martha J. 221
  Mary J. 149
  Mary Jane 28, 129
  Sarah E. 69
  Sophia E. 131
  Willamina 67
  Wm. A. 221
Boyer, Ann 2
  Anna Maria 86
  Jacob 86

Boyer (cont.)
  Mary (Mrs.) 1
  Rezin 56
  Sarah Ann 56
  Susan A. 60
Boyle, Frances A. 185
  Isabella M. 38
  John F. 38
Braceland, Rose 188
Brack, Louisa Caroline 214
Bracken, Mary Ann 109
Brackin, Mary Jane 163
Braddock, Elizabeth S. 29
Braddox, Emily A. 198
Braden, Mary Elizabeth 159
  Noble S. 159
Bradenbaugh, Laura H. 13
Bradford, A. M. 4
  Elizabeth Jane 72, 119
  Ellen 89
  Margaret 89
  Matilda 76
  S. A. (Mrs.) 129
  Sallie A. 136
Bradix, Lucinda 198
Bradley, Alice 136
  Jane 191
  Maggie 168
  Margaret 79
  Margaret Ann 159
  Mary Ann 118
  Mary Virginia 184
  Persusia A. 80
  Rosa 15
Bradshaw, Lucy E. 122
Brady, Ellen 55
  Lotta 28
  Margaret (Mrs.) 115
  Margaret D. 39
  Mary 104
  Mary C. 125
  Sarah C. 173
  Susan 15, 80
Braley, Mollie 170
Brambell, Louisa 111
Brambill, Rebecca 176
Bramble, Laura Jane 64
  Mary Jane 174
  Permelia 222
  Sarah A. 222
  T. (Capt.) 222
Branan, Catharine 15
Brandau, G. H. (Rev.) 179
  Louisa M. 179
Brandon, Girard C. 78
  Varina S. 78
Brannan, Julia F. 105
  Margaret A. 86
  Sarah Y. 176
Brannon, Mary Jane 86
Branson, Joseph 133
  Ruth Hannah 133
Brant, Mary Caroline 66
Brashear, S. L. 110
Brashears, J. B. 199
  J. Bradley 136
  Mary E. 60, 107
  Sarah F. 99
  Susan 199
  Zorah 136
Bratt, Ann Maria 170
  Henrietta M. 22
  Sarah Ann 91
Braudwick, Johanna Ann 132
Braughton, Julia 199
Braun, Caroline 14
Brauns, Emma J. 84
  F. L. 58

Pensons, Matilda A. 113
Nicholas 113
Pentland, Lizzie M. 25
Pentz, Daniel 11
Julia A. 11
Mary C. 160
Peregoy, Anne M. 69
Catharine A. 174
James C. 174
Jerusha E. 30
John W. 5
Mary E. 101
Nora E. 17
R. Elizabeth 66
Rosa B. 5
Pereira, Luzinha Jantha
153
Perine, Micha A. 221
Thos. J. 221
Perkins, Almira 24
John D. (Rev.) 68
Julia A. 99
Lizzie 223
Sarah Ann 223
Susan C. 206
Susan M. 68
Susannah V. 176
Thatcher 99
Perne, Maulden 182
Rachel P. 182
Perrie, Susan A. 143
Perry, Abbie C. 120
Ann E. 61
Bridget 137
Jane Miller 77
Elizabeth D. 124
Harriet V. 211
Isabel 185
Jeremiah 185
Kate T. 27
Kezia 54
Mary Ann 154
Susan Emeline Louisa 159
Perryman, George H. 46
Isabella 46
Personette, Marcelleaner
99
Margaret E. 167
Pervines, Hannah 188
Peterkin, Ellen A. 130
George W. 130
Peterman, John 4
Nannie E. 4
Peters, Catharine 173
Eliza 120
Henrietta 81
Jane 156
Mary A. 209
Mary Jane 223
Mary R. 116
Sarah A. 34
Susannah 187
William 120, 187
Peterson, Adelia A. 86
E. (Capt.) 86
F. (Capt.) 92
Matilda 92
Petherbridge, Fannie 221
Sarah Frances (Mrs.) 95
Petis, Ann Matilda 89
Petri, Nina R. 204
Pettett, Rachel 117
Petticord, Cassandra 147
Sarah A. 128
Pettit, Amanda 146
James 146
Lizzie Olive 120
Peyne, Benj. N. 30

Peyne (cont.)
Mary 30
Peyton, Caroline Y. 146
Velverton (Rev.) 146
Pfaff, Hannah R. 140
Pfeiffer, Mary 101
Pfeltz, G. A. 56
Maria F. 56
Pffifer, Christina 184
Phelan, Ann C. 212
Phelps, Ellen 185
Julia Maria 11
Louisa 132
Sarah A. 11
Phenix, Elizabeth 30
Philbert, Anna M. 136
Philips, Elizabeth R. 52
Phillips, Anna 186
Belle 11
C. C. 66
Elizabeth 41, 135
Elizabeth Ann 197
Ella 105
Ellennor P. 164
Emily Jane 76
Emily Virginia 185
Emma J. 38
Gracey Ann 109
Harriet 97
Jacob 97
Jane 137
Louisa L. 64
Margaret J. 139, 215
Mary E. 67, 162
Matilda 97
Olevia Augusta 120
S. H. 97
Sarah R. 66
Thomas 105
Thos. 162
Wm. B. 120
Phipps, Mary Ann (Mrs.) 129
Mary L. 41
Phoebus, Margaret 68
Sallie E. 15
Pic, Sallie V. 118
Pickens, Mary Abby 60
Pickett, Cordelia A. 28
Julia A. 223
Mary Lavenia 136
Picquet, Amelia 140
James 140
Pielert, Christine M. 75
Pierce, Annie 126, 190
Delia J. 38
Ellen C. V. 4
Frances R. 34
Jane 179
Josephine 163
Louisa 122
Mary E. 163, 185
Matilda A. 61
Peter P. 126, 190
Sallie O. 67
Sarah E. 63
Stephen A. 38
Virginia 225
Piersol, Sarah Elizabeth
49
Pierson, Emily K. 21
Piet, John 20
Maria Meredith 200
Nannie H. 20
Piggott, Margaret E. 202
Pigman, Hattie B. 112
Pilkington, Elizabeth A.
127
Pilsch, Barbara F. 136

Pimm, John M. 155
Mary E. 155
Pinar, Rebecca 111
Pinckard, Mary D. 121
Robert (Rev.) 121
Pincknaur, Mollie A. 175
Pindell, Annie E. 125
Louis 177
Martha Ann 14
R. G. 125
Sophia C. 177
Thomas (Col.) 14
Thos. (Col.) 161
Pindle, Lizzie D. 116
Thos. 116
Pine, Maria 62
Pinkett, Litham 106
Pinkney, Mary A. 19
Priscilla 130
Pitcher, Laura V. 58
Rebecca 42
Pitt, Kesiah G. 131
Mary Magaline 155
Thos. 131
Pittenger, Agnes Clementine
94
Pitts, Mary Ann 151
Place, Mary C. 150
Placide, Louise F. 60
Plain, Maria 168
Plant, Elizabeth V. 39
Planter, Elizabeth 147
Pleasants, Anne Cleaves
217
Wm. A. 217
Plowman, Catherine 148
Mary Ann 138
Penelope 20
Plummer, Elizabeth A. 34
Georgianna 43
Hannah 43
John 43
Louisa 10
Marriam A. B. 145
Mary A. 141
Mollie M. 191
Sarah E. 54
Sarah Elizabeth 192
Plungett, Annie M. 156
Plunkett, Bridget L. 80
Plyman, John 171
John (Rev.) 27
Julia C. 171
Sarah E. 27
Poblitte, Elizabeth 207
Pochon, Laura 159
Pocock, P. L. 132
Poe, Josephine C. 32
Neilson 32
Pohlen, Anna 54
Charlotte 117
Emma 58
Pole, Annie V. 192
Virginia 192
Polk, Arreana 23
James (Col.) 23
Polkinhorn, Carrie E. 12
Charles 12
Pollard, Mary Teresa 42
Pollock, Elizabeth 125
Mary 171
Pomeroy, Mary H. 215
Pool, Emma 68
John 125
Mary J. 125
Poole, Aliceanna 123
Kate 73
Lucretia 77

FAMILY INDEX

182758